STUDENT TESTED, FACULTY APPROVED

THE ACCT SOLU[…]N

Every 4LTR Press solution [includes]:

Visually Engaging Textbook

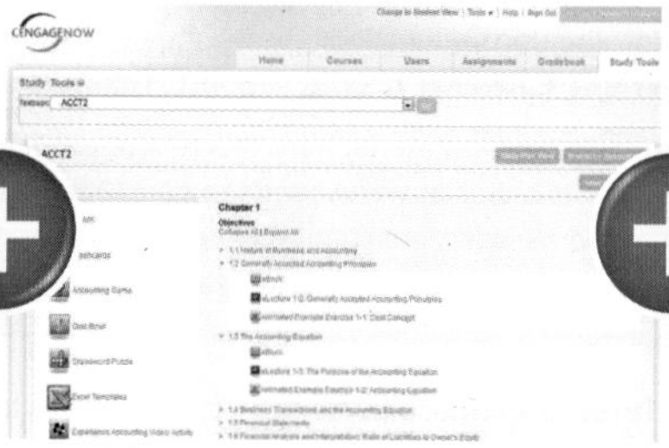

Online Study Tools

Tear-out Review Cards

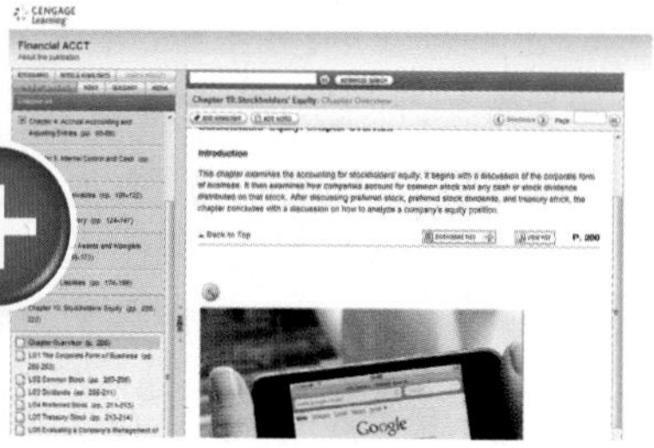

Interactive eBook

STUDENT RESOURCES:

- Interactive eBook
- Pre- and Post-Tests
- Personalized Study Plan
- Flashcards
- Games: Crossword Puzzles, Beat the Clock, & Quiz Bowl
- Animations
- PowerPoint® Slides
- Videos
- E-Lectures

Students sign in at **www.cengagebrain.com**

INSTRUCTOR RESOURCES:

- All Student Resources
- First Day of Class Instructions
- Custom Options through 4LTR+ Program
- Instructor's Manual
- Test Bank
- PowerPoint® Slides
- Instructor Prep Cards
- Solutions Manual

Instructors sign in at **www.cengage.com/login**

"4LTR Press rocks. You understand my brain and my budget."

– **Samantha Jerabek**, Student, *University of Cincinnati*

JULY 2010

4LTR Press adds eBooks in response to a 10% uptick in digital learning preferences.

AUGUST 2010

Engagement Tracker launches, giving faculty a window into student usage of digital tools.

1 out of every 3 (1,400) schools has adopted a 4LTR Press solution.

750,000 students are IN.

NOVEMBER 2010

Third party research confirms that 4LTR Press digital solutions improve retention and outcomes.

IN 2011

60 unique solutions across multiple course areas validates the 4LTR Press concept.

IN 2011

CourseMate

Students access the 4LTR Press website at 4x's the industry average.

APRIL 2011

1 out of every 2 (2,000) schools has a 4LTR Press adoption.

2,000

AUGUST 2011

Over 1 million students are IN.

2012 AND BEYOND

We're always evolving. Join the 4LTR Press In-Crowd on Facebook at www.facebook.com/4ltrpress

SOUTH-WESTERN
CENGAGE Learning™

Financial ACCT2
Norman Godwin and Wayne Alderman

Editor-in-Chief: Rob Dewey

Sr. Acquisitions Editor: Matt Filimonov

Supervising Developmental Editor: Aaron Arnsparger

Editorial Assistant: Ann Loch

Production Manager: Patricia Matthews Boies

Content Project Manager: Darrell E. Frye

Media Editor: Anita Verma

Manufacturing Planner: Doug Wilke

Associate Marketing Manager: Heather Mooney

Marketing Communications Manager: Libby Shipp

Production Service: MPS Limited, a Macmillan Company

Sr. Art Director: Stacy Jenkins Shirley

Cover Designer: KeDesign, Mason, Oh

Cover Image: ©LWA/Larry Williams/ Getty Images

Rights Acquisitions Director: Audrey Pettengill

Rights Acquisitions Specialist: Deanna Ettinger

Library of Congress Control Number: 2011935438
Student Edition ISBN-13: 978-1-111-53077-8
Student Edition ISBN-10: 1-111-53077-7
Student Edition package ISBN-13: 978-1-111-53076-1
Student Edition package ISBN-10: 1-111-53076-9

South-Western
5191 Natorp Boulevard
Mason, OH 45040
USA

Cengage Learning products are represented in Canada by Nelson Education, Ltd.

For your course and learning solutions, visit **www.cengage.com**
Purchase any of our products at your local college store or at our preferred online store **www.cengagebrain.com**

Printed in the United States of America
1 2 3 4 5 6 7 16 15 14 13 12

ACCT

Brief Contents

Dean Mitchell, 2010/Used under license from Shutterstock.Com

iStockphoto

Kristian Sekulic/Shutterstock.com

quavondo/iStockphoto.com

ACCT

Contents

izusekizusek

Acct

wavebreakmedia ltd/Shutterstock.com

pixdeluxe/iStockphoto

Dmitriy Shironosov, 2010/Used under license from Shutterstock.com

Yuri Arcurs/Shutterstock.com

Jacob Wackerhausen/iStockphoto

Monkey Business Images/Shutterstock.com

Hill Street Studios/Getty Images

ACCT

Financial Accounting

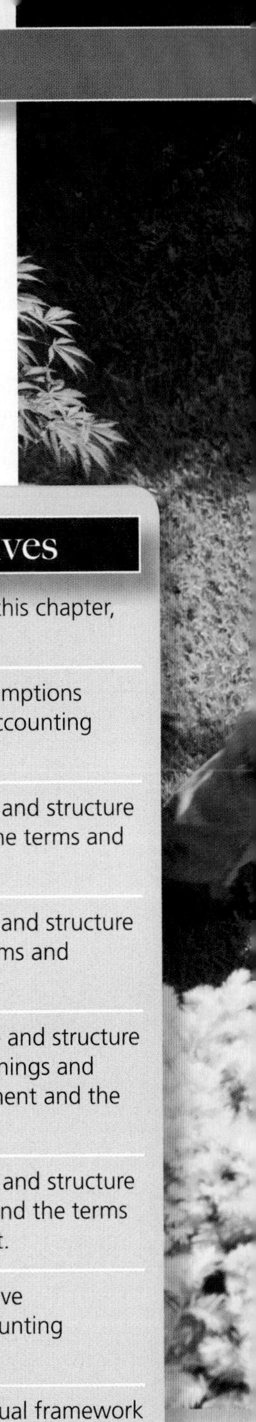

Learning Objectives

After studying the material in this chapter, you should be able to:

LO1 Describe the four assumptions made when communicating accounting information.

LO2 Describe the purpose and structure of an income statement and the terms and principles used to create it.

LO3 Describe the purpose and structure of a balance sheet and the terms and principles used to create it.

LO4 Describe the purpose and structure of a statement of retained earnings and how it links the income statement and the balance sheet.

LO5 Describe the purpose and structure of a statement of cash flows and the terms and principles used to create it.

LO6 Describe the qualitative characteristics that make accounting information useful.

LO7 Describe the conceptual framework of accounting.

Introduction

Imagine for a moment that you are home for the summer and decide to mow lawns to make some money. With $50 of your own money and $100 borrowed from a relative, you pay $130 to rent a lawn mower and a gas can for June and purchase $20 of gas. During June, you mow 40 lawns at $10 each, buy $175 of additional gasoline, and pay your relative $1 of interest. At the end of June, you have $194 in cash, $10 of gasoline, and $30 due from customers.

Given this information, can you tell what happened to your business in June? Were you profitable? What do you have to show for your efforts? How can you tell? Getting answers to such questions requires accounting.

Accounting is the process of identifying, measuring, and communicating economic information to permit informed judgments and decisions. Put more simply, accounting is the "language of business." When you want to know about the financial results of a business, you must understand and speak accounting. The purpose of this book is to teach you this language.

With this overall purpose in mind, the current chapter introduces the basic terms, principles, and rules that comprise the grammar of the accounting language. It does so by creating the June financial statements of the lawn service scenario described above. At the end of the chapter, you should be familiar with the four main financial statements of accounting. You should also have a working accounting vocabulary that can be built upon in the following chapters.

LO1 Beginning Assumptions

Accounting The process of identifying, measuring, and communicating economic information to permit informed judgments and decisions.

The purpose of accounting is to identify, measure, and communicate economic information about a particular entity to interested users. As a foundation for accomplishing this purpose, accountants make the following four assumptions: economic entity, time period, monetary unit, and going concern.

Accounting, the "language of business," would describe this picture as a guy using an asset (the lawn mower) to generate a revenue (the money he will be paid).

Uripos/eStock Photo/Alamy

Economic Entity Assumption

The **economic entity assumption** states that the financial activities of a business can be separated from the financial activities of the business's owner(s). This assumption allows a user to examine a company's accounting information without concern that the information includes the personal affairs of the owner(s). For the lawn service example in the introduction, this means that personal activities such as buying gasoline for your automobile should not be included with the business activities of buying

Economic entity assumption Accountants assume that the financial activities of a business can be separated from the financial activities of the business's owner(s).

MAKING IT REAL

After conducting its 2008 audit of **General Motors Corporation**, the public accounting firm **Deloitte & Touche LLP** wrote the following in its auditor's report:

Jim R. Bounds/Bloomberg via Getty Images

"[General Motors'] recurring losses from operations, stockholders' deficit, and inability to generate sufficient cash flow to meet its obligations and sustain its operations raise substantial doubt about its ability to continue as a going concern."

This language is commonly known as a going concern opinion. The auditor uses it to inform the public of its opinion that the company's continued operations are in doubt. Going concern opinions are therefore designed to protect a company's stakeholders and allow them to make decisions with the most accurate information available.

While no company wants to receive a going concern opinion, receiving one does not always mean that the company will cease operations. But, it does mean that there is substantial doubt that the company will continue without significant changes. In the case of General Motors, these significant changes began on June 1, 2009 when the company filed for Chapter 11 bankruptcy protection. With the help of governmental financing, the company then emerged from bankruptcy on July 10, 2009. Since that time, General Motors has improved its financial position and has paid off its debt to the federal government ahead of schedule. As a result, Deloitte and Touch LLP did not include a going concern opinion in its most recent auditor's report for General Motors.

gasoline for the lawn mower. These activities can and should be accounted for separately.

Time Period Assumption

Business owners and other interested parties usually do not want to wait long before they receive information about how a business is doing. They want periodic measurements of the business's success or failure. Accountants therefore assume that economic information can be meaningfully captured and communicated over short periods of time, even if those time periods are somewhat artificial, such as one month or one quarter. This is known as the **time period assumption**.

Time period assumption Accountants assume that economic information can be meaningfully captured and communicated over short periods of time.

Monetary unit assumption Accountants assume that the dollar is the most effective means to communicate economic activity.

Going concern assumption Accountants assume that a company will continue to operate into the foreseeable future.

Most companies communicate to users on both a quarterly and annual basis. In fact, publicly traded companies such as **Starbucks** are required by law to file quarterly and annual financial statements with the Securities and Exchange Commission (SEC). For the lawn service example, the time period is the month of June.

Monetary Unit Assumption

The **monetary unit assumption** assumes that the dollar is the most effective means to communicate economic activity. If an economic activity cannot be expressed in dollars, then it is not recorded in the accounting system. It assumes further that the dollar is reasonably stable with respect to inflation and deflation. As a result, accountants do not adjust economic values based on inflation or deflation. A dollar earned in 1982 is the same as a dollar earned in 2012.

Going Concern Assumption

The **going concern assumption** states that a company will continue to operate into the foreseeable future. This assumption enables accountants to use certain techniques that will be described later in the chapter. Unless

HOME DEPOT ANALYSIS

On Home Depot's income statement in Appendix C, you can find the following four descriptions: 1) The Home Depot, Inc. and Subsidiaries, 2) amounts in millions, 3) Fiscal Year Ended January 30, 2011. Which assumption does each description best relate?

1) economic entity, 2) monetary unit, 3) time period

there is evidence to the contrary, most companies are assumed to be going concerns. Those that are not going concerns are often in the process of liquidation (that is, selling their resources and paying off their obligations). Because the lawn service will continue through the summer, it is a going concern at the end of June.

LO2 Reporting Profitability: The Income Statement

One of the first questions asked of any business is whether it makes money. Stated differently in "accounting" words, is the business profitable? Does it generate more resources than it uses? Accounting provides answers to these questions with a financial statement called an *income statement*. An income statement reports a company's *revenues* and *expenses*.

Revenues

A **revenue** is an increase in resources resulting from the sale of goods or the provision of services. Receiving $10 for mowing a lawn is an example of a revenue. You have $10 more than you did previously because you provided a service. Other revenue common to businesses is investment income.

Revenues are recorded according to the revenue recognition principle. The **revenue recognition principle** states that a revenue should be recorded when a resource has been earned. A resource is earned when either the sale of the good or the provision of the service is substantially complete and cash collection is reasonably assured.

Given these definitions, total June revenues for the lawn service are as follows. You have only one source of revenue—mowing lawns. Assuming that your customers will pay you, your lawn service creates a revenue each time a lawn is mowed. So, if you mowed 40 lawns at $10 each, revenues total $400 for the month. Note from the previous information that you have yet to collect $30 of that $400. However, revenues are still $400 because cash collection is reasonably assured.

Expenses

An **expense** is a decrease in resources resulting from the sale of goods or provision of services. The gasoline consumed while mowing lawns is an example of an expense. Other expenses common to businesses are wages, taxes, advertising, and utilities.

Expenses are recorded according to the matching principle. The **matching principle** states that expenses should be recorded in the period resources are used to generate revenues. For example, since fuel is used to mow lawns in June, June expenses should include the fuel used.

Given these definitions, total June expenses for the lawn service are as follows. Unlike the revenue side, the lawn service has three sources of expenses. The first is fuel. The amount of fuel used during June can be calculated as follows from the given information:

Amount on hand on June 1	$ 20
+ Amount purchased during June	175
− Amount on hand on June 30	(10)
Amount used during June	$185

Therefore, fuel expense is $185.

Revenue An increase in resources resulting from the sale of goods or the provision of services.

Revenue recognition principle The principle that a revenue should be recorded when a resource has been earned.

Expense A decrease in resources resulting from the sale of goods or provision of services.

Matching principle The principle that expenses should be recorded in the period resources are used to generate revenues.

The second expense relates to your borrowing. You paid your relative $1 at the end of June to compensate her for loaning you $100. Paying for the use of someone else's money is called interest. Therefore, interest expense is $1.

The third expense relates to your use of the rented equipment—the lawn mower and the gas can. You paid $130 for the right to use the equipment during the month. The cost of renting equipment is usually called rent expense. Therefore, rent expense for June is $130.

The Income Statement

Once a company's revenues and expenses are calculated, they are reported on an income statement. An **income statement** is a financial statement that shows a company's revenues and expenses over a specific period of time. Its purpose is to demonstrate the financial success or failure of the company over that specific period of time. When revenues exceed expenses, a company generates net income. When expenses exceed revenues, a company generates a net loss. The basic structure of the statement is as follows:

Revenues − Expenses = Net Income or Net Loss

Given the revenues and expenses determined previously, the lawn service's June income statement would appear as Exhibit 1-1. It contains the company name, the statement name, and the time reference, which for this example is the month of June. It also shows that the lawn service generated $84 of net income during June.

> The income statement's purpose is to demonstrate the financial success or failure of the company over a specific period of time.

Exhibit 1-1 Income Statement for Lawn Service, Inc.

Lawn Service, Inc.
Income Statement
For the Month Ending June 30

Revenues		$400
Expenses:		
Fuel	$185	
Interest	1	
Rent	130	
Total expenses		316
Net income		$ 84

Income statement A financial statement that reports a company's revenues and expenses over a specific period of time.

LO3 Reporting Financial Position: The Balance Sheet

Another important issue for any business is its current financial position. What does the business own? What does it owe? Accounting provides answers

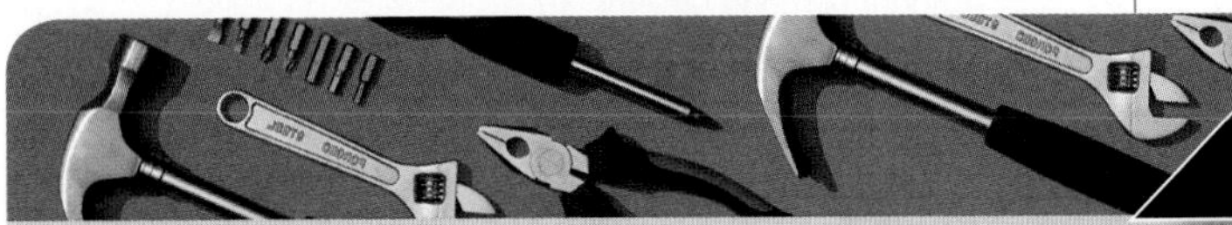

HOME DEPOT ANALYSIS

Look at Home Depot's income statement in Appendix C. The statement contains two revenues and six expenses. Can you identify them? What was the company's net income for the most current year?

Revenues: net sales; interest and investment income

Expenses: cost of sales; selling, general and administrative; depreciation and amortization; interest expense; other; provision for income taxes

Net income (called net earnings): $3,338 million

to these questions with a financial statement called a *balance sheet*. A balance sheet reports a company's *assets*, *liabilities*, and *equity*.

Assets

An asset is a resource of a business. More formally, an **asset** is an economic resource that is objectively measurable, that results from a prior transaction, and that will provide future economic benefit. Cash is a good example of an asset. It can be counted, it is received through a transaction with someone else, and it can be used to buy things in the future. Other common assets include merchandise inventory, equipment, supplies, and investments.

Assets are recorded and reported according to the historical cost principle, which is often shortened to the cost principle. The **cost principle** states that assets should be recorded and reported at the cost paid to acquire them.

Given these definitions, the lawn service has three assets at the end of June—$194 of cash, $10 of remaining fuel, and $30 of receivables from customers. Note that although the lawn service uses a lawnmower and gas can, it rents them from another entity. Therefore, the lawnmower and gas can are assets of the rental company, not the lawn service.

Liabilities

A liability is an obligation of a business. More formally, a **liability** is an obligation of a business that results from a past transaction and will require the sacrifice of economic resources at some future date. Examples of liabilities common to businesses include notes payable to creditors, accounts payable to vendors, salaries payable to employees, and taxes payable to governments. The only liability of the lawn service at the end of June is the $100 borrowed from your relative, who is considered a creditor. As will be explained below, the business does not have a liability for the $50 of your own money that was contributed to the company. You are an owner, not a creditor.

Equity

Equity is the difference between a company's assets and liabilities and represents the share of assets that are claimed by the company's owners. An example of equity with which you may be familiar is home equity. A homeowner's equity refers to the difference between the value of the home and the amount owed to the bank. Equity in accounting is the same principle except that it refers to the difference between the cost of the business's assets and its liabilities.

A company can generate equity in two ways. The first is through contributed capital. **Contributed capital** is defined as the resources that investors contribute to a business in exchange for an ownership interest. The $50 that you, the owner, put into the lawn service is contributed capital. Note here that contributed capital is not a revenue. The increase of $50 did not result from the lawn service providing a service or selling a product. It came by selling an ownership interest. The most common method that companies use to generate contributed capital is the sale of common stock to investors.

The second way a company generates equity is through profitable operations. When a company generates net income, it can either distribute those profits to owners or retain them in the business to grow the business further. Profits that are distributed to owners are called **dividends**. Note here that dividends are not an expense of a company. They are simply a distribution of company assets to owners. Profits that are retained in the business are called **retained earnings**. A company's retained earnings therefore represent the equity generated and retained from profitable operations. Since the lawn service did not distribute any assets to you, the owner, it retained the entire $84 of June profits.

Asset An economic resource that is objectively measurable, results from a prior transaction, and will provide future economic benefit.

Cost principle The principle that assets should be recorded and reported at the cost paid to acquire them.

Liability An obligation of a business that results from a past transaction and will require the sacrifice of economic resources at some future date.

Equity The difference between a company's assets and liabilities, representing the share of assets that is claimed by the company's owners.

Contributed capital The resources that investors contribute to a business in exchange for ownership interest.

Dividends Profits that are distributed to owners.

Retained earnings Profits that are retained in the business.

Because a balance sheet is reported at a specific point in time, it is often referred to as a snapshot of a business.

The Balance Sheet

A company's assets, liabilities, and equity are reported on a balance sheet. A **balance sheet** is a financial statement that shows a company's assets, liabilities, and equity at a specific point in time. Its purpose is to show, at a given point in time, a company's resources and the claims against those resources. Because a balance sheet is reported at a specific point in time, it is often referred to as a snapshot of a business. The basic structure of the statement is as follows:

Assets = Liabilities + Equity

Given the assets, liabilities, and equity determined previously, the lawn service's balance sheet would appear as Exhibit 1-2. It contains the company name, the statement name, and the time reference, which for this example is June 30.

Notice that total assets equal total liabilities plus total equity. This will always be the case for any business. An entity's assets are always claimed by someone. Either they are owed to someone (in this case, your relative) or claimed by an owner (in this case, you). No asset of any business is ever unclaimed. This relationship between assets, liabilities, and equity is represented by the following equation, known as the fundamental accounting equation: **Assets = Liabilities + Equity**. This fundamental accounting equation is what the balance sheet reports. That is why it is called a *balance* sheet.

Exhibit 1-2 Balance Sheet for Lawn Service, Inc.

Lawn Service, Inc.
Balance Sheet
June 30

Cash	$194	
Accounts receivable	30	
Supplies (fuel)	10	
Total assets		$234
Note payable to relative	$100	
Total liabilities		$100
Contributed capital	$ 50	
Retained earnings	84	
Total equity		134
Total liabilities and equity		$234

Balance sheet A financial statement that reports a company's assets, liabilities, and equity at a specific point in time.

Statement of retained earnings A financial statement that reports the change in a company's retained earnings over a specific period of time.

LO4 Reporting Equity: The Statement of Retained Earnings

Owners of a business are usually interested in how their equity is growing as a result of profitable operations. They are also interested in how that equity is distributed in the form of dividends. Such information is reported on the statement of retained earnings. A **statement of retained earnings** shows the

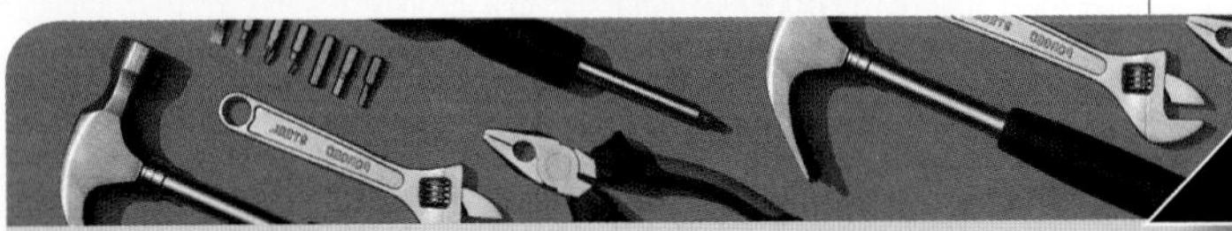

HOME DEPOT ANALYSIS

Look at Home Depot's balance sheet in Appendix C. Write out in numbers the company's accounting equation (A = L + E) for the most current year. How many different assets does the company disclose?

1) $40,125 = $21,236 + $18,889 (in millions)

2) Thirteen different assets are listed on the company's balance sheet.

change in a company's retained earnings over a specific period of time. The basic structure of the statement is as follows:

	Retained Earnings, Beginning Balance
+/−	Net Income/Loss
−	Dividends
=	Retained Earnings, Ending Balance

The lawn service's statement of retained earnings would appear as Exhibit 1-3. It contains the company name, the statement name, and the time reference, which for this example is the month of June.

Exhibit 1-3 Statement of Retained Earnings for Lawn Service, Inc.

Lawn Service, Inc.
Statement of Retained Earnings
For the Month Ending June 30

Retained earnings, June 1	$ 0
+ Net income	84
– Dividends	0
Retained earnings, June 30	$ 84

Your business started with no retained earnings but generated net income of $84 in June. Since none of that income was distributed through dividends, the business retained all of those profits. Therefore, retained earnings increased from $0 to $84.

Linking the Income Statement and the Balance Sheet

In addition to showing the change in retained earnings, the statement of retained earnings links the income statement and the balance sheet. A company cannot calculate its retained earnings balance at the end of the period without factoring in the income earned during the period. The statement of retained earnings provides this link by including net income in the calculation of retained earnings, which is then reported on the balance sheet. This means that when preparing financial statements for any business, the income statement must be prepared first, followed by the statement of retained earnings and then the balance sheet. A graphical depiction of these links is included in Exhibit 1-4.

When preparing financial statements, the income statement must be prepared first, followed by the statement of retained earnings and then the balance sheet.

Exhibit 1-4 Relationship Among Financial Statements

Income Statement

Revenues	$400
– Expenses	316
Net income	$ 84

Statement of Retained Earnings

Retained earnings, June 1	$ 0
+ Net income	84
– Dividends	0
Retained earnings, June 30	$ 84

Balance Sheet

Total assets	$234
Liabilities	100
Contributed capital	50
Retained earnings	84
Total liabilities and equity	$234

LO5 Reporting Cash Flows: The Statement of Cash Flows

Another important issue for any business is its management of cash. Where does a company get its cash? Where does its cash go? Will there be enough cash to pay bills? Accounting provides answers to these questions with a financial statement called a *statement of cash flows*. A statement of cash flows reports

HOME DEPOT ANALYSIS

Look at Home Depot's statement of stockholders' equity in Appendix C. Which column of the statement contains the statement of retained earnings? For the most recent year presented, is the amount for net income the same as net income on the income statement? Is the balance in retained earnings the same as the balance on the balance sheet?

The statement of stockholders' equity has nine columns of numerical data. The fourth numerical column from the left with "Retained Earnings" as the header is the company's statement of retained earnings. The bottom third of the statement is the most recent year. For that year, the amount for net earnings (which is another name for net income) is $3,338 million. That is the same amount shown on the income statement. The balance for retained earnings is $14,995 million. That is the same amount shown on the balance sheet.

a company's cash inflows and outflows from its *operating*, *investing*, and *financing activities*.

Financing Activities

Most businesses must raise funds to get started. Borrowing money from creditors and receiving contributions from investors are both ways to finance a business's operations. Therefore, generating and repaying cash from creditors and investors are considered *financing activities*. In the lawn service example, you contributed $50 of your own money and borrowed $100 from a relative. Both of these inflows are from financing activities. Therefore, the cash inflow in June from financing activities is $150.

Investing Activities

Once a company has raised sufficient capital from creditors and investors, it usually acquires the revenue-generating assets (for example, equipment) that it needs for operations. The buying and selling of such assets are considered *investing activities*. In the lawn service example, you rented the lawn mower and gas can instead of buying them. Therefore, there were no cash flows from investing activities. The cash flows associated with renting equipment are reported as operating activities.

Statement of cash flows A financial statement that reports a company's sources and uses of cash over a specific period of time.

Operating Activities

After the proper equipment is acquired, a business can begin operations. Operating a business includes activities such as the purchase of supplies, the payment of employees, and the sale of products. These transactions are considered *operating activities*. In the lawn service example, cash flows from operations in the month of June included $370 received from customers for mowing their lawns, $195 ($20 + $175) paid for gasoline to operate the lawn mower, $130 paid for equipment rental, and $1 paid to your relative for the right to use her $100. As a result, the net cash inflow from operating activities for the month was $44 ($370 − $195 − $130 − $1).

The Statement of Cash Flows

The details of a business' cash inflows and outflows are reported on a *statement of cash flows*. The **statement of cash flows** is a financial statement that shows a company's sources and uses of cash over a specific period of time. Its purpose is to inform users about how and why a company's cash changed during the period. The basic structure of the statement is as follows:

	Cash Flows Provided (Used) by Operating Activities
+/−	Cash Flows Provided (Used) by Investing Activities
+/−	Cash Flows Provided (Used) by Financing Activities
=	Net Increase (Decrease) in Cash

Given the cash inflows and outflows described previously, the lawn service's June statement of cash flows

An important issue for any business is its management of cash. Where does a company get its cash? Where does its cash go? Will there be enough cash to pay bills?

would appear as Exhibit 1-5. It contains the company name, the statement name, and the time reference, which for this example is the month of June. It also shows a net change in cash from June 1 to June 30 of $194. Note that the ending cash balance on the statement agrees with the cash balance shown on the balance sheet in Exhibit 1-2.

Exhibit 1-5 Statement of Cash Flows for Lawn Service, Inc.

Lawn Service, Inc.
Statement of Cash Flows
For the Month Ending June 30

Operating activities		
Cash received from customers	$ 370	
Cash paid for fuel	(195)	
Cash paid for equipment rental	(130)	
Cash paid for interest	(1)	
Net cash provided by operating activities		$ 44
Investing activities		
Net cash used by investing activities		0
Financing activities		
Cash received from borrowing	$ 100	
Cash received from contributions	50	
Net cash provided by financing activities		150
Net increase in cash		$ 194
Cash balance, June 1		0
Cash balance, June 30		$ 194

LO6 Qualitative Characteristics of Accounting Information

Even though accounting is a very quantitative process and the financial statements introduced thus far are full of numbers, accounting information must possess certain qualitative characteristics to be considered useful. The following qualitative characteristics help ensure that accounting information is indeed useful.

Understandability

Accounting information should first and foremost be understandable. **Understandability** refers to the ability of accounting information to "be comprehensible to those who have a reasonable understanding of business . . . and are willing to study the information with reasonable diligence" (SFAC No. 2, par. 40). Notice that this definition puts much of the responsibility on the user of accounting information. Users must be willing to spend a "reasonable" amount of time studying the information. No specifics are given on what is a "reasonable" amount of time, but it is obvious that the more time you spend studying accounting information, the more you will understand.

Understandability The ability of accounting information to "be comprehensible to those who have a reasonable understanding of business . . . and are willing to study the information with reasonable diligence."

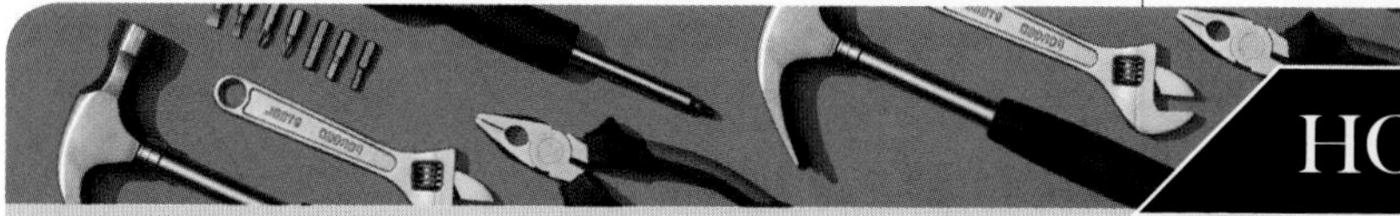

HOME DEPOT ANALYSIS

Look at Home Depot's statement of cash flows in Appendix C. How much cash did the company generate or use for operating, investing, and financing activities during the most recent year?

Operating Activities: Generated $4,858 million
Investing Activities: Used $1,012 million
Financing Activities: Used $4,451 million

IFRS

According to the conceptual framework of the International Accounting Standards Board, the components of relevance are predictive value, feedback value, and materiality.

Relevance

Relevance refers to the capacity of accounting information to make a difference in decisions. Accounting information has this capacity when it possesses feedback value or predictive value. *Feedback value* refers to the ability to assess past performance, while *predictive value* refers to the ability to form expectations of future performance. In the lawn service example, four financial statements were created to demonstrate the financial activities for June. The statements provided feedback on the success of the business, but they also provided the data to generate expectations about July. As a result, the financial statements are relevant to our decision making, which makes them useful.

In addition to having feedback or predictive value, accounting information must be *timely* to be relevant. Information that helps you forecast August revenues is relevant when it is received in July, not when it is received in September. Information is relevant only if it is generated on a timely basis.

Reliability

Reliability refers to the extent to which accounting information can be depended upon to represent what it purports to represent, both in description and in number. To be considered reliable, accounting information should be verifiable, should have representational faithfulness, and should be neutral.

Relevance The capacity of accounting information to make a difference in decisions.

Reliability The extent to which accounting information can be depended upon to represent what it purports to represent, both in description and in number.

Comparability The ability to use accounting information to compare or contrast the financial activities of different companies.

IFRS

According to the conceptual framework of the International Accounting Standards Board, the components of reliability are neutrality, representative faithfulness, substance over form, prudence, and completeness.

Information is *verifiable* if it can be proven to be free from error. One can often prove that accounting information is free from error by comparing the information to an original source document such as an invoice or a contract. For example, the rental cost of the lawn mower in your lawn service is verifiable because you could check the cost against the amount included on the rental agreement. If the two agree, the information is free from error and you can depend on it.

Information has *representational faithfulness* when the description corresponds to the underlying phenomenon. For example, in your lawn service, you purchased fuel to operate the business. In your balance sheet, the remaining fuel was reported as an asset. This reporting was a faithful representation of what the item truly was—a resource.

Information is *neutral* if it is presented in a way that is unbiased toward or against the reporting entity. In other words, neutral information does not portray an entity in a more or less favorable light than the information requires. In the lawn service example, income was reported to be $84, not more or less. The $84 figure was a neutral measure of the activities of the service.

Comparability

Comparability refers to the ability to use accounting information to compare or contrast the financial activities of different companies. Being able to compare information across companies allows an entity to assess its market position within an industry, to gauge its success against a competitor, and/or to set future goals based on industry standards.

As a company gets larger, its materiality threshold usually gets larger as well.

Comparability does not imply uniformity. Accounting rules allow for some discretion in the manner in which accounting is applied to economic phenomenon. As a result, two businesses with the same economic phenomenon could have different accounting information because they use different acceptable accounting methods. Because such differences in accounting methods are a challenge to comparability, accounting rules require that entities disclose the accounting methods that they use so that information can be more easily compared across entities. Usually, such methods are disclosed in the notes to the financial statements, which are discussed in Chapter 2.

Consistency

Consistency refers to the ability to use accounting information to compare or contrast the financial activities of the same entity over time. Consistency is obviously highest when an entity uses the same accounting methods year after year. In such a case, year-to-year comparisons can be very useful because they can reveal trends that help in generating expectations about future performance. However, entities sometimes change the manner in which they account for a particular economic event. Because such changes hinder consistency, accounting rules require that changes be disclosed by the company so that interested parties can assess the effect of the change. Such disclosures are usually found in the notes to the financial statements.

Materiality

Materiality is a concept that is closely related to relevance in that it refers to the threshold at which an item begins to affect decision making. Items meeting or exceeding the threshold are said to be material—that is, they are large enough to possibly affect decision making. Items below the threshold are said to be immaterial—that is, they are small enough that they will not affect decision making. The threshold varies across different companies and across different settings. As a company gets larger, its materiality threshold usually gets larger as well. Often, the materiality threshold is set at some percentage of assets or sales.

To see how materiality is applied, consider the following example from the lawn service. Suppose that an error occurred in the accounting for June transactions such that net income was incorrectly reported as $85 instead of $84. Would such an error affect your decision making about the service? Probably not. In other words, the error is immaterial because $1 is not large enough to affect your decision making.

While materiality is largely quantitative in nature, the materiality threshold is not always solely a function of dollar amounts. For example, an error of $1,000 in a routine transaction may be considered immaterial while a $1,000 error in a nonroutine transaction may be considered material. In addition, transactions that a company may consider immaterial may be considered material by users of the information. Materiality judgments are just that—judgments—and should be made with caution. Furthermore, just because something is immaterial does not mean that errors in accounting should be accepted and condoned. Accounting information must be reliable, so it should be free from error as much as possible.

Consistency The ability to use accounting information to compare or contrast the financial activities of the same entity over time.

Materiality The threshold at which a financial item begins to affect decision making.

Conservatism

Conservatism refers to the manner in which accountants deal with uncertainty regarding economic situations. When accountants are faced with uncertainty about how to account for or report a particular transaction or situation, conservatism dictates that they use the accounting that is least likely to overstate the company's assets and revenues or to understate the company's liabilities and expenses. A common example of conservatism in action is the lower-of-cost-or-market rule for inventory. According to this rule, inventory must be recorded and reported at the lower of its cost or its current market value. This ensures that the value of inventory is not overstated. Other applications of conservatism will be discussed in subsequent chapters.

Conservatism The manner in which accountants deal with uncertainty regarding economic situations.

Conceptual framework of accounting The collection of concepts that guide the manner in which accounting is practiced.

LO7 The Conceptual Framework

This chapter introduced many of the terms, principles, assumptions, and qualitative characteristics that are necessary to communicate the financial activities and position of a business. While they were initially described as the grammar of the financial accounting language, they are more formally known as components of the conceptual framework of accounting. The **conceptual framework of accounting** is the collection of concepts that guide the manner in which accounting is practiced.

The following tables summarize the elements of this conceptual framework. They will provide a good reference for you as you proceed through the remaining chapters. As you tackle more complex accounting methods and procedures, keep in mind that they are simply extensions of the basic grammar presented in the tables. So, with a good understanding of the conceptual framework, you have the grammar necessary to begin your study of accounting.

Terms Used to Identify and Describe Economic Information

Term	Definition	Reported on the
Asset	A resource of a business	Balance sheet
Liability	An obligation of a business	Balance sheet
Equity	The difference between assets and liabilities	Balance sheet
Contributed capital	Equity resulting from contributions from owners	Balance sheet
Retained earnings	Equity resulting from profitable operations	Balance sheet and statement of retained earnings
Revenue	An increase in assets resulting from selling a good or providing a service	Income statement
Expense	A decrease in assets resulting from selling a good or providing a service	Income statement
Dividend	A distribution of profits to owners	Statement of retained earnings

Principles Used to Measure Economic Information

Principle	Definition	Ramification
Revenue recognition	Revenues are recorded when they are earned.	The receipt of cash is not required to record a revenue.
Matching	Expenses are recorded in the time period when they are incurred to generate revenues.	For many assets, the cost of the asset must be spread over the periods that it is used.
Cost	Assets are recorded and maintained at their historical costs.	Except in a few cases, market values are not used for reporting asset values.

Assumptions Made When Communicating Economic Information

Assumption	Definition	Ramification
Economic entity	The financial activities of a business can be accounted for separately from the business's owners.	We do not have to worry that the financial information of the owner is mixed with the financial information of the business.
Monetary unit	The dollar, unadjusted for inflation, is the best means of communicating accounting information in the United States.	All transactions in foreign currencies are converted to dollars.
Time period	Accounting information can be communicated effectively over short periods of time.	Most businesses prepare quarterly and annual financial statements.
Going concern	The company for which we are accounting will continue its operations indefinitely.	If an entity is not selling its assets, then the cost principle is appropriate.

Qualitative Characteristics that Make Accounting Information Useful

Term	Definition	Ramification
Understandability	Accounting information should be comprehensible by those willing to spend a reasonable amount of time studying it.	Users must spend a reasonable amount of time studying accounting information for it to be understandable.
Relevance	Accounting information should have the capacity to affect decisions.	Information should have predictive or feedback value and should be timely.
Reliability	Accounting information should be dependable to represent what it purports to represent.	Information should be free from error, a faithful representation, and neutral.
Comparability	Accounting information should be comparable across different companies.	Entities must disclose the accounting methods that they use so that comparisons across companies can be made.
Consistency	Accounting information should be comparable across different time periods within a company.	An entity should use the same accounting methods year to year and disclose when they change methods.
Materiality	The threshold over which an item could begin to affect decisions.	Small errors, while not condoned, usually do not affect overall decision making.
Conservatism	When uncertainty exists, accounting information should present the least optimistic alternative.	An entity should choose accounting techniques that guard against overstating revenues or assets.

Financial Statements Used to Communicate Economic Information

Statement	Purpose	Structure	Links to Other Statements
Balance sheet	Shows a company's assets, liabilities, and equity at a specific point in time	Assets = Liabilities + Equity	The balance in retained earnings comes from the statement of retained earnings. The balance in cash should agree with the ending cash balance on the statement of cash flows.
Income statement	Shows a company's revenues and expenses over a specific period of time	Revenue − Expenses = Net Income or Net Loss	Net income goes to the statement of retained earnings to compute retained earnings.
Statement of retained earnings	Shows the changes in a company's retained earnings over a specific period of time	Beginning Retained Earnings +/− Net Income/Loss − Dividends = Ending Retained Earnings	Ending retained earnings goes to the balance sheet.
Statement of cash flows	Shows a company's inflows and outflows of cash over a specific period of time	Operating Cash Flows +/− Investing Cash Flows +/− Financing Cash Flows = Net change in cash	The ending cash balance on the statement of cash flows should agree with the balance in cash on the balance sheet.

STUDY TOOLS 1

Chapter review card

- Learning Objective and Key Concept Reviews
- Key Definitions and Formulas

Online (Located at www.cengagebrain.com)

- Flash Cards and Crossword Puzzles
- Games and Quizzes
- E-Lectures
- Homework Assignments (as directed by your instructor)

CONCEPT QUESTIONS

1. (LO1) What is the definition of accounting?
2. (LO1) What is the going concern assumption of accounting and why is it necessary for accounting?
3. (LO1) What is the economic entity assumption of accounting and why is it important?
4. (LO2) What two terms are used to determine and describe the profitability of an entity?
5. (LO2) When are revenues recognized?
6. (LO2) What does the matching principle state about the recording of revenues and expenses?
7. (LO2, 3) How are revenues different from assets?
8. (LO3) What five terms are used to describe the financial position of an entity?
9. (LO2, 3) How are liabilities different from expenses?
10. (LO3) Explain the difference between contributed capital and equity.
11. (LO2, 3) What are the three principles used in recording revenues, expenses, and assets?
12. (LO3) How are assets recorded?
13. (LO4) How are the balance sheet and income statement linked?
14. (LO2, 3, 4, 5) Explain why the different financial statements are used in accounting, and what purpose each statement serves.
15. (LO6) What are the qualitative characteristics of accounting and why are they necessary to accounting information?
16. (LO6) How are relevance and materiality related?
17. (LO7) What is the conceptual framework of accounting and what purpose does it serve?

MULTIPLE CHOICE

1. (LO1) Which of the following is not included in the definition of accounting?
   a. Identifying economic information
   b. Measuring economic information
   c. Developing economic information
   d. Communicating economic information
2. (LO1) Which assumption states that an economic entity will continue its operations indefinitely?
   a. Monetary unit
   b. Time period
   c. Going concern
   d. Economic entity
3. (LO2) Net income is created in a time period when:
   a. assets exceed liabilities.
   b. revenues exceed expenses.
   c. revenues are less than expenses.
   d. liabilities are greater than assets.
4. (LO2) Which financial statement reports revenues and expenses?
   a. Statement of retained earnings
   b. Balance sheet
   c. Statement of cash flows
   d. Income statement

5. (LO2) The revenue recognition principle states that:
   a. assets are recorded and maintained at their historical costs.
   b. revenues are recorded when they are earned.
   c. the dollar, unadjusted for inflation, is the best means of accounting in the U.S.
   d. revenues are recorded when cash is received.
6. (LO2) During the year, Callie's Bagel Shop had revenues of $125,000. Rent expense was $12,000. Salaries expense was $25,000. Short-term investments were $35,000. Other expenses totaled $40,000. What was Callie's net income?
   a. $85,000
   b. $13,000
   c. $48,000
   d. $60,000
7. (LO2) Which of the following accurately describes the matching principle?
   a. Matches assets and liabilities
   b. Matches income and dividends
   c. Matches retained earnings and income
   d. Matches revenues and expenses
8. (LO3) The basic accounting equation states:
   a. assets and liabilities equal equity.
   b. assets equal liabilities plus equity.
   c. liabilities equal equity plus assets.
   d. revenues minus expenses equals net income.
9. (LO3) Which financial statement reports assets, liabilities, and equity?
   a. Statement of cash flows
   b. Balance sheet
   c. Income statement
   d. Statement of retained earnings
10. (LO3) Retained earnings is defined as:
    a. the difference between assets and liabilities.
    b. equity generated from profitable operations and retained in the business.
    c. a decrease in assets resulting from selling a good or providing a service.
    d. equity resulting from contributions from owners.
11. (LO3) As of December 31, Lurie Company has assets of $18,400 and equity of $6,500. What are the liabilities for Lurie Company as of December 31?
    a. $24,900
    b. $11,900
    c. $14,200
    d. $8,600
12. (LO3) Maker's Company had the following account totals: cash $25,000; inventory $15,000; accounts payable $15,000; retained earnings $25,000; equipment $80,000; investments $10,000; and other assets $40,000. What is Maker's total assets?
    a. $170,000
    b. $190,000
    c. $85,000
    d. $210,000
13. (LO4) The statement of retained earnings links which two financial statements?
    a. The income statement and the balance sheet
    b. The balance sheet and the statement of cash flows
    c. The income statement and the statement of cash flows
    d. The statement of retained earnings does not link any statements
14. (LO4) A company begins a period with a $5,000 retained earnings balance. The company generates $12,000 of revenues and $10,000 of expenses during the period and pays $1,000 of dividends. What is the retained earnings balance at the end of the period?
    a. $7,000
    b. $5,000
    c. $6,000
    d. $1,000
15. (LO5) Which of the following is not one of the sections on the statement of cash flows?
    a. Investing activities
    b. Financing activities
    c. Operating activities
    d. Income activities
16. (LO6) Which of the following is not a qualitative characteristic of accounting?
    a. Understandability
    b. Relevance
    c. Pertinence
    d. Consistency

BRIEF EXERCISES

1. Calculate Net Income LO2

Ted's Typing Service generated $4,000 in revenue in the month of January. Salaries were $1,500 for the month, and supplies used were $200. Additionally, Ted's incurred $50 for advertising during the month.

Required
Calculate Ted's net income for the month of January.

2. Calculate Net Income LO2

A manager of a small company has a goal of generating $13,000 in net income. He is confident that his expenses will be approximately $82,500.

Required
Calculate the amount of revenue the manager must generate to reach his goal.

3. Calculate Equity LO3

A company reports assets of $10,000 and liabilities of $6,000.

Required
Calculate the company's equity.
Identify which principle relates to each statement.

4. Identify Accounting Principles LO2, 3

Each of the following statements is an application of the revenue recognition principle, the matching principle, or the cost principle.

1. A company records Equipment for the purchase price of $10,000 although the "suggested retail price" was $13,000.
2. A company receives $2,000 for a service to be performed but records only $1,000 as Service Revenue because it earned only half in the current period.
3. A company pays $6,000 for insurance but uses only $4,000 during the period. Therefore, it records only $4,000 as Insurance Expense.

5. Calculate Retained Earnings LO4

At the beginning of the year, a company has retained earnings of $175,000. During the year, the company generates $110,000 of net income and distributes $10,000 in dividends.

Required

Calculate the company's retained earnings at year end.

6. Calculate Cash Flows LO5

A company starts the year with $175,000 in cash. During the year, the company generates $680,000 from operations, uses $516,000 in investing activities, and uses $98,000 in financing activities.

Required

Calculate the company's cash at year end.

7. Identify Accounting Assumptions and Qualitative Characteristics LO1, 6

Consider the following independent scenarios:

1. Luigi's Pizza has been in business for 25 years. All of its operations are profitable, and the accountants believe that the company will operate into the foreseeable future.
2. A bank used the information presented in Tiger Auto's financial statements to determine if it should extend a $300,000 loan to Tiger. The information in the financial statements made a difference in the bank's lending decision.
3. Jim Furio, manager of Martha's Antiques, does not like to change accounting procedures because it hinders his ability to make year-to-year comparisons.
4. Lynn Hagood, owner of Jonesboro Animal Hospital, informs his accountant that he does not want to review any accounting issue that is smaller than 1% of net income.

Required

Identify the accounting assumption or qualitative characteristic that relates to each scenario.

EXERCISES

8. Principles and Assumptions LO1, 3

The following basic accounting principles and assumptions were discussed in the chapter:

- Economic entity
- Going concern
- Monetary unit
- Cost principle
- Time period

________ 1. Lester Company has a division in Germany. Before preparing the financial statements for the company and the foreign division, Lester translates the financial statements of its Germany division from the euro to U.S. dollars.

________ 2. Matt enters into a partnership to start a bike shop with a friend. Each partner makes an initial cash investment of $8,000. Matt opens a checking account in the name of the company and transfers $8,000 from his personal account into the new account.

________ 3. Dreamland Inc. has always prepared financial statements with a year-end of May 31. However, the company is going to sell stock to the public for the first time and is required by the SEC to give quarterly financial reports.

________ 4. Platt Corp. purchases a fifty acre plot of land to build the world's largest factory. The company recorded the property at the amount of cash given to acquire it.

________ 5. Lockbox Corp. is in its ninetieth year of business. The owner of the company is going to retire in two months and turn the company over to his son.

Required

Fill in the blank with the appropriate principle or assumption.

9. Identify Income Statement Accounts LO2

The following accounts are taken from a company's financial statements:

1. Rent expense
2. Service revenue
3. Dividends
4. Interest revenue
5. Interest expense
6. Accounts receivable

Required

Indicate whether each account is a revenue (R), expense (E), or neither (N).

10. Accounting Terms LO3

Consider the following information:

a. Accounts receivable
b. Salaries payable
c. Office supplies
d. Land
e. Contributed capital
f. Notes payable

Required

Indicate whether each of the above items is an asset (A), a liability (L), or part of equity (E).

11. Accounting Terms LO2, 3

Consider the following information:

Item	Appears On	Classified As
1. Salaries expense	______	______
2. Equipment	______	______
3. Cash	______	______
4. Accounts payable	______	______
5. Buildings	______	______
6. Contributed capital	______	______
7. Retained earnings	______	______
8. Interest revenue	______	______
9. Advertising expense	______	______

Required

Classify each of the items above according to (1) whether it appears on the income statement or balance sheet and (2) whether it is classified as a revenue, expense, asset, liability, or equity.

12. Accounting Terms LO2, 3, 4

The following items were taken from the financial statements of Tiger Inc.:

a. Income tax expense
b. Interest expense
c. Service revenue
d. Accounts receivable
e. Retained earnings
f. Inventory
g. Accounts payable
h. Contributed capital
i. Dividends

Required

Identify whether each item would appear on the balance sheet, the income statement, or the statement of retained earnings.

13. Classify Cash Flows LO5

A company entered into the following cash transactions:

1. Cash paid to suppliers
2. Cash received from issuing new common stock
3. Cash paid to purchase new office furniture
4. Cash paid in dividends to owners
5. Cash received from customers

Required

Indicate the section of the statement of cash flows in which each item would appear: operating activities (O), investing activities (I), or financing activities (F).

14. Accounting Terms LO2, 3, 4, 5

Consider the following information:

a. Revenues during the period
b. Supplies on hand at the end of the year
c. Cash received from borrowings during the year
d. Total liabilities at the end of the period
e. Dividends paid during the year
f. Cash paid for a building
g. Cost of buildings owned at year end

Required

Indicate whether you would find each of the above items on the income statement (IS), the balance sheet (BS), the statement of retained earnings (SRE), or the statement of cash flows (SCF).

15. Financial Statements LO2, 3, 4, 5

Listed below are questions posed by various users of a company's financial statements.

User	Questions	Financial Statement
Stockholder	How did this year's sales figures compare with last year's sales figures?	______
Banker	How much in borrowings does the company currently owe?	______
Supplier	How much does the company owe its suppliers in total?	______
Stockholder	Did the company have any dividends in the prior year?	______
Advertising agent	How much advertising did the company incur in order to generate sales?	______
Banker	What was the company's total interest cost last year?	______

Required

Fill in the blank with the financial statement(s) (income statement, balance sheet, statement of retained earnings, and/or statement of cash flows) the user would most likely use to find this information.

16. Net Income and Retained Earnings LO2, 4

Nova Corporation reports the following as of December 31:

Revenues	$10,000
Beginning retained earnings	20,000
Expenses	8,000
Dividends	1,000

Required
Calculate net income and ending retained earnings for the year ending December 31.

17. Balance Sheet Equation LO3

Consider the following information:

Assets	Liabilities	Equity
50,000	25,000	?
30,000	?	17,000
?	45,000	15,000
68,000	?	13,000
?	14,000	6,000

Required
Use the accounting equation to fill in the missing amounts.

18. Balance Sheet Equation LO3

Consider the following information:

a. Jenkins Company starts the year with $50,000 in assets and $40,000 in liabilities. Net income for the year is $12,500, and no dividends are paid. How much is Jenkins' equity at the end of the year?
b. McCay Inc. doubles the amount of its assets from the beginning to the end of the year. At the end of the year, liabilities are $50,000, and equity is $30,000. What is the amount of McCay's assets at the beginning of the year?
c. During the year the liabilities of Hudson Corp. triple. At the beginning of the year, assets were $40,000, and equity was $20,000. What is the amount of liabilities at the end of the year?

Required
Use the accounting equation to answer each of the independent questions above.

19. Statement of Retained Earnings LO4

War Eagle Company's retained earnings on January 1 is $245,800. The following information is available for the first two months of the year:

	January	February
Revenues	$80,000	$102,000
Expenses	85,000	80,000
Dividends	0	7,000

Required
Prepare a statement of retained earnings for the month ending February 28.

20. Statement of Cash Flows LO5

The following information is for Pasture Corp.:

Cash received from customers	$65,000
Cash received from lenders	20,000
Cash paid to suppliers	20,000
Cash paid for new equipment	50,000
Cash paid for dividends	4,000

Required
Indicate on what section of the statement of cash flows each item would appear and calculate Pasture's net change in cash.

21. Links Between Financial Statements LO2, 3, 4

Below are incomplete financial statements for Sterling Inc.:

Balance Sheet	
Assets	
Cash	$ 8,000
Inventory	22,000
Building	40,000
Total assets	$70,000
Liabilities	
Accounts payable	$7,000
Equity	
Contributed capital	(a)
Retained earnings	(b)
Total liabilities & equity	$70,000

Income Statement	
Service revenue	$90,000
Salaries expense	(c)
Utilities expense	20,000
Net income	$ (d)

Statement of Retained Earnings	
Retained earnings, beginning balance	$20,000
Net income	(e)
Dividends	10,000
Retained earnings, ending balance	$60,000

Required
Calculate the missing amounts.

22. Complete Financial Statements LO2, 3, 4

The following are incomplete financial statements for Mackabee Inc.:

Balance Sheet	
Assets	
Cash	$ 6,000
Inventory	20,000
Building	(a)
Total assets	$64,000
Liabilities	
Accounts payable	$ 7,000
Equity	
Contributed capital	(b)
Retained earnings	(c)
Total liabilities and equity	$64,000

Income Statement	
Service revenue	$120,000
Salaries expense	70,000
Administrative expense	30,000
Net income	$ (d)

Statement of Retained Earnings	
Beginning retained earnings	$20,000
Net income	(e)
Dividends	(f)
Ending retained earnings	$40,000

Required
Calculate the missing amounts.

23. Qualitative Characteristics LO6

The following qualitative characteristics of accounting were discussed in the chapter:

- Consistency
- Understandability
- Conservatism
- Reliability
- Relevance
- Comparability
- Materiality

________ 1. The ability of accounting information to be comprehensible to those who have a reasonable understanding of business and are willing to study the information with reasonable diligence.

________ 2. The capacity to affect business decisions.

________ 3. The dependability of accounting information.

________ 4. The ability to compare and contrast the financial activities of the same company over a period of time.

________ 5. The threshold over which an item begins to affect decision making.

________ 6. The way in which accountants deal with uncertainty.

________ 7. The ability to compare and contrast the financial activities of different companies.

Required
Fill in the blank with the appropriate characteristic.

24. Assumptions and Principles LO1, 2, 3

Harbor Corp. had the following situations during the year:

a. Inventory with a cost of $186,400 is reported at its market value of $235,600.
b. Harbor added four additional weeks to its fiscal year so that it could make its income look stronger. Past years were 52 weeks.
c. Harbor's CEO purchased a yacht for personal use and charged it to the company.
d. Revenues of $25,000 earned in the prior year were recorded in the current year.

Required
In each situation, identify the assumption or principle that has been violated and discuss how Harbor should have handled the situation.

PROBLEMS

25. Prepare Financial Statements LO2, 4

This information relates to York Inc. for the year:

Advertising expense	$ 2,400
Dividends paid	7,000
Rent expense	10,400
Retained earnings, January 1	57,000
Salaries expense	28,000
Service revenue	61,000
Utilities expense	1,800

Required
Prepare an income statement and a statement of retained earnings for the year.

26. Prepare Financial Statements LO2, 3, 4

The following items are available from the records of Honky Tonk Records Inc. at the end of the year:

Accounts payable	$27,000
Accounts receivable	21,000
Advertising expense	6,000
Buildings	76,000
Contributed capital	30,000
Cash	6,320
Notes payable	70,000
Salaries expense	9,500
Service revenue	16,820
Equipment	25,000

Required
Prepare Honky Tonk's income statement and statement of retained earnings for the year and its balance sheet at the end of the year.

27. Identify and Correct Income Statement Errors LO2

Muncie Group was organized on January 1. At the end of the year, the company used a first-year accounting student to prepare the following income statement:

Muncie Group Income Statement December 31	
Income from services	$170,000
Accounts receivable	40,000
Total income	$210,000
Less: Expenses	
Salaries	$ 57,000
Advertising	(14,000)
Dividends	10,000
Utilities	22,000
Total expenses	$ 75,000
Net income	$135,000

Required
List all of the deficiencies that you can identify in this income statement and prepare a proper income statement.

28. Identify and Correct Balance Sheet Errors LO3

Bizilia's Inc. was organized on January 1. At the end of the year, an employee with a mathematics degree prepared the following balance sheet:

Bizilia's Inc. Balance Sheet For the Year Ending December 31	
Resources:	
Cash	$ 30,000
Stuff we can sell	40,000
Land	53,000
Retained earnings	17,000
Grand total	$146,000
Debts:	
Money we owe to vendors	$ 43,000
Contributed capital	63,000
Grand total	$106,000

Required
List all of the deficiencies that you can identify in this balance sheet and prepare a proper balance sheet.

29. Errors in Accounting LO1, 2, 3

The Mock Corporation was formed on January 1. At December 31, William Mock, CEO and sole owner, prepared the company's balance sheet as follows:

Mock Corporation Balance Sheet December 31	
Assets	
Cash	$25,000
Accounts receivable	40,000
Inventory	35,000
Building	20,000
Liabilities and Equity	
Accounts payable	$40,000
Building loan	15,000
Retained earnings	37,000

William is not an accountant by trade, and he believes there may be some mistakes in his balance sheet. He has provided you with the following additional information:

1. The building is William's personal beach house. However, he plans on using it for company retreats and for hosting some large clients. He decided to list the asset and the corresponding liability for this reason.
2. The inventory was originally purchased at $12,000, but due to a recent increase in demand, he believes he could sell it for at least $35,000. He thought that $35,000 would best portray the economic reality of his inventory.
3. William included $5,000 in accounts receivable and retained earnings for a service that he will provide next year. Since he is an honest man and will provide the service, he decided to record the amount in this year's balance sheet.

Required
Comment on what accounting assumptions or principles are violated, briefly describe how each item should be accounted for, and prepare a correct balance sheet.

30. Preparing Financial Statements LO2, 3, 4

On June 1 you begin an ocean tour business for the summer by contributing $600 of contributed capital and borrowing $600 from your parents. With your money, you pay $480 in June to rent a boat and supplies consisting of snorkels, fins, masks, and life-jackets. You also purchase advertising in a local paper for $25 and gasoline for $135. You decide to charge $25 per passenger. At the end of the month of June, you have serviced 240 customers and purchased and used an additional $200 in gasoline. Included in those 240 customers were two neighbors who promised future payment which you have not received (totaling $225). You also pay your parents $5 for monthly interest.

Required
Prepare an income statement and a statement of retained earnings for the month ending June 30 and a balance sheet at June 30.

31. Preparing Financial Statements LO2, 3, 4

During the month of April, you conduct art seminars for children. On April 1, you borrow $500 from your parents, buy $400 of supplies, and pay $50 for advertising on the radio and $25 to rent a room in a local recreation center. You charge $20 per child per seminar. At the end of the month, you have held seminars for 80 children, of which you have received payment for 76. You have $30 of supplies remaining, and you pay your parents $5 for the use of their money during the month.

Required
Prepare an income statement and a statement of retained earnings for the month ending April 30 and a balance sheet at April 30.

CASES

32. Read, Locate, and Compare Financial Statements LO2, 3, 5

Access the financial statements in the 2010 annual report for **CVS Caremark Corp.** by clicking on the *Investors* and *Annual Reports* links at www.cvs.com.

Required

a. For CVS Caremark's current year, identify the amounts reported for net revenues, net earnings, total assets, and cash flows from operating activities. Also, identify the date on which the financial statements are prepared.
b. Locate **Walgreens** financial statements for the same year. Identify the same information as in the previous requirement.
c. Compare Walgreens and CVS Caremark. Identify which company is (1) the largest, (2) the most profitable, and (3) the best able to generate cash from its operations.

33. Ethics in Accounting LO1, 2, 6

As the top accountant at Blaire's Costume Jewelry Company, you discover that net income in each of the previous five years has been overstated due to an error in accounting. After much thought, you decide to approach the company president. His response is, "What the public doesn't know won't hurt them. We'll just adjust this year's income to make up for the mistakes. We had a pretty good year, and I think our income for this year can absorb the errors."

Required
Identify the ethical dilemma of this situation, identify the ways that you could respond, and explain the possible consequences of your responses.

34. Written Communication Skills LO2, 3, 4, 5

Your Uncle Ted just won the lottery. He is trying to find companies in which to invest his winnings. However, he is having trouble reading the financial statements because he has no idea what they are saying. Knowing you are in an accounting class, Uncle Ted asks for your advice.

Required
Prepare a written response to your Uncle Ted explaining what information is contained in each financial statement and how it is relevant to investors.

Corporate Financial Statements

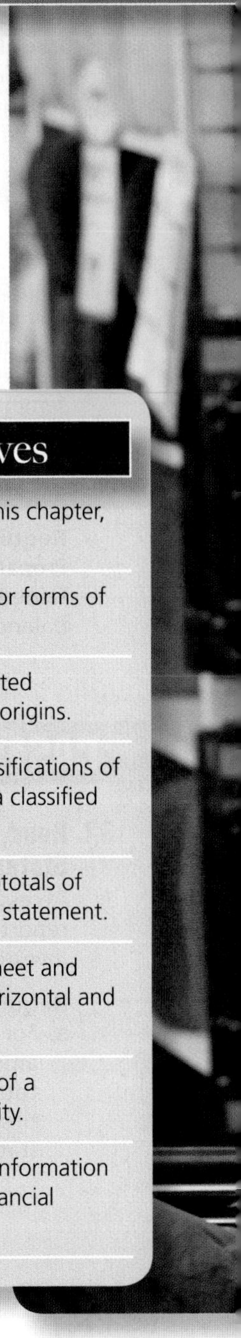

Learning Objectives

After studying the material in this chapter, you should be able to:

LO1 Describe the three major forms of business.

LO2 Define generally accepted accounting principles and their origins.

LO3 Describe the main classifications of assets, liabilities, and equity in a classified balance sheet.

LO4 Describe the main subtotals of income on a multi-step income statement.

LO5 Analyze the balance sheet and the income statement using horizontal and vertical analyses.

LO6 Describe the purpose of a statement of stockholders' equity.

LO7 Describe the types of information usually disclosed along with financial statements.

Introduction

Chapter 1 introduced the terms, assumptions, principles, and statements that accounting uses to capture and communicate a company's economic activities. This chapter takes a more detailed look at the accounting information provided by companies, particularly public corporations such as **Bed Bath & Beyond**. Specifically, the chapter introduces the classified balance sheet, the multi-step income statement, and the statement of stockholders' equity. Each of these three financial statements represents a more detailed version of the balance sheet, the income statement, and the statement of retained earnings covered in Chapter 1. The chapter also introduces two analysis techniques, horizontal and vertical analyses, that are simple but powerful tools for generating a more thorough understanding of a company's balance sheet and income statement. At the end of this chapter, you should be comfortable reading through and using the financial statements of almost any company.

LO1 Business Forms

One of the first decisions that any new business faces is the form that it will take. Businesses have the following three basic options:

- Sole proprietorship
- Partnership
- Corporation

A **sole proprietorship** is a business owned by one person and is the most common type of business in the United States. In a sole proprietorship, the owner maintains complete control of the business, bears all the risk of failure, and reaps all the rewards of success. For

Sole proprietorship A business owned by one person.

Inventory is one of the biggest assets for retailers like Bed Bath & Beyond. Because of its importance, it is reported separately on the company's classified balance sheet.

KEVORK DJANSEZIAN/ASSOCIATED PRESS

accounting purposes, a sole proprietorship is accounted for separately from the proprietor's personal affairs. This is an application of the economic entity assumption. For tax purposes, though, a sole proprietor's business is not separated from the proprietor. The income from the business is reported on Schedule C of the owner's personal tax return.

A **partnership** is a business that is formed when two or more proprietors join together to own a business. Partnerships can be established by either a written or oral agreement and can include any number of partners. Partnerships are formed for various reasons, such as joining proprietors with different skills, combining resources, and spreading the financial risk of the business among several people. Like sole proprietorships, a partnership is considered a

Partnership A business that is formed when two or more proprietors join together to own a business.

One of the first decisions that any new business faces is the form that it will take.

separate accounting entity from the individual partners. Also like sole proprietorships, a partner's share of partnership income is reported on the partner's individual tax return.

A **corporation** is a separate legal entity that is established by filing articles of incorporation in a state, usually with the secretary of state's office. Once a corporation is formed, it sells stock to individuals who want to own part of the corporation. This is one of the main reasons that corporations are formed—the ability to raise capital through the sale of ownership interests. It is also why corporation owners are called stockholders. Like a sole proprietorship and a partnership, a corporation is accounted for separately from its owners. However, it is also taxed separately. Income generated by a corporation is taxed on a corporate tax return, not on the stockholders' individual tax returns.

Corporations can be either private or public. A **public corporation** is one in which ownership is available to the public at large. The stock of a public corporation is usually bought and sold on an open exchange such as the New York Stock Exchange (NYSE) or the National Association of Securities Dealers Automated Quotes (NASDAQ). Such corporations are said to be *publicly traded*. Examples of publicly traded corporations are **Microsoft**, **Kellogg**, and **Bed Bath & Beyond**. From this point forward, this text will focus on the accounting for publicly traded corporations. This will allow you to see accounting issues in companies with which you may be familiar.

Corporation A separate legal entity that is established by filing articles of incorporation in a state.

Public corporation A separate legal entity in which ownership is available to the public at large.

Generally accepted accounting principles The accounting standards, rules, principles, and procedures that comprise authoritative practice for financial accounting.

Securities and Exchange Commission The federal agency charged to protect investors and maintain the integrity of securities markets.

LO2 Generally Accepted Accounting Principles

When accounting for their economic activities, public corporations must follow *generally accepted accounting principles*. **Generally accepted accounting principles (GAAP)** are the accounting standards, rules, principles, and procedures that comprise authoritative practice for financial accounting. These principles have been developed over time by several regulatory bodies, the most significant of which are listed as follows.

- Securities and Exchange Commission
- Financial Accounting Standards Board
- American Institute of Certified Public Accountants

The **Securities and Exchange Commission (SEC)** is the federal agency charged to protect investors and maintain the integrity of securities markets. Established by Congress after the 1929 stock market crash, the SEC was given the authority to determine the rules by which publicly traded companies would disclose information to their owners. However, instead of writing all of the rules itself, the SEC delegated much of its accounting

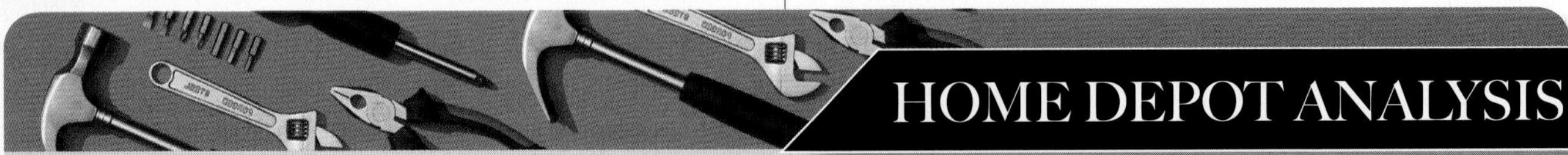

HOME DEPOT ANALYSIS

Look at the full company name at the top of any of **Home Depot's** financial statements in Appendix C. Can you tell from the name what form of business the company uses?

The full company name is "The Home Depot, Inc. and Subsidiaries." Inc. stands for incorporated. Thus, Home Depot is a corporation.

rule-making authority to the accounting profession. Today, the accounting organization that sets major accounting standards in the United States is the Financial Accounting Standards Board.

The **Financial Accounting Standards Board (FASB)** is a standard-setting body whose mission is "to establish and improve standards of financial accounting and reporting for the guidance and education of the public, including issuers, auditors, and users of financial information." The FASB usually tackles large issues, such as the accounting for pensions, leases, stock options, and derivatives. It also maintains the conceptual framework discussed in Chapter 1. The Board consists of seven full-time voting members who oversee a standard-setting process of research, deliberation, public input, and board approval. Once the FASB establishes a rule or standard, it is then enforced by the SEC.

While the FASB is accounting's main standard-setting body, the **American Institute of Certified Public Accountants (AICPA)** also plays a role in establishing accounting rules. The AICPA, which is the professional organization of certified public accountants, maintains a board that establishes rules that are often more technical and more specific to certain industries. For example, the AICPA has issued rules for determining profits in the film industry. The rules set by the AICPA are also enforced by the SEC.

Each of these organizations are based in the United States. However, accounting is practiced throughout the world, and there is a movement to develop one set of international accounting standards to be used by all countries. The **International Accounting Standards Board (IASB)** is a board, similar to the FASB, whose mission is to develop a single set of high-quality standards requiring transparent and comparable information. Those standards, which have both similarities to and differences from GAAP, are called **International Financial Reporting Standards (IFRS)**. Because adoption of IFRS is voluntary, the effectiveness of the IASB at accomplishing its mission has been somewhat limited. However, the IASB and the FASB have both agreed to a commitment to the convergence of U.S. and international standards. At some time in the future, the world may very well use one set of global accounting standards set by a global board. But for now, public companies traded on U.S. exchanges must use generally accepted accounting principles.

IFRS

*The accounting organization that **sets major accounting standards** in the United States is the Financial Accounting Standards Board. International standards are set by the International Accounting Standards Board.*

Financial Accounting Standards Board The standard-setting body whose mission is "to establish and improve standards of financial accounting and reporting for the guidance and education of the public, including issuers, auditors, and users of financial information."

American Institute of Certified Public Accountants The professional organization of certified public accountants whose board establishes rules that are often more technical and more specific to certain industries.

International Accounting Standards Board A board, similar to the FASB, whose mission is to develop a single set of high-quality standards requiring transparent and comparable information.

International Financial Reporting Standards Standards issued by the International Accounting Standards Board.

HOME DEPOT ANALYSIS

Look in Appendix C at the Report of Independent Registered Public Accounting Firm in which the accounting firm is describing its audit of **Home Depot's** financial statements. According to the auditor, are Home Depot's financial statements prepared in accordance with GAAP?

Yes. As the Report states, the financial information is presented "in conformity with U.S. generally accepted accounting principles."

LO3 The Classified Balance Sheet

Chapter 1 introduced the balance sheet. A balance sheet is a financial statement that summarizes a company's assets, liabilities, and equity at a given point in time. The balance sheet shown in Chapter 1 reported every account of the company. However, most public corporations are much too large to report every account, so they prepare a classified balance sheet instead. A **classified balance sheet** groups together accounts of similar nature and reports them in a few major classifications.

The following sections discuss the various asset, liability, and equity classifications commonly used on classified balance sheets. The February 26, 2011, classified balance sheet of **Bed Bath & Beyond** in Exhibit 2-1 will be used as an illustration. As you review the statement, note that all numbers except per share data are in thousands, meaning that each reported number has three 0's missing. Note also that two years of data are presented, with the most recent year listed first. This is the normal format for most corporate balance sheets. It is also why such statements are often called *comparative* balance sheets.

Assets

An asset is a resource of a business. Assets are generally grouped into five main categories on a classified balance sheet:

- Current assets
- Long-term investments
- Fixed assets
- Intangible assets
- Other assets

Classified balance sheet A type of balance sheet that groups together accounts of similar nature and reports them in a few major classifications.

Current asset Any asset that is reasonably expected to be converted to cash or consumed within one year of the balance sheet date.

Long-term investments The investments in the common stock or debt of another entity that will not be sold within a year.

Fixed assets The tangible resources that are used in a company's operations for more than one year and are not intended for resale.

IFRS

SEC rules require balance sheet subtotals for both current assets and current liabilities. International standards do not explicitly require such subtotals.

Current Assets A **current asset** is any asset that is reasonably expected to be converted to cash or consumed within one year of the balance sheet date. Common examples include cash, investments that will mature or be sold within a year, accounts receivable from customers, inventories, and other assets such as prepaid insurance. Current assets are listed in order of their liquidity, which refers to the speed with which a resource can be converted to cash. Cash is listed first, followed by short-term investments, receivables, inventories, and then finally other current assets.

Bed Bath & Beyond reports four current assets totaling over $4 billion on its February 26, 2011, balance sheet. As you might expect from a retailer, the vast majority of those assets (over $1.9 billion) is in *Merchandise inventories,* with a substantial amount also in *Cash and cash equivalents.* The company also reports some *Short-term investment securities* and *Other current assets.*

Long-Term Investments **Long-term investments** are a company's investments in the common stock or debt of another entity that will not be sold within a year. Companies typically list any long-term investments as their first noncurrent asset. Bed Bath & Beyond reports $121 million in *Long-term investment securities.*

Fixed Assets **Fixed assets** are the tangible resources that are used in a company's operations for more than one year and are not intended for resale. Examples include land, buildings, equipment, furniture, and fixtures.

Bed Bath & Beyond reports over $1.1 billion of fixed assets on its February 26, 2011, balance sheet, making them one of the company's largest assets, which makes sense for a retailer. Note, however, that the company uses the term *Property and equipment, net* rather than fixed assets. This is a common name for fixed assets. Note also the word "net" in the description. Most fixed assets are subject to depreciation, which is the process of expensing the cost of an asset over its useful life. Therefore, fixed assets are reported "net" of any depreciation to date. Chapter 8 will discuss depreciation in much more detail.

Exhibit 2-1 Bed Bath & Beyond Classified Balance Sheet

Bed Bath & Beyond Inc. and Subsidiaries
Consolidated Balance Sheets
(in thousands, except per share data)

	February 26, 2011	February 27, 2010
Assets		
Current assets:		
Cash and cash equivalents	$ 1,183,587	$ 1,096,100
Short-term investment securities	605,608	431,476
Merchandise inventories	1,968,907	1,759,703
Other current assets	315,736	276,066
Total current assets	4,073,838	3,563,345
Long-term investment securities	121,446	132,860
Property and equipment, net	1,116,297	1,119,292
Other assets	334,612	336,633
Total assets	$ 5,646,193	$ 5,152,130
Liabilities and Shareholders' Equity		
Current liabilities:		
Accounts payable	$ 709,550	$ 611,163
Accrued expenses and other current liabilities	306,847	281,730
Merchandise credit and gift card liabilities	193,061	172,804
Current income taxes payable	112,982	83,857
Total current liabilities	1,322,440	1,149,554
Deferred rent and other liabilities	292,364	246,273
Income taxes payable	99,730	103,399
Total liabilities	1,714,534	1,499,226
Shareholders' equity:		
Preferred stock—$0.01 par value; authorized 1,000 shares; no shares issued or outstanding	—	—
Common stock—$0.01 par value; authorized 900,000 shares; issued 314,678 and 312,229 shares, respectively;	3,253	3,206
Additional paid-in capital	1,191,123	1,020,515
Retained earnings	5,546,287	4,754,954
Treasury stock, at cost	(2,814,104)	(2,126,499)
Accumulated other comprehensive loss	5,100	728
Total shareholders' equity	3,931,659	3,652,904
Total liabilities and shareholders' equity	$ 5,646,193	$ 5,152,130

Intangible Assets An **intangible asset** is a resource that is used in operations for more than one year, is not intended for resale, and has no physical substance. Examples include trademarks, patents, franchise rights, copyrights, and goodwill. Like fixed assets, intangible assets are subject to depreciation (although it is actually called amortization instead of depreciation) and are reported net of amortization to date. **Bed Bath & Beyond** does not separately report any intangible assets.

Other Assets **Other assets** are those resources that do not fit well into one of the other classifications. The classification can also include those assets that are small enough that they do not warrant separate reporting. Bed Bath & Beyond reports over $334 million in *Other assets*. According to additional information provided by the company, the balance includes the company's intangible assets.

Liabilities

A liability is an obligation of a business. Liabilities are generally classified into two main categories on a classified balance sheet:

- Current liabilities
- Long-term liabilities

Intangible asset A resource that is used in operation for more than one year, is not intended for resale, and has no physical substance.

Other assets Resources that do not fit well into one of the other asset classifications or are small enough that they do not warrant separate reporting.

Current Liabilities A **current liability** is an obligation that is reasonably expected to be satisfied within one year. Examples include accounts payable to vendors, salaries payable to employees, and taxes payable to taxing authorities. Even long-term debt, if maturing within one year, is classified as a current liability.

Bed Bath & Beyond reports four current liabilities totaling over $1.3 billion on its February 26, 2011, balance sheet. The largest is over $709 million in *Accounts payable,* which is the amount owed to suppliers. Over $306 million is listed in *Accrued expenses and other current liabilities,* which likely represents obligations relating to employees, advertising, or other operating matters. Also, over $193 million is reported in *Merchandise credit and gift card liabilities.* This represents the value of unredeemed gift cards and other credits. Finally, the company reports almost $113 million of *Current income taxes payable,* which is the amount owed to taxing authorities based on the income earned previously.

Long-Term Liabilities A **long-term liability** is an obligation that is not expected to be satisfied within one year. Examples include notes payable, mortgage payable, and bonds payable. Bed Bath & Beyond has very few long-term liabilities at February 26, 2011. It reports $292 million in *Deferred rent and other liabilities* and over $99 million in *Income taxes payable.*

Equity

Equity is the difference between a company's assets and its liabilities. It is generated from the following two sources:

- Retained earnings
- Contributed capital

Current liability An obligation that is reasonably expected to be satisfied within one year.

Long-term liability An obligation that is not expected to be satisfied within one year.

Retained earnings The amount of equity a company generates by being profitable and retaining those profits in the business.

Contributed capital The amount of equity a company generates through the sale of stock to investors.

Single-step income statement Calculates total revenues and total expenses and then determines net income in one step by subtracting total expenses from total revenues.

Multi-step income statement Calculates income by grouping certain revenues and expenses together and calculating several subtotals of income.

Retained earnings is the amount of equity a company generates by being profitable and retaining those profits in the business. **Contributed capital** is the amount of equity a company generates through the sale of stock to investors. Such equity is often referred to as capital stock. Examples of capital stock include common stock and preferred stock.

Like most publicly traded companies, Bed Bath & Beyond reports its equity accounts in one general section called *Shareholders' equity*. The company reports five balances, the largest of which is $5.5 billion in *Retained earnings*. Such a large balance indicates a very strong record of generating profits in previous years. The other two large balances are *Additional paid-in capital* (over $1.1 billion) and *Treasury stock* (over $2.8 billion). The Additional paid-in capital account represents capital that the company has received through the sale of stock to investors and owners. The Treasury stock account represents capital that the company has paid to owners to buy back the company's stock. Together, these accounts show than Bed Bath & Beyond has paid out more capital than it has received. A more in-depth analysis of treasury stock and equity in general will be left for Chapter 10.

LO4 The Multi-Step Income Statement

Chapter 1 also introduced the income statement. The income statement is a financial statement that summarizes a company's revenues and expenses over a period of time. Companies generally use one of two forms for their income statements—a single-step statement or a multi-step statement.

A **single-step income statement** calculates total revenues and total expenses and then determines net income in one step by subtracting total expenses from total revenues. The income statement prepared in Chapter 1 was a single-step income statement. The major advantage of a single-step statement is its simplicity. However, the disadvantage is that it does not present the information in a manner that is very useful. As a result, most companies prepare multi-step income statements.

A **multi-step income statement** calculates income by grouping certain revenues and expenses together and calculating several subtotals of income. These subtotals provide information on the profitability of various aspects of the company's operations. While most companies prepare multi-step statements, there is some variation in how they are prepared. However, most include either some or all of the following four subtotals of income.

- **Gross profit**
- **Operating profit**
- **Income before taxes**
- **Net income**

The following sections discuss these subtotals that are commonly used by companies. For illustration purposes, Exhibit 2-2 contains **Bed Bath & Beyond's** income statement for the fiscal year ended February 26, 2011. Note that the company uses the title, *Consolidated Statements of Earnings,* rather than income statement. Note also that like the balance sheet, the numbers are in thousands. However, unlike the balance sheet, the income statement reports three years of data. The presentation of multiple years of data therefore yields comparative income statements.

Gross Profit

For a retailer like Bed Bath & Beyond, the first line item of a multi-step statement is the revenue generated from sales. **Sales**, which is often labeled net sales, is the resources that a company generates during a period from selling its inventory. Listed next is cost of sales. **Cost of sales**, which is sometimes called cost of goods sold, represents the cost of the inventory that was sold during a period. Subtracting cost of sales from net sales then yields the first subtotal of income, gross profit. **Gross profit**, which is sometimes called gross margin, represents the profit that a company generates when considering only the sales price and the cost of the product sold. It therefore represents the gross dollar markup that a company is able to achieve when selling its inventory. Note that unlike a retailer, a service company will not report gross profit as a subtotal of income.

For the fiscal period ended February 26, 2011, Bed Bath & Beyond generated over $8.7 billion in *Net sales*. With *Cost of sales* of over $5.1 billion, the company generated a *Gross profit* of over $3.6 billion for the year. Note that with a profit of $3.6 billion on inventory costing $5.1 billion, the average markup on inventory was around 70% of its cost ($3.6 ÷ $5.1). That is, on average, an inventory item costing the company $100 sold for $170.

Operating Profit

After gross profit is reported, operating expenses are listed. **Operating expenses** are the expenses that a company incurs during normal operations. Such expenses are recurring, meaning that they are incurred year after year as the company runs its business. Examples include advertising, salaries, utilities, depreciation, and insurance.

In most multi-step statements, operating expenses are summed together and subtracted from gross profit to yield the second subtotal of income, operating profit.

Sales The resources that a company generates during a period from selling its inventory.

Cost of sales The cost of the inventory sold during a period.

Gross profit The profit that a company generates when considering only the sales price and the cost of the product sold.

Operating expenses Recurring expenses that a company incurs during normal operations.

Exhibit 2-2 Bed Bath & Beyond Multi-step Income Statement

Bed Bath & Beyond Inc. and Subsidiaries
Consolidated Statements of Earnings
(in thousands)

	FISCAL YEAR ENDED		
	February 26, 2011	**February 27, 2010**	**February 28, 2009**
Net sales	**$8,758,503**	$7,828,793	$7,208,340
Cost of sales	**5,135,574**	4,620,674	4,335,104
Gross profit	**3,622,929**	3,208,119	2,873,236
Selling, general and administrative expenses	**2,334,471**	2,227,432	2,199,340
Operating profit	**1,288,458**	980,687	673,896
Interest income	**4,520**	4,568	9,412
Earnings before provision for income taxes	**1,292,978**	985,255	683,308
Provision for income taxes	**501,645**	385,222	258,185
Net earnings	**$ 791,333**	$ 600,033	$ 425,123

Albert Lozano/iStockphoto.com

Operating profit represents the profit that a company generates when considering both the cost of the inventory and the normal expenses incurred to operate the business. Other names for operating profit include income from operations or operating income.

Bed Bath & Beyond reports over $2.3 billion of operating expenses in one expense line labeled *Selling, general and administrative expenses.* This is a common description for general operating expenses. Subtracting these operating expenses from gross profit yields an *Operating profit* of over $1.2 billion. So, after considering its two major expenses—cost of inventory and operating expenses—Bed Bath & Beyond's $8.7 billion in sales yielded about $1.3 billion in profits.

Operating profit The profit that a company generates when considering both the cost of the inventory and the normal expenses incurred to operate the business.

Other revenue and expenses Revenues and expenses generated outside of normal operations.

Income before taxes The profit that a company generates when considering all revenues and expenses except for income taxes.

Provision for income taxes The amount of income tax expense for a given period.

Just like individuals do, corporations must pay taxes on their incomes.

Income Before Taxes

In addition to cost of sales and operating expenses, companies sometimes generate revenues and expenses that are outside of their normal operations. Common examples include interest revenue and interest expense. Such items are listed separately as **other revenues and expenses** and are netted against operating profit to yield the third subtotal of income, income before taxes. **Income before taxes,** also called earnings before income taxes and other similar titles, represents the profit that a company generates when considering all revenues and expenses except for income taxes.

After reporting its operating profit, Bed Bath & Beyond reports *Interest income* of over $4 million. This $4 million, which likely represents the revenues generated from the company's investment portfolios, is added to operating profit to yield *Earnings before provision for income taxes* of $1.3 billion.

Net Income

Like individuals, corporations must pay taxes on their incomes. Usually, the amount of tax in a given period is listed separately on a multi-step statement as provision for income taxes. **Provision for income taxes** is the amount of income tax expense for a given period. When this provision is subtracted from income before taxes,

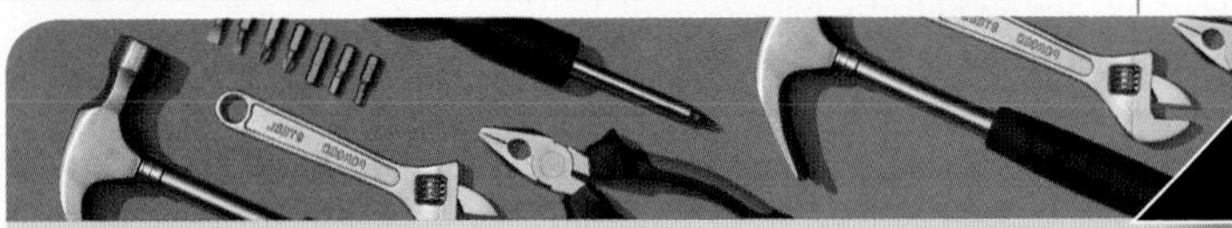

HOME DEPOT ANALYSIS

Look at **Home Depot's** income statement in Appendix C. What form of income statement does the company use?

The company uses a multi-step income statement. It shows several subtotals of income, including Gross Profit, Operating Income, Earnings From Continuing Operations Before Provision for Income Taxes, Earnings From Continuing Operations, and Net Earnings.

IFRS

Under US GAAP, an unusual and infrequent expense can be reported on the income statement as an extraordinary item. Under IFRS, extraordinary items are prohibited from the income statement.

the final income measure, **net income**, is determined. **Bed Bath & Beyond** reports a $501 million *Provision for income taxes.* Subtracting that from income before taxes yields *Net earnings* of approximately $791 million.

In summary, Bed Bath & Beyond's multi-step income statement provides a picture of how the company generated its profits in the last period. It generated $3.6 billion in profits due to its inventory markups. Once it subtracted its operating expenses, it had profits of $1.3 billion remaining. After considering other revenues and taxes, $791 million of profits remained from the original sales of $8.7 billion.

LO5 Horizontal and Vertical Analyses

The previous sections demonstrate that financial statements communicate economic information about a company to interested parties. For example, investors and creditors learn from Bed Bath & Beyond's income statement that the company earned $791 million of income in the most recent year. This is useful information because it demonstrates that the company was profitable during the year. However, the information can be even more useful if it is compared to something else. For example, is $791 million better or worse than last year? Is it high enough given sales for the period? How does it compare to competitors? Such comparisons provide the necessary context for a more thorough understanding of a company's financial activities. Such context can be easily generated through two techniques called horizontal and vertical analyses.

Horizontal Analysis

Horizontal analysis is a method of analyzing a company's account balances over time. It is normally conducted on both the balance sheet and the income statement. The analysis calculates both the dollar and percentage change in each account balance on a financial statement. As a result, it is very useful in identifying promising or troubling trends in a company. The analysis is called "horizontal" because the calculation compares an account's balance across the columns of yearly data—that is, horizontally across the financial statement.

Horizontal analysis is calculated as follows. First, the dollar change in an account is determined. This is defined as the current-year balance less the prior-year balance. The dollar change is then divided by the prior-year balance to yield a percentage change. These two calculations are shown below.

$$\text{Dollar change in account balance} = \text{Current-year balance} - \text{Prior-year balance}$$

$$\text{Percentage change in account balance} = \frac{\text{Dollar change}}{\text{Prior-year balance}}$$

To illustrate, consider the *Merchandise inventories* balance from Bed Bath & Beyond's balance sheet in Exhibit 2-1:

	February 26, 2011	February 27, 2010
Merchandise inventories	$1,968,907	$1,759,703

The company's inventory increased $209,204 from February 27, 2010, to February 26, 2011. Dividing that increase by the February 27, 2010, balance yields a percentage change of 11.9%. These calculations are shown in the following table. Also shown are similar calculations for a horizontal analysis of *Net earnings* from the company's income statement in Exhibit 2-2.

	Inventories	*Net earnings*
Current-year balance	$1,968,907	$791,333
− Prior-year balance	− $1,759,703	− $600,033
Dollar change	$ 209,204	$191,300
Dollar change / Prior-year balance	$209,204 / $1,759,703	$191,300 / $600,033
= Percentage change	= 11.9%	= 31.9%

Net income The final income measure after the provision for income taxes is subtracted from income before taxes.

Horizontal analysis A method of analyzing a company's account balances over time by calculating dollar and percentage changes in each account.

For a full horizontal analysis, both dollar and percentage changes are calculated for each account on both the balance sheet and the income statement. Exhibit 2-3 contains a horizontal analysis of **Bed Bath & Beyond's** balance sheet and income statement. The column headings show the general calculations, with CY and PY representing current year and prior year, respectively.

An examination of the balance sheet shows overall growth. *Total assets* in the most recent year were $494,063, or 9.6%, higher than the prior year. All of this growth was generated in current assets, with the largest

Exhibit 2-3 Horizontal Analysis of Bed Bath & Beyond's Balance Sheet and Income Statement

	CY	PY	(CY – PY)	(CY – PY) / PY
Balance Sheet	**Feb 26, 2011**	**Feb 27, 2010**	**$ Change**	**% Change**
Assets				
Current assets:				
Cash and cash equivalents	$1,183,587	$1,096,100	$ 87,487	8.0%
Short-term investment securities	605,608	431,476	174,132	40.4%
Merchandise inventories	1,968,907	1,759,703	209,204	11.9%
Other current assets	315,736	276,066	39,670	14.4%
Total current assets	4,073,838	3,563,345	510,493	14.3%
Long-term investment securities	121,446	132,860	(11,414)	(8.6%)
Property and equipment, net	1,116,297	1,119,292	(2,995)	(0.3%)
Other assets	334,612	336,633	(2,021)	(0.6%)
Total assets	$5,646,193	$5,152,130	$494,063	9.6%
Liabilities and Shareholders' Equity				
Current liabilities:				
Accounts payable	$ 709,550	$ 611,163	$ 98,387	16.1%
Accrued expenses and other current liabilities	306,847	281,730	25,117	8.9%
Merchandise credit and gift card liabilities	193,061	172,804	20,257	11.7%
Current income taxes payable	112,982	83,857	29,125	34.7%
Total current liabilities	1,322,440	1,149,554	172,886	15.0%
Deferred rent and other liabilities	292,364	246,273	46,091	18.7%
Income taxes payable	99,730	103,399	(3,669)	(3.5%)
Total liabilities	1,714,534	1,499,226	$215,308	14.4%
Shareholders' equity:				
Common stock	3,253	3,206	47	1.5%
Additional paid-in capital	1,191,123	1,020,515	170,608	16.7%
Retained earnings	5,546,287	4,754,954	791,333	16.6%
Treasury stock, at cost	(2,814,104)	(2,126,499)	(687,605)	32.3%
Accumulated other comprehensive loss	5,100	728	4,372	600.5%
Total shareholders' equity	3,931,659	3,652,904	278,755	7.6%
Total liabilities and shareholders' equity	$5,646,193	$5,152,130	$494,063	9.6%

Income Statement	**Feb 26, 2011**	**Feb 27, 2010**	**$ Change**	**% Change**
Net sales	$8,758,503	$7,828,793	$929,710	11.9%
Cost of sales	5,135,574	4,620,674	514,900	11.1%
Gross profit	3,622,929	3,208,119	414,810	12.9%
Selling, general and administrative expenses	2,334,471	2,227,432	107,039	4.8%
Operating profit	1,288,458	980,687	307,771	31.4%
Interest income	4,520	4,568	(48)	(1.1%)
Earnings before provision for income taxes	1,292,978	985,255	307,723	31.2%
Provision for income taxes	501,645	385,222	116,423	30.2%
Net earnings	$ 791,333	$ 600,033	$191,300	31.9%

Common-size statements allow investors and creditors to compare companies of vastly different sizes.

dollar increases in *Short-term investment securities* and *Merchandise inventories*. Overall, the growth in assets was generated through additional liabilities and additional equity. *Total liabilities* increased $215,308, or 14.4%, while *Total shareholders' equity* increased $278,755, or 7.6%. Note that the largest dollar increase in either liabilities or equity was the $791,333 increase to *Retained earnings*. This indicates significant profitability and is a sign of a strong balance sheet.

An examination of the income statement also shows growth. *Net sales* were 11.9% higher than the prior year. With *Cost of sales* increasing slightly less at 11.1%, *Gross profit* was 12.9% higher than the prior year. Moreover, *Selling, general and administrative expenses* increased only 4.8% during the year. This resulted in a $191,300, or 31.9%, increase in *Net earnings* for the year.

In summary, horizontal analysis of the balance sheet and income statement shows that **Bed Bath & Beyond** is a company that is growing and becoming more profitable over time. Horizontal analysis has provided the context for a more thorough understanding of the financial statements.

Vertical Analysis

Vertical analysis is a method of comparing a company's account balances within one year. It also is normally conducted on both the balance sheet and the income statement. The analysis is calculated by dividing each account balance by a base account, yielding a percentage. The base account is total assets for balance sheet accounts and net sales or revenues for income statement accounts. These two calculations are shown below.

	For the Balance Sheet	For the Income Statement
Percentage	Account balance / Total assets	Account balance / Net sales or Revenue

The product of a vertical analysis is sometimes called a common-size financial statement. A **common-size financial statement** is a statement in which all accounts have been standardized by the overall size of the company. Common-size statements are very useful because they allow investors and creditors to determine the importance of each account to the overall company and to compare that importance to other companies, even those of vastly different sizes.

To illustrate, consider again the *Merchandise inventories* balance from Bed Bath & Beyond's balance sheet in Exhibit 2-1 (see page 29). Also shown are the company's *Total assets*.

	February 26, 2011	February 27, 2010
Merchandise inventories	$1,968,907	$1,759,703
Total assets	$5,646,193	$5,152,130

A vertical analysis divides each inventory balance by total assets for that year. These calculations are shown in the following table. Also shown are similar calculations that would be made for a vertical analysis of *Net earnings* from the company's income statement in Exhibit 2-2. The only difference is that *Net earnings* is divided by *Net sales*, not *Total assets*.

	Current Year	*Prior Year*
Merchandise inventories	$1,968,907	$1,759,703
Total assets	$5,646,193	$5,152,130
= Percentage of total assets	= 34.9%	= 34.2%
Net earnings	$791,333	$600,033
Net sales	$8,758,503	$7,828,793
= Percentage of net sales	= 9.0%	= 7.7%

For a full vertical analysis, percentages are calculated for every account on each financial statement.

Vertical analysis A method of comparing a company's account balances within one year by dividing each account balance by a base amount to yield a percentage.

Common-size financial statement A statement in which all accounts have been standardized by the overall size of the company.

Exhibit 2-4 contains a vertical analysis of **Bed Bath & Beyond's** balance sheet and income statement. The column headings show the general calculations, with CY and PY representing current year and prior year, respectively.

An examination of the balance sheet shows that the bulk of Bed Bath & Beyond's assets are held in *Merchandise inventories*, *Cash and cash equivalents*, and *Property and equipment*. Together, these three assets make up over 75% of the company's total assets, which makes sense for a retailer like Bed Bath & Beyond. It also shows that the company generated about 30% of its assets through liabilities and about 70% through equity. This shows a relatively low-risk balance sheet.

An examination of the income statement shows that *Cost of sales* was 58.6% of *Net sales* and *Selling*,

Exhibit 2-4 Vertical Analysis of Bed Bath & Beyond's Balance Sheet and Income Statement

Balance Sheet	CY Feb 26, 2011	CY / CY Total Assets	PY Feb 27, 2010	PY / PY Total Assets
Assets				
Current assets:				
Cash and cash equivalents	$1,183,587	21.0%	$1,096,100	21.3%
Short-term investment securities	605,608	10.7%	431,476	8.4%
Merchandise inventories	1,968,907	34.9%	1,759,703	34.2%
Other current assets	315,736	5.6%	276,066	5.4%
Total current assets	4,073,838	72.2%	3,563,345	69.2%
Long-term investment securities	121,446	2.2%	132,860	2.6%
Property and equipment, net	1,116,297	19.8%	1,119,292	21.7%
Other assets	334,612	5.9%	336,633	6.5%
Total assets	$5,646,193	100.0%	$5,152,130	100.0%
Liabilities and Shareholders' Equity				
Current liabilities:				
Accounts payable	$ 709,550	12.6%	$ 611,163	11.9%
Accrued expenses and other current liabilities	306,847	5.4%	281,730	5.5%
Merchandise credit and gift card liabilities	193,061	3.4%	172,804	3.4%
Current income taxes payable	112,982	2.0%	83,857	1.6%
Total current liabilities	1,322,440	23.4%	1,149,554	22.3%
Deferred rent and other liabilities	292,364	5.2%	246,273	4.8%
Income taxes payable	99,730	1.8%	103,399	2.0%
Total liabilities	1,714,534	30.4%	1,499,226	29.1%
Shareholders' equity:				
Common stock	3,253	0.1%	3,206	0.1%
Additional paid-in capital	1,191,123	21.1%	1,020,515	19.8%
Retained earnings	5,546,287	98.2%	4,754,954	92.3%
Treasury stock, at cost	(2,814,104)	(49.8%)	(2,126,499)	(41.3%)
Accumulated other comprehensive loss	5,100	0.1%	728	0.0%
Total shareholders' equity	3,931,659	69.6%	3,652,904	70.9%
Total liabilities and shareholders' equity	$5,646,193	100.0%	$5,152,130	100.0%

Income Statement	Feb 26, 2011	CY / CY Net Sales	Feb 27, 2010	PY / PY Net Sales
Net sales	$8,758,503	100.0%	$7,828,793	100.0%
Cost of sales	5,135,574	58.6%	4,620,674	59.0%
Gross profit	3,622,929	41.4%	3,208,119	41.0%
Selling, general and administrative expenses	2,334,471	26.7%	2,227,432	28.5%
Operating profit	1,288,458	14.7%	980,687	12.5%
Interest income	4,520	0.1%	4,568	0.1%
Earnings before provision for income taxes	1,292,978	14.8%	985,255	12.6%
Provision for income taxes	501,645	5.7%	385,222	4.9%
Net earnings	$ 791,333	9.0%	$ 600,033	7.7%

MAKING IT REAL

A company's balance sheet often reflects its business model, and a vertical analysis can help you identify one model from another. For example, take the following vertical analyses of selected assets from the 2010 balance sheets of two well-known retailers—**Amazon** and **Wal-Mart**. Can you tell which company is which?

	Company A	Company B
Cash and cash equivalents	20.0%	4.6%
Accounts receivable	8.4%	2.4%
Inventories	17.0%	19.4%
Fixed assets, net	12.8%	58.3%

Both Amazon and Wal-Mart are in the business of selling inventory, but their models are different. Wal-Mart is a traditional "bricks and mortar" company that sells its inventory in stores, while Amazon is a dot com company that sells its inventory online. Therefore, Wal-Mart should have a greater percentage of its total assets in fixed assets. Company B has 58.3% of its assets in fixed assets. Therefore, Company B is Wal-Mart.

AP Photo/Paul Sakuma

general and administrative expenses were 26.7%. Taken together, these two major expense categories consumed over 85% of the company's sales revenues. After taxes, the result was that *Net earnings* were 9% of *Net sales*. This means that the company earned 9 cents of profit for every dollar of sales. Note that this percentage is higher than the 7.7% achieved in the prior year. As seen in the horizontal analysis, **Bed Bath & Beyond** is not only profitable, but its profitability is increasing.

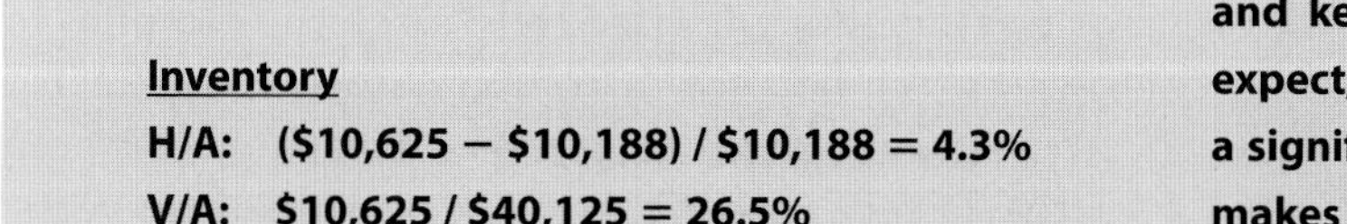

HOME DEPOT ANALYSIS

Conduct and interpret horizontal and vertical analyses of **Home Depot's** inventory and cost of sales found in Appendix C.

Inventory
H/A: ($10,625 − $10,188) / $10,188 = 4.3%
V/A: $10,625 / $40,125 = 26.5%
Cost of Sales
H/A: ($44,693 − $43,764) / $43,764 = 2.1%
V/A: $44,693 / $67,997 = 65.7%

The horizontal analyses indicate that both inventory and cost of sales increased during the year. This reveals that the company is growing. It is selling more and keeping more inventory on hand. As you might expect, the vertical analyses indicate that inventory is a significant part of the company's business. Inventory makes up over one-fourth of total assets. Moreover, for every dollar of sales, the company spends almost 66 cents on the merchandise sold. This leaves only 34 cents to cover all other expenses and generate a profit.

The statement of retained earnings links a company's income statement and balance sheet.

LO6 The Statement of Stockholders' Equity

Chapter 1 introduced the statement of retained earnings. The statement of retained earnings links a company's income statement and balance sheet by showing how net income and dividends change the company's retained earnings balance. All corporations prepare a statement of retained earnings, but most show it as a component of a more comprehensive statement of stockholders' equity.

A **statement of stockholders' equity** is a financial statement that shows how and why each equity account in the company's balance sheet changed from one year to the next. It therefore focuses not only on retained earnings, but also on other equity accounts relating to a company's contributed capital.

For illustration purposes, Exhibit 2-5 contains **Bed Bath & Beyond's** statement of shareholders' equity for the fiscal year ended February 26, 2011. Like the income statement, this statement reports three years of data. However, unlike the income statement, each column reflects the activity in a specific equity account rather than a period of time. The five columns of the statement refer to the five equity accounts from the classified balance sheet. That is, the balances at the bottom of the statement of stockholders' equity are the same balances from the most recent balance sheet. Note that the numbers are in thousands. Note also that Bed Bath & Beyond uses the word *shareholders'* in the title rather than stockholders'.

The first two accounts, *Common Stock* and *Additional Paid-In Capital,* represent the capital that has been contributed to the company through the issuance of stock. Chapter 10 will discuss in more detail why contributed capital is divided into two accounts. For now, you simply need to add the balances together to yield the total amount received to date. The activity in these accounts for the fiscal year ending February 26, 2011, is located on the bottom third of the statement. The columns of information indicate that the company generated contributed capital during the year primarily through transactions with employees.

The third account, *Retained Earnings,* represents the equity that has been generated through profitable operations and retained in the business. The retained earnings column is in fact Bed Bath & Beyond's statement of retained earnings. In each year presented, net income is added to the beginning retained earnings balance, but no dividends are subtracted. This is because Bed Bath & Beyond elects not to pay dividends.

The fourth account is *Treasury Stock*. Treasury stock is common stock that the company has purchased back from stockholders. Since the purchase of treasury stock is effectively a return of capital to owners, the balance in treasury stock is subtracted from stockholders' equity. The company has been active in repurchasing its stock over the three years. Treasury stock will be covered in more detail in Chapter 10.

The last account, *Accumulated Other Comprehensive Income (Loss),* is beyond the scope of this chapter.

Statement of stockholders' equity A financial statement that shows how and why each equity account in the company's balance sheet changed from one year to the next.

Exhibit 2-5 Bed Bath & Beyond's Statement of Shareholders' Equity

Bed Bath & Beyond Inc. and Subsidiaries
Consolidated Statements of Shareholders' Equity
(in thousands)

	Common Stock		Additional Paid-in Capital	Retained Earnings	Treasury Stock		Accumulated Other Comprehensive Income (Loss)	Total
	Shares	Amount			Shares	Amount		
Balance at March 1, 2008	312,229	$3,122	$ 813,568	$3,729,766	(53,309)	$(1,983,590)	$1,038	$2,561,828
Net earnings				425,123				425,123
Adjustments to comprehensive income							(3,502)	(3,502)
Shares sold under employee stock option plans	1,218	12	19,910					19,922
Issuance of restricted shares	1,224	13	(13)					—
Stock-based compensation			44,906					44,906
Director fees paid in stock	7		197					197
Repurchase of common stock					(1,668)	(48,052)		(48,052)
Change in pension plan				32				32
Balance at February 28, 2009	**314,678**	**3,147**	**878,568**	**4,154,921**	**(54,977)**	**(2,031,642)**	**(4,540)**	**3,000,454**
Net earnings				600,033				600,033
Adjustments to comprehensive income							5,268	5,268
Shares sold under employee stock option plans	4,503	45	96,431					96,476
Issuance of restricted shares	1,369	14	(14)					—
Stock-based compensation			45,411					45,411
Director fees paid in stock	3		119					119
Repurchase of common stock					(2,678)	(94,857)		(94,857)
Balance at February 27, 2010	**320,553**	**3,206**	**1,020,515**	**4,754,954**	**(57,655)**	**(2,126,499)**	**728**	**3,652,904**
Net earnings				791,333				791,333
Adjustments to comprehensive income							4,372	4,372
Shares sold under employee stock option plans	3,804	38	125,058					125,096
Issuance of restricted shares	863	9	(9)					—
Stock-based compensation			45,465					45,465
Director fees paid in stock	2		94					94
Repurchase of common stock					(15,901)	(687,605)		(687,605)
Balance at February 26, 2011	**325,222**	**$3,253**	**$1,191,123**	**$5,546,287**	**(73,556)**	**$(2,814,104)**	**$5,100**	**$3,931,659**

LO7 Information Beyond the Financial Statements

A company's financial statements contain a significant amount of information about the financial activities and position of the company. However, they are not exhaustive, and much information that is useful to creditors and investors is not included on the statements. As a result, companies like **Bed Bath & Beyond** prepare and report additional information beyond the financial statements. These items are normally included in a company's annual report that is distributed to all shareholders. Three items of significance are the following:

- **Notes to the financial statements**
- **Auditor's report**
- **Management's Discussion and Analysis**

Notes to the Financial Statements

At the bottom of each of Bed Bath & Beyond's financial statements is the following quote: *See accompanying Notes to the Consolidated Financial Statements.* A company's financial statements cannot communicate or disclose to users all the information necessary to adequately understand the financial activities and condition of an entity. Additional information, both quantitative and qualitative, is necessary and can be found in the notes to the financial statements.

The **notes to the financial statements** are the textual and numerical information immediately following the financial statements that (1) disclose the accounting methods used to prepare the financial statements, (2) disclose additional detail and explanation of account balances, and (3) provide information not recognized in the financial statements. Financial statements should not be examined without considering the notes to the financial statements.

Notes to the financial statements The additional textual and numerical information immediately following the financial statements.

Independent auditor's report A report, prepared by a certified public accountant for the public shareholder, stating an opinion on whether the financial statements present fairly, in conformity with GAAP, the company's financial condition and results of operations and cash flows.

The content of the notes to the financial statements varies by company, but there are some similarities across companies. First, the first note of practically all companies summarizes the significant accounting policies used to prepare the financial statements. For example, you can find how a company accounted for its inventory, how the company uses estimates, and how the company recognizes its revenue. This note is especially useful in maintaining the comparability of financial statements across companies. Second, most companies include a note for each of their significant accounts. These notes can vary depending on the type of business, but most companies have notes for significant items such as property and equipment, income taxes, and employee benefit plans, among other things. Exhibit 2-6 contains the titles of the notes to Bed Bath & Beyond's most recent financial statements.

Exhibit 2-6 Bed Bath & Beyond's Notes to the Financial Statements

Bed Bath & Beyond Notes:

1. Summary of significant accounting policies and related matters
2. Property and equipment
3. Lines of credit
4. Fair value measurements
5. Investment securities
6. Provision for income taxes
7. Transactions and balances with related parties
8. Leases
9. Employee benefit plans
10. Commitments and contingencies
11. Supplemental cash flow information
12. Stock-based compensation
13. Summary of quarterly results (unaudited)

Auditor's Report

How do you know if Bed Bath & Beyond's financial statements and notes can be depended upon to be a fair depiction of its financial condition? Since you don't have the ability to determine whether the reported numbers are reliable, you must rely on a third party to provide assurance that the information is reliable. This is why all annual reports contain an *independent auditor's report.*

An **independent auditor's report** is a report, prepared by a certified public accountant for the public shareholder, stating an opinion on whether the financial statements present fairly, in conformity with GAAP, the company's financial condition and results of operations and cash flows. Exhibit 2-7 contains **Bed Bath & Beyond's** most recent auditor's report.

Exhibit 2-7 Bed Bath & Beyond's Auditor's Report

REPORT OF INDEPENDENT REGISTERED PUBLIC ACCOUNTING FIRM

The Board of Directors and Shareholders
Bed Bath & Beyond Inc.:

We have audited the accompanying consolidated balance sheets of Bed Bath & Beyond Inc. and subsidiaries as of February 26, 2011 and February 27, 2010, and the related consolidated statements of earnings, shareholders' equity, and cash flows for each of the fiscal years in the three-year period ended February 26, 2011. In connection with our audits of the consolidated financial statements, we have also audited the financial statement schedule. These consolidated financial statements and financial statement schedule are the responsibility of the Company's management. Our responsibility is to express an opinion on these consolidated financial statements and financial statement schedule based on our audits.

We conducted our audits in accordance with the standards of the Public Company Accounting Oversight Board (United States). Those standards require that we plan and perform the audit to obtain reasonable assurance about whether the financial statements are free of material misstatement. An audit includes examining, on a test basis, evidence supporting the amounts and disclosures in the financial statements. An audit also includes assessing the accounting principles used and significant estimates made by management, as well as evaluating the overall financial statement presentation. We believe that our audits provide a reasonable basis for our opinion.

In our opinion, the consolidated financial statements referred to above present fairly, in all material respects, the financial position of Bed Bath & Beyond Inc. and subsidiaries as of February 26, 2011 and February 27, 2010, and the results of their operations and their cash flows for each of the fiscal years in the three-year period ended February 26, 2011, in conformity with U.S. generally accepted accounting principles. Also in our opinion, the related financial statement schedule, when considered in relation to the basic consolidated financial statements taken as a whole, presents fairly, in all material respects, the information set forth therein.

We also have audited, in accordance with the standards of the Public Company Accounting Oversight Board (United States), the Company's internal control over financial reporting as of February 26, 2011, based on criteria established in Internal Control—Integrated Framework issued by the Committee of Sponsoring Organizations of the Treadway Commission (COSO), and our report dated April 26, 2011 expressed an unqualified opinion on the effectiveness of the Company's internal control over financial reporting.

KPMG LLP

Short Hills, New Jersey
April 26, 2011

As you can see in the above report, **KPMG LLP**, one of the largest public accounting firms in the world, performed the audit. KPMG's opinion is stated in the first sentence of the third paragraph—"the consolidated financial statements . . . present fairly, in all material respects, the financial position of Bed Bath & Beyond Inc. . . . and the results of their operations and their cash flows. . . ." This type of opinion, which is known as an unqualified opinion, is what all companies hope to receive. With this assurance from KPMG, users can consider the financial statements reliable.

Management's Discussion and Analysis

In addition to financial statements, notes, and the auditor's report, all annual reports contain a section called Management's Discussion and Analysis. **Management's Discussion and Analysis (MD&A)** is a discussion and analysis of the financial activities of the company by the company's management. The MD&A normally precedes the financial statements in the annual report and contains, among other things, comments on the company's results of operations, its ability to satisfy its current obligations, and its expansion plans.

Management's Discussion and Analysis A discussion and analysis of the financial activities of the company by the company's management.

In some areas, the MD&A is useful in understanding past performance. For example, management usually compares the current year's operating results to the prior year's and explains the reasons for any differences. In other areas, the MD&A is useful in generating expectations for the future. For example, management often discloses how many stores it plans to open or how much in new property and equipment it plans to purchase in the coming year.

Given that the MD&A provides feedback value and predictive value, it is therefore relevant information and should be read along with the financial statements. Exhibit 2-8 contains two excerpts from **Bed Bath & Beyond's** most recent MD&A.

Exhibit 2-8 Excerpts from Bed Bath & Beyond's Management's Discussion and Analysis

Net Sales

Net sales in fiscal 2010 increased $929.7 million to $8.759 billion, representing an increase of 11.9% over $7.829 billion of net sales in fiscal 2009, which increased $620.5 million or 8.6% over the $7.208 billion of net sales in fiscal 2008. For fiscal 2010, approximately 65.2% of the increase in net sales was attributable to an increase in the Company's comparable store sales and the balance of the increase was primarily attributable to an increase in the Company's new store sales. For fiscal 2009, approximately 51.4% of the increase in net sales was attributable to an increase in the Company's new store sales and the balance of the increase was primarily attributable to an increase in the Company's comparable store sales.

Expansion Program

The Company is engaged in an ongoing expansion program involving the opening of new stores in both new and existing markets, the expansion or relocation of existing stores and the continuous review of strategic acquisitions. In the 19-year period from the beginning of fiscal 1992 to the end of fiscal 2010, the chain has grown from 34 to 1,139 stores. Total square footage grew from 0.9 million square feet at the beginning of fiscal 1992 to 35.1 million square feet at the end of fiscal 2010. During fiscal 2010, the Company opened a total of 40 new stores, including 18 BBB stores throughout the United States and Canada, five CTS stores, one Harmon store and 16 buybuy BABY stores, and closed one BBB store, all of which resulted in the aggregate addition of approximately 1.3 million square feet of store space. In May 2008, the Company became a partner in a joint venture which operates two stores in the Mexico City market under the name "Home & More."

The Company plans to continue to expand its operations and invest in its infrastructure to reach its long term objectives. In fiscal 2011, the Company expects to open approximately 45 new stores across all concepts.

STUDY TOOLS 2

Chapter review card

- Learning Objective and Key Concept Reviews
- Key Definitions and Formulas

Online (Located at www.cengagebrain.com)

- Flash Cards and Crossword Puzzles
- Games and Quizzes
- E-Lectures
- Homework Assignments (as directed by your instructor)

CONCEPT QUESTIONS

1. (LO1) What are the three main forms of business?
2. (LO1) What are the advantages and disadvantages to each form of business?
3. (LO2) To what does the term GAAP refer?
4. (LO2) Who has the authority to determine GAAP?
5. (LO3) How are accounts classified in a classified balance sheet?
6. (LO3) What is the difference between a fixed asset and an intangible asset?
7. (LO3) What are the differences and similarities between the categories of liabilities in the classified balance sheet?
8. (LO3) How is equity classified in a classified balance sheet, and what are the differences in each category?
9. (LO4) Why is a multi-step income statement divided into multiple sections?
10. (LO4) What are the characteristics of each subtotal of income on a multi-step income statement?
11. (LO5) How is horizontal analysis used?
12. (LO5) How is vertical analysis used?
13. (LO5) How is horizontal analysis different from vertical analysis?
14. (LO6) What is shown on the statement of stockholders' equity?
15. (LO6) How is retained earnings calculated? How are retained earnings and stockholders' equity related?
16. (LO7) What information do companies disclose in addition to the financial statements?

MULTIPLE CHOICE

1. (LO1) The form of business in which one individual bears all risk is a:
   a. partnership.
   b. sole proprietorship.
   c. corporation.
   d. none of the above.
2. (LO1) Which form of business issues shares of ownership to the public?
   a. Partnership
   b. Sole proprietorship
   c. Corporation
   d. None of the above
3. (LO2) Which of the following institutions does not play a role in determining GAAP?
   a. Securities and Exchange Commission
   b. Financial Accounting Standards Board
   c. The American Institute of Certified Public Accountants
   d. All of the above play a role in determining GAAP
4. (LO2) GAAP stands for:
   a. Generally Accepted Auditing Procedures.
   b. Governmental Auditing and Accounting Procedures.
   c. Generally Accepted Accounting Principles.
   d. Guidelines for All Accounting Professionals.
5. (LO3) In a classified balance sheet, assets are usually classified as:
   a. current assets, long-term investments, fixed assets, intangible assets, other assets.
   b. current assets, property and equipment, long-term investments, short-term investments, other assets.
   c. short-term assets, long-term assets, tangible assets, intangible assets.
   d. fixed assets, movable assets, long-term assets, short-term assets, other assets.
6. (LO3) Which of the following would not be a current asset?
   a. Inventory
   b. Accounts receivable
   c. Equipment
   d. Supplies
7. (LO4) Which of the following is not included in a calculation of net income?
   a. Operating expenses
   b. Cost of sales
   c. Sales
   d. Goodwill
8. (LO4) Mayer Corporation had sales of $24,000, cost of sales of $10,000, advertising expense of $8,500, and income tax expense of $1,500. What is *gross profit*?
   a. $4,000
   b. $14,000
   c. $5,500
   d. $12,500
9. (LO4) Mayer Corporation had sales of $24,000, cost of goods sales of $10,000, advertising expenses of $8,500, and income tax expense of $1,500. What is *operating profit*?
   a. $4,000
   b. $14,000
   c. $5,500
   d. $12,500
10. (LO5) Horizontal analysis:
    a. states each account balance as a percentage of a base account.
    b. compares account balances within a year.
    c. does not show trends over time.
    d. compares account balances over time.
11. (LO5) The base account for a vertical analysis of the income statement is:
    a. net income.
    b. income before taxes.
    c. net sales.
    d. operating profit.

12. (LO5) A horizontal analysis of inventory yields 5.5%. This means that:
    a. inventory was 5.5% of total assets.
    b. inventory was 5.5% of net sales.
    c. inventory increased 5.5% from the prior year to the current year.
    d. inventory decreased 5.5% from the prior year to the current year.
13. (LO5) A vertical analysis of depreciation expense yields 5.5%. This means that:
    a. depreciation expense was 5.5% of total assets.
    b. depreciation expense was 5.5% of net sales.
    c. depreciation expense increased 5.5% from the prior year to the current year.
    d. depreciation expense decreased 5.5% from the prior year to the current year.
14. (LO5) Last year J&M had assets of $100,000. This year assets are $120,000. A horizontal analysis of assets would yield:
    a. (20.0%).
    b. 16.7%.
    c. 20.0%.
    d. 16.7%.
15. (LO5) Miller Corporation has current assets of $15,000, total assets of $85,000, and net sales of $132,000. A vertical analysis of current assets would yield:
    a. 17.6%.
    b. 11.4%.
    c. 64.4%.
    d. 21.8%.
16. (LO5) McGee Inc. has administrative expenses of $12,000, total assets of $76,000, and net sales of $90,000. A vertical analysis of administrative expenses would yield:
    a. 10.6%.
    b. 15.8%.
    c. 25.1%.
    d. 13.3%.
17. (LO5) Jones Services generated $123,000 in net income in its first year and $115,000 in its second year. A horizontal analysis of net income would yield:
    a. 7.0%.
    b. (6.5%).
    c. 8.7%.
    d. (7.0%).
18. (LO6) Which of the following would not be included on a statement of stockholders' equity?
    a. Common stock
    b. Treasury stock
    c. Retained earnings
    d. Investments in common stock
19. (LO7) Notes to the financial statements do not include:
    a. additional detail and explanation of financial statement account balances.
    b. accounting methods used in the preparation of the financial statements.
    c. information such as contingencies and future commitments.
    d. discussion and analysis of the company's financial activities by the company's management.
20. (LO7) The auditor's report states an opinion on whether a company's financial statements are:
    a. completely error free.
    b. presented fairly in accordance with GAAP.
    c. better than competitor financial statements.
    d. none of the above.

BRIEF EXERCISES

1. Miscellaneous Terms LO1, 7

The following definitions were discussed in the chapter:

1. A form of business in which multiple entities join together.
2. Information following the financial statements that provides additional information and disclosures.
3. A form of business that is established by filing proper forms in a state.
4. A report that attests to the fair presentation of a company's financial statements.
5. The most common form of business.
6. Analysis of a company's financial activities that focuses on results of operations, ability to pay debts, and expansion plans.

Required

Match each definition with one of the following terms: Sole proprietorship; Management's Discussion and Analysis; Notes to the financial statements; Partnership; Auditor's Report; Corporation.

2. Generally Accepted Accounting Principles LO2

The following definitions were discussed in the chapter:

1. The accounting rules followed by U.S. corporations.
2. The governmental entity whose mission is to protect investors.
3. The accounting organization that contributes rules for more technical issues.
4. The major accounting rule-making body in the United States.
5. The international accounting rule-making body.

Required

Match each definition with one of the following terms: FASB; AICPA; SEC; IASB; GAAP.

3. Classified Balance Sheet LO3

The following accounts were taken from a company's balance sheet:

Supplies	Interest payable
Retained earnings	Equipment
Prepaid insurance	Salaries payable

Required

For each account, indicate whether the account is an asset, a liability, or an equity account. Also indicate the specific asset, liability, or equity classification the account would be reported under on the balance sheet. For example, cash is an asset that would be reported as a current asset.

4. Classified Balance Sheet LO3

The following is a list of accounts taken from Jim's Uniforms:

Accounts receivable	$ 1,200
Sales	18,000
Inventory	3,150
Accounts payable	4,620
Cash	7,330
Prepaid insurance	2,800
Equipment	13,500
Short-term investments	800

Required

Prepare the current asset section of Jim's balance sheet. Make sure to list the accounts in the proper sequence.

5. Calculating Gross Profit LO4

During the month, a retailer generates $15,000 of sales, $2,500 of operating expenses, and $11,500 in cost of sales. At the end of the month, the company had $7,000 of merchandise inventory on hand.

Required

Calculate the company's gross profit for the month.

6. Calculating Operating Profit LO4

Johnson Clothing Supercenter generated a gross profit of $7,750,000 during the year. Also during the year, Johnson incurred advertising expense of $1,500,000, salaries expense of $2,100,000, and income tax expense of $2,000,000.

Required

Calculate the company's operating profit and net income for the year.

7. Horizontal and Vertical Analyses LO5

A company reports the following information from its financial statements:

	Current Year	Prior Year
Inventory	$ 66,540	$ 63,180
Sales	190,405	201,450
Total assets	270,450	240,680

Required

Conduct horizontal and vertical analyses of inventory for the current year. Round percentages to one decimal point (i.e., 10.1%).

8. Horizontal and Vertical Analyses LO5

The following information (in millions) was taken from a recent income statement of **The J.M. Smucker Company**:

	Current Year	Prior Year
Net sales	$4,605	$3,758
Cost of sales	2,818	2,506
Gross profit	$1,787	$1,252

Required

Conduct horizontal and vertical analyses of gross profit. Was the company more or less profitable in the current year? Do both horizontal and vertical analyses indicate that? For your calculations, round percentages to one decimal point (i.e., 10.1%).

9. Horizontal Analysis LO4, 5

A horizontal analysis of a company's sales resulted in a $1.5 million increase, which equaled a percentage change of 22.8%.

Required

Interpret the dollar change and percentage change and identify which item(s) from the following list would potentially explain the results of the analysis.

a. A sales promotion was highly successful.
b. A manufacturing plant was offline for much of the year due to maintenance.
c. The company opened several new stores.
d. The company lost market share to a new competitor.
e. The company issued $1.5 million of stock during the year.

10. Statement of Stockholders' Equity LO6

A company provides the following account balances for the current year:

Common stock	$ 20,600
Retained earnings, beginning of year	62,496
Additional paid-in capital	100,000
Dividends	9,500
Treasury stock	(22,000)
Net income	22,133

Required

Prepare a statement of stockholders' equity at year-end.

EXERCISES

11. Classified Balance Sheet LO3

The following is a list of accounts:

- Mortgage payable, due in 15 years
- Short-term investments
- Cash
- Prepaid rent
- Patents
- Common stock
- Accounts payable
- Buildings
- Notes payable, due in 6 months

Required

Identify each account as a Current asset, Long-term investment, Fixed asset, Intangible asset, Other asset, Current liability, Long-term liability, Contributed capital, or Retained earnings.

12. Classified Balance Sheet LO3

A company reports the following accounts on its classified balance sheet:

Additional paid-in capital	Accounts receivable
Land	Bonds payable, due in 10 years
Treasury stock	Copyrights
Income taxes payable	Dividends payable
Long-term investments	Notes payable, due in 20 months

Required

Identify each account as a Current asset, Long-term investment, Fixed asset, Intangible asset, Other asset, Current liability, Long-term liability, Contributed capital, or Retained earnings.

13. Classified Balance Sheet Terms LO3

The following is a list of balance sheet classifications and descriptions:

a. Current asset
b. Long-term investment
c. Fixed asset
d. Intangible asset
e. Other asset
f. Current liability
g. Long-term liability
h. Capital stock
i. Retained earnings

1. An obligation that is reasonably expected to be satisfied within the normal operations of business.
2. An investment in the common stock or bonds of another entity that the company does not intend to sell within one year.
3. Assets that do not fit into a particular classification of assets (for example, deferred tax liability).
4. An obligation that is not expected to be satisfied within one year.
5. The portion of equity contributed by stockholders through the purchase of stock, which includes common stock and preferred stock.
6. Resources that are reasonably expected to be converted to cash or consumed during the normal operations of business.
7. Tangible resources that are used in the company's operations for more than one year and are not intended for resale.
8. The profits that a company earns over time and retains in the business.
9. Resources to be used in the company's operations for more than one year that have no physical substance.

Required

Match each classification with the appropriate description.

14. Classified Balance Sheet LO3

The following are independent cases:

	Sally's Fish & Chips	Brina's Bar & Grill	Ely's Tanning Salon
ASSETS			
Current assets	3,000	2,500	4,500
Long-term investments	45,500	______	60,000
Fixed assets	125,750	100,000	150,000
Intangible assets	32,250	55,250	15,000
Other assets	______	35,500	6,500
Total assets	**220,000**	**225,750**	______
LIABILITIES			
Current liabilities	15,500	7,000	______
Long-term liabilities	45,000	______	65,500
Total liabilities	______	**75,000**	**69,000**
STOCKHOLDERS' EQUITY			
Capital stock	55,000	______	67,500
Retained earnings	______	105,000	______
Total liabilities and stockholders' equity	**220,000**	______	______

Required

Fill in each blank with the appropriate dollar amount.

15. Classified Balance Sheet LO3

The following items were taken from the December 31 balance sheet of Auburn Bowling Lanes:

Buildings, net	$60,200
Accounts receivable	14,520
Prepaid insurance	4,680
Cash	20,840
Equipment, net	63,680
Land	61,200
Mortgage payable	103,040
Common stock	66,000
Retained earnings	40,000
Interest payable	3,600
Accounts payable	12,480

Required
Recreate the company's classified balance sheet, assuming that $13,600 of the mortgage payable balance will be paid within three months of the balance sheet date.

16. Prepare a Classified Balance Sheet LO3

The following information was taken from the February 26, 2011, balance sheet of **Best Buy**:

(in millions)	
Accounts payable	$ 4,894
Accounts receivable	2,348
Additional paid-in capital	18
Cash	1,103
Short-term investments	22
Common stock	39
Intangible assets	2,587
Long-term liabilities	1,894
Other current assets	1,103
Other current liabilities	3,769
Other equity	863
Other assets	966
Fixed assets	3,823
Retained earnings	6,372
Inventory	5,897

Required
Prepare Best Buy's classified balance sheet at February 26, 2011.

17. Balance Sheet and Income Statement Classifications LO3, 4

A company uses the following pairs of accounts for its financial statements:

- Sales and Accounts receivable
- Interest payable and Interest expense
- Supplies expense and Supplies
- Inventory and Cost of sales
- Salaries payable and Salaries expense
- Income tax expense and Income tax payable

Required
For each pair of accounts, identify which account would be reported on the balance sheet and which would be reported on the income statement. For each balance sheet account, identify its classification. For each income statement account, identify which subtotal(s) of income would be affected by the account.

18. Multi-Step Income Statement LO4

The following are all independent cases:

	The Bike Shop	The Rental Center	The Uniform Center
Sales	$ _____	$ 78,000	$ 35,000
Cost of sales	45,000	_____	_____
Gross profit	18,000	_____	7,000
Selling expenses	_____	9,000	3,000
Administrative expenses	2,800	_____	_____
Total operating expenses	8,800	13,600	_____
Operating profit	9,200	25,400	_____
Income tax expense	_____	11,000	1,000
Net income	7,700	_____	1,500

Required
Fill in each blank with the appropriate dollar amount.

19. Multi-Step Income Statement LO4

These items were taken from the financial records of Brown's Used Cars:

Utilities expense	$ 17,650
Interest expense	50
Selling expense	14,600
Administrative expense	15,230
Interest revenue	500
Cost of sales	75,620
Net sales	154,900

Required
Prepare a multi-step income statement assuming Brown's falls into the 30% tax bracket and has a December 31 year end.

20. Multi-Step Income Statement LO4

The following income statement items are taken from the records of Matthews Music Group for the year ending December 31:

Advertising expense	$ 6,210
Cost of sales	83,910
Income tax expense	2,250
Insurance expense	3,960
Interest expense	4,115
Interest revenue	6,055
Rent expense	11,410
Salaries expense	28,525
Sales	153,010
Supplies expense	5,600

Required
Prepare a multi-step income statement for the year ending December 31.

21. Completing a Multi-Step Income Statement LO4

The following multi-step income statement was provided by Reece Corp.:

Reece Corp. Income Statement For the Year Ending December 31	
Net sales	$ (a)
(b)	96,000
(c)	$92,000
Insurance expense	(d)
Salaries expense	11,500
(e)	$52,500
Interest revenue	9,200
Interest expense	(f)
(g)	$ (h)
(i)	14,990
Net income	$28,310

Required
Identify the missing amounts and descriptions.

22. Financial Statement Accounts LO3, 4, 6

The following is a list of accounts:

Treasury stock	Interest payable
Interest revenue	Common stock
Buildings	Cost of sales
Dividends	Administrative expense
Accounts payable	Additional paid-in capital
Retained earnings	Cash

Required
Identify if each account would appear on the balance sheet, income statement, and/or statement of stockholders' equity.

23. Horizontal and Vertical Analyses LO4, 5

Comparative income statements are available for Johanna's Fine Furs:

	2012	2011
Sales	$850,000	$800,000
Cost of sales	325,000	275,000
Gross profit	525,000	525,000
Operating expenses	175,000	120,000
Operating profit	350,000	405,000
Income tax expense	105,000	121,500
Net income	$245,000	$283,500

Required
Perform horizontal and vertical analyses on each of the items in the above comparative income statements. Round percentages to one decimal point (i.e., 10.1%).

24. Horizontal and Vertical Analyses LO4, 5

The following condensed balance sheets are available for Delta Electronics:

	2012	2011
Cash	$ 142	$ 160
Accounts receivable	35	30
Inventory	428	382
Current assets	605	572
Equipment, net	880	790
Total assets	$1,485	$1,362
Accounts payable	$ 201	$ 220
Salaries payable	169	162
Current liabilities	370	382
Bonds payable	350	300
Total liabilities	720	682
Retained Earnings	382	300
Common Stock	383	380
Total equity	765	680
Total liabilities and equity	$1,485	$1,362

Required
Perform horizontal and vertical analyses on each of the items in the above comparative balance sheets. Round percentages to one decimal point (i.e., 10.1%).

25. Horizontal and Vertical Analyses LO3, 5

Comparative balance sheet data is available for Ellis Enterprises:

	2012	2011
Total assets	$850,000	$700,000
Total liabilities	$240,000	$280,000
Total equity	$610,000	$420,000

Required
Perform horizontal and vertical analyses on each of the items above. Round percentages to one decimal point (i.e., 10.1%). If generating assets through debt is considered more risky than generating assets through equity, is Ellis more or less risky in 2012?

26. Horizontal and Vertical Analyses LO5

A company provides the following information:

	Current Year	Prior Year
Net sales	$121,345	$119,872
Accounts receivable	$ 30,192	$ 12,676
Total assets	$246,933	$250,361

Required
Should the company be concerned about its performance? Use horizontal and vertical analyses to "prove" why or why not. Round percentages to one decimal point (i.e., 10.1%).

27. Financial Accounting Terms LO5, 7

The following are various terms and definitions from financial accounting:

a. Common-size financial statement
b. Notes to the financial statements
c. Management's Discussion and Analysis
d. Auditor's Report
e. Vertical analysis
f. Horizontal analysis

1. A technique that compares account balances within one year by stating each account balance as a percentage of a base amount.
2. Textual and numerical information immediately following the financial statement's disclosing information such as accounting methods used, detail and explanation of account balances, and information not recognized in the financial statements.
3. A statement in which all accounts have been standardized by the overall size of the company.
4. A discussion and analysis of the financial activities of the company by the company's management.
5. A report, prepared by a certified public accountant for the public shareholder, stating an opinion on whether the financial statements present fairly in conformity with GAAP the company's financial condition and results of operations and cash flows.
6. A technique that calculates the change in an account balance from one period to the next and expresses that change in both dollar and percentage terms.

Required
Match each term with the appropriate definition.

PROBLEMS

28. Prepare a Classified Balance Sheet LO3

Bay Company thinks there may be a problem with its balance sheet:

Bay Company Classified Balance Sheet For the Year Ending December 31	
Assets	
Current assets	
Buildings	$ 70,000
Interest revenue	11,000
Equipment	41,000
Cash	8,000
Other current assets	4,000
Total current assets	134,000
Accounts receivable	12,000
Land	20,000
Interest payable	14,000
Total noncurrent assets	46,000
Total assets	$180,000
Liabilities and Stockholders' Equity	
Current liabilities	
Accounts payable	$ 16,000
Interest expense	39,000
Total current liabilities	55,000
Stockholders' equity	
Retained earnings	50,000
Common stock	35,000
Bonds payable	40,000
Total stockholders' equity	125,000
Total liabilities and stockholders' equity	$180,000

Required
Prepare a corrected classified balance sheet.

29. Prepare a Multi-Step Income Statement LO4

The auditor for Foshee Corporation noticed that its income statement was incorrect:

Foshee Corporation Income Statement December 31		
Sales		$130,000
Cost of sales		80,000
Accounts receivable		19,500
Gross profit		30,500
Interest expense	$15,000	
Selling expense	13,000	
Total operating expenses		28,000
Operating profit		2,500
Interest revenue	16,500	
Interest payable	4,000	8,500
Income before taxes		11,000
Income tax expense		12,850
Net income (loss)		$ (1,850)

Required

Prepare a corrected multi-step income statement.

30. Multi-Step Income Statement and Classified Balance Sheet LO3, 4

The following items were taken from the financial statements of Wilson Inc. for 2012:

Accounts payable	$15,780
Accounts receivable	8,470
Advertising expense	4,200
Cash	16,080
Common stock	15,400
Cost of sales	41,250
Dividends	2,310
Equipment, net	45,420
Income tax expense	3,260
Insurance expense	4,680
Long-term liabilities	9,920
Prepaid insurance	5,970
Retained earnings, Jan. 1	28,450
Salaries expense	17,420
Salaries payable	5,210
Sales	78,420
Utilities expense	4,180

Required

Prepare a multi-step income statement for the year ending December 31, 2012, and a classified balance sheet at December 31, 2012. Hint: You must calculate ending retained earnings.

31. Prepare and Analyze the Classified Balance Sheet LO3, 5

The following balance sheet items are available from Carnell Inc. as of December 31, 2012:

	2012	2011
Accounts payable	$ 75,500	$ 35,035
Accounts receivable	50,000	85,065
Bonds payable, due 12/31/2016	125,000	25,000
Buildings, net	240,000	300,000
Capital stock, $5 par	100,000	80,000
Cash	15,000	25,635
Equipment, net	24,000	24,000
Income taxes payable	12,250	16,465
Interest payable	13,755	7,550
Inventory	25,650	27,270
Land	300,000	200,000
Long-term investments	125,000	100,000
Notes payable, due 6/30/2013	100,000	100,000
Supplies	12,500	13,500
Additional paid-in capital	200,000	190,000
Patents	6,000	6,000
Prepaid rent	10,150	12,275
Retained earnings	146,295	306,135
Salaries payable	35,500	33,560

Required

a. Prepare a comparative, classified balance sheet for Carnell Inc.
b. Perform horizontal and vertical analyses and interpret the results. Round percentages to one decimal point (i.e., 10.1%).
c. Assume the same information above except that in 2012, Bonds payable is $0 while Retained earnings is $271,295. Does this new information change any interpretations previously made?

32. Prepare and Analyze the Multi-Step Income Statement LO4, 5

The following income statement items are available from Dansby Inc. for the years ending December 31:

	2012	2011
Advertising expense	$ 7,765	$ 9,789
Commissions expense	4,879	6,010
Cost of sales	48,596	58,896
Income tax expense	2,217	2,684
Insurance expense	4,897	5,236
Interest expense	2,584	2,695
Interest revenue	4,287	4,189
Sales	95,950	106,569
Supplies expense	1,654	2,106
Salaries expense	19,320	21,012
Rent expense	7,634	7,856

Required

a. Prepare a comparative, multi-step income statement for Dansby Inc.
b. Perform horizontal and vertical analyses and interpret the results. Round percentages to one decimal point (i.e., 10.1%).
c. Assume the following change in information: Cost of sales in 2012, $62,470 and in 2011, $45,670. Does this new information change any interpretations previously made?

33. Horizontal Analysis of the Income Statement LO5

The following items were taken from a recent income statement of **PepsiCo**:

	Current Year	Prior Year
Net sales	$43,251	$39,474
Cost of sales	20,351	18,038
Selling and administrative expenses	15,965	14,266
Operating income	6,935	7,170
Other income	86	461
Income before taxes	7,021	7,631
Provision for income taxes	1,879	1,973
Net income	5,142	5,658

Required

Perform a horizontal analysis on each account. Round percentages to one decimal point (i.e., 10.1%). What conclusions can you make about PepsiCo?

34. Using Horizontal and Vertical Analyses LO5

The president of ABC Inc. is disappointed that the company was less profitable this year than last year. Comparative income statements for ABC Inc. are as follows:

	Current Year	Prior Year
Sales	$800,000	$500,000
Cost of sales	300,000	200,000
Gross profit	$500,000	$300,000
Operating expenses	167,000	130,000
Operating income	$333,000	$170,000
One-time gain		180,000
Net income	$333,000	$350,000

Required

Why was ABC's net income lower in the current year? Use horizontal and vertical analyses to show the ways in which ABC was more profitable in the current year. Round percentages to one decimal point (i.e., 10.1%).

CASES

35. Reading and Analyzing Financial Statements LO3, 4, 5

Refer to **Home Depot's** Annual Report contained in Appendix C of the textbook.

Required

a. Identify the company's current-year and prior-year balances in total current assets, net property and equipment, total assets, total current liabilities, total liabilities, and total stockholders' equity.
b. Conduct horizontal analysis on each account balance in part a. What broad trend is indicated by the calculations? Round percentages to one decimal point (i.e., 10.1%).
c. Identify the company's current-year and prior-year gross profit, operating income, earnings before income taxes, and net earnings.
d. Conduct horizontal analysis on each account balance in part c. What broad trend is indicated by the calculations? Round percentages to one decimal point (i.e., 10.1%).

36. Understanding Financial Statements LO3

Refer to Home Depot's classified balance sheet contained in Appendix C of the textbook.

Required

a. The current liability section contains an account entitled "Current Installments of Long-Term Debt." Explain what this account represents and why it is included in current liabilities if it relates to long-term debt.
b. The liability section contains an account entitled "Long-Term Debt, excluding current installments." Examine the fifth note to the financial statements and identify how many different "Senior Notes" are included in the account balance.
c. The current liability section contains an account entitled "Deferred Revenue." Read the "Revenues" and "Services Revenue" paragraphs in the first note to the financial statements. What two general activities are captured in the "Deferred Revenue" account?

37. Understanding Financial Statements LO4

Refer to Home Depot's income statement contained in Appendix C of the textbook.

Required

a. Identify the line item just above Net Earnings. Explain in your own words what you think this line item represents.
b. Look at the fourth note to the financial statements. What was the item that gave rise to the line on the income statement?
c. Do you think that this item should be reported separately on the income statement? Why or why not?

38. Research and Analysis LO4, 5

Access the 2010 annual report for **AnnTaylor Stores** by clicking on the *Investors* and *Annual Reports* links at www.anninc.com.

Required

Conduct horizontal analysis of the company's net sales, cost of sales, and gross profit for the current year and vertical analysis for the same accounts for both the current and prior year. Round percentages to one decimal point (i.e., 10.1%). What conclusions can you draw about the company's ability to earn a profit from its sales?

39. Communication in Accounting LO4, 5

You and some friends have decided to start an investment club. Several of the new members of the club, however, have no knowledge of financial statements, particularly the income statement. They understand that a company must "make money," but they get confused when they read a multi-step income statement.

Required

Prepare a short memo for current and future members that describes the subtotals of income on a multi-step income statement.

ACCT

Recording
Accounting Transactions

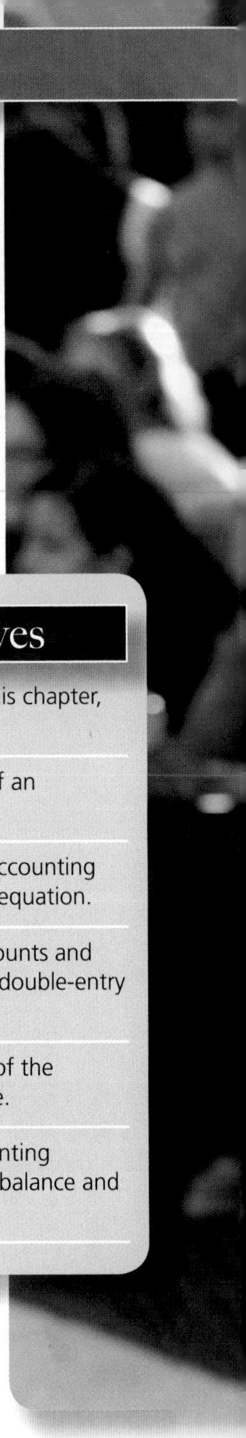

Learning Objectives

After studying the material in this chapter, you should be able to:

LO1 Describe the purpose of an accounting information system.

LO2 Analyze the effect of accounting transactions on the accounting equation.

LO3 Understand how T-accounts and debits and credits are used in a double-entry accounting system.

LO4 Describe the purpose of the journal, ledger, and trial balance.

LO5 Record and post accounting transactions and prepare a trial balance and financial statements.

Introduction

The first two chapters of this book focused on how economic information is communicated to users through financial statements: the balance sheet, the income statement, the statement of stockholders' equity, and the statement of cash flows. This chapter and Chapter 4 focus on how the activities of a business are captured by the accounting system so that these financial statements can be prepared. More specifically, Chapters 3 and 4 describe the accounting cycle. Because financial statements must be prepared periodically, the process of capturing and reporting information is a repetitive process, or cycle. This chapter explores the first three steps in the accounting cycle. The next chapter explores the remaining steps.

LO1 The Accounting Information System

A company's **accounting information system** is the system that identifies, records, summarizes, and communicates the various transactions of a company. Accounting information systems vary widely, ranging from manual, pencil-and-paper systems in some organizations to highly complex electronic systems in other organizations. However different their forms, though, all accounting systems are built to capture and report the effects of a company's *accounting transactions*.

An **accounting transaction** is any economic event that affects a company's assets, liabilities, or equity at the time of the event. Examples include the purchase of equipment, the consumption of supplies in operations, and the issuance of debt or stock. In each of these examples, the event increases or decreases a specific asset, liability, or equity account of the company. Accounting transactions between a company and an external party (for example, an equipment purchase or the issuance of stock) are *external* transactions, while transactions within a company (the consumption of supplies) are *internal* transactions.

Accounting information system The system that identifies, records, summarizes, and communicates the various transactions of a company.

Accounting transaction Any economic event that affects a company's assets, liabilities, or equity at the time of the event.

Much like a video camera, an accounting information system captures business activity so that others can view it.

Jeff Greenberg/Alamy

To record accounting transactions and summarize the resulting information, companies use accounts. An **account** is an accounting record that accumulates the activity of a specific item and yields the item's balance. For example, a company's cash account is increased and decreased as cash is received and paid, and it shows the amount of cash held at any point in time. The various accounts that a company uses to capture its business activities are often listed in a **chart of accounts**. An example chart of accounts, complete with numerical references for each account, is found in Exhibit 3-1.

Charts of accounts will vary across companies. For example, a bank will have accounts relating to customer deposits while a biotech company will have accounts relating to research and development. Of course, there certainly will be many

Account An accounting record that accumulates the activity of a specific item and yields the item's balance.

Chart of accounts The list of accounts that a company uses to capture its business activities.

You can tell a lot about what a company does if you have its chart of accounts.

Exhibit 3-1 Chart of Accounts

100–199	ASSETS
100	Cash
101	Accounts Receivable
110	Supplies
120	Equipment
200–299	LIABILITIES
210	Accounts Payable
211	Unearned Revenues
230	Notes Payable
300–399	EQUITY
300	Common Stock
350	Retained Earnings
400–499	REVENUES
400	Service Revenue
500–599	EXPENSES
501	Administrative Expense
502	Advertising Expense
600–699	DIVIDENDS

commonalities across charts of accounts—for example, practically every company will have an account for cash—but there will be differences depending on the company's activities. As a result, you can tell a lot about what a company does if you have its chart of accounts.

Dual nature of accounting Every accounting transaction must affect at least two accounts.

LO2 Accounting Transactions and the Accounting Equation

All accounting transactions must be recorded in the accounting information system. To understand the nature of recording transactions, it is best to start with the fundamental accounting equation:

$$\text{Assets} = \text{Liabilities} + \text{Equity}$$

The equation states that a company's assets must always equal the sum of its liabilities and equity. This means that any change to one part of the equation must be accompanied by a second change to another part. For example, suppose that a transaction increases an asset account. For the equation to stay in balance, the transaction must also either decrease another asset account or increase a liability or equity account. This means that every accounting transaction must affect at least two accounts. This is known as the **dual nature of accounting**.

Transaction Analysis

To illustrate how accounting transactions affect the accounting equation, consider the following ten transactions in the first month of operations of Circle Films, a company that documents weddings, birthdays, and other significant life events. Although the example is a small hypothetical company, the transactions would be treated in the same way by all companies, large or small.

HOME DEPOT ANALYSIS

Look at **Home Depot's** balance sheet in Appendix C and determine how many accounts it uses to report its assets, liabilities, and equity. Also, consider the scenario when one stockholder of Home Depot sells his or her stock to another stockholder. Is this an economic event relating to Home Depot? Is it an accounting transaction?

Home Depot's balance sheet reports 29 different accounts: 14 asset accounts, 10 liability accounts, and 5 equity accounts.

When Home Depot's stock is sold on the New York Stock Exchange, the sale is an economic event of interest to Home Depot. However, because Home Depot is not involved in the transaction, it is not an accounting transaction.

TRANSACTION #1: Circle Films incorporates in the state of Texas and issues 3,000 shares of common stock to investors for $15,000 cash. Because Circle Films receives cash of $15,000, assets increase. Its equity also increases because investors have contributed cash for an ownership interest in the company. More specifically, Circle Films' common stock increases.

	Assets	=	Liabilities	+	Equity
	Cash	=		+	Common Stock
Prior Bal.	$ 0				$ 0
#1	+$15,000				+$15,000
New Bal.	$15,000				$15,000
	$15,000	=	$0	+	$15,000

TRANSACTION #2: Circle Films purchases a video camera for $9,000 and memory cards for $1,000. In this transaction, the company is exchanging one asset (cash) for other assets (equipment and supplies). Therefore, assets both increase and decrease by $10,000. The net effect is no change in total assets.

	Assets			=	Liabilities	+	Equity
	Cash	Supplies	Equipment	=		+	Common Stock
Prior Bal.	$15,000	$ 0	$ 0				$15,000
#2	−$10,000	+$1,000	+$9,000				
New Bal.	$ 5,000	$1,000	$9,000				$15,000
	$15,000			=	$0	+	$15,000

TRANSACTION #3: Circle Films receives a $1,500 payment immediately after filming a customer's wedding. Because Circle Films is receiving cash, assets increase. But unlike the previous transaction in which assets were exchanged, the increase in assets in this transaction results from filming the wedding. Recall from Chapter 1 that an inflow of assets from providing a service is a revenue. Revenues increase net income and therefore retained earnings. As a result, Circle Films' equity increases.

	Assets			=	Liabilities	+	Equity	
	Cash	Supplies	Equipment	=		+	Common Stock	Retained Earnings
Prior Bal.	$5,000	$1,000	$9,000				$15,000	$ 0
#3	+$1,500							+$1,500
New Bal.	$6,500	$1,000	$9,000				$15,000	$1,500
	$16,500			=	$0	+	$16,500	

TRANSACTION #4: Circle Films receives a $2,000 deposit from a customer to film her parents' fiftieth wedding anniversary. In this transaction, Circle Films again receives cash from a customer, so assets increase. However, it has not yet provided the service, so it has an obligation to the customer. As a result, Circle Films' liabilities increase for the amount of cash received.

	Assets			=	Liabilities	+	Equity	
	Cash	Supplies	Equipment	=	Unearned Revenue	+	Common Stock	Retained Earnings
Prior Bal.	$6,500	$1,000	$9,000		$ 0		$15,000	$1,500
#4	+$2,000				+$2,000			
New Bal.	$8,500	$1,000	$9,000		$2,000		$15,000	$1,500
	$18,500			=	$2,000	+	$16,500	

TRANSACTION #5: Circle Films paid $250 cash to run an ad in the local paper. Because Circle Films paid cash, assets decrease. The decrease in assets results from advertising its business. Recall from Chapter 1 that a decrease in assets from operating a business is an expense. Expenses decrease net income and therefore retained earnings. As a result, Circle Films' equity decreases.

	Assets			=	Liabilities	+	Equity	
	Cash	Supplies	Equipment	=	Unearned Revenue	+	Common Stock	Retained Earnings
Prior Bal.	$8,500	$1,000	$9,000		$2,000		$15,000	$1,500
#5	−$ 250							−$ 250
New Bal.	$8,250	$1,000	$9,000		$2,000		$15,000	$1,250
	$18,250			=	$2,000	+	$16,250	

TRANSACTION #6: Circle Films films a dance competition, leaving a $3,500 invoice with the customer. Because Circle Films receives no cash at the time of the competition, it is tempting to conclude that there is no accounting transaction and therefore no effect on the accounting equation. However, not all accounting transactions affect cash. By completing the job and leaving an invoice with the customer, Circle Films now has a receivable from the customer. Therefore, assets increase. And because the receivable is generated by providing a service, the firm has additional revenues and therefore more equity. So, equity increases as well. Note that this transaction is very similar to transaction #3, with the only difference being the type of asset that increases.

	Assets				=	Liabilities	+	Equity	
	Cash	Accounts Receivable	Supplies	Equipment	=	Unearned Revenue	+	Common Stock	Retained Earnings
Prior Bal.	$8,250	$ 0	$1,000	$9,000		$2,000		$15,000	$1,250
#6		+$3,500							+$3,500
New Bal.	$8,250	$3,500	$1,000	$9,000		$2,000		$15,000	$4,750
	$21,750				=	$2,000	+	$19,750	

TRANSACTION #7: Circle Films purchases another $9,000 video camera by signing a two-year promissory note requiring the payment of principal and interest at maturity. Interest is charged at a 6% annual rate. Like transaction #2, Circle Films receives equipment, so assets increase. Unlike transaction #2, though, Circle Films promises to pay in two years rather than today. Therefore, its liabilities increase.

	Assets				=	Liabilities		+	Equity	
	Cash	Accounts Receivable	Supplies	Equipment	=	Unearned Revenue	Notes Payable	+	Common Stock	Retained Earnings
Prior Bal.	$8,250	$3,500	$1,000	$ 9,000		$2,000	$ 0		$15,000	$4,750
#7				+$ 9,000			+$9,000			
New Bal.	$8,250	$3,500	$1,000	$18,000		$2,000	$9,000		$15,000	$4,750
	$30,750				=	$11,000		+	$19,750	

TRANSACTION #8: Circle Films receives $3,500 from the customer in payment of the open invoice from transaction #6. In this transaction, Circle Films exchanges one asset for another. It receives cash in satisfaction of the receivable that was created when the service was performed. As a result, cash increases while receivables decrease. There is no change in total assets.

	Assets				=	Liabilities		+	Equity	
	Cash	Accounts Receivable	Supplies	Equipment	=	Unearned Revenue	Notes Payable	+	Common Stock	Retained Earnings
Prior Bal.	$ 8,250	$3,500	$1,000	$18,000		$2,000	$9,000		$15,000	$4,750
#8	+$ 3,500	−$3,500								
New Bal.	$11,750	$ 0	$1,000	$18,000		$2,000	$9,000		$15,000	$4,750
	$30,750				=	$11,000		+	$19,750	

TRANSACTION #9: Circle Films pays salaries of $2,000 to its employees. In this case, its cash decreases by $2,000, so its assets decrease. Since the payments are an outflow of assets from operating the business, the payments are an expense, which is a reduction to equity. Therefore, equity decreases.

	Assets				=	Liabilities		+	Equity	
	Cash	Accounts Receivable	Supplies	Equipment	=	Unearned Revenue	Notes Payable	+	Common Stock	Retained Earnings
Prior Bal.	$11,750	$0	$1,000	$18,000		$2,000	$9,000		$15,000	$4,750
#9	−$ 2,000									−$2,000
New Bal.	$ 9,750	$0	$1,000	$18,000		$2,000	$9,000		$15,000	$2,750
	$28,750				=	$11,000		+	$17,750	

TRANSACTION #10: At the end of the month, Circle Films pays its owners a $1,500 cash dividend. In this transaction, cash and therefore assets decrease. Payments to a company's owners are dividends. Recall from Chapter 1 that dividends decrease retained earnings, so equity decreases as well.

	Assets				=	Liabilities		+	Equity	
	Cash	Accounts Receivable	Supplies	Equipment	=	Unearned Revenue	Notes Payable	+	Common Stock	Retained Earnings
Prior Bal.	$9,750	$0	$1,000	$18,000		$2,000	$9,000		$15,000	$2,750
#10	−$1,500									−$1,500
New Bal.	$8,250	$0	$1,000	$18,000		$2,000	$9,000		$15,000	$1,250
		$27,250			=	$11,000		+	$16,250	

Summary of Transactions

The ten transactions of Circle Films are summarized in Exhibit 3-2. Circle Films started the month with nothing but an idea and ended the month with $27,250 in assets, $11,000 in liabilities, and $16,250 in equity. As you review the exhibit, note that changes to the left side of the equation equaled changes to the right side of the equation for all transactions. As a result, the accounting equation was always in balance. Note also that every transaction affected at least two specific accounts. Sometimes the transaction affected two asset accounts (#2 and #8), sometimes an asset and a liability account (#4 and #7), and sometimes an asset and an equity account (#1, #3, #5, #6, #9, and #10). Any combination affecting assets, liabilities, and equity can occur, as long as the equation stays in balance.

Exhibit 3-2 Transaction Summary for Circle Films

	Assets				=	Liabilities		+	Equity	
	Cash	**Accounts Receivable**	**Supplies**	**Equipment**	=	**Unearned Revenue**	**Notes Payable**	+	**Common Stock**	**Retained Earnings**
#1	+15,000				=			+	+15,000	
#2	−10,000		+1,000	+9,000	=			+		
#3	+1,500				=			+		+1,500
#4	+2,000				=	+2,000		+		
#5	−250				=			+		−250
#6		+3,500			=			+		+3,500
#7				+9,000	=		+9,000	+		
#8	+3,500	−3,500			=			+		
#9	−2,000				=			+		−2,000
#10	−1,500				=			+		−1,500
	$8,250	$0	$1,000	$18,000	=	$2,000	$9,000	+	$15,000	$1,250
		$27,250			=	$11,000		+	$16,250	

LO3 The Double-Entry Accounting System

While the preceding analysis is an excellent way to understand and visualize the effect of accounting transactions, accounting information systems do not record transactions using plusses and minuses in a tabular format since such an approach, while accurate, would be very cumbersome. Rather, they use a *double-entry system* that traces its origins back to a mathematical treatise written in the fifteenth century by a Franciscan monk, Luca Pacioli. The double-entry system is based on the dual nature of accounting demonstrated in the preceding transaction analyses. That is, every accounting transaction affects at least two accounts, so accounting systems record those transactions with a "double" or "two-fold" entry. The following sections explain the mechanics of this double-entry system, starting with the T-account.

The T-Account

All accounts can be characterized or represented in the following form known as a T-account due to its resemblance to a capital T.

Account Name	
Debit Side	Credit Side

The name of the account is listed at the top with two columns appearing below. The left column is the *debit* side while the right column is the *credit* side. The term **debit** simply means left side of an account while the term **credit** simply means right side of an account.

T-accounts work as follows. When a transaction affects an account balance, the amount of the transaction is entered on the account's debit side or credit side, depending on the transaction. You will see how transactions are recorded shortly. An entry on the debit side is called a "debit," while an entry on the credit side is called a "credit." Once all entries are made, the balance in an account is determined by separately adding up all debits and all credits and subtracting the smaller total from the larger, leaving the difference as the account balance. The following three examples illustrate this process.

Examples of T-Account Mechanics

Asset		Liability		Equity	
1,000	5,000	2,000	6,000	7,000	2,000
4,000	3,000	1,000	4,000		3,000
8,000		3,000			3,000
5,000			4,000		1,000

The areas between the horizontal lines contain the activity in each account, with the account balance below. The asset account has three debit entries totaling $13,000 and two credit entries totaling $8,000, leaving a debit balance of $5,000. The liability account has debit entries totaling $6,000 and credit entries totaling $10,000, resulting in a $4,000 credit balance. The equity account has a $1,000 credit balance after having $7,000 of debit entries and $8,000 of credit entries.

It is no coincidence that in this example the asset account has a debit balance while the liability and equity accounts have credit balances. In a double-entry system, asset accounts should normally have debit balances while liability and equity accounts should normally have credit balances. Such "normal" balances mirror the accounting equation, where assets are on the left side of the equal sign and liabilities and equity are on the right side.

Normal Account Balances

Asset Accounts		Liability Accounts		Equity Accounts	
Normal Balance			Normal Balance		Normal Balance

Accounting Equation

Assets = Liabilities + Equity

This arrangement of normal balances is the key to how a double-entry system works. To keep the accounting equation balanced, a double-entry system must keep debit balances equal to credit balances. This means that every accounting transaction must be recorded with equal changes to debit and credit balances. That, again, is why the system is "double-entry." How debits and credits are used to change account balances is discussed next.

Debit The left side of an account.

Credit The right side of an account.

Any change to the accounting equation must be accompanied by a second change.

Debit and Credit Rules

In a double-entry system, changes in account balances are recorded according to the following basic rules.

To *increase* an account balance	Record transaction on the same side as the normal balance.
To *decrease* an account balance	Record transaction on the opposite side as the normal balance.

These two rules seem simple enough, but their application can be confusing at first because different accounts have different normal balances. The following sections demonstrate how these rules are applied to asset, liability, and equity accounts. Also demonstrated is how these rules are applied to the three types of accounts that affect equity: revenues, expenses, and dividends. Once you have mastered the mechanics of these six types of accounts, you should be able to record most any accounting transaction correctly.

Asset Accounts Asset accounts have normal debit balances. Therefore, increases to assets are recorded on the debit side while decreases are recorded on the credit side.

Asset Accounts

Record increases on debit side	Record decreases on credit side
Balance	

To illustrate, suppose that a company starts the day with $5,000 in cash, receives $300 from a customer, and pays $250 to a vendor. The beginning balance of $5,000 is recorded on the debit side of the cash T-account. The increase of $300 is also recorded on the debit side, but the $250 decrease in cash is recorded on the side opposite of the normal balance—the credit side. Netting the debit and credit sides yields a debit balance of $5,050.

Cash

5,000	250
300	
5,050	

Liability and Equity Accounts Liability and equity accounts have normal credit balances. Therefore, increases are recorded on the credit side, while decreases are recorded on the debit side.

Liability and Equity Accounts

Record decreases on debit side	Record increases on credit side
	Balance

To illustrate a liability account, suppose that a company owing $2,500 to a vendor buys an additional $150 of product on account and then pays $850 of its obligation. The beginning balance of $2,500 is recorded on the credit side of the Accounts Payable T-account. The additional payable of $150 is also recorded on the credit side. In contrast, the $850 payment, which is a reduction to the payable, is recorded on the debit side. Netting the debit and credit sides yields a credit balance of $1,800.

Accounts Payable

850	2,500
	150
	1,800

To illustrate an equity account, suppose that a company has $34,000 of common stock outstanding. The company then issues additional common stock for $10,000 and later buys back and retires $6,000 of stock. The original $34,000 balance appears on the credit side of the Common Stock T-account. Since the Common Stock account has a normal credit balance, the $10,000 increase is recorded on the credit side while the $6,000 decrease is recorded on the opposite or debit side of the account. Netting the debit and credit sides yields a credit balance of $38,000.

Common Stock

6,000	34,000
	10,000
	38,000

Revenue Accounts When a company generates a revenue, it is increasing its equity. As demonstrated previously, increasing an equity account requires a credit entry. Therefore, revenue accounts are set up so that they also are increased with a credit entry. That is, revenue accounts have normal credit balances and are increased with credit entries and decreased with debit entries.

Revenue Accounts

Record decreases on debit side	Record increases on credit side
	Balance

To illustrate, suppose that a company has $115,000 in existing service revenue. The company then earns an additional $13,000 in revenue. Since the Service Revenue account has a normal credit balance, both the existing $115,000 balance and the $13,000 increase are shown on the credit side, resulting in a balance of $128,000.

Service Revenue

	115,000
	13,000
	128,000

Expense and Dividend Accounts When a company incurs expenses or pays dividends, it is decreasing its equity. As demonstrated previously, decreasing equity requires a debit entry. Therefore, for expense and dividend accounts to effectively reduce equity, they have normal debit balances. Expense and dividend accounts are therefore increased with debit entries and decreased with credit entries.

Expense and Dividend Accounts

Record increases on debit side	Record decreases on credit side
Balance	

To illustrate an expense, suppose that a company has $66,000 in salaries expense when it incurs an additional $6,000 in salaries expense. Since the Salaries Expense account has a normal debit balance, both the $66,000 in existing expense and the $6,000 increase should be recorded on the debit side of the account, yielding a balance of $72,000.

Salaries Expense

66,000	
6,000	
72,000	

Summary of Debit and Credit Rules

You have now seen each major type of account and how the debit and credit columns are used to increase or decrease those accounts. For asset, expense, and dividend accounts, increases are recorded in the debit column and decreases are recorded in the credit column. For liability, equity, and revenue accounts, increases are recorded in the credit column and decreases are recorded in the debit column. A summary of these rules is presented in Exhibit 3-3.

Exhibit 3-3 Summary of Debit and Credit Rules

Type of Account	Normal Balance	Increase with a	Decrease with a
Asset	Debit	Debit	Credit
Liability	Credit	Credit	Debit
Equity	Credit	Credit	Debit
Revenue	Credit	Credit	Debit
Expense	Debit	Debit	Credit
Dividend	Debit	Debit	Credit

HOME DEPOT ANALYSIS

Look at Home Depot's income statement in Appendix C. Which of the accounts would be increased with a credit entry? Would the remaining accounts be increased with a debit entry?

Home Depot's income statement lists eight different accounts. Of those accounts, Net Sales and Interest and Investment Income would be increased with a credit entry. Both of these accounts are revenue accounts. The other six accounts are expense accounts and are increased with a debit entry.

In a double-entry system, asset accounts have debit balances while liability and equity accounts have credit balances.

LO4 Recording Transactions in the Accounting System

This section examines the actual process of recording accounting transactions in a double-entry system. Accounting transactions are not recorded directly in T-accounts. Instead, accounting transactions are first recorded in a journal. Once recorded, the information is transferred or posted to a ledger. Information in the ledger is then summarized in a worksheet known as a trial balance. Financial statements are then prepared from the information in the trial balance.

The Journal

A **journal** is a chronological record of transactions. Because the journal is where transactions are first recorded into the accounting system, it is often called the book of original entry. Entries recorded in the journal are called *journal entries*. Companies can have various types of journals in which they record transactions, but since the mechanics of all journals are the same, we will focus on the most basic of journals, the general journal. The general journal and an example journal entry take the form shown in Exhibit 3-4.

Exhibit 3-4 General Journal Form

Date	Accounts and Explanation	Debit	Credit
Date of transaction	Account(s) Debited	Amount	
	Account(s) Credited		Amount
	(Explanation of transaction)		

Journal A chronological record of transactions.

Ledger A collection of accounts and their balances.

At the far left of the journal is a column for the transaction date. To the right of the date is a column to record the names of the accounts affected by the transaction and an explanation. The account(s) receiving debit entries are listed first followed by the account(s) receiving credit entries, which are slightly indented. To the right of the account names are debit and credit columns to record the monetary amounts of the transaction. As explained previously, the totals in the debit and credit columns should be the same for each transaction. When an accounting transaction is recorded in the general journal, we often say that the transaction has been *journalized*.

The general journal is useful in that it contains in one place a chronological record of all the accounting transactions of a company. Thus, a company can examine its journal if it has a question about whether a transaction was recorded or whether it was recorded correctly. However, the general journal is not very useful if a company is trying to determine the balance in a particular account. To get an account balance, one would have to find all journal entries affecting that account and then compute a balance. To avoid such a time-consuming task, the information recorded in the general journal is transferred to a *ledger*.

The Ledger

A **ledger** is a collection of accounts and their balances. While most companies have various types of ledgers containing different accounts, we will focus on the most basic type of ledger, the general ledger. The general ledger is nothing more than a collection of T-accounts for a company, which means that the general ledger contains both the activity and balances of all company accounts.

Account balances in the general ledger are updated as follows. When an accounting transaction is recorded in the general journal, the amounts recorded in the debit and credit columns are transferred to the debit and credit columns of the respective T-accounts in the ledger. This process of copying or transferring the information from the journal to the ledger is called *posting* and results in up-to-date account balances. Thus, companies look to the ledger for balances in their accounts.

When an accounting transaction is recorded in the general journal, we often say that the transaction has been *journalized.*

Jacob Wackerhausen/iStockphoto

The Trial Balance

After accounting transactions are recorded in the journal and posted to the ledger, companies prepare a trial balance. A **trial balance** is a listing of accounts and their balances at a specific point in time. In a trial balance, all accounts in a company's ledger are listed in a column on the left. Asset accounts are listed first, followed by liability accounts, equity accounts, and then revenue, expense, and dividend accounts. Each account's balance from the ledger is listed in the appropriate debit or credit column. At the bottom of each column, a total is calculated. The form of the trial balance is shown in Exhibit 3-5.

Exhibit 3-5 Trial Balance Form

	Debit	Credit
Asset Account(s)	Amount	
Liability Account(s)		Amount
Equity Account(s)		Amount
Revenue Account(s)		Amount
Expense Account(s)	Amount	
Dividends	Amount	
Totals	Total Debits	Total Credits

Trial balance A listing of accounts and their balances at a specific point in time.

MAKING IT REAL

Although the text primarily discusses a manual accounting system, there are several popular computerized accounting information systems utilized by small businesses. Two of the most popular are QuickBooks® and Peachtree®.

QuickBooks is favored largely for its simplicity and ease of use for individuals with little to no accounting experience. Peachtree is a more sophisticated accounting system designed for a user with more accounting knowledge than the average person.

David Young-Wolff/PhotoEdit

Both systems provide banking, general ledger, accounts payable, accounts receivable, payroll, and inventory features and can keep track of income and expenses by customer, job, and department. Many reports can be created by both systems to analyze business performance. Both systems also provide security features to ensure only authorized users are accessing the businesses' accounting information.

Overall, such computerized systems are a great tool for businesses because they help ensure that a company's accounting information is captured and communicated effectively and efficiently.

A trial balance serves several functions. First and foremost, a trial balance proves that total debit balances equal total credit balances. If they are unequal, then the accounting equation is out of balance and a correction is warranted. Second, a trial balance summarizes in one place all accounts of an entity and their respective balances. Financial statements are then prepared from those balances. Finally, a trial balance is helpful in making any necessary adjustments to account balances at the end of an accounting period. We will see this function in Chapter 4.

LO5 Comprehensive Example: Journal Entries to Financial Statements

The following section uses the Circle Films transactions to demonstrate the recording of transactions in the journal, the posting of information to the ledger, the preparation of a trial balance, and the preparation of financial statements.

Recording Transactions in the Journal and Posting to the Ledger

Circle Films entered into ten transactions. A four-step process will be used to demonstrate how to properly record each transaction and post it to the ledger. First, the accounts affected by the transaction will be identified. Second, the relevant debit/credit rules for those accounts will be identified. Third, the transaction will be recorded in the journal. Fourth, the transaction will be posted to the ledger. This four-step process can be followed when recording and posting any accounting transaction.

Transaction #1 Circle Films issued 3,000 shares of common stock for $15,000.

Step 1—What accounts are affected and how?
Circle Films receives cash, so cash increases. Circle Films issues common stock, so common stock increases.

Step 2—What debit and credit entries are required?
Cash is an asset, so debit the Cash account to increase it. Common Stock is an equity account, so credit the Common Stock account to increase it.

Step 3—Record the journal entry.

#1	Cash	15,000	
	Common Stock		15,000
	(Owners invest cash in business)		

Assets	=	Liabilities	+	Equity
+15,000				+15,000

Step 4—Post the information to the ledger.

Cash (Dr.)	Cash (Cr.)	Common Stock (Dr.)	Common Stock (Cr.)
15,000			15,000
15,000			15,000

Transaction #2 Circle Films buys a $9,000 video camera and $1,000 of memory cards for $10,000 cash.

Step 1—What accounts are affected and how?
Circle Films receives a camera and some tapes, so both equipment and supplies increase. Circle Films pays with cash, so cash decreases.

Step 2—What debit and credit entries are required?
Equipment and supplies are assets, so debit the Equipment and Supplies accounts to increase them. Cash is also an asset, so credit the Cash account to decrease it.

Step 3—Record the journal entry.

#2	Equipment	9,000	
	Supplies	1,000	
	Cash		10,000
	(Purchase video camera and tapes)		

Assets	=	Liabilities	+	Equity
+9,000				
+1,000				
−10,000				

Step 4—Post the information to the ledger.

Cash (Dr.)	Cash (Cr.)	Supplies (Dr.)	Supplies (Cr.)	Equipment (Dr.)	Equipment (Cr.)
15,000	10,000	1,000		9,000	
5,000		1,000		9,000	

Transaction #3 Circle Films films a wedding for $1,500 cash.

Step 1—What accounts are affected and how?
Circle Films receives cash, so cash increases. The increase in cash results from Circle Films providing its service, so service revenue increases.

Step 2—What debit and credit entries are required?
Cash is an asset, so debit the Cash account to increase it. Revenues increase equity, so credit the Service Revenue account to increase it.

Step 3—Record the journal entry.

#3	Cash	1,500	
	Service Revenue		1,500
	(Provide service to customer)		

Assets	=	Liabilities	+	Equity
+1,500				+1,500

Step 4—Post the information to the ledger.

Cash	
15,000	10,000
1,500	
6,500	

Service Revenue	
	1,500
	1,500

Transaction #4 Circle Films receives $2,000 to film a future reception.

Step 1—What accounts are affected and how? Circle Films receives cash, so cash increases. Because Circle Films has not yet performed the required service, it has a new liability to the customer called unearned revenue.

Step 2—What debit and credit entries are required? Cash is an asset, so debit the Cash account to increase it. Unearned Revenue is a liability, so credit the Unearned Revenue account to increase it.

Step 3—Record the journal entry.

#4	Cash	2,000	
	Unearned Revenue		2,000
	(Cash received in advance of providing service to customer)		

Assets	=	Liabilities	+	Equity
+2,000		+2,000		

Step 4—Post the information to the ledger.

Cash	
15,000	10,000
1,500	
2,000	
8,500	

Unearned Revenue	
	2,000
	2,000

Transaction #5 Circle Films pays $250 cash for advertising.

Step 1—What accounts are affected and how? Circle Films pays cash, so cash decreases. The decrease in cash results from Circle Films' advertising its service, so advertising expense increases.

Step 2—What debit and credit entries are required? Cash is an asset, so credit the Cash account to decrease it. Expenses decrease equity, so debit the Advertising Expense account to increase it.

Step 3—Record the journal entry.

#5	Advertising Expense	250	
	Cash		250
	(Pay for advertising)		

Assets	=	Liabilities	+	Equity
−250				−250

Step 4—Post the information to the ledger.

Cash	
15,000	10,000
1,500	250
2,000	
8,250	

Advertising Expense	
250	
250	

Transaction #6 Circle Films films an event for $3,500 and leaves an invoice with the customer.

Step 1—What accounts are affected and how? Circle Films performed a service for a customer, so its service revenue increases. Circle Films has not yet received any payment from the customer, so its accounts receivable also increases.

Step 2—What debit and credit entries are required? Accounts Receivable is an asset, so debit the Accounts Receivable account to increase it. Revenues increase equity, so credit the Service Revenue account to increase it.

Step 3—Record the journal entry.

#6	Accounts Receivable	3,500	
	Service Revenue		3,500
	(Provide service to customer on account)		

Assets	=	Liabilities	+	Equity
+3,500				+3,500

Step 4—Post the information to the ledger.

Accounts Receivable	
3,500	
3,500	

Service Revenue	
	1,500
	3,500
	5,000

Transaction #7 Circle Films buys another camera by signing a $9,000 promissory note.

Step 1—What accounts are affected and how? Circle Films receives a camera, so equipment increases. It signs a note for payment, so notes payable increases.

Step 2—What debit and credit entries are required? Equipment is an asset, so debit the Equipment account to increase it. Notes Payable is a liability, so credit the Notes Payable account to increase it.

Step 3—Record the journal entry.

#7	Equipment	9,000	
	Notes Payable		9,000
	(Purchase of a video camera with a promissory note)		

Assets	=	Liabilities	+	Equity
+9,000		+9,000		

Step 4—Post the information to the ledger.

Equipment

9,000	
9,000	
18,000	

Notes Payable

	9,000
	9,000

Transaction #8 Circle Films receives $3,500 from a customer in payment of services provided.

Step 1—What accounts are affected and how? Circle Films receives cash, so cash increases. Circle Films collects a receivable from a customer, so its accounts receivable decreases.

Step 2—What debit and credit entries are required? Cash is an asset, so debit the Cash account to increase it. Accounts Receivable is also an asset account, so credit the Accounts Receivable account to decrease it.

Step 3—Record the journal entry.

#8	Cash	3,500	
	Accounts Receivable		3,500
	(Receive payment from customer)		

Assets	=	Liabilities	+	Equity
+3,500				
−3,500				

Step 4—Post the information to the ledger.

Cash

15,000	10,000
1,500	250
2,000	
3,500	
11,750	

Accounts Receivable

3,500	3,500
0	

Transaction #9 Circle Films pays $2,000 in salaries to employees.

Step 1—What accounts are affected and how? Circle Films pays cash, so cash decreases. This reduction in cash results from salaries paid to employees, so salaries expense increases.

Step 2—What debit and credit entries are required? Cash is an asset, so credit the Cash account to decrease it. Expenses decrease equity, so debit the Salaries Expense account to increase it.

Step 3—Record the journal entry.

#9	Salaries Expense	2,000	
	Cash		2,000
	(Pay salaries to employees)		

Assets	=	Liabilities	+	Equity
−2,000				−2,000

Step 4—Post the information to the ledger.

Cash

15,000	10,000
1,500	250
2,000	2,000
3,500	
9,750	

Salaries Expense

2,000	
2,000	

Transaction #10 Circle Films pays $1,500 in dividends to the owners.

Step 1—What accounts are affected and how? Circle Films pays cash, so cash decreases. The cash payment is a distribution of company assets to the owners, so dividends increase.

Step 2—What debit and credit entries are required? Cash is an asset, so credit the Cash account to decrease it. Dividends decrease equity, so debit the Dividends account to increase it.

Step 3—Record the journal entry.

#10	Dividends	1,500	
	Cash		1,500
	(Pay dividends to owners)		

Assets	=	Liabilities	+	Equity
−1,500				−1,500

Step 4—Post the information to the ledger.

Cash	
15,000	10,000
1,500	250
2,000	2,000
3,500	1,500
8,250	

Dividends	
1,500	
1,500	

Summary After recording and posting the ten transactions, Circle Films' complete Journal and Ledger would appear as follows:

General Journal

Transaction	Accounts	Debit	Credit
#1	Cash	15,000	
	Common Stock		15,000
#2	Equipment	9,000	
	Supplies	1,000	
	Cash		10,000
#3	Cash	1,500	
	Service Revenue		1,500
#4	Cash	2,000	
	Unearned Revenue		2,000
#5	Advertising Expense	250	
	Cash		250
#6	Accounts Receivable	3,500	
	Service Revenue		3,500
#7	Equipment	9,000	
	Notes Payable		9,000
#8	Cash	3,500	
	Accounts Receivable		3,500
#9	Salaries Expense	2,000	
	Cash		2,000
#10	Dividends	1,500	
	Cash		1,500

General Ledger

Cash	
15,000	10,000
1,500	250
2,000	2,000
3,500	1,500
8,250	

Accounts Receivable	
3,500	3,500
0	

Supplies	
1,000	
1,000	

Equipment	
9,000	
9,000	
18,000	

Unearned Revenue	
	2,000
	2,000

Notes Payable	
	9,000
	9,000

Common Stock	
	15,000
	15,000

Service Revenue	
	1,500
	3,500
	5,000

Advertising Expense	
250	
250	

Salaries Expense	
2,000	
2,000	

Dividends	
1,500	
1,500	

Preparing a Trial Balance

Once all transactions are recorded in the journal and posted to the ledger, a trial balance can be prepared. Recall that a trial balance is a listing of all accounts

Circle Films
Trial Balance
May 31

	Debit	Credit
Cash	$ 8,250	
Supplies	1,000	
Equipment	18,000	
Unearned Revenue		$ 2,000
Notes Payable		9,000
Common Stock		15,000
Service Revenue		5,000
Advertising Expense	250	
Salaries Expense	2,000	
Dividends	1,500	
Totals	$31,000	$31,000

and their balances at a specific point in time, starting with assets and followed by liabilities, equity, revenues, expenses, and dividends. Therefore, it is a summary of the balances in the ledger. You can confirm that the trial balance includes only the balances from the general ledger by reviewing again Circle Films' ledger on the previous page. As expected, total debit balances of $31,000 equal total credit balances of $31,000 in the trial balance.

Preparation of Financial Statements

Once the trial balance is finished, the final product of the accounting system can be prepared—the financial statements. As demonstrated in Chapter 1, the income statement must be prepared first, followed by the statement of retained earnings, and then the balance sheet.

The income statement shows a company's revenues and expenses. Circle Films' May 31 trial balance contains only one revenue account and two expense accounts. Therefore, its income statement for the month of May would appear as follows:

Circle Films
Income Statement
For the Month Ending May 31

Service revenue		$5,000
Expenses		
Advertising expense	$ 250	
Salaries expense	2,000	
Total expenses		2,250
Net income		$2,750

With net income calculated, Circle Films' statement of retained earnings can be prepared. Recall from Chapter 1 that the statement of retained earnings takes the beginning balance in retained earnings, adds net income, and subtracts dividends to yield the current balance in retained earnings. Its May 31 trial balance shows no balance in beginning retained earnings because it just started its business. It also shows a $1,500 balance in dividends. Combining these two balances with net income yields the following statement of retained earnings for the month of May:

Circle Films
Statement of Retained Earnings
For the Month Ending May 31

Retained earnings, May 1	$ 0
+ Net income	2,750
− Dividends	1,500
Retained earnings, May 31	$1,250

Scott Kochsiek/iStockphoto.com

With retained earnings calculated, the company's balance sheet can be prepared. A balance sheet shows a company's assets, liabilities, and equity at a point in time. Circle Films' May 31 trial balance shows three asset accounts, two liability accounts, and one equity account (Common Stock). These six accounts, along with the amount of retained earnings from the May statement of retained earnings, should be included on the balance sheet. Therefore, its May 31 balance sheet would appear as follows:

Circle Films
Balance Sheet
May 31

Cash		$ 8,250
Supplies		1,000
Equipment		18,000
Total assets		$27,250
Unearned revenue	$ 2,000	
Notes payable	9,000	
Total liabilities		$11,000
Common stock	15,000	
Retained earnings	1,250	
Total stockholders' equity		16,250
Total liabilities and stockholders' equity		$27,250

STUDY TOOLS 3

Chapter review card

- Learning Objective and Key Concept Reviews
- Key Definitions and Formulas

Online (Located at www.cengagebrain.com)

- Flash Cards and Crossword Puzzles
- Games and Quizzes
- E-Lectures
- Homework Assignments (as directed by your instructor)

CONCEPT QUESTIONS

1. (LO1) What is an accounting information system?
2. (LO1) What is an accounting transaction?
3. (LO1) What is the main function of an account?
4. (LO1) What does a chart of accounts contain?
5. (LO2) What is the fundamental accounting equation?
6. (LO2) Do accounting transactions have to affect both sides of the fundamental accounting equation? Explain.
7. (LO3) Does the double entry system mean that each transaction is recorded twice? Explain.
8. (LO3) True or false: debit means "increase" and credit means "decrease." Why?
9. (LO3) What are the normal account balances for the following accounts: a) Equipment; b) Unearned Revenue; c) Supplies Expense; d) Accounts Payable; e) Retained Earnings?
10. (LO3) What is used to decrease an asset account, a liability account, a revenue account, and an expense account?
11. (LO4) Where are transactions first recorded?
12. (LO4) What is a ledger, and from where does the input for a ledger come?
13. (LO4) In what order are accounts listed in a trial balance?
14. (LO4) To what does the term "posting" refer?
15. (LO4) What are the three main purposes of a trial balance?

MULTIPLE CHOICE

1. (LO1) When considering accounting information systems, which of the following is false?
   a. Accounting information systems vary in size across companies
   b. An accounting information system records and summarizes economic events
   c. All accounting information systems use the same basic procedures to identify, record, and communicate the effects of economic events
   d. Accounting information systems record all economic events
2. (LO1) Which of the following would be considered an accounting transaction?
   a. Hiring a new CEO
   b. Selling an in-house developed patent
   c. Establishing a new company dress code
   d. Posting journal entries to the general ledger
3. (LO1) Which of the following would not be an account found in the financial statements?
   a. Equipment
   b. Salaries Payable
   c. Employees' Personal Data
   d. Dividends
4. (LO1) Which of the following is false regarding a chart of accounts?
   a. The total number of asset accounts must equal the total number of liability accounts
   b. A chart of accounts is a listing of all the accounts that a company uses to record accounting information

c. Each account listing contains an account name and a numerical reference
d. Charts of accounts will vary across companies

5. (LO2) Which of the following is false?
   a. A company can have a transaction that affects only the left side of the fundamental accounting equation
   b. In each accounting transaction, total debits to assets must equal total credits to liabilities
   c. The fundamental accounting equation will always balance after each correctly recorded accounting transaction
   d. All of the above are true

6. (LO3) Which of the following is true?
   i. In the double-entry system, each accounting transaction is recorded twice
   ii. Each journal entry will at least affect two accounts.
   a. i. only
   b. ii. only
   c. Both i. and ii.
   d. Neither i. nor ii.

7. (LO3) Which of the following groups of accounts shows only accounts that are increased with a debit?
   a. Assets, Liabilities, Dividends
   b. Assets, Equity, Dividends
   c. Assets, Expenses, Dividends
   d. Assets, Equity, Expenses

8. (LO3) Which of the following is true?
   i. Paying out a dividend of $1,000 would result in a debit to the Dividends account.
   ii. In the general ledger, this $1,000 would be entered on the right side of the Dividends T-account.
   a. i. only
   b. ii. only
   c. Both i. and ii.
   b. Neither i. nor ii.

9. (LO3) What would be the result of a credit to these accounts?

	Cash	Service Revenue	Common Stock
a.	Increase	Increase	Decrease
b.	Decrease	Increase	Increase
c.	Decrease	Increase	Decrease
d.	Increase	Decrease	Increase

10. (LO4) The general journal:
   a. pulls all information from the general ledger.
   b. only contains revenue and expense accounts.
   c. is where transactions are recorded.
   d. is a collection of all of the accounts maintained by a company.

11. (LO4) The general ledger:
   a. is the first place a transaction is recorded.
   b. records economic events as well as accounting transactions.
   c. shows the activity in, and balances for, all of the company's accounts.
   d. requires adjusting entries in order for total debit balances to equal total credit balances.

12. (LO4) Which of the following is false?
   a. A trial balance is considered to be a financial statement
   b. In a trial balance, total debit balances must equal total credit balances
   c. A trial balance summarizes in one place all accounts of an entity and their respective balances
   d. Preparation of a trial balance is part of the accounting cycle

13. (LO4) Which of the following would cause a trial balance not to balance?
   a. Recording a $350 purchase of supplies on account as a debit to Supplies and a credit to Cash
   b. A $425 payment on account is unrecorded
   c. A $400 purchase on account is debited to Supplies for $400 and credited to Accounts Payable for $4,000
   d. A $500 purchase of supplies on account is credited to Supplies and debited to Accounts Payable

14. (LO4) Which of the following is not a purpose of the trial balance?
   a. To summarize in one place all accounts of an entity and their respective balances
   b. To provide a chronological order of a company's transactions
   c. To serve as a helpful tool in preparing financial statements
   d. To prove that total debit balances equal total credit balances

15. (LO4) A journal entry does not contain:
   a. the date of the transaction.
   b. the balance of the accounts involved.
   c. an explanation of the transaction.
   d. at least two accounts.

16. (LO2, 5) Incurring $500 in salaries while earning $1,500 of revenue would result in a:
   a. $1,500 net increase in net income.
   b. $1,000 net increase in net income.
   c. $2,000 net increase in net income.
   d. none of the above.

17. (LO5) Which of the following properly demonstrates the flow of information through the accounting system?
   a. Journal ⇒ Ledger ⇒ Trial Balance ⇒ Financial Statements
   b. Ledger ⇒ Journal ⇒ Trial Balance ⇒ Financial Statements
   c. Journal ⇒ Trial Balance ⇒ Ledger ⇒ Financial Statements
   d. Trial Balance ⇒ Ledger ⇒ Journal ⇒ Financial Statements

BRIEF EXERCISES

1. Chart of Accounts LO1

The following accounts were taken from the charts of accounts of a retailer, a bank, and/or a chemical company:

Cash	Property and Equipment
Research and Development Expense	Dividends Payable
Retained Earnings	Salaries Expense
Mortgage Receivable	Sales Returns

Required
Indicate whether each account would likely appear in the chart of accounts of the retailer (R), the bank (B), the chemical company (C), or all three (A).

2. Accounting Transactions LO1

A company enters into the following economic events:

1. Hired a new receptionist.
2. Billed customers for services performed.
3. Announced the signing of a contract that should produce $100,000 of new revenue.
4. Paid for insurance that will not be used until next year.

Required
Indicate whether each economic event would be considered an accounting transaction.

3. Analyze Transactions LO2

EA Systems entered into the following transactions during the month of August:

1. Received $6,350 for services performed during August.
2. Purchased $1,200 of supplies on account.
3. Paid employee salaries of $3,280 for the first week of August.
4. Paid $900 towards the previous purchase of supplies.

Required
Indicate whether each transaction increases, decreases, or has no effect on assets, liabilities, and equity. If a transaction affects equity, indicate whether the transaction affects revenues or expenses.

4. Journalize Transactions LO3

Review the EA Systems information in the preceding Brief Exercise.

Required
Prepare journal entries for each transaction (omitting explanations).

5. T-Accounts LO3

A company reports the following asset and liability T-accounts:

Account #1		Account #2		Account #3	
1,000	6,000	8,400	3,250	4,280	3,600
4,000	3,000		2,120	1,660	1,120

Required
Determine the balance in each account and identify whether each account would most likely be an asset account or a liability account.

6. Normal Balances LO 3

The following is a list of possible accounts found in a trial balance:

1. Equipment
2. Notes Payable
3. Dividends
4. Supplies
5. Rent Expense
6. Service Revenue
7. Unearned Revenue

Required
Indicate each account's normal balance and the effect of a debit and credit to the account.

7. Posting Transactions LO3

A company records the following transactions during November:

Date	Account Title	Debit	Credit
Nov. 1	Accounts Receivable	3,200	
	Service Revenue		3,200
Nov. 6	Cash	1,000	
	Accounts Receivable		1,000
Nov. 15	Utilities Expense	250	
	Cash		250
Nov. 26	Inventory	2,360	
	Accounts Payable		2,360

Required
Post the transactions to appropriate T-accounts and prepare a Trial Balance.

8. Recording Transactions LO2, 3, 5

Barrett Fisher, a clerk for Naval Supplies, received a payment from a customer and recorded the following journal entry:

Date	Account Title	Debit	Credit
Mar. 1	Cash	1,000	
	Accounts Payable		1,000

Required
Is this entry correct or not? Explain why it is or is not correct.

9. Trial Balance LO4

Harris Consulting provides the following incomplete trial balance:

Harris Consulting Trial Balance September 30		
	Debit	**Credit**
(a)	$ 8,850	
Accounts Receivable	(b)	
Supplies	1,625	
Notes Payable		$ 3,000
Common Stock		10,000
Retained Earnings		(c)
Service Revenue		15,630
Salaries Expense	10,560	
Utilities Expense	2,350	
Totals	$33,765	$ (d)

Required
Determine the missing values.

10. Prepare Financial Statements LO4

Review the Harris Consulting information in the preceding Brief Exercise.

Required
Using the given information and your answers for a-d, prepare Harris' income statement and statement of retained earnings for September and its balance sheet at September 30.

EXERCISES

11. Transaction Analysis LO2

The following is a list of independent economic events:

1. Purchased inventory on account.
2. Paid dividends at the end of the year.
3. Received cash in payment for services.
4. Issued common stock for cash.
5. Paid rent in cash.
6. Received a bill for utilities incurred.
7. Bought equipment for cash.
8. Billed customers for services.

Required
Indicate a) the accounts that would be affected by each transaction and b) whether each transaction increases, decreases, or has no effect on assets, liabilities, and stockholders' equity.

12. Transaction Analysis LO2

The following are a few possible ways in which the accounting equation can be affected by a transaction:

Assets	= Liabilities	+ Stockholders' Equity
1. Increase	Increase	
2. Decrease		Decrease
3. Increase		Increase
4. Increase/Decrease		
5. Decrease	Decrease	

Required
Describe at least two situations that could result in each of the five scenarios listed.

13. Transaction Analysis LO2

Handyman Services was founded on January 1 and entered into the following transactions during January:

1. Issued common stock of $30,000 in exchange for cash.
2. Purchased an old warehouse for $50,000 by issuing notes payable.
3. Purchased a truck for $15,000 cash.
4. Purchased shop supplies for $5,000 on account.
5. Provided services of $15,325, receiving $12,200 in cash.
6. Paid $1,000 for local advertising for January.
7. Received payment of $3,125 from customers in #5.
8. Paid $4,000 on open account from #4.
9. Paid dividends of $1,000 to stockholders.
10. Paid employee salaries of $4,000 for January.
11. Billed customers $3,500 for services provided during January.
12. Paid $100 interest on notes payable.

Required
a. Show the effects of each transaction on the accounting equation by preparing a tabular analysis using the following column headings: Cash, Accounts Receivable, Supplies, Property and Equipment, Accounts Payable, Notes Payable, Common Stock, Retained Earnings.
b. Calculate Handyman's net income for the month of January.

14. Normal Balances LO3

The following is a list of possible accounts found in a trial balance:

1. Accounts Receivable
2. Common Stock
3. Cash
4. Retained Earnings
5. Accounts Payable
6. Salaries Expense
7. Long-term Investments
8. Service Revenue
9. Dividends

Required
Indicate each account's normal balance and the effect of a debit and a credit to the account.

15. T-account Mechanics LO3

The general ledger for TPC Company contains the following accounts:

Cash	
2,000	3,000
8,000	(a)
4,000	

Notes Payable	
10,000	5,500
	18,100
	(b)

Salaries Expense	
13,500	
(c)	
15,900	

Accounts Payable	
23,850	45,300
(d)	12,775
	17,300

Service Revenue	
	(e)
	33,210
	88,690

Accounts Receivable	
(f)	3,500
2,500	9,570
7,660	

Required
Determine the missing values.

16. Transaction Analysis LO2, 3

Tsunami, Inc., entered into the following transactions during one month of operations:

1. Purchased $3,000 of computer equipment on account.
2. Issued $7,500 of common stock to investors in exchange for cash.
3. Purchased supplies for $300 in cash.
4. Billed customers $25,000 for services rendered.
5. Paid salaries of $3,500 to employees.
6. Paid dividends to stockholders in the amount of $1,000.
7. Received $5,000 cash in payment of services earned and billed in the previous month.
8. Paid cash for the purchase in #1.
9. Borrowed $50,000 from the bank.

Required

a. Indicate the specific accounts affected by each transaction.
b. Indicate whether those accounts were increased or decreased.
c. Designate the normal balances for each of the specific accounts.

17. Recording Transactions LO3, 4, 5

Prepare journal entries for the transactions listed in the preceding exercise (omitting explanations).

18. Recording Transactions LO3, 4, 5

The following information pertains to York Rafting Company:

Jan. 2 Issued common stock to investors for $25,000.
3 Bought $3,500 of supplies on account.
4 Paid rent for January in the amount of $1,200.
9 Billed a customer $7,000 for services provided.
16 Paid $1,500 cash to vendor for the January 3 purchase.
24 Borrowed $10,000 from local bank.
26 Received payment for billing made on January 9.

Required
Prepare journal entries for each transaction (omitting explanations).

19. Posting Transactions LO4, 5

Post the journal entries prepared in the preceding exercise to their appropriate T-accounts and prepare a trial balance at January 31.

20. Recording Transactions LO3, 4, 5

In the month of March, C. D. Goose, Inc. entered into the following transactions:

Mar. 2 Bought a new building for $135,000.
3 Paid February utility bill of $860.
11 Issued common stock to investors in return for $5,000.
13 Hired a new administrative assistant for a $35,000 salary.
19 Received payment in the amount of $750 for service billed in February.
31 Paid dividends of $1,000.

Required
Prepare all necessary journal entries for March (omitting the explanations).

21. Recreate Journal Entries LO3, 4

The general ledger for King Consulting contains the following accounts:

Cash	
23,500	7,200
13,000	10,500
15,000	1,000
32,800	

Accounts Receivable	
14,200	13,000
19,300	15,000
5,500	

Salaries Expense	
10,500	
10,500	

Accounts Payable	
7,200	8,100
	900

Service Revenue	
	14,200
	19,300
	33,500

Supplies	
8,100	
8,100	

Dividends	
1,000	
1,000	

Common Stock	
	23,500
	23,500

Required
Recreate the nine journal entries that resulted in King's ledger balances.

22. Transaction Analysis LO2, 4, 5

The following is a tabular analysis of transactions in the month of September for the Fresh Company:

	Cash	+	Accounts Receivable	+	Supplies	+	Equipment	=	Accounts Payable	+	Stockholders' Equity	Additional Information
1.	+2,000		+7,000								+9,000	Service Revenue
2.					+1,000				+1,000			
3.	−500								−500			
4.	−1,500										−1,500	Dividends
5.	−750										−750	Advertising
6.	+10,000										+10,000	Common Stock
7.	+5,000		−5,000									
8.	−2,000										−2,000	Rent
9.									+2,500		−2,500	Utilities
10.							+5,000		+5,000			

Required

a. Provide a probable explanation for each individual event.
b. Recreate the appropriate journal entries.
c. Prepare an income statement for the month of September.
d. Prepare a statement of retained earnings for the month of September. Assume beginning Retained Earnings is $1,000.

23. Accounting Terms LO1, 2, 3, 4

The following is a list of various terms and definitions associated with accounting information systems:

a. Accounting information system
b. Accounting transaction
c. Account
d. Double-entry accounting
e. Chart of accounts
f. Debit
g. Credit
h. Journal
i. Ledger
j. Trial balance

1. A listing containing a name and a numerical reference for all the accounts that a company uses to record accounting information.
2. A recording system in which at least two accounts will be affected when recording every accounting transaction.
3. The system that identifies economic events to be recorded, measures and records those events, and then processes the resulting information so that financial statements can be prepared.
4. An accumulation of the activity and balance for a specific item.
5. Any economic event that affects specific asset, liability, or equity accounts at the time of the event.
6. The right side of an account.
7. The left side of an account.
8. A collection of accounts and their balances.
9. A listing of all accounts and their balances at a specific point in time.
10. A chronological record in which transactions are first recorded.

Required

Match terms a–j with their appropriate definitions.

24. Errors in Recording Transactions LO4, 5

Chappy's Chapstick, Inc. recently hired a new accountant, who made the following errors:

1. Recorded a $200 cash purchase of inventory as a debit to inventory and a credit to accounts payable.
2. Failed to record the payment of $300 for advertising for the period.
3. Debited supplies for $150 and credited cash for invoice amount of $510.
4. Recorded $100 cash received for services but forgot to record the service revenue.

Required

a. Recreate each entry that was made and prepare each entry that should have been made.
b. Which of the four errors would result in the trial balance being out of balance?

25. Posting Information LO4, 5

The following is the general journal of Dee's Fur Company for the month of November:

Date	Account Titles	Debit	Credit
Nov. 1	Cash	15,000	
	Common Stock		15,000
8	Equipment	5,000	
	Accounts Payable		3,000
	Cash		2,000
11	Accounts Receivable	7,500	
	Service Revenue		7,500
18	Accounts Payable	1,700	
	Cash		1,700
21	Cash	5,000	
	Notes Payable		5,000
24	Dividends	1,500	
	Cash		1,500
25	Cash	3,500	
	Accounts Receivable		3,500

Required

a. Post the journal entries to the appropriate T-accounts assuming Dee's Fur starts its business in November.
b. Prepare a trial balance for the month ending November 30.

26. Trial Balance LO4, 5

Saxon Company provides the following account balances as of July 31:

Accounts Payable	$12,445
Accounts Receivable	12,300
Buildings	99,840
Cash	33,200
Common Stock	15,000
Dividends	4,000
Notes Payable	33,000
Salaries Expense	45,205
Retained Earnings	45,700
Service Revenue	49,700
Supplies	6,980

Required

Prepare a trial balance as of July 31.

27. Trial Balance LO4, 5

During the audit of Hines Brewery, the auditor discovered the following errors:

1. A purchase of equipment in the amount of $3,500 was recorded as a debit to Equipment for $350 and a credit to Accounts Payable for $350.
2. A credit of $5,600 to Service Revenue in the general journal was posted to the general ledger at $6,500.
3. $1,000 cash paid for salaries incurred in previous months was recorded as a debit to Salaries Expense and a credit to Cash.
4. A journal entry recording a purchase of $1,200 of supplies on account was posted twice to the general ledger.
5. A credit posting to Service Revenue of $4,000 was omitted.

Required

For each error, indicate whether or not the trial balance will still balance after the error is made. Also, indicate the manner in which the trial balance will be incorrect (for example, Service Revenue will be overstated by $500).

PROBLEMS

28. Transaction Analysis LO2

Gels and Shells, Inc., was established on January 1 and entered into the following transactions during its first month of business:

1. Issued common stock of $50,000 in exchange for cash.
2. Purchased equipment for $24,000 cash.
3. Purchased supplies of $6,000 on account.
4. Received $235 bill for January advertising in the newspaper.
5. Billed customers $14,680 for services.
6. Paid salaries of $2,015.
7. Received payment of $6,023 from customers for bills in #5.
8. Received $5,000 cash for services to be performed in March.
9. Paid $4,500 to suppliers for purchase in #3.
10. Received bill for January utilities in the amount of $175.
11. Paid dividends of $300 to stockholders.
12. Borrowed $10,000 from bank on a long-term basis.
13. Paid $100 interest on the bank loan.

Required

a. Show the effects of each transaction on the accounting equation by preparing a tabular analysis using the following column headings: Cash, Accounts Receivable, Supplies, Property and Equipment, Accounts Payable, Unearned Revenue, Notes Payable, Common Stock, Retained Earnings.
b. Prepare an income statement for the month of January.
c. Prepare a statement of retained earnings for the month of January.
d. Prepare a balance sheet at January 31.

29. Recording Transactions LO3, 4, 5

Darby Consulting, Inc., was established on March 1, and during March, Darby entered into the following transactions:

Mar. 1 Issued $10,000 common stock in exchange for cash.
3 Purchased $300 of supplies on account.
7 Prepaid $1,500 total for April, May, and June rent.
8 Paid $175 towards the March 3 purchase of supplies.
11 Billed customers $5,780 for services rendered.
12 Paid $700 for March advertising.
25 Received $4,500 from customers billed on March 11.
28 Paid $200 in dividends to stockholders.
29 Paid $1,200 for March salaries.
29 Paid $760 for March utilities.

Required
a. Prepare journal entries for each transaction (omitting explanations).
b. Post journal entries to appropriate T-accounts.
c. Prepare a trial balance at March 31.
d. Prepare an income statement and a statement of retained earnings for the month of March. Prepare a balance sheet at the end of March.

30. Recording Transactions LO3, 4, 5

The trial balance for ShirtCraft, Inc., at January 31 is shown as follows:

ShirtCraft, Inc. Trial Balance January 31		
	Debit	**Credit**
Cash	$ 5,600	
Accounts Receivable	12,890	
Supplies	9,235	
Prepaid Rent	1,500	
Equipment	30,500	
Accounts Payable		$ 7,625
Unearned Revenue		6,400
Notes Payable		15,000
Common Stock		25,000
Service Revenue		9,650
Salaries Expense	2,300	
Utilities Expense	650	
Dividends	1,000	
Totals	$63,675	$63,675

During February the following transactions occurred:

Feb. 1 Billed customers $2,500 for services rendered.
1 Paid $150 interest on note from bank.
4 Received $4,500 from customers billed in January.
8 Bought $560 of office supplies on account.
12 Completed a $3,500 service for which payment was received in January.
18 Paid $1,895 towards a January purchase of supplies on account.
26 Paid $1,000 in dividends to stockholders.
27 Paid $2,100 for February salaries and $775 for February utilities.

Required
a. Prepare opening T-accounts for the month of February.
b. Prepare journal entries for transactions in the month of February.
c. Post journal entries to appropriate T-accounts.
d. Prepare a trial balance at February 28.

31. Recording Transactions LO3, 4, 5

On November 1, Josh White started an amusement park. The park experienced the following transactions during the first month of operations:

Nov. 1 Stockholders contributed $50,000 in exchange for common stock.
2 Hired six employees to staff the park.
3 Purchased go-carts for $12,500 on account.
3 Borrowed $10,000 from bank.
3 Purchased arcade games for $4,000.
4 Paid $1,000 to advertise the park's opening.
7 Purchased bumper boats for $11,750 on account.
10 Billed Mr. Jones $1,100 for his son's birthday party.
11 Received cash of $2,200 for entry fees into the park.
15 Paid $5,000 cash towards go-cart bill.
20 Received $3,400 for entry fees into the park.
25 Received full payment from Mr. Jones.
28 Paid utilities in the amount of $560.
30 Paid $100 interest on loan.

Required
Prepare journal entries for each transaction, including explanations.

32. Recording and Posting Journal Entries LO3, 4, 5

Carbon Company entered into the following transactions during November:

Nov. 1 Issued common stock in exchange for $15,000 cash.
4 Purchased $6,500 of equipment, paying $4,000 in cash and the remainder on account.
8 Paid $5,000 for investments, which will mature in six months.
12 Billed customers $12,550 for services rendered.
16 Hired office assistant at a salary equal to being paid $1,000 every two weeks.
21 Received $8,950 from customers billed on Nov. 12.
22 Purchased $1,500 of supplies on account.
24 Paid $1,000 towards the remaining balance on the equipment purchase.
29 Paid $500 in dividends to stockholders.
30 Paid $3,400 for November salaries.

After journalizing these transactions, Carbon Company's general ledger appeared as follows:

Cash			
1st	15,000	4th	4,000
21st	8,950	8th	5,000
		24th	1,000
		30th	3,400

Accounts Payable			
24th	1,000	4th	2,500
		16th	1,000
		22th	1,500

Accounts Receivable			
12th	12,550		

Common Stock			
29th	500	1st	15,000

Supplies			
22th	1,500		

Service Revenue			
		12th	12,550
		21th	8,950

Short-Term Investments			
8th	5,000		

Salaries Expense			
16th	1,000		
30th	4,300		

Equipment			
4th	6,500		

Dividends			
		29th	500

Required

a. Reproduce Carbon Company's journal entries for November.
b. Post the journal entries to the appropriate T-accounts.
c. Compare your postings to those of Carbon Company and identify Carbon's recording errors.
d. Prepare a trial balance at November 30.

CASES

33. Read and Interpret Financial Statements LO3, 4, 5

Access **Walgreens'** balance sheet in its 2010 annual report by clicking on the *Investor Relations* and *Annual Report/Proxies* links at www.walgreens.com.

Required

a. Identify the dollar change in the following subtotals: total current assets; total non-current assets; total current liabilities; total non-current liabilities; and total shareholders' equity. (For example, total current assets increased $1,616.)
b. Identify whether the accounting system would debit or credit each subtotal to achieve the change. Treat each subtotal description as if it were an account. (For example, an increase of $1,616 in total current assets would be accomplished with a debit to that account.)
c. Prepare one journal entry that records the changes in all subtotals. Again, use the subtotal descriptions as if they were actual accounts.
d. Does the entry in part c balance? Should it? Explain why or why not.

34. Ethics in Accounting LO3, 4, 5

You are a staff accountant at a large service provider. Your company is under tremendous pressure to meet earnings targets so that the company stock price can continue to grow and the company can continue to acquire other companies. For the current year, it appears that the company will miss its earnings targets. Your boss, who has been a mentor to you, asks you to prepare a journal entry to record $100,000 of revenue for a fictitious job. He provides a fabricated invoice as documentation. He states that as soon as the new year begins, he will make a reversing entry that removes the receivable from the books. He asks you to do this as a personal favor to him.

Required

a. Identify the ethical issues associated with this scenario.
b. What factors other than accounting are at play here?
c. What are your alternatives?

35. Written Communication LO3, 4

Since you are enrolled in an introductory accounting class, a friend asks you the following: "I've never understood debits and credits. All I know is that debit means bad and credit means good."

Required

Write a brief explanation of the terms *debit* and *credit* and how they are used in an accounting information system. Explain why debit and credit cannot mean good and/or bad.

Accrual Accounting and Adjusting Entries

Learning Objectives

After studying the material in this chapter, you should be able to:

LO1 Describe how income is measured and reported under the accrual and cash bases of accounting.

LO2 Identify the four major circumstances in which adjusting journal entries are necessary.

LO3 Record and post adjusting journal entries, and prepare an adjusted trial balance and financial statements.

LO4 Describe the purpose of the closing process and prepare closing entries.

LO5 Describe the steps of the accounting cycle.

Introduction

Chapter 3 introduced the first three steps in the accounting cycle—recording transactions, posting information to the ledger, and preparing a trial balance from which financial statements are prepared. This chapter explores the remaining steps in the cycle. This includes the adjusting process that leads to accrual-based financial statements and the closing process that prepares the accounting system for the next period. Both the adjusting and closing processes occur at the end of each accounting period.

LO1 Accrual and Cash Bases of Accounting

One of the main functions of the accounting information system is to record the revenues and expenses that a business generates. In accounting, there are two possible bases for recording revenues and expenses—the cash basis and the accrual basis. The main difference between the two is the timing of when revenues and expenses are recorded.

The **cash basis of accounting** records revenues when cash is received and records expenses when cash is paid. The best example of a cash basis accounting system is your personal checking account. Revenues such as job wages are recorded only when you are paid. Expenses such as utilities are recorded only when you write the check.

In contrast, the **accrual basis of accounting** records revenues when they are earned and records expenses when they are incurred. This is an application of the revenue recognition and matching principles, respectively, discussed in Chapter 1. In an accrual accounting system, revenues such as job wages are recorded when earned, regardless of when payment is received. Likewise, expenses such as utilities are recorded when used, regardless of when payment is made. A summary of each basis is as follows.

Cash basis of accounting Records revenues when cash is received and records expenses when cash is paid.

Accrual basis of accounting Records revenues when they are earned and records expenses when they are incurred.

When a retailer like American Eagle Outfitters sells a gift card, it records a liability. It records a revenue when the customer redeems the card.

AP Photo/Gene J. Puskar

	Cash Basis	Accrual Basis
Record revenues when:	Cash is received	Revenue is earned
Record expenses when:	Cash is paid	Expense is incurred

To illustrate the difference between the cash and accrual bases, suppose that a neighbor leaves town for the months of June and July and asks you to collect his mail and newspapers. Before he leaves, he pays you $100. Suppose further that you agree to pay a friend $40 to do the work, but you pay him at the end of July after the work is completed. Income for June and July under each basis would be calculated as follows.

The best example of a cash basis accounting system is your personal checking account.

Under the cash basis, June revenues are $100 because you received $100 during the month. Likewise, June expenses are $0 because you paid nothing during the month. As a result, June income is $100. For July, you received no money but paid your friend $40, so revenues are $0 and expenses are $40. Therefore, July income is a loss of $40.

	Cash Basis			Accrual Basis		
	June	July	Total	June	July	Total
Revenues	$100	$ 0	$100	$50	$50	$100
– Expenses	0	40	40	20	20	40
Net Income	$100	$(40)	$ 60	$30	$30	$ 60

Under the accrual basis, revenues for June are $50 because you earned half of the $100 during June. And, even though you don't pay your friend until July, he provided half of the agreed labor in June, so June expenses are $20. As a result, June income is $30. Because the exact same circumstances occur in July, income for July is also $30.

The comparative income statements show that although each basis results in the same $60 of cumulative income, monthly income varies considerably. The cash-based statement reports that you generated a $100 profit one month and a $40 loss the next, while the accrual-based statement reports that you generated $30 in profits each month. Given that your activities were exactly the same each month, accrual-based income of $30 each month makes more sense than a $100 profit and a $40 loss. Even though both bases result in the same $60 income over the long term, the accrual basis provides a better representation of income over the two shorter periods of time. As a result, the accrual basis is required by Generally Accepted Accounting Principles.

Reporting Accrual- and Cash-Based Income

Because Generally Accepted Accounting Principles require the accrual basis, income statements report accrual-based income. However, cash basis information is also useful in understanding the financial condition of a company. A company that generates accrual income but never generates cash is a company that will soon fail. As a result, cash-based income is reported on the statement of cash flows. Recall from Chapter 1 that the operating activities section of a company's statement of cash flows calculates and reports the cash generated from operating the business. Cash generated from operations is the same as cash-based income.

To illustrate, consider the following condensed version of the operating activities section of **American Eagle Outfitters'** statement of cash flows shown in Exhibit 4-1.

American Eagle Outfitters uses the indirect method of reporting operating cash flows, which means that it calculates cash-based income by adjusting accrual-based income. The top line shows income on an accrual basis. For the current year, American Eagle Outfitters generated over $140 million of income under the accrual basis. This number would also be found on American Eagle Outfitters' income statement. After $220 million of adjustments, cash basis income is determined to be over $402 million. As you can see, American Eagle Outfitters' cash-based income is greater than its accrual-based income in all three years reported. The nature of these differences will be explored further in Chapter 11.

Exhibit 4-1 American Eagle Outfitters' Condensed Statement of Cash Flows—Operating Activities

(in thousands) **For the Years Ended**	**01/29/11**	**01/30/10**	**01/31/09**
Operating activities:			
Net income	$140,647	$169,022	$179,061
Adjustments to reconcile net income to cash provided:			
Depreciation and amortization	145,548	139,832	126,362
⋮	⋮	⋮	⋮
Accrued liabilities	(12,457)	(1,993)	(1,930)
Total adjustments	220,660	186,928	115,128
Net cash provided by operating activities	$402,594	$400,326	$345,112

LO2 Adjusting Journal Entries

To ensure that revenues and expenses are properly recorded under an accrual basis, accounting information systems use adjusting journal entries. **Adjusting journal entries** are entries made in the general journal to record revenues that have been earned but not recorded and expenses that have been incurred but not recorded. The process of recording and posting adjusting entries is the fourth step in the accounting cycle and occurs at the end of each accounting period after the trial balance is prepared. After adjusting entries are journalized and posted, an "adjusted" trial balance is then prepared, from which financial statements are generated.

While adjusting entries can vary significantly across companies, they all arise because the exchange of cash does not always coincide with the earning of a revenue or incurrence of an expense. For example, sometimes cash is received *before* a revenue is earned while at other times cash is received *after* a revenue is earned. Likewise, sometimes cash is paid *before* an expense is incurred while at other times cash is paid *after* an expense is incurred. These four basic scenarios are the reasons that adjusting journal entries are necessary. Each scenario is listed in the following table and is discussed in the following sections.

The process of recording and posting adjusting entries is the fourth step in the accounting cycle and occurs at the end of each accounting period after the trial balance is prepared.

Scenario	Classification of Adjusting Entry
1. Cash is received before revenue is earned	Deferred Revenue
2. Cash is received after revenue is earned	Accrued Revenue
3. Cash is paid before expense is incurred	Deferred Expense
4. Cash is paid after expense is incurred	Accrued Expense

Adjusting journal entries Entries made in the general journal to record revenues that have been earned but not recorded and expenses that have been incurred but not recorded.

HOME DEPOT ANALYSIS

In Appendix C, look at the Revenues paragraph in **Home Depot's** Note 1: Summary of Significant Accounting Policies. How can you tell from that paragraph that Home Depot uses the accrual basis of accounting?

Also, look at Home Depot's statement of cash flows in Appendix C. Over the three years presented, what was the total net income on a cash basis and how does that compare to total net income on an accrual basis?

The Revenues paragraph states that the company recognizes revenues when the customer takes possession of the merchandise or receives the service (that is, when the revenue is earned). It further states that when a customer pays in advance, the company records a "Deferred Revenue" because it has not yet earned the revenue, even though cash has been received.

The company's statement of cash flows shows that cash basis income was greater than accrual basis income in all years presented.

	2011	2010	2009	Total
Net income (cash basis):	$4,585	$5,125	$5,528	$15,238
Net income (accrual basis):	$3,338	$2,661	$2,260	$ 8,259

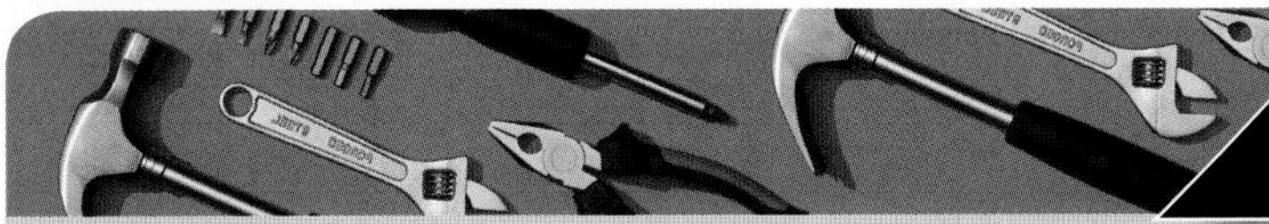

HOME DEPOT ANALYSIS

Look at the Revenues, Prepaid Advertising, and Self-Insurance paragraphs in **Home Depot's** Note 1: Summary of Significant Accounting Policies, found in Appendix C. Do these paragraphs represent examples of deferred revenues, accrued revenues, deferred expenses, or accrued expenses?

The Revenues paragraph explains the example of receiving payment before providing the good or service (deferred revenue). The Prepaid Advertising paragraph explains the example of making payment before consuming the advertising (deferred expense). The Self-Insurance paragraph explains the recording of a liability before payment of claims against the company (accrued expense).

Scenario 1: Deferred Revenue

Companies sometimes receive cash before they earn the revenue. For example, airlines get your money before you fly. When a company receives cash before it provides the service, it has a *deferred revenue*. The term *deferred* is used because at the time of cash receipt, the company has not yet provided the promised service and therefore cannot record a revenue in its accounting system. Instead, it must record a liability. Recording of the revenue must be *deferred* until the revenue is earned.

Subscription Revenue To illustrate a deferred revenue adjustment, suppose that a company sells 12-month subscriptions to its monthly magazine. On October 1, the company receives a total of $1,200 for 20 subscriptions. To record this transaction, the company would record the following entry in its general journal:

Oct. 1	Cash	1,200	
	Unearned Revenue		1,200
	(To record cash received for future magazines)		

Assets	=	Liabilities	+	Equity
+1,200		+1,200		

This entry first increases the Cash account by the amount received. And, because the company now has an obligation to its customers to deliver the magazines, the entry also increases a liability account called Unearned Revenue. As a result, both assets and liabilities are increasing. The entry would then be posted to the relevant T-accounts as follows:

Cash		Unearned Revenue		Service Revenue	
1,200			1,200		0
1,200			1,200		0

Suppose further that the company prepares financial statements at the end of each month. As of October 31, the company has provided one month of magazines and has therefore earned one month of revenue, or $100 ($1,200 ÷ 12 months). Because the accounting system does not yet reflect this earned revenue, the following adjusting journal entry should be made on October 31:

Oct. 31	Unearned Revenue	100	
	Service Revenue		100
	(To record revenue earned during October)		

Assets	=	Liabilities	+	Equity
		−100		+100

This entry increases the Service Revenue account by the amount earned during the month and decreases the liability account Unearned Revenue by the same amount. As a result, liabilities are decreasing and equity is increasing. The entry would be posted to the relevant T-accounts as follows:

Cash		Unearned Revenue		Service Revenue	
1,200			1,200		0
		100			100
1,200			1,100		100

After posting, the Service Revenue T-account reflects the $100 earned in the current period while the Unearned Revenue T-account reflects the remaining $1,100 to be earned over the next 11 months. These two accounts have been *adjusted* so that they properly reflect revenues earned during October and liabilities owed on October 31. The Cash account is not affected by the adjusting journal entry. Cash was exchanged and recorded on October 1.

General Rule When a company receives cash before it provides a service, the company should always increase a liability account for the amount received. As the company provides the service, the liability account is adjusted down (decreased) and the related revenue account is adjusted up (increased). So, the adjusting journal entry for this scenario will always be a reduction to a liability account and an increase to a revenue account, as shown in Exhibit 4-2.

Scenario 2: Accrued Revenue

Companies often provide a service and then collect the cash. When a company earns a revenue before it receives cash, it has an *accrued revenue*. The term *accrue* means to accumulate or increase. An accrued revenue is another name for a receivable.

Exhibit 4-2 Entries in a Deferred Revenue Scenario

MAKING IT REAL

Although gift cards have existed for many years, their ever-growing popularity in recent times is causing some accounting issues for retailers.

Many people would assume that retailers record revenue with each gift card purchased. However, the transfer of merchandise is required for revenue to be recognized. Therefore, gift card sales represent a deferred revenue, which is a liability. Revenue is not generated until the gift card is redeemed. For companies like American Eagle Outfitters, this liability is significant and, as a result, is a separate line item on the balance sheet. American Eagle Outfitters reports over $41 million in unredeemed gift cards at January 29, 2011.

© Mark erickson/Getty Images

Gift cards create another accounting challenge because of "breakage"—gift cards that are never redeemed. When a retailer determines that a card will not be redeemed, it can reduce its liability and increase its revenue for the breakage estimate. American Eagle Outfitters follows this practice. In the notes to its financial statements, the company states that it "determines an estimated gift card breakage rate by continuously evaluating historical redemption data and the time when there is a remote likelihood that a gift card will be redeemed. The Company recorded gift card breakage of $5.5 million, $6.8 million, and $12.2 million during Fiscal 2010, Fiscal 2009, and Fiscal 2008, respectively."

Service Revenue To illustrate an accrued revenue adjustment, suppose that an accounting firm agrees to provide a service to a client for a $1,000 fee. The firm completes its work on September 23, bills the client on October 10, and receives payment on October 21. Suppose further that the accounting firm prepares its own financial statements at the end of each month, which in this case is September 30.

Because the accrual basis requires that revenues be recorded in the period in which they are earned, the accounting firm must record the $1,000 of revenue on September 30 with the following adjusting journal entry:

Sept. 30	Accounts Receivable	1,000	
	Service Revenue		1,000
	(To record revenue earned during September)		

Assets	=	Liabilities	+	Equity
+1,000				+1,000

The entry increases the Accounts Receivable account for the amount that the client owes the firm and increases the Service Revenue account for the amount that the firm has earned. As a result, both assets and equity are increasing. The preceding entry would be posted to the relevant T-accounts as follows:

Cash (Dr.)	Cash (Cr.)	Accounts Receivable (Dr.)	Accounts Receivable (Cr.)	Service Revenue (Dr.)	Service Revenue (Cr.)
0		1,000			1,000
0		1,000			1,000

After posting, the Service Revenue T-account reflects the $1,000 earned in the current period while the Accounts Receivable T-account reflects the $1,000 of expected cash receipts from the client. These two accounts have been *adjusted* so that they properly reflect revenues earned during September and receivables held on September 30.

When the customer pays cash on October 21, the following entry is made:

Oct. 21	Cash	1,000	
	Accounts Receivable		1,000
	(To record receipt of cash)		

Assets	=	Liabilities	+	Equity
+1,000				
−1,000				

This entry increases the Cash account and decreases the Accounts Receivable account for the amount collected. As a result, although specific asset accounts are changing, total assets remain unchanged. No revenue is recorded because it was recorded in the prior period when it was earned. The entry would be posted to the relevant T-accounts as follows:

Cash (Dr.)	Cash (Cr.)	Accounts Receivable (Dr.)	Accounts Receivable (Cr.)
0		1,000	
1,000			1,000
1,000		0	

General Rule When a company earns a revenue before it receives cash, the company should always increase a receivable account and a revenue account for the amount earned. In other words, the receivable account should be adjusted up (increased) and the revenue account should also be adjusted up (increased). When the company collects the receivable, the receivable account is decreased and the cash account is increased. So, the adjusting journal entry for this scenario will always be an increase to an asset account and an increase to a revenue account, as shown in Exhibit 4-3.

Exhibit 4-3 Entries in an Accrued Revenue Scenario

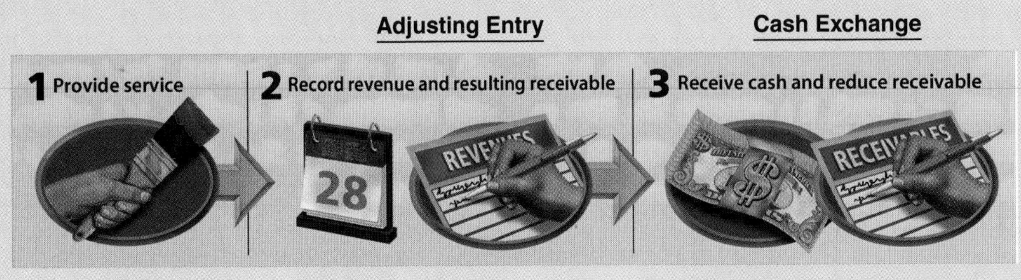

Scenario 3: Deferred Expense

Companies often pay cash before they incur an expense. You need look no further than your own personal expenses to find numerous examples of payments made before you use the service. One example is insurance. You pay for insurance for several months in advance and are then covered.

When a company pays for a resource before it uses or consumes it, the company has a *deferred expense.* We use the term *deferred* because at the time of cash payment for the resource, the company has yet to use or consume the resource it is acquiring and therefore cannot record an expense in the accounting system. Instead, it records an asset. Recording of the expense must be *deferred* until the expense is incurred. You should note that a *deferred expense* is nothing more than an asset—a resource to be used.

Insurance Expense To illustrate a deferred expense adjustment, suppose that on March 1, a company purchases a 12-month general liability insurance policy for $36,000. To record this transaction, the company would record the following entry in its general journal:

Mar. 1	Prepaid Insurance	36,000	
	Cash		36,000
	(To record purchase of insurance)		

Assets	=	Liabilities	+	Equity
−36,000				
+36,000				

This entry increases the asset account Prepaid Insurance to reflect the amount of insurance bought and decreases the Cash account for the same. Since both of these accounts are assets, this entry does not change total assets. The entry would then be posted to the relevant T-accounts as follows. For illustration purposes, assume that the Cash account has a $100,000 balance prior to the entry.

Cash		Prepaid Insurance		Insurance Expense	
100,000	36,000	36,000		0	
64,000		36,000		0	

Suppose further that the company prepares financial statements at the end of March. As of March 31, the company has been covered for one month and has therefore consumed one month of insurance, or $3,000 ($36,000 ÷ 12 months). Because the accounting system does not yet reflect this expense, the following adjusting journal entry should be made on March 31:

Mar. 31	Insurance Expense	3,000	
	Prepaid Insurance		3,000
	(To record expense incurred during March)		

Assets	=	Liabilities	+	Equity
−3,000				−3,000

This entry increases the Insurance Expense account by the amount consumed during the month and decreases the asset account Prepaid Insurance by the same amount. As a result, both assets and equity are decreasing. The entry would be posted to the relevant T-accounts as follows:

Cash		Prepaid Insurance		Insurance Expense	
100,000	36,000	36,000		0	
			3,000	3,000	
64,000		33,000		3,000	

After posting, the Insurance Expense T-account reflects the $3,000 of insurance that was consumed in the current period while the Prepaid Insurance T-account reflects the remaining $33,000 of insurance to be consumed over the next eleven months. These two accounts have been *adjusted* so that they properly reflect expenses incurred during March and unexpired assets on March 31. The Cash account is not affected by the adjusting journal entry. Cash was exchanged and recorded on March 1.

Depreciation Expense Another example of an expense where cash is paid before the expense is incurred is depreciation. Depreciation is the process of spreading out over their useful lives the cost of non-current assets such as equipment and buildings. For example, suppose that on August 1, a company purchases a delivery truck for $40,000. This transaction would be recorded into the accounting system as follows:

Aug. 1	Equipment	40,000	
	Cash		40,000
	(To record purchase of truck)		

Assets	=	Liabilities	+	Equity
−40,000				
+40,000				

This entry increases the asset account Equipment to reflect the cost of the truck and decreases the Cash account for the same. Since both of these accounts are assets, this entry does not change total assets. The entry would then be posted to the relevant T-accounts as follows. We will assume that the Cash account has a $70,000 balance prior to the entry.

Cash		Equipment		Depreciation Expense	
70,000	40,000	40,000		0	
30,000		40,000		0	

Suppose further that the company prepares financial statements at the end of August. As of August 30, the company has used the truck for one month and should therefore record some amount of expense associated with the use of the truck. If we assume for simplicity that the amount of expense to be recognized in the current month is $1,000, the following adjusting journal entry should be made on August 31:

Aug. 31	Depreciation Expense	1,000	
	Accumulated Depreciation		1,000
	(To record expense incurred during August)		

Assets	=	Liabilities	+	Equity
−1,000				−1,000

This entry increases the Depreciation Expense account by the amount of expense allocated to the current month. However, instead of decreasing the Equipment account directly, the entry increases Accumulated Depreciation. We discuss accumulated depreciation in detail in Chapter 8, but for now you should know that the account is a contra-asset account that accumulates depreciation expense to date and is subtracted from the Equipment account to yield the net balance of the asset. As a result of the entry, both assets and equity are decreasing. Equity is decreasing because the company recorded an expense. Assets are decreasing because the net balance of Equipment and Accumulated Depreciation at the end of August is now $39,000 ($40,000 – $1,000). The entry would be posted to the relevant T-accounts as follows:

Equipment		Accumulated Depreciation		Depreciation Expense	
40,000			0	0	
			1,000	1,000	
40,000			1,000	1,000	

The Depreciation Expense and Accumulated Depreciation accounts have been *adjusted* so that they properly reflect the $1,000 of expenses incurred during August and the $39,000 of net unexpired balance of Equipment on August 31.

General Rule When a company pays cash before it incurs an expense, the company should always increase an asset account for the amount paid. As the company consumes the asset, the asset account is adjusted down (decreased) and the related expense account is adjusted up (increased). Depending on the type of asset, either the actual asset account will be decreased or a related contra-asset account will be increased. So, the adjusting journal entry for this scenario will always be a reduction to an asset account and an increase to an expense account, as shown in Exhibit 4-4.

Exhibit 4-4 Entries for a Deferred Expense Scenario

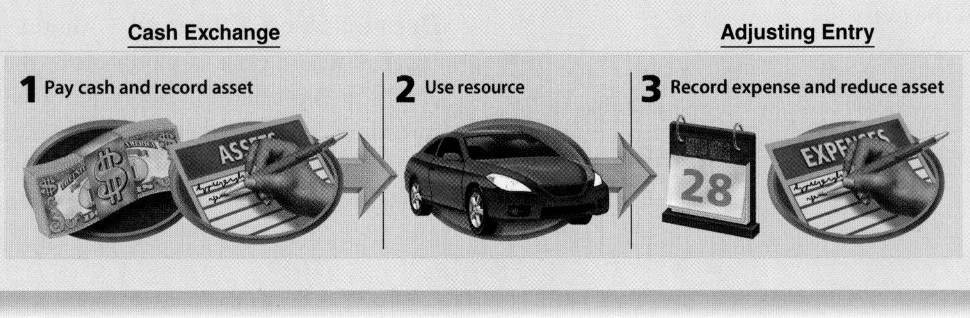

Scenario 4: Accrued Expense

Companies often incur expenses and pay for them later. A good example is employee salaries. Practically all companies pay their employees after the employees have provided labor for the company. When this occurs, the company has an *accrued expense*. An accrued expense is another name for a liability.

Salaries Expense To illustrate an accrued expense adjustment, suppose that a company's daily payroll is $1,000. The company pays its employees via direct deposit every Saturday for the work the employees have provided Monday through Friday. Suppose further that the company prepares its financial statements on April 30, which is a Friday.

Because the accrual basis requires that expenses be recorded in the period in which they are incurred, the company must record $5,000 of expense on April 30 with the following adjusting journal entry:

Apr. 30	Salaries Expense	5,000	
	Salaries Payable		5,000
	(To record salaries incurred during April)		

Assets	=	Liabilities	+	Equity
		+5,000		−5,000

The preceding entry increases the Salaries Expense account for the $5,000 of salaries incurred for the week and increases the Salaries Payable account for the same since it owes the employees those salaries. As a result, liabilities are increasing and equity is decreasing. The preceding entry would be posted to the relevant T-accounts as follows:

Cash (Dr.)	Cash (Cr.)	Salaries Payable (Dr.)	Salaries Payable (Cr.)	Salaries Expense (Dr.)	Salaries Expense (Cr.)
8,000			5,000	5,000	
8,000			5,000	5,000	

After posting, the Salaries Expense T-account reflects the $5,000 incurred in the current period while the Salaries Payable T-account reflects the $5,000 owed to employees on April 30. These two accounts have been *adjusted* so that they properly reflect expenses incurred during April and the payable owed on April 30.

The Cash account is not affected by the adjusting journal entry. Cash, which has an $8,000 balance for illustrative purposes, will be paid on Saturday, May 1. When the company pays its employees, the following entry would be made:

May 1	Salaries Payable	5,000	
	Cash		5,000
	(To record payment of cash)		

Assets	=	Liabilities	+	Equity
−5,000		−5,000		

The entry decreases the Cash account for the $5,000 paid to employees and decreases the Salaries Payable account by the same $5,000. No expense is recorded because it was recorded in the prior period when the expense was incurred. As a result, both assets and liabilities are decreasing. The entry would be posted to the relevant T-accounts as follows:

Cash (Dr.)	Cash (Cr.)	Salaries Payable (Dr.)	Salaries Payable (Cr.)
8,000			5,000
	5,000	5,000	
3,000			0

Interest Expense Interest is another example of incurring an expense before cash is paid. For example, suppose that a company borrows $10,000 on November 1. The annual interest rate on the loan is 6%, and interest is payable on the first day of each month. Suppose further that the company prepares its financial statements on November 30.

As of November 30, the company has used the borrowed money for one month, so it has incurred one month's worth of interest. To calculate the amount of interest, we simply multiply the principal amount ($10,000) by the annual interest rate (6%) and by the relevant number of periods (1 month out of 12, or 1/12). So, interest for the month of November is:

$$\text{Principal} \times \text{annual rate} \times \text{time} = \$10{,}000 \times 0.06 \times 1/12 = \$50$$

Therefore, the following adjusting journal entry should be made on November 30:

Nov. 30	Interest Expense	50	
	Interest Payable		50
	(To record interest incurred during November)		

Assets	=	Liabilities	+	Equity
		+50		−50

The preceding entry increases the Interest Expense account for the $50 of interest for November and increases the Interest Payable account for the same. As a result, liabilities are increasing and equity is decreasing. The preceding entry would be posted to the relevant T-accounts as follows:

Cash		Interest Payable		Interest Expense	
1,000			50	50	
1,000			50	50	

After posting, the Interest Expense T-account reflects the $50 incurred in the current period and the Interest Payable T-account reflects the $50 owed to the bank on November 30. These two accounts have been *adjusted* so that they properly reflect expenses incurred during November and the payable owed on November 30.

The Cash account is not affected by the adjusting journal entry. Cash, which has a $1,000 balance for illustrative purposes, will be paid on December 1. On that date, the following entry would be made:

Dec. 1	Interest Payable	50	
	Cash		50
	(To record payment of cash)		

Assets	=	Liabilities	+	Equity
−50		−50		

The preceding entry decreases the Cash account for the $50 paid to the bank and decreases the Interest Payable account by the same $50. As a result, both assets and liabilities are decreasing. The entry would be posted to the relevant T-accounts as follows:

Cash		Interest Payable	
1,000			50
	50	50	
950			0

General Rule When a company incurs an expense before it pays cash, the company should always increase a payable account and an expense account for the amount incurred. In other words, the payable account should be adjusted up (increased) and the expense account should also be adjusted up (increased). When the company pays the liability, the liability account is reduced and the cash account is decreased. So, the adjusting journal entry for this scenario will always be an increase to a liability account and an increase to an expense account, as shown in Exhibit 4-5.

Summary of Adjusting Journal Entries

Exhibit 4-6 summarizes the four scenarios that give rise to adjusting journal entries and the characteristics of the relevant entries.

As you review this exhibit, consider the following generalizations of all adjusting entries:

1. The purpose of adjusting entries is to record revenues that have been earned but not recorded and expenses that have been incurred but not recorded.

Exhibit 4-5 Entries in an Accrued Expense Scenario

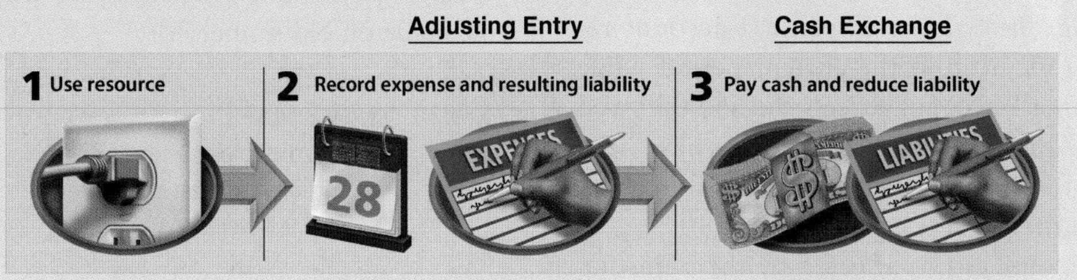

Exhibit 4-6 Summary of Adjusting Journal Entry Scenarios

Scenario	Classification	Entry Before End of Period	Adjusting Entry at End of Period	Entry After End of Period
Cash is received *before* revenue is earned	Deferred Revenue	Cash $$ Liability $$	Liability $$ Revenue $$	
Cash is received *after* revenue is earned	Accrued Revenue		Receivable $$ Revenue $$	Cash $$ Receivable $$
Cash is paid *before* expense is incurred	Deferred Expense	Asset $$ Cash $$	Expense $$ Asset $$	
Cash is paid *after* expense is incurred	Accrued Expense		Expense $$ Payable $$	Payable $$ Cash $$

2. Every adjusting journal entry will affect at least one revenue or one expense account. In addition, every adjusting journal entry will affect at least one asset or liability account. This means that every adjusting entry will affect at least one account from the income statement and one account from the balance sheet.
3. Adjusting journal entries arise because the timing of revenue and expense recognition differs from the exchange of cash. Therefore, cash will never be increased or decreased in an adjusting entry.

LO3 Comprehensive Example: Adjusting Journal Entries

To illustrate the process of making adjusting journal entries from a trial balance and then preparing an adjusted trial balance, the Circle Films example from Chapter 3 will be continued. As a result of the transactions entered into by Circle Films during its first month of operations, the following unadjusted trial balance was prepared at May 31. Notice that it is an *unadjusted* trial balance because adjusting entries have not yet been made.

Circle Films
Unadjusted Trial Balance
May 31

	Debit	Credit
Cash	$ 8,250	
Supplies	1,000	
Equipment	18,000	
Unearned Revenue		$ 2,000
Notes Payable		9,000
Common Stock		15,000
Service Revenue		5,000
Advertising Expense	250	
Salaries Expense	2,000	
Dividends	1,500	
Totals	$31,000	$31,000

In addition to these accounts and balances, the following information was available on May 31:

1. On May 31, Circle Films filmed the retirement reception for the customer who paid $2,000 on May 10 (see transaction #4 in Chapter 3 on page 58).
2. On May 31, Circle Films filmed the first night of a two-night local play. The second night will be filmed on June 1, at which time Circle Films will bill the customer. The customer has agreed to pay Circle Films $1,500 for each night.

3. After a physical count, Circle Films determined that it had $650 of supplies remaining.

4. The interest rate for the promissory note is 6%.

5. Circle Films estimates that depreciation for May on its two cameras totals $600.

Given this information, the following adjusting entries can be prepared.

Journalizing and Posting Adjusting Entries

Adjustment #1 (Deferred Revenue) Circle Films has now filmed the retirement reception, so it no longer has a liability to the customer. It has a revenue instead. However, the trial balance still shows the $2,000 liability. Thus, the adjusting entry to adjust the liability down and the revenue up is as follows:

May 31	Unearned Revenue	2,000	
	Service Revenue		2,000
	(To record revenue earned)		

Assets	=	Liabilities	+	Equity
		−2,000		+2,000

The entry would be posted to the relevant T-accounts as follows:

Unearned Revenue		Service Revenue	
	2,000		5,000
2,000			2,000
	0		7,000

Adjustment #2 (Accrued Revenue) Circle Films filmed one night of a local play. Therefore, it has earned revenue for one night, or $1,500. The trial balance does not reflect this because Circle Films has not issued a bill, so the adjusting journal entry to adjust receivables and revenues up is as follows:

May 31	Accounts Receivable	1,500	
	Service Revenue		1,500
	(To record revenue earned)		

Assets	=	Liabilities	+	Equity
+1,500				+1,500

The entry would be posted to the relevant T-accounts as follows:

Accounts Receivable		Service Revenue	
0			5,000
1,500			2,000
			1,500
1,500			8,500

Adjustment #3 (Deferred Expense) Circle Films has $650 in supplies on hand. However, the trial balance shows $1,000 in the Supplies account, which is the amount that Circle Films originally purchased. Therefore, Circle Films must have used $350 of supplies ($1,000 – $650). To adjust the Supplies account down from $1,000 to $650 and to record the $350 in expense, the following adjusting journal is required.

May 31	Supplies Expense	350	
	Supplies		350
	(To record expense incurred)		

Assets	=	Liabilities	+	Equity
−350				−350

The entry would be posted to the relevant T-accounts as follows:

Supplies		Supplies Expense	
1,000		0	
	350	350	
650		350	

Adjustment #4 (Accrued Expense) Circle Films must pay interest on the promissory note at a 6% annual rate. Therefore, after one month, Circle Films has incurred $45 of interest expense ($9,000 × 6% × 1/12). This expense and the related obligation are not reflected in the trial balance because they have not yet been recorded. To record them, the following adjusting entry is required:

May 31	Interest Expense	45	
	Interest Payable		45
	(To record expense incurred)		

Assets	=	Liabilities	+	Equity
		+45		−45

Once an adjusted trial balance is prepared, financial statements can be generated.

The entry would be posted to the relevant T-accounts as follows:

Interest Payable	
	0
	45
	45

Interest Expense	
0	
45	
45	

Adjustment #5 (Deferred Expense) Circle determines that depreciation on its cameras should be $600 for the month of May. To record this depreciation, the following adjusting entry is required:

May 31	Depreciation Expense	600	
	Accumulated Depreciation		600
	(To record expense incurred)		

Assets	=	Liabilities	+	Equity
−600				−600

The entry would be posted to the relevant T-accounts as follows:

Equipment	
18,000	
18,000	

Depreciation Expense	
0	
600	
600	

Accumulated Depreciation	
	0
	600
	600

Preparing an Adjusted Trial Balance

Once all of the preceding adjusting entries are journalized and posted to the ledger, an adjusted trial balance can be prepared. Like the previous trial balance, the adjusted trial balance simply lists all balances from the ledger. Since the ledger now reflects several adjustments, so does the adjusted trial balance.

Zeffss1/iStockphoto.com

The following is Circle Films' May 31 adjusted trial balance. The accounts that were either created or adjusted by the adjusting entries are highlighted.

Circle Films
Adjusted Trial Balance
May 31

	Debit	Credit
Cash	$ 8,250	
Accounts Receivable	1,500	
Supplies	650	
Equipment	18,000	
Accumulated Depreciation		$ 600
Interest Payable		45
Unearned Revenue		0
Notes Payable		9,000
Common Stock		15,000
Service Revenue		8,500
Advertising Expense	250	
Depreciation Expense	600	
Interest Expense	45	
Salaries Expense	2,000	
Supplies Expense	350	
Dividends	1,500	
Totals	$33,145	$33,145

Preparing Financial Statements

Once all revenues and expenses are recorded and an adjusted trial balance is prepared, financial statements can be generated. Recall from Chapter 1 that the income statement should be prepared first. Using the adjusted revenue and expense account balances from the adjusted trial balance, Circle Films' income statement for the month of May would appear as follows:

Circle Films
Income Statement
For the Month Ending May 31

Service revenue		$ 8,500
Expenses		
Advertising expense	$ 250	
Depreciation expense	600	
Interest expense	45	
Salaries expense	2,000	
Supplies expense	350	
Total expenses		3,245
Net income		$ 5,255

After a period ends and financial statements are prepared, all temporary accounts must be reset to zero for the start of the next period.

With net income calculated, Circle Films' statement of retained earnings can be prepared. Recall that the statement of retained earnings takes the beginning balance in Retained Earnings, adds net income, and subtracts dividends to yield the current balance in Retained Earnings. Circle Films' May 31 adjusted trial balance shows no balance in beginning Retained Earnings and a $1,500 balance in dividends. Therefore, Circle Films' statement of retained earnings for the month of May would appear as follows:

Circle Films
Statement of Retained Earnings
For the Month Ending May 31

Retained earnings, May 1	$ 0
+ Net income	5,255
− Dividends	1,500
Retained earnings, May 31	$ 3,755

With Retained Earnings calculated, Circle Films' balance sheet can be prepared. Circle Films' May 31 adjusted trial balance shows several balance sheet accounts, starting with Cash and continuing through Common Stock. These accounts, along with the amount of Retained Earnings from the May statement of retained earnings, should be included on the balance sheet. Therefore, Circle Films' May 31 balance sheet would appear as follows.

Circle Films
Balance Sheet
May 31

Cash		$ 8,250
Accounts receivable		1,500
Supplies		650
Equipment	$18,000	
Less: Accumulated depreciation	600	17,400
Total assets		$27,800
Interest payable	$ 45	
Notes payable	9,000	
Total liabilities		$ 9,045
Common stock	$15,000	
Retained earnings	3,755	
Total stockholders' equity		18,755
Total liabilities and stockholders' equity		$27,800

LO4 Closing Process

After financial statements are prepared, companies conduct the closing process. The **closing process** is the process of transferring all revenue, expense, and dividend account balances to the Retained Earnings account. This transfer is necessary for two reasons.

First, revenue, expense, and dividend accounts are **temporary accounts**, meaning that they accumulate balances only for the current period. After the period ends and financial statements are prepared, all temporary accounts must be reset to zero for the start of the next period.

Second, the transfer updates the Retained Earnings account to its proper end-of-period balance. In the preceding example, the balance in Retained Earnings

Closing process The process of transferring all revenue, expense, and dividend account balances to the Retained Earnings account.

Temporary accounts Accounts that accumulate balances only for the current period.

is generated from the statement of retained earnings, not the adjusted trial balance. The closing process is the mechanism that updates the actual Retained Earnings account balance in the ledger.

The closing process is accomplished with several entries. **Closing entries**, which are made in the journal and posted to the ledger, eliminate the balances in all temporary accounts and transfer those balances to the Retained Earnings account. Usually, one entry is made for revenues, one for expenses, and a final entry for dividends. To illustrate, the temporary accounts from Circle Films' adjusted trial balance are shown in the following partial adjusted trial balance:

Circle Films
Partial Adjusted Trial Balance
May 31

	Debit	Credit
Service Revenue		$8,500
Advertising Expense	$ 250	
Depreciation Expense	600	
Interest Expense	45	
Salaries Expense	2,000	
Supplies Expense	350	
Dividends	1,500	

Circle Films has one revenue account with an $8,500 credit balance. To eliminate that balance and transfer it to the Retained Earnings account, the following closing entry is required:

May 31	Service Revenue	8,500	
	Retained Earnings		8,500
	(To close revenue account)		

In this entry, the revenue balance is eliminated while the Retained Earnings account is increased.

Expense and dividend accounts are closed in a similar fashion. To eliminate those balances and transfer them to Retained Earnings, the following closing entries are required:

May 31	Retained Earnings	3,245	
	Advertising Expense		250
	Depreciation Expense		600
	Interest Expense		45
	Salaries Expense		2,000
	Supplies Expense		350
	(To close expense accounts)		

May 31	Retained Earnings	1,500	
	Dividends		1,500
	(To close dividend account)		

In the first entry, all expense accounts are eliminated, and the Retained Earnings account is decreased for the same. In the second entry, the dividend account is eliminated, and the Retained Earnings account is decreased for the same.

All three closing entries would be posted to the appropriate T-accounts as follows:

Retained Earnings		Service Revenue		Advertising Expense	
	8,500		8,500	250	
3,245		8,500			250
1,500					
	3,755		0	0	

Depreciation Exp.		Interest Expense		Salaries Expense	
600		45		2,000	
	600		45		2,000
0		0		0	

Supplies Expense		Dividends	
350		1,500	
	350		1,500
0		0	

Notice that after the closing entries are posted, all revenue, expense, and dividend accounts have zero balances as desired. They are now ready to begin the next reporting period. Also, Retained Earnings has a $3,755 credit balance. This is the balance reported on Circle Films' statement of retained earnings and balance sheet. In other words, the Retained Earnings account now has the proper balance at the end of the period.

As a final check that all accounts have been properly closed, a new trial balance is prepared. Appropriately called a post-closing trial balance, it contains all account balances for the beginning of the next accounting period. Circle Films' post-closing trial balance is as follows:

Closing entries Entries made in the journal and posted to the ledger that eliminate the balances in all temporary accounts and transfer those balances to the Retained Earnings account.

Circle Films
Post-Closing Trial Balance
May 31

	Debit	Credit
Cash	$ 8,250	
Accounts Receivable	1,500	
Supplies	650	
Equipment	18,000	
Accumulated Depreciation		$ 600
Interest Payable		45
Notes Payable		9,000
Common Stock		15,000
Retained Earnings		3,755
Totals	$28,400	$28,400

LO5 The Accounting Cycle—A Summary

This and the previous chapter covered the accounting cycle. The **accounting cycle** is the sequence of steps in which an accounting information system captures, processes, and reports a company's accounting transactions during a period. Chapter 3 demonstrated the first three steps—how to record journal entries in the journal, post the information to the ledger, and prepare a trial balance. This chapter demonstrated the two major processes that occur at the end of the period—adjusting and closing. The adjusting process includes the recording and posting of adjusting entries and the preparation of an adjusted trial balance, from which financial statements are prepared. The closing process includes the recording and posting of closing entries and the preparation of a post-closing trial balance. Once closing is completed, the accounting information system is prepared to begin the next period. Exhibit 4-7 summarizes these steps.

Accounting cycle The sequence of steps in which an accounting information system captures, processes, and reports a company's accounting transactions during a period.

Exhibit 4-7 The Accounting Cycle

1. Journalize and post accounting transactions.
2. Prepare a trial balance.
3. Journalize and post adjusting entries.
4. Prepare an adjusted trial balance.
5. Prepare financial statements.
6. Journalize and post closing entries.
7. Prepare a post-closing trial balance.

STUDY TOOLS 4

Chapter review card

- Learning Objective and Key Concept Reviews
- Key Definitions and Formulas

Online (Located at www.cengagebrain.com)

- Flash Cards and Crossword Puzzles
- Games and Quizzes
- E-Lectures
- Homework Assignments (as directed by your instructor)

CONCEPT QUESTIONS

1. (LO1) When are revenues and expenses recognized under the cash basis of accounting?
2. (LO1) When are revenues and expenses recognized under the accrual basis of accounting?
3. (LO1) Which basic accounting principle(s) does the cash basis of accounting violate?
4. (LO1) Income under the cash basis of accounting is not reported at all under Generally Accepted Accounting Principles. Do you agree or disagree? Explain.
5. (LO1) Why will income under the cash basis and the accrual basis be the same in the long run?
6. (LO2) What is the purpose of adjusting journal entries, and when are they made?
7. (LO2) What circumstances give rise to a deferred revenue? a deferred expense?
8. (LO2) What circumstances give rise to an accrued revenue? an accrued expense?
9. (LO2) List the four basic classifications of adjusting entries and describe the nature of each adjusting entry.
10. (LO2) Deferred expense and accrued expense are interchangeable terms. Explain why this statement is false.
11. (LO3) Is it possible for adjusting entries to affect only the balance sheet? Why or why not?
12. (LO3) How is the adjusted trial balance used to prepare financial statements?
13. (LO4) What does the term "temporary accounts" mean? List the general types of accounts that fall under this classification.
14. (LO4) At the beginning of an accounting period, a company's revenue, expense, and dividend accounts will always have zero balances. Do you agree or disagree? Explain.
15. (LO4) Describe the three possible closing entries.

MULTIPLE CHOICE

1. (LO1) The cash basis of accounting:
   a. is a basis for when to record revenues and expenses.
   b. is required by Generally Accepted Accounting Principles.
   c. records expenses when they are incurred.
   d. records revenues only when they have been earned.
2. (LO1) On December 31, a company receives a $5,000 payment for services not yet rendered and a $500 electric bill for the month of December. Under the cash basis of accounting, this company would recognize:
   a. $4,500 of revenue and $500 of expense.
   b. $5,000 of revenue and $0 of expense.
   c. $5,000 of revenue and $500 of expense.
   d. $0 of revenue and $500 of expense.
3. (LO1) On December 31, a company receives a $5,000 payment for services not yet rendered and a $500 electric bill for the month of December. Under the accrual basis of accounting, this company would recognize:
   a. $4,500 of revenue and $500 of expense.
   b. $5,000 of revenue and $0 of expense.
   c. $5,000 of revenue and $500 of expense.
   d. $0 of revenue and $500 of expense.
4. (LO2) Which of the following situations would likely not require an adjusting entry?
   a. Revenue is earned before cash is received
   b. Expense is incurred before cash is paid
   c. Cash is received before revenue is earned
   d. Cash is paid before equipment is received
5. (LO2) Which of the following accounts is most likely associated with a deferred revenue?
   a. Depreciation Expense
   b. Salaries Payable
   c. Unearned Revenue
   d. Accounts Receivable
6. (LO2) Which of the following accounts is most likely associated with an accrued expense?
   a. Depreciation Expense
   b. Salaries Payable
   c. Unearned Revenue
   d. Accounts Receivable
7. (LO2) Which of the following is false?
   a. Adjusting entries are made at the end of an accounting period
   b. Adjusting entries are not necessary under the cash basis of accounting
   c. The cash account will always be affected by adjusting journal entries
   d. Adjusting journal entries always affect at least one revenue or expense account and at least one asset or liability account
8. (LO1, 2) A company prepays rent of $500 and receives a $3,000 payment for services not yet rendered. Under the accrual basis of accounting, these two transactions will:
   a. increase net income $2,500.
   b. increase net income $3,000.
   c. decrease net income $500.
   d. have no effect on net income.
9. (LO2) A company has $3,000 of supplies on hand at the beginning of the year. During the year, the company buys $7,500 of supplies. At the end of the year, supplies on hand total $4,000. What is the amount of Supplies Expense reported on the company's income statement?
   a. $4,000
   b. $7,500
   c. $6,500
   d. $10,500
10. (LO2) On December 1, Smiles, Inc. prepays $2,400 for three months of rent. On December 31, Smiles prepares financial statements. After the appropriate

adjusting entry for rent, Smiles' balance sheet would show:
a. prepaid Rent of $2,400.
b. rent Expense of $800.
c. prepaid Rent of $1,600.
d. prepaid Rent of $800.

11. (LO2) A company has a $4,000 balance in Unearned Revenue on its unadjusted trial balance. At the end of the year, the company has earned all but one-fourth of the revenue. The adjusting journal entry necessary at year-end would include:
a. a debit to Service Revenue of $4,000.
b. a credit to Unearned Revenue for $3,000.
c. a debit to Unearned Revenue for $3,000.
d. a credit to Service Revenue of $1,000.

12. (LO2) A company fails to record the expiration of insurance that it purchased previously. Because of this error, the company's assets and equity are:
a. overstated.
b. understated.
c. unaffected.
d. cannot tell from the given information.

13. (LO2, 3) A company's unadjusted trial balance shows a $12,000 balance in Salaries Expense while the adjusted trial balance shows a balance of $13,000. Which of the following best describes the reason for the difference?
a. An adjusting entry to reduce Salaries Expense by $1,000 was prepared
b. An adjusting entry to reduce Salaries Payable by $1,000 was prepared
c. An adjusting entry to record the payment of $1,000 of salaries was prepared
d. An adjusting entry to increase Salaries Expense by $1,000 was prepared

14. (LO2, 3) Tom and Judy's Bed and Breakfast received the following bills for December utilities:
i. Electricity - $500 on December 31, 2011
ii. Water - $750 on December 29, 2011
iii. Telephone - $375 on January 1, 2012
On the December 31, 2011, financial statements, Tom and Judy's should show accrued expenses of:
a. $1,625.
b. $1,250.
c. $500.
d. None of the above.

15. (LO4) The closing process:
a. updates the retained earnings account.
b. prepares all revenue and expense accounts for the next period.
c. puts any dividend account to zero.
d. all of the above.

16. (LO4) Claw's Irrigation, Inc. paid $2,000 of dividends in the prior year and $4,500 of dividends in the current year. The closing entry for the current year would include:
a. a debit to Retained Earnings for $6,500.
b. a credit to Dividends for $6,500.
c. a credit to Dividends for $4,500.
d. a credit to Retained Earnings for $4,500.

17. (LO4) Collins Construction Co. uses the accrual basis of accounting. During the year, Collins reported $45,000 of revenue, $12,500 of expenses, and $1,200 of dividends. On December 31, Collins prepares all closing entries. The net effect on Retained Earnings is a:
a. decrease of $1,200.
b. increase of $42,500.
c. increase of $31,300.
d. decrease of $13,700.

18. (LO4) Which of the following is not a possible closing entry?
a. A debit to Retained Earnings and a credit to Dividends
b. A debit to Revenue and a credit to Retained Earnings
c. A debit to Retained Earnings and a credit to Expense
d. A debit to Expense and a credit to Retained Earnings

19. (LO5) Which of the following is not a step in the accounting cycle?
a. Prepare an adjusted trial balance
b. Prepare and post closing entries
c. Prepare financial statements
d. Each of the above is a step in the accounting cycle

20. (LO5) Which of the following best summarizes the order of the accounting cycle?
a. Journalize, post, adjust, close
b. Journalize, adjust, post, close
c. Journalize, close, adjust, post
d. Journalize, post, close, adjust

BRIEF EXERCISES

1. Cash and Accrual Basis LO1

During the year, Black Diamond Company earned $86,500 in revenue. At year-end, only $65,000 of that revenue had been collected. Also, Black Diamond incurred $44,000 of expenses of which only $35,000 had been paid.

Required

Determine net income for the year under (a) the cash basis of accounting and (b) the accrual basis of accounting.

2. Adjusting Journal Entries LO2, 3

Consider the following incomplete adjusting journal entries:

1. Utilities Expense	2,900	
(a)		2,900
2. (b)	19,500	
Service Revenue		19,500
3. (c)	7,000	
Prepaid Insurance		7,000
4. Unearned Revenue	4,650	
(d)		4,650

Required
Identify the likely account(s) that would complete each adjusting journal entry.

3. Adjusting Journal Entries LO2
Consider the four entries in the preceding brief exercise.

Required
Identify each entry as an accrued expense, an accrued revenue, a deferred expense, or a deferred revenue.

4. Adjusting Journal Entry—Revenue LO2, 3
On March 1, Global Airlines received $3,500 cash from customers who bought tickets. Only half of the tickets were used by the end of March, and the remaining tickets were expected to be used in April. Global prepares adjusting entries monthly.

Required
a. Determine whether the revenue is a deferred or accrued revenue and explain why.
b. Prepare the journal entries that Global would make on March 1 and March 31.

5. Adjusting Journal Entry—Expense LO2, 3
White Star Enterprises records salaries expense each Friday when employees are paid. The company is preparing its financial statements on June 30, which is a Wednesday. Salaries are $5,000 a week.

Required
a. Prepare any adjusting journal entry necessary on June 30.
b. Explain if this situation is a deferred or accrued expense.
c. Show the T-accounts with the adjusting journal entry posted to them.

6. Adjusting Journal Entry—Expense LO2, 3
On January 1, PGD Corporation bought equipment for $20,000 cash. For the year, PGD calculates a total of $1,250 of depreciation on the equipment. PGD records depreciation annually on December 31.

Required
a. Prepare all journal entries relating to the purchase and depreciation of the equipment.
b. Post the December 31 journal entry to the relevant T-accounts.

7. Adjusting Journal Entry Errors LO2, 3
Suppose that a company fails to make the proper adjusting journal entries associated with the following expenses and revenues:
1. Prepaid insurance that has expired
2. Interest that has accrued on notes payable
3. Unearned revenue that has now been earned

Required
Determine the likely accounts that are affected by each error and whether those accounts are understated or overstated as a result of the error.

8. Calculate Expenses and Revenues LO2, 3
The current- and prior-year balance sheets of Banter Company show the following account balances:

	Current Year	Prior Year
Supplies	$3,000	$4,500
Unearned Revenue	7,200	7,000

During the current year, Banter purchased $11,300 of supplies and received $9,200 of cash for services to be performed later.

Required
Using T-accounts, determine Banter Company's supplies expense and service revenue for the current year.

9. Adjusting Journal Entries LO2, 3
Big E Services provides the following selected information from its trial balance and adjusted trial balance at August 31:

Big E Services
Trial Balance
August 31

	Unadjusted		Adjusted	
	Debit	Credit	Debit	Credit
Accounts Receivable	$8,910		$9,240	
Supplies	3,400		2,200	
Service Revenue		$17,480		$17,810
Supplies Expense	5,320		6,520	

Required
Prepare the adjusting journal entries that Big E must have made at August 31.

10. Prepare Financial Statements from Trial Balance LO3
The adjusted trial balance for Handle Coffee is as follows:

Handle Coffee
Adjusted Trial Balance
November 30

	Debit	Credit
Cash	$2,500	
Accounts Receivable	350	
Supplies	1,800	
Accounts Payable		$ 750
Salaries Payable		2,000
Retained Earnings		1,000
Service Revenue		4,400
Salaries Expense	2,900	
Supplies Expense	600	
Total	$8,150	$8,150

Required
Prepare Handle's income statement and statement of retained earnings for the month of November and its balance sheet at November 30.

11. Closing Entries LO4

Ivey Publishing generates and records $15,000 of revenues and $12,000 of expenses during the month. It also pays and records $500 in dividends for the month.

Required
Prepare Ivey's closing entries for the month and determine the net change in Retained Earnings as a result of those entries.

12. Adjusting and Closing Process LO3, 4, 5

Consider the following accounts:

Cash
Accounts Receivable
Interest Payable
Common Stock
Service Revenue
Salaries Expense

Required
Determine which accounts fall into the following categories: A) Accounts that can be adjusted and closed; B) Accounts that can be adjusted but not closed; C) Accounts that are not normally adjusted nor closed.

EXERCISES

13. Cash and Accrual Income LO1

During 2012, Stacker Enterprises earned $55,000 from services provided and incurred $15,500 of expenses. At the end of the year, Stacker had received cash for $35,750 of the revenues and had paid $11,600 of the expenses. Also during 2012, Stacker received $3,500 cash for services to be performed in 2013 and paid $4,500 for rent for the first six months of 2013.

Required
Determine 2012 net income under (a) the cash basis and (b) the accrual basis of accounting.

14. Adjusting Journal Entries LO2, 3

Following are several independent accounting situations:

1. Interest of $1,500 on a loan outstanding during 2012 is due on January 1, 2013.
2. Received $100,000 in 2012 for a service project that is 45% complete at year-end.
3. Received a $450 utility bill for the month of December on January 3, 2013.
4. $750 of prepaid rent for the month of December has expired.
5. $5,000 of revenue for services performed on December 14, 2012, is uncollected.
6. Prepay $6,500 of insurance on December 31, 2012, for the entire year of 2013.
7. Intend to buy a warehouse on January 1, 2013, for $125,000.
8. Equipment depreciation is $5,000 for the year.

Required
For each independent situation, determine the basic type of adjustment, if any, that is needed on December 31, 2012 (deferred revenue, deferred expense, accrued revenue, accrued expense). What would be the cumulative effect on 2012 net income of all adjustments made in situations 1–8?

15. Adjusting Journal Entries LO2, 3

The following selected accounts were taken from the general ledger of the Cone Corporation on September 30 before adjusting entries have been made. Cone makes adjusting entries *quarterly*.

	Debit	Credit
Supplies	4,000	
Prepaid Rent	5,400	
Building	100,000	
Notes Receivable	25,000	
Accumulated Depreciation		20,000
Unearned Revenue		8,500

Additional Information:

1. Rent expires at a rate of $900 per month.
2. Supplies on hand total $2,000.
3. Utilities incurred in September but not yet recorded or paid are $500.
4. The building depreciates at a rate of $2,700 per quarter.
5. $5,000 of the $8,500 unearned revenue has been earned during the quarter.
6. Interest of $250 on the notes receivable has been earned but not yet recorded.

Required
Prepare the necessary adjusting journal entries at September 30.

16. Adjusting Journal Entries LO2, 3

For each of the transactions for Cone Corporation in Exercise 15, indicate the amount of the increase or decrease on the appropriate element of the balance sheet or income statement. The first transaction has been completed as an example.

Transaction	Balance Sheet: Assets	Liability	Equity	Income Statement: Revenues	Expenses	Net Income
1.	−2,700	NE	−2,700	NE	+2,700	−2,700
2.						
3.						
4.						
5.						
6.						

17. Adjusting Journal Entries LO2, 3

In its first year of operations, Lien Corporation entered into the following transactions, among others:

1. January 1: Bought equipment, $105,000.
2. March 31: Prepaid one year's rent, $24,000.
3. July 1: Took out a one year loan from the bank at an annual interest rate of 8%, $20,000.
4. August 1: Received payment for services not yet rendered, $12,000.

On December 31, Lien has earned $8,000 of the $12,000 in transaction 4 and has incurred but not recorded $450 of utilities. Lien prepares adjusting entries on an annual basis.

Required

Prepare journal entries for transactions 1–4. Prepare any adjusting journal entries needed at December 31. Assume that the equipment depreciates $15,000 annually.

18. Adjusting Journal Entries LO 2,3

Mikato Company's annual accounting period ends on June 30, 2012. Mikato makes adjusting journal entries semiannually, and the following information applies to all necessary adjusting journal entries at June 30, 2012:

1. Mikato carries the following two insurance policies:

Policy	Purchase Date	Policy Length	Cost at Purchase Date
A	July 1, 2010	5 years	$48,000
B	July 1, 2011	2 years	16,000

2. At January 1, 2012, office supplies totaled $1,800. In the past six months, additional supplies of $2,700 were purchased, and a count revealed $2,150 available supplies at June 30, 2012.
3. Mikato owns one building:

Cost	Useful Life	Annual Depreciation
$150,000	25	$6,000

4. Mikato decides to rent out a portion of its building. On June 1, 2012, Mikato received a prepayment of $5,700 for rent for the months of June, July, and August.
5. The Mikato staff consists of seven employees. Each employee earns a total of $1,200 a week and is paid each Monday for the previous week's work. June 30, 2012, falls on Thursday.

Required

Prepare all necessary adjusting entries at June 30, 2012, and indicate whether each entry relates to a deferred revenue, deferred expense, accrued revenue, or accrued expense.

19. Errors in Adjusting Journal Entries LO2, 3

Consider the following independent situations.

1. A company provides a service but has not yet received payment. Therefore, the company does not record any revenue for the service.
2. A company receives cash in advance of providing a service and properly records a liability to the customer. At year-end, the company has not provided any of the service. The company does not adjust the liability at year-end.
3. Half of a company's prepaid insurance expires during the year, but the company does not adjust the prepaid insurance account to reflect the expiration.
4. A company incurs legal expenses associated with defending a lawsuit. No bill has been received at year-end, so the company does not record any expenses associated with the lawsuit.

Required

For each independent scenario, determine whether the company's accounting was correct or incorrect. If it was incorrect, determine whether the error resulted in the company's assets, liabilities, equity, revenues, and expenses being correct, understated, or overstated.

20. Adjusting Journal Entries LO2, 3

Coy Williams, a first-year accountant at Protein Plus, has asked you to review the following items for potential errors. Protein Plus has a December 31 year-end.

1. Did not adjust the Prepaid Insurance account for the $6,600 of insurance that expired during the year.
2. Recorded a full year of accrued interest on a $20,000, 10% note payable that was entered into on July 1. Interest is payable each July 1.

3. Did not record $8,500 of depreciation on an office building.
4. Recorded revenues of $12,000 when payment was received for a job that will be completed next year.
5. Recorded $600 of utilities expense for December utilities even though Protein Plus will not pay the bill until January of next year.

Required
Determine if Coy made any errors in the five items. For those in which an error was made, prepare the entry that Coy should have made. What was the net effect of Coy's errors on the net income of Protein Plus?

21. Closing Entries LO4

Ivey Publishing provides the following trial balance at March 31:

Ivey Publishing Trial Balance March 31		
	Debit	**Credit**
Cash	$ 4,280	
Prepaid Insurance	3,500	
Unearned Revenue		$ 3,000
Retained Earnings		2,380
Service Revenue		14,820
Insurance Expense	2,300	
Salaries Expense	8,920	
Dividends	1,200	
Totals	$20,200	$20,200

Required
Prepare Ivey's closing entries at March 31 and its Post-Closing Trial Balance.

22. Closing Process LO4

A partial adjusted trial balance is shown as follows for Sparks Electricity:

Sparks Electricity Partial Adjusted Trial Balance June 30		
	Debit	**Credit**
Retained Earnings		$17,150
Service Revenue		30,500
Advertising Expense	$ 1,200	
Depreciation Expense	10,750	
Interest Expense	560	
Salaries Expense	5,000	
Supplies Expense	2,500	
Utilities Expense	2,080	
Dividends	1,000	

Required
a. Prepare Sparks' income statement and statement of retained earnings for the month of June.
b. Prepare the appropriate closing entries at June 30.
c. What is the purpose of "closing the books" at the end of an accounting period?

23. Closing Process LO4

The following T-accounts contain the December postings to the general ledger of Swoops, Inc. The December 1 postings are beginning balances, while the December 31 postings are closing entries.

Service Revenue

12/31	75,000	12/1	64,000
		12/8	4,000
		12/24	3,000
		12/30	4,000

Salaries Expense

12/1	15,000	12/31	17,000
12/15	1,000		
12/30	1,000		

Supplies Expense

12/1	1,800	12/31	2,500
12/30	700		

Depreciation Expense

12/1	4,400	12/31	4,800
12/30	400		

Interest Expense

12/1	1,500	12/31	1,800
12/24	300		

Retained Earnings

12/31	2,500	12/1	51,550
12/31	26,100	12/31	75,000

Dividends

12/1	2,000	12/31	2,500
12/15	500		

Required
Recreate the closing journal entries made by Swoops on December 31.

24. Errors in Closing Entries LO4

Landers Manufacturing prepares the following three closing entries at the end of the year:

#1 Retained Earnings	45,550	
Service Revenue		45,550
#2 Retained Earnings	39,200	
Advertising Expense		10,400
Rent Expense		4,500
Salaries Expense		18,800
Supplies Expense		4,500
#3 Retained Earnings	2,000	
Dividends Payable		2,000

Required

Identify the potential error(s) in Landers' closing entries.

25. Match Terms and Definitions LO1, 2, 3, 4

The following is a list of various accounting terms and definitions:

1. Accrual basis of accounting
2. Cash basis of accounting
3. Adjusting journal entries
4. Deferred revenue
5. Accrued revenue
6. Deferred expense
7. Accrued expense
8. Closing process

a. The final step in the accounting cycle whereby all revenue, expense, and dividend account balances are transferred to the Retained Earnings account.

b. Cash is received before revenue is earned.

c. Entries made into the general journal at the end of an accounting period that record previously unrecorded revenues or expenses.

d. Expense is incurred before cash is paid.

e. Revenues are recorded only when cash is received, and expenses are recorded only when cash is paid.

f. Cash is paid before expense is incurred.

g. Revenues are recorded only when they are earned, and expenses are recorded only when they are incurred.

h. Revenue is earned before cash is received.

Required

Match each accounting term with the appropriate definition.

PROBLEMS

26. Cash and Accrual Income LO1, 2

Olga Industries keeps records under the cash basis of accounting rather than the accrual basis. Olga's 2012 income statement and additional data from 2011 and 2012 are as follows:

Olga Industries
Cash-Basis Income Statement
For the Year Ending December 31, 2012

Revenues		$54,000
Expenses		35,000
Net income		$19,000
Additional Information:		
	12/31/11	**12/31/12**
Accrued Revenues	6,000	8,000
Deferred Revenues	13,000	4,500
Accrued Expenses	5,000	4,000
Deferred Expenses	10,000	9,500

All accrued revenues and expenses as of 12/31/11 were collected and paid, respectively, in 2012. All deferred revenues and expenses as of 12/31/11 were earned and used, respectively, in 2012.

Required

Convert revenues and expenses from the cash basis to the accrual basis and recalculate income. Briefly explain why each adjustment is made.

27. Adjusting Entries and Trial Balance LO2, 3

The unadjusted trial balance of Sweet Cheeks Facial Spa is shown as follows:

Sweet Cheeks Facial Spa
Unadjusted Trial Balance
September 30

	Debit	Credit
Cash	$ 4,300	
Supplies	2,250	
Equipment	18,000	
Accumulated Depreciation		$ 2,400
Unearned Revenue		1,500
Notes Payable		10,000
Common Stock		10,000
Service Revenue		4,000
Advertising Expense	650	
Depreciation Expense	1,200	
Interest Expense	400	
Salaries Expense	600	
Dividends	500	
Totals	$27,900	$27,900

Additional Information:

1. On September 30, Sweet Cheeks completed a service for which it had received payment in August, \$1,500.
2. On September 30, Sweet Cheeks determined that it had earned but not yet billed revenues of \$500.
3. Monthly depreciation on Sweet Cheeks' equipment is \$150.
4. The interest rate on the promissory note is 6%.
5. A count of the supplies revealed \$500 of supplies remaining on September 30.
6. Assume the trial balance was last adjusted on August 31.

Required

Prepare all necessary adjusting entries for the month of September and prepare an adjusted trial balance as of September 30.

28. Adjusting Entries and Closing Entries LO2, 3, 4

The unadjusted and adjusted trial balances of HD Rizzle, Inc. are as follows:

HD Rizzle, Inc. Trial Balance December 31	Unadjusted		Adjusted	
	Debit	Credit	Debit	Credit
Cash	\$ 3,500		\$ 3,500	
Accounts Receivable	8,250		10,750	
Prepaid Insurance	4,600		3,400	
Supplies	600		200	
Buildings	165,000		165,000	
Land	75,000		75,000	
Accumulated Depreciation		\$ 15,000		\$ 31,500
Accounts Payable		9,950		11,000
Salaries Payable		0		1,800
Unearned Revenue		12,050		10,050
Notes Payable		50,000		50,000
Common Stock		100,000		100,000
Retained Earnings		34,600		34,600
Service Revenue		48,550		53,050
Advertising Expense	5,600		5,600	
Depreciation Expense			16,500	
Insurance Expense			1,200	
Salaries Expense	7,600		9,400	
Supplies Expense			400	
Utilities Expense			1,050	
Totals	\$270,150	\$270,150	\$292,000	\$292,000

Required

a. Compare the two trial balances and recreate all adjusting journal entries that were made at December 31.
b. What is the net effect of the adjusting journal entries on net income?

29. Adjusting Entries and Financial Statements LO2, 3

The June 30 unadjusted trial balance of Prime Realty appears as follows:

Prime Realty Unadjusted Trial Balance June 30	Debit	Credit
Cash	\$ 6,900	
Accounts Receivable	4,500	
Prepaid Rent	6,300	
Supplies	2,250	
Equipment	18,000	
Accumulated Depreciation		\$ 900
Unearned Revenue		1,500
Notes Payable		10,000
Common Stock		8,000
Retained Earnings, Jan. 1		12,200
Service Revenue		11,200
Advertising Expense	650	
Depreciation Expense	900	
Interest Expense	150	
Rent Expense	2,100	
Salaries Expense	1,700	
Dividends	350	
Totals	\$43,800	\$43,800

Additional Information:

1. Rent expires at a rate of \$700 per month.
2. Monthly depreciation on equipment is \$300.
3. Interest on the 6% promissory note is paid quarterly on April 1, July 1, October 1, and January 1.
4. Performed services for which payment was received in April, \$800.
5. Received utility bill to be paid next month, \$500.
6. Services to customers earned during June but unrecorded at June 30, \$2,500.
7. Supplies on hand totaled \$1,500 at June 30.
8. Owed employees for salaries for the last week of June to be paid in July, \$800.
9. Prime Realty prepares adjusting entries each quarter. Adjustments were last made on March 31.

Required

a. Prepare all adjusting journal entries for the quarter ending June 30.
b. Post journal entries to T-accounts using totals on the unadjusted trial balance as the opening balances.
c. Prepare an adjusted trial balance as of June 30.
d. Prepare an income statement and a statement of retained earnings for the six months ending June 30.
e. Prepare a classified balance sheet as of June 30.

30. Adjusting Entries and Closing Entries LO2, 3, 4

The unadjusted and adjusted trial balances of Wang, Inc. are shown as follows:

Wang, Inc. Trial Balance December 31				
	Unadjusted Trial Balance		Adjusted Trial Balance	
	Debit	Credit	Debit	Credit
Cash	$ 8,000		$ 8,000	
Accounts Receivable	12,250		16,250	
Prepaid Insurance	6,400		5,600	
Supplies	2,400		1,200	
Buildings	250,000		250,000	
Land	75,000		75,000	
Accumulated Depreciation		$ 25,000		$ 50,000
Salaries Payable				2,000
Unearned Revenue		9,500		7,000
Utilities Payable		15,450		20,950
Notes Payable		75,000		75,000
Common Stock		150,000		150,000
Retained Earnings		22,100		22,100
Service Revenue		75,500		82,000
Advertising Expense	8,500		8,500	
Depreciation Expense			25,000	
Insurance Expense			800	
Salaries Expense	8,000		10,000	
Supplies Expense			1,200	
Utilities Expense			5,500	
Dividends	2,000		2,000	
Totals	$372,550	$372,550	$409,050	$409,050

Required

a. Compare the unadjusted trial balance and the adjusted trial balance and recreate all adjusting journal entries that were made at December 31.
b. Prepare the income statement and a statement of retained earnings for the year. Also prepare a classified balance sheet at December 31.
c. Prepare necessary closing entries.

31. The Accounting Cycle LO2, 3, 4, 5

Ruberstein, Inc. was founded on April 1 and entered into the following transactions:

Apr. 1 Issued common stock to shareholders in exchange for cash, $20,000.
1 Purchased a delivery van (equipment), $13,000.
1 Purchased a one-year insurance policy to be consumed evenly over the next 12 months, $4,800.
1 Took out a loan from First Bank, $20,000.
6 Hired two new employees on salary of $1,000 a month each.
6 Received prepayment for a contracted job to be performed in May, $4,500.
7 Purchased office supplies on credit, $1,200.
8 Billed customers for services provided, $7,500.
12 Paid to have an ad placed on a billboard during April, $1,300.
18 Billed customers for services provided, $8,600.
24 Paid dividends to stockholders, $1,000.
30 Received utility bills for the month of April to be paid next month, $740.
30 Prepaid the next six months of rent starting with May, $3,600.

Additional Information:

1. April depreciation for the delivery van is $217.
2. Interest on the loan from the bank is paid annually at a rate of 6%.
3. An inventory count of office supplies at April 30 showed $500 of supplies on hand.
4. Prepaid insurance has expired.
5. Employees' salaries earned during April but to be paid in May, $2,000.

Required

a. Journalize the transactions for the month of April.
b. Post the journal entries to the general ledger using T-accounts.
c. Prepare a trial balance as of April 30.
d. Prepare all necessary adjusting journal entries and post the entries to the appropriate T-accounts.
e. Prepare an adjusted trial balance as of April 30.
f. Prepare an income statement and a statement of retained earnings for the month of April. Also prepare a classified balance sheet as of April 30.
g. Prepare all closing entries for the temporary accounts and post the entries to the appropriate T-accounts.
h. Prepare a post-closing trial balance as of April 30.

CASES

32. Locate and Understand Accounting Information

Access the latest annual report for **Starbucks Corporation** by clicking on the *Investor Relations* and *Annual Reports* links at www.starbucks.com.

Required

Review the first note to the financial statements and answer the following questions.

a. When does Starbucks recognize revenue from stored value cards? Where does it report outstanding customer balances? Is this an example of a deferred or accrued revenue?
b. When does Starbucks recognize retail revenues?
c. When does Starbucks recognize revenues from product sales such as coffee, tea, and related products?
d. Does Starbucks recognize all advertising costs as they are incurred? If not, does it treat those advertising costs as a deferred or accrued expense?

33. Communication Activity

You are the chief financial officer of a small corporation, and the date is December 31. You recently asked the new accountant to prepare the initial draft of the financial statements for your review. However, when you receive the draft, you quickly notice that no adjusting journal entries were made.

Required

Write a short memo explaining the importance of adjusting entries and the potential misstatements that can result from their exclusion.

34. Ethics and Adjusting Entries

Traction Tires is a large producer of automobile tires. During the current year, Traction was on pace to have record revenues and profits. However, towards the end of the current year, a string of accidents linked to Traction's tires resulted in numerous lawsuits and a product recall of Traction's Premiere line. Traction's President, Hal Marker, recently approached chief accountant Ronnie Williams about the inevitable losses next year and asked Ronnie to defer all possible revenue until next year and to accrue all possible expenses to the current year. "We have so much revenue to spare this year," Hal said, "but next year, we will need all the help we can get."

Required

a. What ethical issues are involved in this scenario?
b. If Hal gets his way, what accounting principles would be violated?
c. Some may say that Hal is simply managing his earnings like he manages all other aspects of his business. What is your opinion of "earnings management"?

35. Ethics and Adjusting Entries

You are a service associate with a major company. When you sell a service, the customer pays cash and you provide the service. At the end of each year, you are required to estimate how much of each outstanding service contract has been earned. At year-end, you have $100,000 of outstanding contracts. You estimate that you have earned somewhere between 40% and 60% of those contracts.

Required

Under the following independent conditions, identify the amount of outstanding contracts that you would report earned. Explain why you would report those amounts.

a. Your compensation is based on performance, and you are $80,000 short of your quota before your estimate.
b. Your compensation is based on performance, and you are $50,000 short of your quota before your estimate.
c. Your compensation is based on your group's performance, and while you have met your quota before your estimate, the group needs $60,000 to meet the group quota.

REVIEW!

ACCT2 puts a multitude of study aids at your fingertips. After reading the chapters, check out these resources for further help:

- **Review Cards,** found in the back of your book, include all learning objectives, key terms and definitions, and visual summaries for each chapter.
- **Online Printable Flash Cards** give you additional ways to check your comprehension of key accounting concepts.
- **Animations**, found in the **CengageNOW™** Personalized Study Plan, offer dynamic, visual examples based around key concepts. One example is the "Make-or-Buy Decision" based on Birdie Maker Golf Company in Chapter 7.
- **Interactive games** include Beat the Clock, a timed quiz for each chapter, and Quiz Bowl—a Jeopardy-style game that helps test your knowledge and understanding of the critical concepts within the chapter.

Find these and other great resources online as part of **CengageNOW™** for **ACCT2**. Sign on at www.cengagebrain.com.

Andersen Ross/Getty Images

Internal Control
and Cash

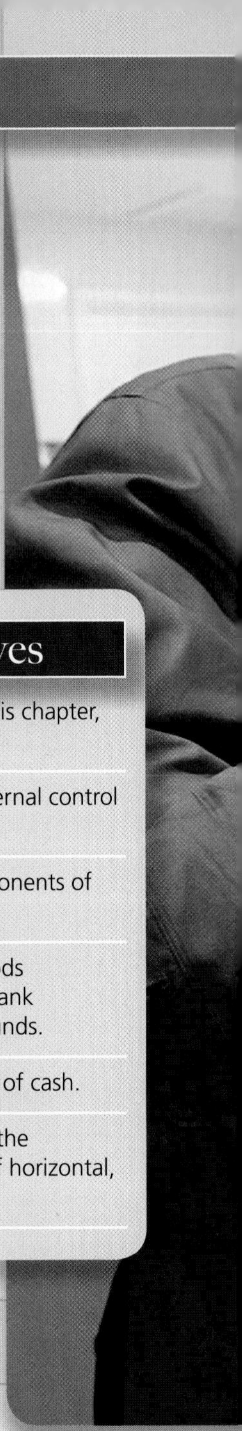

Learning Objectives

After studying the material in this chapter, you should be able to:

LO1 Describe the role of internal control in a business.

LO2 Describe the five components of internal control.

LO3 Understand two methods of internal control over cash—bank reconciliations and petty cash funds.

LO4 Describe the reporting of cash.

LO5 Evaluate cash through the calculation and interpretation of horizontal, vertical, and ratio analyses.

Introduction

This chapter examines the concepts of internal control and how those concepts affect the accounting for cash. Internal control is a company-wide process that seeks to improve a company's operations and its financial reporting. Among other things, internal control helps a company protect its assets. There are few assets that are more prone to theft than cash, so internal control is quite relevant and important to the accounting for cash.

This chapter begins with the role and overall concepts of internal control and then examines two control activities relating to cash—bank reconciliations and petty cash funds. The chapter concludes with how cash is reported and how a company's cash position can be analyzed.

LO1 Internal Control

In recent years, there have been numerous widely publicized accounting frauds. Major corporations such as **Enron**, **WorldCom**, and **HealthSouth** failed due to fraudulent activity. As a result, investors, regulators, politicians, and the general public began to question the reliability and integrity of financial reporting of publicly traded companies.

Faced with this crisis, the United States Congress passed the Sarbanes-Oxley Act (SOX) in July 2002. The act sought to restore public confidence in financial reporting by enacting major changes in the manner in which accounting is practiced in the United States. Several of those changes focused on *internal control.*

Internal control The system of policies and procedures used in a company to promote efficient and effective operations, reliable financial reporting, and compliance with laws and regulations.

In its broadest sense, internal control is the process that a company's management uses to help the company meet its operational and financial reporting objectives. More specifically, **internal control** is

Making pizza is probably the most prominent process at a Domino's location, but equally important are internal control processes, especially in the collection of customer payments.

AP Photo/Paul Sancya

the system of policies and procedures that a company puts in place to provide reasonable assurances that:

- the company's operations are effective and efficient,
- the company's financial reporting is reliable, and
- the company is complying with applicable laws and regulations.

All companies have systems of internal control. The only question is how strong or weak those systems are.

Recognizing that internal control affects a company's success or failure, Section 404 of SOX contained several requirements for publicly traded companies regarding internal control.

One of the most important requirements is that corporations include in their annual reports to stockholders an **internal control report** containing the following two items:

- A statement that it is management's responsibility to establish and maintain an adequate internal control structure and procedures for financial reporting.
- An assessment of the effectiveness of the internal control structure and procedures for financial reporting for the most recent year.

These requirements publicly place the burden of internal controls squarely on management. Management must take responsibility for, as well as provide an assessment of, internal control. This forces management to be engaged with respect to its internal control.

In addition to requiring an internal control report, SOX also requires management to obtain an annual audit of its internal control structure and its assessment. In other words, SOX requires an independent, third-party evaluation of management's assessment. This evaluation is performed by the public accounting firm conducting the company's financial audit.

Internal control report Annual report in which management states its responsibility for internal control and provides an assessment of its internal control.

To illustrate these requirements, Exhibit 5-1 contains **Domino's Pizza's** most recent internal control report as well as excerpts from the audit report of Domino's auditor, **PricewaterhouseCoopers LLP**. The highlighted sections of the internal control report show that Domino's management (1) takes responsibility for its internal control, (2) states that it has conducted an evaluation of the effectiveness of its internal control, and (3) concludes that its internal control is effective. The highlighted portion of the audit report shows that the audit firm agrees. Based on its audit of Domino's internal controls, PricewaterhouseCoopers' opinion is that Domino's maintained effective internal control over financial reporting during the most recent period. This is the opinion that management wants to receive.

Before leaving Exhibit 5-1, note that both reports contain an italicized reference to *Internal Control—Integrated Framework*. This title refers to an influential report released in 1992 by the Committee of Sponsoring Organizations (COSO) of the Treadway Commission. The report was the culmination of the committee's exhaustive research and deliberation on the elements of sound internal control. The

Exhibit 5-1 Internal Control Reporting by Domino's Pizza

Management Report on Internal Controls

The management of Domino's Pizza, Inc. is responsible for establishing and maintaining adequate internal control over financial reporting. Internal control over financial reporting is defined in Rule 13a-15(f) promulgated under the Exchange Act, as a process designed by, or under the supervision of, the Company's principal executive and principal financial officers and effected by the Company's board of directors, management and other personnel, to provide reasonable assurance regarding the reliability of financial reporting and the preparation of financial statements for external purposes in accordance with generally accepted accounting principles.

Because of its inherent limitations, internal control over financial reporting may not prevent or detect misstatements. Also, projections of any evaluation of effectiveness to future periods are subject to the risk that controls may become inadequate because of changes in conditions, or that the degree of compliance with the policies or procedures may deteriorate.

Under the supervision and with the participation of the Company's management, including its Chief Executive Officer and Chief Financial Officer, the Company conducted an evaluation of the effectiveness of its internal control over financial reporting as of January 2, 2011 based on the framework in *Internal Control—Integrated Framework* issued by the Committee of Sponsoring Organizations of the Treadway Commission. Based on that evaluation, management concluded that its internal control over financial reporting was effective as of January 2, 2011.

The effectiveness of the Company's internal control over financial reporting as of January 2, 2011, has been audited by PricewaterhouseCoopers LLP, an independent registered public accounting firm, as stated in their report which appears herein.

Excerpt from the Report of Independent Registered Public Accounting Firm

To the Stockholders and Board of Directors of Domino's Pizza, Inc.:

In our opinion, the consolidated financial statements . . . present fairly, in all material respects, the financial position of Domino's Pizza, Inc. and its subsidiaries at January 2, 2011 and January 3, 2010, and the results of their operations and their cash flows for each of the three years in the period ended January 2, 2011 in conformity with accounting principles generally accepted in the United States of America . . . Also in our opinion, the Company maintained, in all material respects, effective internal control over financial reporting as of January 2, 2011, based on criteria established in *Internal Control—Integrated Framework* issued by the Committee of Sponsoring Organizations of the Treadway Commission (COSO).

PricewaterhouseCoopers LLP
Detroit, Michigan
March 1, 2011

The *COSO Framework* is the standard for understanding what good internal control looks like in an organization.

committee's objective was to provide a common understanding of internal control—a framework for implementing good internal control practices. Its success is clear. The *Framework* has become the standard for understanding what good internal control looks like in an organization, and it is the basis for the discussion in this chapter.

LO2 Components of Internal Control

The broad purpose of internal control is to help management achieve effective and efficient operations, reliable financial reporting, and compliance with laws and regulations. *Internal Control—Integrated Framework* states that good internal control consists of the following five interrelated components:

- Control Environment
- Risk Assessment
- Control Activities
- Information and Communication
- Monitoring

Control Environment

The **control environment** is the foundation for all other components of internal control. It is the atmosphere in which the members of an organization conduct their activities and carry out their responsibilities. The control environment is often called the "tone at the top" because it reflects the overall control consciousness of an organization.

Many factors affect an organization's control environment. One of the most important is the overall integrity and ethical values of personnel. These attributes translate into standards of behavior that can permeate throughout an organization's operations. Other factors include management's philosophy and operating style, the assignment of authority and responsibility, and the general structure of an organization. Each of these factors contributes to the overall corporate culture within which internal control operates. Without a sound control environment, the remaining elements of internal control suffer.

Risk Assessment

All organizations face a variety of risks that threaten the achievement of organizational objectives. **Risk assessment** refers to the identification and analysis of these risks, with the goal of effectively managing them. Because business conditions change throughout time, risk assessment is an ongoing organizational activity.

Organizational risks can arise from both external and internal sources. External sources might include new competitors, changing customer expectations, or even natural catastrophes. Internal sources might include inadequate workforce training, errors in financial reporting of activities, or theft of assets by employees.

Control environment The atmosphere in which the members of an organization conduct their activities and carry out their responsibilities.

Risk assessment The identification and analysis of the risks that threaten the achievement of organizational objectives.

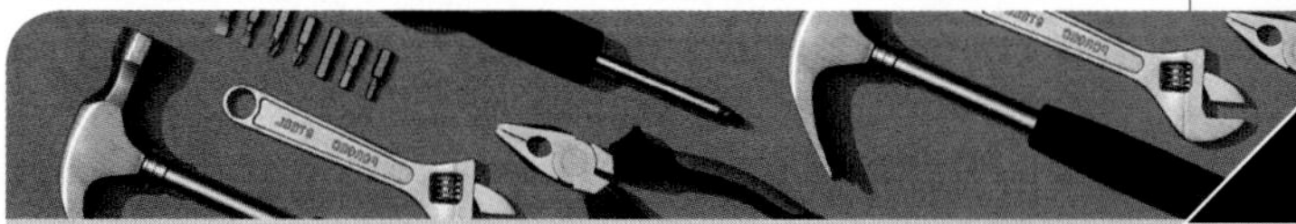

HOME DEPOT ANALYSIS

Look at the Report of Independent Registered Public Accounting Firm accompanying **Home Depot's** financial statements in Appendix C. What was the auditor's opinion regarding the effectiveness of Home Depot's internal control?

In the auditor's opinion, The Home Depot, Inc. maintained, in all material respects, effective internal control over financial reporting as of January 30, 2011, based on criteria established in *Internal Control—Integrated Framework* issued by the Committee of Sponsoring Organizations of the Treadway Commission.

The control environment is often called the "tone at the top" because it reflects the overall control consciousness of an organization.

Once an organization identifies its risks, the risks can be analyzed with the following general process:

- Estimate the significance of a risk
- Assess the likelihood of the risk occurring
- Consider what actions should be taken to manage the risk

Risks of minor significance or those with a lower likelihood of occurrence generally do not warrant serious concern. For example, the risk of a meteorite destroying a company's warehouse can likely be ignored. In contrast, significant risks with higher likelihood demand considerable attention. For example, the risk of an employee stealing cash from customer collections likely requires some attention. That attention comes in the form of control activities.

Control Activities

Control activities are the policies and procedures management establishes to address the risks that might prevent the organization from achieving its objectives. Although specific control activities vary widely across organizations, they generally fall into one of several categories.

Establishing Responsibility A critical factor in good internal control is establishing responsibility for the performance of a given task. When responsibility is clear, two benefits arise. First, the employee knows that he or she will be held accountable for completion of the task. Second, management knows who to consult if the task is not completed satisfactorily.

A good example is a retailer's cashiers. Each cashier is assigned sole responsibility over a specific cash drawer. No other cashier has access to or responsibility for that drawer. If a drawer is returned to the company short of cash, management knows exactly who to speak to. As a result, cashiers are motivated to perform their tasks well, and the risk of theft or error is reduced.

Maintaining Adequate Documentation Accounting information is useful only when it is reliable, which means that it must be free from error. Control activities are necessary in all organizations to promote error-free accounting records. Consider the sale of a company's inventory as an example. Good control practices would require that the sale be documented on a sales invoice, preferably a sequentially numbered one so that the sale will neither be lost nor recorded twice. The invoice might also require the employee's initials to establish responsibility for the sale, and it will have multiple copies to be sent throughout the organization for proper fulfillment and recording of the sale. Such invoices and processes are increasingly computerized, which brings additional controls that further reduce the introduction of errors into the accounting system.

Segregation of Duties Segregation of duties is a technique that limits one person's control over a particular task or area of a company. Often called separation of duties, it is accomplished by spreading responsibility among multiple employees so that one employee's work can serve as a check against another's work. For example, consider the process of ordering, receiving, and paying for merchandise. If one employee handles all three tasks, there is greater risk of error and possibly theft of assets. However, if these three tasks are handled by different employees, errors by one employee can be caught by another employee. Moreover, unless the employees work unethically together, company assets are more protected against theft.

Physical Security Good internal control includes an effort to safeguard company assets and records. Most of these safeguarding controls are meant to prevent the loss of assets. Examples include secured facilities, fire and alarm systems, computer passwords and encryption, video monitors, and door sensors that signal when product is inappropriately taken from a store. Other controls are meant to detect the loss of assets. An example is the periodic counting of inventory for comparison to accounting records. Significant discrepancies can then be investigated.

Independent Verification Independent verification is the process of reviewing and reconciling information within an organization. This is particularly useful when reconciling an asset balance with the accounting records for that asset. An example would be a bank reconciliation, where the bank's balance and the company's

Control activities The policies and procedures established to address the risks that threaten the achievement of organizational objectives.

balance are reconciled. Often, the most effective verifications are conducted on a surprise basis and are conducted by individuals who have no connection to the process or the employee being verified. Internal audit divisions of organizations commonly perform such verifications.

Information and Communication

Information and communication is another element of sound internal control. **Information and communication** refers to the need for the open flow of relevant information throughout an organization. Information must be captured and communicated in a form and a timeframe that enables employees to complete their responsibilities. This requires information systems that produce relevant and reliable reports. It also requires both upward and downward lines of communication. Management must communicate with employees, and employees must communicate with management.

Monitoring

Monitoring refers to the assessment of the quality of an organization's internal control. Monitoring can be accomplished in two ways. The first is through ongoing activities. For example, in his recurring daily responsibilities, a supervisor can check for evidence that a control activity is functioning properly. He or she can also ask employees if they understand the controls in place and if those controls are being completed. The second is through a separate evaluation. The audit of internal controls required by SOX is an example of a separate evaluation. In both ways, the purpose of monitoring is to continuously improve internal control.

Limitations of Internal Control

Regardless of how well internal control is designed within an organization, it can provide only reasonable assurances that a company is meeting its objectives. Internal control systems are limited in their effectiveness because of (1) the human element and (2) cost-benefit analysis.

The *human element* refers to the fact that internal controls are often based on human judgment and action.

Information and communication Required for the open flow of relevant information throughout an organization.

Monitoring The assessment of the quality of an organization's internal control.

MAKING IT REAL

The monitoring of internal control is an ongoing process, and a company never knows when a problem might be found and what the effect might be.

George Spade

Consider the case of Weatherford International Ltd., an oilfield services company. The company was due to file its annual report to the Securities and Exchange Commission (SEC) on March 1, 2011. However, instead of filing its annual report, it filed a *Notification of Late Filing*, in which it advised the SEC that it would file its annual report at a later date.

The reason for the late filing was the identification of a material weakness in the company's internal control over the financial reporting associated with income taxes. During its final assessment of its internal controls, the company determined that its controls were not effective enough to ensure the accuracy of several tax-related accounts and footnote disclosures. As a result, the company delayed its annual report filing to give it time to ensure the accuracy of the accounts and disclosures. The additional work resulted in adjustments of approximately \$500 million to the financial statements over the period 2007 to 2010.

In addition to the financial statement adjustments, the company disclosed a remediation plan to address the internal control weakness. The plan included a redesign of the control processes for tax-related accounts, more frequent testing to identify errors more quickly, and the hiring of additional personnel.

Weatherford ultimately filed its annual report with the SEC one week late on March 8, 2011.

Collusion among employees can be very effective at defeating a company's internal controls.

Despite our best efforts, we all make mistakes at times, and internal control cannot eliminate them all. Furthermore, employees can purposefully circumvent controls for personal gain. Sometimes this will be a manager who overrides the control activities in place. Other times this will be multiple employees working together to circumvent existing controls. Such collusion among employees can be very effective at defeating a company's internal controls.

Cost-benefit analysis refers to the cost of implementing a control activity versus the benefit that the control provides. For example, a company could install retina-scanning security systems for its warehouses to decrease the risk of theft. However, the cost of the installation may far outweigh the marginal advantage that retina-scanning security provides over normal lock-and-key security. In such a case, security would be limited to lock-and-key because the cost of the extra security would far outweigh its benefit.

LO3 Cash Controls

The best asset to use in demonstrating internal control is cash. Cash is a highly desired asset. It is easily concealed, taken, and converted into other assets with only a small chance of detection. As a result, companies normally institute many controls to safeguard their cash and to report it properly. Two of these controls are bank reconciliations and petty cash funds. Each is discussed in the following sections.

Bank Reconciliations

Most companies keep the majority of their cash in a bank. This in itself is a good control procedure because it limits opportunities for theft. It is difficult to steal cash when it is locked up in the bank. The use of a bank also

Monkey Business Images/Shutterstock.com

provides two sources of independent record keeping. That is, both the company and the bank keep a record of all cash transactions between them. As a result, a company can compare these records to verify its cash balance. This comparison is called a bank reconciliation.

A **bank reconciliation** is the process of reconciling the differences between the cash balance on a bank statement and the cash balance in a company's records. The purpose of a bank reconciliation is twofold. First, it confirms the accuracy of both the bank's and the company's cash records. Second, it determines the actual cash balance to be reported on the company's balance sheet. A bank reconciliation is prepared as follows:

- Reconcile the bank balance to the actual cash balance
- Reconcile the company's book balance to the actual cash balance
- Adjust the company's book balance to the actual cash balance

Reconciling the Bank Balance The first step in a bank reconciliation is to reconcile the cash balance reported on the bank statement to the company's actual cash balance. The bank balance may differ from the actual cash balance for two main reasons.

The first reason relates to deposits and payments made by the company that are not reflected on the bank statement. For example, a **deposit in transit** is a deposit that has been made by the company but does not appear on the bank statement because it had not cleared the bank as of the statement date. Because the cash is now in the bank, deposits in transit should be added to the bank's cash balance. An **outstanding check** is a check that has been distributed by the company but does not appear on the bank statement because it had not cleared the bank as of the statement date. Because the cash is no longer in the bank, outstanding checks should be subtracted from the bank cash balance.

Bank reconciliation The process of reconciling the differences between the cash balance on a bank statement and the cash balance in a company's records.

Deposit in transit A deposit that has been made by the company but has not cleared the bank as of the statement date.

Outstanding check A check that has been distributed by the company but has not cleared the bank as of the statement date.

A bank reconciliation confirms the accuracy of a company's cash records and determines the actual balance to be reported on the balance sheet.

The second reason the bank balance may differ from the actual cash balance relates to errors made by the bank. Although bank errors are rare, they can occur and must also be reconciled. An error can result in the need to add to or subtract from the bank balance. For example, suppose that the bank erroneously records a $1,450 deposit as $1,540. The bank balance is overstated by $90 and should therefore be reduced by $90. In contrast, suppose that the bank records a $10 check as $100. In that case, the bank balance is understated by $90 and should be increased $90.

Once all adjustments to the bank balance are made, the adjusted bank balance should equal the actual cash balance to be reported on the balance sheet.

Reconciling the Company Book Balance The second step in a bank reconciliation is to reconcile the cash balance reported on the company's books to the actual cash balance. The company book balance may differ from the actual cash balance for two main reasons.

The first reason relates to bank activities that change a company's cash balance but have not been recorded by the company. Usually, companies are notified of these changes through bank memoranda. More specifically, a **credit memorandum** is notification of an addition to the cash balance on the bank statement. Credit memoranda arise when the bank collects cash on behalf of the company—often through the collection of a company receivable or interest on a note. Credit memoranda should be added to the company's book balance. A **debit memorandum** is notification of a subtraction from the cash balance on the bank statement. Common examples are fees charged for banking services and customer checks returned for insufficient funds. Both of these examples reflect cash that the company no longer has, so they should be subtracted from the company's book balance.

The second reason that the book balance may differ from the actual cash balance relates to errors made in the company's cash records. For example, suppose that during the reconciliation a company discovers that it erroneously recorded for $100 a check written as $1,000. The company's balance is overstated by $900 and should be reduced by $900.

Adjusting the Cash Balance Once the bank balance and the company's book balance are reconciled, the company's cash balance must be adjusted to the actual cash balance determined by the reconciliations. Therefore, the third step in a bank reconciliation is to record the journal entries necessary to adjust the company's book balance to the actual cash balance. The journal entries are based on the credit and debit memoranda and errors identified during the reconciliation of the company's balance.

Bank Reconciliation Example

To illustrate a bank reconciliation, suppose that Chapman Enterprises maintains an account with Great Plains Bank. At the end of March, Chapman shows a cash balance of $54,567 while Great Plains shows a balance of $49,880. The differences result from the following:

1. Deposits of $6,450 on March 30 and $1,236 on March 31 do not appear on the March 31 bank statement since they had not cleared the bank as of March 31.

   Resolution: These are deposits in transit. Add them to the bank balance.

2. Checks written in late March for $589 (#1987), $900 (#1990), and $1,180 (#1991) do not appear on the March 31 bank statement since they had not cleared the bank as of March 31.

   Resolution: These are outstanding checks. Subtract them from the bank balance.

3. The March 31 bank statement shows the collection of a $550 receivable from one of Chapman's customers and a $50 monthly service fee. Chapman had not recorded either of these two items.

   Resolution: The collection is a credit memorandum. Add it to Chapman's cash balance. The fee is a debit memorandum. Subtract it from Chapman's cash balance.

4. The March 31 bank statement shows that a $220 customer check was returned to the bank for nonsufficient funds (NSF). Chapman had not recorded this item.

   Resolution: The NSF check is a debit memorandum because no cash was received from the customer's check that Chapman deposited earlier. Subtract it from Chapman's cash balance.

Credit memorandum An addition to the cash balance on the bank statement for items such as the collection of interest.

Debit memorandum A subtraction from the cash balance on the bank statement for items such as service charges.

5. A check clearing the bank for $400 was erroneously recorded in Chapman's records at $450. The check was written to pay off an open account payable.

Resolution: Chapman recorded $50 too much for the check. Therefore, Chapman's cash is understated by $50. Add the $50 to Chapman's cash balance.

Chapman's resulting bank reconciliation is shown as follows. The top half shows the reconciliation of the bank balance while the bottom half shows the reconciliation of the company's book balance.

Chapman Bank Reconciliation
March 31

Balance per bank statement		$49,880
Add deposits in transit:		
March 30	$6,450	
March 31	1,236	7,686
Deduct outstanding checks:		
No. 1987	$ 589	
No. 1990	900	
No. 1991	1,180	2,669
Actual cash balance		$54,897
Balance per company records		$54,567
Add:		
Collection of receivable	$ 550	
Error by Chapman	50	600
Deduct:		
Monthly service charge	$ 50	
NSF check	220	270
Actual cash balance		$54,897

Both reconciliations correctly show an actual cash balance of $54,897. To adjust the company's cash balance to that actual balance, the following entries must be made. Note that each of the four entries comes from the four adjustments made in the reconciliation of the book balance to the actual balance.

Entry 1—Collection of the Receivable Chapman updates its cash balance to reflect the bank's collection of the receivable.

Mar. 31	Cash	550	
	Accounts Receivable		550
	(To record the collection of a receivable by the bank)		

Assets	=	Liabilities	+	Equity
+550				
−550				

Entry 2—Correction of Error Chapman corrects the error made when the $400 check was recorded for $450. This requires Chapman to add back to both cash and accounts payable.

Mar. 31	Cash	50	
	Accounts Payable		50
	(To correct error)		

Assets	=	Liabilities	+	Equity
+50		+50		

Entry 3—Monthly Service Charge Chapman records the monthly service charge as an expense. As a result, both assets and equity decrease.

Mar. 31	Service Charge Expense	50	
	Cash		50
	(To record monthly expense for bank account)		

Assets	=	Liabilities	+	Equity
−50				−50

Entry 4—NSF Check Chapman records the effect of a check returned for non-sufficient funds by reinstating the receivable and reducing its cash balance. Since the check was no good, the receivable has not yet been collected. Chapman must now try to collect again.

Mar. 31	Accounts Receivable	220	
	Cash		220
	(To reinstate customer receivable)		

Assets	=	Liabilities	+	Equity
+220				
−220				

After these four entries are recorded, the company's cash balance is updated to the actual cash balance.

Petty Cash Funds

Most companies require that all disbursements of cash be made with a check. This is a basic control activity that allows a company to better monitor its cash outflows. However, there are many instances when only a small amount of cash is needed and the process of writing a check is burdensome. Examples would include postage for small mailings and the purchase of miscellaneous office supplies. To handle such cases, companies often establish a petty cash fund.

Ultrashock/Shutterstock.com

A **petty cash fund** is an amount of cash kept on hand to pay for minor expenditures. While the size and scope of a petty cash fund will vary across companies, its operation will involve the following three activities:

- Establishing the fund
- Making payments from the fund
- Replenishing the fund

Establishing the Fund A petty cash fund is established by writing a check for the amount of the fund, cashing the check, and placing the cash under the care of an employee designated as custodian. A journal entry is then made to record the establishment of the fund.

To illustrate, suppose that on May 1, Barnett Design Group cashes a $100 check to establish a petty cash fund and gives the cash to John Stephens, the custodian. On this date, Barnett would record the following entry:

May 1	Petty Cash	100	
	Cash		100
	(To establish $100 petty cash fund)		

Assets	=	Liabilities	+	Equity
+100				
−100				

The entry increases Petty Cash and decreases Cash. Notice that there is no change in total assets because Petty Cash is an asset account that would be reported as Cash. Barnett has simply designated $100 to be used in a petty cash fund. Barnett still has its cash. It has not yet disbursed any cash outside of the company.

Making Payments from the Fund After the fund is established, the cash is used to pay for qualifying expenditures. Payments are usually made in one of two ways. Cash can be taken from the fund to make payment, or employees can seek reimbursement from the fund for payments they have personally made. In either case, the custodian should collect receipts for the use of any cash. As payments are made from petty cash, no journal entries are made. Journal entries are recorded only when the fund is replenished.

Replenishing the Fund As the cash in the fund decreases, the fund must be replenished. To do so, the remaining cash in the fund is counted, and the company cashes a check for the amount that brings the total cash in the fund back to the original balance. The receipts in the fund are then used as documentation for recording expenses.

To illustrate, suppose that on May 31, Stephens examines the petty cash fund and prepares the following report:

Petty Cash Fund Replenishment Report

Petty cash fund	$100
Less: cash remaining in the fund	15
Cash requested to replenish fund	$ 85
Receipts in the fund:	
Postage	$ 25
Supplies	47
Miscellaneous	13
Total receipts	$ 85

The report shows that the fund needs $85 to be fully replenished. It also shows that there are receipts totaling $85. As a result, Barnett would cash a check for $85 to replenish the fund and record expenses as follows:

May 31	Postage Expense	25	
	Supplies Expense	47	
	Miscellaneous Expense	13	
	Cash		85
	(To replenish petty cash fund and record various expenses)		

Assets	=	Liabilities	+	Equity
−85				−25
				−47
				−13

The entry increases the three expense accounts related to the expenditures and decreases the Cash account for the amount of the check. Because Barnett is recording the expenses resulting from fund use, the entry reduces both assets and equity. This same type of entry would be repeated each time the fund is replenished.

Cash Over and Short When a petty cash fund is replenished, the amount of cash needed for replenishment should equal the total amount of receipts. However,

Petty cash fund An amount of cash kept on hand to pay for minor expenditures.

this will not always be the case. Sometimes, the custodian may not obtain all receipts or may give incorrect change, resulting in a discrepancy between the cash needed for replenishment and the amount of receipts. In such cases, the discrepancy is charged to an account called Cash Over and Short. Cash Over and Short is a temporary account that can have either a debit or credit balance, depending on the situation. A debit balance increases expenses while a credit balance decreases expenses.

To illustrate, assume the same facts as previously except that Stephens counts only $13 of cash in the fund before replenishment.

Petty Cash Fund Replenishment Report

Petty cash fund	$100
Less: Cash remaining in the fund	13
Cash requested to replenish fund	$ 87
Receipts in the fund:	
Postage	$ 25
Supplies	47
Miscellaneous	13
Total receipts	$ 85

In this case, a check must be written for $87 to fully replenish the fund. However, there is only $85 of receipts. The $2 difference is charged to the Cash Over and Short account as follows:

May 31	Postage Expense	25	
	Supplies Expense	47	
	Miscellaneous Expense	13	
	Cash Over and Short	2	
	Cash		87
	(To replenish petty cash fund and record various expenses)		

Assets	=	Liabilities	+	Equity
−87				−25
				−47
				−13
				− 2

In this entry, the Cash Over and Short account is debited, which indicates an increase to expenses. Most likely, the balance would be reported as a miscellaneous expense.

Cash A medium of exchange.

Cash equivalent Any investment that is readily convertible into cash and has an original maturity of three months or less.

Restricted cash Cash a company has restricted for a specific purpose.

Cash takes many forms—the coins and dollar bills in your pocket, your checking and savings accounts, even a check from a friend that has not yet been deposited.

LO4 Reporting Cash and Cash Equivalents

At its most basic level, **cash** is a medium of exchange. A general rule is that something is cash if you can deposit it into a bank and readily use it to pay someone. Cash takes many forms—the coins and dollar bills in your pocket, your checking and savings accounts, even a check from a friend that has not yet been deposited. Money orders and travelers checks are other examples of cash.

In addition to these forms of cash, companies often hold investments that are so much like cash that they are deemed to be *equivalent to cash*. A **cash equivalent** is any investment that (1) is readily convertible into a known amount of cash and (2) has an original maturity of three months or less. Examples of cash equivalents can include Treasury bills, certificates of deposit, money market accounts, and commercial paper, as long as they mature in three months or less. Cash equivalents are so much like cash that they are combined with cash for reporting purposes.

Cash and cash equivalents are reported on the balance sheet as a current asset. Most companies report their balances in the first line of the balance sheet.

In some cases, though, a company will restrict some of its cash for a specific purpose. For example, a company may designate a certain amount of cash for the payment of interest. To inform investors and creditors of such restrictions, companies will report such **restricted cash** separately from cash and cash equivalents.

An example of such a company is **Domino's Pizza**. Shown below are the first two accounts of Domino's 2010 balance sheet as well as the notes to the financial statements addressing the company's cash balances.

As you can see, Domino's has almost $48 million in cash and cash equivalents at the end of 2010. It reports even more in restricted cash—over $85 million.

Cash Information from Domino's 2010 Annual Report

Balance Sheet

(in thousands)	2010	2009
Cash and cash equivalents	$47,945	$42,392
Restricted cash	85,530	91,141

Notes to the financial statements

Cash and Cash Equivalents

Cash equivalents consist of highly liquid investments with original maturities of three months or less at the date of purchase. These investments are carried at cost, which approximates fair value.

Restricted Cash

Restricted cash includes $37.2 million of cash held for future interest payments, $35.4 million of cash held in trust or as collateral for outstanding letters of credit, $6.6 million of cash held in interest reserves, $6.0 million cash held for capitalization of entities, and $0.3 million of other restricted cash.

Domino's notes disclose the purpose of this restriction. The majority of restricted cash is intended for future interest payments and for collateral on outstanding letters of credit.

LO5 Analyzing Cash

A company's management of cash is critical to its success. If a company can't keep enough cash, it can quickly run into major problems. The following sections examine the cash position of **Papa John's International**. The examination will require the cash balance from the company's balance sheet and various items from its statement of cash flows. The required information is found in Exhibit 5-2, excerpted from Papa John's 2010 Annual Report.

Exhibit 5-2 Account Balances from Papa John's 2010 Annual Report

Source	Accounts	2010	2009	2008
Balance Sheet	Cash and cash equivalents	$ 46,225	$ 25,457	
	Total assets	$415,941	$393,726	
Statement of Cash Flows	Net cash provided by operating activities	$ 89,096	$100,070	$ 73,063
	Net cash used in investing activities	(28,657)	(36,407)	(26,232)
	Net cash used in financing activities	(39,733)	(49,298)	(44,129)
	Specific investing activity cash flows:			
	Purchase of property and equipment	(31,125)	(33,538)	(29,271)
	Specific financing activity cash flows:			
	Acquisition of Company common stock	(46,936)	(28,477)	(37,697)

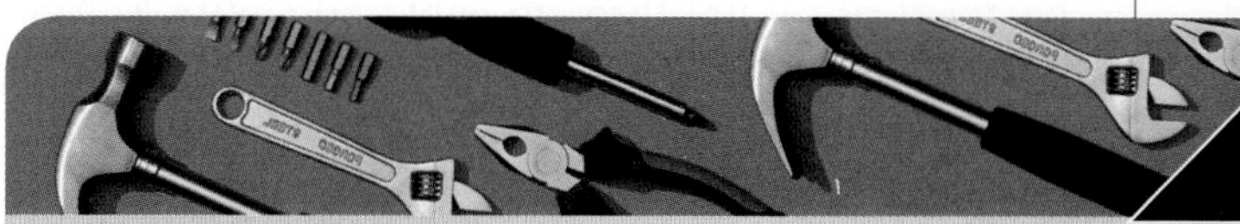

HOME DEPOT ANALYSIS

Home Depot's balance sheet in Appendix C reports Cash and Cash Equivalents of $545 million. Looking at the Cash Equivalents paragraph in Home Depot's first note, what types of investments does the company include in cash equivalents?

Home Depot's Cash Equivalents note states that its cash equivalents include high-grade commercial paper, money market funds, and U.S. government agency securities.

Horizontal and Vertical Analyses

A good place to start the analysis of any asset account is horizontal and vertical analyses. Recall from Chapter 2 that horizontal analysis calculates the dollar change in an account balance, defined as the current-year balance less the prior-year balance, and divides that change by the prior-year balance to yield the percentage change. Vertical analysis divides each account balance by a base account, yielding a percentage. The base account for an analysis of cash is total assets. These calculations are summarized as follows:

Horizontal Analysis

$$\text{Dollar change in account balance} = \text{Current-year balance} - \text{Prior-year balance}$$

$$\text{Percentage change in account balance} = \frac{\text{Dollar change}}{\text{Prior-year balance}}$$

Vertical Analysis

$$\text{Percentage} = \frac{\text{Cash}}{\text{Total Assets}}$$

Given **Papa John's** information in Exhibit 5-2, horizontal and vertical analyses of cash result in the following:

Horizontal Analysis

	Change	*Percentage Change*
Cash and cash equivalents	46,225 − 25,457 = 20,768	$\frac{20,768}{25,457} = 81.6\%$

Vertical Analysis

	2010	*2009*
Cash and cash equivalents	$\frac{46,225}{415,941} = 11.1\%$	$\frac{25,457}{393,726} = 6.5\%$

The horizontal analysis shows that Papa John's cash balance increased a little under $21 million in 2010, which equals an 81.6% increase over the prior year. The vertical analysis shows that cash made up about 11.1% of total assets in 2010. This was also an increase from the prior year, when cash made up only 6.5% of total assets.

While the preceding analysis shows that Papa John's cash increased during 2010, it does not indicate why cash increased. To find out why, investors and

Stephen Coburn/Shutterstock.com

creditors can look at the information on a company's statement of cash flows. Recall from Chapter 1 that the statement of cash flows classifies a company's cash inflows and outflows into three main categories—operating activities, investing activities, and financing activities.

Operating activities include those transactions necessary to run the business. This would include selling a product, paying employees, and advertising. According to Exhibit 5-2, Papa John's generated over $89 million in cash from operations during 2010.

Investing activities include the buying and selling of revenue-generating assets such as buildings and equipment. Papa John's reports a net cash outflow of almost $29 million from investing activities in 2010. The additional investing activity detail in Exhibit 5-2 shows that the majority of that outflow was due to the purchase of property and equipment.

Financing activities include the raising and repayment of capital through debt and equity. During 2010, Papa John's reports just under $40 million in cash outflows from financing activities. The additional financing activity detail in Exhibit 5-2 shows that the outflow was due mostly to the acquisition of its own common stock.

With this information, you can conclude that Papa John's cash increased by about $21 million during 2010 because its operating cash flows significantly exceeded its primary use of cash in purchasing property and equipment and acquiring its own common stock. This seems to be a good situation with respect to cash.

Free Cash Flow

A company needs to generate enough cash to pay its bills. It also needs to generate enough to maintain its operational assets and to reward its shareholders with dividends. If a company can generate more cash than it needs for these commitments, it is generating free cash flow.

Free cash flow is the excess cash a company generates beyond what it needs to invest in productive capacity and pay dividends to stockholders. That is, free cash flow is a measure of a company's ability to generate cash for expansion, for other forms of improved operations, or for increased returns to stockholders. While free cash flow can be defined in many ways, the most straightforward definition is as follows:

Free Cash Flow
Cash Flows from Operating Activities
Less: Capital Expenditures
Less: Dividends
Free Cash Flow

The ratio starts with cash flows from operating activities, which is a measure of a company's ability to generate cash from its current operations. Capital expenditures refers to the amount a company spends on fixed assets during the year. Dividends are payments to stockholders during the year. Each of these items is found on the statement of cash flows.

From the information in Exhibit 5-2, **Papa John's** free cash flow for the most recent two years is calculated as follows:

Free Cash Flow	**2010**	**2009**
Cash Flows from Operating Activities	$89,096	$100,070
Less: Capital Expenditures	(31,125)	(33,538)
Less: Dividends	0	0
Free Cash Flow	$57,971	$ 66,532

In each year, Papa John's produces positive free cash flow. And, from the statement of cash flow information in Exhibit 5-2, you can get an idea of how it has used that free cash flow. Notice the large cash outflows in the additional financing activity detail. In the three years reported, the company paid out $46,936, $28,477, and $37,697 for "Acquisition of Company common stock." Papa John's has been buying back its common stock from its shareholders.

Free cash flow The excess cash a company generates beyond what it needs to invest in productive capacity and pay dividends to stockholders.

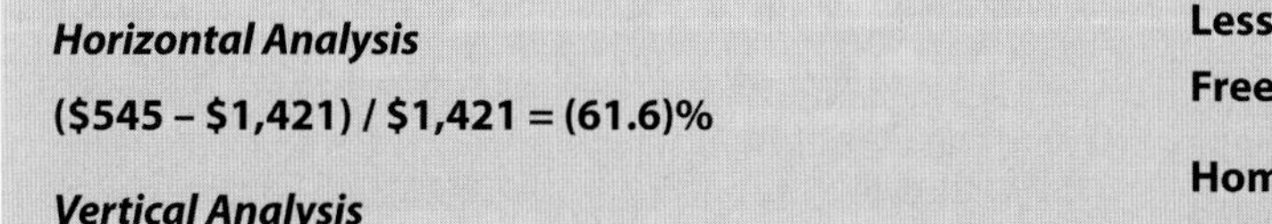

HOME DEPOT ANALYSIS

Using **Home Depot's** financial statements in Appendix C, calculate and interpret (1) horizontal and vertical analyses of cash and (2) free cash flow.

Horizontal Analysis

($545 – $1,421) / $1,421 = (61.6)%

Vertical Analysis

$545 / $40,125 = 1.4%

The (61.6)% horizontal analysis indicates that cash decreased during the year by more than 61%. The 1.4% vertical analysis indicates that a very small portion of Home Depot's assets are in the form of cash.

Free Cash Flow

Cash Flows from Operating Activities	**$4,585**
Less: Capital Expenditures	**(1,096)**
Less: Dividends	**(1,569)**
Free Cash Flow	**$1,920**

Home Depot generated enough cash from operations to fund its capital expenditures and its dividends and to have over $1.9 billion of free cash flow. This amount shows that Home Depot is able to generate cash for other company purposes.

STUDY TOOLS 5

Chapter review card

- Learning Objective and Key Concept Reviews
- Key Definitions and Formulas

Online (Located at www.cengagebrain.com)

- Flash Cards and Crossword Puzzles
- Games and Quizzes
- E-Lectures
- Homework Assignments (as directed by your instructor)

CONCEPT QUESTIONS

1. (LO1) What did the Sarbanes-Oxley Act seek to do?
2. (LO1) Internal control is supposed to provide reasonable assurance about what three things?
3. (LO1) What two items should management's internal control report contain?
4. (LO2) What are the five components of the *Internal Control—Integrated Framework*?
5. (LO2) What phrase is often used to describe the control environment of a company?
6. (LO2) What three general processes will an organization use to analyze risk?
7. (LO2) What are two benefits that arise from establishing responsibility?
8. (LO2) What are two limitations of internal control?
9. (LO3) What is the purpose of a bank reconciliation?
10. (LO 3) What are the steps in preparing a bank reconciliation?
11. (LO 3) What are three ways in which the bank balance may need to be adjusted to reach the actual cash balance?
12. (LO 3) Why do credit and debit memorandums arise?
13. (LO 3) The operation of a petty cash fund involves what three activities?
14. (LO 4) Where are cash and cash equivalents reported?
15. (LO 5) When is a company generating free cash flow?

MULTIPLE CHOICE

1. (LO1) Which of the following is not normally included in an internal control report?
   a. An assessment of the effectiveness of internal control
   b. A statement that it is management's responsibility to *establish* the internal control structure and procedures for financial reporting
   c. A statement that it is management's responsibility to *maintain* the internal control structure and procedures for financial reporting
   d. Suggestions on how the company can improve the internal control structure

2. (LO1) Which of the following is not true of the Sarbanes-Oxley Act?
   a. It required an internal control report
   b. It was passed after many major corporations failed as a result of fraudulent activity
   c. It required that management obtain an audit of internal control
   d. It sought to restore management's confidence over financial reporting
3. (LO 2) "Tone at the top" is a phrase used to describe which component of internal control?
   a. Control Environment
   b. Monitoring
   c. Control Activities
   d. Information and Communication
4. (LO2) Which of the following is not an example of a good control activity?
   a. Establishing responsibility for the performance of a given task
   b. Using computer passwords and encryption
   c. Having the same employee receive and pay for merchandise
   d. Using sequentially numbered sales invoices
5. (LO2) Internal control systems are limited in their effectiveness by:
   a. the human element.
   b. cost-benefit analysis.
   c. both a and b.
   d. neither a nor b.
6. (LO3) Which of the following would you see on a reconciliation of the bank balance to the actual cash balance?
   a. Outstanding check
   b. NSF check
   c. Bank service fee
   d. Collection of a receivable
7. (LO3) Which of the following would you most likely see on a reconciliation of the book balance to the actual cash balance?
   a. Deposit in transit
   b. Collection of interest
   c. Outstanding check
   d. None of the above
8. (LO3) Austin Corporation's ending cash book balance was $14,560. The bank statement showed the following reconciling items:

Bank service fee	$150
NSF check from customer	$180
Collection of receivable	$500

   What is Austin's actual cash balance?
   a. $14,560
   b. $14,730
   c. $15,090
   d. $13,730
9. (LO3) The month-end bank statement showed a $42,600 ending balance for Hurry Corporation's cash balance. Use the following items to calculate Hurry's actual ending cash balance:

Outstanding checks	$4,240
Bank service fee	$150
Deposit in transit	$780

   a. $46,060
   b. $37,430
   c. $47,620
   d. $37,580
10. (LO3) Which of the following represents an item that would likely be paid from petty cash?
    a. A manager's salary
    b. Utilities for a warehouse
    c. Miscellaneous office supplies
    d. Insurance
11. (LO4) Which of the following would least likely qualify as a cash equivalent?
    a. Treasury bills
    b. Commercial paper
    c. Certificate of deposit
    d. U.S. Savings Bond
12. (LO5) Nickel Corporation's cash and cash equivalents balances for the current and prior year are presented below:

Current year	$22,500
Prior year	$19,350

    Perform a horizontal analysis on Nickel's cash and cash equivalents.
    a. 16.3%
    b. 14.0%
    c. (14.0)%
    d. 13.9%
13. (LO5) Using the following information taken from Reebals Incorporated's balance sheet, prepare a vertical analysis of Reebals' cash balance.

Cash and cash equivalents, current year	$1,345
Cash and cash equivalents, prior year	$1,267
Total assets, current year	$38,500

    a. 3.5%
    b. 3.3%
    c. 6.2%
    d. 2.2%
14. (LO5) Free cash flow is not affected by:
    a. dividends.
    b. purchase of an office building.
    c. purchase of a warehouse.
    d. purchase of raw materials.
15. (LO5) Using the following information from Walker Enterprises, calculate free cash flow.

Cash flows from operating activities	$75,200
Cash flows from investing activities	$43,550
Dividends paid	$7,500
Capital expenditures	$25,320
Cost of goods sold	$45,300

    a. $10,730
    b. $42,380
    c. ($2,920)
    d. $49,880

BRIEF EXERCISES

1. Internal Control LO1, 2

The following items relate to internal control:

1. Sarbanes-Oxley Act of 2002
2. Management's Report on Internal Control
3. *Internal Control—Integrated Framework*
4. Five elements of internal control

Required
Provide a brief explanation of each of these items.

2. Internal Control LO2

Consider the following independent scenarios:

1. A company's top management team promotes an atmosphere of ethical behavior within the organization.
2. A company discovers the need to increase measures taken to mitigate the risk of employee theft.

Required
Which element of internal control does each of the above scenarios best relate?

3. Internal Control Activities LO1, 2

Douglas Company has the following internal control procedures:

1. A pre-numbered shipping document is used for each shipment to customers.
2. The employee who writes checks cannot make entries in the general ledger.
3. An internal auditor reconciles the bank statement each month.
4. The company stores inventory in a room that is monitored by cameras.
5. The manager is required to authorize purchases before they are made by employees.

Required
For each item, identify the internal control principle that is being followed.

4. Bank Reconciliation Items LO3

The following items may or may not be relevant to a company's bank reconciliation:

1. The company recorded a deposit as $540, but it correctly cleared the bank for $450.
2. A check recorded for $1,000 is shown on the bank statement as a $1,000 reduction to the cash balance.
3. The bank statement shows a $25 monthly service fee.
4. A $3,250 deposit made by the company is not reflected on the bank statement.
5. Payment received from a customer is reflected on the bank statement but not on the company's books.

Required
Identify whether each item is (a) an addition to or subtraction from the book balance, (b) an addition to or subtraction from the bank balance, or (c) not included on a bank reconciliation.

5. Petty Cash LO3

On June 1, CWA Enterprises established a petty cash fund for $250. On June 30, the fund's custodian prepares a report showing $76.25 in cash remaining and receipts of $36.50 for postage, $76.45 for office supplies, and $60.80 for miscellaneous items. The custodian presents the report to the company accountant, who replenishes the fund.

Required
Prepare all necessary journal entries for the month of June.

6. Reporting Cash and Cash Equivalents LO4

At the end of 2012 a company has a $10,000 certificate of deposit that matures in 120 days, $60,000 of cash in a checking account, and $100,000 of one-month T-bills.

Required
At what amount would the company report cash and cash equivalents on its 2012 balance sheet?

7. Calculate Free Cash Flow LO5

During the year, a company had net income of $145,000 and cash flow from operations of $195,000. During the year the company also bought a new piece of equipment for $45,000, and $10,000 of dividends were paid.

Required
What is the company's free cash flow for the year?

8. Evaluate Cash LO5

Howard Manufacturing strives to keep a "consistent" amount of cash on hand. Its latest balance sheet provides the following information:

Cash and cash equivalents, current year	$ 5,959
Cash and cash equivalents, prior year	6,011
Total assets, current year	77,410
Total assets, prior year	68,744

Required
Using horizontal and vertical analyses, determine whether Howard is maintaining a "consistent" amount of cash. Round percentages to one decimal point (i.e., 9.4%).

EXERCISES

9. Internal Control Activities LO1, 2

Percy Printers uses the following control procedures:

1. Checks are not pre-numbered because the purchasing manager must approve payments before checks are signed.
2. The company's accountant records the receipt of cash and checks and makes deposits at the bank.
3. The employee who works the register reconciles cash to receipts at the end of the day.
4. Employees know that the internal auditor will perform a bank reconciliation at the end of each month.
5. Petty cash is kept in a back room but is not monitored during the day.
6. A cashier lets another employee work his assigned register while he helps a customer.

Required
Identify the problem with each internal control procedure.

10. Internal Control LO1, 2

Suppose that a company's president engages in the following independent behaviors:

1. Holds monthly meeting with staff during which the importance of internal control is stressed.
2. Signs documents without reading them.
3. Occasionally visits staff and reviews their work.
4. Requests contingency plans for every conceivable threat to the organization.

Required
For each behavior, identify the component of internal control that is affected and whether that component is strengthened or weakened by the behavior. Each behavior may affect multiple components.

11. Internal Control Activities LO1, 2

Lee County Medical Group is a medical practice that distributes several expensive and popular medications to patients. You are tasked with developing control procedures for distribution of the medications.

Required
For each of the following areas, provide one possible example control activity that could be implemented: Establishing responsibility, Maintaining adequate documentation, Segregation of duties, Physical security, and Independent verification.

12. Internal Control Activities LO1, 2

A company is considering implementing internal control procedures for the following processes:

1. The collection of significant amounts of cash from customers.
2. Employee use of small office supplies such as pens and paper clips.
3. The documentation of medical procedures performed to protect against malpractice claims and to ensure proper revenue collection.

Required
Using risk analysis and cost-benefit analysis, comment on the appropriateness of implementing control activities for the above scenarios.

13. Bank Reconciliation Items LO3

Luther's Grille is preparing a bank reconciliation for the month of March and needs help with the following items:

1. A customer's $125 check was deposited on March 31 but does not appear on the bank statement.
2. A check clearing for $35 was recorded by Luther's Grille for $53.
3. The bank statement shows a $45 NSF check.
4. A service charge of $50 was reported on the bank statement.
5. The bank statement shows that the bank collected $80 of interest on Luther's Grille's behalf.
6. A charge of $30 for Internet banking was reported on the bank statement.
7. A $100 check written on March 31 does not appear on the bank statement.

Required
Identify whether each item is (1) an addition to the book balance, (2) a deduction from the book balance, (3) an addition to the bank balance, or (4) a deduction from the bank balance.

14. Bank Reconciliation Items LO3

Consider the following two independent situations:

1. A company's January 31 bank reconciliation shows deposits in transit of $1,500. The company's books indicate deposits of $23,000 for the month of February, but the bank statement indicates deposits of $21,750 for February.
2. A company's January 31 bank reconciliation indicates outstanding checks of $2,500. The company's books indicate disbursements of $17,950 for the month of February, but the bank statement shows $18,900 of disbursements for February.

Required
For situation 1, determine deposits in transit at February 28. For situation 2, determine outstanding checks at February 28.

15. Prepare Bank Reconciliation LO3

McKnight Company's June 30 bank statement shows a balance of $14,750. McKnight's books show a June 30 cash balance of $13,600. McKnight also has the following information:

1. Deposits in transit as of June 30, $1,000
2. Outstanding checks as of June 30, $2,500
3. $100 service charge reported on the bank statement
4. NSF check returned with bank statement, $1,500
5. Interest on note receivable collected by the bank, $1,250

Required
Prepare McKnight's bank reconciliation as of June 30 and prepare any necessary journal entries resulting from the reconciliation. What is the actual cash balance that should be reported on the June 30 balance sheet?

16. Prepare Bank Reconciliation LO3

Hayley Company's September 30 bank statement shows a balance of $53,810. Hayley's September 30 cash balance is $45,800. Hayley also has the following information:

1. Deposits made but not appearing on the September bank statement, $5,500.
2. Check written but not appearing on the September bank statement, $12,200.
3. One check written for the purchase of Supplies was erroneously recorded for $890 but appears on the bank statement at $980.
4. Monthly service charges listed on the bank statement are $230. Hayley had already recorded the effect of $130 of those charges.
5. A customer payment for a $1,500 receivable was collected by the bank but not yet recorded by Hayley.

Required
Prepare Hayley's bank reconciliation as of September 30, and prepare any necessary journal entries resulting from the reconciliation.

17. Prepare Bank Reconciliation LO3

The following bank statement for the month of May is for El Guapo Industries:

Bank Statement			
	Checks	**Deposits**	**Balance**
Balance, May 1			$ 12,000
Deposits recorded during May		$ 46,000	
Checks cleared during May	$ 34,000		
NSF checks—Hugo Company	2,500		
Interest collected on note receivable		5,600	
Bank service charge	35		
Service charge for new checks	65		
Balance, May 31			27,000

The following information was taken from the books at El Guapo:

Balance, May 1	$ 12,000
Deposits during May	48,500
Checks written during May	36,500

Required
Prepare El Guapo's May bank reconciliation and prepare any necessary journal entries resulting from the reconciliation.

18. Bank Reconciliation Items LO3

A company makes the following journal entries after preparing a bank reconciliation:

1. Accounts Receivable	340	
Cash		340
2. Service Charge Expense	45	
Cash		45
3. Cash	1,100	
Notes Receivable		1,000
Interest Revenue		100

Required
Explain the likely circumstance behind each of the entries.

19. Petty Cash LO3

On September 1, Anders Properties establishes a petty cash fund for $200. On September 30, the fund's custodian prepares a report showing $130 in cash remaining and receipts of $12 for miscellaneous items, $20 for postage, and $35 for supplies. The custodian presents the report to the company accountant, who replenishes the fund.

Required
Prepare all necessary journal entries for the month of September.

20. Petty Cash LO3

On January 1, Martin Co. establishes a petty cash fund in the amount of $500. On January 31, the fund is replenished. Before replenishment, there was $128.75 remaining in the petty cash drawer and the following receipts: parking fees, $103.50; postage, $50; office supplies, $198; and miscellaneous expenses, $22.

Required
Prepare all journal entries necessary to record the establishment and replenishment of the fund.

21. Petty Cash LO3

Malone Gifts makes the following two entries to establish and replenish its petty cash fund.

Petty Cash	100	
Cash		100
Miscellaneous Expense	35	
Postage Expense	10	
Supplies Expense	30	
Cash Over and Short	2	
Cash		77

Required
Determine the effect on the accounting equation for each entry. Determine how much cash was in the petty cash fund when established, immediately before replenishment, and immediately after replenishment. Were receipts equal to the cash needed for replenishment?

22. Reporting Cash and Cash Equivalents LO4

The following is a list of items that may or may not be included in the cash and cash equivalents total on the balance sheet:

1. Cash in checking account
2. Petty cash on hand
3. Shares of Coca-Cola common stock
4. Certificate of deposit maturing in 45 days
5. Certificate of deposit that matures in 120 days
6. One-month Treasury bills
7. Undeposited check from a customer
8. A customer's check returned by the bank and marked NSF

Required
For each of the stated items, indicate whether the item should be included or excluded from the Cash and Cash Equivalents total.

23. Reporting Cash and Cash Equivalents LO4

The CPA Company invested in the following items during November and December of 2012:

November	
60-day Treasury bills	$15,000
Preferred stock	25,500
Certificate of deposit, maturing 1/31/2014	34,000
Certificate of deposit, maturing 2/1/2013	50,000
December	
Common stock	$60,000
Commercial paper, maturity date of 1/15/2013	90,000

Required
Determine the total of cash and cash equivalents that should be reported on the December 31, 2012, balance sheet, assuming that cash on hand was $5,500.

24. Evaluate Cash LO5

In a recent annual report, **Kraft Foods** reported the following account balances (in millions):

Cash and cash equivalents, current year	$ 1,244
Cash and cash equivalents, prior year	567
Total assets, current year	63,078
Cash flows from operating activities	4,141
Capital expenditures	1,367
Dividends	1,663

Required

a. Prepare horizontal and vertical analyses of Kraft's cash balance. Round percentages to one decimal point (i.e., 9.4%).
b. Calculate free cash flow.
c. Interpret the results of your calculations.

25. Free Cash Flow LO5

A company provides the following information regarding cash flows:

Cash flows provided by operating activities	$67,505
Cash flows used in investing activities	30,599
Cash flows used by financing activities	22,700
Cash paid for fixed assets	13,686
Cash paid for dividends	5,118
Cash received from issuing notes payable	8,000
Cash paid to purchase treasury stock	10,500

Required
Calculate free cash flow. Given the company's free cash flow and the additional cash flow information provided, does it appear that the company is in a position to expand?

PROBLEMS

26. Prepare Bank Reconciliation LO3

Helms Foundation's bank statement for the month of September and its general ledger cash account at September 30 are as follows:

Bank Statement

Date	Disbursements	Deposits	Balance
Sept. 1			33,450
3	560		32,890
4		4,000	36,890
6	910		35,980
9	150		35,830
13		13,500	49,330
15	900		48,430
16	875		47,555
18	8,000		39,555
19	775		38,780
22	450		38,330
25		6,000	44,330
26	5,000		39,330
27	650		38,680
30		1,000	39,680
30	75		39,605
30	65		39,540

Cash

Sept. 1	35,980	Sept. 5	150
12	13,500	8	875
24	6,000	9	900
30	9,000	10	8,000
		11	775
		17	5,000
		19	450
		22	650
		23	850
		25	900
		28	1,200

Additional information: At the end of August, Helms had two outstanding checks ($560 and $910) and one $4,000 deposit in transit. On Helms' September bank statement, the two Sept. 30 disbursements were bank service charges. The Sept. 30 deposit of $1,000 was the result of the bank collecting a note receivable on behalf of Helms.

Required

Prepare a bank reconciliation for the month of September, and prepare any journal entries required at September 30.

27. Prepare Bank Reconciliation LO3

Murphy Cotton Company's bank statement for the month of June and its general ledger cash account at the end of June are as follows:

Bank Statement

Date	Disbursements		Deposits	Other	Balance
June 1					$8,250
3	# 200	$1,220			7,030
4			$2,100		9,130
6	# 203	365			8,765
9	# 204	840			7,925
15	# 202	900			7,025
16	# 207	1,400			5,625
18	# 205	2,000			3,625
18			3,500		7,125
19	# 208	1,620			5,505
22	# 209	150			5,355
25			2,220		7,575
26	# 211	355			7,220
27	# 212	3,650			3,570
28			5,100		8,670
30				$100	8,770
30				130	8,640

Cash

June 1	9,130	June 5 # 201	790
June 17	3,500	June 6 # 202	900
June 24	2,220	June 6 # 203	365
June 27	5,100	June 8 # 204	840
June 30	1,750	June 11 # 205	2,000
		June 15 # 206	1,180
		June 16 # 207	1,400
		June 18 # 208	1,260
		June 20 # 209	150
		June 22 # 210	560
		June 23 # 211	355
		June 26 # 212	3,650

Other information: Murphy had one deposit in transit of $2,100 and one outstanding check (#200) of $1,220 at May 31. All canceled check amounts agree with the bank statement.

Required

a. Identify all deposits in transit and outstanding checks at June 30.

b. Prepare a bank reconciliation for the month of June.

c. Prepare all journal entries required by Murphy at June 30. Assume any debit memorandum is a service charge, any credit memorandum is a collection of an account receivable, and any error relates to an account payable.

28. Evaluate Cash LO5

In their recent annual reports, **Walgreens** and **CVS** reported the following account balances:

	Walgreens	CVS
Cash and cash equivalents, 12/31/10	$ 1,880	1,427
Cash and cash equivalents, 12/31/09	2,087	1,086
Total assets	26,275	62,169
Cash flows from operating activities	3,744	4,779
Capital expenditures	1,014	2,005
Dividends	541	479

Required

For both companies, calculate and interpret (a) horizontal and vertical analyses of cash balance and (b) free cash flow. How do the cash positions compare? Round percentages to one decimal point (i.e., 9.4%).

CASES

29. Research and Analysis LO1, 4, 5

Access the 2010 annual report for **WD-40 Company** by clicking on the *Investors* and *Financial Reports* links at www.wd40company.com.

Required

a. Conduct horizontal and vertical analyses of WD-40 Company's cash balance. Round percentages to one decimal point (i.e., 9.4%).
b. Examine the company's statement of cash flows and determine the major ways in which the company has been using its cash in the past three years.
c. Examine the Report of Independent Registered Public Accounting Firm and locate **PricewaterhouseCoopers'** opinion of WD-40 Company's internal control over financial reporting.
d. Based on your answers above, write a paragraph explaining your opinion of WD-40 Company's cash position. Use your answers as supporting facts.

30. Written Communication LO1, 2

You are the owner of Curry's, a small retail company in a college town. You have a store manager who supervises employees. Most employees are part-time college students, and your manager is having a difficult time getting the employees to follow internal control procedures. Most of the employees think that the procedures are "a waste of time" and that they don't relate to the main purpose of the company, which is to "sell stuff."

Required

Prepare a memo that can be given to incoming employees explaining to them the importance of the control environment in general and control activities specifically.

Receivables

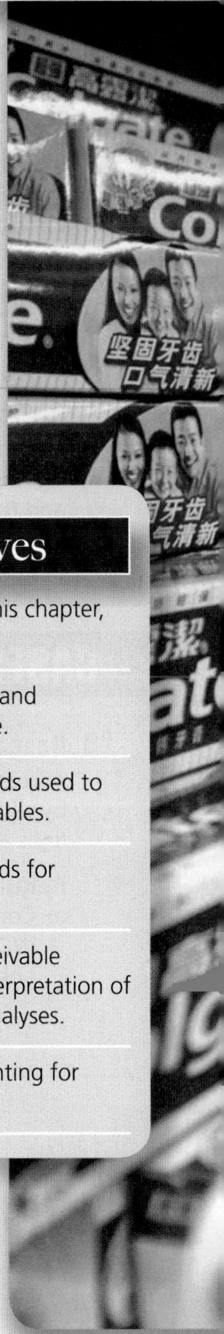

Learning Objectives

After studying the material in this chapter, you should be able to:

LO1 Describe the recording and reporting of accounts receivable.

LO2 Understand the methods used to account for uncollectible receivables.

LO3 Understand the methods for estimating bad debt expense.

LO4 Evaluate accounts receivable through the calculation and interpretation of horizontal, vertical, and ratio analyses.

LO5 Understand the accounting for notes receivable.

Introduction

This chapter examines the accounting for receivables. Specifically, the chapter focuses on how companies account for the recording, the collection, and the noncollection of accounts receivable. After a discussion of how to analyze a company's receivable position, the chapter concludes with the accounting for a second type of receivable, notes receivable.

LO1 Recording and Reporting Accounts Receivable

A receivable represents a company's claim on the assets of another entity. The most common type of receivable is an account receivable. An **account receivable** is an amount owed by a customer who has purchased the company's product or service. Sometimes these receivables are referred to as trade receivables because they arise from the trade of the company.

Recording Accounts Receivable

Receivables are recorded at the time of the sale. To illustrate, suppose that on June 4 Furio Company sells $1,000 of product to a customer on account. Furio would record the revenue and receivable arising from the sale with the following entry. Note that this example ignores the effects on Furio's inventory and cost of goods sold. These will be covered in Chapter 7.

Jun. 4	Accounts Receivable	1,000	
	Sales		1,000
	(To record sale on account)		

Assets	=	Liabilities	+	Equity
+1,000				+1,000

Account receivable An amount owed by a customer who has purchased the company's product or service.

Companies like Colgate-Palmolive commonly sell their products on account. Unfortunately, the receivables that are created are not always collected.

Shou Sheng/epa/Corbis

Both assets and equity increase as a result of this sale. When Furio collects the receivable, it will increase its cash and eliminate the receivable.

In some cases, a customer will return a product instead of paying for it, and this affects the accounts receivable balance. To illustrate, suppose that on June 10, the customer returns a $150 product because it is not needed. Furio would record the return with the following entry. Again, the example focuses only on the effect on receivables and ignores the effects on inventory and cost of goods sold.

Jun. 10	Sales Returns and Allowances	150	
	Accounts Receivable		150
	(To record sales return)		

Assets	=	Liabilities	+	Equity
−150				−150

The entry decreases Accounts Receivable for the sales price of the product. However, instead of decreasing the Sales account directly, the entry increases Sales Returns and Allowances. Sales Returns and Allowances is a contra-revenue account, meaning that its balance is subtracted from sales when calculating a company's net sales. Companies use this account to maintain a record of returns each period. Like the Sales account, Sales Returns and Allowances is a temporary account whose balance is zeroed-out during the closing process at the end of each period.

In addition to returns, companies sometimes provide discounts to customers if they pay within a certain time period. For example, sales are commonly made with terms 2/10, n/30. Such terms mean that while the net receivable is due in 30 days, customers can receive a 2% discount if they pay within 10 days of the invoice. To illustrate, suppose that Furio grants terms of 2/10, n/30. On June 12 the customer pays the remaining $850 bill. By qualifying for a 2% discount, the customer saves $17 ($850 × 2%) and pays only $833. Furio would record the receipt of payment as follows:

Jun. 12	Cash	833	
	Sales Discounts	17	
	Accounts Receivable		850
	(To record payment)		

Assets	=	Liabilities	+	Equity
+833				−17
−850				

The entry increases Cash for the $833 payment and decreases Accounts Receivable for the full $850 balance. The difference, which equals the discount of $17 for timely payment, goes into the Sales Discounts account. Like Sales Returns and Allowances, the Sales Discounts account is a contra-revenue account that is subtracted from sales when calculating net sales. Companies use this account to maintain a record of discounts each period. It is a temporary account whose balance is zeroed-out at the end of each period.

Reporting Accounts Receivable

Because accounts receivable are expected to be collected quickly, they are classified and reported as current assets. However, companies do not normally collect all of their receivables because customers do not always pay their bills. Among other reasons, customers have financial hardships, relocate without paying, or simply refuse to pay. As a result, companies must follow the principle of conservatism and report their accounts receivable at net realizable value.

Companies must follow the principle of conservatism and report their accounts receivable at net realizable value.

Net realizable value The amount of cash that a company expects to collect from its total accounts receivable.

Net realizable value is the amount of cash that a company expects to collect from its total or gross accounts receivable balance. It is calculated by subtracting from gross receivables the amount that a company does not expect to collect. For example, a company that has $1,000 of gross receivables but does not expect to collect $50 of them has receivables with a net realizable value of $950. The amount that a company does not expect to collect is usually called an allowance. How companies estimate and record the allowance will be examined later in the chapter.

To illustrate the reporting of receivables, consider the following receivables balances from **Colgate-Palmolive's** 2010 balance sheet:

Receivables Balances from Colgate-Palmolive's 2010 Balance Sheet

(in millions)	2010	2009
Receivables (net of allowances of $53 and $52, respectively)	1,610	1,626

Colgate-Palmolive reports a net realizable value of receivables of approximately $1.6 billion in both years. It also states textually that its receivables are net of allowances of $53 million and $52 million. Again, the term *allowances* refers to the amount of receivables that Colgate-Palmolive expects to be uncollectible. At the end of 2009, the company was allowing for $52 million of uncollectible receivables. At the end of 2010, the allowance had grown to $53 million.

To demonstrate the relation among gross receivables, the allowance, and net realizable value of receivables, Colgate-Palmolive's numbers are recast as follows. Note that gross accounts receivable is the one value that is not reported by the company.

	2010	2009
Gross accounts receivable	$1,663	1,678
Less: Allowance	53	52
Net realizable value	$1,610	$1,626

While **Colgate-Palmolive** provides the allowance balance on the face of the balance sheet, many companies do not. They simply report their receivables at "net" and disclose the allowance for uncollectible accounts in their notes to the financial statements. An example is **The Clorox Company**. The following shows both the company's receivables balances from its 2010 balance sheet and its Revenue Recognition note:

Receivables Balances and Revenue Recognition Note from The Clorox Company's 2010 Balance Sheet and Notes

(amounts in millions)	2010	2009
Receivables, net	$544	$486

Revenue Recognition
The Company provides an allowance for doubtful accounts based on its historical experience and a periodic review of its accounts receivable. Receivables were presented net of an allowance for doubtful accounts of $6 at June 30, 2010 and 2009.

As you can see, The Clorox Company provides the same information as Colgate-Palmolive. You just have to look in a different place to find it. As in the previous example, these numbers are recast to demonstrate how they were calculated.

	2010	2009
Gross accounts receivable	$550	$492
Less: Allowance	6	6
Net realizable value	$544	$486

LO2 Uncollectible Receivables

As stated in the previous section, most companies are unable to collect all of their accounts receivable. Losses from the inability to collect accounts receivable are recorded in the accounting system as **bad debt expense**.

Because uncollectible accounts are a normal part of any business, bad debt expense is considered an operating expense. It is included in the calculation of net income but is usually combined with other operating expenses on the income statement. Thus, you will rarely find a company's bad debt expense listed separately on its income statement. If you do, it is likely bad news because the amount was large enough to warrant individual reporting.

There are two methods to account for bad debt expense:

- direct write-off method
- allowance method

Each method is discussed in the following sections.

Bad debt expense The expense resulting from the inability to collect accounts receivable.

HOME DEPOT ANALYSIS

Look at **Home Depot's** balance sheet in Appendix C. How can you tell whether the company's receivables are reported at net realizable value?

Home Depot reports the following for receivables: "Receivables, net." The "net" indicates that the reported balance is gross receivables less the allowance balance. The Accounts Receivable paragraph in Note 1 discloses that the allowance balance (Home Depot refers to it as the "valuation reserve") is not material. That is, the balance is small enough that it will not affect the evaluation of Home Depot's reported receivables. Therefore, the actual allowance value is not reported.

Direct Write-off Method

Under the **direct write-off method**, bad debt expense is recorded when a company determines that a receivable is uncollectible. The receivable is eliminated or "written off" the company's accounting records, and bad debt expense is recorded for the amount of the receivable.

To illustrate, suppose that Thompson Inc. makes a $4,000 credit sale to Brandon LLC on October 10, 2012. Ignoring the effects on inventory, Thompson would make the following entry to record the sale:

Oct. 10 2012	Accounts Receivable	4,000	
	Sales		4,000
	(To record sale on account)		

Assets	=	Liabilities	+	Equity
+4,000				+4,000

Now suppose that on April 3, 2013, Thompson determines that it will be unable to collect from Brandon. Once that determination is made, Thompson would record the following entry:

Apr. 3 2013	Bad Debt Expense	4,000	
	Accounts Receivable		4,000
	(To record bad debt expense and write off receivable)		

Assets	=	Liabilities	+	Equity
−4,000				−4,000

This entry increases Bad Debt Expense to reflect the loss incurred from the inability to collect from Brandon. It also decreases Accounts Receivable to remove the receivable from Thompson's records. As a result of this write-off, both assets and equity decrease. All write-offs under the direct method will result in the same basic entry. The only difference will be the dollar amount.

The major advantage of the direct write-off method is its simplicity. When an account is deemed uncollectible, it is written off and an expense is recorded. The major disadvantage is that it can violate the matching principle. The matching principle requires that expenses be matched as closely as possible to the period in which the related revenues are recognized. In the preceding example, the revenue is recorded in 2012, but the expense is recorded in 2013. Assuming that Thompson prepares financial statements at the end of December, the expense is not matched to the year of the sale.

Direct write-off method Method in which bad debt expense is recorded when a company determines that a receivable is uncollectible and removes it from its records.

Allowance method Method in which companies use two entries to account for bad debt expense—one to estimate the expense and a second to write off receivables.

IFRS

GAAP and IFRS contain similar requirements that must be met to record a credit sale, but they are worded differently. GAAP states that collectibility should be reasonably assured while IFRS states that it must be probable that the economic benefits will flow to the company.

Because the direct write-off method violates the matching principle, Generally Accepted Accounting Principles prohibit its use. The only exception to this prohibition is when bad debt expense is immaterial to the company. An expense is immaterial if it is small enough that failure to report it properly does not alter decision making. For example, if a company's bad debt expense totals $100 when it has $1 million in sales, failure to follow the matching principle will not likely affect decisions about the company. For most companies, though, bad debt expense is material, so they must use the allowance method.

Allowance Method

While the direct write-off method accounts for uncollectible receivables with one entry, the **allowance method** splits the accounting into two entries—one to record an estimate of bad debt expense and another to write off receivables when they become uncollectible. Both of these entries are described in the following sections.

Recording Bad Debt Expense The purpose of the allowance method is to match the expense from uncollectible receivables to the period in which those receivables were created. To achieve this purpose, a company must record bad debt expense *at the end of each accounting period*. However, at the end of the period, the company does not yet know which receivables will be uncollectible. As a result, bad debt expense must be *estimated*.

Because the direct method violates the matching principle, generally accepted accounting principles prohibit its use.

Because of this inability to know which specific receivables will turn out to be uncollectible, the allowance method requires a company to set up an "allowance" for uncollectible receivables when recording bad debt expense. That is, instead of writing off specific receivables at year end, a company increases a contra-asset account called Allowance for Bad Debts. **Allowance for bad debts** represents the dollar amount of receivables that a company estimates will ultimately be uncollectible. As described earlier, its balance is subtracted from gross receivables to yield the receivables' net realizable value.

To illustrate, suppose that Duncan Sports makes credit sales of $800,000 during 2012. Based on past experience, Duncan estimates on December 31 that $8,000 of these sales will not be collected. Duncan would therefore make the following entries to record this activity:

During 2012	Accounts Receivable	800,000	
	Sales		800,000
	(To record sales on account)		

Assets	=	Liabilities	+	Equity
+800,000				+800,000

Dec. 31 2012	Bad Debt Expense	8,000	
	Allowance for Bad Debts		8,000
	(To record bad debt expense)		

Assets	=	Liabilities	+	Equity
−8,000				−8,000

The first entry increases Accounts Receivable and Sales for the credit sales during the year. This increases both assets and equity. The second entry at year end increases both Bad Debt Expense and Allowance for Bad Debts by $8,000. This effectively matches the expense of future uncollectible receivables to 2012 sales. It also reduces Duncan's net realizable value of receivables by $8,000 because it is now allowing for $8,000 of those receivables to be uncollectible. As a result, both assets and equity decrease.

Note here that whenever bad debt expense is estimated and recorded under the allowance method, an entry similar to Duncan's December entry will be prepared. The only difference will be the amount of the estimate, which will depend on various circumstances as well as the estimation method a company uses. Methods of estimating bad debt expense are covered later in the chapter.

Recording a Write-Off Regardless of the method used to account for uncollectible receivables, a company must write off a receivable when it is deemed to be uncollectible. Under the direct write-off method, the company writes off the receivable and records bad debt expense. However, under the allowance method, the company writes off the receivable and reduces the balance in the allowance account that was created when bad debt expense was recorded.

To illustrate, suppose that on February 8, 2013, Duncan Sports determines that a $2,500 receivable from William Johnson is uncollectible and decides to write it off the books. Duncan would make the following entry:

Feb. 8 2013	Allowance for Bad Debts	2,500	
	Accounts Receivable		2,500
	(To record write-off)		

Assets	=	Liabilities	+	Equity
−2,500				
+2,500				

The entry decreases Accounts Receivable and decreases an equal amount of Allowance for Bad Debts. Note that the entry has no effect on total assets or net income. More specifically, the entry has no effect on Duncan's net realizable value of receivables. This is because both the asset account and the contra-asset account are decreasing by the same amount, thereby offsetting one another. Duncan now knows that Johnson will not pay, but Duncan had already allowed for that possibility at the end of 2012 when it recorded bad debt expense. Therefore, Duncan's expected cash receipts are unchanged. This will be the case for all write-offs under the allowance method.

Recording the Recovery of a Write-Off Occasionally, a company will collect a receivable that it had previously written off. For example, suppose that Johnson pays his bill in full later on March 22, 2013. When this payment occurs, the following two entries are made:

Allowance for bad debts The dollar amount of receivables that a company believes will ultimately be uncollectible.

The allowance method requires a company to estimate its bad debt expense and to set up an "allowance" for uncollectible receivables.

Mar. 22 2013	Accounts Receivable	2,500	
	Allowance for Bad Debts		2,500
	(To reverse the original write-off)		

Assets	=	Liabilities	+	Equity
+2,500				
−2,500				

Mar. 22 2013	Cash	2,500	
	Accounts Receivable		2,500
	(To collect the receivable)		

Assets	=	Liabilities	+	Equity
+2,500				
−2,500				

The first entry simply reverses the original entry writing off the receivable. The second entry records the collection of cash and the reduction of the receivable. Notice that once again there is no effect on total assets by either of these two entries.

LO3 Estimating Bad Debt Expense

The previous section demonstrated how to record bad debt expense under the allowance method. This section demonstrates how to estimate the amount of bad debt expense to be recorded.

When estimating bad debt expense companies may use one of two different approaches:

- percentage-of-sales approach
- percentage-of-receivables approach

Both approaches use information such as past experience, industry norms or trends, and current customer credit ratings to make the estimate as accurate as possible. Each approach is discussed in the following sections.

MAKING IT REAL

Most companies have a good idea of how long it takes them to collect their receivables. However, sometimes shocks to the economy can cause significant delays in collections. Take the recent recession and economic downturn. Customer payments have slowed significantly. The reduced cash flow is especially damaging to small businesses that might not have sufficient cash on hand to pay their own suppliers. This turns into a never-ending cycle where buyers and sellers are both past due on their bills and reduces the cash flow to the entire economy.

wavebreakmedia ltd/Shutterstock.com

To combat this, companies are being forced to alter their collections policies. Traditionally, buyers with delinquent accounts would have their credit slashed or cancelled. Now, companies are considering alternative approaches which do not place undue pressure on the customer in the hopes of maintaining an agreeable relationship. The CEO of The UnitedCompanies Inc., a Houston-based company, began making personal calls to buyers with accounts more than 60 days past due. Some companies stop shipping to buyers until their accounts are made current. Others are implementing technology into the collections process to facilitate faster and easier payment.

The bottom line is that delayed collection of accounts receivable affects both the business and the customer. Longer collection cycles mean that businesses have a diminished cash flow and have to struggle to make do with less cash on hand. Without timely collections, many businesses are put in a situation where they might face delinquency with their own vendors or even bankruptcy from lack of liquidity.

Percentage-of-Sales Approach

Under the **percentage-of-sales approach**, bad debt expense is a function of a company's sales. It is calculated by multiplying sales for the period by some percentage set by the company. For example, suppose a company with 2012 sales of $250,000 estimates at its December 31 year end that it will not collect 4% of those sales. The estimate for bad debt expense would be $10,000 ($250,000 × 4%) and would be recorded as follows:

Dec. 31 2012	Bad Debt Expense	10,000	
	Allowance for Bad Debts		10,000
	(To record bad debt expense)		

Assets	=	Liabilities	+	Equity
−10,000				−10,000

The advantages of this approach are its simplicity and the fact that it results in very good matching. Bad debt expense for a period is primarily a function of sales for that period. The main disadvantage is that no consideration is given to the resulting balance in the Allowance for Bad Debts account. It is simply the existing balance plus the current estimate. Since the allowance account is used to compute net realizable value, the percentage-of-sales approach results in a less meaningful net realizable value of receivables.

Percentage-of-Receivables Approach

Under the **percentage-of-receivables approach**, bad debt expense is a function of a company's receivables balance. It is calculated in two steps. The first step is to calculate what the balance in the Allowance for Bad Debts account should be. This is accomplished by multiplying accounts receivable by a percentage set by the company. The second step is to adjust the allowance account to that calculated balance. The amount of the adjustment is bad debt expense for the period.

To illustrate, suppose that a company has a receivables balance of $24,000 at December 31, 2012. Based on past experience, the company expects that 2% of its receivables balance will be uncollectible. As a result, the balance in the allowance account at December 31 should be 2% of receivables, or a $480 credit balance ($24,000 × 2%). The next step is to make the adjustment.

Since the allowance method for bad debts relies on estimates, a company's allowance balance prior to adjustment can have either a debit or credit balance. A debit balance means that the company has experienced greater write-offs during the year than expected. A credit balance indicates that write-offs have been less than expected. Whether the balance is a debit or credit does not require a company to correct its bad debt expense from the prior year. However, it does affect the adjustment for the current year.

To illustrate, assume that the allowance account has a $100 credit balance prior to adjustment. To get the balance to a $480 credit requires a $380 credit entry. Therefore, bad debt expense for 2012 is $380. This calculation and the resulting entry are as follows:

Allowance for Bad Debts

Debit	Credit	
	100	Existing balance
	380	Adjustment required = Bad Debt Expense
	480	Desired balance ($24,000 × 2%)

Dec. 31 2012	Bad Debt Expense	380	
	Allowance for Bad Debts		380
	(To record bad debt expense)		

Assets	=	Liabilities	+	Equity
−380				−380

In contrast, assume that the allowance account has a $50 debit balance prior to adjustment. In that case, the necessary adjustment is a $530 credit entry. Therefore, bad debt expense for 2012 is $530. This calculation and the resulting entry are as follows:

Allowance for Bad Debts

Debit	Credit	
50		Existing balance
	530	Adjustment required = Bad Debt Expense
	480	Desired balance ($24,000 × 2%)

Dec. 31 2012	Bad Debt Expense	530	
	Allowance for Bad Debts		530
	(To record bad debt expense)		

Assets	=	Liabilities	+	Equity
−530				−530

The major advantage of the percentage-of-receivables approach is that it results in a very meaningful net realizable value. This is because the allowance account is determined as a set percentage of receivables. The disadvantage is that it does not match expenses as well as the

Percentage-of-sales approach Method that estimates bad debt expense as a percentage of sales.

Percentage-of-receivables approach Method that estimates bad debt expense as a percentage of receivables.

percentage-of-sales approach. This is because the adjustment necessary is a function of both the set percentage and a company's prior experience with write-offs. As a result, current expenses are affected by prior-year experiences.

Aging of Accounts Receivable Many companies use a more refined version of the percentage-of-receivables approach. Recognizing that receivables become less collectible as they get older, companies often prepare aging schedules for their receivables. An **aging schedule** is a listing and summation of accounts receivable by their ages. Normally, receivables that are outstanding for 30 days or less are considered current and are grouped together. Receivables outstanding longer than 30 days are considered past due and are grouped together in 30-day increments. Companies then apply increasing uncollectible percentages to older receivables.

To illustrate, suppose that SC Works prepares an aging schedule at December 31, 2012 as shown in Exhibit 6-1. SC Works reports $66,600 of receivables and breaks them into Current and several categories of Past Due. Each category is assigned an expected percentage of uncollectable receivables that rises as the age of the receivables increases. The necessary allowance balance is then calculated by summing the totals from each category.

Exhibit 6-1 Aging Schedule of Accounts Receivable—SC Works

		Number of Days Past Due				
Customer	Current	1–30	31–60	61–90	Over 90	Total
Ellis Manufacturing			$4,100			$ 4,100
Clayburn Company					$2,400	$ 2,400
MAG, Incorporated				$2,750		$ 2,750
Others	$44,450	$10,400	$1,000	$1,200	$ 300	$57,350
Totals	$44,450	$10,400	$5,100	$3,950	$2,700	$66,600
* % Uncollectible	1%	3%	15%	30%	50%	
Allowance Balance	$ 4,450	$ 312	$ 765	$1,185	$1,350	$ 8,062

Assuming that SC Works has a credit balance of $870 in the allowance account prior to recording bad debt expense, the company would calculate and record bad debt expense as follows:

Allowance for Bad Debts		
	870	Existing balance
	7,192	Adjustment required = Bad Debt Expense
	8,062	Desired balance

Aging schedule A listing of accounts receivable by their ages.

Dec. 31 2012	Bad Debt Expense	7,192	
	Allowance for Bad Debts		7,192
	(To record bad debt expense)		

Assets	=	Liabilities	+	Equity
−7,192				−7,192

As you can see, the entry to record bad debt expense is the same as previously described. The difference is that an aging schedule provides a more accurate estimate of the allowance for bad debts and therefore a better estimate of bad debt expense. But an aging schedule has another benefit. It is a good internal control activity.

Recall from Chapter 5 that control activities are one of the five elements of a good internal control system. They are procedures put in place to assist companies in operating and reporting efficiently and effectively. Keeping track of receivables and their ages helps meet these objectives. For example, an aging schedule provides the information a company needs to pursue its receivables effectively. It also provides information for future credit decisions. A company may hesitate to provide credit to customers who have past due receivables.

LO4 Analyzing Accounts Receivable

Any investor, creditor, or manager of a company should be interested in how well a company manages its accounts receivable. Because a receivable is an uncollected sale, the main question that should be asked of a company is how well it collects its receivables. In general, better collection means better management of receivables.

The following sections examine how well **Colgate-Palmolive** collects its receivables. The examination

An aging schedule provides a more accurate estimate of the allowance for bad debts and therefore a better estimate of bad debt expense.

will require information from the company's balance sheet and its income statement. The required information is found in Exhibit 6-2, excerpted from **Colgate-Palmolive's** 2010 Annual Report.

Exhibit 6-2 Account Balances from Colgate-Palmolive's 2010 Annual Report

Source	Accounts	2010	2009
Income Statement	Net sales	$15,564	$15,327
	Net accounts receivable	$ 1,610	$ 1,626
Balance Sheet	Allowance for bad debts	53	52
	Total assets	11,172	11,134

Horizontal and Vertical Analyses

A good place to start the analysis of accounts receivable is with horizontal and vertical analyses. Recall from Chapter 2 that horizontal analysis calculates the dollar change in an account balance, defined as the current-year balance less the prior-year balance, and divides that change by the prior-year balance to yield the percentage change. Vertical analysis divides each account balance by a base account, yielding a percentage. The base account is total assets for balance sheet accounts and net sales or total revenues for income statement accounts. These calculations are summarized as follows:

Horizontal Analysis

$$\text{Dollar change in account balance} = \text{Current-year balance} - \text{Prior-year balance}$$

$$\text{Percentage change in account balance} = \frac{\text{Dollar change}}{\text{Prior-year balance}}$$

Vertical Analysis

For the Balance Sheet / *For the Income Statement*

$$\text{Percentage} = \frac{\text{Account Balance}}{\text{Total Assets}} \qquad \frac{\text{Account Balance}}{\text{Net Sales or Revenue}}$$

Martin Lee/mediablitzimages (UK) Limited/Alamy

Given Colgate-Palmolive's financial information in Exhibit 6-2, horizontal and vertical analyses of accounts receivable and sales result in the calculations shown below. Note that the net realizable value of receivables, as reported on the balance sheet, is used in the calculations.

The calculations show slight improvement in Colgate-Palmolive's receivables position. Horizontal analysis shows that the company's receivables balance decreased $16 million, or 1.0%, in 2010. Horizontal analysis of net sales shows growth in sales of $237 million, or 1.5%, during the year, so it does not appear that receivables are lower because sales have fallen. Vertical analysis shows that receivables as a percentage of assets were down slightly, from 14.6% in 2009 to 14.4% in 2010.

For comparison purposes, the 2010 horizontal and vertical analyses of **The Clorox Company** are provided.

Horizontal Analysis

	Change	*Percentage Change*
Accounts receivable	1,610 − 1,626 = (16)	$\frac{(16)}{1,626} = (1.0\%)$
Net sales	15,564 − 15,327 = 237	$\frac{237}{15,327} = 1.5\%$

Vertical Analysis

	2010	*2009*
Accounts receivable	$\frac{1,610}{11,172} = 14.4\%$	$\frac{1,626}{11,134} = 14.6\%$
Net sales	$\frac{15,564}{15,564} = 100\%$	$\frac{15,327}{15,327} = 100\%$

Because a receivable is an uncollected sale, the main question that should be asked of a company is how well it collects its receivables.

		Horizontal Analysis	Vertical Analysis
Accounts receivable	*Colgate*	(1.0%)	14.4%
	Clorox	11.9%	11.9%
Net sales	*Colgate*	1.5%	100%
	Clorox	1.5%	100%

The calculations show that **The Clorox Company** maintains less receivables as a percentage of assets than **Colgate-Palmolive**. They also show that while both companies generated the same percentage growth in sales, The Clorox Company experienced a much larger increase in receivables. This is a trend that the company may wish to monitor.

Receivables Turnover Ratio

The preceding analysis indicates that Colgate-Palmolive appears to be managing its receivables well. Another means to assess the management of receivables is to calculate a company's receivables turnover ratio. The **receivables turnover ratio** compares a company's credit sales during a period to its average receivables balance during that period. It is calculated as follows:

$$\text{Receivables Turnover Ratio} = \frac{\text{Credit Sales}}{\text{Average Receivables}}$$

where average receivables is:

$$\frac{\text{Beginning Receivables} + \text{Ending Receivables}}{2}$$

Receivables turnover ratio A comparison of credit sales to receivables that measures a company's ability to generate and collect receivables.

Days-in-receivables ratio A conversion of the receivables turnover ratio that expresses a company's ability to generate and collect receivables in days.

Allowance ratio A comparison of the allowance account to receivables that measures the percentage of receivables that are expected to be uncollectible in the future.

Because the ratio divides credit sales during a period by the average receivables balance during the period, it indicates how many times during a period a company generates and collects receivables. In general, companies want this ratio to be higher rather than lower because a higher ratio indicates that the company collects, or turns over, its receivables faster.

Colgate-Palmolive's 2010 receivables turnover ratio is calculated as follows from the information in Exhibit 6-2. Note that net sales is used instead of net credit sales. While net credit sales would be preferable, it is infrequently reported by companies, so net sales is used as a substitute.

$$\frac{15{,}564}{(1{,}610 + 1{,}626)/2} = 9.6$$

The 9.6 ratio indicates that Colgate-Palmolive's 2010 sales were 9.6 times its average receivables balance. In other words, the company was able to generate and collect its receivables balance close to ten times in 2010.

Because the receivables turnover ratio is sometimes difficult to interpret, it is often converted into the days-in-receivables ratio. The **days-in-receivables ratio** divides the receivables turnover ratio into 365 days to express, in days, how long it takes a company to generate and collect its receivables. Thus, the days-in-receivables ratio is calculated as follows:

$$\text{Days-in-Receivables Ratio} = \frac{365}{\text{Receivables Turnover Ratio}}$$

$$\frac{365}{9.6} = 38.8$$

A ratio of 38.0 indicates that it takes Colgate-Palmolive 38 days to generate and collect the average receivable. Whether this is good or bad requires some comparison. In the prior year, Colgate-Palmolive's ratio was 38.4. The Clorox Company's 2010 ratio was 34.0 days. Thus, you can conclude that while Colgate-Palmolive's ability to collect its receivables is fairly stable, it lags behind The Clorox Company's collection by about 4 days.

Allowance Ratio

One additional ratio that is useful in analyzing a company's management of receivables is the allowance ratio. The **allowance ratio** compares the allowance account to gross accounts receivable to determine the percentage

HOME DEPOT ANALYSIS

Using **Home Depot's** financial statements in Appendix C, calculate and interpret (1) horizontal and vertical analyses of accounts receivable and net sales, (2) receivables turnover and days-in-receivables ratios, and (3) the allowance ratio.

(1) Horizontal Analysis

Accounts Receivable: ($1,085 − $964)/$964 = 12.6%

Net Sales: ($67,997 − $66,176)/$66,176 = 2.8%

Vertical Analysis

Accounts Receivable: $1,085/$40,125 = 2.7%

Net Sales: $67,997/$67,997 = 100%

The 12.6% horizontal analysis indicates that receivables increased during the year by over 12%. With the company's increase in sales of 2.8%, an increase in receivables is not alarming. The 2.7% vertical analysis indicates that a very small portion of Home Depot's assets are in the form of receivables.

(2) Receivables Turnover Ratio:

$67,997/[($1,085 + $964)/2] = 66.4

Days-in-Receivables: 365/66.4 = 5.5 days

The 66.4 receivables turnover ratio indicates that Home Depot generates and collects its receivables very quickly—about 64 times each year. The days-in-receivables ratio of 5.5 also indicates that receivables are collected rapidly. We should note here that Home Depot sells very little merchandise on credit. Rather, it accepts third-party credit cards, which pay Home Depot each day for the charges made by cardholders. This helps the company to keep receivables balances extremely low given its large sales volume.

(3) Allowance Ratio: Not applicable

In its first note, Home Depot discloses that its "valuation reserve related to accounts receivable was not material..." This means that Home Depot's allowance balance is effectively zero, which yields an allowance ratio of 0%. Home Depot expects to collect virtually all of its outstanding accounts receivable.

of receivables that are expected to be uncollectible in the future. It is calculated as follows:

$$\text{Allowance Ratio} = \frac{\text{Allowance for Bad Debts}}{\text{Gross Accounts Receivable}}$$

where gross accounts receivable is:

Net Accounts Receivable + Allowance for Bad Debts

A higher ratio indicates that a company expects more receivables to be uncollectible. In general, a company would want this ratio to be as low as possible. **Colgate-Palmolive's** allowance ratio for 2010 and 2009 is calculated as follows from the information in Exhibit 6-2:

2010	**2009**
$\frac{53}{1{,}610 + 53} = 3.2\%$	$\frac{52}{1{,}626 + 52} = 3.1\%$

For both years, Colgate-Palmolive expected that it would not collect slightly over 3% of its receivables, or about 3 cents per dollar of receivables. For comparison purposes, **The Clorox Company's** 2010 ratio was 1.1%. Again, like the receivables turnover ratio, this shows that Colgate-Palmolive collects its receivables at a high rate, but not as high as The Clorox Company.

LO5 Notes Receivable

An account receivable is an amount owed by a customer who has purchased the company's product or service. Sometimes, because of a customer's poor credit rating or because of the size of the transaction, a company will enter into a more formal agreement with the customer beyond a normal account receivable. This is often accomplished through a promissory note.

Promissory notes can be used to formalize a receivable or to loan money to another entity.

A **promissory note** is a written promise to pay a specific sum of money on demand or at some specific date in the future. Promissory notes can be used to formalize a receivable or to loan money to another entity. In most cases, promissory notes require the payment of both principal and interest. The company that will receive the principal and interest is called the *payee*. The customer or borrower who will pay the interest and principal is called the *maker* of the note. This chapter focuses on the accounting of the payee.

When a company accepts a promissory note, it has a **note receivable**. Like other assets, a note receivable is reported on the balance sheet. However, its classification depends on its terms. If the note is due within a year of the balance sheet date, it is classified as a current asset. Otherwise, it is a non-current asset.

Accounting for a note receivable usually requires entries to record the following:

- Issuance of the note
- Interest earned on the note
- Collection of the note

To illustrate, suppose that on October 1, 2011, Bentonville Machine Works sells a lathe to Tilbury Designs for $12,000. Bentonville accepts a six-month, 8% promissory note from Tilbury for payment. The note stipulates that Bentonville will receive both principal and interest from Tilbury on March 31, 2012.

Promissory note A written promise to pay a specific sum of money on demand or at some specific date in the future.

Note receivable An asset created when a company accepts a promissory note.

Recording the Note

A note receivable is recorded at its face value, which is $12,000 in this example. Therefore, Bentonville would record the sale of the lathe and the resulting note receivable as follows:

Oct. 1 2011	Notes Receivable	12,000	
	Sales		12,000
	(To record sale in exchange for a promissory note)		

Assets	=	Liabilities	+	Equity
+12,000				+12,000

In this entry, Bentonville increases Notes Receivable to reflect the receipt of the promissory note and increases Sales to reflect the inflow of assets resulting from the sale. As a result, both assets and equity increase. As in previous examples in this chapter, the effects on inventory and cost of goods sold are ignored.

Recording Interest

Most promissory notes require that the maker pay interest to the payee. The amount of interest is a function of (1) the principal or face value of the note, (2) the annual interest rate, and (3) the length of time the note is outstanding. The calculation is as follows:

$$\text{Interest} = \text{Principal} \times \text{Annual Rate of Interest} \times \text{Time Outstanding}$$

In this example, Bentonville's note receivable is outstanding for six months. As a result, interest of 8% will be charged for only six out of twelve months. Therefore, interest over the life of the note is $480, calculated as follows:

$$\begin{aligned}\text{Interest} &= \text{Principal} \times \text{Annual Rate of Interest} \times \text{Time Outstanding}\\ &= \$12{,}000 \times .08 \times 6/12 \text{ months}\\ &= \$480\end{aligned}$$

According to the calculation, Bentonville will receive $480 of interest at the maturity of the note. However, the revenue recognition principle requires companies to record interest revenue when it is earned, even if cash will not be received until later. Assuming that Bentonville has a fiscal year end prior to the maturity of the note, it must make an adjusting journal entry to record interest earned during the year. Recall from Chapter 4 that such an entry is an accrual adjusting entry.

To illustrate, suppose that Bentonville prepares financial statements on December 31. Bentonville has not yet received any interest payment from Tilbury because payment is not required until March 31, 2012. However, Bentonville has earned three months of interest, calculated as follows:

$$\begin{aligned}\text{Interest earned} &= \text{Principal} \times \text{Annual Rate of Interest} \times \text{Time Outstanding}\\ &= \$12{,}000 \times .08 \times 3/12 \text{ months}\\ &= \$240\end{aligned}$$

On December 31, Bentonville would record this interest revenue as follows:

Dec. 31 2011	Interest Receivable	240	
	Interest Revenue		240
	(To record interest earned on note)		

Assets	=	Liabilities	+	Equity
+240				+240

This entry increases Interest Receivable to reflect the additional receivable Bentonville now has from Tilbury. Bentonville will report this receivable on its balance sheet until the interest is paid in March 2012. The entry also increases Interest Revenue to reflect the inflow of assets attributable to the year 2011. As a result, both assets and equity increase.

Collecting the Note

The collection of a note receivable is much like the collection of an account receivable. When a note is collected, the note receivable is decreased and cash is increased. However, when a note receivable requires interest to be paid, the collection of the note often includes the collection of interest as well. This is the case for Bentonville.

On March 31, 2012, Bentonville collects cash and interest from Tilbury. The total interest over the six months Bentonville held the note is $480. The principal is $12,000. Therefore, Bentonville receives $12,480 in cash, recorded as follows:

Mar. 31 2012	Cash	12,480	
	Interest Receivable		240
	Notes Receivable		12,000
	Interest Revenue		240
	(To record collection of note and interest)		

Assets	=	Liabilities	+	Equity
+12,480				+240
−12,000				
−240				

This entry has four parts. First, the entry increases Cash for the amount of cash collected by Bentonville. Second, it decreases Interest Receivable to eliminate the asset that was created by the December 31 adjusting entry. Third, the entry decreases Notes Receivable by its principal value because the note has been collected and is no longer outstanding. Finally, the entry increases Interest Revenue for the three months of interest (January, February, and March) earned in the current period ($12,000 × 8% × 3/12). This interest revenue will be reported on Bentonville's 2012 income statement. The result of the entry is a net increase to assets of $240 and an increase to equity of $240. If this seems low to you, remember that equity was increased substantially when the sale was made and the note created. When Bentonville collects the note, it is simply exchanging one asset for another. The net $240 increase to assets and equity results from the interest earned during the three months of the current year.

STUDY TOOLS 6

Chapter review card

- Learning Objective and Key Concept Reviews
- Key Definitions and Formulas

Online (Located at www.cengagebrain.com)

- Flash Cards and Crossword Puzzles
- Games and Quizzes
- E-Lectures
- Homework Assignments (as directed by your instructor)

CONCEPT QUESTIONS

1. (LO1) When is an account receivable recorded?
2. (LO1) Describe how accounts receivable are reported on the balance sheet.
3. (LO2) What method of accounting for uncollectible receivables is recommended by GAAP?
4. (LO2) When is bad debt expense recorded under the direct write-off method? Under the allowance method?
5. (LO2) What happens when a receivable that previously had been written off is collected?
6. (LO3) Identify the two ways to estimate bad debt expense under the allowance method.
7. (LO3) What are the benefits of preparing an aging schedule?
8. (LO4) Explain the logic of comparing the percentage increase in receivables to the percentage increase in sales.
9. (LO4) State the formula for receivables turnover ratio and describe what this ratio tells an analyst.
10. (LO4) State the formula for the allowance ratio and describe what this ratio tells an analyst.
11. (LO5) Who is considered the *maker* of a promissory note?
12. (LO5) How does one determine whether a note receivable will be classified as a current asset or a non-current asset?
13. (LO5) The amount of interest earned on a note receivable is a function of what three factors?

MULTIPLE CHOICE

1. (LO1) Which of the following statements is true?
   i. Accounts receivable may be reported as a current asset or a current liability.
   ii. Accounts receivable are reported at net realizable value on the balance sheet.
   a. i only
   b. ii only
   c. Both i and ii
   d. Neither i nor ii
2. (LO1) Accounts receivable are:
   a. recorded at the time cash is received.
   b. netted with a liability account to be presented on the balance sheet at net worth.
   c. recorded when a revenue is earned but cash has not yet been received.
   d. reported as unearned revenue until payment is received.
3. (LO1) Which of the following is not true of the Sales Returns and Allowances account?
   a. It is a contra-revenue account
   b. It is increased when sales are returned
   c. It is a contra-expense account
   d. It is a temporary account that is zeroed-out during the closing process
4. (LO2) Under the direct write-off method:
   a. bad debt expense increases only when a receivable is deemed uncollectible.
   b. a contra-asset account is used to estimate the amount of receivables that will be uncollectible.

c. the matching principle of accounting is not violated.
d. the income statement approach is used to estimate Bad Debt Expense.

5. (LO2) The allowance method:
   a. requires only one journal entry to write off uncollectible accounts and record bad debt expense.
   b. uses a contra-asset account to report accounts receivable at net realizable value.
   c. is not recommended by GAAP.
   d. is only used if the amount of accounts receivable is immaterial.
6. (LO6) The percentage-of-sales approach to estimating bad debt expense:
   a. is considered a balance sheet approach.
   b. focuses on getting the allowance for bad debts account as accurate as possible.
   c. matches expenses and revenues better than the percentage-of-receivables approach.
   d. is calculated using gross margin.
7. (LO3) Which is not true of the percentage-of-receivables approach to estimating bad debt expense?
   a. It is calculated in two steps
   b. It is a function of a company's receivables balance
   c. It results in a meaningful net realizable value
   d. It always results in less bad debt expense compared to the percentage-of-sales approach
8. (LO4) Horizontal analysis of accounts receivable:
   a. calculates accounts receivable as a percentage of total assets.
   b. highlights the change in accounts receivable as a percentage of the prior year's receivables balance.
   c. calculates accounts receivable as a percentage of net sales.
   d. both "a" and "b" are correct.
9. (LO4) Vertical analysis of accounts receivable:
   a. calculates accounts receivable as a percentage of total assets.
   b. highlights the change in accounts receivable as a percentage of the prior year's receivables balance.
   c. calculates accounts receivable as a percentage of net sales.
   d. both "a" and "b" are correct.
10. (LO4) Which of the following statements is correct?
    i. The receivables turnover ratio is indicative of a company's ability to collect its receivables
    ii. Companies normally strive to maintain a high receivables turnover ratio.
    a. i only
    b. ii only
    c. Both i and ii
    d. Neither i nor ii
11. (LO4) The allowance ratio:
    a. is calculated by dividing Bad Debt Expense by Gross Accounts Receivable.
    b. is normally a ratio that companies try to keep as high as possible.
    c. indicates how much of a company's receivables is estimated to be uncollectible.
    d. is calculated using income statement accounts.
12. (LO5) Which of the following is not true of a note receivable:
    a. A note receivable can be reported as a current asset or a non-current asset depending on the maturity date of the receivable
    b. A note receivable is normally acquired through the acceptance of a promissory note in settlement of a debt
    c. When a note receivable is received for services rendered, the revenue is not reported until the maturity date of the note
    d. The entity borrowing the money is considered the maker of the note
13. (LO5) When accounting for a note receivable:
    a. interest revenue is never recorded until payment is received.
    b. interest receivable is normally reported as a current asset.
    c. interest rates are normally stated at semi-annual rates.
    d. the note receivable is recorded at issuance with a credit entry.

BRIEF EXERCISES

1. Recording Sales Discounts LO1

On July 1, Pam's Pizza Supply sold 100 pounds of pepperoni for $800 on account to a local pizza parlor. The terms of the sale were 2/10, n/30. The pizza parlor pays Pam's Pizza Supply in full on July 7.

Required
Prepare the entries that Pam would make to record the sale and the receipt of the payment.

2. Recording Sales Returns LO1

On March 5, Monica's Cooking Company sells inventory to a customer for $2,000. On March 13, the customer returns $750 of merchandise. The accountant recorded the return with the following entry:

March 13	Sales	750	
	Accounts Receivable		750

Required
Prepare the entry the accountant should have made when the merchandise was returned on March 13 and explain why the accountant's entry was incorrect. Ignore any effect on cost of goods sold or inventory.

3. Compute Net Realizable Value LO2

At the end of the year a company has gross accounts receivable of $65,500. The allowance for doubtful accounts has a balance of $7,600, and sales discounts for the year were $5,400.

Required
What is the net realizable value of accounts receivable that the company will report on its balance sheet?

4. Direct Write-off Method LO2

Chandler Inc. sells $3,500 of goods to Tribbiani Company during January. In April, Chandler determines that it will be unable to collect the receivable from Tribbiani.

Required
Prepare the journal entries to record the sale and the bad debt expense if Chandler uses the direct write-off method. Ignore any effect on cost of goods sold or inventory.

5. Recording Bad Debt Expense LO2

While reviewing outstanding accounts receivables, John's Tractor Supply Company determines that a receivable of $15,000 is now uncollectable.

Required
Journalize the entry to record bad debt expense assuming that John uses a) the direct write-off method or b) the allowance method. Is the use of the direct write-off method allowed under GAAP? If so, under what circumstances?

6. Estimating Bad Debt Expense LO3

A company uses the percentage-of-sales approach to estimate bad debts. Sales for the year were $750,000, and gross profit was $450,000. The company estimates that 5% of sales are uncollectible.

Required
What is the company's estimated bad debt expense for the year? Would your answer change if the company was able to increase its gross profit from its sales?

7. Allowance Method LO2, 3

Phoebe's Massage Company uses the allowance method to account for bad debt expense. Phoebe makes credit sales of $70,000 during the year. At year end, Phoebe estimates that $7,000 of those sales will not be collected. The next year, Phoebe determines that a $1,500 receivable is uncollectible and should be written off.

Required
Prepare the journal entries to record the credit sales, bad debt expense, and the write-off of uncollectible accounts.

8. Estimating Bad Debt Expense LO3

Rachel's Clothing Company has a receivables balance of $15,000 at the end of the year. Based on past history, Rachel estimates that it will not collect 2% of its receivables balance. Prior to any year-end adjustment, the balance in the allowance account is a $200 debit.

Required
a. Prepare the journal entry to record bad debt expense for the year. Show your calculation of bad debt expense in T-account form.
b. Assume that the balance in the allowance account was a $100 credit instead of the $200 debit. What is bad debt expense in this situation? Show your calculation in T-account form.

9. Horizontal and Vertical Analyses LO4

The following information pertains to Moose Corporation:

	2012	2011
Net sales	$350,000	$342,000
Net accounts receivable	189,000	197,000
Bad debt expense	8,200	7,000
Total assets	410,000	425,000

Required
Prepare horizontal and vertical analyses of all four accounts. Round percentages to one decimal point (i.e., 23.9%).

10. Analyzing Receivables LO4

The following information pertains to Skelton Resorts:

Credit sales	$450,000
Net accounts receivable, beginning	63,000
Net accounts receivable, ending	54,000
Allowance for bad debts, ending	5,000

Required
Compute Skelton's receivables turnover ratio, days-in-receivables ratio, and allowance ratio.

11. Effects of Recording Bad Debt Expense LO2, 3, 4

You are the accountant for a company, and you are preparing the entry to record bad debt expense for the year under the allowance method. Your boss is not an accountant and provides you with the following grid to fill out so that he can understand the effect of the expense entry:

	Net Income	Amount in accounts receivable account	Amount of accounts receivables reported on the financial statements	Receivables turnover ratio
Effect of bad debt expense entry				

Required
Fill out the grid with Increase, Decrease, or No Effect.

12. Accounting for Notes Receivable LO5

On March 1, Auburn Actuarial Services accepted from Meadows Inc. a six-month, 5%, $12,000 note receivable and $3,000 in cash in exchange for services. The note and interest were paid at maturity on September 1. Auburn has a December 31 year end.

Required
Prepare all journal entries Auburn would make to properly account for the sale and note.

13. Record Interest on Note Receivable LO5

On July 1, West Tennessee Supply Group sold $15,000 of supplies to Russell Research Labs in exchange for a 7 month, 8% note receivable.

Required
Assuming that West Tennessee Supply Group prepares adjusting journal entries monthly, prepare all entries necessary in July to account for the note. Ignore any effects on inventory or cost of goods sold.

14. Calculating Interest on Notes Receivable LO5

Bowers Technology is in the process of converting a customer's $10,000 account receivable into a note receivable. Bowers is considering the following three options in establishing the terms of the note:

1. 4% 9-month note
2. 6% 6-month note
3. 8% 3-month note

Required
Which option(s) should Bowers choose if it wants to maximize interest revenue? What reasons might Bowers have for choosing the options that results in the least amount of interest revenue?

EXERCISES

15. Recording Accounts Receivable LO1

On February 4, Campbell Company sells inventory to a customer for $6,000. Terms of the sale are 1/15, net 30. On February 10, the customer returns $500 of merchandise. The customer pays on February 15.

Required
Prepare all journal entries to record the merchandise sale, its return, and the collection of the receivable. Ignore any effects on inventory or cost of goods sold.

16. Reporting Accounts Receivable LO1

A company reports the following for accounts receivable:

	2012	2011
Accounts receivable, net of allowance of $234 and $267	$5,432	$4,905

Required
For each year, determine the company's total or gross accounts receivable, net realizable value of accounts receivable, and allowance for bad debts balance. What does net realizable value represent?

17. Uncollectible Receivables LO2

Carnes Inc. reported the following information in its latest annual report:

Allowance for bad debts, beginning balance	$1,775
Bad debt expense for the year	325
Accounts receivable written off during the year	256

Required
Determine which method of accounting for bad debts Carnes uses, record all journal entries associated with the allowance account for the year, and determine the ending balance in the allowance account.

18. Accounting for Uncollectible Receivables LO2

The following information pertains to Godwin Motors, which uses the allowance method for receivables:

	2012	2011
Gross receivables	$ 648,750	$ 580,498
Allowance for bad debts	33,560	24,650
Net sales	7,555,000	6,325,000

Required

a. Assuming that Godwin Motors recorded bad debt expense of $25,600 in 2012, what amount of accounts receivable were written off in 2012?
b. Prepare the journal entries to record the 2012 bad debt expense and the 2012 write-offs of uncollectible accounts.
c. Assuming that Godwin made all sales on credit, what amount of cash was collected in 2012?

19. Uncollectible Receivables LO2, 3

At December 31, Vicki's Designers had gross accounts receivable of $346,000. Historically, Vicki's Designers has estimated bad debt expense as 5% of gross receivables.

Required

a. Calculate bad debt expense for the year, assuming that the allowance account currently has (1) a credit balance of $5,000 and (2) a debit balance of $1,200.
b. Assume that on January 14, an account receivable of $2,000 is deemed uncollectible and written off. Prepare the journal entry to record this event. What effect does this have on (1) net income and (2) the net realizable value of receivables?

20. Estimating Bad Debt Expense LO3

Buster's Furniture provides the following information for the year:

Net credit sales for the year	$985,750
Accounts receivable at year end	450,000
Allowance for bad debts at year end	18,000 credit

Required
Estimate bad debt expense for the year as (a) 5% of accounts receivable and (b) 2% of net credit sales. Discuss why Buster's Furniture might choose one approach over the other.

21. Aging Schedule for Accounts Receivable LO3

Outdoor Living has the following accounts receivable at year end, broken down by age:

Age	Amount
Current	$150,000
One month overdue	40,000
Two months overdue	18,000
Three months overdue	8,000

Prior experience has shown that the company will probably collect 95% of its current receivables. Furthermore, the collection percentage will fall by 15% for each additional month an account receivable remains outstanding past its due date.

Required
Develop an estimate of Outdoor Living's allowance account balance and prepare the journal entry for bad debt expense, assuming that the allowance has an existing (a) $4,000 credit balance and (b) $1,000 debit balance.

22. Analyzing Receivables LO4

The following information was taken from the annual report of SC Enterprises:

	2012	2011
Sales	$240,000	$250,000
Total assets	840,000	825,000
Accounts receivable	125,000	78,000

Required
Prepare and interpret horizontal and vertical analyses of all three accounts. Round percentages to one decimal point (i.e., 23.9%). Should the owners of the business be concerned?

23. Analyzing Receivables LO4

The following information was taken from the annual report of Sparky Foundation:

	2012	2011
Gross receivables	$ 784,560	$685,000
Allowance for bad debts	56,895	45,600
Net sales	8,100,000	

Required
Compute and interpret Sparky's receivables turnover ratio and its days-in-receivables ratio.

24. Analyzing Receivables LO4

The following information is from Canning Company:

2012	Allowance for bad debts	$ 500
	Net accounts receivable	21,000
2011	Allowance for bad debts	350
	Net accounts receivable	19,500

Required
Calculate the allowance ratio for both years. Is Canning Company getting better or worse at collecting its receivables?

25. Recording Notes Receivable LO5

On April 1, Fly Corporation accepted cash of $15,000 and a six-month, 6%, $75,000 interest-bearing note from Gonzo, Inc., as settlement of an account receivable. Fly has a fiscal year end of June 30, and Gonzo paid the principal and the interest at maturity.

Required
Identify the note's maker and payee and prepare all appropriate journal entries from the acceptance of the note to the maturity date.

26. Accounting for Notes Receivable LO5

Brandon Enterprises makes the following entries regarding a note receivable:

Sep. 1	Notes receivable	6,000	
	Accounts receivable		6,000
Sep. 30	Interest receivable	40	
	Interest revenue		40
Dec. 1	Cash	6,120	
	Interest receivable		40
	Interest revenue		80
	Notes receivable		6,000

Required
Identify (a) whether Brandon is the maker or the payee, (b) the terms of the note (issuance date, maturity date, interest rate), and (c) Brandon's year end.

27. Interest on Notes Receivable LO5

Consider the following independent scenarios.

1. On 9/1, a company accepts a $10,000, 5%, 8-month note receivable.
2. On 3/1, a company accepts a $20,000, 8%, 6-month note receivable.
3. On 6/15, a company accepts a $15,000, 10%, 4-month note receivable.

Required
Assuming a December 31 year end, calculate current-year interest revenue for each scenario.

28. Accounting Terms LO2, 3, 5

The following is a list of terms and definitions associated with receivables:

1. Direct write-off method
2. Maker
3. Allowance method
4. Maturity value
5. Promissory note
6. Aging schedule
7. Payee
8. Maturity date
9. Notes receivable

a. An asset resulting from accepting a promissory note as payment for products sold or services rendered.
b. A schedule used to organize accounts receivable according to the length of time each has been outstanding.
c. The amount of cash the maker is to pay the payee on the maturity date of the note.
d. The date the promissory note is due.
e. Recognition of bad debts expense at the point in time at which the accounts receivable is deemed uncollectible and written off.
f. The party that will receive the money from a promissory note at some future date.
g. A method of estimating bad debts expense on the basis of either net credit sales or accounts receivable at the end of period.
h. A written promise to pay a specific sum of money on demand or at some specific date in the future.
i. The party that agrees to repay the money for a promissory note at some future date.

Required

Match each term with the appropriate definition.

PROBLEMS

29. Accounts Receivable Entries LO1, 2, 3

During 2012, CE Electronics entered into the following transactions:

Sales on account	$1,400,000
Collections of credit sales	1,225,000
Wrote off accounts deemed uncollectible	20,000
Received payments on accounts previously written off	7,500

On its 2011 balance sheet, CE reported gross accounts receivable of $707,000 and an allowance account of $43,000.

Required

Prepare all journal entries to record each of the transactions that occurred in 2012 and the journal entry to record bad debt expense at the end of 2012, assuming that 7% of accounts receivable at the end of 2012 are uncollectible.

30. Comparing Methods for Uncollectible Receivables LO2, 3

The following data pertains to the operations of Knight Corporation for 2012:

Net credit sales	$725,000
Net income (before bad debt expense)	135,000
Write-offs of uncollectible accounts	17,500
Estimated uncollectible percentage of net credit sales	3%

The controller is trying to decide which method of accounting for bad debts to use. The company is attempting to maximize its net income to meet projected figures. The bad debt expense is material to the company's financial statements.

Required

a. Calculate bad debt expense for 2012 under the direct write-off method and the allowance method.
b. Compute net income under both methods (assume a tax bracket of 30%).
c. Does Knight have the option of which method to use under GAAP?

31. Account Receivable Entries LO1, 2, 3

The following financial information pertains to Sleepy Company:

Accounts receivable, 12/31/11	$ 275,000
Allowance for bad debts, 12/31/11	8,400
Net credit sales, 2012	1,980,000
Collections on credit sales during 2012	1,730,000
Accounts receivable written off in 2012	6,500

Required

a. Prepare all the necessary journal entries for 2012 sales, collections, and write-offs (using the direct write-off method).
b. Using the allowance method, prepare 2012 journal entries to record write-offs and to estimate bad debt expense assuming bad debt expense is estimated on a (i) percentage of net credit sales approach (2%) and (ii) percentage of accounts receivable approach (5%).
c. What is the net realizable value of accounts receivable in parts b(i) and b(ii)?
d. Explain the rationale for each of the approaches in part b.

32. Analyzing Receivables LO4

The following information was taken from the annual reports of two high-end jewelry retailers:

	Company A	Company B
Net accounts receivable, 2012	$ 584,000	$ 460,000
Net accounts receivable, 2011	505,000	398,000
Net sales, 2012	2,425,000	2,195,000
Net sales, 2011	2,200,000	1,500,000

Required

a. Calculate the 2012 receivables turnover ratio for both companies.
b. Compare the two companies. Which one is more efficient with their receivables?
c. What other methods and factors would one consider when evaluating receivables? What one other comparison demonstrates one company's efficiency over the other?

33. Analyzing Receivables LO4

The following information pertains to Rocky Foundation:

	2012	2011
Net sales	$600,000	$582,000
Net accounts receivable	465,000	450,000
Allowance for bad debts	14,000	13,200
Total assets	630,000	653,000

Required

a. Prepare and interpret horizontal and vertical analyses of all four accounts. Round percentages to one decimal point (i.e., 23.9%).
b. Calculate and interpret the receivables turnover ratio and days-in-receivables ratio.
c. Calculate and interpret the allowance ratio for both years.

34. Recording Notes Receivable LO5

On February 15, Harpool Inc. sold equipment to Adams Corporation on account for $40,000. On November 1, Harpool deemed the account uncollectible and wrote it off. On December 31, Adams offered Harpool a six-month, 10%, $40,000 promissory note in payment of its obligation, which Harpool accepted. Adams paid the principal and the interest at the maturity date. Harpool uses the allowance method for bad debts.

Required

a. Prepare all of Harpool's necessary journal entries from the date of the equipment sale to the maturity date of the note. Ignore any effect on inventory or cost of goods sold.
b. What would be Adams' motives for offering a promissory note in settlement of such an old debt?

CASES

35. Research and Analysis LO1, 4

Access the 2010 annual report for **Under Armour, Inc.** by clicking on the *Investor Relations, Financials,* and *Annual Report & Proxy* links at www.underarmour.com.

Required

a. Examine the company's income statement and balance sheet and conduct horizontal and vertical analyses of net revenues and accounts receivable. Round percentages to one decimal point (i.e., 23.9%).
b. Examine the company's Allowance for Doubtful Accounts paragraph in its Summary of Significant Accounting Policies (second note). What is the company's 2010 and 2009 balances in its allowance for bad debts account? What factors are considered when estimating the balance? How often is the balance reviewed?
c. With the gathered information, calculate the company's receivables turnover and days-in-receivables ratios for 2010 and the company's allowance ratio for 2010 and 2009.
d. Based on your answers above, write a paragraph explaining your opinion of Under Armour's accounts receivable position. Use your answers as supporting facts.

36. Ethics in Accounting LO2, 3

The Hines Corporation is in the process of closing its books for the year. The company has been growing at an unexpected rate. The chief accountant at the Hines Corporation is currently determining the applicable percentage for the allowance for bad debts and believes it should be based on 2% of net credit sales. The president of the company, Jay Hines, has expressed concerns about living up to the expectations established by the growth in the current year. The president approached the controller and has made a request to increase the allowance for bad debts to 5% of net credit sales with the expectation that the lower net income will decrease the pressure to perform in future years.

Required

a. What factors should one consider when determining the applicable percentage to apply when using the income statement or balance sheet approach?
b. Should the controller be concerned with the company's growth rate when determining the allowance for bad debts? Explain.

37. Entrepreneurial Decision Making LO2, 3

Valley Clothing Shop is a small clothing retailer now in its fourth year of business. Through its first year of operations, Valley has operated on a pure cash or check basis. Currently, Valley has averaged $275,000 of annual cash sales with an average profit margin of 40%. Lately, many customers have expressed frustration over the fact that Valley does not accept credit sales, and Valley believes that this is beginning to have a substantial negative impact on the business. Valley is contemplating two plans of action, neither of which will impact the company's current cash sales.

Plan 1

Offer qualified customers the opportunity to purchase merchandise on account. Valley believes this will create new credit sales of 18% of current cash sales. Increased expenses would include 4% of net credit sales related to bad debts, 2% of net credit sales for billing, and 1% of net credit sales for increased recordkeeping.

Plan 2

Begin accepting credit cards. Valley believes this will create new credit sales of 23% of current cash sales. Increased expenses would include 5.5% of net credit sales-related credit card fees and 0.5% of net credit sales for increased recordkeeping.

Required

a. Compute net income under each plan assuming a tax rate of 30%.
b. Which plan would you recommend Valley accept?
c. What other factors should Valley consider when evaluating these options?

38. Written Communication LO2, 3

Assume you are the controller of a manufacturing plant that sells light machinery to businesses in the surrounding area. You are currently training new employees, and in a recent training session, you report that total credit sales for the year is $300,000, accounts receivable total $40,000 less a $2,000 allowance for bad debts, and bad debt expense is $3,500. After the session, a trainee approaches somewhat confused about why bad debt expense and the allowance balance differ.

Required

Prepare a written explanation to the trainee on the difference between bad debt expense and the allowance for bad debts.

39. Reading and Analyzing Financial Statements LO3, 4, 5

Access the 2010 annual report for **Green Mountain Coffee Company** by clicking on the *Investor Services, Financial Information* and *Annual Reports links* at www.greenmountaincoffee.com.

Required

a. Examine the company's current-year and prior-year balances in accounts receivable. Calculate the percentage change in the account. Round percentages to one decimal point (i.e., 23.9%).
b. Calculate the company's allowance ratio for 2010 and 2009.
c. Do your calculations indicate a positive or negative trend in receivables?
d. Examine the fifth note to the financial statements. Would the company's accounts receivable balance increase due to the described activity?

Inventory

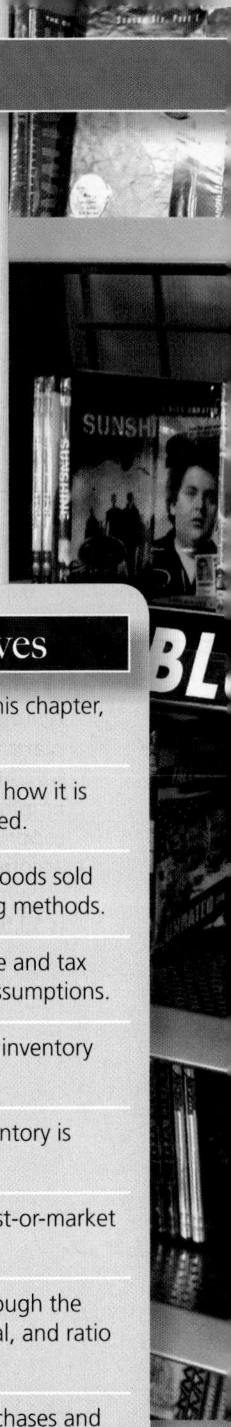

Learning Objectives

After studying the material in this chapter, you should be able to:

LO1 Describe inventory and how it is recorded, expensed, and reported.

LO2 Calculate the cost of goods sold using different inventory costing methods.

LO3 Understand the income and tax effects of inventory cost flow assumptions.

LO4 Analyze the effects of inventory errors.

LO5 Demonstrate how inventory is estimated.

LO6 Apply the lower-of-cost-or-market rule to inventory.

LO7 Evaluate inventory through the calculation of horizontal, vertical, and ratio analyses.

LO8 Appendix: Record purchases and calculate the cost of goods sold under a periodic system.

Introduction

This chapter examines the accounting for inventory. In particular, it examines how companies record their inventory and how they determine the cost of the inventory that is sold. It also examines how errors in inventory can affect income for multiple periods, how inventory can be estimated if needed, and how inventory must be adjusted if its market value falls below its cost. The chapter concludes with how to analyze a company's inventory position. The appendix covers inventory accounting under a periodic system.

LO1 Recording, Expensing, and Reporting Inventory

Inventory is a tangible resource that is held for resale in the normal course of operations. For a retailer, inventory is the merchandise on the shelves or in the warehouse. For a manufacturer, inventory also includes the raw materials and work in process related to producing a finished product. This chapter focuses exclusively on the merchandise inventory of a retailer. You will study the issues concerning raw materials, work in process, and finished goods when you take a managerial accounting course.

As you consider the definition of inventory, note that the phrase "intended for resale" differentiates inventory from other operational assets. A tractor that **Caterpillar Corp.** intends to sell is classified as inventory, while an identical tractor used in Caterpillar's operations is classified as equipment. Furthermore, the phrase "in the normal course of operations" means that some assets intended for sale are not classified as inventory. For example, **Wal-Mart** may vacate a store to relocate within a community. Although the vacated building is put up for sale, it is not classified as inventory because Wal-Mart is not in the business of selling buildings.

Inventory A tangible resource that is held for resale in the normal course of operations.

CHAPTER

For a retailer, inventory is an important asset, and accounting for it properly affects both the balance sheet and the income statement.

Justin Sullivan/Getty Images

Recording Inventory

Following the cost principle, inventory is recorded at its acquisition cost. This includes all costs incurred to get the inventory delivered and, if necessary, prepared for resale. It also includes any reductions granted by the vendor or supplier after purchase. Examples of items affecting the cost of inventory would include, but not be limited to, the following:

- purchase price
- taxes paid
- costs for shipping the product
- insurance during transit
- labor required to assemble the product
- returns to and allowances from the vendor
- purchase discounts from the vendor

For a retailer, inventory is the merchandise on the shelves or in the warehouse. For a manufacturer, inventory also includes the raw materials and work in process related to producing a finished product.

When inventory is purchased, a company will use one of two approaches to record the inventory into its accounting system—a perpetual inventory system or a periodic inventory system. A **perpetual inventory system** updates the inventory account each time inventory is bought or sold—that is, perpetually. Therefore, purchases of inventory are recorded directly into the Inventory account. In contrast, a **periodic inventory system** updates the inventory account only at the end of an accounting period—that is, periodically. Instead of recording purchases into the inventory account, they are recorded in an account called Purchases, which is a temporary account that is closed into Inventory at the end of the period. This chapter will demonstrate inventory accounting under a perpetual system. The periodic system is demonstrated in the appendix to the chapter.

To illustrate the recording of inventory, suppose that Snowy Owl Outfitters purchases $20,000 of inventory on account on October 10. The purchase would be recorded as follows:

Oct. 10	Inventory	20,000	
	Accounts Payable		20,000
	(To record purchase of inventory)		

Assets	=	Liabilities	+	Equity
+20,000		+20,000		

Perpetual inventory system A recording system that updates the inventory account each time inventory is bought or sold.

Periodic inventory system A recording system that updates the inventory account only at the end of an accounting period.

Both assets and liabilities increase as a result of this transaction.

In some cases, a company must pay for the transportation necessary to obtain the inventory. Such additional costs are called *transportation-in* and are added to the overall cost of the inventory. To illustrate, suppose that Snowy Owl pays a third-party carrier $300 to transport the inventory to its warehouse. Snowy Owl would record the payment with the following entry:

Oct. 10	Inventory	300	
	Cash		300
	(To record transportation-in)		

Assets	=	Liabilities	+	Equity
+300				
−300				

Sometimes, a company will return inventory to the vendor or seek some reduction in the cost of the inventory due to defective merchandise. The former is called a *purchase return*, while the latter is a *purchase allowance*. Both reduce the cost of the inventory purchased.

To illustrate, suppose that on October 12 Snowy Owl is granted a $1,000 reduction in the cost of the inventory due to blemishes on the merchandise. Even though Snowy Owl keeps the inventory, its cost has decreased due to the purchase allowance. Therefore, Snowy Owl would reduce the cost of the inventory and its payable to the vendor with the following entry:

Oct. 12	Accounts Payable	1,000	
	Inventory		1,000
	(To record purchase allowance granted by vendor)		

Assets	=	Liabilities	+	Equity
−1,000		−1,000		

In addition to returns and allowances, companies sometimes receive discounts from vendors if payment is made within a certain time period. Such *purchase discounts* reduce the cost of the inventory. To illustrate, suppose that Snowy Owl pays its remaining $19,000 bill to the vendor on October 15, which qualifies Snowy Owl for a 1% discount. As a result, Snowy Owl would save $190 ($19,000 × 1%) and pay only $18,810. The entry to record payment would be as follows:

Oct. 15	Accounts Payable	19,000	
	Inventory		190
	Cash		18,810
	(To record payment)		

Assets	=	Liabilities	+	Equity
−190		−19,000		
−18,810				

The entry decreases Accounts Payable for the full $19,000 (since the debt is paid in full) and decreases Cash for the $18,810 payment. The difference is a reduction to Inventory because the purchase discount of $190 has reduced the cost of the inventory. Both assets and liabilities decrease.

Given the preceding activity, Snowy Owl's *net purchases* of inventory can be calculated as follows:

Gross purchases	$20,000
Add: Transportation-in	300
Less: Purchase returns and allowances	(1,000)
Purchase discounts	(190)
Net purchases	$19,110

Expensing Inventory

Inventory becomes an expense when it is sold. The account Cost of Goods Sold or Cost of Sales is used to capture the amount of inventory expensed during a period. Like the recording of inventory purchases, the recording of cost of goods sold depends on a company's inventory system. Under a perpetual system, cost of goods sold is updated each time inventory is sold—that is, perpetually. Under a periodic system, cost of goods sold is calculated and recorded only at the end of the period—that is, periodically. Again, this chapter will demonstrate inventory accounting under a perpetual system, with the periodic system demonstrated in the appendix to the chapter.

To illustrate the recording of cost of goods sold, suppose that on November 2 Snowy Owl sells inventory costing $400 for $600 cash. Snowy Owl would record the sale with the following two entries:

Nov. 2	Cash	600	
	Sales		600
	(To record sale of inventory)		

Assets	=	Liabilities	+	Equity
+600				+600

Nov. 2	Cost of Goods Sold	400	
	Inventory		400
	(To record sale of inventory)		

Assets	=	Liabilities	+	Equity
−400				−400

The first entry records the effect of the sale on Snowy Owl's cash and revenues. Both Cash and Sales increase for the amount of the sale. As a result, both assets and equity increase by $600.

The second entry records the effect of the sale on Snowy Owl's inventory and expenses. Cost of Goods Sold increases for the cost of the inventory sold. Inventory decreases for the same amount. As a result, both assets and equity decrease by $400.

The net effect of both entries on assets and equity is a $200 increase, which is equal to the gross profit that Snowy Owl earned on the sale.

Reporting Inventory and Cost of Goods Sold

Inventory is expected to be sold within a year. Therefore, it is reported on the balance sheet as a current asset. Because cost of goods sold is usually a large and important expense for a retailer, it is normally reported as a separate line item on the income statement just below sales.

To illustrate, consider the following excerpts from **Wal-Mart's** 2010 balance sheet and income statement. As you might expect from the world's largest retailer, inventory is an important asset. Wal-Mart reported Inventories of over $36 billion on its 2010 balance sheet—by far its largest current asset. It also reported over $315 billion in Cost of Sales on its 2010 income statement, by far its largest expense. The same importance is found in the 2010 financial statements of Wal-Mart's smaller rival, **Target.** Target reported $7.5 billion in inventory, and cost of sales of $45.7 billion is easily its largest expense.

Because cost of goods sold is usually a large expense for a retailer, it is normally reported separately on the income statement.

Excerpts from Wal-Mart's 2010 Financial Statements

amounts in millions	
From the Balance Sheet:	
Current assets	
Cash and cash equivalents	$ 7,395
Receivables	5,089
Inventories	36,318
Prepaid expenses and other	2,960
Current assets of discontinued operations	131
Total current assets	$ 51,893
From the Income Statement:	
Revenues:	
Net sales	$418,952
Membership and other income	2,897
Total revenues	$421,849
Cost and expenses:	
Cost of sales	$315,287
Operating, selling, general and admin. expenses	81,020
Operating income	$ 25,542

LO2 Inventory Costing Methods

The previous section demonstrated how inventory and cost of goods sold *are recorded* under a perpetual system. This section demonstrates how companies *determine the cost* of the inventory sold.

quavondo/iStockphoto.com

To determine the cost of inventory sold, companies can use one of the following four inventory costing methods:

- specific identification
- first-in, first-out (FIFO)
- last-in, first-out (LIFO)
- moving average

To illustrate each method, suppose that Nell Farms sells a specialty maple syrup that it purchases from Waverly Manufacturing. During the month of September, Nell experiences the following inventory activity:

		Units	Unit Cost	Total
Sept. 1	Beginning inventory	40	$12	$480
Sept. 4	Purchase	60	$13	$780
Sept. 10	Sale	(65)		
Sept. 15	Purchase	30	$14	$420
Sept. 23	Purchase	45	$15	$675
Sept. 30	Sale	(50)		

The table shows that Nell sold a total of 115 units during September. However, it does not show the cost of

HOME DEPOT ANALYSIS

Look at **Home Depot's** balance sheet and income statement in Appendix C. What name does the company use for its inventory and cost of goods sold? Is inventory the company's largest current asset? What is its cost? Is cost of goods sold the company's largest expense?

Home Depot uses the names Merchandise Inventories and Cost of Sales. Merchandise Inventories is the company's largest current asset and second largest asset only to Buildings. Its cost is $10,625 million. Cost of Sales of $44,693 million is by far the largest expense of the company.

Exhibit 7-1 Calculations for Specific Identification Method

	Transaction	Inventory Purchased			Inventory Sold			Inventory on Hand		
Sept. 1	Beginning Inventory							40	$12	$ 480
Sept. 4	Purchase #1	60	$13	$780				40 60 100	$12 $13	$ 480 780 $1,260
Sept. 10	Sell 65 units				30 35 65	$12 $13	$360 455 $815	10 25 35	$12 $13	$ 120 325 $ 445
Sept. 15	Purchase #2	30	$14	$420				10 25 30 65	$12 $13 $14	$ 120 325 420 $ 865
Sept. 23	Purchase #3	45	$15	$675				10 25 30 45 110	$12 $13 $14 $15	$ 120 325 420 675 $1,540
Sept. 30	Sell 50 units				10 20 10 10 50	$12 $13 $14 $15	$120 260 140 150 $670	0 5 20 35 60	$12 $13 $14 $15	$ 0 65 280 525 $ 870

those inventory items sold. That is because the cost of the inventory sold in September depends on the inventory costing method Nell uses. Each method is described below.

Specific Identification

The **specific identification method** determines cost of goods sold based on the actual cost of each inventory item sold. To use this method, a retailer must know which inventory item is sold and the exact cost of that particular item. As a result, the method is most likely to be used by companies whose inventory is unique. Examples might include an antiques store or a fine jeweler.

For illustration purposes, suppose that Nell specifically identifies each of its inventory items and provides the detailed inventory activity as shown in Exhibit 7-1.

The Inventory Sold column of Exhibit 7-1 shows that the September 10 sale consisted of thirty $12 units and thirty-five $13 units for a total cost of $815. The September 30 sale consisted of ten $12 units, twenty $13 units, ten $14 units, and ten $15 units, for a total cost of $670. Together, cost of goods sold for September is $1,485 ($815 + $670). The 60 units remaining in ending inventory, as shown in the bottom right corner of Exhibit 7-1, have a cost of $870.

Because most companies cannot track the actual cost of every inventory item that is sold, they cannot use the specific identification method. Instead, they must make an *assumption* about the cost of inventory sold. They can assume that the cost of the inventory sold is the cost of the first unit purchased, the last unit purchased, or an average of all purchases. Each of these three assumptions is described as follows.

First-In, First-Out (FIFO)

The **first-in, first-out (FIFO) method** calculates cost of goods sold based on the assumption that the first unit of inventory available for sale is the first unit sold. That is, inventory is assumed to be sold in the order that it is purchased. For most companies, the FIFO assumption

Specific identification method Inventory costing method that determines cost of goods sold based on the actual cost of each inventory item sold.

First-in, first-out method Inventory costing method that determines cost of goods sold based on the assumption that the first unit of inventory available for sale is the first unit sold.

matches the actual physical flow of their inventory. Note, however, that companies are not required to choose the assumption that matches their physical flow.

Exhibit 7-2 illustrates the calculation of cost of goods sold under the FIFO method.

At each sale, the FIFO method requires Nell to assign to cost of goods sold the costs of the *first units purchased*. On September 10, Nell sold 65 units. It therefore assumes that it sold all 40 units of beginning inventory and 25 of the units in Purchase #1. The total cost of those 65 units was $805.

For the September 30 sale, Nell assumes that it sold the 35 units remaining from Purchase #1 and 15 units of Purchase #2. The total cost of those 50 units was $665.

As a result of these two calculations, cost of goods sold for September is $1,470 ($805 + $665). The 60 units remaining in ending inventory, as shown in the bottom right corner of Exhibit 7-2, have a cost of $885.

Last-in, first-out method Inventory costing method that determines cost of goods sold based on the assumption that the last unit of inventory available for sale is the first unit sold.

IFRS

International accounting standards do not allow the LIFO method in determining cost of goods sold and inventory.

Last-In, First-Out (LIFO)

The **last-in, first-out (LIFO) method** calculates cost of goods sold based on the assumption that the last unit of inventory available for sale is the first unit sold. That is, inventory is assumed to be sold in the opposite order of its purchase. Exhibit 7-3 illustrates the calculations under the LIFO method.

At each sale, the LIFO method requires Nell to assign to cost of goods sold the costs of the *last or most recent units purchased*. On September 10, Nell sold 65 units. It therefore assumes that it sold all 60 units of

Exhibit 7-2 Calculations for FIFO Method

	Transaction	Inventory Purchased			Inventory Sold			Inventory on Hand		
Sept. 1	Beginning Inventory							40	$12	$ 480
								40	$12	$ 480
Sept. 4	Purchase #1	60	$13	$780				60	$13	780
								100		$1,260
					40	$12	$480	0	$12	$ 0
					25	$13	325	35	$13	455
Sept. 10	Sell 65 units				65		$805	35		$ 455
								35	$13	$ 455
Sept. 15	Purchase #2	30	$14	$420				30	$14	420
								65		$ 875
								35	$13	$ 455
								30	$14	420
Sept. 23	Purchase #3	45	$15	$675				45	$15	675
								110		$1,550
					35	$13	$455	0	$13	$ 0
					15	$14	210	15	$14	210
					0	$15	0	45	$15	675
Sept. 30	Sell 50 units				50		$665	60		$ 885

Exhibit 7-3 Calculations for LIFO Method

	Transaction	Inventory Purchased			Inventory Sold			Inventory on Hand		
Sept. 1	Beginning Inventory							40	$12	$ 480
Sept. 4	Purchase #1	60	$13	$780				40 60 100	$12 $13	$ 480 780 $1,260
Sept. 10	Sell 65 units				5 60 65	$12 $13	$ 60 780 $840	35 0 35	$12 $13	$ 420 0 $ 420
Sept. 15	Purchase #2	30	$14	$420				35 30 65	$12 $14	$ 420 420 $ 840
Sept. 23	Purchase #3	45	$15	$675				35 30 45 110	$12 $14 $15	$ 420 420 675 $1,515
Sept. 30	Sell 50 units				0 5 45 50	$12 $14 $15	$ 0 70 675 $745	35 25 0 60	$12 $14 $15	$ 420 350 0 $ 770

Purchase #1 and 5 of the units from beginning inventory. The total cost of those 65 units was $840.

For the September 30 sale, Nell assumes that it sold all 45 units of Purchase #3 and 5 units of Purchase #2. The total cost of those 50 units was $745.

As a result, cost of goods sold for September is $1,585 ($840 + $745). Ending inventory, as shown in the bottom right corner of Exhibit 7-3, has a cost of $770.

Moving Average

The **moving average method** calculates cost of goods sold based on the average unit cost of inventory available for sale. That is, the cost of each inventory item sold is assumed to be the average cost of all inventory available for sale at that time.

To calculate cost of goods sold at each sale date, a retailer must calculate the average unit cost of the inventory available for sale on that date. This calculation is conducted as follows:

$$\text{Average Unit Cost} = \frac{\text{Cost of Goods Available for Sale}}{\text{Units Available for Sale}}$$

Once the average unit cost is known, it is multiplied by the units sold to determine cost of goods sold. Exhibit 7-4 contains Nell's calculations under the moving average method. Note that the average unit cost is rounded to the nearest penny, while inventory sold and inventory on hand is rounded to the nearest dollar.

At the September 10 sale, Nell has 100 units available for sale at a total cost of $1,260. Therefore, the average unit cost is $12.60 ($1,260 ÷ 100). Nell uses that unit cost to determine the costs of the inventory sold and the inventory that remains. Having sold 65 units, Nell's cost of goods sold on September 10 is $819 (65 × $12.60). The cost of the 35 units on hand after the sale is therefore $441 (35 × $12.60).

For the September 30 sale, Nell must recalculate the average unit cost because it has purchased additional units of inventory. This is why the term "moving

Moving average method Inventory costing method that determines cost of goods sold based on the average unit cost of inventory available for sale.

Exhibit 7-4 Calculations for Moving Average Method

	Transaction	Inventory Purchased			Inventory Sold			Inventory on Hand		
Sept. 1	Beginning Inventory							40	$12.00	$ 480
Sept. 4	Purchase #1	60	$13	$780				40 60 100	$12.00 $13.00	$ 480 780 $1,260
Sept. 10	Sell 65 units				65	$12.60	$819	35	$12.60	$ 441
Sept. 15	Purchase #2	30	$14	$420				35 30 65	$12.60 $14.00	$ 441 420 $ 861
Sept. 23	Purchase #3	45	$15	$675				35 30 45 110	$12.60 $14.00 $15.00	$ 441 420 675 $1,536
Sept. 30	Sell 50 units				50	$13.96	$698	60	$13.96	$ 838

average" is used—because the average cost per unit can change during the period as new purchases are made.

At September 30, Nell has 110 units available for sale at a total cost of $1,536. Therefore, the new average unit cost, rounded to the nearest cent, is $13.96 ($1,536 ÷ 110). Having sold 50 units, Nell's cost of goods sold on September 30 is $698 (50 × $13.96).

As a result of these two calculations, cost of goods sold for September is $1,517 ($819 + $698). Ending inventory, as shown in the bottom right corner of Exhibit 7-4, has an average unit cost of $13.96, for a total cost of $838 (60 × $13.96).

LO3 Comparing Inventory Costing Methods

The previous sections show that a company's choice of inventory costing methods affects both its cost of goods sold and its ending inventory. To summarize these effects, Exhibit 7-5 puts Nell's inventory data in a form known as the cost of goods sold model and compares the results of each of the three cost flow assumptions. The specific identification method is omitted from the comparison because of its infrequent use.

HOME DEPOT ANALYSIS

Look at the Merchandise Inventories paragraph of **Home Depot's** first note in Appendix C. What cost flow assumption does the company use? As a result, which inventory units are represented by the $10,625 million balance on the company's balance sheet, and which units are represented by the $44,693 million cost of sales on the company's income statement?

The note indicates that the company uses the FIFO method. Therefore, the $10,625 million balance in inventory represents the last inventory units that the company purchased. The $44,693 million balance in cost of sales represents the cost of the first inventory units purchased.

Exhibit 7-5 Comparison of Inventory Costing Methods

	Units	FIFO	Moving Average	LIFO
Beginning Inventory	40	$ 480	$ 480	$ 480
Add: Net Purchases	135	1,875	1,875	1,875
Cost of Goods Available for Sale	175	$2,355	$2,355	$2,355
Less: Ending Inventory	60	885	838	770
Cost of Goods Sold	115	$1,470	$1,517	$1,585

Because inventory costing methods affect both income statement and balance sheet accounts, a company must disclose the method that it uses. It must also use the same method consistently.

The cost of goods sold model summarizes a company's inventory activity during a period by adding net purchases to beginning inventory to yield cost of goods available for sale. This represents the total cost of the inventory that could have been sold during the period. That cost is then allocated to either what was sold (cost of goods sold) or what was not sold (ending inventory).

In Nell's case, it began the month of September with 40 units costing $480 and bought an additional 135 units costing $1,875 during the month. So, it could have sold up to 175 units with a total cost of $2,355. This is the case regardless of the inventory costing system chosen. However, the cost of the 115 units sold and the 60 units unsold depends on the cost flow assumption.

The FIFO method assigns the costs of the first and, in this case, less expensive units purchased to cost of goods sold, thereby yielding the lowest cost of goods sold ($1,470). It also assigns the costs of the last and more expensive units to ending inventory, thereby yielding the highest ending inventory ($885).

In contrast, the LIFO method assigns the costs of the last and, in this case, more expensive units to cost of goods sold, resulting in the highest cost of goods sold ($1,585). The costs of the first and less expensive units are assigned to ending inventory, resulting in the lowest ending inventory ($770).

The moving average assigns the average costs of all units purchased to cost of goods sold. Therefore, it yields cost of goods sold ($1,517) and ending inventory ($838) that fall in between the FIFO and LIFO extremes.

When a company experiences rising prices for its inventory, these relative differences will continue. These relationships are summarized as follows:

	Ending Inventory	Cost of Goods Sold
FIFO yields:	Highest	Lowest
Moving average yields:	Middle	Middle
LIFO yields:	Lowest	Highest

Because inventory costing methods yield different balances in income statement accounts and balance sheet accounts, a company must disclose the inventory costing method that it uses. It must also use the same method consistently. These requirements allow for meaningful comparisons of inventory activity across different companies and across different time periods within the same company.

While companies can use any of the four costing methods, some choose the LIFO method because of the resulting tax deferral. A **tax deferral** is a temporary delay in the payment of income taxes. Tax deferrals are beneficial because a company can keep and use its cash for a longer period of time.

To illustrate, suppose that Nell generated revenues of $5,240 from its sale of inventory during September. Suppose further that Nell incurred $1,850 in operating expenses during the month and that it is subject to a tax rate of 40%. Exhibit 7-6 contains

Exhibit 7-6 Comparative Income Statements

	FIFO	Moving Average	LIFO
Sales	$5,240	$5,240	$5,240
− Cost of goods sold	1,470	1,517	1,585
Gross profit	$3,770	$3,723	$3,655
− Operating expenses	1,850	1,850	1,850
Income before taxes	$1,920	$1,873	$1,805
− Income taxes (40%)	768	749	722
Net income	$1,152	$1,124	$1,083

Tax deferral A temporary delay in the payment of income taxes.

comparative multi-step income statements prepared under the FIFO, moving average, and LIFO inventory costing methods.

Comparing the income tax obligations under the LIFO and FIFO assumptions (which are the two extremes), you can see that Nell can defer $46 in taxes ($768 − $722) if it uses the LIFO method rather than the FIFO method. In other words, it can write a $722 check to the taxing authority instead of a $768 check. Keep in mind, though, that this deferral is only temporary. If Nell sold its entire inventory in the next period, the deferral would be eliminated.

The general amount of tax deferral a company generates from using LIFO can be determined from information found in the notes to the financial statements. Companies that use the LIFO method must disclose the LIFO reserve. The **LIFO reserve** is the difference between the inventory reported on a LIFO basis and what inventory would be if reported on a FIFO basis. The reserve is cumulative, meaning that it represents the cumulative difference between LIFO and FIFO over the years. As a result, the amount of taxes deferred over time can be calculated by multiplying the reserve by the company's tax rate.

To illustrate, consider the following excerpt from Safeway's 2010 inventory note.

LIFO reserve The difference between inventory reported on a LIFO basis and what inventory would be if reported on a FIFO basis.

Excerpts from Safeway's 2010 Inventory Note

Merchandise inventory of $1,685 million at year-end 2010 and $1,629 million at year-end 2009 is valued . . . on a last-in, first-out ("LIFO") basis . . . Such LIFO inventory had a replacement or current cost of $1,720 million at year-end 2010 and $1,692 million at year-end 2009 . . . The FIFO cost of inventory approximates replacement or current cost.

The note explains that while Safeway's inventory balance as determined under the LIFO method was $1,685 million at the end of 2010, the balance would have been $1,720 had the company used the FIFO method. Therefore Safeway's 2010 LIFO reserve in millions is calculated as follows:

	2010
Inventories valued at FIFO	$1,720
Inventories valued at LIFO	1,685
LIFO reserve	$ 35

Assuming a tax rate of 30%, the taxes that Safeway has deferred as of the end of 2010 are $10.5 million ($35 × 30%).

LO4 Inventory Errors

Most companies take a physical count of inventory at least once a year to confirm that the inventory balance from the accounting system matches the actual inventory on hand. Taking a physical inventory is

MAKING IT REAL

AP Photo/Charlie Neibergall

Inventory errors can originate from many different sources. Consider what happened at Winnebago Industries in its second quarter of 2005. During a review of its physical inventory counts, it was determined that a formula in an electronic worksheet was incorrect. The error in the formula resulted in an overstatement of quarter-ending inventory of approximately $2.8 million, which led to an equal understatement of cost of goods sold for the quarter. The error in cost of goods sold resulted in a $1.8 million after-tax overstatement of quarterly earnings. Since actual earnings were $12.6 million and reported earnings were $14.4 million, the mistake was a 14% overstatement of actual earnings. After finding the problem, the company corrected its financial statements and released them to the public with a statement that the previously released financial statements could not be relied upon due to the inventory counting error.

By counting inventory, a company can determine if it has lost inventory due to theft, damage, or errors in accounting.

an example of an internal control procedure discussed in Chapter 5. By counting inventory, a company can determine if it has lost inventory due to theft, damage, or errors in accounting. However, sometimes errors are introduced into the accounting system by incorrectly counting inventory.

Errors in the counting of inventory affect both the balance sheet (through inventory) and the income statement (through cost of goods sold). Moreover, because ending inventory in one period becomes beginning inventory in the next period, an error can affect not only the current period, but also the next period. To understand the effect of errors, consider the following scenario.

Suppose that Baggett Company has 3,000 units of inventory on January 1, 2012, and purchases an additional 34,000 units during the year. Included in those purchases are 1,000 units that ship on December 30. According to the shipping terms, Baggett owns the units while in transit, so they are properly included in its purchases. However, when Baggett counts its inventory on December 31, 2012, the 1,000 units are erroneously omitted from the count.

To demonstrate the effect of this error, Baggett's information is put into the cost of goods sold model. For simplicity purposes, each unit of inventory is assumed to cost Baggett $1.

In the year of the error (2012)

	As Counted	Correct	Effect
Beginning inventory	$ 3,000	$ 3,000	Not affected
Add: Net purchases	34,000	34,000	Not affected
Cost of goods available for sale	$37,000	$37,000	Not affected
Less: Ending inventory	4,000	5,000	Understated
Cost of goods sold	$33,000	$32,000	Overstated

The model shows that the counting error does not affect beginning inventory or purchases during 2012. These were recorded correctly. However, because 1,000 units were incorrectly omitted from the count, ending inventory of 4,000 units is understated by 1,000 units. This, in turn, results in cost of goods sold being calculated at 33,000 units, which is an overstatement of 1,000 units. In the period of the error, assets are therefore understated by $1,000 and cost of goods sold is overstated by $1,000. As a result, net income, and therefore equity, are also understated by $1,000.

The effect of the counting error is not limited to the year of the error. Because Baggett's ending inventory becomes beginning inventory in the next period, the effects of the 2012 counting error spill into 2013. To demonstrate, suppose that in 2013 Baggett purchases an additional 41,000 units of inventory and properly counts ending inventory at 6,000 units. The following cost of goods sold model shows how the error in 2012 affects 2013, even though no error is made in 2013.

In the period after the error (2013)

	As Counted	Correct	Effect
Beginning inventory	$ 4,000	$ 5,000	Understated
Add: Net purchases	41,000	41,000	Not affected
Cost of goods available for sale	$45,000	$46,000	Understated
Less: Ending inventory	6,000	6,000	Unaffected
Cost of goods sold	$39,000	$40,000	Understated

Beginning inventory of 4,000 units for 2013 is understated by 1,000 units. As a result, the 45,000 units of inventory available for sale are also understated by 1,000 units. If ending inventory for 2013 is properly counted, then the 39,000 units of inventory sold are understated by the same 1,000 units. If it is assumed that all units were purchased for $1 each, then the cost of goods sold model shows that the ending inventory account has the correct balance of $6,000, while the cost of goods sold balance is understated by $1,000 ($39,000 versus the correct $40,000 balance). Thus, while the balance sheet in 2013 is not affected by the 2012 counting error (since inventory is now correctly counted), the 2013 income statement is affected since the beginning inventory value in the cost of goods sold model is understated.

The preceding scenario is an example of a counterbalancing inventory error. A counterbalancing error is an error whose effect on net income is corrected in the period after the error. Note that there was only one error in this scenario—the failure to include 1,000 units of inventory in the final inventory count of 2012. However, the error affected cost of goods sold in two years.

In 2012, cost of goods sold was overstated by $1,000 because *ending* inventory was incorrect. Cost of goods sold was reported as $33,000 when it should have been $32,000. In 2013, cost of goods sold was understated by $1,000 because *beginning* inventory was incorrect. Cost of goods sold was reported as $39,000 when it should have been $40,000. The overstatement in cost of goods sold in 2012 was followed by an equal understatement in 2013. In this way, the inventory error is counterbalancing.

The effects of such errors on inventory, cost of goods sold, and related financial measures are listed in in Exhibit 7-7.

A company must sometimes estimate its inventory balance. One example is when inventory is destroyed by a natural catastrophe. Another example is when a company prepares interim financial statements.

Exhibit 7-7 Effect of Counterbalancing Inventory Errors

	If inventory is understated		If inventory is overstated	
	Current period	**Next period**	**Current period**	**Next period**
Inventory	Understated	Correct	Overstated	Correct
Cost of goods sold	Overstated	Understated	Understated	Overstated
Net income	Understated	Overstated	Overstated	Understated
Total assets	Understated	Correct	Overstated	Correct

Not all inventory errors are counterbalancing. For example, if a particular warehouse of inventory is not counted year after year, the error will not work itself out. However, a discussion of noncounterbalancing errors will be left to future accounting courses.

LO5 Estimating Ending Inventory

A company must sometimes estimate its inventory balance. One example is when inventory is destroyed by a natural catastrophe. Another example is when a company prepares interim financial statements. In such cases, a company can estimate its ending inventory with the gross profit method.

The **gross profit method** of estimating inventory uses a company's gross profit percentage to estimate cost of goods sold and then ending inventory. To apply the method, a company first subtracts its normal gross profit from its sales to yield an estimate of its cost of goods sold. That estimate is then put into the cost of goods sold model to estimate ending inventory.

To illustrate, assume that Alsup Hardware is preparing interim financial statements at the end of its first quarter and needs to estimate cost of goods sold and ending inventory. Alsup has generated quarterly sales of $400,000. In past quarters, Alsup's gross profit percentage has averaged 45%. Assuming that this quarter is similar to prior quarters, Alsup can estimate that gross profit on current-quarter sales is $180,000.

Current-quarter sales (actual)	$400,000
Historical gross profit percentage	× 45%
Gross profit (estimated)	$180,000

Alsup can then estimate cost of goods sold for the period as $220,000.

Current-quarter sales (actual)	$400,000
Less: Gross profit (estimated)	180,000
Cost of goods sold (estimated)	$220,000

Now that Alsup has estimated cost of goods sold, it can calculate its ending inventory by plugging the cost of goods sold estimate into the cost of goods sold model. Based on past financial reports and purchase records, Alsup knows that it started the quarter with $200,000 in inventory and bought $90,000 of inventory during the quarter. This means that Alsup had $290,000 in inventory available for sale during the period. With $220,000 in estimated cost of goods sold, the cost of

Gross profit method A method of estimating inventory using a company's gross profit percentage to estimate cost of goods sold and then ending inventory.

goods sold model yields a $70,000 estimate for ending inventory.

Beginning inventory (actual)	$200,000
Add: Net purchases (actual)	90,000
Cost of goods available for sale (actual)	$290,000
Less: Cost of goods sold (estimated)	220,000
Ending inventory (estimated)	$ 70,000

IFRS

Under US GAAP, an LCM inventory adjustment cannot be reversed. Under international standards, an LCM adjustment can be reversed if the reason(s) for the adjustment no longer exist.

LO6 Lower-of-Cost-or-Market

The cost principle requires that inventory be recorded at its cost. However, because of the principle of conservatism, accounting rules require that inventory be reported on the balance sheet at its market value if the market value is lower than the inventory's cost. This is known as the **lower-of-cost-or-market (LCM) rule**.

The lower-of-cost-or-market rule is applied at the end of each accounting period by comparing inventory costs to market values. For purposes of our comparison, an inventory's market value is equal to the cost to replace the inventory. Companies have some discretion in how LCM is applied. For example, they can compare costs and market values of (1) inventories in total, (2) major groups of inventories, or (3) individual inventory items. When the cost is lower than the market value, nothing further is done. However, when the market value is lower than the cost, the company must adjust its inventory down to the lower market value.

To illustrate, suppose that Dryden Company provides the December 31 inventory information shown in Exhibit 7-8.

Lower-of-cost-or-market rule Requires inventory to be reported on the balance sheet at its market value if the market value is lower than the inventory's cost.

Exhibit 7-8 LCM Calculation for Dryden Company as of December 31

						Lower-of-Cost-or-Market Calculation		
Item	Units	Unit Cost	Unit Market	Total Cost	Total Market	Total	Two Groups	Individual Items
A	5	$ 40	$ 80	$ 200	$ 400			$ 200
B	8	$ 65	$ 50	520	400			400
Group 1				$ 720	$ 800		$ 720	
C	4	$100	$160	$ 400	$ 640			400
D	10	$ 30	$ 50	300	500			300
Group 2				$ 700	$1,140		700	
Total				$1,420	$1,940	$1,420	$1,420	$1,300

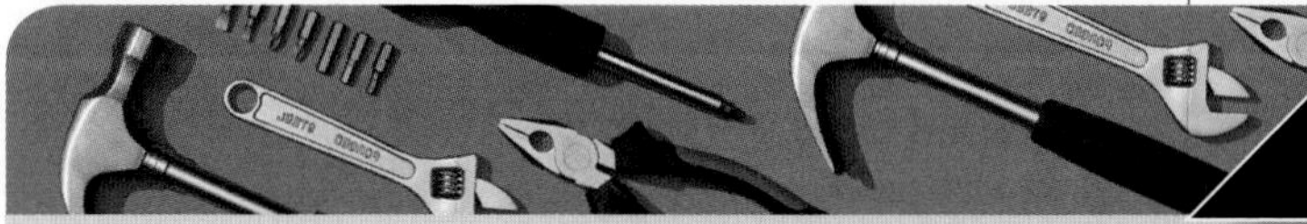

HOME DEPOT ANALYSIS

Look at the Merchandise Inventories paragraph of Home Depot's first note in Appendix C. Does the company follow the lower-of-cost-or-market rule?

Home Depot discloses that its inventory is reported at the lower-of-cost-or-market value. Cost is determined on a FIFO basis.

Any investor, creditor, or manager of a company should be interested in how well a company manages its inventory. A company manages its inventory by buying and selling efficiently and effectively.

Dryden has four types of inventory (A, B, C, and D) separated into two groups (1 and 2). Cost and market values are computed for each inventory type, each inventory group, and total inventory. The three right columns show the value that should be reported for inventory when applying LCM to total inventories, to the two groups of inventory, and to each individual inventory item.

When applied to total inventories, the total cost of $1,420 is lower than the total market value of $1,940. Therefore, the LCM value for total inventory is the cost of $1,420, and no adjustment to inventory is needed.

When applied to Groups 1 and 2, the $720 and $700 group costs are lower than than the respective group market values of $800 and $1,140. Therefore, the LCM value is $1,420, and no adjustment to inventory is needed.

When applied to individual items, an adjustment is needed. The comparison of costs and market values of each item yields an LCM value of $1,300. Since this is lower than the inventory's cost of $1,420, the inventory must be adjusted down to $1,300. This is accomplished with the following entry:

Dec. 31	Cost of Goods Sold	120	
	Inventory		120
	(To adjust inventory to market)		

Assets	=	Liabilities	+	Equity
−120				−120

The journal entry increases Cost of Goods Sold to reflect the loss in value of the inventory and decreases Inventory to adjust the account down to the $1,300 market value. As a result, both assets and equity decrease. Dryden's inventory is now ready to be reported on the balance sheet at its more conservative market value.

LO7 Evaluating a Company's Management of Inventory

Any investor, creditor, or manager of a company should be interested in how well a company manages its inventory. A company manages its inventory by buying and selling efficiently and effectively.

The following sections examine the effectiveness of **Target Corporation** in managing its inventory. The examination will require information from the company's balance sheet and income statement. The required information is found in Exhibit 7-9, excerpted from Target's 2010 annual report.

Exhibit 7-9 Account Balances from Target's 2010 Annual Report

Source	Accounts	2010	2009
Income Statement	Net sales	$65,786	$63,435
	Cost of sales	$45,725	$44,062
Balance Sheet	Inventory	$ 7,596	$ 7,179
	Total assets	$43,705	$44,533

Horizontal and Vertical Analyses

An easy and useful place to start an examination of inventory is with horizontal and vertical analyses. Recall from Chapter 2 that horizontal analysis calculates the dollar change in an account balance, defined as the current-year balance less the prior-year balance, and divides that change by the prior-year balance to yield the percentage change. Vertical analysis divides each account balance by a base account, yielding a percentage. The base account is total assets for balance sheet accounts and net sales or total revenues for income statement accounts. These calculations are summarized as follows:

Horizontal Analysis

$$\text{Dollar change in account balance} = \text{Current-year balance} - \text{Prior-year balance}$$

$$\text{Percentage change in account balance} = \frac{\text{Dollar change}}{\text{Prior-year balance}}$$

Vertical Analysis

$$\text{Percentage} = \frac{\text{Account Balance}}{\text{Total Assets}}\ (\textit{Balance Sheet}) \quad \text{or} \quad \frac{\text{Account Balance}}{\text{Net Sales or Revenue}}\ (\textit{Income Statement})$$

MAKING IT REAL

R. Gino Santa Maria/Shutterstock

Companies examine all aspects of their inventory management to find ways to increase their profits. Consider the case of SuperValu Inc., owner of Albertsons, Acme Markets, and Jewel-Osco stores. The company recently embarked on a rigorous training program designed to reduce the cost of bagging groceries.

Throughout its stores, the company uses more than 1.5 billion bags (plastic and paper) in a given year. At anywhere from 2 to 5 cents per bag, this expense adds up to a significant amount of money. To reduce bag use, employees are taught bagging techniques and are instructed to skip bagging of items with handles (for example, a gallon of milk) and to forgo double bagging. The company makes use of bagging quizzes during employee training and has developed the following slogan: "When you're done, add one."

The results have been positive. The company was averaging about 3 to 5 items per bag on annual sales of about 10 billion items. Since mid-2009, the company has saved approximately $4 to $6 million dollars annually by increasing items per bag by 5%. The company has then passed the savings onto its customers by lowering its prices on items such as bread.

Given **Target's** financial information in Exhibit 7-9, horizontal and vertical analyses of inventory and cost of sales result in the following:

	Horizontal Analysis	
	Change	*Percentage Change*
Inventory	7,596 − 7,179 = 417	$\frac{417}{7,179} = 5.8\%$
Cost of sales	45,725 − 44,062 = 1,663	$\frac{1,663}{44,062} = 3.8\%$

	Vertical Analysis	
	2010	*2009*
Inventory	$\frac{7,596}{43,705} = 17.4\%$	$\frac{7,179}{44,533} = 16.1\%$
Cost of sales	$\frac{45,725}{65,786} = 69.5\%$	$\frac{44,062}{63,435} = 69.5\%$

The calculations show a sound inventory position. Horizontal analysis of inventory shows a $417 million, or 5.8%, increase from 2009 to 2010. Vertical analysis indicates that inventories made up 16.1% of Target's total assets in 2009 and 17.4% of total assets in 2010. So, inventory is growing both in total and as a percentage of assets.

The analysis of cost of goods sold shows an increase of $1,663 million, which equals a 3.8% increase. Furthermore, vertical analysis indicates that cost of goods sold was 69.5% of sales in both 2009 and 2010. Thus, while cost of goods sold increased during the year, Target kept its cost of goods sold as a percentage of sales steady, which is a good sign.

For comparison purposes, the 2010 horizontal and vertical analyses of **Wal-Mart** are listed in Exhibit 7-10. While the horizontal analysis shows similar changes between the two companies, the vertical analysis shows a significant difference. Cost of goods sold as a percentage of sales is 69.5% for Target and 75.3% for Wal-Mart. Since a lower percentage means greater profits on sales, the comparison shows that Target outperformed Wal-Mart in 2010. This also is a good sign.

Exhibit 7-10 Target versus Wal-Mart Comparison

	Account	Horizontal Analysis	Vertical Analysis
Target	*Inventory*	5.8%	16.1%
	Cost of goods sold	3.8%	69.5%
Wal-Mart	*Inventory*	11.0%	20.1%
	Cost of goods sold	3.6%	75.3%

Inventory Turnover Ratio

While horizontal and vertical analyses are useful for generating information about inventory, a more direct way to assess a company's ability to sell its inventory is to calculate the inventory turnover ratio. The **inventory turnover ratio** compares the cost of goods sold during a period to the average inventory balance during that period. It is calculated as follows:

$$\text{Inventory Turnover Ratio} = \frac{\text{Cost of Goods Sold}}{\text{Average Inventory}}$$

Where average inventory is:

$$\frac{\text{Beginning Inventory} + \text{Ending Inventory}}{2}$$

Because this ratio compares the cost of all inventory sold to the average cost of inventory on hand, it indicates how many times a company is able to sell its inventory balance in a period. All other things being equal, a higher ratio indicates that the company sold more inventory while maintaining less inventory on hand. This means that the company generated more sales revenue while reducing the costs of stocking inventory on the shelves.

Inventory turnover ratio Compares cost of goods sold during a period to the average inventory balance during that period and measures the ability to sell inventory.

Days-in-inventory ratio Converts the inventory turnover ratio into a measure of days by dividing the turnover ratio into 365 days.

Target's 2010 inventory turnover ratio is calculated as follows:

$$\frac{45{,}725}{(7{,}596 + 7{,}179)/2} = 6.2$$

The 6.2 ratio indicates that Target's cost of goods sold for 2010 was 6.2 times its average inventory balance. For every dollar of inventory on its shelves, on average, Target was able to sell over $6.00 of inventory during the period.

Because the turnover ratio is sometimes difficult to interpret, it is often converted into the days-in-inventory ratio. The **days-in-inventory ratio** converts the inventory turnover ratio into a measure of days by dividing the turnover ratio into 365 days. Thus, the days-in-inventory ratio is calculated as follows:

$$\frac{365}{6.2} = 58.9$$

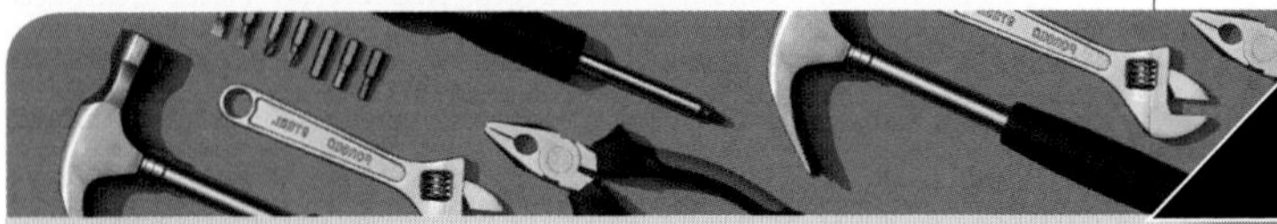

HOME DEPOT ANALYSIS

Using **Home Depot's** information in Appendix C, calculate and interpret (1) horizontal and vertical analyses of inventory and cost of goods sold, (2) inventory turnover ratio, and (3) days-in-inventory ratio.

(1) *Horizontal Analysis*

Inventory: ($10,625 − $10,188)/10,188 = 4.3%

Cost of Goods Sold: ($44,693 − $43,764)/43,764 = 2.1%

Vertical Analysis

Inventory: $10,625/$40,125 = 26.5%

Cost of Goods Sold: $44,693/$67,997 = 65.7%

The 4.3% and 2.1% horizontal analysis of inventory and cost of goods sold shows that Home Depot sold and stocked more inventory during this year compared to the previous year. The 26.5% vertical analysis of inventory shows that over a quarter of the company's assets are tied up in inventory. This seems reasonable, given that Home Depot is a "big box" retailer. The 65.7% vertical analysis of cost of goods sold indicates that inventory cost is a very large expense for the company. For the average dollar of sales, the cost of the inventory sold was about 66 cents.

(2) *Inventory Turnover Ratio*

$44,693/[($10,625 + $10,188)/2] = 4.3

(3) *Days-in-Inventory*

365/4.3 = 84.9 days

The 4.3 inventory turnover ratio indicates that Home Depot buys and sells its inventory about 4 times each year. The days in inventory ratio of 84.9 indicates that it takes the company almost three months to sell through its inventory.

When purchases are made in a periodic inventory system, they are recorded in a temporary account called Purchases. When sales are made, the resulting revenue is recorded, but not the cost of goods sold.

A ratio of 58.9 indicates that it takes **Target** about 59 days to sell as much inventory as it keeps on hand. Naturally, Target wants this ratio to be as low as possible. Its rival **Wal-Mart** generated a 40.1 ratio in 2010. This means it takes Target about 19 days longer than Wal-Mart to sell as much inventory as it has on hand.

LO8 Appendix—Periodic Inventory System

A periodic inventory system does not update the inventory and cost of goods sold accounts during the period. When purchases are made, they are recorded in a temporary account called Purchases. When sales are made, the resulting revenue is recorded, but not the cost of goods sold. As a result, companies that use a periodic system must calculate and update the inventory and the cost of goods sold accounts at the end of the period. The following sections demonstrate the recording of purchases and the determination of ending inventory and cost of goods sold under a periodic system.

Recording Inventory

A periodic system uses the following four temporary accounts to capture the cost of inventory purchases during a period. The **Purchases** account accumulates the cost of all purchases. The **Transportation-in** account accumulates the transportation costs of obtaining the inventory. Both of these increase the cost of inventory. The **Purchases Returns and Allowances** account accumulates the cost of all inventory returned to vendors as well as the cost reductions from vendor allowances. The **Purchase Discounts** account accumulates the cost reductions generated from vendor discounts granted for prompt payment. Both of these reduce the cost of inventory. Each of the four accounts is closed at the end of the period when the inventory and the cost of goods sold accounts are updated.

To illustrate the recording of inventory with these accounts, the example used in the chapter is repeated. Suppose that Snowy Owl Gifts purchases $20,000 of inventory on account on October 10. The purchase would be recorded as follows:

Oct. 10	Purchases	20,000	
	Accounts Payable		20,000
	(To record purchase of inventory)		

Assets	=	Liabilities	+	Equity
+20,000		+20,000		

Suppose further that Snowy Owl pays a third-party carrier $300 cash to transport the inventory to its warehouse. Snowy Owl would record the payment with the following entry:

Oct. 10	Transportation-in	300	
	Cash		300
	(To record transportation-in)		

Assets	=	Liabilities	+	Equity
+300				
−300				

Suppose further that on October 12 Snowy Owl is granted a $1,000 reduction in the cost of the inventory due to blemishes on the merchandise. Snowy Owl would reduce its payable to the vendor and record the allowance as follows:

Oct. 12	Accounts Payable	1,000	
	Purchase Returns and Allowances		1,000
	(To record purchase allowance granted by vendor)		

Assets	=	Liabilities	+	Equity
−1,000		−1,000		

Purchases An account used to accumulate the cost of all purchases.

Transportation-in An account that accumulates the transportation costs of obtaining the inventory.

Purchase Returns and Allowances An account that accumulates the cost of all inventory returned to vendors as well as the cost reductions from vendor allowances.

Purchase Discounts An account that accumulates the cost reductions generated from vendor discounts granted for prompt payments.

Finally, suppose that Snowy Owl pays its remaining $19,000 bill to the vendor on October 15, which qualifies Snowy Owl for a 1% discount. As a result, Snowy Owl would save $190 ($19,000 × 1%) and pay only $18,810. The entry to record payment would be as follows:

Oct. 15	Accounts Payable	19,000	
	Purchase Discounts		190
	Cash		18,810
	(To record payment)		

Assets	=	Liabilities	+	Equity
−190		−19,000		
−18,810				

The entry decreases Accounts Payable for the full $19,000 and decreases Cash for the $18,810 payment. The difference is an addition to Purchase Discounts.

Given the preceding activity, Snowy Owl's **net purchases** of inventory can be calculated as follows:

Purchases	$20,000
Add: Transportation-in	300
Less: Purchase returns and allowances	(1,000)
Purchase discounts	(190)
Net purchases	$19,110

This is the same cost of net purchases as calculated under the perpetual system discussed in the chapter. Whether using a periodic or perpetual system, the cost of net purchases is the same. It is just captured in different accounts.

Inventory Costing Methods

A periodic system does not update the Inventory and the Cost of Goods Sold accounts during the period. Thus, the balances in these accounts must be calculated at the end of the period. This is accomplished in the following three steps:

1. Count the inventory on hand at the end of the period.
2. Use an inventory costing method to assign a cost to the ending inventory.
3. Calculate cost of goods sold using the cost of goods sold model.

Net purchases The value of inventory purchased and transportation-in less purchase returns and allowances and purchase discounts.

To illustrate this process, the example used in the chapter is repeated. Suppose that during the month of September, Nell Farms experiences the following inventory purchases:

		Units	Unit Cost	Total
Sept. 1	Beginning inventory	40	$12	$480
Sept. 4	Purchase	60	$13	$780
Sept. 15	Purchase	30	$14	$420
Sept. 23	Purchase	45	$15	$675

At the end of the month, Nell counts 60 units on hand. Nell's cost of goods sold model for September is therefore as follows:

	Units	Cost
Beginning inventory	40	$ 480
Add: Net purchases	135	1,875
Cost of goods available for sale	175	$2,355
Less: Ending inventory	60	???
Cost of goods sold	115	???

To calculate the cost of the 60 units in ending inventory and therefore the cost of the 115 units sold, Nell must use one of the four inventory costing methods.

Specific Identification

Under the specific identification method, Nell determines the cost of ending inventory based on the actual cost of the units on hand. Suppose that Nell knows that the costs of the 60 units are five $13 units, twenty $14 units, and thirty-five $15 units. It can therefore calculate the cost of ending inventory as follows:

	Units	Unit Cost	Total Cost
Sept. 4 purchase	5	$13	$ 65
Sept. 15 purchase	20	$14	280
Sept. 23 purchase	35	$15	525
Ending inventory	60		$870

Plugging this cost of ending inventory into the cost of goods sold model yields Nell's cost of goods sold of $1,485.

	Units	Cost
Cost of goods available for sale	175	$2,355
− Ending inventory	60	870
= Cost of goods sold	115	$1,485

First-In, First-Out (FIFO)

Under the FIFO method, Nell assumes that the first units of inventory purchased are the first units sold. As a result, the costs of the last (most recent) purchases are assigned to ending inventory. It can therefore calculate the cost of ending inventory as follows:

	Units	Unit Cost	Total Cost
Sept. 23 purchase	45	$15	$675
Sept. 15 purchase	15	$14	210
Ending inventory	60		$885

The cost of all 45 units purchased on September 23 and 15 of the units purchased on September 15 are assigned to ending inventory, yielding a cost of $885. Plugging this into the cost of goods sold model yields Nell's cost of goods sold of $1,470.

	Units	Cost
Cost of goods available for sale	175	$2,355
− Ending inventory	60	885
= Cost of goods sold	115	$1,470

Last-In, First-Out (LIFO)

Under the LIFO method, Nell assumes that the last units of inventory purchased are the first units sold. As a result, the costs of the first purchases are assigned to ending inventory. Nell can therefore calculate the cost of ending inventory as follows:

	Units	Unit Cost	Total Cost
Beginning inventory	40	$12	$480
Sept. 4 purchase	20	$13	260
Ending inventory	60		$740

The cost of all 40 units of beginning inventory and 20 of the units purchased on September 4 are assigned to ending inventory, yielding a cost of $740. Plugging this into the cost of goods sold model yields Nell's cost of goods sold of $1,615.

	Units	Cost
Cost of goods available for sale	175	$2,355
− Ending inventory	60	740
= Cost of goods sold	115	$1,615

Weighted Average

Under the weighted average method, Nell assumes that the cost of each unit in ending inventory is the average cost of all units available for sale during the period. The weighted average cost per unit is calculated as follows:

$$\text{Weighted Average Unit Cost} = \frac{\text{Cost of Goods Available for Sale}}{\text{Units Available for Sale}}$$

Note here that under a periodic system, the average unit cost is based on all the inventory available to be sold during the period. As a result, the average unit cost does not change during the period. Therefore, it is called a weighted average instead of a moving average (as under the perpetual system).

Nell's weighted average cost per unit, rounded to the nearest cent, is calculated as follows:

$$\frac{\$2{,}355}{175} = \$13.46$$

Nell can therefore calculate the cost of ending inventory as follows, rounded to the nearest dollar:

	Units	Unit Cost	Total Cost
Ending inventory	60	$13.46	$808

Plugging this into the cost of goods sold model yields Nell's cost of goods sold of $1,547.

	Units	Cost
Cost of goods available for sale	175	$2,355
− Ending inventory	60	808
= Cost of goods sold	115	$1,547

STUDY TOOLS 7

Chapter review card

- Learning Objective and Key Concept Reviews
- Key Definitions and Formulas

Online (Located at www.cengagebrain.com)

- Flash Cards and Crossword Puzzles
- Games and Quizzes
- E-Lectures
- Homework Assignments (as directed by your instructor)

CONCEPT QUESTIONS

1. (LO1) On which financial statement would inventory be listed as a line item? How would it be classified on that financial statement?
2. (LO1) When inventory is purchased, at what value is it recorded?
3. (LO1) What accounts are used to record the purchase of inventory under perpetual and periodic inventory systems? Which method results in the inventory account being updated continually?
4. (LO1) When inventory is sold, into what expense account is it transferred?
5. (LO2) Which inventory costing method(s) is based on actual costs of the inventory sold and which method(s) is based on an assumption of which inventory is sold?
6. (LO2) For each inventory costing method—LIFO, FIFO, and Moving Average—which costs are presumed to be in ending inventory? Which costs are presumed to be in cost of goods sold?
7. (LO3) Why might a company choose to use the LIFO cost flow assumption? The FIFO assumption? The Moving Average assumption?
8. (LO3) What is the LIFO reserve? What can be learned from it?
9. (LO4) If ending inventory is incorrectly overstated, how will the current year's net income be affected? Current year retained earnings? Next year's net income?
10. (LO4) Explain what is meant by a counterbalancing inventory error.
11. (LO5) Explain how the gross profit method of estimating inventory works and why a company would use it.
12. (LO6) Under what circumstances should a company adjust the carrying value of its inventory on its balance sheet to the inventory's market value?
13. (LO7) List four common inventory analysis techniques (including ratios) that can be used to evaluate a company's inventory management.
14. (LO8) Under a periodic inventory system, what four accounts are used to record the acquisition of inventory?
15. (LO8) Under a periodic inventory system, what are the three steps in determining cost of goods sold for a period?

MULTIPLE CHOICE

1. (LO1) The cost of inventory under a perpetual system does not include which of the following?
   a. Inventory price
   b. Freight charges
   c. Sales commissions
   d. Sales taxes on inventory purchase

2. (LO1) The Cost of Goods Sold account represents the cost of inventory:
   a. remaining in a company's inventory account at year end and classified as ending inventory.
   b. purchased during the year plus inventory sold.
   c. sold during the year.
   d. available for sale at the beginning of the year.
3. (LO1) When inventory is bought under a perpetual inventory system, what happens to the Inventory and Cost of Goods Sold accounts, respectively?
   a. No change, Increase
   b. Increase, No change
   c. Increase, Increase
   d. Decrease, No change
4. (LO1) When an inventory item is sold under a perpetual inventory system:
   a. the Inventory account is not affected.
   b. inventory is decreased and Cost of Goods Sold is increased.
   c. inventory is increased and Cost of Goods Sold is increased.
   d. neither Inventory nor Cost of Goods Sold is affected until the end of the current period.
5. (LO2) A company purchases a unit of inventory for $1.50 and then later purchases a second for $2.00. The company then sells one unit for $4.50. After the sale, the company purchases an additional unit for $2.50. The company uses a perpetual inventory system. Given these facts, which of the following is true?
   a. Cost of Goods Sold under FIFO is $1.50
   b. Ending Inventory under LIFO is $4.00
   c. Cost of Goods Sold under Moving Average is $1.75
   d. All of the above are true
6. (LO2) A company purchases a unit of inventory for $1.50, another for $2.00 and then a third for $2.50. The company then sells one unit for $4.50. The company uses a perpetual inventory system. Given these facts, which of the following is true?
   a. Ending Inventory under FIFO is $1.50
   b. Cost of Goods Sold under LIFO is $2.50
   c. Cost of Goods Sold under Moving Average is $4.50
   d. Ending Inventory under LIFO is $4.50
7. (LO2) Which of the following inventory costing methods is not based on an assumption about the cost of inventory sold?
   a. FIFO
   b. LIFO
   c. Specific Identification
   d. Moving Average
8. (LO3) In a period of rising prices, under which inventory valuation method would ending inventory have the highest assigned value?
   a. FIFO
   b. LIFO
   c. Moving average
   d. All methods will result in the same value
9. (LO3) Which inventory costing method generally results in less current taxes paid by the company?
   a. LIFO
   b. FIFO
   c. Moving Average
   d. All methods result in the same taxes paid
10. (LO3) Which inventory costing method should a grocer use?
    a. LIFO
    b. FIFO
    c. Moving Average
    d. A grocer can use any of the inventory costing methods
11. (LO3) A company that uses the FIFO costing method reports cost of goods sold for the year of $10,000. Had it used the LIFO method, cost of goods sold would have been $12,000. How much in taxes could the company have deferred in the current year if it had used the LIFO method? Assume a 30% tax rate.
    a. $2,000
    b. $600
    c. $1,400
    d. Cannot tell from the given information
12. (LO4) A company overstates its ending inventory by $2,000. Which of the following is true concerning the effect of this error on cost of goods sold in the year of the error?
    a. Cost of goods sold will be unaffected
    b. Cost of goods sold will be understated
    c. Cost of goods sold will be overstated
    d. Cannot tell from given information
13. (LO4) A company understates its ending inventory by $2,000. Which of the following is true concerning the effect of this error on cost of goods sold in the year after the error (assuming no other errors)?
    a. Cost of goods sold will be unaffected
    b. Cost of goods sold will be understated
    c. Cost of goods sold will be overstated
    d. Cannot tell from given information
14. (LO4) A counterbalancing inventory error will result in:
    a. an overstatement of income.
    b. an understatement of income.
    c. both an overstatement and understatement of annual income that offset each other such that total net income over the two years is correct.
    d. cannot tell from given information.
15. (LO5) Suppose that Lee Enterprises usually generates a 25% gross profit on sales. If Lee's annual sales are $100,000, what is Lee's estimated cost of goods sold using the gross profit method?
    a. $0
    b. $25,000
    c. $75,000
    d. $100,000

16. (LO5) Suppose that Lee Enterprises usually generates a 40% gross profit on sales. If Lee's annual sales are $130,000 and cost of goods available for sale is $90,000, what is Lee's estimated ending inventory using the gross profit method?
    a. $38,000
    b. $90,000
    c. $78,000
    d. $12,000
17. (LO6) What principle or assumption results in the use of lower-of-cost-or-market?
    a. Historical cost
    b. Conservatism
    c. Going concern
    d. Materiality
18. (LO6) Under the lower-of-cost-or-market rule, an inventory item with a selling price of $6.00, a historical cost of $2.50, and a replacement cost of $3.50 would be reported at:
    a. $6.00.
    b. $3.50.
    c. $2.50.
    d. cannot tell from given information.
19. (LO7) A horizontal analysis of Cost of Goods Sold yields a percentage of 14.0%. Given that change, which of the following would cause the greatest concern for the company?
    a. Sales increased 20.1%
    b. Operating Expenses increased 14.2%
    c. Sales decreased 10.8%
    d. Inventory increased 12.4%
20. (LO7) CG Films generates Cost of Goods Sold of $135,000 for the year. Inventory at the beginning and ending of the year was $40,000 and $46,000, respectively. Calculate CG's inventory turnover ratio.
    a. 3.1
    b. 3.4
    c. 116.2
    d. 0.3
21. (LO7) Horizontal analysis of inventory:
    a. calculates inventory as a percentage of total assets.
    b. calculates cost of goods sold as a percentage of revenues.
    c. highlights the change in inventory as a percentage of the prior year's inventory balance.
    d. both "a" and "b" are correct.
22. (LO7) Vertical analysis of inventory:
    a. calculates inventory as a percentage of total assets.
    b. calculates cost of goods sold as a percentage of revenues.
    c. highlights the change in inventory as a percentage of the prior year's inventory balance.
    d. both "a" and "b" are correct.
23. (LO8) If a company uses a periodic inventory system and returns an inventory item to a vendor, the company would record the return as:
    a. a decrease to the Inventory account.
    b. an increase to the Cost of Goods Sold account.
    c. an increase to the Purchase Returns and Allowances account.
    d. an increase to the Purchase Discounts account.
24. (LO8) Which of the following is not a part of the process to calculate costs of goods sold under a periodic inventory system?
    a. Count the ending inventory on hand at the end of the period
    b. Assign a cost to the ending inventory using an inventory costing method
    c. Use the cost of goods sold model to calculate cost of goods sold
    d. Each of the above is part of the process

BRIEF EXERCISES

1. Determining Inventory Costs LO1

Matthews Electronics purchased 100 laptop computers from a vendor for $75,000. The vendor gave Mathews a $1,500 discount because of scratches on the screens of some of the laptops. The cost to ship the computers was $500.

Required
Determine Matthews' cost of inventory.

2. Recording Inventory Purchases LO1

On March 20, Shelton Fireworks purchases on account $12,000 of fireworks with a list price of $13,000. Shelton pays the vendor on March 30, which qualifies Shelton for a 2% discount. Shelton uses a perpetual inventory system.

Required
Record all entries associated with Shelton's purchase of the inventory.

3. Reporting Inventory LO1

Asheton Supplies Inc. purchases 1,000 fax machines from its main supplier for $100,000 cash. Asheton plans to resell 900 of them to customers for use in homes and offices. The additional fax machines will be used in Asheton's offices.

Required
Prepare the entry that Asheton would make to record the purchase. Explain your reasoning for the account(s) you use to record the new fax machines.

4. Inventory Costing Methods LO2

A company with no inventory buys the following three inventory items:

Date	Item	Cost
January 7	A	$6
January 9	B	$7
January 12	C	$8

On January 10, the company sells one item for $10. On January 15, the company sells a second item $10. The company uses a perpetual inventory system.

Required
Calculate the company's cost of goods sold under the a) FIFO, b) LIFO, and c) moving average inventory costing methods.

5. **Effects of Inventory Methods** LO3
Assume that you are an accountant at a local retailer and your boss asks you to explain the financial statement impact of inventory costing methods. In particular, she is interested in whether the company should use the FIFO or LIFO method. She would like to use the method that results in the highest net income, the highest inventory balance, and the lowest taxes.

Required
Assuming that the company is experiencing rising prices, explain the effects of using the LIFO and FIFO methods on income, inventory, and taxes. Can your boss get all that she wants?

6. **LIFO Reserve** LO3
A company's ending inventory balance is $140,000 using the LIFO method. If the company used the FIFO method, the balance would have been $172,000. If the company used the Moving Average method, the balance would have been $158,000. The company uses a perpetual inventory system and is subject to a 35% corporate tax rate.

Required
Calculate a) the company's LIFO Reserve and b) the total taxes deferred over time by using the LIFO method.

7. **Inventory Errors** LO4
Suppose that a company's preliminary financial statements show net income of $230,000 and ending inventory of $39,500. Before finalizing the financial statements, management discovers that ending inventory should be $42,500.

Required
Describe the error in the inventory account (for example, inventory was overstated by $1,000) and calculate the company's correct net income for the year.

8. **Estimating Inventory** LO5
Johnson Enterprises uses the gross profit method to estimate ending inventory. Current-year sales and cost of inventory available for sale were $700,000 and $540,000, respectively. Johnson's historical gross profit percentage is 40%.

Required
Estimate Johnson's ending inventory.

9. **Applying Lower-of-Cost-or-Market** LO6
Alpaca Enterprises Inc. has an inventory balance of $156,000. At year end, the market value of Alpaca's inventory has fallen to $151,500.

Required
Prepare the journal entry that Alpaca should make at year end regarding its inventory balance and identify the accounting principle that makes the entry necessary.

10. **Analyzing Inventory** LO7
A company's cost of goods sold for the year was $97,500. Ending inventory was $12,000 and $13,500 in the current and prior years, respectively.

Required
Calculate the company's inventory turnover ratio. If the company's ratio was 6.2 in the prior year, has the company become more or less efficient in selling its inventory?

11. **Appendix—Recording Inventory Purchases** LO8
On March 20, Shelton Fireworks purchases on account $10,000 of fireworks. On March 25, Shelton returns $1,000 of the merchandise to the vendor. Shelton then pays the remaining bill, less a 3% discount for early payment, on March 30.

Required
Record all entries associated with the purchase of the inventory assuming that Shelton uses a periodic inventory system.

12. **Appendix—Inventory Costing Methods** LO8
A company with no inventory purchases the following three inventory items:

Date	Item	Cost
January 7	A	$6
January 9	B	$7
January 12	C	$8

On January 15, the company sells two items for $10 each. The company uses a periodic inventory system.

Required
Calculate the company's cost of goods sold under the a) FIFO, b) LIFO, and c) weighted average inventory costing methods. How would your answers change if one item was sold on January 10 while the second was sold on January 15?

EXERCISES

13. Determine Inventory Costs LO1

Mary Cosmetics sells specialty lipstick for a retail price of $12.25 each. Mary purchases each tube for $5.00 and pays the following additional amounts: $1.50 per tube in freight charges, $0.40 per tube in taxes, and $2 per tube in commissions to employees for sales.

Required

Compute the cost of each tube of lipstick.

14. Record Inventory Purchases LO1

Heston Company purchases inventory with a list price of $7,000 for $6,300 on account. Heston pays a transportation company $200 to deliver the inventory. Upon receipt, Heston notices some defects, contacts the vendor, and receives a $500 allowance. Heston pays the vendor three days later, which qualifies Heston for a 2% discount. Heston uses a perpetual inventory system.

Required

Prepare all journal entries Heston would make to record the preceding activity and calculate Heston's net purchases.

15. Recording Purchases and Sales of Inventory LO1, 2

Lowder Company purchased 275 units of inventory on account for $5,775. Due to early payment, Lowder received a discount and paid only $5,225. Lowder then sold 150 units for cash at $55 each, purchased an additional 65 units for cash at a cost of $1,430, and then sold 100 more units for cash at $55 each. Lowder uses a perpetual inventory system.

Required

a. Prepare all journal entries to record Lowder's purchases and sales assuming the FIFO inventory costing method.
b. Which journal entries would be different if Lowder used the LIFO inventory costing method? How would they be different?

16. Inventory Costing Methods LO2

Avant Corporation's November inventory activity is as follows. Avant uses a perpetual inventory system.

Date	Transaction	Units	Unit Cost	Total Cost
11/1	Beginning inventory	32	$55	$1,760
11/7	Purchase	45	$60	$2,700
11/9	Sale	50		
11/14	Purchase	52	$65	$3,380
11/30	Sale	61		

Required

Compute the ending inventory and cost of goods sold under the FIFO, LIFO, and moving average costing methods. Round average unit costs to the nearest cent and cost of goods sold and inventory values to the nearest dollar.

17. Inventory Costing Methods LO2

Hahn Hardware provides the following information relating to its June inventory activity. Hahn uses a perpetual inventory system.

Date	Transaction	Units	Unit Cost	Total Cost
June 1	Inventory	13	$ 8.00	$104.00
June 7	Purchase	22	$ 9.50	$209.00
June 12	Sale	20		
June 18	Purchase	10	$10.25	$102.50
June 20	Sale	14		
June 26	Purchase	16	$11.00	$176.00
June 30	Sale	15		

Required

a. Put Hahn's given information into a cost of goods sold model. What is unknown?
b. Compute the ending inventory and cost of goods sold using the FIFO, LIFO, and moving average costing methods. Round dollar amounts to the nearest penny.
c. Calculate the sum of the ending inventory and cost of goods sold for each method. What do you notice about the answer for each method?

18. Inventory Costing Methods LO2, 8

Harrison, Charles & Company Inc. sells flower planters for $7 each. On its first day of business in January, the company purchased 2,000 planters for $3 each. The company sold 300 units during the first month of operations and sold an additional 1,300 units the next month. To prevent inventory stock-outs during summertime, the company bought an additional 700 units for $4.50 each in May. The company sold 850 units from May through December. The company uses a perpetual inventory system and the FIFO inventory costing method.

Required

a. Compute Harrison, Charles & Company's ending inventory balance at the end of the year and its cost of goods sold balance for the year.
b. Would those balances be different if the company had used the FIFO costing method under a periodic inventory system?

19. Choosing an Inventory Costing Method LO3

LAN Corporation uses the LIFO inventory costing method to account for its inventory. In the most recent year, LAN had net sales of $4,000, cost of goods sold of $1,685, and operating expenses of $1,750. LAN is subject to a tax rate of 30%. Had LAN used the FIFO inventory costing method, its cost of goods sold for the year would have been $1,495.

Required

a. Prepare comparative income statements under LIFO and FIFO and identify the amount of taxes that LAN deferred in the current year by using LIFO rather than FIFO.

b. Explain why the term "tax deferral" is used in association with inventory costing methods rather than the term "tax savings."

20. Inventory Errors LO4

Goodwin Grocery reported the following financial facts for 2011 and 2012:

	2011	2012
Beginning inventory	$ 20,000	$ 30,000
Cost of goods purchased	150,000	175,000
Cost of goods available for sale	$170,000	$205,000
Ending inventory	30,000	35,000
Cost of goods sold	$140,000	$170,000

Goodwin made two accounting errors during the years:
1. 2011 ending inventory was understated by $3,000.
2. 2012 ending inventory was overstated by $4,000.

Required
Compute Goodwin's correct cost of goods sold for each year.

21. Inventory Errors LO4

Apollo Company reported the following financial information for the years 2011 and 2012. At the end of 2011, $1,500 of inventory that was in transit and owned by Apollo was included in purchases but not counted in ending inventory. The inventory was received in 2012 and was ultimately sold during 2012.

	2011	2012
Beginning inventory	$13,000	$11,500
Purchases	16,000	17,000
Cost of goods available for sale	$29,000	$28,500
Ending inventory	11,500	12,500
Cost of goods sold	$17,500	$16,000

Required
a. Identify whether Apollo made an error in the accounting for its inventory. Specifically, was Apollo in error by including the inventory in transit in its 2011 purchases or by excluding it from its 2011 ending inventory?
b. If Apollo made an error, prepare corrected cost of goods sold models for 2011 and 2012. Use the models to demonstrate why some inventory errors are said to be counterbalancing.

22. Inventory Errors LO4

FMA Company reported the following income statement data:

	2011	2012
Sales	$210,000	$250,000
Beginning inventory	32,000	40,000
Cost of goods available for sale	205,000	242,000
Ending inventory	40,000	52,000
Cost of goods sold	165,000	190,000
Gross profit	45,000	60,000

Inventory balances at January 1, 2011, and December 31, 2012, are correct. However, the ending inventory at December 31, 2011, is overstated by $5,000.

Required
Prepare corrected data for 2011 and 2012, identify all accounts that were affected by the error and whether they were overstated or understated, and calculate the cumulative two-year effect of the inventory error on gross profit.

23. Estimating Inventory LO5

Clayburn Enterprises reported the following information for the current year:

Sales	$800,000
Beginning inventory	25,000
Purchases	502,000
Gross profit percentage	40%

Required
Using the gross profit method, estimate Clayburn's cost of goods sold for the year and the ending inventory at year end. Explain why a company might need to estimate its ending inventory.

24. Estimating Inventory and Cost of Goods Sold LO5

Marshall Inc. experiences a fire in its warehouse at the end of the year, which destroys its entire inventory. Marshall's records show that it started the year with $35,000 of inventory and purchased $150,000 during the year. It also shows sales of $310,000 for the year. Normally, Marshall's experiences a 55% gross profit percentage on sales.

Required
Use the gross profit method to estimate Marshall's cost of goods sold and ending inventory.

25. Applying Lower-of-Cost-or-Market LO6

Kay Mart Company is preparing financial statements and provides the following information about several of its major inventory items at year end:

Item	Quantity on Hand	Unit Cost When Acquired	Replacement Cost (Market Value) as of December 31
R	25	$15	$19
S	60	$22	$20
T	34	$30	$33
U	50	$10	$11
V	13	$50	$55

Required
If Kay Mart uses the lower-of-cost-or-market rule (LCM), what should it report as the balance of inventory if (1) one market value is computed for all inventories or (2) a market value is computed for each inventory type?

26. Applying Lower-of-Cost-or-Market LO6

Azalea Garden Center provides the following information about its inventory:

Group	Item	Units	Unit Cost	Unit Market
1	A	5	$15	$13
1	B	14	$10	$11
2	C	8	$ 5	$ 7
2	D	15	$12	$11

Required

a. If Azalea uses the lower-of-cost-or-market rule, what should it report as the balance of inventory if (1) one market value is computed for all inventories, (2) market value is computed by group, and (3) market value is computed for each inventory type?
b. Prepare any journal entries necessary based on your answers in part (a).

27. Accounting Terms LO1, 2, 3, 4, 5, 6

The following is a list of terms and definitions associated with inventory:

1. Perpetual inventory system
2. Periodic inventory system
3. LIFO costing method
4. FIFO costing method
5. Tax deferral
6. LIFO reserve
7. Counter-balancing error
8. Specific identification costing method
9. Lower-of-cost-or-market rule
10. Gross profit method

a. Updates the inventory account only at the end of an accounting period.
b. Calculates the cost of goods sold based on the assumption that the first unit of inventory available for sale is the first unit sold.
c. Determines the cost of goods sold based on the actual cost of each inventory item sold.
d. Updates the inventory account each time inventory is bought or sold.
e. A method of estimating inventory using a company's gross profit percentage.
f. Calculates the cost of goods sold based on the assumption that the last unit of inventory available for sale is the first one sold.
g. A temporary delay in the payment of income taxes.
h. The difference between the LIFO inventory reported on the balance sheet and what inventory would be if reported on a FIFO basis.
i. Requires inventory to be reported at its market value if market value is lower than the inventory's cost.
j. An error whose effect on net income is corrected in the period after the error.

Required

Match each term with the appropriate definition.

28. Analyzing Inventory LO7

Available information from Panosian Company for the years 2012 and 2011 is as follows:

	2012	2011
Inventory	$105,000	$ 85,000
Other assets	385,000	315,000
Cost of goods sold	76,000	55,000
Sales	129,000	80,000
Retained earnings	135,000	100,000
Long term liabilities	120,000	135,000

Required

Prepare a horizontal analysis of Panosian Company's balances. Round percentages to one decimal point (i.e., 4.8%). Can you make a general conclusion about the direction of the company? How?

29. Analyzing Inventory LO7

During the current year, Norlander Inc. implemented an inventory management system that it believes will result in greater efficiencies and profits. Norlander's CEO was therefore disappointed when he saw the following condensed income statement showing no increase in net income:

	2012	2011
Sales	$650,000	$775,000
Cost of goods sold	372,500	451,800
Operating expenses	232,500	278,200
Net income	45,000	45,000

Required

Using horizontal and vertical analyses, provide reasoning to the CEO that the inventory management system was effective. Round percentages to one decimal point (i.e., 4.8%).

30. Analyzing Inventory LO7

The following information is provided for three different companies: A, B, and C:

in millions	A	B	C
Beginning inventory	$ 569	$ 774	$ 989
Ending inventory	423	214	356
Cost of goods sold	1,376	1,232	1,771
Sales	2,232	1,836	3,025

Required

Calculate the inventory turnover ratio and days-in-inventory ratio for each company. How do the companies compare?

31. Analyzing Inventory LO7

Comparative income statements for Berg Company are given as follows:

Berg Company Comparative Income Statements For the Years Ending December 31		
	2012	2011
Net sales	$812,000	$812,000
Cost of goods sold	649,600	664,364
Gross profit	$162,400	$147,636
Operating expenses	84,448	79,724
Net income	$ 77,952	$ 67,912

Required

Prepare horizontal and vertical analyses of Berg's income statement data and comment on the current status of the company. Round percentages to one decimal point (i.e., 4.8%)

32. Appendix—Inventory Purchases LO8

Consider the following separate situations:

	William's Widgets	Sarah's Sofas	Clay's Cars
Beginning inventory	$4,000	$2,350	$ (e)
Purchases (gross)	4,230	(c)	7,340
Purchase returns	470	800	550
Purchase discounts	(a)	458	310
Transportation-in	150	500	420
Cost of goods available for sale	(b)	7,320	8,790
Ending inventory	1,890	1,750	(f)
Cost of goods sold	5,220	(d)	7,590

Required

Compute the missing amounts.

33. Appendix—Inventory Costing Methods (Periodic System) LO8

Hahn Hardware provides the following information relating to its June inventory. Hahn uses a periodic inventory system and sold 49 units during the month.

Date	Transaction	Units	Unit Cost	Total Cost
June 1	Inventory	13	$ 8.00	$104.00
June 7	Purchase	22	$ 9.50	$209.00
June 18	Purchase	10	$10.25	$102.50
June 26	Purchase	16	$11.00	$176.00
	Totals	61		$591.50

Required

a. Put Hahn's given information into a cost of goods sold model. What is unknown?
b. Compute the ending inventory and cost of goods sold using the FIFO, LIFO, and weighted average costing methods.
c. Calculate the sum of the ending inventory and cost of goods sold for each method. What do you notice about the answer for each method?

34. Appendix—Inventory Costing Methods LO8

Avant Corporation's November inventory activity follows. Avant uses a periodic inventory system.

Date	Transaction	Units	Unit Cost	Total Cost
11/1	Beginning inventory	32	$55	$1,760
11/7	Purchase	45	$60	$2,700
11/14	Purchase	52	$65	$3,380
11/30	Ending inventory	18		

Required

a. Compute the ending inventory and cost of goods sold under the FIFO, LIFO, and weighted average costing assumptions. For the weighted average method, round the unit average to the nearest penny and the cost of goods sold and ending inventory values to the nearest dollar.
b. Which costing assumption gives the highest ending inventory? Highest cost of goods sold? Why?
c. Explain why the average item cost is not $60 under the weighted average costing assumption.

35. Appendix—Recording and Reporting Inventory LO8

Lowder Company purchased 275 units of inventory on account for $5,775. Due to some defects in the merchandise, Lowder received a $2 per unit allowance and paid only $5,225. Lowder then sold 150 units for cash at $55 each, purchased an additional 65 units for cash at a cost of $1,430, and then sold 100 more units for cash at $55 each. Lowder uses a periodic inventory system.

Required

a. Prepare all journal entries to record Lowder's purchases of inventory.
b. Compute Lowder's cost of goods sold and ending inventory under the FIFO, LIFO, and weighted average inventory costing methods. For the weighted average method, round all values to the nearest cent.

PROBLEMS

36. Effects of Inventory Costing Methods on Income LO2, 3

Martin Merchandising has hired you to examine whether the company should use the LIFO or FIFO inventory costing method. The company uses a perpetual inventory system and has supplied the following information for the month:

Beginning inventory, 2,000 units at $40	$ 80,000
Purchases on June 4, 12,000 units at $45	540,000
Sales on June 18, 10,500 units at $77	808,500
Operating expenses (excluding taxes)	148,000
Company tax rate	35%

Required

Prepare multi-step income statements under the LIFO and FIFO costing methods. Explain to Martin the advantages and disadvantages of using each inventory costing method. Use the income statements to support your explanation.

37. Analyzing Different Inventory Costing Methods LO2, 7

Farmville Tools sells shovels nationwide to farmers. For March, Farmville had beginning inventory of 270 shovels with a per-shovel cost of $15. During March, Farmville made the following purchases of additional shovels.

March 8	50 @ $16.25	March 22	115 @ $ 18.00
March 13	130 @ $17.50	March 29	60 @ $ 18.50

Farmville uses a perpetual inventory system. During March, 525 shovels were sold on the following dates:

March 10	100	March 21	175
March 17	120	March 30	130

Required

a. Determine the appropriate balance in ending inventory and cost of goods sold under each of the inventory cost flow assumptions (LIFO, FIFO, and moving average). Round all values to the nearest penny.
b. Compute the inventory turnover and days-in-inventory ratios under each inventory costing method.
c. Which method yields ratios that show the most effective turnover of inventory? Are the company's inventory sales different depending on the costing method chosen? If not, why are the ratios different?

38. Recording Inventory Activity LO1, 2, 6

Campbell Candy Company starts the month of January with 40 boxes of Tiger Bars costing $20 each. The following transactions occurred during the month:

Jan. 2	Purchased 15 additional boxes for $22 each. Paid with cash.
Jan. 4	Paid freight costs of $30 on January 2 purchase.
Jan. 10	Sold 45 boxes for $40 each.
Jan. 27	Purchased 10 additional boxes on account for $23 each.

Campbell uses a perpetual inventory system and the FIFO inventory costing method.

Required

a. Prepare all necessary journal entries related to Campbell's inventory activity.
b. Suppose that the inventory has a replacement value of $375 at the end of the month. What entry, if any, is required?

39. Analyzing Inventory LO7

The following is comparative financial data for JK Martin Company and Stratton Company:

	JK Martin Company		Stratton Company	
	2012	2011	2012	2011
Net sales	$2,000,000		$550,000	
Cost of goods sold	1,100,000		240,000	
Operating expenses	305,000		75,000	
Income tax expense	52,000		6,500	
Cash	85,070	$82,508	16,100	$15,777
Inventory	250,000	225,000	70,000	65,600
Equipment	525,000	500,000	140,000	125,000
Current liabilities	65,000	75,000	35,000	30,000
Long-term liabilities	109,000	88,000	29,000	24,800
Common stock, $10 par	490,000	490,000	115,000	115,000
Retained earnings	173,000	147,520	40,756	30,289

Required

a. Prepare a vertical analysis of the 2012 income data. Round percentages to one decimal point (i.e., 4.8%). Is one company more profitable than the other?
b. Prepare a horizontal analysis of all accounts. Round percentages to one decimal point (i.e., 4.8%). What does this analysis show?
c. Compute the inventory turnover and days-in-inventory ratios for 2012. Do these ratios change your conclusions about these companies?

40. Appendix—Analyzing Different Inventory Costing Methods LO7, 8

Farmville Tools sells shovels nationwide to farmers. For March, Farmville had beginning inventory of 270 shovels with a per-shovel cost of $15. During March, Farmville made the following purchases of additional shovels.

March 8	50 @ $16.25	March 22	115 @ $ 18.00
March 13	130 @ $17.50	March 29	60 @ $18.50

Farmville uses a periodic inventory system. During March, 525 shovels were sold on the following dates:

March 10	100	March 21	175
March 17	120	March 30	130

Required

a. Determine ending inventory and cost of goods sold under each of the inventory cost flow assumptions (LIFO, FIFO, and weighted average).
b. Compute the inventory turnover and days-in-inventory ratios under each inventory costing method.
c. Which method yields ratios that show the most effective turnover of inventory? Are the company's inventory sales different depending on the costing method chosen? If not, why are the ratios different?

41. Appendix—Recording Inventory Activity LO8

Campbell Candy Company starts the month of January with 40 boxes of Tiger Bars costing $20 each. The following transactions occurred during the month:

Jan. 2	Purchased 15 additional boxes for $22 each. Paid with cash.
Jan. 4	Paid freight costs of $30 on January 2 purchase.
Jan. 10	Sold 45 boxes for $40 each.
Jan. 27	Purchased 10 additional boxes on account for $23 each.

Campbell uses a periodic inventory system and the FIFO inventory costing method.

Required

Prepare all necessary journal entries related to Campbell's inventory activity. Calculate the cost of goods sold and the ending inventory under the FIFO, LIFO, and weighted average costing methods. Round all values to the nearest penny.

CASES

42. Research and Analysis LO1, 3, 6, 7

Access the 2010 annual report for **Safeway Inc.** by clicking on the *Investors* and *Financial Reports* links at www.safeway.com.

Required

a. Examine the company's income statement and balance sheet and conduct horizontal and vertical analyses of the company's cost of goods sold and inventory balances. Round percentages to one decimal point (i.e., 4.8%).
b. Examine the company's merchandise inventories note to its financial statements. What inventory costing method(s) does the company use to account for its inventory? How often does the company take a physical count of its inventory? Does the company follow the lower-of-cost-or-market rule?
c. Using the LIFO reserve disclosed on the balance sheet and assuming a 35% marginal income tax rate, determine how much in taxes the company has deferred at the end of 2010.
d. Calculate the inventory turnover and days-in-inventory ratios for 2010.
e. Based on your answers above, write a paragraph explaining your opinion of Safeway's inventory position. Use your answers as supporting facts.

43. Research and Analysis LO3, 4, 5, 7

Access the 2010 annual report of **American Eagle Outfitters** by clicking on the *About AEO Inc., AE Investment Info,* and *Historical Annual Reports* links at www.ae.com. Also, access the 2010 annual report of **Gap Inc.** by clicking on the *Investors, Financial Information,* and *Annual Reports & Proxy* links at www.gapinc.com.

Required

a. Conduct horizontal and vertical analyses of sales, cost of goods sold, gross profit, inventory, and total assets for each company.
b. Compute the inventory turnover and days-in-inventory ratios for each company.
c. Compare each company's management of inventory. Is one company better than the other?
d. Look in the notes to the financial statements. Do the companies use the same or different inventory costing methods? Do the methods used match the companies' actual physical flow of inventory?

44. Ethics in Accounting LO5

As a newly hired staff accountant for Jordan Designs, you have been asked to conduct the year-end physical inventory count. During the process, you observe that much of the inventory is outdated and therefore could not be sold for the recorded cost. You recommend to your manager that the inventory be written down, based upon the lower-of-cost-or-market principle. However, the manager informs you that you should leave the inventory value at the cost value. She insists that the company frequently experiences inventory value changes and that the inventory will be marketable again in the future. Until that time, the company plans to leave the merchandise in its warehouse.

Required

a. Why would the manager want to keep the inventory at its current cost?
b. Who is affected by the decision to, or not to, write the inventory down to its market value?
c. What things should you consider when evaluating whether you should recommend an inventory write-down to your manager's boss?

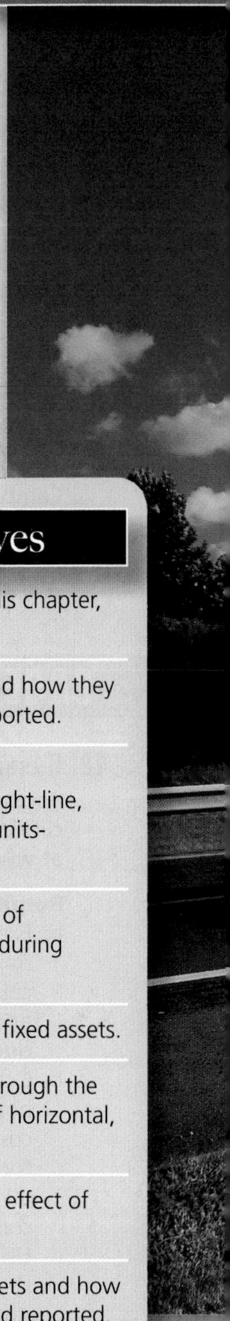

Fixed Assets and Intangible Assets

Learning Objectives

After studying the material in this chapter, you should be able to:

LO1 Describe fixed assets and how they are recorded, expensed, and reported.

LO2 Calculate and compare depreciation expense using straight-line, double-declining-balance, and units-of-activity methods.

LO3 Understand the effects of adjustments that may be made during a fixed asset's useful life.

LO4 Record the disposal of fixed assets.

LO5 Evaluate fixed assets through the calculation and interpretation of horizontal, vertical, and ratio analyses.

LO6 Describe the cash flow effect of acquiring fixed assets.

LO7 Describe intangible assets and how they are recorded, expensed, and reported.

Introduction

This chapter examines the accounting for property and equipment, which is otherwise known as "fixed assets." For most companies, the objectives associated with fixed assets are fairly simple. They want to acquire fixed assets, use them productively for some period of time, and then dispose of them. Thus, the chapter examines these three activities—the acquisition of fixed assets, the depreciation of fixed assets over their useful lives, and the disposal of fixed assets. It also examines a few issues that arise during the life of a fixed asset, such as additional expenditures and revisions of original estimates. The chapter then focuses on how to analyze a company's fixed asset position. It concludes with the accounting for intangible assets.

LO1 Recording, Expensing, and Reporting Fixed Assets

A **fixed asset** is any tangible resource that is expected to be used in the normal course of operations for more than one year and is not intended for resale. Examples include land, buildings, equipment, furniture, fixtures, etc. Fixed assets are reported on the balance sheet and are classified as noncurrent assets because they are used for more than one year.

As you consider the definition of a fixed asset, note that the phrase "not intended for resale" differentiates a fixed asset from inventory. A computer that **Dell Corporation** makes for sale is classified as inventory, while an identical computer used by an employee in business operations is classified as a fixed asset. Also, note that the phrase "used in the normal course of operations" differentiates a fixed asset from an investment. Land on which a company builds a manufacturing plant is classified as a fixed asset, while land bought to be sold to a developer is classified as an investment. The company's intended use of the asset dictates how the asset is classified.

Fixed asset A tangible resource that is expected to be used in operations for more than one year and is not intended for resale.

Accounting for fixed assets like this truck involves recording the purchase, depreciating the asset over its life, and then disposing of it.

Elena Elisseeva/iStockphoto.com

Recording Fixed Assets

Following the cost principle, fixed assets should be recorded at the cost of acquiring them. This includes all costs incurred to get the asset delivered, installed, and ready to use. Examples of expenditures to include in the cost of a fixed asset would therefore include, but not be limited to, the following:

- purchase price
- taxes paid on the purchase
- fees such as closing costs paid to attorneys
- delivery costs
- insurance costs during transit
- installation costs

To illustrate, suppose that Dozier Building Supply buys a delivery truck with a purchase price of $60,000, additional state sales taxes of $3,600, and a county fee of $400. Prior to receiving the truck, Dozier has the dealer paint the company's logo on the doors and install a specialized GPS. The dealer charges an additional $1,000 for this. Finally, Dozier pays an insurance company an additional $1,400 in premiums to add the truck to its coverage for the coming year. Given the preceding items, the cost of Dozier's truck is determined as follows:

Purchase price	$60,000
Sales taxes	3,600
County fee	400
Installation of logo and GPS	1,000
Total cost	$65,000

All of the costs except for the insurance are necessary to get the asset into its condition and location for intended use and are therefore included in the cost of the truck. The insurance covers the truck during its operations and is therefore an operating expense during the year. Assuming that Dozier paid cash to the dealer on January 5, the entry to record the purchase of the truck would be as follows:

Jan. 5	Equipment	65,000	
	Cash		65,000
	(To record the purchase of truck)		

Assets	=	Liabilities	+	Equity
+65,000				
−65,000				

Consider another example. Suppose a company purchases a tract of land for a new building site. The purchase price is $500,000 plus $25,400 in taxes and fees paid to the realtor, the bank, and the attorneys. Included on the land are four small buildings that must be removed at a total cost of $12,000. Also, the land requires $100,000 in logging, grading, and filling before it can be used. The timber harvested from the logging is sold for $20,000. The total cost of the land is as follows:

Purchase price	$500,000
Taxes and fees	25,400
Removal of buildings	12,000
Logging, grading, and filling	100,000
Less: Sales of timber	(20,000)
Total cost	$617,400

In this case, each cost is included in the asset because the land is not in the condition for use until each of the activities is completed. Notice also that the proceeds from the sale of the timber reduce the cost of the land.

Expensing Fixed Assets

A fixed asset converts to an expense as it is used or consumed. The expensing of fixed assets is accomplished through *depreciation*. **Depreciation** is the process of allocating the cost of a fixed asset over its useful life. Depreciation is an application of the matching principle. Because a fixed asset is used to generate revenues period after period, some of its cost should be expensed in, or matched to, those same periods. The amount of expense recognized each period is known as **depreciation expense**. The cumulative amount of depreciation expense recognized to date is known as **accumulated depreciation.**

Some students experience some confusion with depreciation because of its everyday use in our language. For example, it is often said that a new car "depreciates" in value once it is driven off the dealer's lot. When utilized in this way, the term depreciation implies a decline or loss in value because the car is used. For our purposes, depreciation is a process of allocating an asset's cost, not a method of determining an asset's market value.

While depreciation applies to fixed assets, not all fixed assets are depreciated. Depreciation applies only to those fixed assets with limited useful lives. An asset has a limited useful life when its revenue-generating potential is limited by wear and tear and/or obsolescence. Most fixed assets such as equipment and buildings have limited useful lives and are therefore subject to depreciation. The major exception to this is land, which has an unlimited useful life. As a result, land is not subject to depreciation.

Depreciation expense is normally calculated at the end of an accounting period and recorded with an adjusting journal entry. Regardless of the fixed asset being

Depreciation The process of systematically and rationally allocating the cost of a fixed asset over its useful life.

Depreciation expense The portion of a fixed asset's cost that is recognized as an expense in the current period.

Accumulated depreciation The cumulative amount of depreciation expense recognized to date on a fixed asset.

For accounting purposes, depreciation is a process of allocating an asset's cost, not a method of determining an asset's market value.

depreciated or the facts of the calculation, the general form of the entry is the same: Depreciation Expense and Accumulated Depreciation are increased.

To illustrate, suppose that Dozier calculates its truck's depreciation as $10,000 for the first year. At year-end, Dozier would make the following entry:

Year-end	Depreciation Expense	10,000	
	Accumulated Depreciation		10,000

Assets	=	Liabilities	+	Equity
−10,000				−10,000

This entry increases Depreciation Expense for the $10,000 of cost allocated to the current period. However, instead of decreasing Equipment, the entry increases Accumulated Depreciation, which is a contra-asset account that accumulates all depreciation recorded to date. Its balance is subtracted from the fixed asset account to yield the net book value of the fixed asset. We will see an example of this later in the chapter. The result of this entry is a decrease to both equity and assets.

Like other expenses, depreciation expense is reported on the income statement. Some companies, such as the **Wendy's/Arby's Group**, report it as a separate line item. Shown below is a condensed version of Wendy's/Arby's Group's 2010 expenses with depreciation expense highlighted:

Wendy's/Arby's Group 2010 Condensed Expenses

in thousands	
Cost of sales	$2,610,761
General and administrative	416,606
Depreciation and amortization	182,172
Impairment of long-lived assets	69,477
Other	5,010
Total	$3,284,026

Other companies, such as **McDonald's Corporation** and **Burger King Holdings**, do not separately disclose depreciation expense. Rather, they include it in a larger expense category, usually in Administrative Expenses. The operating expense portion of McDonald's 2010 income statement is shown as follows:

McDonald's 2010 Condensed Operating Expenses

in millions	
OPERATING COSTS AND EXPENSES	
Company-operated restaurant expenses:	
Food & paper	$ 5,300.1
Payroll & employee benefits	4,121.4
Occupancy & other operating expenses	3,638.0
Franchised restaurants—occupancy expenses	1,377.8
Selling, general & administrative expenses	2,333.3
Impairment and other charges, net	29.1
Other operating (income) expense, net	(198.2)
Total operating costs and expenses	$16,601.5

No reference is made to depreciation expense on the statement, but this does not mean that McDonald's had no depreciation expense. To find it, we must consult the notes to the financial statements. The following is an excerpt from McDonald's Property and Equipment note:

Excerpt from McDonald's 2010 Property and Equipment Note

Depreciation and amortization expense was (in millions): 2010—$1,200.4; 2009—$1,160.8; 2008—$1,161.6.

This note shows that over $1.2 billion in depreciation expense is included in one of the six operating expense subtotals in McDonald's 2010 income statement. Even though you don't see it on the income statement, it is there as a component of the reported expenses.

Reporting Fixed Assets

Fixed assets are reported on the balance sheet, usually as a separate line item just below current assets.

Shown below is a condensed version of the assets section of **Wendy's/Arby's** 2010 balance sheet with fixed assets highlighted:

Wendy's/Arby's Group 2010 Condensed Assets	
in thousands	
Total current assets	$ 754,788
Properties, net	1,551,261
Other assets	2,426,605
Total assets	$4,732,654

IFRS

International accounting standards permit companies to revalue their fixed assets to current cost. US GAAP requires companies to maintain their fixed assets at historical cost.

Notice first that Wendy's/Arby's uses "Properties" instead of "Fixed Assets." Because the bulk of fixed assets for most companies is property, buildings, and equipment, most companies use some variation of the term "property, plant and equipment" to describe their fixed assets. Notice also that Wendy's/Arby's description includes the word "net." The term "net" is an abbreviation for the phrase *net book value*. **Net book value** represents the cost of a fixed asset that has not yet been depreciated. It is calculated by subtracting the accumulated depreciation to date from the cost of the fixed asset. For example, an asset costing $5,000 with $1,000 of accumulated depreciation would have a net book value of $4,000.

Net book value The unexpired cost of a fixed asset, calculated by subtracting accumulated depreciation from the cost of the fixed asset.

Because Wendy's/Arby's only reports the net number on the balance sheet, those interested in how the net book value was calculated would need to consult the notes to the financial statements. Wendy's/Arby's discloses the following condensed data in its property and equipment note:

Wendy's/Arby's 2010 Properties Note	
in thousands	
Properties, at cost	$2,006,691
Accumulated depreciation and amortization	(455,430)
Properties, net	$1,551,261

At the end of 2010, Wendy's/Arby's held fixed assets with a total cost of $2 billion and accumulated depreciation of approximately $455 million. Netting those together yields the $1.55 billion net book value reported on the balance sheet.

HOME DEPOT ANALYSIS

Look at **Home Depot's** balance sheet in Appendix C. What general name does the company use for its fixed assets and what specific fixed asset accounts does it list? What is the historical cost of its fixed assets, how much depreciation expense has been accumulated to date, and what is the net book value of those fixed assets? What does the company report for depreciation expense for the current year?

Home Depot uses the name Property and Equipment for fixed assets. It lists the following six specific accounts: Land; Buildings; Furniture, Fixtures and Equipment; Leasehold Improvements; Construction in Progress; and Capital Leases. It reports a cost of $38,385 for its Property and Equipment. It also reports Accumulated Depreciation and Amortization to date of $13,325 million. Together, these result in a net book value of $25,060 million. Depreciation and Amortization for the current year is reported as $1,616 million on the income statement.

While **Wendy's/Arby's** reports the cost and accumulated depreciation amounts in its notes, other companies, such as **McDonald's**, report both amounts directly on their balance sheets.

McDonald's 2010 Fixed Assets Section of Balance Sheet	
in millions	
Property and equipment, at cost	$34,482.4
Accumulated depreciation and amortization	(12,421.8)
Net property and equipment	$22,060.6

McDonald's lists over $34 billion in cost of fixed assets and over $12 billion in accumulated depreciation of those assets. Thus, the net book value of its fixed assets is about $22 billion.

LO2 Calculating Depreciation Expense

When a company owns depreciable assets, it must calculate depreciation expense each period. Doing so requires the following information about the asset:

- Cost
- Salvage value
- Useful life
- Depreciation method

Cost refers to the historical cost of the asset being depreciated. This is the amount that was recorded when the asset was purchased. **Salvage value** refers to the market value of the asset at the end of its useful life. It is the amount the company expects to receive when the asset is sold, traded-in, or scrapped. The difference between an asset's cost and its salvage value is the asset's net cost to the company, or its **depreciable cost**. The depreciable cost is the total amount that should be depreciated over time. **Useful life** refers to the length of time the asset will be used in operations.

Depreciation method refers to the method used to calculate depreciation expense. Generally accepted accounting principles allow the use of several different methods for calculating depreciation expense. This chapter focuses on the following three methods:

- Straight-line
- Double-declining-balance
- Units-of-activity

To illustrate how depreciation expense is calculated under each method, the Dozier Building Supply example will be continued. The following information about Dozier's delivery truck is available:

- Purchase date: January 1, 2012
- Cost: $65,000
- Estimated salvage value: $15,000
- Estimated useful life: 5 years or 100,000 miles

Straight-Line Method

The **straight-line method** of depreciation spreads depreciation expense evenly over each year of the asset's useful life. It is a very simple calculation. The depreciable cost of the asset is divided by the useful life of the asset (in years) to yield the amount of depreciation expense per period. This calculation is shown below:

Straight-Line Method

$$\text{Depreciation Expense} = \frac{\text{Cost} - \text{Salvage Value}}{\text{Useful Life}}$$

For Dozier's delivery truck, annual depreciation expense under the straight-line method would therefore be:

$$\text{Depreciation Expense} = \frac{\$65{,}000 - \$15{,}000}{5} = \$10{,}000$$

Cost The historical cost of a fixed asset being depreciated.

Salvage value An estimate of the value of a fixed asset at the end of its useful life.

Depreciable cost The difference between an asset's cost and its salvage value.

Useful life The length of time a fixed asset is expected to be used in operations.

Depreciation method The method used to calculate depreciation expense, such as the straight-line method, the double-declining-balance method, and the units-of-activity method.

Straight-line method A depreciation method that results in the same amount of depreciation expense each year of the asset's useful life.

Dozier would record the depreciation expense with the following adjusting journal entry at the end of the first year:

Dec. 31 2012	Depreciation Expense	10,000	
	Accumulated Depreciation		10,000

Assets	=	Liabilities	+	Equity
−10,000				−10,000

The same entry would be made at the end of each year through 2016. Exhibit 8-1 illustrates depreciation for the entire useful life of the asset.

Exhibit 8-1 Depreciation Schedule—Straight-Line Method

Year	Calculation	Depreciation Expense	Accumulated Depreciation	Net Book Value
			$ 0	$65,000
2012	($65,000 − $15,000) / 5	$10,000	10,000	55,000
2013	($65,000 − $15,000) / 5	10,000	20,000	45,000
2014	($65,000 − $15,000) / 5	10,000	30,000	35,000
2015	($65,000 − $15,000) / 5	10,000	40,000	25,000
2016	($65,000 − $15,000) / 5	10,000	50,000	15,000

The depreciation schedule highlights several items. First, depreciation expense is the same each period. This will always be true under the straight-line method.

Second, the accumulated depreciation account grows each year by $10,000 until the balance equals the depreciable cost of the asset. This is no coincidence. The final balance in accumulated depreciation is the total of all depreciation expense recorded during the asset's life. Therefore, the balance should equal the asset's depreciable cost. This will be true regardless of the depreciation method used.

Finally, the net book value decreases each year by $10,000 until it equals the salvage value estimated for the asset. This is no coincidence either. Net book value represents the remaining unexpired cost of the asset. Therefore, an asset's final net book value should always equal the estimated salvage value at the end of the asset's useful life. This will be true regardless of the depreciation method used.

Double-declining-balance method A depreciation method that accelerates depreciation expense into the early years of an asset's life.

Double-Declining-Balance Method

The **double-declining-balance method** of depreciation is an accelerated method that results in more depreciation expense in the early years of an asset's life and less depreciation expense in the later years of an asset's life. As a result, the double-declining-balance method often matches expenses to revenues better than the straight-line method. More depreciation expense is recorded when the asset is more useful.

To calculate depreciation expense under the double-declining-balance method, the rate of depreciation is determined first by taking the straight-line rate of depreciation and doubling it (hence, the word *double* in the name). For example, if an asset has a four-year life, it has a straight-line rate of 25% (calculated by dividing 100% by four years). The straight-line rate is then doubled to 50%. An asset with a five-year life would have a 20% straight-line rate, which would be doubled to 40%. The doubled rate is then multiplied by the net book value of the asset to yield the amount of depreciation expense for the period. This calculation is shown as follows:

Double-Declining-Balance Method

Depreciation Expense = Depreciation Rate × Net Book Value
= (Straight-Line Rate × 2)
× (Cost − Accumulated Depreciation)

Before depreciation expense for Dozier is calculated, note again that the depreciation rate is applied to the net book value of the asset, not its depreciable cost. Because an asset's net book value declines as the asset is depreciated, the amount of depreciation expense will therefore differ each period. In fact, depreciation expense will become smaller and smaller each period as the depreciation rate is applied to a smaller net book value. This stands in contrast to the straight-line method and is why the name of this method contains the words *declining balance*.

Under the double-declining-balance method, Dozier's depreciation expense for the first year of the asset's life is calculated as follows:

$$\text{Depreciation Expense for 2012} = (20\% \times 2) \times (\$65{,}000 - \$0) = \$26{,}000$$

You can now see how the double-declining-balance method *accelerates* the depreciation. Instead of $10,000 of expense as under the straight-line method, depreciation expense in the first year is $26,000. In other words, $16,000 of depreciation expense is accelerated to the first year by using the double-declining-balance method instead of the straight-line method.

In the second year of the asset's life, the same formula is used. However, the resulting depreciation expense is lower because the depreciation rate is applied to a lower net book value. With $26,000 in depreciation to date, the accumulated depreciation balance is $26,000, yielding a net book value of $39,000 ($65,000 – $26,000). Therefore, depreciation expense in the second year would be:

$$\text{Depreciation Expense for 2013} = (20\% \times 2) \times (\$65{,}000 - \$26{,}000) = \$15{,}600$$

As you can see, depreciation expense for the second year is lower than the first year, but it is still more than would be calculated under the straight-line method. In other words, depreciation expense is still being accelerated to the early years of the asset's life.

In the third year of the asset's life, the same formula is used again, but this time the net book value is $23,400 (cost of $65,000 less accumulated depreciation of $41,600). Therefore, the calculation of depreciation expense for the third year is as follows:

$$\text{Depreciation Expense for 2014} = (20\% \times 2) \times (\$65{,}000 - \$41{,}600) = \$9{,}360$$

Now, at this point we need to be careful. Over an asset's life, an entity cannot record more total depreciation than the asset's depreciable cost. Regardless of how much depreciation expense is calculated to be, an asset's accumulated depreciation balance should never exceed the asset's depreciable cost. In our example, Dozier's depreciable cost is $50,000. Accumulated depreciation after 2013 is $41,600. Therefore, depreciation expense in 2014 is limited to $8,400. This calculation is as follows:

Depreciable cost of asset ($65,000 – $15,000)	$50,000
Less: Accumulated depreciation at the end of 2013	41,600
Remaining depreciation to be taken	$ 8,400

Even though the calculation yields $9,360, depreciation expense for 2014 is limited to $8,400. And, because Dozier's truck is fully depreciated after 2014, there is no depreciation expense for the remaining two years of the truck's life.

A schedule of depreciation for all five years is shown in Exhibit 8-2. The calculated amounts in 2014 are struck through and are replaced with the necessary amounts.

Exhibit 8-2 Depreciation Schedule—Double-Declining-Balance Method

Year	Calculation	Depreciation Expense	Accumulated Depreciation	Net Book Value
			$ 0	$65,000
2012	(20% × 2) × ($65,000 – $0)	$26,000	26,000	39,000
2013	(20% × 2) × ($65,000 – $26,000)	15,600	41,600	23,400
2014	(20% × 2) × ($65,000 – $41,600)	~~9,360~~	~~50,960~~	~~14,040~~
		8,400	50,000	15,000
2015		0	50,000	15,000
2016		0	50,000	15,000

Note that, as expected, depreciation expense is accelerated to the early years of the asset's life. Note also that, like the straight-line method, the double-declining-balance method results in a total of $50,000 of depreciation expense and a resulting net book value that is equal to the estimated salvage value of $15,000. The only difference between the methods is when depreciation expense is recognized.

Units-of-Activity Method

Both the straight-line and double-declining-balance methods are a function of the passage of time rather than the actual use of the asset. Each method assumes that the calculated depreciation is a reasonable representation of the actual usage of the asset. In contrast, the **units-of-activity method** of depreciation calculates depreciation based on actual asset activity. Because it relies on an estimate of an asset's lifetime activity, the method is limited to those assets whose units of activity can be determined with some degree of accuracy.

Calculating depreciation expense under the units-of-activity method starts by calculating depreciation per unit of expected activity. Depreciation per unit of expected activity is the depreciable cost of the asset divided by the estimated units of activity over the life of the asset.

$$\text{Depreciation Expense per Unit} = \frac{\text{Cost} - \text{Salvage Value}}{\text{Useful Life in Units}}$$

For Dozier's truck, depreciation expense per unit will be a function of miles driven. Since Dozier estimates that the truck will be driven 100,000 miles, its estimated depreciation per mile would be $0.50 per mile.

$$\text{Depreciation Expense per Unit} = \frac{\$65{,}000 - \$15{,}000}{100{,}000 \text{ miles}} = \$0.50 \text{ per mile}$$

With a $0.50 per mile rate, the actual miles driven in a given year is needed to calculate depreciation expense. Assume that the truck is driven 24,000 miles in 2012. Its depreciation expense for 2012 would therefore be $12,000.

$$\text{Depreciation Expense} = \$0.50 \times 24{,}000 = \$12{,}000$$

Similar calculations would be made for the next four years of the asset's life. A depreciation schedule, complete with the actual miles driven in each of the five years, is shown in Exhibit 8-3.

Exhibit 8-3 Depreciation Schedule—Units-of-Activity Method

Year	Calculation	Depreciation Expense	Accumulated Depreciation	Net Book Value
			$ 0	$65,000
2012	$0.50 × 24,000 miles	$12,000	12,000	53,000
2013	$0.50 × 22,000 miles	11,000	23,000	42,000
2014	$0.50 × 27,000 miles	13,500	36,500	28,500
2015	$0.50 × 17,000 miles	8,500	45,000	20,000
2016	$0.50 × 10,000 miles	5,000	50,000	15,000

Note that this calculation is very similar to the straight-line calculation. Depreciable cost is divided by estimated life. But, instead of calculating depreciation expense per year, depreciation expense per unit is calculated. Once depreciation expense per unit is known, depreciation expense is determined by multiplying the per unit rate by the actual units of activity during the period. The calculation is as follows:

Units-of-Activity Method

$$\text{Depreciation Expense} = \text{Depreciation Expense per Unit} \times \text{Actual Units of Activity}$$

Units-of-activity method A depreciation method in which depreciation expense is a function of the actual usage of the asset.

As you review the schedule, note that depreciation expense fluctuates as the asset's activity fluctuates. As a result, depreciation expense is a function of usage. Second, note that the total number of miles driven over the five years equals 100,000 miles. This assumption is made for simplicity. However, had Dozier driven the truck more than 100,000 miles, total depreciation expense over the life of the asset would still be limited to $50,000, the asset's depreciable cost.

Comparing Depreciation Methods

The calculations in the previous sections demonstrate that a company's depreciation expense in a given year will depend on the depreciation method chosen. For comparative purposes, Exhibit 8-4 summarizes the annual depreciation for Dozier's truck as well as the resulting net book values under the three methods.

One of the most common reasons that companies choose one depreciation method over another is the effect on taxes.

Exhibit 8-4 Comparison of Three Depreciation Methods

Straight-Line			Double-Declining-Balance			Units-of-Activity		
Year	Depr. Exp.	NBV	Year	Depr. Exp.	NBV	Year	Depr. Exp.	NBV
2012	$10,000	$55,000	2012	$26,000	$39,000	2012	$12,000	$53,000
2013	10,000	45,000	2013	15,600	23,400	2013	11,000	42,000
2014	10,000	35,000	2014	8,400	15,000	2014	13,500	28,500
2015	10,000	25,000	2015	0	15,000	2015	8,500	20,000
2016	10,000	15,000	2016	0	15,000	2016	5,000	15,000
	$50,000			$50,000			$50,000	

The summary demonstrates that total depreciation expense over the life of the asset is $50,000 regardless of the method chosen. However, each method arrives at $50,000 differently. The straight-line method depreciates the same amount each year. The double-declining-balance method accelerates depreciation into the early years of the asset's life. The units-of-activity method depreciates different amounts each year depending on the asset's usage. No depreciation method is right. They are just different, and companies choose to use one over another for different reasons. One of the most common reasons is the effect on taxes.

Like all expenses, depreciation expense reduces net income, which in turn reduces income taxes. Assuming a 40% tax rate in the example above, the $50,000 of depreciation on the truck will lower taxes by $20,000. The advantage of the double-declining-balance method is that all of the tax savings are realized in three years rather than five. This is beneficial to a company because the company can temporarily use the cash that would otherwise be paid to the government.

Many companies take advantage of this tax effect by using one method of depreciation for tax purposes and another for financial reporting purposes. The Internal Revenue Service (IRS) allows companies to use a depreciation method known as the Modified Accelerated Cost Recovery System (MACRS). As its name implies, MACRS is an accelerated method much like the double-declining-balance method. However, the IRS does not require that a company use the same method on its tax return that it does for its financial statements. As a result, many companies that use MACRS for taxes use the straight-line method for financial reports.

Regardless of the method chosen, companies must disclose their choices in the notes to their financial statements so that comparisons can be made among different companies. This is an application of the qualitative characteristic of comparability. The disclosure is sometimes found in a note dedicated solely to fixed assets. However, most companies like **McDonald's** put it in the first note summarizing the significant accounting policies used to prepare financial statements.

McDonald's 2010 Disclosure of Depreciation Method

Property and equipment are stated at cost, with depreciation and amortization provided using the straight-line method over the following estimated useful lives: buildings—up to 40 years; leasehold improvements—the lesser of useful lives of assets or lease terms, which generally include option periods; and equipment—three to 12 years.

LO3 Adjustments Made During a Fixed Asset's Useful Life

Since fixed assets are used for multiple years, companies sometimes must make adjustments to fixed asset accounts as new information is available or as new activity occurs. These adjustments can arise from the following:

- Changes in estimates
- Additional expenditures to improve the fixed asset
- Significant declines in the asset's market value

Changes in Depreciation Estimates

Calculating depreciation expense requires that a company estimate the asset's useful life and its salvage value. These estimates are normally based on previous company experience with similar assets as well as factors such as the manufacturer's recommendations. As a result, they are usually fair and reasonable. However, estimates can differ from actual experience. When such errors are small and will not affect decision making, they are usually deemed to be immaterial and ignored. When the estimates are materially wrong, though, revisions can be made. We call this a change in estimate.

When an estimate is changed, the change is made prospectively, meaning that the change affects only the calculation of current and future depreciation expense. Depreciation expense for prior years is not retroactively corrected. Calculating depreciation expense after a revision is made is accomplished by (1) determining the remaining depreciable cost of the asset at the time of the revision and (2) depreciating that cost over the remaining useful life using the same depreciation method.

To illustrate, suppose that Thomas Supply purchases a machine for $90,000 on January 1, 2012. Thomas estimates that the machine will have a 10-year useful life and a $10,000 salvage value. Thomas uses the straight-line method of depreciation and records $8,000 of depreciation expense [($90,000 − $10,000) ÷ 10] each year as follows:

Dec. 31	Depreciation Expense	8,000	
	Accumulated Depreciation		8,000
	(To record depreciation expense)		

Assets	=	Liabilities	+	Equity
−8,000				−8,000

When actual experience shows that a past estimate was incorrect, accountants change the estimate going forward instead of correcting the past.

Now suppose that on January 1, 2016, Thomas decides that the machine will last only eight years rather than the ten years originally estimated and will have a salvage value of only $6,000 rather than $10,000. When these revisions are made, Thomas does not correct the four previous depreciation expense entries of $8,000 because they were based on reasonable estimates at the time. Instead, Thomas calculates the remaining depreciable cost of the asset and spreads it out over the remaining useful life.

To calculate the asset's remaining depreciable cost, Thomas must first determine the asset's net book value at the date of revision, which represents the unexpired cost of the asset. Thomas must then subtract the asset's salvage value (in this case the revised value) to yield the remaining depreciable cost of the asset. These calculations are as follows:

Cost of the asset, January 1, 2012	$90,000
Less: Accumulated depreciation for four years	32,000
Net book value on January 1, 2016	$58,000
Less: Revised estimated salvage value	6,000
Remaining depreciable cost	$52,000

Once the depreciable cost is determined, Thomas calculates depreciation expense by dividing the remaining depreciable cost by the remaining useful life. In this case, the total useful life is now estimated to be eight years instead of ten, which means that there are only four years remaining instead of six.

Remaining depreciable cost	$52,000
Divided by remaining useful life	÷ 4
Annual depreciation expense	$13,000

With this new depreciation expense calculated, Thomas would make the following journal entry at the end of Years 5 through 8.

Dec. 31	Depreciation Expense	13,000	
	Accumulated Depreciation		13,000
	(To record depreciation expense)		

Assets	=	Liabilities	+	Equity
−13,000				−13,000

So, Thomas depreciates $8,000 per year in Years 1 through 4 and $13,000 per year in Years 5 through 8. This results in $84,000 of total depreciation over the life of the asset, which is equal to the original cost of the asset less its revised salvage value ($90,000 − $6,000 = $84,000).

When a company has a material change in a fixed asset estimate, it will disclose the change in the notes to its financial statements. Exhibit 8-5 is an example from **IBM**, which in 1999 reduced income $404 million due to a change in useful life estimates on computers.

Exhibit 8-5 Change in Estimate—IBM

Change in Estimate
As a result of a change in the estimated useful life of personal computers from five years to three years, the company recognized a charge in the second quarter of 1999 of $404 million ($241 million after tax, $0.13 per diluted common share). In the second quarter of 1999, the company wrote off the net book value of personal computers that were three years old or older and, therefore, had no remaining useful life. The remaining book value of the assets will be depreciated over the remaining new useful life.

Expenditures After Acquisition

Most fixed assets require expenditures throughout their useful lives. You have to think no further than your personal automobile to see this. The purchasing price is only the first cost. Expenditures for oil changes, tune ups, minor repairs, and even major repairs come later. So, how are these additional expenditures treated from an accounting standpoint?

The accounting treatment for expenditures made during the useful life of a fixed asset depends on whether they are classified as *capital* or *revenue* expenditures.

Because classifying expenditures as capital or revenue is subjective, two accountants may classify the same expenditure differently.

A **capital expenditure** increases the expected useful life or productivity of the asset. An example would be a new engine for an automobile. Capital expenditures are added to the cost of the asset and depreciated over the asset's remaining useful life. A **revenue expenditure** maintains the expected useful life or productivity of the asset. An example would be an oil change. Revenue expenditures are expensed in the period in which they are incurred. They are not added to the cost of the asset.

To illustrate, suppose that a company purchases equipment for $50,000 on January 1, 2012. The company estimates the asset's useful life and salvage value at five years and $0, respectively. Using the straight-line depreciation method, the company records $10,000 of depreciation expense each year. Now suppose that on January 1, 2016, during the fifth and last year of the asset's life, the company incurs $1,000 in ordinary maintenance and $8,000 for upgrades. The upgrades allow the equipment to be used productively in years six and seven (2017 and 2018).

Given this information, the $1,000 is a revenue expenditure and should be expensed as follows:

Jan. 1	Maintenance Expense	1,000	
2016	Cash		1,000
	(To record normal maintenance)		

Assets	=	Liabilities	+	Equity
−1,000				−1,000

In contrast, the $8,000 for upgrades is a capital expenditure since the asset's useful life is extended two

Capital expenditure An expenditure that increases the expected useful life or productivity of a fixed asset.

Revenue expenditure An expenditure that maintains the expected useful life or productivity of a fixed asset.

IFRS

Under international standards, expenditures related to a major inspection of fixed assets should be capitalized. Under GAAP, such expenditures may be either capitalized or expensed as incurred.

years. It should therefore be capitalized with the following entry:

Jan. 1 2016	Equipment	8,000	
	Cash		8,000
	(To record upgrade to asset)		

Assets	=	Liabilities	+	Equity
+8,000				
−8,000				

Notice that this entry results in an increase and decrease to assets rather than a change in equity. This is because the company is capitalizing the expenditure rather than expensing it.

With this addition to the cost of the asset, depreciation expense for 2016 must be recalculated. To do so, the company follows the same general procedures used in the change of estimate scenario. It first calculates the asset's remaining depreciable cost. This is accomplished by determining the asset's net book value at the time of the expenditure, adding the capital expenditure to yield an updated net book value, and then subtracting the asset's salvage value to yield depreciable cost. These calculations are as follows:

Cost of the asset, January 1, 2012	$50,000
Less: Accumulated depreciation for four years	(40,000)
Add: Capital expenditure	8,000
Updated net book value on January 1, 2016	$18,000
Less: Estimated salvage value	0
Remaining depreciable cost	$18,000

Next, the company calculates depreciation expense under the straight-line method by dividing the remaining depreciable cost by the remaining useful life which is three years. In 2016, 2017, and 2018, the company will record $6,000 of depreciation expense each year.

The classification of expenditures as capital expenditures rather than revenue expenditures was the source of one of the largest frauds in recent history.

Remaining depreciable cost	$18,000
Divided by remaining useful life	÷ 3
Annual depreciation expense	$ 6,000

While the classification of post-acquisition expenditures may seem rather unimportant, it is actually an area of great interest because of the potential for fraudulent behavior by companies. One of the largest corporate frauds in recent history centered on the treatment and reporting of revenue expenditures. In 2002, it was discovered that **WorldCom** was treating operating expenses associated with telecommunication lines as capital expenditures. Instead of appearing on the income statement as expenses, these costs were recorded as assets on the balance sheet. This resulted in a gross understatement of current expenses and overstatement of net income. Over the seven quarters that it committed this fraud, the company overstated its results by several billion dollars. After several years of investigation and prosecution, the chief executive officer of the company was found guilty of nine counts of securities fraud, conspiracy, and filing false documents.

Asset Impairment

Sometimes, a fixed asset's market value will fall substantially due to changing market conditions, technological improvements, or other factors. When a fixed asset's market value falls materially below its net book value and the decline in value is deemed to be *permanent*, the asset is considered *impaired*. Accounting rules require companies to write impaired assets down from their book values to their

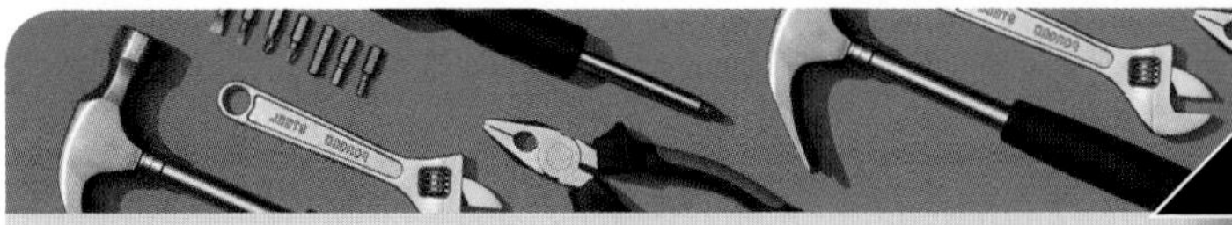

HOME DEPOT ANALYSIS

Look at **Home Depot's** first note to its financial statements in Appendix C. There is one paragraph describing expenditures for a certain type of activity where the treatment of the expenditures is very similar to the capital and revenue expenditures described in this text. What is this activity?

The activity is software costs. Home Depot describes in the Capitalized Software Costs paragraph that certain expenditures associated with the development of software are capitalized into Furniture, Fixtures, and Equipment and then amortized over the software's useful life, which is three to six years. All expenditures not meeting the requirements for capitalization are expensed in the period incurred.

market values. This, like the lower-of-cost-or-market rule with inventory, is an application of the concept of conservatism.

To illustrate, suppose a company has equipment that makes a unique toy that becomes extremely popular. The equipment has a net book value of $140,000 and a higher market value. Suppose further that the toy suddenly loses its popularity, and the company is unable to alter the machine to produce anything else. As a result, the market value of the machine plummets to $40,000. The company deems this decline in market value to be permanent and declares that the asset is impaired on March 23. The asset impairment would be recorded as follows:

Mar. 23	Loss on Impairment	100,000	
	Equipment		100,000
	(To record permanent impairment of asset)		

Assets	=	Liabilities	+	Equity
−100,000				−100,000

In the above entry, a Loss on Impairment is increased to reflect the decline in value of the asset. This reduces equity. In addition, the Equipment account is decreased to reflect the reduced value. This reduces assets. After the impairment entry, depreciation expense would be calculated based on the revised depreciable cost and remaining useful life.

Asset impairments are not uncommon. In fact, current accounting rules require companies to periodically assess whether any of their fixed assets are impaired. Consider the following excerpt from **Wendy's/Arby's** 2010 Impairment of Long-Lived Assets note:

Excerpt from Wendy's/Arby's 2010 Impairment of Long-Lived Assets Note

Impairment of company-owned Wendy's restaurants:	$21,201
Impairment of company-owned Arby's restaurants:	$37,264
Total Wendy's/Arby's	$58,465

The . . . company-owned restaurant impairment losses . . . reflected impairment charges on all restaurant level assets resulting from the deterioration in operating performance of certain restaurants, additional charges for capital improvements in restaurants impaired in a prior year which did not subsequently recover, and write-downs in the carrying value of surplus properties and properties held for sale.

The note discloses that the company experienced over $58 million in impairment losses during 2010. The losses were the result of decreasing value due to deteriorating performance, unrecovered capital improvements, and general loss in value of surplus properties.

LO4 Disposing of Fixed Assets

When a company decides that it no longer needs a fixed asset, it usually disposes of the asset in one of three ways. When the asset has no value, it will simply be discarded. When the asset still has value, it

MAKING IT REAL

The value of a company's equipment can be impaired or reduced for many reasons. One of those is a decrease in demand for the product that the equipment makes. Take Crocs, Inc., as an example.

AP Photo/Frank Augstein

Crocs, Inc., is well known for its lightweight and colorful ventilated clogs. The company burst onto the scene in 2002 with the launch of its Beach™ model, and demand grew quickly. The company responded by rapidly diversifying into different styles and increasing production capacity and warehouse space. By 2007, the company was generating record profits of $168 million.

But things quickly changed. Demand for Crocs' products fell in 2008, resulting in a $185 million overall loss. Approximately 12% of that loss, or nearly $22 million, was attributable to impairment charges on its manufacturing equipment. Specifically, projections of product demand indicated that the company had significant excess capacity. It simply had too much equipment and too many shoe molds given demand. As a result, the company abandoned the equipment and molds and took a $22 million charge to income.

And unfortunately for the company, the impairments continued into 2009. The company recognized an additional $26 million in impairment charges, for a two-year total of $48 million.

will either be sold or traded in for another asset, often a newer model. Since the accounting for trading an asset is beyond the scope of this book, we will focus on the first two cases—discarding or selling the asset.

The accounting for the disposal of a fixed asset consists of the following three steps:

1. Update depreciation on the asset.
2. Calculate gain or loss on the disposal.
3. Record the disposal.

The first step is to record any necessary depreciation expense to update the accumulated depreciation account. Usually, this means that depreciation expense must be recorded for a partial period. For example, a company that records annual depreciation expense on December 31 and sells equipment on the following February 15 must record depreciation expense for one and one-half months at the time of disposal.

The second step is to calculate any gain or loss on the disposal by comparing the asset's net book value to the proceeds from the asset's sale, if any. When the proceeds exceed the net book value, a gain on disposal is recognized. When the net book value exceeds the proceeds, a loss on disposal is recognized. This is summarized below:

$$\text{Gain on Disposal} = \text{Proceeds from Sale} > \text{Net Book Value}$$
$$\text{Loss on Disposal} = \text{Proceeds from Sale} < \text{Net Book Value}$$

The third and final step is to prepare a journal entry that decreases the asset account and its related accumulated depreciation account. If the asset is sold and cash is received, the entry must also record the increase in cash. Finally, any gain or loss on the disposal must be recorded.

To illustrate, suppose that a company purchases a machine on January 1, 2012, for $30,000. The company estimates the useful life and salvage value to be four years and $2,000, respectively. The company uses the straight-line method of depreciation and records depreciation expense annually on December 31. Given these facts, annual depreciation expense for the machine is $7,000 [($30,000 – $2,000) / 4].

Loss Example

Suppose further that the company sells the machine on June 30, 2014, for $12,000. To account for this sale, the company must first update the accumulated depreciation account. The asset has been used for six months since the last time depreciation was recorded (December 31), so the company must record six months of depreciation expense. Since annual depreciation expense is $7,000, six months of depreciation would be half of that, or $3,500. Therefore, the following entry would be made on June 30, 2014:

June 30 2014	Depreciation Expense	3,500	
	Accumulated Depreciation		3,500

Assets	=	Liabilities	+	Equity
−3,500				−3,500

As a result of this entry, the accumulated depreciation account is updated to a balance of $17,500 ($7,000 in 2012, $7,000 in 2013, and $3,500 in 2014). With this balance, the gain/loss on disposal can be calculated as follows:

Proceeds from sale		$12,000
Cost of machine	$30,000	
Less: Accumulated depreciation	17,500	
Net book value at June 30, 2014		12,500
Loss on sale		$ (500)

Because the asset's net book value of $12,500 exceeds the sale proceeds of $12,000, the company generates a $500 loss. With this information, the company can prepare the following journal entry to record the disposal:

June 30 2014	Cash	12,000	
	Accumulated Depreciation	17,500	
	Loss on Disposal	500	
	Equipment		30,000

Assets	=	Liabilities	+	Equity
+12,000				−500
+17,500				
−30,000				

The entry first decreases the Equipment account by $30,000 to eliminate the account. A common mistake is to think that the Equipment account should be decreased by its net book value of $12,500. But remember that fixed assets are recorded and maintained at their costs, so the balance in the Equipment account is $30,000 prior to disposal. Second, the entry decreases Accumulated Depreciation by $17,500. Because the company no longer has the asset, it should no longer maintain accumulated depreciation for the asset. Third, the entry increases the Cash account to reflect the asset received from selling the machine. Finally, the entry increases a Loss on Disposal account to reflect the loss on sale. This account is reported on the income statement among Other Revenues and Expenses. As a result of the entry, assets and equity decrease by $500, the amount of the loss.

A loss on the sale of a fixed asset is reported in other expenses so that operating expenses include only those expenses related to normal operations.

Gain Example

To illustrate a gain example, suppose that the company sells the machine on March 31, 2015, for $8,000. After updating depreciation, the Accumulated Depreciation account would have a balance of $22,750:

Three full years (2012, 2013, 2014)	$21,000
One-fourth of 2015 ($7,000 × ¼)	1,750
Accumulated depreciation at March 31, 2015	$22,750

Therefore, the machine's net book value and the gain/loss on disposal at March 31, 2015, can be calculated as follows:

Proceeds from sale		$8,000
Cost of machine	$30,000	
Less: Accumulated depreciation	22,750	
Net book value at March 31, 2015		7,250
Gain on sale		$ 750

Because the sale proceeds of $8,000 exceed the asset's net book value of $7,250, the company generates a $750 gain. With this information, the following journal entry can be prepared to record the disposal:

Mar. 31 2015	Cash	8,000	
	Accumulated Depreciation	22,750	
	Gain on Disposal		750
	Equipment		30,000

Assets	=	Liabilities	+	Equity
+ 8,000				+750
+22,750				
−30,000				

Like the loss example, the entry decreases the Equipment account by $30,000. It also decreases the machine's Accumulated Depreciation account by $22,750 to eliminate the account and increases the Cash account by $8,000 to reflect the asset received from selling the machine. Finally, the entry increases a Gain on Disposal account to reflect the gain on sale. Like the loss example, the net effect on the accounting equation is an equal change in assets and equity, with this example resulting in a $750 increase to both.

LO5 Evaluating a Company's Management of Fixed Assets

Because fixed assets comprise the largest category of assets for most companies, it is usually a good idea to evaluate a company's management of its fixed assets. A company manages fixed assets by acquiring them, using them productively, and then replacing them. Therefore, two issues of importance for any company with fixed assets would be as follows:

- How productive are the company's fixed assets in generating revenues?
- What is the condition of the company's fixed assets?

The following sections examine these issues for the fixed assets of **McDonald's**. The examination will require information from the company's balance sheet, income statement, and notes to the financial statements. The required information is found in Exhibit 8-6, excerpted from McDonald's 2010 Annual Report.

Horizontal and Vertical Analyses

A good place to start an analysis of fixed assets is with horizontal and vertical analyses. Recall from Chapter 2 that horizontal analysis calculates the dollar change in an account balance, defined as the current-year balance less the prior-year balance, and divides that change by the prior-year balance to yield the percentage change. Vertical analysis divides each account balance by a base account, yielding a percentage. The base account is total assets for balance sheet accounts and net sales or total revenues for income statement accounts. These calculations are summarized as follows:

Horizontal Analysis

$$\text{Dollar change in account balance} = \text{Current-year balance} - \text{Prior-year balance}$$

$$\text{Percentage change in account balance} = \frac{\text{Dollar change}}{\text{Prior-year balance}}$$

Vertical Analysis

For the Balance Sheet / *For the Income Statement*

$$\text{Percentage} = \frac{\text{Account Balance}}{\text{Total Assets}} \text{ or } \frac{\text{Account Balance}}{\text{Net Sales or Revenue}}$$

Exhibit 8-6 Account Balances from McDonald's 2010 Annual Report

Source	Accounts	2010	2009
Income Statement	Total revenues	$ 24,074.6	$ 22,744.7
Balance Sheet	Property and equipment, at cost	$ 34,482.4	$ 33,440.5
	Less: Accumulated depreciation	(12,421.8)	(11,909.0)
	Net property and equipment	$ 22,060.6	$ 21,531.5
	Total assets	$ 31,975.2	$ 30,224.9
Notes to Financial Statements	Depreciation expense	$ 1,200.4	$ 1,160.8

Given **McDonald's** financial information in Exhibit 8-6, horizontal and vertical analyses of fixed assets and depreciation expense result in the following. Note that the net book value of property and equipment is used in the calculations. Note also that vertical analysis is conducted on both years of data.

Horizontal Analysis

	Dollar Change	*Percentage Change*
Property and equipment	22,060.6 − 21,531.5 = 529.1	$\frac{529.1}{21,531.5} = 2.5\%$
Depreciation expense	1,200.4 − 1,160.8 = 39.6	$\frac{39.6}{1,160.8} = 3.4\%$

Vertical Analysis

	2010	*2009*
Property and equipment	$\frac{22,060.6}{31,975.2} = 69.0\%$	$\frac{21,531.5}{30,224.9} = 71.2\%$
Depreciation expense	$\frac{1,200.4}{24,074.6} = 5.0\%$	$\frac{1,160.8}{22,744.7} = 5.1\%$

The calculations show a fairly stable fixed asset position. Horizontal analysis shows a slight increase of 2.5% in fixed assets and an increase of 3.4% in depreciation expense from 2009 to 2010. Vertical analysis shows that fixed assets make up a large part of McDonald's asset base. In both years, around 70% of the company's assets are fixed assets. Furthermore, depreciation expense is shown to be about 5% in each year. This tells us that for every dollar in sales revenue, the company incurs about a nickel in depreciation expense. Overall, both of these analyses indicate fairly stable fixed assets over the two-year period.

For comparison purposes, the following table lists the 2010 horizontal and vertical analyses of **Burger King Holdings**:

		Horizontal Analysis	Vertical Analysis
Fixed Assets	*McDonald's*	2.5%	69.0%
	Burger King	0.1%	37.0%
Depreciation Expense	*McDonald's*	3.4%	5.0%
	Burger King	13.9%	4.5%

The comparison shows that McDonald's holds a larger percentage of its total assets in fixed assets. However, for both companies, depreciation expense consumes around 5% of total revenues, with Burger King's depreciation expense increasing faster than McDonald's.

Fixed Asset Turnover Ratio

The preceeding analyses indicate that McDonald's fixed assets were stable. But they do not indicate whether the company is using those fixed assets productively to generate revenues. One means to find out is to calculate the fixed asset turnover ratio. The **fixed asset turnover ratio** compares total revenues during a period to the average net book value of fixed assets during that period. It is calculated as follows:

$$\text{Fixed Asset Turnover Ratio} = \frac{\text{Total Revenues}}{\text{Average Net Book Value of Fixed Assets}}$$

where average net book value is:

$$\frac{\text{Beginning Net Book Value} + \text{Ending Net Book Value}}{2}$$

Because this ratio compares total revenues to fixed assets, it indicates the productivity of every dollar invested in fixed assets. In general, companies want this ratio to be higher rather than lower. All other things equal, a higher ratio indicates that the company is using its fixed assets more effectively to produce more revenue.

McDonald's 2010 fixed asset turnover ratio is calculated as follows.

$$\frac{24,074.6}{(22,060.6 + 21,531.5)/2} = 1.10$$

The 1.10 ratio shows that McDonald's total revenues for 2010 were 1.10 times the average net book value of its fixed assets. In other words, for every dollar of fixed assets, on average, McDonald's was able to generate \$1.10 in revenue during the period. Whether this is good or bad requires some comparison. **Wendy's/Arby's** 2010 fixed asset turnover ratio was 2.16, while Burger King's was 2.47. McDonald's trails its two rivals in generating revenues from its fixed assets.

Fixed asset turnover ratio A comparison of total revenues to the average net book value of fixed assets that measures the productivity of fixed assets.

HOME DEPOT ANALYSIS

Using **Home Depot's** information in Appendix C, calculate and interpret (1) horizontal and vertical analyses of fixed assets and depreciation expense, (2) fixed asset turnover ratio, and (3) average life and average age of fixed assets.

(1) Horizontal Analysis

Fixed assets: ($25,060 − $25,550) / $25,550 = 1.9%

Depreciation Expense: ($1,616 − $1,707) / $1,707 = (5.3%)

Vertical Analysis

Fixed assets: $25,060 / $40,125 = 62.5%

Depreciation Expense: $1,616 / $67,997 = 2.4%

The horizontal analysis shows that while fixed assets increased slightly, depreciation expense actually decreased during the year. The 62.5% vertical analysis of fixed assets shows how important fixed assets are to the company. Almost two-thirds of its assets are in fixed assets. The 2.4% vertical analysis of depreciation expense indicates that although the company has large fixed assets, depreciation expense consumes less than three cents per dollar of sales in the most recent year.

(2) Fixed Asset Turnover Ratio:

$67,997 / [($25,060 + $25,550)/2] = 2.69

The 2.69 fixed asset turnover ratio indicates that Home Depot generates $2.69 in sales for every $1 of fixed assets that it owns. This could provide Home Depot with a benchmark expectation for stores. For example, a store with $10 million of fixed assets could be expected to generate about $27 million in sales.

***(3) Average Life Ratio:* $25,060 / $1,616 = 15.5 years**

***Average Age Ratio:* $13,325 / $1,616 = 8.2 years**

The 15.5 average life ratio shows that Home Depot's average fixed asset has about a 15-year life. The 8.2 average age ratio indicates that the company's fixed assets have been used for a little over half that time. Taken together, these two ratios indicate that Home Depot will not need significant fixed asset replacement in the near term.

Average Life and Age of Fixed Assets

In addition to understanding the productivity of fixed assets, it is a good idea to understand the condition of a company's fixed assets. Fixed assets in poor condition are usually less productive and normally require significant expenditures either to repair or replace. While a user of **McDonald's** financial statements cannot physically examine the company's fixed assets, one way to get a rough idea of the general condition of a company's fixed assets is to look at the age of the assets in comparison to their useful lives. This can be accomplished by calculating the average useful life and average age of the assets.

The **average useful life of fixed assets** represents the number of years, on average, that a company expects to use its fixed assets. It is calculated as follows:

$$\text{Average Useful Life} = \frac{\text{Cost of Fixed Assets}}{\text{Depreciation Expense}}$$

The ratio divides the total cost of fixed assets by the amount of annual depreciation expense to approximate the number of years that it will take to fully depreciate the assets. A higher number represents a longer useful life. You may notice that this ratio is basically a rearrangement of the calculation of straight-line depreciation. Therefore, the ratio works best when the company uses the straight-line method.

The **average age of fixed assets** represents the number of years, on average, that the company has used its fixed assets. It is calculated as follows:

Average useful life of fixed assets A comparison of the cost of fixed assets to depreciation expense that estimates the number of years, on average, that a company expects to use its fixed assets.

Average age of fixed assets A comparison of accumulated depreciation to depreciation expense that estimates the number of years, on average, that the company has used its fixed assets.

$$\text{Average Age} = \frac{\text{Accumulated Depreciation}}{\text{Depreciation Expense}}$$

The ratio divides the accumulated depreciation balance by the amount of annual depreciation expense to approximate the number of years that the assets have already been depreciated. A higher number means that the assets are older. Like the average useful life ratio, the average age ratio works best when the company uses the straight-line method.

Calculating **McDonald's** 2010 ratios requires the cost of the fixed assets and their accumulated depreciation balances at the end of 2010. These are found on the balance sheet. It also requires depreciation expense for 2010. This is found in the company's Property and Equipment note to its financial statements. Each account balance is shown in Exhibit 8-6.

$$\text{Average Life} = \frac{34{,}482.4}{1{,}200.4} = 28.7$$

$$\text{Average Age} = \frac{12{,}421.8}{1{,}200.4} = 10.3$$

The ratios show that McDonald's fixed assets, on average, have about a 29-year expected life and are currently about 10 years old. Now, we have to be careful here not to read too much into these numbers. In its first note to its financial statements, McDonald's reports that it assumes lives of up to 40 years for buildings, up to 15 years for restaurant equipment, and up to 10 years for other equipment. Like many companies, McDonald's has various fixed assets with various useful lives. While this makes the average life and age ratios very general estimates, the calculations do allow us to draw the general conclusion that the company's fixed assets are relatively new. On average, the company has used its fixed assets for about one-third of their useful lives. Thus, we would not expect McDonald's to have abnormally high expenditures for repairing or replacing fixed assets in the near future.

LO6 Fixed Assets and Cash Flows

Another important aspect of fixed assets is their effect on a company's cash flows. Fixed assets affect cash flows the most when they are purchased. Because companies often purchase significant amounts of fixed assets each year, the cash paid for them is reported as a separate line item in the investing activities section of the statement of cash flows. The line item is often labeled as Capital Expenditures or something similar. McDonald's is a little more specific, reporting the following on the first line of its investing activities section:

A negative number for capital expenditures indicates that a company is investing in operating assets.

McDonald's 2010 Capital Expenditures from the Statement of Cash Flows

in millions	2010	2009	2008
Property and equipment expenditures	$(2,135.5)	$(1,952.1)	$(2,135.7)

The negative number signifies a cash outflow. In 2010, McDonald's spent over $2.1 billion in cash to purchase fixed assets. In the two previous years, the company spent about $1.9 billion and $2.1 billion. For the three years combined, this totals over $6.1 billion in cash paid for fixed assets.

A natural question arising from this data is where the company got the $6.1 billion it needed for these investments in fixed assets. Did it borrow the money or did it have it on hand? We can get an idea of where the money came from by looking one line above the capital expenditures. There we find the cash provided by operating activities, which is summarized as follows:

McDonald's 2010 Operating Cash Flows from the Statement of Cash Flows

in millions	2010	2009	2008
Cash provided by operations	$6,341.6	$5,751.0	$5,917.2

In each year, McDonald's generated more cash from operating activities than it spent for fixed assets. For example, in 2010 the company generated $6.3 billion in cash from operations while it paid out $2.1 billion for fixed assets. This means that the company was able to finance its growth with money generated from profitable operations. When a company's capital expenditures exceed its cash from operating activities, the company

HOME DEPOT ANALYSIS

Look at **Home Depot's** statement of cash flows in Appendix C. How much cash has the company spent to acquire fixed assets over the past three years in total? Compare Home Depot's capital expenditures in the most recent year to its cash from operations.

According to the investing activities section of its statement of cash flows, Home Depot spent a total of \$3,909 capital expenditures over the past three years (\$1,096 + \$966 + \$1,847 = \$3,909).

Home Depot's capital expenditures in the most recent year were \$1,096 million while its cash generated from operations was \$4,585. Thus, it appears that Home Depot generated enough cash to pay for its growth in fixed assets without having to borrow the cash or dip into its reserves.

must get the needed cash from some other place. Either it must use its cash reserves or borrow the money from a creditor. Being able to generate enough cash to pay for new fixed assets is a good sign for **McDonald's**.

LO7 Intangible Assets

In addition to fixed assets, companies often possess other long-term assets known as intangible assets. An **intangible asset** is a resource that is used in operations for more than one year but has no physical substance. A patent is a good example. A **patent** is the right, granted by the United States Patent Office, for the holder of the patent to manufacture, sell, or use a particular product or process exclusively for a limited period of time. Although the right of exclusive use has no physical properties, it can be a very valuable resource to the holder. Consider the pharmaceutical industry. When a company develops a new drug that is approved by the Food and Drug Administration, which will be more valuable—the equipment that manufactures the drug or the patent that provides for exclusive manufacturing and selling of the drug? Pharmaceutical companies will likely tell you that the patent is most valuable to them.

You are probably familiar with other intangible assets. For example, a **trademark** or **trade name** is the right, granted by the United States Patent Office, for a company to use exclusively a name, symbol, or phrase to identify the company. Often, you can tell if something is registered as a trademark if it has a small ™ or ® beside the name or symbol. **Wendy's/Arby's** Frosty™ is an example. No other company, without permission from Wendy's/Arby's, can lawfully use the name Frosty™ in association with an ice cream drink. The **Nike** swoosh™ is another example, as is the script Coca-Cola™.

Another recognizable intangible is a copyright. A **copyright** is the right, granted by the United States Copyright Office, to reproduce or sell an artistic or published work. The publisher of this book owns the copyright to the material in the book and can reproduce and sell it as it pleases. The material cannot be reproduced by someone else lawfully without the permission of the publisher.

A third intangible with which you may be familiar is a franchise. A **franchise** is the right, granted by the franchisor, to operate a business under the trade name of the franchisor. Examples of franchises are all around you. For example, whenever you visit a McDonald's, you may be entering into a restaurant that is owned

Intangible asset A resource that is used in operations for more than one year but that has no physical substance.

Patent The right to manufacture, sell, or use a particular product or process exclusively for a limited period of time.

Trademark (trade name) The right to use exclusively a name, symbol, or phrase to identify a company.

Copyright The right to reproduce or sell an artistic or published work.

Franchise The right to operate a business under the trade name of the franchisor.

The Nike swoosh is a well-known example of a trademark.

PRNewsFoto/Nike/AP Photos

by an individual (the franchisee) who has purchased from **McDonald's Corporation** (the franchisor) the right to operate the restaurant.

Recording Intangible Assets

Like all other assets, intangible assets are recorded at their acquisition costs. However, what is included as an acquisition cost can vary given the type of intangible asset and how it is acquired.

Externally Acquired The easiest case is when an intangible asset is acquired through an external transaction. For example, suppose that a company purchases a product patent from another company for $100,000. Because the patent is purchased in an arm's-length transaction with another company, the cost of the patent is the purchase price. In general, if an intangible asset is acquired through an external transaction, its cost is the purchase price.

A common example of an intangible that is created through an external transaction is goodwill. Goodwill is created when one company buys another company and pays more than the value of the net assets of the purchased company. **Goodwill** is equal to the excess of the purchase price over the value of the purchased net assets. For example, suppose that in December 8 Buyer Company purchases Seller Company for $8 million when the value of Seller Company's net assets is $6 million. In this transaction, Buyer Company pays $8 million and records $6 million of new assets and $2 million of goodwill. A condensed form of the entry Buyer Company would make to record this transaction would be as follows:

Dec. 8	Net Assets of Seller Company	6,000,000	
	Goodwill	2,000,000	
	Cash		8,000,000
	(To record the purchase of Seller)		

Assets	=	Liabilities	+	Equity
+6,000,000				
+2,000,000				
−8,000,000				

The above entry records the decrease in cash resulting from the purchase and the increase in net assets acquired through the purchase. The difference of $2 million is debited to Goodwill, which increases that asset account. The result of the entry is an increase and decrease to assets.

To understand what goodwill represents, think about why a company would pay a premium for another company. The purchasing company might want to acquire the other company's customers, its reputation, its employees, its market share, or its research. Whatever the reason, the purchasing company is paying for something intangible that the other company possesses. This intangible value is what goodwill represents. Note here that goodwill can be recorded by a company *only* when it purchases another company. Goodwill created internally by a company cannot be recorded as an asset because its cost cannot be reliably determined. Only through an independent purchase can the value of goodwill be objectively measured.

Goodwill can be a large asset on the balance sheets of companies that have acquired other companies. **Wendy's/Arby's** is a good example. On its 2010 balance sheet, the company reports over $888 million in goodwill. Most of this goodwill was created when Wendy's International was purchased by **Triarc**, the parent company of Arby's. With total assets of approximately $4.4 billion, goodwill represents over 20% of assets. McDonald's also has a large balance in goodwill. It reports about $2.6 billion in goodwill on total assets of just under $32 billion. Goodwill makes up about 8% of McDonald's assets.

Internally Generated In the previous two examples, intangible assets were purchased externally and therefore recorded at their purchase prices. When an intangible asset is developed internally, the accounting is slightly different. The initial cost of an internally generated intangible asset is limited to the legal and administrative fees to establish the asset.

To illustrate, suppose that a company's researchers spend $150,000 creating a patentable product. To register the patent, the company spends $10,000. In this case, the cost of the patent is only $10,000. The $150,000 of research and development must be expensed in the period it is incurred, not added to the cost of the asset. While many disagree with this accounting treatment, it is another application of conservatism. It is very difficult to know whether particular research and development costs will result in productive assets and how long those assets might last. Given this uncertainty, excluding research and development costs from the cost of an internally developed intangible asset reduces the likelihood that the intangible asset is overstated.

Once an intangible asset is acquired and recorded, it is often challenged by other companies. For example, patent holders often must defend their rights against companies

Goodwill An intangible asset equal to the excess that one company pays to acquire the net assets of another company.

manufacturing similar products. When a company incurs costs to successfully defend the legality of its assets, such costs should be added to the cost of the asset. You can see this treatment in company disclosures. For example, **eSpeed, Inc.**, a provider of business-to-business electronic solutions, discloses in its notes that "[i]ntangible assets consist of purchased patents, costs incurred in connection with the filing and registration of patents and *the costs to defend and enforce our rights under patents.*"

Amortizing Intangible Assets

Like fixed assets that are depreciated, intangible assets with limited useful lives are amortized. **Amortization** is the process of spreading out the cost of an intangible asset over its useful life. Two examples of intangible assets with limited lives are patents and copyrights. Patents are granted for up to 20 years, and copyrights are granted for the life of the creator plus 70 years. Companies usually use the straight-line method for amortization.

To illustrate, suppose that a company possesses a $60,000 patent that has the maximum legal life of 20 years. The company believes that the patent will be useful for only 12 years and will then be worthless.

Amortization The process of spreading out the cost of an intangible asset over its useful life.

Amortization expense at the end of each year would be $5,000 ($60,000 ÷ 12) and would be recorded as follows:

End of year	Amortization Expense	5,000	
	Patent		5,000

Assets	=	Liabilities	+	Equity
−5,000				−5,000

The result of this entry is an increase to expenses and a decrease to assets. Notice that the entry records amortization expense based on the 12-year useful life, not the 20-year legal life. Amortization should be based on the shorter of the legal life or useful life. Notice also that the entry directly reduces the patent account. Unlike fixed assets, the amortization of intangible assets does not require the use of an accumulated amortization contra-account.

Amortization applies only to intangible assets with limited lives. Assets with indefinite lives such as trademarks and goodwill are instead examined periodically to check for impairment. This is similar to the impairment of fixed assets. In general, if the market value of the intangible asset permanently falls below its cost, then the asset is impaired. In such a case, the company records a loss on impairment and reduces the asset to its market value. As you can imagine, determining whether an intangible asset is impaired is a very subjective process and requires a great deal of judgment. In such cases, it is important for accountants to follow guiding principles such as conservatism, relevance, and reliability.

STUDY TOOLS 8

Chapter review card

- Learning Objective and Key Concept Reviews
- Key Definitions and Formulas

Online (Located at www.cengagebrain.com)

- Flash Cards and Crossword Puzzles
- Games and Quizzes
- E-Lectures
- Homework Assignments (as directed by your instructor)

CONCEPT QUESTIONS

1. (LO1) Define the term "fixed asset."
2. (LO1) How and where are fixed assets recorded in the financial statements?
3. (LO1) Define the term "depreciation."
4. (LO2) List the three methods of depreciation and state the formula for each method.
5. (LO2) Compare and contrast the three methods of depreciation.
6. (LO3) A change in accounting estimate is said to be made "prospectively." What does this mean?
7. (LO3) What is the effect of a change in estimate of the useful life of a fixed asset?
8. (LO3) What are the two possible methods of accounting for expenditures made during the useful life of a fixed asset? How does one determine which method to apply?
9. (LO3) What does it mean for an asset to be considered "impaired?"
10. (LO3) What action is taken when an asset is considered impaired?
11. (LO4) List the steps required to calculate the disposal of a fixed asset.
12. (LO5) State the formula for fixed asset turnover ratio and describe what this ratio tells an analyst.
13. (LO5) State the formula for the average age and average useful life of fixed assets and describe what they tell an analyst.
14. (LO6) How is the cash paid for fixed assets reported on the statement of cash flows?
15. (LO7) What is normally included in the cost of an internally developed intangible asset? How are research and development costs treated?

MULTIPLE CHOICE

1. (LO1) A fixed asset is classified as a/an:
   a. current asset.
   b. non-current asset.
   c. intangible asset.
   d. contra-asset.
2. (LO1) Which of the following is not a characteristic of a fixed asset?
   a. Recorded at cost
   b. Used for less than one year
   c. Used in the normal course of operations
   d. Not intended for resale
3. (LO1) Which of the following would not be included in the cost of purchased equipment?
   a. Taxes paid on the equipment
   b. Shipping costs to have equipment delivered
   c. Insurance premiums for the next month of use
   d. Installation costs of equipment
4. (LO1) Teel, Inc., bought a new forklift and incurred the following costs in association with the purchase:

Purchase price	$25,000
State sales tax	$ 2,100
Delivery fees	$ 350
Liability insurance for year 1	$ 1,200

   At what value will the forklift be reported on Teel's balance sheet?
   a. $28,650
   b. $25,000
   c. $27,100
   d. $27,450
5. (LO2) Which of the following is not an acceptable method of depreciation?
   a. Total cost
   b. Straight-line
   c. Double-declining-balance
   d. Units-of-activity
6. (LO2) If Alcorn Industries purchases for $20,000 a new delivery truck with an estimated 5-year useful life and $2,500 salvage value, what is the depreciation expense for year one using the straight-line depreciation method?
   a. $3,500
   b. $4,000
   c. $4,500
   d. $5,000
7. (LO2) Assume the same facts as the question above except that Alcorn Industries uses the double-declining-balance method of depreciation. What would Alcorn Industries record as depreciation expense for year one?
   a. $5,000
   b. $6,000
   c. $7,000
   d. $8,000
8. (LO2) Which of the following statements about depreciation is false?
   a. Depreciation is necessary because of the matching principle
   b. Depreciation expense is reported as a reduction to income on the income statement
   c. All three methods of depreciation result in the same total depreciation over the life of an asset
   d. All of the above statements are true

9. (LO1, 2) Which of the following statements are true?
   i. All assets have a limited useful life
   ii. Net Book Value = Cost − Accumulated Depreciation
   a. i only
   b. ii only
   c. Both i and ii
   d. Neither i nor ii
10. (LO3) A change in the estimate of the useful life of a fixed asset affects:
    a. depreciation expense of the prior years.
    b. the current total in the accumulated depreciation account.
    c. depreciation expense in the period of the change and all future periods.
    d. depreciation expense in past, current, and future periods.
11. (LO3) An expenditure that extends the useful life of a fixed asset should be:
    a. expensed in the period in which it was incurred.
    b. capitalized and depreciated over the remaining useful life of the asset.
    c. recorded in the repairs and maintenance account.
    d. ignored.
12. (LO3) An expenditure that maintains the useful life of a fixed asset should be:
    a. expensed in the period in which it was incurred.
    b. capitalized and depreciated over the remaining useful life of the asset.
    c. added to the historical cost of the asset.
    d. ignored.
13. (LO4) A fixed asset has a historical cost of $20,000, a net book value of $12,000, and a salvage value of $2,500. What is the gain (loss) on the disposal of the fixed asset if it is sold for $15,000?
    a. $5,000 loss
    b. $3,000 gain
    c. $12,500 gain
    d. $15,000 gain
14. (LO3) Which of the following statements is false?
    a. The impairment of a fixed asset is an application of conservatism
    b. When an asset is considered impaired, its book value must be reduced to its fair market value
    c. Impairment of a fixed asset results in a gain on the income statement
    d. An asset is considered impaired if its market value is materially below its net book value and the difference is considered permanent
15. (LO4) The following account totals appear in the general ledger of the Boston Company:

Equipment	$12,000
Accumulated Depreciation	$ 4,500

    If the equipment is sold to an outside party for $5,500, what amount of gain (loss) will the Boston Company record on the disposal of the equipment?
    a. $2,000 loss
    b. $1,000 gain
    c. $2,500 gain
    d. $4,000 gain
16. (LO5) Horizontal analysis of fixed assets:
    a. calculates fixed assets as a percentage of total assets.
    b. calculates depreciation expense as a percentage of revenues.
    c. calculates the change in fixed assets as a percentage of the prior year's fixed assets balance.
    d. both "a" and "b" are correct.
17. (LO5) Vertical analysis of fixed assets and depreciation:
    a. calculates fixed assets as a percentage of total assets.
    b. calculates depreciation expense as a percentage of revenues.
    c. calculates the change in fixed assets as a percentage of the prior year's fixed assets balance.
    d. both "a" and "b" are correct.
18. (LO5) The results of the fixed asset turnover ratio communicates to management:
    a. how quickly a fixed asset is depreciated.
    b. how many fixed assets were bought in the current period.
    c. how much depreciation expense was recorded compared to total fixed assets.
    d. how effectively a company is using its fixed assets to produce revenue.
19. (LO5) The average useful life of a company's fixed assets is calculated by the formula:
    a. Average Useful Life = Total Useful Lives of Assets/Cost of Fixed Assets.
    b. Average Useful Life = Depreciation Expense/Cost of Fixed Assets.
    c. Average Useful Life = Costs of Fixed Assets/Accumulated Depreciation.
    d. Average Useful Life = Costs of Fixed Assets/Depreciation Expense.
20. (LO6) Which of the following statements is true?
    i. Cash paid for fixed assets is normally reported as a separate line item on the statement of cash flows
    ii. Capital expenditures are normally reported as a cash outflow in the operating section of the statement of cash flows
    a. i only
    b. ii only
    c. Both i and ii
    d. Neither i nor ii
21. (LO7) Which of the following is not an intangible asset?
    a. Patent
    b. Goodwill
    c. Franchise
    d. All of the above are intangible assets

22. (LO7) Company A purchases Company B for a total of $2,800,000. Company B has total assets of $2,500,000, total liabilities of $400,000, and total equity of $2,100,000. How much Goodwill will Company A record as a result of the purchase of Company B?
    a. $0
    b. $300,000
    c. $400,000
    d. $700,000
23. (LO7) Which of the following statements is true?
    a. All intangible assets have an indefinite life
    b. Spreading the cost of an intangible asset over its estimated useful life is called depreciation
    c. The cost of an externally acquired intangible asset is its purchase price
    d. Internally generated intangible assets cannot be recorded as an asset

BRIEF EXERCISES

1. Acquisition Cost LO1

Orange & Blue, Inc., incurred the following expenditures when purchasing land: $47,000 purchase price; $4,500 in taxes; $2,000 of sales commissions; and $13,000 for clearing and grading, of which $8,000 was for removing an old building.

Required
Determine the acquisition cost of the land.

2. Reporting Fixed Assets LO1

At the end of the year, The Puppy Emporium had property and equipment with a historical cost of $100,000. Collectively, these assets had been depreciated $25,000.

Required
Show two ways in which the property and equipment could be reported on The Puppy Emporium's balance sheet.

3. Depreciation Expense: Straight-Line LO2

Garrett Deliveries purchases a truck for $18,000. The truck has an estimated salvage value of $4,000 and is expected to be driven for seven years. Garrett uses the straight-line method of depreciation.

Required
Calculate annual depreciation expense.

4. Determine Net Book Value LO2

Suppose that an asset is purchased for $86,000. The asset has an estimated useful life of ten years and a salvage value of $4,000.

Required
Assuming straight-line depreciation, determine the net book value of the asset after two years.

5. Depreciation Expense: Double-Declining-Balance LO2

Sanders Catering purchases a van for $32,000. The van has an estimated salvage value of $6,000 and is expected to be driven for four years. Garrett uses the double-declining-balance method of depreciation.

Required
Calculate depreciation expense for each of the four years of the asset's life.

6. Depreciation Expense: Units-of-Activity LO2

City Taxi purchases a new taxi cab for $25,000. The cab has an estimated salvage value of $1,000 and is expected to be driven for approximately 120,000 miles over its useful life of five years.

Required
a. Calculate the depreciation expense per mile.
b. Prepare a deprecation schedule assuming that the actual miles driven for years one through five were as follows: 25,000; 27,000; 21,000; 28,000; and 19,000.

7. Change in Useful Life LO3

A company purchases a fixed asset with an estimated useful life of 15 years and a salvage value of $10,000. When the asset has 7 years of life remaining, the company decides that the remaining useful life should be 5 years. The asset's net book value at the time of revision is $60,000.

Required
Using the straight-line method, calculate depreciation expense for the first year after the revision.

8. Expenditures After Acquisition LO3

Tiger Logistics acquired a new truck for $75,000 in 2008. At the end of 2011, accumulated depreciation on the truck was $25,000. On January 1, 2012, Tiger paid $2,000 for routine service on the truck and $8,000 to overhaul the engine. The engine work is anticipated to extend the useful life of the truck by 5 years.

Required
Calculate the net book value of Tiger's truck immediately after the service and overhaul.

9. Impairment Entry LO3

Jenford Factories acquired equipment for $350,000. On March 15, 2012, Jenford determines that the equipment is impaired by $65,000.

Required
Prepare the entry to record the impairment of the equipment.

10. Calculating Gains and Losses on Disposal LO4

Chris' Crispy Chicken sold one of its used deep fryers for $5,000. The original cost of the fryer was $15,000, and related accumulated depreciation at the time of the sale was $7,000.

Required
Calculate the gain or loss on the sale of the deep fryer. For what amount would Chris need to sell the equipment to generate no gain or loss?

11. Recording a Disposal LO4

A company sells a building with a cost of $350,000 and accumulated depreciation of $270,000 and records the entry for the sale as follows:

Cash	70,000	
Loss on Disposal	10,000	
Building		80,000

Required
a. Did the company prepare the entry correctly? If not, prepare the correct entry.
b. What would the gain or loss on sale be if the sale price was $97,000?

12. Analyze Fixed Assets LO5

In its annual report, Phono Corporation reported beginning total assets of $360,000, ending total assets of $406,000, beginning fixed assets of $300,000 (at cost), ending fixed assets of $311,000 (at cost), ending accumulated depreciation of $106,000, depreciation expense of $16,500, and net revenues of $120,000.

Required
Calculate Phono's fixed asset turnover ratio for the year and its average useful life and age of fixed assets at year-end.

13. Recording Intangible Assets LO7

Gentry Software, Inc., incurred $400,000 in research costs and $500,000 in salaries to develop a new tablet application. Gentry paid $12,000 to register the patent protecting the application.

Required
Should Gentry record the patent as an asset, and if so, at what value?

14. Recording Amortization Expense LO7

In 2012 Buckeye Research Labs patented a new polymer. The patent was capitalized at $55,000, but the market value is $800,000. Buckeye determines that the legal life of the patent is 8 years, although it knows that the useful life is only 5 years.

Required
Record the entry for amortization expense for 2012. Assume that Buckeye records a full year of expense.

EXERCISES

15. Acquisition Cost LO1

Prince's Pipe Co. purchases equipment with a list price of $22,000. Regarding the purchase, Prince:

- Received a 2% discount off the list price
- Paid shipping costs of $800
- Paid $1,750 to install the equipment, $1,200 of which was for a unique stand for the equipment
- Paid $2,800 to insure the equipment, $300 for delivery transit, and $2,500 for a two-year policy to cover operations
- Paid $600 to have the manufacturer train employees on safety features

Required
Determine the acquisition cost of the equipment.

16. Acquisition Costs LO1

Knight Company acquired a new tract of land for $250,000. Knight also paid $20,000 in taxes and fees, $23,000 to remove an old building, and $75,000 for logging, grading, and filling the land prior to its use. Proceeds from the sale of timber as a result of logging were $40,000.

Required
Determine the amount that Knight would record as the cost of the land.

17. Depreciation Methods LO2

Phigam Steel purchases a machine on January 1 for $30,000. The machine has an estimated useful life of seven years, during which time it is expected to produce 114,800 units. Salvage value is estimated at $1,300. The machine produces 15,500 and 16,200 units in its first and second years of operation, respectively.

Required
Calculate depreciation expense for the machine's first two years using the straight-line, double-declining-balance, and units-of-activity methods of depreciation. Round values to the nearest dollar.

18. Depreciation Methods LO2

Xing, Inc., purchases a delivery truck on January 1 for $25,000. The truck has an estimated useful life of five years and an estimated salvage value of $2,500.

Required
For both the straight-line and double-declining-balance methods of depreciation, prepare a schedule of depreciation expense, accumulated depreciation, and net book value over the life of the asset. Advise Xing, Inc., of the advantages/disadvantages of the two depreciation methods.

19. Depreciation Methods and Taxes LO2

On January 1, 2012, Scout Manufacturing purchased new equipment for $145,000. The equipment was estimated to have a five-year useful life and a salvage value of $15,000. Scout estimates that the equipment will produce 81,250 units over its useful life. However, it actually produces 18,000 units in 2012, 17,500 units in 2013, 17,750 units in 2014, 17,000 units in 2015, and 15,000 units in 2016.

Required

a. Prepare a depreciation schedule for Scout for each of the five years using the straight-line method, the double-declining-balance method, and the units-of-activity method.
b. Assuming a tax rate of 30%, how much more could Scout defer in taxes in the first year by using the double-declining-balance method versus the straight-line method?

20. Acquisition Costs and Depreciation LO1, 2

On January 1, Jones Company acquired a new delivery truck for $40,000 cash. Additional cash payments during the year were as follows.

- Taxes and fees on delivery truck, $3,200
- Installation of GPS system and painting of logo for truck, $3,000
- Auto and liability insurance premiums paid on truck, $1,500.

Required

a. Prepare all journal entries Jones would make regarding the delivery truck.
b. Assume that the delivery truck has an estimated useful life of five years and an estimated salvage value of $2,000. Calculate depreciation expense on the delivery truck for the current year, assuming Jones uses the double-declining-balance method of depreciation.
c. Show how Jones would report the truck on its current-year balance sheet.

21. Change in Estimates LO2, 3

On January 1, 2012, Roosters Co. purchases equipment for $30,000 and estimates a useful life of eight years and a salvage value of $2,000. On January 1, 2014, Roosters revises the equipment's useful life from eight years to five years. Roosters uses the straight-line method of depreciation.

Required

a. Calculate depreciation expense for 2012, 2013, and 2014.
b. Recalculate 2014 depreciation expense assuming that Roosters leaves the useful life at eight years but reduces the salvage value to $0.

22. Capital/Revenue Expenditures LO3

A company incurs the following expenditures related to currently owned fixed assets:

- Annual pressure washing of building, $5,000
- New engine in delivery truck, $4,500
- Repair of water damage caused by leaking roof, $3,500
- New tires on tractor, $2,000
- Addition of 1,000 square feet of office space, $22,000
- Modifications to machinery to improve efficiency, $7,200

Required

Identify each expenditure as a capital or revenue expenditure.

23. Adjustments to Fixed Assets LO2, 3

A company that uses the straight-line method of depreciation experiences the following independent items:

- Increases a useful life estimate from 5 years to 8 years
- Pays for maintenance of equipment
- Reduces a salvage value estimate by $10,000
- Pays $50,000 to significantly increase the productivity of an existing fixed asset
- Records an impairment on a fixed asset

Required

Identify whether each independent item would increase, decrease, or not affect depreciation expense for the underlying fixed asset.

24. Capital Expenditure LO2, 3

On January 1, 2013, Moran Manufacturing has a building with a net book value of $357,000, no salvage value, and a remaining useful life of 7 years. During January, major renovations in the amount of $73,000 are conducted and add five more years to the building's useful life and increase the salvage value to $40,000. Moran uses the straight-line method of depreciation.

Required

a. Determine the amount of depreciation that Moran recorded in 2012. Hint: think about how straight-line depreciation works.
b. Determine the net book value of the building immediately after the repairs were completed.
c. Calculate depreciation expense for the year 2013. Assume that the cost of the renovation is depreciated for a full year in 2013.

25. Disposal LO4

Ellis Industries sells a building that has an original cost of $200,000 and an accumulated depreciation balance of $100,000.

Required

Prepare the journal entry to record the sale assuming the sales price was (a) $100,000, (b) $95,000, and (c) $108,000.

26. Disposal LO2, 4

On January 1, 2012, A&G Company pays $40,000 for equipment with a 10-year estimated life and a $5,000 estimated salvage value. On January 1, 2016, A&G sells the equipment for $18,500.

Required

Calculate the gain or loss on the sale assuming A&G uses the straight-line method of depreciation. Where should the gain or loss on the sale be presented on the income statement?

27. Depreciation and Disposal LO2, 4

On January 1, 2012, the Von Schoppe Company purchased a delivery truck for $20,000. The truck had an estimated useful life of six years and a salvage value of $2,000. On September 30, 2014, Von Shoppe sold the truck for $13,000. Von Shoppe uses the straight-line method of depreciation and records depreciation on December 31.

Required

a. Calculate the gain or loss on the disposal of the delivery truck.
b. Prepare all entries necessary on September 30, 2014.

28. Evaluate Fixed Assets LO5

In a recent annual report, **Nike** reported the following information (in millions): beginning total assets $6,821; ending total assets $7,891; beginning property, plant, and equipment $2,988 (at cost); ending property, plant, and equipment $3,132 (at cost); beginning accumulated depreciation $1,293; revenues $12,253; and depreciation expense of $252.

Required

Calculate the following ratios for Nike: fixed asset turnover, average useful life, and average age.

29. Evaluate Fixed Assets LO5

The following data was taken from the annual financial statements of Grizzle Company:

	Revenues	Fixed Asset NBV
2006	4,889	150
2007	5,897	201
2008	6,583	245
2009	8,563	395
2010	10,589	524
2011	13,584	687
2012	14,555	793

Required

Calculate the fixed asset turnover ratio for the years presented. What does the trend in the ratio tell you about the company's performance?

30. Intangible Assets LO7

Phoebe, Inc., incurred the following expenditures:

- Research and development costs of $60,000 were incurred to develop a new patentable product.
- Paid $1,000 in application fees for the patent.
- Paid $12,000 in legal fees to register the awarded patent.
- Incurred $5,000 in legal fees to successfully defend the patent against a competitor.

Required

Determine the total cost of the patent.

31. Amortization of Intangible Assets LO7

Ramon Productions purchased the copyright to a film script for $264,000 on July 1. The copyright protects the owners' legal rights for the next 20 years, but producers at Ramon estimate they will only be able to use the copyright for the next 15 years. Ramon Productions uses the straight-line method of amortization and has a June 30 year-end.

Required

Prepare the journal entry to record amortization expense for the first year.

PROBLEMS

32. Depreciation Methods LO2, 4

Development Industries purchased a depreciable asset for $50,000 on January 1, 2012. The asset has a five-year useful life and a $10,000 estimated salvage value. The company will use the straight-line method of depreciation for book purposes. However, Development will use the double-declining-balance method for tax purposes. Assume a tax rate of 30%.

Required

a. Prepare depreciation schedules using the straight-line and double-declining-balance methods of depreciation for the useful life of the asset.
b. Calculate the 2012 tax savings from the use of the accelerated depreciation method for tax purposes.
c. Under the straight-line method of depreciation, what is the gain or loss if the equipment is sold (1) at the end of 2014 for $30,000 or (2) at the end of 2015 for $16,000?
d. How is the gain or loss on the disposal of the equipment presented in the financial statements? How does this differ from how depreciation expense is presented?

33. Various Transactions LO1, 2, 3, 4

On January 1, 2012, Ravioli, Inc., purchased a building for a cash price of $192,000 and accrued property taxes of $14,950. The building is estimated to have a useful life of 10 years and no salvage value. On the same day, Ravioli paid $25,450 in cash plus sales tax of $2,290 for a new delivery truck that is estimated to have a useful life of five years and a salvage value of $2,200. Another $1,100 was paid to paint the company logo on the truck. Over the next several years, the following events related to these fixed assets occurred:

1/1/2013	Uncovered new information which caused the estimated life of the truck to be reduced to three total years instead of five years.
6/30/2013	Repaired truck's air conditioning system which broke down for one week, $500.
1/1/2014	Renovated bottom floor of the building for $15,000, adding three years of useful life to the building.
1/1/2015	Sold building for $163,000.
9/1/2015	Sold truck for $5,350.

Required

Prepare all entries for 2012 through 2015. Ravioli records annual depreciation expense on 12/31.

34. Recording and Expensing Fixed Assets LO1, 2

At the beginning of the year, Wiggins Co. purchased ten new computers in order to transform an existing café into an Internet café. The following expenditures were related to the purchase of the computers.

- Purchase price, $27,000
- Sales taxes, $2,400
- Freight costs, $1,800
- Installation, $400

The accountant at Wiggins recorded $29,400 in the asset account Equipment and $2,200 in the expense account Delivery Expense. The computers have a three-year life and no salvage value. Wiggins depreciates all fixed assets using the straight-line method.

Required

a. How much depreciation expense will Wiggins record in year one of the computers? Do you agree with this amount? If not, what amount do you think should be recorded as depreciation expense for year one?
b. If income before any expense related to the purchase and depreciation of these computers is $80,000, what will Wiggins report as net income for year one? (Assume a tax rate of 40%.) What amount of income should Wiggins report?
c. Briefly explain to Wiggins' accountant why his net income is incorrect in year one.

35. Fixed Asset Transactions and Reporting LO1, 2, 4

A partial portion of the balance sheet at December 31, 2012, for the Gusto Corporation is presented below:

Land		$500,000
Buildings	$630,000	
Less: Accumulated depreciation	250,000	380,000
Equipment	$ 65,000	
Less: Accumulated depreciation	22,000	43,000
Total property and equipment		$923,000

The following transactions occurred during 2013:

- On January 1, retired equipment with a net book value of $2,000. The equipment was purchased for $8,000. No value was received from the retirement.
- On January 1, Gusto sold a building with an original 30-year useful life and no estimated salvage value for $90,000 cash. The building was originally purchased on December 31, 2002 for $120,000.
- Purchased land for $90,000 on April 30.
- On July 1, Gusto purchased equipment for $30,000 by signing a long-term note payable.
- Prepared depreciation entries on December 31. Depreciation expense for the year was $40,000 for buildings and $4,500 for equipment.

Required

a. Prepare journal entries to record all of the above transactions.
b. Prepare the property and equipment portion of Gusto's balance sheet at December 31, 2013.

36. Evaluate Fixed Assets LO5

The following information was available from recent financial statements of Papa John's Pizza:

	Current year	Prior year
Property and equipment, net	$ 189,992	$ 198,957
Total assets	386,468	401,817
Depreciation expense	31,800	30,600
Property and equipment, at cost	388,080	408,074
Accumulated depreciation	198,088	209,117
Total revenues	1,132,087	1,063,595

Required
Calculate and interpret (1) horizontal and vertical analyses of fixed assets and depreciation expense, (2) fixed asset turnover ratio, and (3) average life and average age of fixed assets. Round percentages to one decimal points (e.g., 45.2%).

37. Evaluate Fixed Assets LO5

The following information comes from an analysis of two competitors, Claw Co. and the Smiles Company:

	Claw	Smiles
Net revenues	$125,000	$110,000
Net income	50,000	68,000
Average total assets	1,245,000	950,000
Average NBV of fixed assets	750,000	645,000
Accumulated depreciation	120,000	240,000
Depreciation expense	25,000	12,000

Required
a. For both competitors, compute the asset turnover ratio, average useful life of the assets, and the average age of the fixed assets.
b. After analysis, which of the two companies is better at using assets to generate revenues?
c. Are there factors that seem to contradict each other in these numbers? What could be some valid reasons for such circumstances?

38. Intangible Assets LO3, 7

During 2012, Haslem, Inc., invested $105,000 to successfully develop a new product, and a patent was granted on December 31, 2012. Haslem incurred $22,000 of legal fees and $1,200 of registration fees to secure the patent. Haslem estimates that the patent will have a useful life of 10 years and no salvage value. On January 1, 2015, Haslem's major competitor announced that it had developed a similar product, which reduced the value of Haslem's patent to $12,000. Haslem considers the loss in value permanent. Haslem has a December 31 year-end.

Required
a. What amount should be recorded as the cost of the patent? How are the remaining costs treated for financial reporting purposes?
b. Compute amortization expense for the patent for years 2013 and 2014 and prepare the appropriate journal entries.
c. What should Haslem do on January 1, 2015, if anything?

CASES

39. Research and Analysis LO1, 5, 6

Access the 2010 annual report for **Columbia Sportswear Company** by clicking on the *Investor Relations, Financial Information,* and *Annual Reports* links at www.columbia.com.

Required
a. Examine the company's balance sheet and conduct horizontal and vertical analyses of net property, plant, and equipment. Round percentages to one decimal points (e.g., 45.2%).
b. Calculate the company's 2010 fixed asset turnover ratio. Also, calculate the company's average age and useful life ratios at the end of 2010. Cost and accumulated depreciation data can be found in Note 6 to the financial statements. Depreciation and amortization expense can be found in Note 18 (Segment Information).
c. Examine the company's statement of cash flows. How much cash did the company spend on property and equipment over the three years presented?
d. Based on your answers above, write a paragraph explaining your opinion of Columbia's fixed asset position. Use your answers as supporting facts.

40. Research and Analysis LO1, 2, 5, 6

Access the 2010 annual report for **Nike, Inc.**, by clicking on the Investors and Annual Reports links at www.nikebiz.com.

Required
a. Examine the balance sheet and identify the name Nike uses for fixed assets. Are fixed assets reported at net book value?
b. Examine Note 3 and identify the original cost of Nike's fixed assets and the current balance in accumulated depreciation.
c. According to Note 1, what method of depreciation does Nike use?
d. According to the statement of cash flows, how much has Nike spent on fixed assets over the past three years? Does the company generate enough cash from operations to sustain that level of investment?
e. Calculate the average age and useful life of Nike's fixed assets. Use "Depreciation" on the statement of cash flows as depreciation expense for the year. What can you conclude from these calculations?

41. Written Communication LO2

Play Hard Fitness Center is a chain of work-out facilities. Play Hard's financial analysts have forecasted sales to remain at a constant level for the next three years, but income taxes are forecasted to grow by 5% a year for the next five years. Play Hard is about to refurnish 50% of its centers with new equipment that will have an estimated useful life of five years. As a CPA, you know that companies can use one method of depreciation for tax purposes and another for book purposes. The two methods under consideration are the double-declining-balance method and straight-line method of depreciation.

Required

Write a short memo recommending the method you would use for tax purposes and the method you would use for book purposes. Be sure to discuss the advantages and disadvantages of both of the methods as well as the associated effects on income, depreciation over time, cash flows, etc.

42. Ethics in Accounting LO1, 3

A friend of yours claims that he likes accounting because there is always a right and wrong answer to a question and therefore there is no temptation for wrongdoing.

Required

Using capital and revenue expenditures as an example, explain how judgment can be involved in accounting decisions and how an individual's ethics can affect the manner in which he or she accounts for a particular item.

ACCT

Liabilities

Learning Objectives

After studying the material in this chapter, you should be able to:

LO1 Describe the recording and reporting of various current liabilities.

LO2 Describe the reporting of long-term liabilities and the cash flows associated with those liabilities.

LO3 Understand the nature of bonds and record a bond's issuance, interest payments, and maturity.

LO4 Account for a bond that is redeemed prior to maturity.

LO5 Understand additional liabilities such as leases and contingent liabilities.

LO6 Evaluate liabilities through the calculation and interpretation of horizontal, vertical, and ratio analyses.

LO7 Appendix: Determine a bond's issuance price.

LO8 Appendix: Record bond interest payments under the effective interest method.

Introduction

The generation and payment of liabilities is common to every business. Some are generated daily and paid quickly. Others are paid over time and often require the payment of interest. Still others must be estimated, and some never come to fruition. This chapter examines the accounting for such liabilities. It focuses first on how some common current liabilities are generated and reported. It then examines long-term liabilities with a specific focus on the issuance of, interest on, and payment of bonds. It also discusses the obligations associated with leases and considers the treatment of potential obligations that may or may not become liabilities. As in previous chapters, the final section of the chapter focuses on the analysis of a company's position regarding its obligations. The appendix covers bond pricing and the effective interest method for bond amortization.

LO1 Current Liabilities

A **current liability** is an obligation of a business that is expected to be satisfied or paid within one year. Current liabilities can arise from regular business operations such as the purchase of inventory, the compensation of employees, the repayment of debt, and the incurrence of taxes. Most current liabilities, such as accounts payable and notes payable, will be satisfied through the payment of cash. Others, such as deferred revenues in which a customer prepays for a service to be performed later, will be satisfied through the performance of the service. The following sections present the accounting for some of the more common types of current liabilities.

Current liability An obligation of a business that is expected to be satisfied or paid within one year.

Taxes Payable

When conducting business, corporations generate a variety of tax obligations to federal, state, and local taxing

CHAPTER

A deposit in a bank is an asset to the customer, but it is a liability to the bank.

Lester Lefkowitz/Stone/Getty Images

authorities. One example is the income tax. Like individuals, corporations are subject to federal taxation of their income. And like individuals, they often wait until later to pay the bill, which creates a current liability. For example, suppose a company computes its annual income tax expense to be $25,000 on December 31 but plans to pay it in the next period. The company would make the following journal entry on December 31 to record the expense in the proper period:

Dec. 31	Income Tax Expense	25,000	
	Income Tax Payable		25,000
	(To record income tax expense)		

Assets	=	Liabilities	+	Equity
		+25,000		−25,000

Current liabilities arise from regular business operations such as the purchase of inventory, the compensation of employees, the repayment of debt, and the incurrence of taxes.

The entry increases both Income Tax Expense and Income Tax Payable. The result of the entry is a reduction to equity and an increase to liabilities.

Another example is sales taxes. Each time a company makes a retail sale, it collects sales tax according to state and/or local regulations. Because the company remits the taxes to the appropriate authority at some later date, the company must record a liability when the sale is made. To illustrate, suppose that a company sells a $1,000 item on July 10 and collects an 8% sales tax. The following entry records the sale and the resulting liability:

Jul. 10	Cash	1,080	
	Sales		1,000
	Sales Tax Payable		80
	(To record sale of merchandise)		

Assets	=	Liabilities	+	Equity
+1,080		+80		+1,000

The entry increases Cash for the $1,080 received from the customer, increases Sales for the $1,000 earned from the sale, and increases Sales Tax Payable for the $80 of tax collected and now owed to the taxing authorities. Notice that the company does not incur any expense related to the sales tax. The sales tax liability is created only because the company has collected sales tax on behalf of the taxing authorities.

A third type of tax that generates a current liability is payroll taxes. When paying employee wages, employers must withhold income taxes and Social Security (FICA) taxes owed by the employee. The employer then remits those taxes to the taxing authorities. To illustrate, suppose that an employee earns a May salary of $10,000. Based on the employee's filing status, the company must withhold 15% of the salary for federal income taxes, 12% for state income taxes, and 7.65% for Social Security taxes. On payday (May 31), the company would prepare the following entry:

May 31	Salaries Expense	10,000	
	Federal Tax Withholdings Payable		1,500
	State Tax Withholdings Payable		1,200
	FICA Taxes Payable		765
	Cash		6,535
	(To record payment of May salary)		

Assets	=	Liabilities	+	Equity
−6,535		+1,500		−10,000
		+1,200		
		+ 765		

The entry increases Salaries Expense for the $10,000 salary earned by the employee for May. However, the employee is paid only $6,535. The difference is the amount that the employee owes in taxes. On behalf of the employee, the employer withholds those taxes and records the resulting liabilities. As a result of this entry, assets decrease, liabilities increase, and equity decreases for the amount of the total salaries expense.

In addition to withholding taxes on behalf of employees, employers must also pay Social Security taxes on employee wages, currently at a rate of 7.65%. These additional taxes are an added expense for the employer. Along with the preceding entry, the employer would make the following entry to record the additional tax expense and the current liability:

May 31	Payroll Tax Expense	765	
	FICA Taxes Payable		765
	(To record employer share of FICA taxes)		

Assets	=	Liabilities	+	Equity
		+765		−765

Unearned Revenues

Many companies have business models in which customers pay in advance for services or products. An example is an airline such as **Delta Airlines**. Customers pay for tickets and then fly at some later date. Another example is a retailer such as **Target**. Customers often purchase gift cards, which are then redeemed for merchandise at a later date.

When a company receives a customer's cash prior to providing the service or product, the company has an obligation known as unearned revenue. Unearned revenue is classified as a current liability when the service or product is expected to be provided within one year.

As shown in Chapter 4, the accounting for unearned revenue requires the initial recording of the liability when cash is exchanged and then the recording of service revenue or sales when the service or product is provided. For example, suppose that Gayden Lawn Service sells annual contracts to customers for year-round lawn service and maintenance. Suppose further that on March 1, Erle Fairly purchases an annual contract for $600 cash. On March 1, Gayden would record the transaction as follows:

Mar. 1	Cash	600	
	Unearned Revenue		600
	(To record unearned revenue)		

Assets	=	Liabilities	+	Equity
+600		+600		

In this entry, Gayden increases Cash for the amount received and increases Unearned Revenue to indicate that it has an obligation to Fairly. As a result, both assets and liabilities increase. Note that Gayden does not record revenue in the entry because it has not yet earned any of Fairly's payment.

As Gayden provides the service to Fairly, it can begin to reduce the unearned revenue and record the resulting revenue. For example, suppose that Gayden provides its service equally over the annual contract such that it earns $50 each month ($600 ÷ 12 = $50). At the end of March, Gayden would therefore record the following entry:

Mar. 31	Unearned Revenue	50	
	Service Revenue		50
	(To record revenue earned)		

Assets	=	Liabilities	+	Equity
		−50		+50

In this entry, Gayden increases Service Revenue by $50 to recognize the amount of the obligation earned during the month. It also reduces Unearned Revenue by $50 to recognize that its obligation to Fairly is now $50 less than it was. After the entry, the remaining balance in Unearned Revenue is $450.

Unearned revenue can be a large liability for many companies. For example, **Delta Airlines, Inc.** recently reported approximately $4.5 billion in deferred revenue related to its frequent flyer program while **Target**, Inc. reported $422 million in unearned revenue related to gift cards.

Notes Payable

Chapter 6 introduced the concept of a promissory note, which is a written promise to pay a specific sum of money at some date in the future. That chapter focused on the party that accepted the note in exchange for cash. That is, chapter 6 demonstrated the accounting for notes *receivable*. This chapter focuses on the party that accepts cash in exchange for the note. That is, this chapter demonstrates the accounting for notes *payable*.

When a company issues a promissory note to borrow money, the company generates a **note payable**. Depending on the terms of the promissory note, a note payable can be classified as either a current liability or a long-term liability. If the note is payable within a year, it is a current liability. Otherwise, it is a long-term liability. The accounting for a note payable consists of recording the note, recording any interest that must be paid to the creditor, and recording the payment of the note.

To illustrate, suppose that on March 1 Brown Company borrows $30,000 by signing an 8%, 6-month note with Miller Street Bank. The note calls for interest to be paid when the note is repaid on August 31. On March 1, Brown would make the following entry to record the note:

Mar. 1	Cash	30,000	
	Note Payable		30,000
	(To record the note)		

Assets	=	Liabilities	+	Equity
+30,000		+30,000		

In this entry, Brown increases both Cash and Note Payable for $30,000. As a result, both assets and liabilities increase. Since this note matures within a year, the note payable would be reported as a current liability.

On August 31, Brown must pay Miller Street Bank the original $30,000 borrowed plus the interest on the note. Interest over the six months is calculated as follows:

Interest = Principal × Annual Rate of Interest × Time Outstanding
= $30,000 × 0.08 × 6/12 months
= $1,200

Note payable A liability generated by the issuance of a promissory note to borrow money.

Therefore, Brown would pay $31,200 to the bank and make the following entry on August 31:

Aug. 31	Note Payable	30,000	
	Interest Expense	1,200	
	Cash		31,200
	(To record payment of note and interest)		

Assets	=	Liabilities	+	Equity
−31,200		−30,000		−1,200

In this entry, Brown increases Interest Expense to reflect the cost of borrowing the $30,000 over the six months. Brown also decreases the Note Payable account because the note is being paid. Finally, Brown decreases Cash for the payment of principal and interest. Because of the entry, Brown's assets, liabilities, and equity decrease.

Current Portion of Long-Term Debt

Companies that borrow money on a long-term basis often pay principal on a short-term basis. The **current portion of long-term debt** represents the portion of a long-term liability that will be paid within one year. To illustrate, suppose that a company borrows $500,000 from a bank through a 10-year promissory note. Because the note is payable in 10 years, the company classifies it as a long-term liability. In year 10, the note is reclassified as a current liability because it will be satisfied in a year.

Suppose instead that the bank requires the company to repay the principal in installments of $50,000 per year plus interest. In that case, when the note is signed, the company has a long-term liability of $450,000 and a current liability of $50,000. Since the company must pay $50,000 each year until the note is repaid, the company will report $50,000 as Current Portion of Long-Term Debt each year.

As you consider these two examples, keep in mind that regardless of how the liability is classified on the balance sheet, the company is borrowing and repaying $500,000. The classification of the note payable as current or long-term does not affect the borrowing or repayment of the note. It only affects how the payable is reported on the balance sheet. However, this balance sheet reporting is important because it tells users of the financial statements what obligations will require payment in the short term.

Current portion of long-term debt The portion of a long-term liability that will be paid within one year.

Reporting Current Liabilities

Current liabilities are reported in a separate section on a classified balance sheet. The following is the current liabilities section of the 2010 balance sheet of **Advance Auto Parts**:

Advance Auto Parts' 2010 Current Liabilities

(in thousands)	
Current portion of long-term debt	$ 973
Financed vendor accounts payable	31,648
Accounts payable	1,292,113
Accrued expenses	404,086
Other current liabilities	119,229
Total	$1,848,049

Advance Auto Parts reports over $1.8 billion in current liabilities. This total is made up mostly of accounts payable and accrued expenses. Accounts payable normally represents what a company owes vendors for inventory that it stocks in its stores. It is not surprising to see a large balance in accounts payable for a retailer like Advance Auto Parts. Accrued expense is another name for a liability that is created when recording an unpaid expense. Advance Auto Parts' balance sheet doesn't report what activities created the accrued expenses. However, Note 10 to the company's financial statements shows that the liabilities arise from various operating activities related to payroll, product returns, insurance, and taxes.

Advance Auto Parts' 2010 Accrued Expense Note

(in thousands)	
Payroll and related benefits	$106,843
Warranty reserves	36,352
Capital expenditures	43,365
Self-insurance reserves	46,778
Taxes payable	55,662
Other	115,086
Total accrued expenses	$404,086

To provide some comparison, the 2010 current liabilities section of **O'Reilly Automotive's** balance sheet is as follows:

O'Reilly Automotive's 2010 Current Liabilities

(in thousands)	
Accounts payable	$ 895,736
Self-insurance reserve	51,192
Accrued payroll	52,725
Accrued benefits and withholdings	45,542
Income Taxes Payable	4,827
Other current liabilities	177,505
Current portion of long-term debt	1,431
Total	$1,228,958

Similar to **Advance Auto Parts'** current liabilities, O'Reilly's is made up of various operating obligations, with the largest being accounts payable.

LO2 Long-Term Liabilities

A **long-term liability** is any obligation of a business that is expected to be satisfied or paid in more than one year. Like current liabilities, the type and size of long-term liabilities can vary across companies. However, the most common and largest long-term liabilities often arise from borrowing money. This is the case for Advance Auto Parts. The following shows the company's condensed liabilities from its 2010 balance sheet:

> The most common and largest long-term liabilities often arise from borrowing money.

Advance Auto Parts' 2010 Condensed Liabilities

(in thousands)	
Total current liabilities	$1,848,049
Long-term debt	300,851
Other long-term liabilities	165,943
Total liabilities	$2,314,843

Advance Auto Parts reports two long-term liabilities. The first and largest is long-term debt. The balance sheet reports a total obligation of over $300 million. However, it does not reveal how or why this long-term debt was generated or when it must be repaid. Such information is disclosed in the notes to the company's financial statements.

Advance Auto Parts' 2010 Condensed Long-term Debt Note

(in thousands)	
5.75% Senior Unsecured Notes due May 2020	$298,824
Other	3,000
	$301,824
Less: Current portion of long-term debt	(973)
Total long-term debt	$300,851

Long-term liability Any obligation of a business that is expected to be satisfied or paid in more than one year.

HOME DEPOT ANALYSIS

Look at **Home Depot's** statement of cash flows in Appendix C. Over the three years presented, did Home Depot receive or pay more cash with respect to long-term debt?

The statement of cash flows shows total repayments of long-term debt of $3,116 million ($1,029 + $1,774 + $313). It also shows cash received of $998 in 2010 from issuing additional long-term debt. As a result, Home Depot repaid a net amount of long-term debt of $2,118 million over the three years presented. Note that this is in addition to the $1,732 repayment of short-term debt in 2008, which means that Home Depot repaid almost $4 billion of total debt during the three years.

Darla Hallmark

The note discloses that the company's total long-term debt is composed primarily of Senior Unsecured Notes issued at a rate of 5.75%. The notes are due to be paid in May of 2020.

While the balance sheet reports the balance in long-term liabilities, the statement of cash flows reports the cash flows associated with those liabilities in the financing activities section. The following are excerpts from **Advance Auto Parts'** financing activities section of its 2010 statement of cash flows. These contain the significant cash flows resulting from the generation and repayment of the company's long-term liabilities.

Excerpts from Advance Auto Parts' 2010 Statement of Cash Flows

(*in thousands*)	2010	2009	2008
Issuance of senior unsecured notes	298,761	—	—
Early extinguishment of debt	($200,000)	—	—
Borrowings under credit facilities	$75,000	$173,400	$438,600
Payments on credit facilities	($75,000)	($424,900)	($488,100)

This information reveals that Advance Auto Parts experienced significant debt-related cash inflows and cash outflows over the three-year period. In 2008 and 2009, the main debt-related cash flows were borrowings from and payments to the company's credit facilities. Such borrowings and payments occurred in 2010 as well. However, in 2010 the company also paid $200,000 to extinguish debt early and received $298,761 by issuing the senior unsecured notes that appear on the 2010 balance sheet. Overall, the statement of cash flows shows significant cash flows associated with long-term liabilities.

LO3 Bonds

A tool that companies such as Advance Auto Parts often use to borrow money on a long-term basis is a bond. A **bond** is a financial instrument in which a borrower promises to pay future interest and principal to a creditor in exchange for the creditor's cash today. The borrower "sells" or "issues" the bond and records a liability. The creditor "buys" the bond and records an investment. This chapter focuses on the borrower.

The terms and features of a bond are determined by the borrowing entity and can vary widely. However, all bonds have a face value, a stated interest rate, and a maturity date.

A bond's **face value** is the amount that the borrowing company wants to borrow. It is also the amount that must be repaid to the creditor upon maturity of the bond. Another name for face value is principal value.

A bond's **stated interest rate** is the contractual rate at which interest is paid to the creditor. Other names for stated rate include face rate, nominal rate, contractual rate, or coupon rate. Along with this stated rate, a bond will specify the timing of interest payments. These will usually be annually or semiannually. A bond's **maturity date** is the date on which the face value must be repaid to the creditor.

These three terms, which do not change over the life of the bond, are disclosed on the certificate that is given to the creditor or the creditor's trustee when the bond is purchased. An example certificate is shown in Exhibit 9-1. The face value is $1,000, the stated interest rate is 4.75%, and the maturity date is 1996.

Although these terms establish both the amount to be paid at maturity (the face value) and the amount of interest to be paid each period (the stated interest rate), they do not establish the issuance price of the bonds. A bond's issuance price is a function of these terms as well as a fourth item, the market rate of interest.

The **market (or effective) rate of interest** is the rate of return that investors in the bond markets demand on bonds of similar risk. The market rate is based on many complicated factors, including current and expected economic conditions. However, its relation to a bond's issuance price is relatively straightforward. To understand why, consider the following three scenarios.

Bond A financial instrument in which a borrower promises to pay future interest and principal to a creditor in exchange for the creditor's cash today.

Face value The amount that is repaid at maturity of a bond.

Stated interest rate The contractual rate at which interest is paid to the creditor.

Maturity date The date on which the face value must be repaid to the creditor.

Market (or effective) rate of interest The rate of return that investors in the bond markets demand for bonds of similar risk.

Exhibit 9-1 Example Bond Certificate

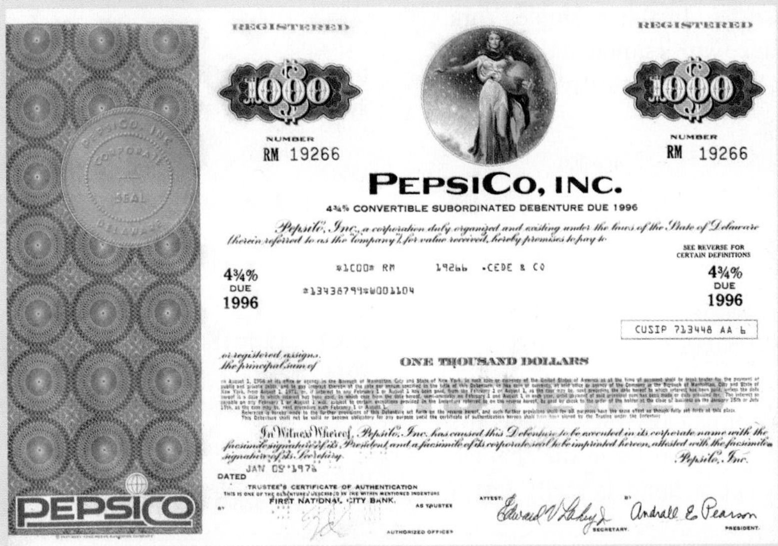

© Terri Miller/E-Visual Communications, Inc.

Scenario 1: Sometimes a bond will pay interest at a rate that is equal to what creditors demand in the market. In such cases, creditors will buy the bond at its face value. Creditors are getting the return that they demand, so no adjustment to price is needed. As a result, the borrower receives face value. We say that such bonds are issued at par value.

Scenario 2: Sometimes a bond will pay interest at a rate that is lower than what creditors demand. In such cases, creditors will purchase the bond only if the price is discounted. By discounting the price, the borrower is effectively increasing the rate of interest that the creditor earns. In fact, the bond will sell only when the price is reduced enough so that the effective interest rate that the creditor earns equals the market rate of interest. Bonds that are issued for less than face value are issued at a *discount*.

Scenario 3: Sometimes a bond will pay interest at a rate that is higher than what creditors demand. In such cases, the borrower will sell the bond only if the price is raised. By raising the price, the borrower effectively lowers the rate of interest that the creditor earns. In fact, the bond will sell only when the price is raised enough so that the effective interest rate that the creditor earns equals the market rate of interest. Bonds that are issued for more than face value are issued at a *premium*.

So, we see that bonds sometimes sell for face value, sometimes at a discount, and sometimes for a premium. The actual price at which a bond sells can be calculated using present value computations. The chapter appendix illustrates these calculations. Here, you should simply understand that bonds sell for whatever price is necessary to make the effective rate of interest equal to the market rate of interest.

The following sections demonstrate how to account for a bond's issuance, the periodic interest payments, and the maturity of bonds under each scenario.

Bonds Issued at Face Value

To illustrate a bond issued at face value, suppose that on January 1, 2012, York Products sells bonds with a face value of $100,000. The bonds carry a 6% interest rate and a January 1, 2027, maturity date. Interest is to be paid semiannually on July 1 and January 1. The

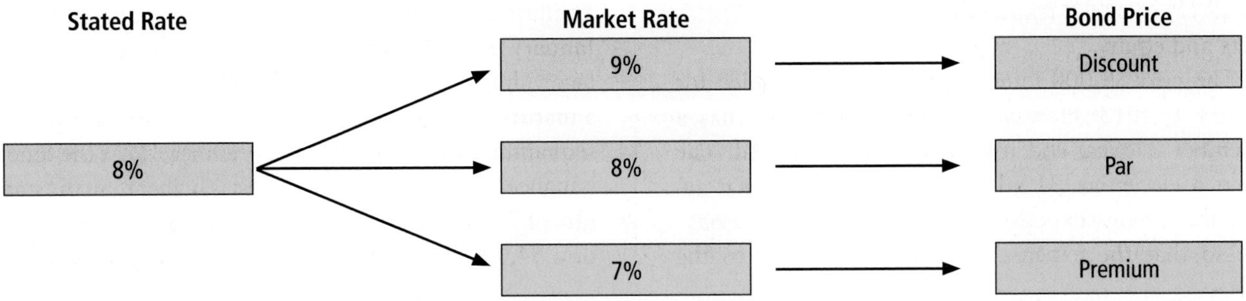

market rate of interest at the time of issuance is also 6%. Therefore, the bonds sell at face value.

Recording the Issuance In this example, York would record the bond issuance with a simple and straightforward entry to increase Cash and Bonds Payable:

Jan. 1 2012	Cash	100,000	
	Bonds Payable		100,000
	(To record bonds issued at face value)		

Assets	=	Liabilities	+	Equity
+100,000		+100,000		

Note that this entry is practically the same as the entry recording the note payable earlier in the chapter. This should make sense since a bond is really just a more formalized note payable.

Recording Interest Payments Once the bond is issued, York must pay interest on July 1 and January 1 of each year. For any bond, the amount of interest paid each period is a product of the face value, the stated interest rate, and the length of the payment period. In this example, interest is paid every six months, or semiannually, so the amount paid is $3,000, calculated as follows:

$$\begin{aligned}\textbf{Interest Paid} &= \textbf{Face Value} \times \textbf{Stated Interest Rate} \\ &\quad \times \textbf{Time Outstanding} \\ &= \$100{,}000 \times 0.06 \times 6/12 \text{ months} \\ &= \$3{,}000\end{aligned}$$

Therefore, on July 1, York would record its interest payment with the following entry:

Jul. 1 2012	Interest Expense	3,000	
	Cash		3,000
	(To record payment of interest)		

Assets	=	Liabilities	+	Equity
−3,000				−3,000

York increases Interest Expense to reflect the cost of borrowing over the six months and decreases Cash to reflect the payment made to the bondholders. The overall effect of the transaction is a decrease to York's assets and equity.

The next $3,000 interest payment is scheduled for January 1, 2013. However, assuming that York has a December 31 year-end, two entries are required. The first is a December 31 adjusting journal entry that accrues the interest expense and records the related payable so that the expense is properly matched to the period in which the money was used. The second entry records York's payment on January 1, 2013. These two entries are shown as follows:

Dec. 31 2012	Interest Expense	3,000	
	Interest Payable		3,000
	(To record accrual of interest)		

Assets	=	Liabilities	+	Equity
		+3,000		−3,000

Jan. 1 2013	Interest Payable	3,000	
	Cash		3,000
	(To record payment of interest)		

Assets	=	Liabilities	+	Equity
−3,000		−3,000		

Note that the interest expense is matched to 2012 and that the overall effect of the two entries is to decrease assets and equity by the amount of the interest paid. This is the same overall effect as the July 1 interest entry.

Interest is paid and recorded in the same manner every July 1 and December 31/January 1 for 15 years through the January 1, 2027, maturity date. Over time, York will make 30 payments of $3,000 for a total of $90,000 of interest paid. Thus, the total cost of borrowing the $100,000 over the 15 years is $90,000.

Recording the Maturity On the January 1, 2027, maturity date, York would record the repayment of the bonds in addition to the last interest payment.

Jan. 1 2027	Bonds Payable	100,000	
	Cash		100,000
	(To record repayment of the bonds)		

Assets	=	Liabilities	+	Equity
−100,000		−100,000		

Bonds Issued at a Discount

To illustrate a bond issued at a discount, suppose that on January 1, 2012, Agnew Company issues bonds with a face value of $200,000, a stated interest rate of 7%, and a maturity date of December 31, 2016. Interest is payable semiannually on June 30 and December 31. At the time of issuance, the market rate of interest is higher than the stated rate of 7% such that the bonds sell at a price of $196,000, or a $4,000 discount. At such a price, the bonds are said to have sold at 98, meaning that they were issued at 98% of face value ($200,000 × 98% = $196,000).

Recording the Issuance Agnew would record the issuance as follows:

Jan. 1 2012	Cash	196,000	
	Discount on Bonds Payable	4,000	
	Bonds Payable		200,000
	(To record bonds issued at a discount)		

Assets	=	Liabilities	+	Equity
+196,000		+200,000 −4,000		

In this entry, Agnew increases Cash for the $196,000 received from the investors. Agnew also increases Bonds Payable to reflect the new obligation that it has. Notice that Bonds Payable is recorded at the bond's face value of $200,000. The Bonds Payable account is *always* recorded at the amount that will ultimately be repaid, which is face value. The difference of $4,000 is recorded in an account called Discount on Bonds Payable, which is a contra-liability account. Its balance is subtracted from the Bonds Payable account to yield the book value or carrying value of the bonds. As a result, both assets and liabilities increase by only $196,000.

After issuance, the bonds would be reported on the balance sheet as follows:

	Jan. 1, 2012
Bonds payable	$200,000
Less: Discount on bonds payable	4,000
Carrying value	$196,000

Notice that the carrying value of $196,000 at the time of issuance is equal to the cash received at issuance. This will always be the case at issuance, regardless of the price of the bond.

Recording Interest Payments Agnew's bonds call for semiannual interest payments over the life of the bonds. Each payment is calculated as follows:

Interest Paid = Face Value × Stated Interest Rate × Time Outstanding
= $200,000 × 0.07 × 6/12 months
= $7,000

Note that this $7,000 interest payment is calculated the same way as the bond issued at face value. Whether a bond is issued at face value, at a discount, or at a premium, interest paid on a bond is always: face value × stated interest rate × time outstanding.

However, unlike the face value scenario, interest expense will not equal interest paid. Recall that Agnew received only $196,000 at issuance but must repay $200,000 at maturity. That $4,000 discount is therefore an additional cost to Agnew that must be amortized over the life of the bond. To amortize the discount is to gradually reduce the discount balance and add the amount amortized to interest expense. Therefore, at each interest payment date, interest expense will be greater than interest paid.

There are two methods to amortize the discount on bonds payable—the straight-line method and the effective interest method. Because the straight-line method is easier to compute and is often close to the results from the effective interest method, the straight-line method is demonstrated here. The effective interest method is demonstrated in the chapter appendix.

Under the **straight-line method of amortization**, an equal amount of the discount is amortized each time interest is paid. The amount amortized is calculated as follows:

$$\text{Discount Amortized} = \frac{\text{Discount at Issuance}}{\text{Number of Interest Payments}}$$

With a $4,000 discount and 10 semiannual interest payments, Agnew must amortize $400 ($4,000 ÷ 10) each payment. As a result, Agnew's interest expense for each period is $7,400 ($7,000 interest paid + $400 discount amortized). With this information, Agnew can make the following entry to record the first semiannual interest payment on June 30:

June 30 2012	Interest Expense	7,400	
	Discount on Bonds Payable		400
	Cash		7,000
	(To record the payment of interest)		

Assets	=	Liabilities	+	Equity
−7,000		+400		−7,400

The entry affects three accounts. First, Cash is decreased for the amount paid to the creditor. Second, the Discount on Bonds Payable account is decreased (or "amortized") by $400, resulting in a remaining balance of $3,600. Third, Interest Expense is increased by $7,400 to record the expense associated with the interest paid and the discount amortized. The effect of this entry is to decrease equity by $7,400 (the amount of expense),

Straight-line method of amortization
Method that amortizes an equal amount of the discount or premium each time interest is paid.

to decrease assets by $7,000 (the cash paid), and to increase liabilities by $400 (the discount amortized).

It may be counterintuitive to you that liabilities would *increase* as a result of the preceding interest entry. However, remember that the contra-liability Discount on Bonds Payable, which was first created for $4,000, is now only $3,600. Therefore, the carrying value of the bonds has increased by $400 because of the interest payment entry. This is illustrated as follows:

	Issuance	June 30, 2012
Bonds payable	$200,000	$200,000
Less: Discount on bonds payable	4,000	3,600
Carrying value	$196,000	$196,400

The carrying value will continue to increase by $400 each interest payment date as the discount is amortized. After ten total payments, the discount will be fully amortized (that is, it will have a zero balance), and the carrying value of the bonds will equal the face value of $200,000.

This movement of the carrying value from issuance price to face value is best illustrated in the schedule found in Exhibit 9-2. It is called an **amortization schedule** because it provides the details of the discount amortization and the resulting expense amounts and carrying values.

As you review the amortization schedule, note that it provides the dollar amounts for each semiannual interest entry. The first three monetary columns provide the amounts of cash to be paid, discount to be amortized, and interest expense to be recognized each six months. Because the straight-line method of amortization is used, the amounts are the same each period. Thus, Agnew would make the same interest entry every six months until the bonds mature.

Note also that the schedule confirms that the total cost of borrowing is a combination of the interest paid and the original discount. Total interest expense over the life of the bonds is $74,000, which is the sum of interest paid ($70,000) and the original discount ($4,000). When bonds are issued at a discount, total interest expense will *always* exceed interest paid by the amount of the discount. An alternate calculation of the total cost of borrowing is as follows:

Interest payments ($200,000 × 7% × 6/12)	$ 7,000
× Number of payments	× 10
= Total interest paid	$70,000
+ Discount at issuance	4,000
Total cost of borrowing	$74,000

Recording the Maturity Agnew must repay $200,000 on December 31, 2016, to satisfy its obligation. The entry to repay the bonds requires a decrease to both Cash and the Bonds Payable account.

Dec. 31 2016	Bonds Payable	200,000	
	Cash		200,000
	(To record repayment of the bonds)		

Assets	=	Liabilities	+	Equity
−200,000		−200,000		

Amortization schedule A schedule that illustrates the amortization of a bond discount or premium over the life of a bond.

Exhibit 9-2 Amortization Schedule—Bonds Issued at a Discount

Interest Payment	Interest Paid	Discount Amortized	Interest Expense	Unamortized Discount	Carrying Value
				$4,000	$196,000
Jun. 30, 2012	$ 7,000	$ 400	$ 7,400	3,600	196,400
Dec. 31, 2012	7,000	400	7,400	3,200	196,800
Jun. 30, 2013	7,000	400	7,400	2,800	197,200
Dec. 31, 2013	7,000	400	7,400	2,400	197,600
Jun. 30, 2014	7,000	400	7,400	2,000	198,000
Dec. 31, 2014	7,000	400	7,400	1,600	198,400
Jun. 30, 2015	7,000	400	7,400	1,200	198,800
Dec. 31, 2015	7,000	400	7,400	800	199,200
Jun. 30, 2016	7,000	400	7,400	400	199,600
Dec. 31, 2016	7,000	400	7,400	0	200,000
	$70,000	$4,000	$74,000		

Bonds Issued at a Premium

To illustrate the accounting for a bond issued at a premium, suppose that on January 1, 2012, McCarthy Company issues bonds with a face value of $50,000, a stated interest rate of 8%, and a maturity date of December 31, 2014. Interest is payable semiannually on June 30 and December 31. At the time of issuance, the market rate of interest is lower than the stated rate of 8% such that the bonds sell at a price of $50,600, or a $600 premium. At such a price, the bonds are said to have sold at 101.2, meaning that they were issued at 101.2% of face value ($50,000 × 101.2% = $50,600).

Recording the Issuance McCarthy would record the issuance as follows:

Jan. 1 2012	Cash	50,600	
	Premium on Bonds Payable		600
	Bonds Payable		50,000
	(To record bonds issued at a premium)		

Assets	=	Liabilities	+	Equity
+50,600		+50,000		
		+600		

In this entry, McCarthy increases Cash for the $50,600 received from creditors. McCarthy also increases Bonds Payable for the face value of $50,000. The $600 received in excess of the face value is recorded in an account called Premium on Bonds Payable. The balance in Premium on Bonds Payable is added to the Bonds Payable account to yield the bond's carrying value. The calculation of McCarthy's carrying value after issuance is shown as follows:

	Jan. 1, 2012
Bonds payable	$50,000
Plus: Premium on bonds payable	600
Carrying value	$50,600

As a result of this entry, McCarthy's assets and liabilities increase by $50,600.

Recording Interest Payments McCarthy's bonds call for semiannual interest payments over the life of the bonds. Each payment is calculated as follows:

Interest Paid = Face Value × Stated Interest Rate × Time Outstanding

= $50,000 × 0.08 × 6/12 months

= $2,000

Like the discount example, McCarthy's interest payment will differ from its interest expense. McCarthy received $50,600 at issuance but must repay only $50,000 at maturity. The $600 premium is a reduction in McCarthy's cost. Like the discount example, the premium should be amortized over the life of the bond. As a result, at each interest payment date, interest expense will be less than interest paid.

The following is the amortization calculation using the straight-line method.

$$\text{Premium Amortized} = \frac{\text{Premium at Issuance}}{\text{Number of Interest Payments}}$$

With a $600 premium and 6 semiannual interest payments, McCarthy must amortize $100 ($600 ÷ 6) each payment. Therefore, interest expense for each period is $1,900 ($2,000 interest paid − $100 premium amortized). This leads to the following entry to record the first semiannual interest payment on June 30.

Jun. 30 2012	Interest Expense	1,900	
	Premium on Bonds Payable	100	
	Cash		2,000
	(To record the payment of interest)		

Assets	=	Liabilities	+	Equity
−2,000		−100		−1,900

The entry affects three accounts. First, Cash is decreased for the $2,000 payment. Second, the Premium on Bonds Payable account is amortized or decreased by $100, leaving a remaining balance of $500. Third, Interest Expense is increased by $1,900 to record the expense associated with the interest paid and the premium amortized. The effect of this entry is to decrease equity by $1,900 (the amount of expense), to decrease assets by $2,000 (the cash paid), and to decrease liabilities by $100 (the premium amortized).

After the entry, the carrying value of the bonds would be reported as follows:

	Issuance	June 30, 2012
Bonds payable	$50,000	$50,000
Plus: Premium on bonds payable	600	500
Carrying value	$50,600	$50,500

The bonds' carrying value is $100 smaller after the first interest payment. The carrying value will continue to decrease by $100 each interest payment date as the premium is amortized. After six total payments, the premium will be fully amortized and the carrying value of the bonds will equal the face value of $50,000. The amortization schedule in Exhibit 9-3 illustrates the change in the carrying value of the bonds over time.

Exhibit 9-3 Amortization Schedule—Bonds Issued at a Premium

Interest Payment	Interest Paid	Premium Amortized	Interest Expense	Unamortized Premium	Carrying Value
				$600	$50,600
Jun. 30, 2012	$ 2,000	$100	$ 1,900	500	50,500
Dec. 31, 2012	2,000	100	1,900	400	50,400
Jun. 30, 2013	2,000	100	1,900	300	50,300
Dec. 31, 2013	2,000	100	1,900	200	50,200
Jun. 30, 2014	2,000	100	1,900	100	50,100
Dec. 31, 2014	2,000	100	1,900	0	50,000
	$12,000	$600	$11,400		

Like the amortization schedule for bonds issued at a discount, the first three monetary columns in the schedule provide the amounts of cash to be paid, premium to be amortized, and interest expense to be recognized each six months. Because of the straight-line method of amortization, the amounts are the same each period. Thus, McCarthy would make the same interest entry every six months until the bonds mature.

The schedule also illustrates that the total cost of borrowing is composed of interest paid and the original premium. Total interest expense over the life of the bonds is $11,400, which is the amount of interest paid ($12,000) less the original premium ($600). When bonds are issued at a premium, total interest paid will *always* exceed interest expense by the amount of the premium. An alternate calculation of the total cost of borrowing is as follows:

Interest payments ($50,000 × 8% × 6/12)	$ 2,000
× Number of payments	× 6
= Total interest paid	$12,000
– Premium at issuance	600
Total cost of borrowing	$11,400

Recording the Maturity McCarthy must repay $50,000 on December 31, 2014, to satisfy its obligation. The entry to repay the bonds requires a decrease to both Cash and Bonds Payable:

Dec. 31 2014	Bonds Payable	50,000	
	Cash		50,000
	(To record repayment of the bonds)		

Assets	=	Liabilities	+	Equity
−50,000		−50,000		

LO4 Redeeming a Bond Before Maturity

Sometimes a bond is redeemed or retired before maturity. This can occur when the bond has a feature that allows the borrowing company to "call" or retire the bonds at a certain price. The call price is usually stated as a percentage of face value. For example, a call price of 105 means that the bonds can be retired by paying the creditor 105% of the face value of the bonds.

Bonds are retired early for various reasons. A company may simply want to reduce future interest expense or take advantage of falling interest rates by replacing existing bonds with less costly bonds. Whatever the reason, the accounting for the early retirement of a bond consists of the following three steps:

1. Update the carrying value of the bond.
2. Calculate gain or loss on the retirement.
3. Record the retirement.

The first step is to update the carrying value of the bond. Often this means that the bond must be amortized

A company may retire bonds early to reduce future interest expense or take advantage of falling interest rates by replacing existing bonds with less costly bonds.

for a partial period. For example, if a bond is retired three months after the last interest payment date, the bond would be amortized for those three months to update the carrying value. Interest payable for the three months would also be recorded and would be paid in addition to the call price.

The second step is to calculate any gain or loss on retirement by comparing the call price to the carrying value. When the call price is less than the carrying value, the company is paying less than the value of the liability. In that case, the company records a gain on the redemption. In contrast, when the call price exceeds the carrying value, the company is paying more than the value of the liability. In that case, the company records a loss on the redemption. This is summarized as follows:

Gain on Redemption = Call price < Carrying value

Loss on Redemption = Call price > Carrying value

To illustrate, suppose that Doyle Township issues a $20,000 eight-year bond on January 1, 2012, to fund the conversion of a warehouse to a youth activity center. The bond has a stated interest rate of 5% and is callable at 103 any time after 2016. The bond pays interest semiannually on June 30 and December 31. The bond sells for $19,200, or an $800 discount. A condensed amortization schedule is presented in Exhibit 9-4.

Now suppose that Doyle decides to retire the bond a year early on December 31, 2018. The bond's call price of 103 means that Doyle can retire the bond by paying the bondholder 103% of face value, or $20,600 ($20,000 × 103%). According to the amortization schedule, the December 31, 2018, carrying value of the bond is $19,900 (after the interest payment). Therefore, the gain or loss on redemption is calculated as follows:

Call price	$20,600
Less: Carrying value on Dec. 31, 2018	19,900
Loss on redemption	$ 700

The third step is to record the redemption. Doyle would do so with the following journal entry:

Dec. 31	Bonds Payable	20,000	
2018	Loss on Redemption	700	
	Discount on Bonds Payable		100
	Cash		20,600
	(To record redemption of the bond)		

Assets	=	Liabilities	+	Equity
−20,600		−$20,000 +100		−700

This entry first decreases the Bonds Payable account by its face value of $20,000. Because Doyle no longer has the bond, it also decreases the remaining $100 balance in the Discount on Bonds Payable. The entry then reduces Cash for the amount paid to retire the bond and records a $700 Loss on Redemption to reflect the loss on retiring the bond. This loss account is reported on the income statement, usually as an other or nonoperating expense.

Exhibit 9-4 Condensed Amortization Schedule—Bond Issued at a Discount

Interest Payment	Interest Paid	Discount Amortized	Interest Expense	Unamortized Discount	Carrying Value
				$800	$19,200
Jun. 30, 2012	$1,000	$50	$1,050	750	19,250
Dec. 31, 2012	1,000	50	1,050	700	19,300
⋮	⋮	⋮	⋮	⋮	⋮
Jun. 30, 2017	1,000	50	1,050	250	19,750
Dec. 31, 2017	1,000	50	1,050	200	19,800
Jun. 30, 2018	1,000	50	1,050	150	19,850
Dec. 31, 2018	1,000	50	1,050	100	19,900
Jun. 30, 2019	1,000	50	1,050	50	19,950
Dec. 31, 2019	1,000	50	1,050	0	20,000

MAKING IT REAL

A financial crisis can often be an advantage to a company, and these current economic conditions are no exception. With interest rates at historic lows, many companies are issuing debt to lock in the rates. One example is Google, Inc.

Denis Doyle/Bloomberg via Getty Images

In May of 2011, when its balance sheet showed a $37 billion cash balance, Google issued bonds for the first time in its history. Issuing three-year, five-year, and ten-year bonds, the company raised $3 billion. And it could have likely raised much more—orders from investors wanting to purchase the bonds exceeded $10 billion. Rates on the bonds were set very close to U.S. Treasury Notes, which were below 4% at issuance.

Why would a company with $37 billion borrow $3 billion more? The company says that it may use the funds to pay off short-term debt. Other analysts guess that it is just too good of a time to borrow to pass on the opportunity. The cash could be used to acquire another company or serve simply as a rather cheap way to maintain flexibility in a volatile economic climate. Regardless of the reason, Google joined many others in the technology industry such as Cisco Systems, Dell, and IBM who issued bonds in 2011.

Source: Cash-Rich Google Sells First Bonds, Wall Street Journal, May 2011.

The overall effect of the entry is to decrease assets, liabilities, and equity.

LO5 Additional Liabilities

The next two sections examine two additional types of liabilities that are common to many organizations: lease liabilities and contingent liabilities.

Leases

When companies acquire fixed assets, they have a few ways to pay for them. One option is to pay with cash on hand. Another option is to issue notes or bonds to raise the necessary capital. A third option, which is the focus of this section of the text, is to use lease financing.

A **lease** is a contractual agreement in which the lessee obtains the right to use an asset by making periodic payments to the lessor. One of the major advantages of lease financing is its flexibility. Terms of usage, time limits, and payments are a few of the many aspects of lease contracts that can vary. As a result, one lease can look very different from another. However, from an accounting perspective, there are only two main types of leases—operating leases and capital leases.

An **operating lease** is a contract in which the lessee obtains the right to use an asset for a limited period of time but does not acquire ownership of the asset. Ownership remains with the lessor. As a result, the lessee does not record any asset or liability associated with the lease but simply records rent expense as lease payments are made. A common example of an operating lease is the leasing of an automobile from a dealership.

Operating leases can be very popular with companies because they are a form of off-balance-sheet financing. **Off-balance-sheet financing** occurs when a company's future obligations regarding an asset are not reported as a liability on the balance sheet. A common example is a noncancelable operating lease. Although

Lease A contractual agreement in which the lessee obtains the right to use an asset by making periodic payments to the lessor.

Operating lease A contract in which the lessee obtains the right to use an asset for a limited period of time but does not acquire ownership of the asset.

Off-balance-sheet financing Occurs when a company's future obligations regarding an asset are not reported as a liability on the balance sheet.

One of the major advantages of lease financing is its flexibility. Terms of usage, time limits, and payments are a few of the many aspects of lease contracts that can vary.

such lease obligations are not reported on the balance sheet, accounting rules require that the future lease payments be disclosed in the notes to the financial statements. The following is a portion of **Advance Auto Parts'** Note 15 that covers Lease Commitments:

Excerpt from Advance Auto Parts' 2010 Lease Commitments Note

At January 1, 2011, future minimum lease payments due under noncancelable operating leases with lease terms ranging from 1 year to 30 years through the year 2039 for all open stores are as follows:

(in thousands)	**Total**
2011	$ 297,315
2012	265,680
2013	239,573
2014	210,722
2015	188,876
Thereafter	887,708
	$2,089,874

The note discloses that Advance Auto Parts is committed to over $2 billion in future operating lease payments, with over $297 million coming due in the current year. This $2 billion in future lease payments is an example of off-balance-sheet financing. Advance Auto Parts is obligated to pay $2 billion in the future to use certain assets, but the obligation does not appear on the balance sheet. If it did, total liabilities for Advance Auto Parts would increase 90%, from $2,314,843 to $4,404,717. As you can see, off-balance-sheet financing can be significant.

IFRS

International standards use the term "finance lease" instead of "capital lease."

In contrast to operating leases, a **capital lease** is a contract in which the lessee obtains enough rights to use and control an asset such that the lessee is in substance the owner of the asset. Because of this effective ownership, accounting rules require that the leased asset and the lease obligation be recorded by the lessee and reported on the balance sheet. This is why such contracts are called *capital* leases—because the asset is capitalized on the balance sheet. The actual entries associated with a capital lease and the criteria for determining whether a contract is a capital lease will be left to more advanced accounting courses.

Contingent Liabilities

A **contingent liability** is an obligation that arises from an existing condition whose outcome is uncertain

Capital lease A contract in which the lessee obtains enough rights to use and control an asset such that the lessee is in substance the owner of the asset.

Contingent liability An obligation that arises from an existing condition whose outcome is uncertain and whose resolution depends on a future event.

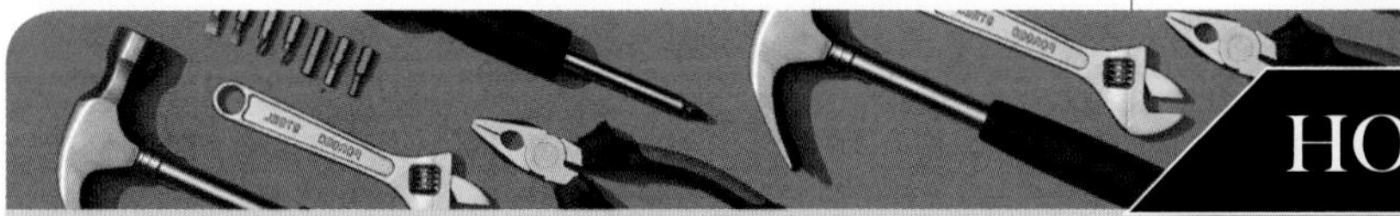

HOME DEPOT ANALYSIS

Look at **Home Depot's** debt and leases notes in Appendix C. How much does the company owe under capital leases? What is the amount of future minimum lease payments under operating leases? Which of the two amounts is reported on the balance sheet?

In its debt note, Home Depot reports a $452 million obligation related to capital leases. In its leases note, it discloses that it has over $8.1 billion in future payments under operating leases. Even though Home Depot will pay out much more in operating leases, only the obligations related to capital leases are reported on the balance sheet as a liability.

IFRS

International standards permit reduced disclosures about a contingent liability if the disclosures seriously prejudice the company's position in a dispute about the related liability. U.S. standards do not allow such reduced disclosures.

and whose resolution depends on a future event. A good example of a contingent liability is a product warranty. The existing condition is the company's promise that it will replace the product or refund the price. The uncertain outcome is whether the product will be defective. Finally, the resolution depends on both the product malfunctioning and the customer returning it. Another example is legal action against a company, which is an uncertain condition whose resolution depends on future events such as a jury verdict.

Accounting rules state that a contingent liability should be recorded and reported on the balance sheet if 1) it is *probable* that the liability will be incurred and 2) the liability can be reasonably estimated. A warranty meets these two conditions. Most merchandisers or manufacturers will have defective products that customers return, and most can reasonably estimate their future warranty claims by reviewing historical claims. As a result, most companies include warranty obligations among their liabilities.

For companies like **Advance Auto Parts**, warranty liabilities are not large enough to be reported as a separate item on the balance sheet. Rather, they are usually combined with other liabilities. To illustrate, consider again Advance Auto Parts' 2008 accrued expenses note to its financial statements:

Advance Auto Parts' 2010 Accrued Expenses Note

(*in thousands*)	
Payroll and related benefits	$106,843
Warranty reserves	36,352
Capital expenditures	43,365
Self-insurance reserves	46,778
Taxes payable	55,662
Other	115,086
Total accrued expenses	$404,086

Advance Auto Parts shows that the 2010 balance in accrued expenses as reported on the balance sheet includes over $36 million of warranty obligations.

While probable contingent liabilities are reported on the balance sheet, those that have only a *remote* probability of occurring can be ignored. Companies are not generally required to record or disclose any information regarding remote contingent liabilities. If they were, companies would likely have to list so many potential liabilities that the notes to the financial statements would be many pages longer.

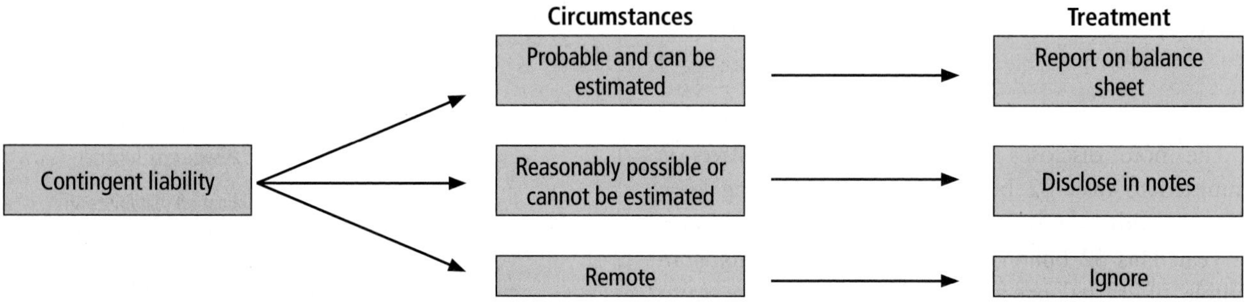

Those contingent liabilities that lie in between probable and remote—that is, those that are *reasonably possible*—are disclosed in the notes to the financial statements. This same treatment is required of liabilities that are probable but cannot be reasonably estimated. Note that disclosing something in the notes brings it to the attention of investors, but it does not result in a change to a company's liabilities.

The following is an excerpt from Advance Auto Parts' contingencies note to its 2010 financial statements. It describes a contingency whose occurrence is at least reasonably possible but whose amount cannot be reasonably estimated:

Excerpt from Advance Auto Parts' 2010 Contingencies Note

The Company is involved in various types of legal proceedings arising from claims of employment discrimination or other types of employment matters as a result of claims by current and former employees. The damages claimed against the Company in some of these proceedings are substantial. Because of the uncertainty of the outcome of such legal matters and because the Company's liability, if any, could vary widely, including the size of any damages awarded if plaintiffs are successful in litigation or any negotiated settlement, the Company cannot reasonably estimate the possible loss or range of loss which may arise.

LO6 Evaluating a Company's Management of Liabilities

As a company operates its business, it will generate liabilities. In fact, the generation of liabilities is usually the easy part of a business. It is the repayment of those liabilities that can create significant problems.

The following sections examine the liabilities of **Advance Auto Parts** to see how well it can meet its obligations. The examination will require information from the company's balance sheet. The required information is found in Exhibit 9-5, excerpted from Advance Auto Parts' 2010 Annual Report.

Exhibit 9-5 Account Balances from Advance Auto Parts' 2010 Annual Report

Source	Accounts	2010	2009
Balance Sheet	Current assets	$2,124,271	$1,887,618
	Total assets	3,354,217	3,072,963
	Current liabilities	1,848,049	1,466,027
	Total liabilities	2,314,843	1,790,598

Horizontal and Vertical Analyses

An easy and useful place to start an examination of liabilities is with horizontal and vertical analyses. Recall from Chapter 2 that horizontal analysis calculates the dollar change in an account balance, defined as the current-year balance less the prior-year balance, and divides that change by the prior-year balance to yield the percentage change. Vertical analysis divides each account balance by a base account, yielding a percentage. The base account is total assets for balance sheet accounts and net sales or total revenues for income statement accounts. These calculations are summarized as follows:

Horizontal Analysis

$$\text{Dollar change in account balance} = \text{Current-year balance} - \text{Prior-year balance}$$

$$\text{Percentage change in account balance} = \frac{\text{Dollar change}}{\text{Prior-year balance}}$$

Vertical Analysis

$$\text{Percentage} = \underset{\textit{Balance Sheet}}{\frac{\text{Account Balance}}{\text{Total Assets}}} \text{ or } \underset{\textit{Income Statement}}{\frac{\text{Account Balance}}{\text{Net Sales or Revenue}}}$$

Given Advance Auto Parts' financial information in Exhibit 9-5, horizontal and vertical analyses of liabilities result in the following:

Horizontal Analysis

Change / *Percentage Change*

$$\text{Total Liabilities} \quad \begin{array}{r} 2,314,843 \\ -1,790,598 \\ \hline 524,245 \end{array} \qquad \frac{524,245}{1,790,598} = 29.3\%$$

Vertical Analysis

2010 / *2009*

$$\text{Total Liabilities} \quad \frac{2,314,843}{3,354,217} = 69.1\% \qquad \frac{1,790,598}{3,072,963} = 58.3\%$$

The calculations show the Advance Auto Parts' liabilities are growing. Horizontal analysis shows that liabilities increased by almost 30% from 2009 to 2010. Vertical analysis shows that liabilities also increased as a percentage of assets. In 2009, 58.3% of assets were generated through liabilities. By the end of 2010, the percentage had risen to 69.1%. This means that liabilities grew faster than assets, which is a trend to watch.

For comparison, the horizontal and vertical analyses of liabilities for Advance Auto Parts, **O'Reilly Automotive**, and **Pep Boys** are shown as follows:

		Horizontal Analysis	Vertical Analysis
Liabilities	*Advance Auto Parts*	29.3%	69.1%
	O'Reilly	(12.3)%	36.4%
	Pep Boys	2.1%	69.3%

You can see that Advance Auto Parts' liabilities grew much more than both of its competitors. Also, you can see that Advance Auto Parts is equal with **Pep Boys** in having the highest percentage of liabilities to assets. Overall, this shows that Advance Auto Parts is on the higher end of the three competitors but still within a reasonable range.

In addition to an analysis of total liabilities, it is usually a good idea to conduct horizontal and vertical analyses on some of the larger individual liabilities to identify any potential areas of concern. For **Advance Auto Parts**, the two largest liabilities are accounts payable and accrued expenses. (These balances are not reported in this text.) In 2010, accounts payable increased 33.7% while accrued expenses increased 2.8%. These changes show that a large part of the increase in total liabilities was caused by growing accounts payable.

Current Ratio

Liquidity refers to a company's ability to pay off its obligations in the near future. Many parties are interested in a company's liquidity. For example, a loan officer would be interested in whether a company could pay monthly interest. A vendor would want to know if it could expect prompt payment. Employees are concerned with their employer's ability to satisfy payroll. One way to measure a company's liquidity is to calculate the current ratio.

mladn61/iStockphoto.com

Liquidity A company's ability to pay off its obligations in the near future.

Current ratio Compares a company's current assets to its current liabilities and measures its ability to pay current obligations.

When interpreting the current ratio, it is a good idea to gauge whether a company can turn its current assets into cash.

The **current ratio** compares a company's current assets to its current liabilities as follows:

$$\text{Current Ratio} = \frac{\text{Current Assets}}{\text{Current Liabilities}}$$

By comparing what a company expects to turn into cash within a year to what it expects to pay within the year, this ratio suggests how well a company can pay its short-term liabilities. A higher current ratio indicates a greater ability to satisfy current obligations.

Advance Auto Parts' 2010 current ratio is calculated as follows:

$$\frac{\$2,124,271}{\$1,848,049} = 1.15$$

The 1.15 ratio shows that at the end of 2010, Advance Auto Parts had $1.15 in current assets for every dollar of current liabilities. That is, Advance Auto Parts had more than enough current assets to satisfy its obligations coming due in the following year. The company's 2009 ratio was similar ($1,887,618/$1,466,027 = 1.29). By way of comparison, **O'Reilly's** 2010 current ratio was 1.87 and Pep Boys' was 1.36. Thus, Advance Auto Parts had the lowest liquidity of the three.

When interpreting the current ratio, it is a good idea to gauge whether a company can turn its current assets into cash. For example, a company that cannot sell its inventory cannot generate cash to pay its obligations. This could be a risk for Advance Auto Parts. Over $1.8 billion of its $2.1 billion of current assets is inventory. One way to gauge the impact of inventory is to calculate the inventory turnover ratio.

Recall from Chapter 7 that the inventory turnover ratio is calculated as follows: Cost of Goods Sold/Average Inventory. Advance Auto Parts' inventory turnover ratio is 1.7, meaning that the company sells through its inventory 1.7 times during the year. This is similar to industry standards, so it appears that Advance Auto Parts should not have a problem turning its inventory into cash and paying off its obligations.

Debt to Assets Ratio

Solvency refers to a company's ability to continue in business in the long term by satisfying its long-term obligations. While predicting whether a company will survive in the long term is very difficult, we can get an idea of a company's prospects by calculating the debt to assets ratio. The **debt to assets ratio** compares a company's total liabilities to its total assets. It is calculated as follows:

$$\text{Debt to Assets Ratio} = \frac{\text{Total Liabilities}}{\text{Total Assets}}$$

This ratio takes all of the obligations a company reports and divides by all of the assets the company reports, yielding the percentage of assets that are provided by debt. Thus, the ratio is a good indicator of a company's capital structure. **Capital structure** refers to the mix of debt and equity that a company uses to generate its assets. Since debt must be repaid, a company that uses more debt has a riskier capital structure and therefore a greater risk of being unable to meet its obligations.

Advance Auto Parts' 2010 debt to assets ratio is calculated as follows:

$$\frac{\$2{,}314{,}843}{\$3{,}354{,}217} = 0.69$$

The 0.69 ratio shows that at the end of 2010, 69.0% of Advance Auto Parts' assets were generated through debt. In comparison, **O'Reilly's** ratio was 0.36 in 2010 and **Pep Boys**' was 0.69. Whether a ratio of 0.69, 0.36, or 0.69 is good or bad for a company depends on many factors. Some companies willingly expose themselves to liabilities and the risk that comes with them in order to provide a greater chance of significant profits. Others purposely reduce their risk by limiting the use of debt. Neither strategy is right or wrong. They are just different. This issue will be discussed in more detail in Chapter 12. At this point, you should simply recognize that Advance

Solvency A company's ability to continue in business in the long term by satisfying its long-term obligations.

Debt to assets ratio Compares a company's total liabilities to its total assets and measures its ability to satisfy its long-term obligations.

Capital structure The mix of debt and equity that a company uses to generate its assets.

HOME DEPOT ANALYSIS

Using **Home Depot's** information in Appendix C, calculate and interpret (1) horizontal and vertical analyses of liabilities, (2) the current ratio, and (3) the debt to assets ratio.

(1) *Horizontal Analysis*

($21,236 − $21,484)/$21,484 = (1.2%)

Vertical Analysis

$21,236/$40,125 = 52.9%

The (1.2%) horizontal analysis reflects a decreasing amount of obligations. The 52.9% vertical analysis of total liabilities shows that a little over half of the company's assets are generated through liabilities, with the rest generated through equity.

(2) *Current Ratio*

$13,449/$10,122 = 1.33

The 1.33 Current Ratio indicates that Home Depot has 1.33 in current assets for every $1 of current liabilities. It appears that the company can pay off its current liabilities with its current assets. Since most of Home Depot's current assets are tied up in inventory, it will be important for the company to continue to sell its inventory.

(3) *Debt to Assets Ratio*

$21,236/$40,125 = 52.9%

The 52.9% Debt to Assets Ratio indicates that Home Depot has 53 cents in liabilities for every $1 of assets. This is a reasonable capital structure, composed of almost half debt and half equity.

A bond's issuance price will always be the present value of future cash flows discounted back at the current market rate of interest.

Auto Parts appears to have more risk of insolvency than O'Reilly and about the same risk as Pep Boys.

As you consider the debt to assets ratios, you may recognize the numbers from earlier in the chapter. They are the same as those generated in the vertical analysis of total liabilities. In fact, the debt to assets ratio is equivalent to a vertical analysis of total liabilities. Both the debt to assets ratio and vertical analysis divide total liabilities by total assets and are interpreted the same. So, when you conduct a vertical analysis, you already have the debt to assets ratio.

LO7 Appendix—Determining a Bond's Issuance Price

Calculating the issuance price of a bond requires the conversion of a bond's future cash flows into today's dollars. A conventional interest-paying bond has two types of future cash flows: the one-time principal payment made at maturity and the periodic interest payments made each year. The bond's issuance price will always be the present value of those future cash flows discounted back at the current market rate of interest.

To illustrate, suppose that the market rate of interest is 8% when Bowman Corporation issues a $100,000 4-year bond that pays interest annually at a rate of 10%. The future cash flows of this bond are represented graphically as follows:

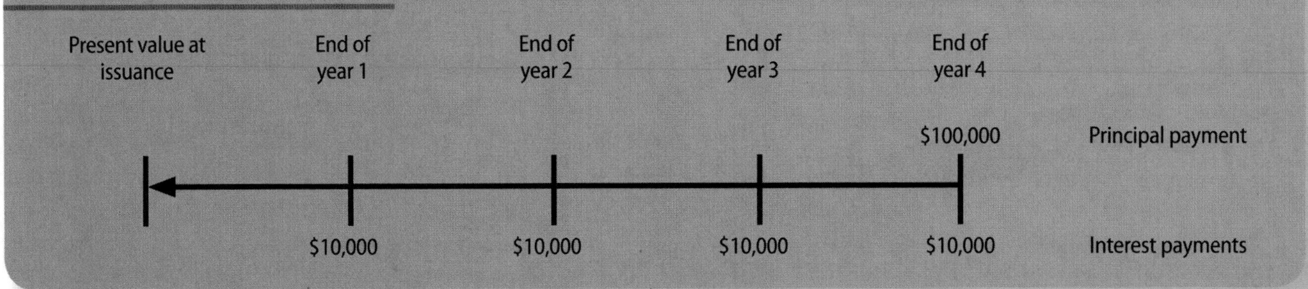

Bowman Bond Future Cash Flows

The $100,000 principal payment is a single payment made at the end of year four. Therefore, it is discounted back four periods at an 8% rate using the appropriate factor found in Exhibit B-4 on page 342, Present Value of $1. The factor for four periods (n = 4) and a rate of 8% (r = 8%) is 0.7350. Therefore, the present value of the $100,000 payment is $73,500 ($100,000 × 0.7350).

The $10,000 interest payments are made at the end of each of the next four years. Therefore, they constitute an annuity that is discounted back four periods at an 8% rate using the appropriate factor found in Exhibit B-9 on page 345, Present Value of an Ordinary Annuity. The factor for four periods (n = 4) and a rate of 8% (r = 8%) is 3.3121. Therefore, the present value of the four $10,000 payments is $33,121 ($10,000 × 3.3121).

Adding these two present values together yields $106,621. So, the bond sells for a premium. This calculation, along with similar calculations for 10% and 12% market rates are shown in Exhibit 9-6:

Exhibit 9-6 Calculations of Bond Issuance Prices

	Premium Case 8% market rate	Par Value Case 10% market rate	Discount Case 12% market rate
Present value of a single payment of $100,000	$ 73,500	$ 68,300	$63,550
Present value of an annuity of $10,000	33,121	31,700	30,373
Issuance price	$106,621	$100,000	$93,923

Note that the prices calculated confirm that bonds are issued for (1) a premium when the stated interest rate exceeds the market rate, (2) face value when the two rates are equal, and (3) a discount when the market interest rate exceeds the stated rate.

When a bond is issued at a discount or premium, the discount or premium must be amortized over the life of the bond.

LO8 Appendix—Effective Interest Method of Amortization

When a bond is issued at a discount or premium, the discount or premium must be amortized over the life of the bond. The following sections demonstrate the effective interest method of amortization.

The **effective interest method of amortization** amortizes the bond discount or premium so that interest expense each period is a constant percentage of the bond's carrying value. Under this method, interest expense is calculated by multiplying the bond's carrying value by the market rate of interest at issuance by the time outstanding.

Interest Expense = Carrying Value × Market Rate of Interest at Issuance × Time Outstanding

Once interest expense is known, the amount of discount or premium amortized is the difference between interest expense and interest paid.

Discount Amount Amortized = Interest Expense − Interest Paid

Premium Amount Amortized = Interest Paid − Interest Expense

To illustrate, refer to the Bowman example, starting first with the discount case.

Discount Example

In the discount case for the Bowman bonds found in Exhibit 9-6, the market rate of interest was 12% and the $100,000 bond was issued for $93,923, resulting in a discount of $6,077. The issuance would be recorded with the following entry:

Jan. 1	Cash	93,923	
	Discount on Bonds Payable	6,077	
	Bonds Payable		100,000
	(To record bonds issued at a discount)		

Assets	=	Liabilities	+	Equity
+93,923		+100,000		
		−6,077		

At the end of the first year, interest expense, interest paid, and the amount of the discount amortized would be calculated as follows. Note that "time outstanding" is omitted from the calculations because interest is paid annually.

Interest Expense	Carrying value × Market rate	$93,923 × 12%	$11,271
Interest Paid	Face value × Stated rate	$100,000 × 10%	$10,000
Discount Amortized	Interest expense − Interest paid	$11,271 − $10,000	$1,271

With these values, Bowman would record the following entry on the first interest payment date:

Payment 1	Interest Expense	11,271	
	Discount on Bonds Payable		1,271
	Cash		10,000
	(To record the payment of interest)		

Assets	=	Liabilities	+	Equity
−10,000		+1,271		−11,271

Because the Discount on Bonds Payable account is reduced by this entry, the carrying value of the bonds will increase. As a result, the amount of interest expense for the second interest payment will increase as well. In fact, interest expense will continue to increase each period as the bond's carrying value increases toward the face value of $100,000. To illustrate this fact, a full amortization schedule for this bond is shown in

Effective interest method of amortization Method that amortizes the bond discount or premium so that interest expense each period is a constant percentage of the bond's carrying value.

Exhibit 9-7 (with the numbers rounded for presentation purposes):

Exhibit 9-7 Amortization Schedule of Bond Discount Using Effective Interest Method

Interest Payment	Interest Paid	Discount Amortized	Interest Expense	Unamortized Discount	Carrying Value
				$6,077	$ 93,923
1	$10,000	$1,271	$11,271	4,806	95,194
2	10,000	1,423	11,423	3,383	96,617
3	10,000	1,594	11,594	1,789	98,211
4	10,000	1,789	11,789	0	100,000
	$40,000	$6,077	$46,077		

Note that, like the straight-line method of amortization, the effective method amortizes the bond discount to zero, resulting in an ending carrying value equal to the face value. But, unlike the straight-line method, interest expense and the amount amortized under the effective interest method are different each period. Again, this is because the effective interest method makes sure that interest expense is a constant percentage (12%) of the current carrying value.

Premium Example

In the premium case from Exhibit 9-6, the market rate of interest was 8% and the $100,000 bond was issued for $106,621, resulting in a premium of $6,621. The issuance would be recorded with the following entry:

Jan. 1	Cash	106,621	
	Premium on Bonds Payable		6,621
	Bonds Payable		100,000
	(To record bonds issued at a premium)		

Assets	=	Liabilities	+	Equity
+106,621		+100,000		
		+6,621		

At the end of the first year, interest expense, interest paid, and the amount of the discount amortized would be calculated as follows:

Interest Paid	Face value × Stated rate	$100,000 × 10%	$10,000
Interest Expense	Carrying value × Market rate	$106,621 × 8%	$8,530
Premium Amortized	Interest paid − Interest expense	$10,000 − $8,530	$1,470

With these values, Bowman would record the following entry on the first interest payment date:

Payment 1	Interest Expense	8,530	
	Premium on Bonds Payable	1,470	
	Cash		10,000
	(To record the first bond payment)		

Assets	=	Liabilities	+	Equity
−10,000		−1,470		−8,530

Because the carrying value of the bonds decreases as a result of this entry, the amount of interest expense for the second interest payment will also decrease. Interest expense will continue to decrease each period as the bond's carrying value decreases toward the face value of $100,000. To illustrate, a full amortization schedule for this bond is shown in Exhibit 9-8 (with the numbers rounded for presentation purposes):

Exhibit 9-8 Amortization Schedule of Bond Premium Using Effective Interest Method

Interest Payment	Interest Paid	Premium Amortized	Interest Expense	Unamortized Discount	Carrying Value
				$6,621	$106,621
1	$10,000	$1,470	$ 8,530	5,151	105,151
2	10,000	1,588	8,412	3,563	103,563
3	10,000	1,715	8,285	1,848	101,848
4	10,000	1,848	8,152	0	100,000
	$40,000	$6,621	$33,379		

Note that like the straight-line method of amortization, the effective method amortizes the bond premium to zero, resulting in an ending carrying value equal to the face value. But, unlike the straight-line method, interest expense and the amount amortized are different each period under the effective method. Again, this is because the effective interest method makes sure that interest expense is a constant percentage (8%) of the current carrying value.

STUDY TOOLS 9

Chapter review card

- Learning Objective and Key Concept Reviews
- Key Definitions and Formulas

Online (Located at www.cengagebrain.com)

- Flash Cards and Crossword Puzzles
- Games and Quizzes
- E-Lectures
- Homework Assignments (as directed by your instructor)

CONCEPT QUESTIONS

1. (LO1) What is a current liability and where are current liabilities reported?
2. (LO1) What are three examples of current liabilities?
3. (LO2) What is a long-term liability?
4. (LO2) Where are cash flows associated with long-term liabilities reported?
5. (LO3) What are the main terms of a bond?
6. (LO3) What is the difference between the stated and market interest rates associated with a bond?
7. (LO3) When does a bond sell for face value, a premium, or a discount?
8. (LO3) For a $100,000 bond, what amount is recorded in the Bonds Payable account? Does it matter whether the bond is issued at face value, a premium, or a discount?
9. (LO3) What is the formula to calculate semiannual interest paid on a bond?
10. (LO3) How will interest expense compare to interest paid if a bond is issued at a) face value, b) a discount or c) a premium?
11. (LO3) What does a bond amortization schedule show?
12. (LO4) What are the three steps in accounting for a bond that is redeemed before maturity?
13. (LO4) What is the calculation for the gain or loss on redemption when a bond is redeemed before maturity?
14. (LO5) What are the two main types of leases? Explain the differences in the two.
15. (LO5) What is off-balance-sheet financing and what is a common example?
16. (LO5) What are the three treatments of a contingent liability and when is each used?
17. (LO6) How is the current ratio calculated and what does it measure?
18. (LO6) How is the debt to assets ratio calculated and what does it measure?
19. (LO7) To what is a bond's issuance price equal?
20. (LO8) What is the effective interest method of amortization and how does it differ from the straight-line method?

MULTIPLE CHOICE

1. (LO1) A current liability is any obligation of a business that:
   a. is expected to be satisfied or paid within six months.
   b. is expected to be satisfied or paid within two years.
   c. a business will not be able to pay off.
   d. is expected to be satisfied or paid within one year.

2. (LO1) Floyd Corporation sells merchandise to a customer who pays $500 for the merchandise and $40 in sales tax. What amount will Floyd Corporation record as sales?
   a. $500
   b. $540
   c. $460
   d. $520
3. (LO1) Which of the following is not a type of tax that is commonly withheld from an employee's paycheck?
   a. Federal Income Tax
   b. FICA Tax
   c. Contribution Tax
   d. State Income Tax
4. (LO1) Which of the following statements is true?
   i. A note payable can be classified as a current or long-term liability.
   ii. Taxes payable are never current liabilities.

   a. i only
   b. ii only
   c. Both i and ii
   d. Neither i nor ii
5. (LO1) A company issues a $2,000 6% note payable due in 4 months. How much interest will the company pay for this note?
   a. $120
   b. $0
   c. $30
   d. $40
6. (LO1) When will Long-Term Debt be considered a current liability?
   a. Never
   b. In the first year of its issuance
   c. Always
   d. Whatever portion of the debt is due within one year of the balance sheet date will be considered current
7. (LO2) Cash flows associated with long-term liabilities are reported:
   a. in the operating activities section of the statement of cash flows.
   b. in the investing activities section of the statement of cash flows.
   c. in the financing activities section of the statement of cash flows.
   d. on the balance sheet.
8. (LO2) Which of the following is a financial instrument used by an entity to borrow money?
   a. Bond
   b. Check
   c. Cash
   d. Note Receivable
9. (LO3) Which of the following is used to determine the amount of interest a company issuing a bond must pay the investor?
   a. Stated Interest Rate
   b. Face Value
   c. Market Interest Rate
   d. Both a and b
10. (LO3) On January 1, Doroh Enterprises issues $200,000, 10-year, 6% bonds at par value with interest payable on July 1 and January 1. The entry on July 1 to record payment of bond interest will include a:
   a. debit to Interest Expense, $6,000.
   b. debit to Interest Expense, $12,000.
   c. credit to Cash, $12,000.
   d. credit to Interest Payable, $6,000.
11. (LO3) Camp Corporation issues bonds with a stated interest rate of 8%. The current market rate of interest is 10%. These bonds likely sold at:
   a. par value.
   b. a discount.
   c. a premium.
   d. none of the above.
12. (LO3) If bonds with a face value of $400,000 are issued at 102, how much cash is received by the borrowing company?
   a. $402,000
   b. $404,000
   c. $408,000
   d. $392,000
13. (LO3) If bonds with a face value of $100,000 are sold for $96,000, how must this $4,000 difference be accounted for?
   a. It must be depreciated
   b. It must be amortized over the life of the bond
   c. It must be recorded as a loss on issuance
   d. It must be ignored
14. (LO3) What does it mean when bonds are issued at a premium?
   a. The market interest rate exceeds the stated interest rate
   b. The market interest rate and the stated rate are the same
   c. The stated interest rate exceeds the market interest rate
   d. None of the above
15. (LO3) Freeman Incorporated issues 5-year bonds with a face value of $300,000 for $288,000. Using the straight-line method of amortization, how much of this discount will be amortized each payment if interest is paid semiannually?
   a. $2,400
   b. $1,200
   c. $1,000
   d. $600
16. (LO3) If bonds with a face value of $200,000 are issued at 102, what amount is recorded in the Bonds Payable account?
   a. $204,000
   b. $202,000
   c. $196,000
   d. $200,000

17. (LO3) The carrying value of a bond issued at a discount is equal to:
    a. the face value less the unamortized discount.
    b. the face value plus the unamortized discount.
    c. the face value.
    d. None of the above.
18. (LO4) A bond with a face value of $80,000 and an unamortized discount of $2,000 is redeemed at a price of $81,000. What is the gain or loss on redemption?
    a. $1,000 loss
    b. $3,000 loss
    c. $1,000 gain
    d. $3,000 gain
19. (LO5) An operating lease:
    a. allows a company to finance an asset without reporting a liability on the balance sheet.
    b. can be disclosed in the notes to the financial statements.
    c. Both a and b
    d. Neither a nor b
20. (LO5) Which of the following is necessary for a contingent liability to exist?
    a. There must be an existing condition
    b. The resolution of the condition must depend on some event in the future
    c. The outcome of the condition must be unknown
    d. All of the above
21. (LO5) Which of the following is a common contingent liability that is often reported on the balance sheet as a liability because of its probable nature?
    a. Warranties
    b. Bonds
    c. Taxes
    d. Salaries
22. (LO6) The debt to assets ratio is a measure of a company's:
    a. liquidity.
    b. solvency.
    c. capital structure.
    d. both b and c.
23. (LO6) A company's current ratio increases. What does this mean?
    a. The company is less liquid.
    b. The company is more liquid.
    c. The company's liquidity is unchanged.
    d. None of the above.
24. (LO7) A company issues bonds. The issuance price will be equal to:
    a. the present value of the interest payments.
    b. the present value of the principal payment.
    c. the present values of both the interest payments and the principal payment.
    d. the sum of the interest payments and the principal payment.
25. (LO8) Under the effective interest method of amortization, interest expense is calculated as:
    a. face value times the stated interest rate.
    b. carrying value times the market interest rate.
    c. face value times the market interest rate.
    d. carrying value times the stated interest rate.
26. (LO8) Under the effective interest method of amortization, the amount of discount or premium amortized each interest payment is equal to:
    a. the difference between interest expense and interest paid.
    b. the original discount or premium divided by the number of interest payments.
    c. the carrying value times the market rate of interest.
    d. None of the above.

BRIEF EXERCISES

1. Sales Tax Payable LO1

A company makes a sale of $2,000. The sales tax rate is 9%.

Required

Prepare the entry to record the sale and related sales tax liability. Ignore any effects on inventory.

2. Current Liabilities LO1

The following list represents liabilities on the December 31 balance sheet of Munday Motor Company.

1. Money owed to employees for work performed the last two weeks in December
2. Money owed to a supplier for goods purchased based on the terms net 30
3. Money owed to the government, based on the annual income of the company
4. Money owed to the bank on a note due in July

Required

Identify the liability account that would likely be used to report each item.

3. Unearned Revenues LO1

Ivey Designs provides internet hosting services to customers who purchase annual maintenance contracts. Ivey charges $1,200 per year. On September 1, Durbin Farms signs a contract with Ivey and pays $1,200.

Required

Prepare a) the September 1 entry that Ivey makes to record the contract and b) the December 31 entry to recognize Ivey's revenues earned to date.

4. Reporting Liabilities LO3

At the end of 2012, Brandon Corporation has total current liabilities of $1,755,000. Long-term debt is $850,000, and other long-term liabilities are $645,000.

Required

Prepare the liability section of Brandon Corporation's 2012 balance sheet.

5. Recording and Reporting Bonds LO2, 3

Johnson Galleries issued $500,000 of 10-year bonds on January 1, 2012. The bonds pay 8% interest semiannually on July 1 and January 1. The market rate of interest on the date of issuance was 8%.

Required

a. Prepare all journal entries necessary in 2012.
b. How would the issue price change if the market rate was lower than 8%? Higher than 8%?
c. What cash flows associated with the bond will be reported in the financing section of the 2012 statement of cash flows?

6. Recording and Reporting Bonds LO2, 3

On January 1, 2012, Mason Company issues $2 million of 5-year, 7% bonds at 98, with interest payable on June 30 and December 31. Mason uses the straight-line method of amortization.

Required

a. Prepare the journal entry to record the issuance of these bonds.
b. Prepare the journal entry to record interest expense and bond discount amortization on June 30, 2012.
c. Where will the issuance of the bond be reported on Mason's 2012 statement of cash flows?

7. Bond Interest and Amortization LO3

Andrews Corporation issued $300,000 of 12%, 3-year bonds on January 1. Interest is payable semiannually on June 30 and December 31. Andrews uses the straight-line method of amortization.

Required

a. Prepare the journal entry to record the issuance of the bonds if they are issued at 101.
b. Prepare the journal entry to record the first payment of interest on June 30.
c. Will Andrews make the same interest payment entry on December 31?

8. Calculating Gain or Loss on Bond Redemption LO4

Fly Corporation issued 10-year bonds on January 1, 2006. On July 1, 2012 Fly Corporation decides to retire the bonds early. The call price is $212,000 and the carrying value of the bonds on the date of redemption is $188,000.

Required

Calculate the gain or loss on redemption recognized by Fly.

9. Contingent Liabilities LO5

Frank's Fireworks has a pending lawsuit because of an accident that a customer had with one of Frank's products. The suit has been filed, and based on similar suits against other fireworks companies, Frank's believes that it is probable that it will lose the lawsuit. However, the cost of the suit to Frank's cannot be accurately estimated.

Required

Describe how Frank's should treat this contingent liability.

10. Analyzing Liabilities LO6

A company has total assets of $18,500,000 and current assets of $9,750,000. Total liabilities are $12,225,000, and current liabilities are $6,850,000.

Required

Calculate the company's current and debt to assets ratios.

11. Appendix—Calculate Bond Issue Price LO7

The market rate of interest was 7% when Greene Corporation issued a $100,000 5-year bond that pays interest annually at a rate of 10%. Present value of the principal is $71,300. The present value of the interest payments is $37,908.

Required

Calculate the amount of premium or discount at the time of issuance.

12. Appendix—Effective Interest Method LO8

On January 1, 2012, a bond has a carrying value of $89,280 and a face value of $100,000. The market rate of interest is 9% and the stated rate of interest on the bond is 10%. Interest is paid on December 31 of each year.

Required

Calculate interest paid and interest expense for 2012 under the effective interest method.

EXERCISES

13. Current Liabilities LO1

The following are accounts commonly used in accounting information systems:

1. Accounts payable
2. Salaries payable
3. Common stock
4. Current portion of long-term debt
5. Unearned revenue
6. Notes payable (due in 60 days)
7. Taxes payable
8. Allowance for doubtful accounts
9. Notes payable (due in 2 years)

Required
Identify whether each item would be classified on a balance sheet as a current liability, a long-term liability, or something else.

14. Current Liabilities LO1

Jones Hardware Store has total receipts for the day of $12,550. This total includes 7% sales tax on all sales.

Required
Calculate sales tax payable and prepare the journal entry to record the sales. Ignore any effects on inventory and round numbers to the nearest dollar.

15. Current Liabilities LO1

On March 1, Azalea Golf borrows $30,000 on a 6-month, 6% note from Augusta Bank. Assume interest is paid at the maturity of the note.

Required
Prepare (a) the journal entry to record the receipt of cash from the note, (b) the journal entry to record the accrual of interest if Azalea prepares financial statements on June 30, and (c) the journal entry to record the repayment of the note at maturity.

16. Current Liabilities LO1

The employees of Pinehurst Company earned wages of $80,000 during the month of June. The following were withholdings related to these salaries: $5,000 for Social Security (FICA), $3,000 for state income tax, and $7,700 for federal income tax. Additional employer-paid FICA taxes are $5,450.

Required
Prepare (a) the journal entry to record the payment of these salaries assuming they are paid on June 30 and (b) the journal entry to record Pinehurst Company's additional payroll tax expense for June.

17. Recording and Reporting Notes Payable LO1, 2

On July 1, 2012, Williams Company borrows $80,000 from the bank by signing an $80,000, 8%, 2-year note payable. Annual interest is paid on June 30. Williams has a December 31 year-end.

Required
a. Prepare the journal entries to record the issuance of the note and accrued interest at December 31, 2012.
b. How would Williams report the note payable on its 2012 and 2013 balance sheets?

18. Bond Terms LO3

The following is a list of terms and definitions associated with liabilities:

1. Face value
2. Market interest rate
3. Stated interest rate
4. Sold at a discount
5. Maturity date
6. Bond certificate
7. Amortization schedule
8. Sold at a premium

a. Amount paid when a bond matures.
b. Rate of return investors who are buying similar bonds demand for their investments.
c. Rate used to determine the amount of interest the issuing company of a bond must pay to the investor.
d. The date on which the face value of the bond must be paid to the investor.
e. Document that contains the terms of the bond.
f. This occurs when the stated rate of a bond is less than the market rate.
g. A schedule that illustrates the amortization of a bond discount or premium over time.
h. This occurs when the stated rate of a bond is greater than the market rate.

Required
Match each term with the appropriate definition.

19. Understanding Bonds LO2, 3

The following items are associated with bonds:

- Face value
- Interest expense
- Carrying value
- Interest paid
- Amortization of discount or premium
- Balance in unamortized discount or premium

Required
Assuming that bonds are issued at (a) a discount and (b) a premium, identify whether each item will increase, decrease, or remain the same as the bond approaches maturity. Assume straight-line amortization of any discount or premium.

20. Recording Bonds at a Premium and a Discount LO3

On January 1, 2012, Hampton, Inc. issues $3 million of 5-year, 10% bonds with interest payable on July 1 and January 1. Hampton prepares financial statements on December 31 and amortizes any discount or premium using the straight-line method.

Required
Prepare all journal entries necessary in 2012 assuming the bonds were issued at (a) 96 and (b) 103.

21. Bond Amortization LO3

On January 1, 2012, Thompson Company issues $4 million of 5-year, 8% bonds with interest payable on June 30 and December 31. Thompson amortizes any discount or premium using the straight-line method.

Required
Prepare a bond amortization schedule assuming the bonds were issued at (a) 101 and (b) 97.

22. Bond Amortization Schedule LO3

Fred Corp. provides the following two lines of a bond amortization schedule:

(A)	Interest Paid	(B)	(C)	(D)	Carrying Value
6/30/2014	$3,200	$200	$3,400	$2,200	$77,800
12/31/2014	$3,200	$200	$3,400	$2,000	$78,000

Required
Answer the following:

a. Identify the column headings A–D.
b. Was the bond issued at a discount, a premium, or at face value?
c. What is the face value of the bonds?
d. What is the stated interest rate?
e. Is the market interest rate greater than, less than, or equal to the stated interest rate?

23. Bond Calculations LO3

Consider the following two bonds:

- $100,000, 5-year, 7% bond issued for $103,000
- $250,000, 8-year, 8% bond issued for $240,000

Required
Calculate the total cost of borrowing for each bond. Assume that the bonds are outstanding through maturity.

24. Bond Errors LO3, 4

Consider the following independent situations. If necessary, assume the straight-line method of amortization.

1. A company issues a $100,000, 5-year, 4% bond for $102,000 and increases the Bond Payable account by $102,000.
2. A company issues a $250,000, 8-year, 8% bond for $240,000. On the first semiannual interest payment, the company amortizes $1,250 of the bond discount.
3. A company redeems an $85,000 bond with a carrying value of $86,000 for $85,000 and records a $1,000 gain on redemption.
4. A company issues $50,000 of bonds with a 6% stated interest rate when the market rate of interest is 7%. At the first semiannual interest payment date, the company pays $1,750.

Required
For each situation, identify whether the company made an error and if so, what the company should have done.

25. Bond Redemption LO3, 4

A company issues $80,000 of 10-year bonds for $86,000. Immediately after the thirteenth semiannual interest payment, the company redeems the bonds for $83,700. The company uses the straight-line method of amortization.

Required
Prepare the journal entry to record the bond redemption.

26. Bond Redemption LO4

Immediately after making a semiannual interest payment, the carrying value of Woods Company's bonds were as follows:

Bonds payable	$1,500,000
Less: Discount on bonds payable	80,000
Carrying value	$1,420,000

Required

a. Calculate the gain or loss on redemption assuming Woods redeems the bonds at 101.
b. Prepare the journal entry to record the redemption.
c. Can a company redeem the bonds it issues at any time? Explain.
d. Why might a company want to redeem its bonds before maturity?

27. Leases LO5

Glennon Incorporated needs a new piece of equipment for its factory. Instead of purchasing the asset, the company chooses to enter into a 5-year operating lease with annual payments of $50,000. Assume each lease payment is made on December 31.

Required

a. Prepare the journal entry to record the first annual lease payment.
b. What are the financial reporting advantages of an operating lease over a capital lease?
c. Why might Glennon have chosen to lease the equipment instead of buying it?

28. Contingent Liabilities LO5

Tanner Toys had sales of $2,500,000 during 2012. In 2011, 5% of sales were returned for a refund, but Tanner believes that recent product changes will reduce warranty expense to about 3% of 2012 sales.

Required

a. What amount is Tanner expecting to refund customers for purchases made in 2012?
b. Should this amount be reported as a liability on the financial statements? Why or why not?
c. Is Tanner using a reasonable means to estimate warranty expense?

29. Contingent Liabilities LO5

Harris Foods had the following independent situations.

1. A court recently found Harris liable for $400,000 in damages due to faulty coatings on paper plates it manufactures. Because Harris plans to appeal the decision and therefore currently accepts no blame, it ignores the $400,000 in its financial reports.
2. Harris buys discontinued utensils and repackages them for sale. Due to differing quality, each year Harris has average warranty returns of 25% of prior-year sales. Harris' policy is to provide full refunds for customers. Harris discloses the potential returns in the notes to its financial statements.
3. Harris prides itself on giving back to its community and considers it an obligation. In the coming year, Harris plans to give $50,000 to the local food bank. It therefore records a $50,000 contingent liability on its balance sheet.

Required

For each situation, identify whether Harris is using proper accounting and if not, how each situation should be handled.

30. Evaluate Liabilities LO6

In a recent balance sheet, Wal-Mart reported the following information (in millions):

	Current year	Prior year
Current assets	$48,949	$48,020
Current liabilities	55,390	58,478

Required

Calculate Wal-Mart's current ratio for each year and answer the following questions:

a. Was the company more or less liquid in the current year?
b. Should an investor be concerned that the current ratio is less than 1.0? Why or why not?
c. What is likely to be the most important factor in Wal-Mart being able to pay its current liabilities in a timely manner? (Hint: Think about its largest current asset.)

31. Evaluate Liabilities LO6

A company needs to raise $10 million to expand its operations. It is considering two options: (1) issuing bonds or (2) issuing common stock. Currently, the company's balance sheet shows the following (in millions):

Assets	Liabilities	Equity
$53.8	$37.9	$15.9

Required

a. Calculate the company's debt to assets ratio prior to raising the $10 million and comment on the riskiness of the company's existing capital structure.
b. Recalculate the company's debt to assets ratio under the two options the company is considering and comment on how this changes the riskiness of the company's capital structure.
c. Can one of the options be considered the "correct" option?

32. Evaluate Liabilities LO6

The following financial data were reported by Verizon Wireless for two recent years (in millions):

Verizon Wireless Balance Sheet (partial)		
	Current	Prior
Current assets	$2,290	$ 669
Current liabilities	2,257	2,172
Total liabilities	9,801	9,854
Total assets	5,131	6,200

Required

Calculate the current and debt to assets ratios for each year. How would the most recent ratios change if Verizon decided to pay off $1 billion of current liabilities with cash?

33. Appendix—Calculate Issuance Price LO7

Suppose that a company issues the following bonds at different times. Interest on the bonds is paid annually.

1. $80,000 of 6%, 10-year bonds when the market rate of interest is 7%
2. $60,000 of 8%, 6-year bonds when the market rate of interest is 6%
3. $120,000 of 10%, 5-year bonds when the market rate of interest is 8%

Required

Calculate the issuance price for each bond.

34. Appendix—Bond Interest and Amortization LO7, 8

On January 1, 2012, Tallakson Company issues a $50,000, 5-year, 8% bond with interest payable annually on December 31. The market interest rate at issuance is 10%. Tallakson uses the effective interest method of amortization.

Required

a. Determine the issuance price of the bond by using the appropriate table(s) in Appendix A.
b. Prepare the entry for the first interest payment on December 31, 2012.
c. Prepare an amortization schedule for the bond.

35. Appendix—Effective Interest Amortization LO8

On January 1, 2012, Big E Electronics issues a $100,000, 8-year, 8% bond for $105,970. The market rate of interest at the time of issuance was 7%. Interest is payable annually on December 31.

Required

a. Prepare entries for the bond issuance and the first three interest payments.
b. Prepare an amortization schedule for the bond.

PROBLEMS

36. Recording and Reporting Current Liabilities LO1

The following is a list of liability accounts on the ledger of Chop House Incorporated on January 1:

Sales Tax Payable	$ 7,500
Accounts Payable	9,500
Unearned Revenue	16,500

The following transactions occurred during the month of January:

Jan. 1 Borrowed $25,000 from Atlanta Bank on a 6-month, 6% note.
9 Provided service for customers who had paid $6,000 in advance.
15 Paid state treasurer for sales taxes collected in December, $7,500.
18 Bought inventory on credit for $12,000.
23 Sold goods on credit for $3,000, plus 7% sales tax.

The employees of the Chop House earned gross salaries of $45,000 during January. Withholdings were $2,500 for Social Security, $4,000 for federal income tax, and $1,900 for state income tax. The employer share of FICA taxes was also $2,500. Salaries earned in January will be paid during February.

Required

a. Prepare journal entries for the January transactions. Assume that purchases are recorded directly into the inventory account.
b. Prepare adjusting entries at January 31 related to salaries, payroll taxes, and notes payable.
c. Create the current liability section of the balance sheet at January 31.

37. Bond Presentation, Interest, and Redemption LO2, 3, 4

The following is an excerpt taken from the December 31, 2011, balance sheet of the Wimbledon Company:

Current liabilities	
Bond interest payable	$ 64,000
Long-term liabilities	
Bonds payable	1,600,000
Less: Discount on bonds payable	30,000
Carrying value	$1,570,000

The bonds have a stated interest rate of 8% and mature on January 1, 2017. Interest is paid semiannually on July 1 and January 1. The bonds are callable at 105 on any semiannual interest date.

Required

a. Prepare the journal entry to record the payment of bond interest on January 1, 2012.
b. Prepare the journal entry to amortize the bond discount and pay the interest on July 1, 2012.
c. Prepare the journal entry to record the redemption of the bonds on July 1, 2012, after the interest has been paid.
d. Prepare the adjusting journal entry for December 31, 2012, assuming that the bonds were not redeemed.
e. Show how all liabilities related to the bonds would be reported on Wimbledon's balance sheet at December 31, 2012.

38. Bond Issuance, Interest, Redemption, and Reporting LO3, 4

Gateway Unlimited sold $2,000,000 of 6-year, 10% bonds on January 1, 2012. The bonds pay interest semiannually on July 1 and January 1. The bonds sell at 97. The straight-line method is used to amortize any bond premium or discount.

Required

a. Prepare all journal entries related to the bonds for 2012 and 2013 and show how the bonds would be reported on the December 31 balance sheets.
b. How would the 2012 statement of cash flows be affected by the bonds?
c. Prepare a bond amortization schedule.
d. On July 1, 2016, after the interest payment, Gateway redeems the bonds for 101. Prepare the entry to record the redemption.
e. How would the 2016 statement of cash flows be affected by the redemption?

39. Analyzing Liabilities LO6

Explorer Corporation's board of directors is having its annual meeting to analyze the performance of the firm. One area the board is focusing on is total liabilities. The following are selected items from the December 31 balance sheet:

	2012	2011
Total assets	$935,870	$902,225
Total liabilities	575,430	562,855
Total equity	360,440	339,370

Required

Conduct horizontal and vertical analyses of total liabilities and interpret the results. Explain whether or not Explorer should be pleased with its financial position based on these calculations.

40. Appendix—Comparing Amortization Methods LO7, 8

On January 1, 2012, LED issues bonds with a face value of $300,000. These bonds have a stated interest rate of 4% and interest is paid annually on December 31. The bonds mature in four years. The market interest rate at the date the bonds are issued is 5%.

Required

a. Determine the amount of discount on the bonds at issuance.
b. How much of the discount will be amortized in the first year under (1) the straight-line method and (2) the effective interest method?
c. Does interest expense each year differ under the straight-line and effective interest methods of amortization?
d. Does total interest expense over the life of the bonds differ under the straight-line and effective interest methods of amortization?

CASES

41. Research and Analysis LO1, 2, 5, 6

Access the 2010 annual report for **Amazon** by clicking on the *Investor Relations* and *Annual Reports and Proxies* links at www.amazon.com.

Required

a. Examine the company's balance sheet and conduct horizontal and vertical analyses of all liability account balances, including total liabilities.
b. Examine the financing activities section of the company's statement of cash flows. Over the past three years, did the company receive or pay more cash related to debt and leases?
c. Calculate the company's current ratio and debt to assets ratios for 2010 and 2009.
d. Examine the company's long-term debt note. What was the weighted average interest rate on its long-term debt for 2010 and 2009?
e. Based on your answers above, write a paragraph explaining your opinion of Amazon's liability position. Use your answers as supporting facts.

42. Research and Analysis LO6

Access the 2010 annual report for **Carmike Cinemas, Inc.** by clicking on the SEC Filings link at www.carmikeinvestors.com.

Required

a. Perform horizontal and vertical analyses on the major subtotals from the company's balance sheet.
b. Calculate current and debt to assets ratios for the most recent two years.
c. Examine the amount of interest expense reported by the company on its income statement.
d. What conclusions can you make about the current health of the company? Would it surprise you that in the last ten years the company entered into and emerged from bankruptcy protection?

43. Written Communication LO5

Bill Deere Tractors manufactures and sells all types of yard equipment. The company was recently sued by a plaintiff who claimed that a defective lawnmower caused a serious injury. The company was made aware of this at the end of its fiscal year but it is not sure how to report it in its financial statements.

Required

Write a brief memo explaining the possible treatments of this lawsuit for financial reporting purposes. Also, provide some ideas on how to estimate the potential liability if the company believes that liability is probable.

44. Ethics in Accounting LO1, 2, 6

You are the accountant for a medium-size manufacturer. Your company has some existing debt that requires the company to maintain a current ratio of 1.50 or higher. If the ratio drops below that value, the lender can increase the interest rate from 6% to 9%. Recently, the company's current ratio has been hovering around 1.50, and the president believes that when some long-term debt maturing in the following year is reported as current, the ratio will fall below 1.50. The president asks you to keep the long-term debt as a long-term liability instead of reclassifying it as a current liability. "After all, "he says, "it is still reported as a liability."

Required

Is there an ethical issue with the president's request? How should you respond?

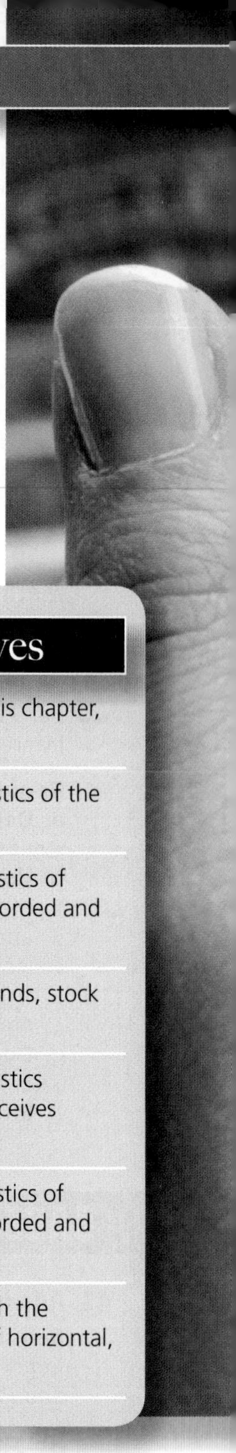

Stockholders' Equity

Learning Objectives

After studying the material in this chapter, you should be able to:

LO1 Describe the characteristics of the corporate form of business.

LO2 Describe the characteristics of common stock and how it is recorded and reported.

LO3 Understand cash dividends, stock dividends, and stock splits.

LO4 Describe the characteristics of preferred stock and how it receives preference in dividends.

LO5 Describe the characteristics of treasury stock and how it is recorded and reported.

LO6 Evaluate equity through the calculation and interpretation of horizontal, vertical, and ratio analyses.

Introduction

This chapter examines the accounting for stockholders' equity. It begins with a discussion of the corporate form of business. It then examines how companies account for common stock and any cash or stock dividends distributed on that stock. After discussing preferred stock, preferred stock dividends, and treasury stock, the chapter concludes with a discussion on how to analyze a company's equity position.

LO1 The Corporate Form of Business

Chapter 2 introduced the three major forms of business—the sole proprietorship, the partnership, and the corporation. The following sections describe some of the characteristics of the corporate form of business that distinguish it from sole proprietorships and partnerships. These corporate characteristics are as follows:

- Separate legal entity
- Ability to raise capital
- Limited liability of owners
- Transferability of ownership
- Double taxation
- Regulation

Separate Legal Entity

A corporation is a separate legal entity. It is formed under state law by submitting articles of incorporation to a state government and requesting the establishment of a corporate entity. The articles describe the business of the corporation and request authority to sell ownership interests (that is, stock) in the corporation. Once the articles are approved, the state grants a corporate charter that effectively creates a new legal entity. In most cases, this new legal entity can buy, own, and sell assets in its name and can also borrow money. It can sue and be sued. In other words, it has most of the rights and responsibilities of an individual in society.

Google became a publicly traded corporation in 2004 when it sold stock to the public for the first time. It raised $1.6 billion in that initial public offering (IPO).

Alex Segre/Alamy

Ability to Raise Capital

Many sole proprietorships and partnerships have limited access to the capital needed to successfully operate or expand their businesses. In contrast, corporations can access capital through the sale of stock to investors, who then become stockholders. Most corporations begin by selling stock privately to a few owners. And while many corporations stay privately owned, others "go public" by offering stock to the public through an initial public offering (IPO). Such public offerings can generate substantial amounts of capital. For example, **Google, Inc.**, raised over $1.6 billion in its 2004 IPO. If needed, a corporation can continue to raise capital in the future by selling additional stock. Google followed its IPO with a second stock offering in 2005, raising another $4.2 billion in capital. The ability to access capital through the sale of stock is certainly an advantage of the corporate form of business.

Stockholders normally have no personal liability for the corporation's obligations beyond their investment in the corporation's stock.

Limited Liability of Owners

Under a sole proprietorship and a general partnership, owners are personally liable for the actions and obligations of their businesses. However, stockholders normally have no personal liability for the corporation's obligations beyond their investment in the corporation's stock. If a corporation defaults and cannot meet its obligations, creditors cannot seek the assets of the stockholders as compensation for the corporate default. They can only pursue the assets of the corporation. As a result of this limited liability, stockholders stand to lose only the amount of their investments. This limited liability of owners is a significant advantage of the corporate form of business.

Transferability of Ownership

Another advantage of the corporate form of business is the ease with which ownership can be transferred. When a sole proprietor wants to transfer his or her ownership to another individual, the business itself must be sold. When a partner wants to transfer an ownership interest to another investor, usually all other partners must agree. Once the transfer occurs, a new partnership is formed. In both of these cases, the transfer of ownership can be burdensome.

In contrast, when stockholders of a publicly traded corporation want to transfer ownership to another investor, they need only to sell the stock to other investors. Such sales usually occur through an open stock exchange such as the New York Stock Exchange (NYSE) or the National Association of Securities Dealers Automated Quotes (NASDAQ). They can be accomplished by calling a broker or logging onto a website such as **E*TRADE** and executing a sell order. Hundreds of millions of shares of stock are bought and sold every day.

Double Taxation

While the corporate form has several advantages over sole proprietorships and partnerships, it does have some disadvantages. One is the double taxation of income.

A corporation's income is taxed at the federal and state levels. Dividends paid to stockholders are also taxed on the stockholders' personal tax returns. As a result, a corporation's income that is paid in dividends is taxed twice—once at the corporate level and a second time at the personal stockholder level. In contrast, the income of sole proprietorships and partnerships is reported only on personal tax returns and is therefore taxed only once—at the personal level.

To illustrate double taxation, suppose that a corporation earns $1.0 billion in pre-tax earnings and is subject to a 40% corporate tax rate. The corporation would pay $400 million in corporate taxes. Suppose further that the corporation distributed all $600 million of its remaining profits to its stockholders, who all had personal tax rates of 25%. The stockholders would pay $150 million in personal taxes. As a result, the corporation's pre-tax income of $1 billion is taxed twice for a total of $550 million in taxes.

HOME DEPOT ANALYSIS

Look at **Home Depot's** balance sheet in Appendix C. What tells you that Home Depot is a corporation?

You can tell in two ways. First, the balance sheet shows balances in common stock, which means that the company has stockholders and is therefore a corporation. Second, the company name refers to Home Depot, Inc. The "Inc." stands for Incorporated. Home Depot does not report where it is incorporated on its balance sheet, but it is incorporated in the state of Delaware.

Common stock is sold in shares. That is, each unit of stock is called a "share" of stock.

Regulation

Another disadvantage of the corporation is the extent of regulation. Consider some of the reporting requirements of a publicly traded corporation such as **Walgreens**. Walgreens must file numerous reports with the Securities and Exchange Commission. These include audited annual financial statements on Form 10-K, unaudited quarterly financial statements on Form 10-Q, and any notifications of significant events, such as the hiring of a new chief executive officer or the announcement of a dividend or the closing of a factory on Form 8-K. There are many other reporting and legal requirements arising from state laws, stock exchange regulations, the Internal Revenue Service, and Congress. Adherence to and compliance with laws and regulations consume significant amounts of the time, labor, and resources of corporations.

LO2 Common Stock

One of the distinguishing characteristics of the corporation is its ability to sell capital stock to investors to raise funds. The amount raised by issuing capital stock is called **contributed capital** because the funds are contributed by investors in exchange for an ownership claim on company assets. The most common type of capital stock is appropriately named **common stock**. Investors who purchase common stock are called stockholders and are the owners of the corporation.

Authorized, Issued, and Outstanding Shares

Common stock is sold in shares. That is, each unit of stock is called a "share" of stock. There are three ways in which a company describes its shares of stock:

- Authorized shares
- Issued shares
- Outstanding shares

Authorized shares refers to the number of shares of stock that a company can legally issue. This capacity is set in the corporate charter filed with the state. Usually, corporations request authority to sell more shares than initially needed so that they do not have to amend the corporate charter to issue additional shares.

Issued shares refers to the number of shares a company has distributed to owners to date. Notice that the description "sold shares" is not used. Common stock is not always distributed via a sale. For example, some stock is issued to employees as part of their compensation. Thus, the description "issued shares" is used.

Outstanding shares refers to the number of shares that have been issued and are still held by someone other than the issuing company. When you hear news about a company's stock price rising or falling, the news is referring to a company's outstanding shares. The difference between a company's issued and outstanding shares is usually the number of shares the company has repurchased from investors, which is called treasury stock. Treasury stock is discussed later in this chapter.

Companies usually disclose the number of authorized, issued, and outstanding shares on their balance sheets or in the notes to their financial statements. You can see an example of the balance sheet disclosure on page 251.

Stockholder Rights

When a corporation issues common stock, it usually grants to stockholders the following four rights:

- the right to vote
- the right to participate proportionally in dividends
- the right to participate proportionally in residual assets
- the right of preemption

Contributed capital The amount of capital raised by issuing stock to investors in exchange for an ownership claim on company assets.

Common stock The most common type of capital stock.

Authorized shares The number of shares of stock that a company can legally issue.

Issued shares The number of shares a company has distributed to owners to date.

Outstanding shares The number of shares that have been issued and are still held by someone other than the issuing company.

The *right to vote* ensures that a stockholder can participate in company governance by voting on issues and actions that require owner consent or approval. An example of such an action is the election of a corporation's board of directors.

The *right to participate proportionally in dividends* ensures that stockholders receive an appropriate amount of any dividends declared by the company. For example, if a stockholder owns 25% of a corporation's common stock, he or she has the right to receive 25% of any dividend the company distributes.

The *right to participate proportionally in residual assets* ensures that stockholders receive an appropriate amount of assets upon liquidation of the company. For example, if a stockholder owns 10% of a corporation's common stock when the company ceases operations and liquidates, he or she has the right to receive 10% of all residual assets.

The *right of preemption* ensures that stockholders can maintain their ownership percentage when new stock is issued. For example, if a company decides to issue additional shares of common stock, a stockholder who owns 15% of all shares of common stock has the right to purchase 15% of the new issuance. Because of the recordkeeping burden of this right and the ease with which an investor can purchase stock in the marketplace, this right may be withheld from stockholders.

Par Value

A corporation normally assigns to its common stock a value known as a par value. **Par value** is an arbitrary value that determines an entity's legal capital. Legal capital is the amount of capital that a state requires a corporation to maintain in order to protect creditor claims. Most companies set par value very low. For example, **Walgreens** has a $0.078125 par value for its common stock, while **CVS Caremark** has a $0.01 par value. Although most states still require corporations to set par values for their stock, the value has lost much of its legal significance over time. However, as the following section demonstrates, par value still affects both the recording and reporting of common stock.

Par value An arbitrary value that determines an entity's legal capital.

Recording Common Stock

Because a stock's par value is usually set very low, most common stock is issued for more than par value. When this occurs, a company uses two equity accounts to record the stock issuance—one account for the par value and a second account for the excess paid over par value.

To illustrate, suppose that a company issues 100 shares of $1 par value stock for $5 per share on April 5. The company would record this issuance as follows:

Apr. 5	Cash	500	
	Common Stock		100
	Additional Paid-In Capital		400
	(To record sale of $1 par stock)		

Assets	=	**Liabilities**	+	**Equity**
+500				+100
				+400

This entry increases Cash for the amount received and divides the increase in equity into two accounts. The Common Stock account is increased for $100, which is the par value of the stock ($1 par × 100 shares issued). The $400 excess paid over par value is recorded in Additional Paid-In Capital. Since both Common Stock and Additional Paid-In Capital are equity accounts, this entry increases the company's assets and equity.

While most companies set a par value for their stock, some do not because their state of incorporation does not require it. Stock without a par value is called no-par stock. For no-par stock, the entire issuance is recorded directly into the common stock account. To illustrate, consider the previous example, except that the stock has no par value. The company would record the issuance as follows:

Apr. 5	Cash	500	
	Common Stock		500
	(To record sale of no-par stock)		

Assets	=	**Liabilities**	+	**Equity**
+500				+500

Everything in the entry is the same as previously, except that Common Stock is increased for the entire issuance price rather than just the par value.

HOME DEPOT ANALYSIS

Look at **Home Depot's** balance sheet in Appendix C. How many shares of common stock does Home Depot have authorized, issued, and outstanding at the end of 2010? What is the stock's par value? Has the company properly recorded the par value of common stock? Calculate the total capital contributed to the company through the issuance of stock.

Home Depot has 10 billion shares authorized, but only 1,722 million issued and 1,623 million outstanding at the end of 2010. The par value of the common stock is $0.05 per share. The common stock account has a balance of $86 million, which is equivalent to 1,722 million issued shares times $0.05 par value per share (1,722 × $0.05 = $86). Adding the $86 million to the $6,556 balance in Paid-In Capital yields the total capital received from the issuance of common stock ($86 + $6,556 = $6,642). Home Depot has received over $6.6 billion from the issuance of common stock.

AP Photo/Douglas C. Pizac

Walgreens has over 938 million shares of common stock outstanding at the end of 2010.

Reporting Common Stock

A company's balances in both common stock and additional paid-in capital are reported in the stockholders' equity section of the balance sheet. Shown below is the stockholders' equity section of **Walgreens'** balance sheet as of August 31, 2010.

Walgreens reports an $80 million balance in common stock and a $684 million balance in paid-in capital at the end of 2010. Adding these two amounts together yields $764 million, which is the amount of contributed capital Walgreens has generated to date from the issuance of common stock. This number is much smaller than the balance in retained earnings, which indicates that Walgreens has generated much more equity from profitable operations than from contributed capital.

The textual description also provides information about Walgreens' shares. It discloses that Walgreens stock has a par value of $0.078125 and that the company has the authority to issue 3.2 billion shares. At the

Stockholders' Equity Section of Walgreens' 2010 Balance Sheet

(In millions, except shares and per share amounts)	2010	2009
Shareholders' Equity		
Preferred stock, $.0625 par value; authorized 32 million shares; none issued	$ —	$ —
Common stock, $.078125 par value; authorized 3.2 billion shares; issued 1,025,400,000 shares in 2010 and 2009	80	80
Paid-in capital	684	605
Employee stock loan receivable	(87)	(140)
Retained earnings	16,848	15,327
Accumulated other comprehensive income (loss)	(24)	37
Treasury stock at cost, 86,794,947 shares in 2010 and 36,838,610 shares in 2009	(3,101)	(1,533)
Total shareholders' equity	$ 14,400	$14,376

end of 2010, Walgreens had issued slightly over 1 billion shares. Note that multiplying the number of shares issued by the par value yields the balance in the common stock account (1,025,400,000 × \$0.078125 = \$80,109,375, which is rounded to \$80 million on the balance sheet). So, Walgreens has recorded its stock issuances as described in the previous example.

One additional reported item that relates to common stock is treasury stock. Treasury stock is common stock that has been repurchased by the company. Treasury stock will be covered in detail later in the chapter, but notice here that **Walgreens** discloses just under 87 million shares in treasury stock. This means that Walgreens has over 938 million shares of common stock outstanding at the end of 2010. The actual calculation of outstanding shares is as follows:

	2010
Common shares issued	1,025,400,000
Less: Shares in treasury stock	86,794,947
Common shares outstanding	938,605,053

LO3 Dividends

The goal of any corporation is to generate profits. Once generated, a company must decide whether or not to distribute those profits to its owners through dividends. A **dividend** is a distribution of profits to owners. The decision to distribute any dividend rests with the company's board of directors, which is the group of individuals elected by stockholders to govern the company and represent the interests of all owners. The board will consider many factors in its decisions, including the financial condition of the company, the cash available for dividends, and the company's past history of dividends. When dividends are distributed, they are normally stated as a per share amount and are paid only on outstanding shares of stock.

The goal of any corporation is to generate profits. Once generated, a company must decide whether or not to distribute those profits to its owners through dividends.

When and how a company distributes dividends is called a company's dividend policy. A company's policy can often be found on its website. Walgreens is an example. It reports in its Frequently Asked Questions that "(h)istorically, dividends have been paid in March, June, September, and December" and that checks are "customarily mailed on the 12th of each of these months." In other words, like many companies, Walgreens pays a dividend each quarter.

Dividends are normally paid in cash, but they can also be paid in other forms such as stock. The following sections discuss the practice of distributing dividends, starting with the most common type—the cash dividend.

Cash Dividends

As the name suggests, a **cash dividend** is a distribution of cash to stockholders. When a corporate board decides that a cash dividend is warranted, it will declare publicly that a dividend will be distributed. The date on which the board declares the dividend is called the **date of declaration.** On this date, the board legally obligates the company to pay the dividend, so a liability is created. The board's declaration will also include the payment date and the date of record. The **payment date** is the date on which the dividend will be distributed. The **date of record** determines who receives the dividend. The stock's owner on the date of record receives the dividend.

Exhibit 10-1 contains a press release from Walgreens announcing the declaration of a quarterly dividend of \$0.1375 per share. Each of the three dates can be identified: declaration (April 12), record (May 20), and payment (June 12).

Dividend A distribution of profits to a corporation's owners.

Cash dividend A distribution of cash to stockholders.

Date of declaration The date on which a corporation's board of directors declares a dividend.

Payment date The date on which a dividend will be distributed.

Date of record The date that determines who receives the dividend; the stock's owner on the date of record receives the dividend.

Exhibit 10-1 Walgreens' Press Release of Quarterly Dividend

Walgreens Declares Regular Quarterly Dividend

DEERFIELD, Ill., April 12, 2010 – The board of directors of Walgreens (NYSE, NASDAQ:WAG) today declared a regular quarterly dividend of 13.75 cents per share, a 22.2 percent increase over the year-ago dividend, payable June 12, 2010, to shareholders of record May 20, 2010.

Recording Cash Dividends The recording of cash dividends usually requires two entries. The first entry records the declaration of the dividend and the resulting liability. The second entry records the actual distribution on the payment date.

To illustrate, suppose that a company with 1,000,000 outstanding shares of stock declares a $0.05 per share dividend on November 3. The dividend is payable on November 30 to stockholders of record on November 21.

On the date of declaration, the company obligates itself to pay a $50,000 dividend (1,000,000 × $0.05). This obligation would be recorded as follows:

Nov. 3	Retained Earnings	50,000	
	Dividends Payable		50,000
	(To record declaration of dividend)		

Assets	=	Liabilities	+	Equity
		+50,000		−50,000

The entry decreases Retained Earnings because dividends reduce retained earnings. The entry also increases Dividends Payable, which is a current liability. The result of the entry is a reduction in equity and an increase in liabilities.

The distribution of cash on the payment date would be recorded as follows:

Nov. 30	Dividends Payable	50,000	
	Cash		50,000
	(To record payment of dividend)		

Assets	=	Liabilities	+	Equity
−50,000		−50,000		

This entry is simply a payment of an obligation. Both Dividends Payable and Cash are decreased for the amount of the payment. As a result, both assets and liabilities decrease.

Note that no entry is made on the date of record because no accounting transaction occurs on that date. The date of record only determines who will receive the dividend. Therefore, it is a date with administrative importance only.

Reporting Cash Dividends Companies usually report their dividends on two financial statements. Dividends *declared* during the year are reported on the statement of stockholders' equity. Recall that dividends reduce retained earnings, so they are reported in the retained earnings column of the statement of stockholders' equity. The following is the retained earnings column of **Walgreens'** 2010 statement of stockholders' equity.

Retained Earnings Column of Walgreens' 2010 Statement of Stockholders' Equity

(In millions, except per share amounts)	
Balance, August 31, 2007	$12,027
Net earnings	2,157
Cash dividends declared ($.3975 per share)	(394)
FIN No. 48 adoption impact	2
Balance, August 31, 2008	$13,792
Net earnings	2,006
Cash dividends declared ($.4750 per share)	(471)
Balance, August 31, 2009	$15,327
Net earnings	2,091
Cash dividends declared ($.5875 per share)	(570)
Balance, August 31, 2010	$16,848

The statement provides both the per share and total dollar value of dividends declared during each year. Notice that dividends per share are increasing each year, from $0.3975 to $0.4750 to $0.5875. This results in greater total dividends each year, from $394 million to $471 million to $570 million. Dividends are presented as negative numbers because they are subtracted from retained earnings.

Dividends *paid* during the year are reported on the statement of cash flows. Because a cash dividend is a distribution of assets to an owner, dividends are considered to be a financing activity. Therefore, they are reported in the financing activities of the statement of cash flows. The following is the financing activities section of Walgreens' 2010 statement of cash flows.

Because dividends are cash outflows, they are shown as negative numbers on the statement of cash

Financing Activities Section of Walgreens' 2010 Statement of Cash Flows

	2010	2009	2008
Cash Flows from Financing Activities			
Net payment from short-term borrowings	$ —	$ (70)	$ (802)
Net proceeds from issuance of long-term debt	—	987	1,286
Payments of long-term debt	(576)	—	(28)
Stock purchases	(1,756)	(279)	(294)
Proceeds related to employee stock plans	233	138	210
Cash dividends paid	(541)	(446)	(376)
Other	(37)	(21)	(29)
Net cash (used for) provided by financing activities	$(2,677)	$ 309	$ (33)

flows. Note that the amount of dividends paid is not the same as the amount of dividends declared. For example, the $541 million of dividends paid in the most recent year is less than the $570 million of dividends declared and reported on the statement of stockholders' equity. In fact, dividends paid are less than dividends declared in each year of the three years presented. This is not an error, but rather a consequence of 1) increasing dividends each year and 2) the fact that **Walgreens'** last quarterly dividend is declared in one fiscal year but paid in the next.

Stock Dividends

While cash dividends are by far the most common type of dividend, some companies distribute stock dividends. A **stock dividend** is a distribution of a company's common stock to existing stockholders. Stock dividends are declared by a company's board of directors and are usually stated in percentage terms. For example, a 10% stock dividend means that the company will issue additional shares equal to 10% of the current outstanding shares. So, an investor owning 10,000 shares will receive 1,000 additional shares (10,000 × 10%).

At first glance, a stock dividend appears to be a great value to stockholders because they receive more shares. However, some argue that a stock dividend has very little value to stockholders. This is because the stockholders receive no assets. Furthermore, because all stockholders receive the same percentage increase in shares, a stock dividend does not change a stockholder's ownership percentage. Finally, a stock dividend usually results in a reduction to the market price of individual shares such that the total market value of a stockholder's holdings remains unchanged. For example, a company distributing a 100% stock dividend will

Stock dividend A distribution of a company's common stock to existing stockholders.

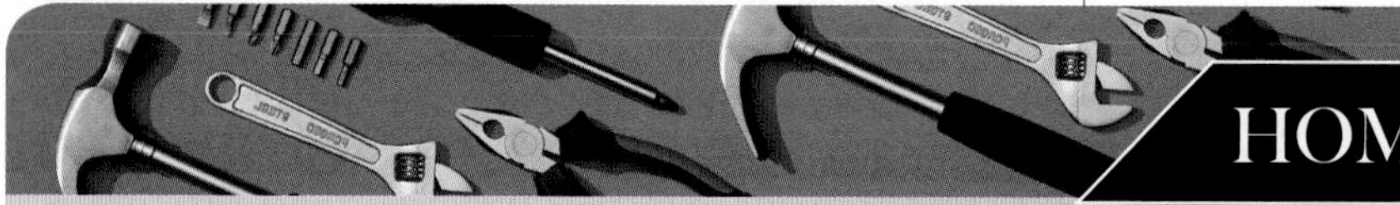

HOME DEPOT ANALYSIS

Look at **Home Depot's** statement of stockholders' equity and statement of cash flows in Appendix C. What was the total and per share amount of dividends declared in the most recent year? What was the total amount of dividends paid during the year?

Home Depot declared $1,569 million, or $0.945 per share, in dividends in the most recent year. It also paid $1,569 million.

double the shares of stock outstanding, but this will usually result in the stock's market value being cut in half. As a result, each stockholder will have a higher number of shares but no additional monetary value.

So why do companies distribute stock dividends? There are a couple of potential reasons. First, a stock dividend can substitute for a cash dividend when a company does not have enough cash on hand. This motivation can be especially strong when a company is trying to maintain a long and uninterrupted streak of declaring dividends. Second, a company may want to reduce the market price of its stock to keep its stock price in an "affordable" range for the average investor. Distributing more shares in the marketplace brings down the price of each individual share.

Like cash dividends, a stock dividend is paid out of retained earnings. However, unlike a cash dividend, a stock dividend is not a distribution of assets. It is a distribution of common stock. As a result, a stock dividend simply transfers an amount from retained earnings to contributed capital (that is, common stock and additional paid-in capital). The amount transferred depends on whether the dividend is considered small or large.

A *small stock dividend* is a distribution of 25% or less of the existing outstanding shares. Small stock dividends are recorded at the market value of the stock on the date of declaration. A *large stock dividend* is a distribution of more than 25% of the existing outstanding shares. Large stock dividends are recorded at the par value of the stock.

Recording Small Stock Dividends To illustrate a small dividend, suppose that Bethany Technologies declares a 15% stock dividend on June 1 to be distributed on June 28 to stockholders of record on June 14. On June 1, Bethany has 100,000 shares of $1 par common stock outstanding, and the stock is trading at $10 per share. Because the dividend is small, it is recorded at the market value of the stock on the date of declaration. Thus, the amount of the dividend would be calculated as follows:

Outstanding shares	100,000
× Stock dividend	× 15%
Shares to be issued	15,000
× Market value per share	× $10
Value of stock dividend	$150,000

On the date of declaration, Bethany would make the following entry:

Jun. 1	Retained Earnings	150,000	
	Common Stock To Be Distributed		15,000
	Additional Paid-In Capital		135,000
	(To record declaration of small stock dividend)		

Assets	=	Liabilities	+	Equity
				−150,000
				+15,000
				+135,000

This entry decreases Retained Earnings for the amount of the dividend and increases two contributed capital accounts. The first is Common Stock To Be Distributed. This account is exactly like Common Stock, except that the words "To Be Distributed" are added to indicate that the stock has yet to be issued. The account is recorded at the par value of the stock. The second is Additional Paid-In Capital, which is increased for the value of the dividend that exceeds par value—in this case, $135,000. The effect of the entry is a change in specific equity accounts, but no change in total equity. That again is the nature of a stock dividend. It is a transfer of equity between accounts, not a distribution of assets.

On the payment date, Bethany would make the following entry:

Jun. 28	Common Stock To Be Distributed	15,000	
	Common Stock		15,000
	(To record distribution of dividend)		

Assets	=	Liabilities	+	Equity
				−15,000
				+15,000

This entry simply decreases Common Stock To Be Distributed and increases Common Stock to reflect that the stock has been issued. Like the first entry, there is no effect on total equity as a result of this second entry.

Recording Large Stock Dividends To illustrate a large dividend, suppose that Bethany Technologies declares a 50% dividend instead of 15%. Because the dividend is large, it is recorded at the par value of the stock. Thus, the amount of the dividend would be calculated as follows:

Outstanding shares	100,000
× Stock dividend	× 50%
Shares to be issued	50,000
× Par value per share	× $1
Value of stock dividend	$50,000

HOME DEPOT ANALYSIS

Look at **Home Depot's** statement of stockholders' equity in Appendix C. Did the company issue any stock during the years presented? Was the issuance a stock dividend?

Home Depot issued stock in each of the years presented. The stock was issued under employee stock plans, not under a stock dividend.

On the date of declaration, Bethany would make the following entry:

Jun. 1	Retained Earnings	50,000	
	Common Stock To Be Distributed		50,000
	(To record declaration of large stock dividend)		

Assets	=	Liabilities	+	Equity
				−50,000
				+50,000

This entry decreases Retained Earnings and increases Common Stock To Be Distributed for the amount of the dividend. Because the dividend is recorded at par value, the entry does not affect Additional Paid-In Capital. As in the case of the small dividend, total equity is not affected by this entry.

On the payment date, Bethany would make the following entry to reflect that the stock has been distributed:

Jun. 28	Common Stock To Be Distributed	50,000	
	Common Stock		50,000
	(To record distribution of dividend)		

Assets	=	Liabilities	+	Equity
				−50,000
				+50,000

Stock split An increase in a company's shares of stock according to some specified ratio.

Stock Splits

When a company wants to decrease the market price of its stock to make it more affordable, it can use a stock split instead of a stock dividend. A **stock split** is

MAKING IT REAL

While companies often split their stock to make the price more affordable to the average investor, one company takes the exact opposite approach. Berkshire Hathaway, the company made famous by its founder, Warren Buffett, has never split its Class A stock. As a result, the value of each share of stock is quite high. During the month of February 2011 the value of one share of stock was approximately $125,000!

AP Photo/Nati Harnik

According to the company's website, the company does not split its stock so that it can attract high-quality investors who "think of themselves as business owners and invest in companies with the intention of staying a long time." The company continues that it wants owners who "keep their eyes focused on business results, not market prices." The company concludes that "(s)plitting the stock would . . . downgrade the quality of our shareholder population and encourage a market price less consistently related to intrinsic business value."

Source: http://www.berkshirehathaway.com/letters/1983.html.

Usually, preferred stockholders relinquish the right to vote in exchange for preference to dividends and preference to assets upon liquidation of the company.

an increase in a company's shares of stock according to some specified ratio. For example, a company that declares a 2-for-1 split recalls all shares from existing stockholders and issues two shares in return, effectively doubling the shares outstanding. As result of this increased supply of shares, the market price of the stock usually falls proportionally. In a 2-for-1 split, the stock price would be cut in half.

Stock splits are very similar to stock dividends in that they both result in additional shares outstanding. In fact, a 2-for-1 stock split is the same as a 100% stock dividend. However, there are important differences. First, a stock split is not an accounting transaction, so no entry is recorded. Second, stock splits apply to all authorized shares, not just outstanding shares. Whether a share is outstanding, is in treasury stock, or is authorized but unissued, it is split according to the ratio. Third, a stock split results in a proportional change in the par value of the stock. For example, a company declaring a 2-for-1 stock split on its $0.50 par value stock would reduce its par value in half to $0.25. The reduction in the per share par value then allows total par value to remain unchanged.

To illustrate, suppose that Constance Enterprises declares a 3-for-1 stock split on its $1.50 par value common stock when it has 50,000 shares outstanding and 200,000 authorized. Before the stock split, the share price is $60. After the stock is split, Constance would have 150,000 shares outstanding, 600,000 shares authorized, and a par value of $0.50. The stock would trade at $20 per share.

LO4 Preferred Stock

While all corporations issue common stock, many also authorize the sale of preferred stock. **Preferred stock** is a form of capital stock that receives one or more priorities over common stock. Usually, preferred stockholders relinquish the right to vote in exchange for preference to dividends and preference to assets upon liquidation of the company. Preference to dividends means that preferred stockholders receive their dividends before common stockholders receive any dividends.

Recording Preferred Stock

Because it is a form of contributed capital, preferred stock is recorded in the same manner as common stock. To illustrate, suppose that a company issues 500 shares of $5 par value preferred stock for $15 per share on August 23. The company would record this issuance as follows:

Aug. 23	Cash	7,500	
	Preferred Stock		2,500
	Additional Paid-In Capital		5,000
	(To record sale of preferred stock)		

Assets	=	Liabilities	+	Equity
+7,500				+2,500
				+5,000

This entry increases Cash for $7,500, which is the amount paid by the investor. Preferred Stock is increased for $2,500, which is the par value of the stock ($5 par × 500 shares issued). Additional Paid-In Capital is then increased for the excess paid over par value, which is $5,000 ($7,500 − $2,500). As a result of this entry, both assets and equity increase.

Reporting Preferred Stock

A company's balances in both preferred stock and additional paid-in capital are reported in the stockholders' equity section of the balance sheet. The following shows **Walgreen's** preferred stock balances from its 2010 balance sheet:

Preferred Stock Reported on Walgreens' 2010 Balance Sheet

	2010	2009
Preferred stock, $.0625 par value; authorized 32 million shares; none issued	$ —	$ —

Walgreens reports a zero balance in preferred stock for both years. Although the company is authorized to issue 32 million shares of $0.0625 par value preferred stock, it has not yet issued any.

Preferred stock A form of capital stock that receives one or more priorities over common stock.

Cash Dividends on Preferred Stock

When a company has both preferred and common stock outstanding, cash dividends must be allocated between the two. Because preferred stockholders have dividend preference, they are paid first, followed by common stockholders. The amount that is allocated to preferred stockholders depends on the dividend rate and whether the stock is cumulative or noncumulative.

The dividend rate refers to the annual dividend amount that preferred stockholders normally receive. The rate is usually set as a dollar amount per share or as a percentage of par value. For example, preferred stock may carry a dividend of $2 per share or a dividend of 6% of par value.

All preferred stock is either cumulative or noncumulative. **Cumulative preferred stock** carries the right to receive current-year dividends and all unpaid dividends from prior years before dividends are paid to common stockholders. This means that if a company fails to pay a dividend one year, the missed dividend will be paid the next time dividends are declared. The accumulated value of unpaid prior-year dividends is called **dividends in arrears.** Note that dividends in arrears is not a liability because dividends are declared at the discretion of the board of directors and become a legal obligation only when declared. Nonetheless, because dividends in arrears are informative, they are disclosed in the notes to the financial statements.

Noncumulative preferred stock carries the right to receive current-year dividends only. If a company does not declare a dividend in a particular year, noncumulative preferred stockholders lose the right to that annual dividend forever. As a result, a company with noncumulative preferred stock will not have dividends in arrears.

To illustrate the allocation of dividends to preferred and common stockholders, suppose that Stover, Inc. has the following two types of stock:

- Common stock, $2 par, 100,000 shares outstanding
- 5% Preferred stock, $10 par, 20,000 shares outstanding

Cumulative preferred stock Stock that carries the right to receive current-year dividends and all unpaid dividends from prior years before dividends are paid to common stockholders.

Dividends in arrears The accumulated value of unpaid prior-year dividends.

Noncumulative preferred stock Stock that carries the right to receive current-year dividends only.

Suppose further that Stover does not pay dividends in 2011 or 2012 but declares $64,000 of dividends in 2013. The allocation of the 2013 dividend depends on whether the preferred stock is cumulative or noncumulative.

Cumulative Preferred Stock If Stover's stock is cumulative, the preferred stockholders receive not only the current-year annual dividend but also the two years of dividends in arrears. The annual dividend on preferred stock is $0.50 per share ($10 par × 5%) and $10,000 in total ($0.50 per share × 20,000 shares). Therefore, $30,000 is allocated to preferred stockholders, with the remainder going to common stockholders. These calculations are illustrated as follows:

Cumulative preferred stock	Preferred	Common
Dividends in arrears—Year 2011	$10,000	
Dividends in arrears—Year 2012	10,000	
Current-year preferred dividend	10,000	
Distribute remainder to common ($64,000 – $30,000)		$34,000
Total allocated in 2013	$30,000	$34,000

Once the allocation of dividends is calculated, Stover would record the declaration and payment of the dividend as follows:

Date of Declaration	Retained Earnings	64,000	
	Dividends Payable-Common		34,000
	Dividends Payable-Preferred		30,000
	(To record declaration of dividend)		

Assets	=	Liabilities	+	Equity
		+34,000		−64,000
		+30,000		

Payment Date	Dividends Payable-Common	34,000	
	Dividends Payable-Preferred	30,000	
	Cash		64,000
	(To record payment of dividend)		

Assets	=	Liabilities	+	Equity
−64,000		−34,000		
		−30,000		

As is the case with any cash dividend, the net overall result of the declaration and payment of the dividend is a decrease in Stover's equity and its assets.

Noncumulative Preferred Stock If Stover's stock is noncumulative, the preferred stockholders receive only the current-year annual dividend. The missed dividends in 2011 and 2012 are irrelevant to the calculation for the current year. Therefore, only $10,000 is allocated to preferred stockholders, with the remainder going to common stockholders. These calculations are illustrated as follows:

Noncumulative preferred stock	Preferred	Common
Current-year preferred dividend	$10,000	
Distribute remainder to common ($64,000 − $10,000)		$54,000
Total allocated in 2013	$10,000	$54,000

LO5 Treasury Stock

Like any investor, a corporation can purchase shares of its own common stock in the marketplace. The common stock that a company reacquires from stockholders is **treasury stock**. Because shares of treasury stock are no longer held by an external investor, they are no longer outstanding. However, they are still considered to be issued.

The practice of purchasing treasury stock is commonplace in publicly traded companies today. One common reason is to acquire shares that can be issued to employees under the company's stock compensation plans. **Walgreens** is an excellent example. The following shows the common stock column of Walgreens' statement of stockholders' equity. This column reports the number of shares of common stock outstanding:

AP Photo/Elise Amendola

One common reason that a company repurchases its common stock is to acquire shares that can be issued to employees under stock compensation plans.

Common Stock Column of Walgreens' 2010 Statement of Stockholders' Equity

	Common Stock Shares
Balance, August 31, 2007	991,141,357
Treasury stock purchases	(8,000,000)
Employees stock purchase and option plans	6,034,861
Balance, August 31, 2008	989,176,218
Treasury stock purchases	(10,270,000)
Employees stock purchase and option plans	9,655,172
Balance, August 31, 2009	988,561,390
Treasury stock purchases	(55,716,733)
Employees stock purchase and option plans	5,760,396
Balance, August 31, 2010	938,605,053

In each year presented, Walgreens reports significant purchases of treasury shares, which reduce the shares outstanding, and significant distributions to employees, which increase shares outstanding. Because Walgreens has purchased more shares than it has distributed during these three years, its total number of outstanding shares has decreased from over 991 million at the end of 2007 to over 938 million at the end of 2010.

Recording Treasury Stock

Companies record the purchase of treasury stock using either the cost method or the par value method. Because most companies use the cost method, it will be demonstrated. Under the **cost method**, treasury stock is recorded at its cost of acquisition.

To illustrate, suppose that Bahakel, Inc. purchases 1,000 shares of its own common stock on May 3 when

Treasury stock Common stock that a company reacquires from its stockholders.

Cost method A method of recording the purchase of treasury stock at its cost of acquisition.

the stock is trading for $32 per share. Bahakel would record the purchase as follows:

May 3	Treasury Stock	32,000	
	Cash		32,000
	(To record purchase of treasury stock)		

Assets	=	Liabilities	+	Equity
−32,000				−32,000

The entry increases Treasury Stock and decreases Cash for the $32,000 paid to acquire the stock. Notice that Treasury Stock is increased with a debit. Treasury Stock is a contra-equity account because it represents a return of capital from the company to the stockholder. Its balance is therefore subtracted from Bahakel's total equity. As a result of this entry, both assets and equity decrease.

Treasury stock is sometimes reissued at a later date. To illustrate how such a reissuance would be recorded, suppose that Bahakel reissued 100 shares of its treasury stock for $40 per share on July 22. Bahakel would record this transaction as follows:

Jul. 22	Cash	4,000	
	Treasury Stock		3,200
	Additional Paid-In Capital		800
	(To record issuance of treasury stock)		

Assets	=	Liabilities	+	Equity
+4,000				+3,200
				+ 800

This entry increases Cash for the $4,000 received from investors. It then decreases Treasury Stock for the cost of the shares that are reissued. The stock was originally repurchased for $32 per share, so Treasury Stock is decreased by $3,200 (100 shares × $32 cost per share).

The difference between the cash received and the cost of the treasury stock represents additional contributed capital beyond the cost of the stock. Therefore, Additional Paid-In Capital is increased for the $800 difference. Note that although it appears that Bahakel has generated a gain on the sale of treasury stock, accounting rules prohibit the recording of a gain or loss on treasury stock transactions. As a result of this entry, both assets and equity increase.

Reporting Treasury Stock

A company's balance in treasury stock is reported in the stockholders' equity section of the balance sheet. The following shows **Walgreen's** treasury stock balances from its 2010 balance sheet:

Treasury Stock Reported on Walgreens' 2010 Balance Sheet

(In millions, except share amounts)	**2010**	**2009**
Treasury stock at cost, 86,794,947 shares in 2010 and 36,838,610 shares in 2009	$(3,101)	$(1,533)

Walgreens reports a little over $3.1 billion in treasury stock in 2010, which is roughly two times the balance of $1.5 billion in 2009. This is a large increase and is the result of a share repurchase program approved by Walgreens' board of directors and described in the company's notes to its financial statements. Because treasury stock is a contra-equity account, the balances are reported as negative numbers. The textual description contains the words "at cost," which indicates that Walgreens uses the cost method to account for its treasury stock. It also discloses that at the end of 2010, Walgreens owned over 86 million shares of treasury stock. This means that Walgreens has paid about $35.73 on average per share of treasury stock ($3,101,000,000 balance ÷ 86,794,947 shares).

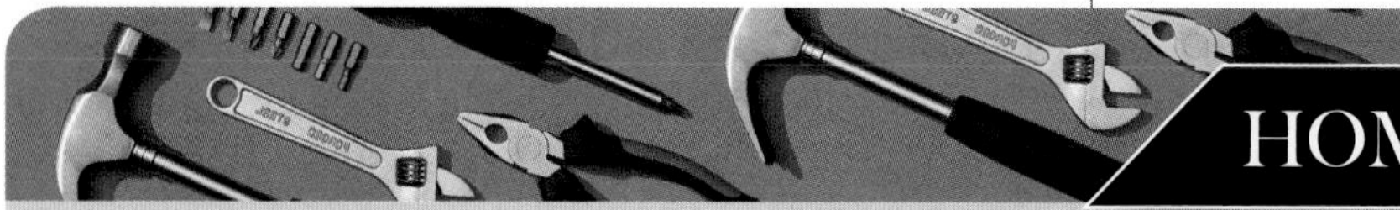

HOME DEPOT ANALYSIS

Look at **Home Depot's** balance sheet in Appendix C. How many shares of treasury stock does Home Depot have at the end of 2010? Does Home Depot use the cost or par value method? What is the average cost of each share of treasury stock?

Home Depot reports 99 million shares of treasury stock at the end of 2010. Home Depot reports its treasury shares "at cost." Thus, Home Depot uses the cost method and spent $3,193 million to acquire the 99 million shares. The average cost per share of treasury stock is therefore $32.25 ($3,193 ÷ 99).

Because a company's equity represents the owners' claim on corporate assets, stockholders are particularly interested in a company's ability to manage its equity.

LO6 Evaluating a Company's Management of Equity

Because a company's equity represents the owners' claim on corporate assets, stockholders are particularly interested in a company's ability to manage its equity. Some of the issues that are important to most stockholders are as follows:

- How does the company generate equity for stockholders?
- How does the company reward its stockholders through dividends?
- How does the company's equity affect its cash flows?

The following sections examine these three issues for **Walgreens**. The examination will require information from the company's balance sheet, income statement, statement of stockholders' equity, and statement of cash flows. The required information is found in Exhibit 10-2, excerpted from Walgreens' 2010 Annual Report. All amounts are in millions except the per share data.

Exhibit 10-2 Account Balances from Walgreens' 2010 Annual Report

Source	Accounts	2010	2009
Balance Sheet	Total assets	\$26,275	\$25,142
	Total equity	\$14,400	\$14,376
Income Statement	Net income	\$ 2,091	\$ 2,006
	Earnings per share	\$ 2.13	\$ 2.03
Statement of Stockholders' Equity	Cash dividends declared	\$ 570	\$ 471
	Dividends per share	\$0.5875	\$0.4750
	Common shares outstanding	939	989

Horizontal and Vertical Analyses

A good place to start the analysis of accounts receivable is horizontal and vertical analyses. Recall from Chapter 2 that horizontal analysis calculates the dollar change in an account balance, defined as the current-year balance less the prior-year balance, and divides that change by the prior-year balance to yield the percentage change. Vertical analysis divides each account balance by a base account, yielding a percentage. The base account is total assets for balance sheet accounts and net sales or total revenues for income statement accounts. These calculations are summarized as follows:

Horizontal Analysis

$$\text{Dollar change in account balance} = \text{Current-year balance} - \text{Prior-year balance}$$

$$\text{Percentage change in account balance} = \frac{\text{Dollar change}}{\text{Prior-year balance}}$$

Vertical Analysis

For the Balance Sheet / *For the Income Statement*

$$\text{Percentage} = \frac{\text{Account Balance}}{\text{Total Assets}} \text{ or } \frac{\text{Account Balance}}{\text{Net Sales or Revenue}}$$

Given Walgreens' financial data in Exhibit 10-2, horizontal and vertical analyses result in the following:

Horizontal Analysis

	Change	Percentage Change
Stockholders' equity	14,400 − 14,376 = 24	$\frac{24}{14,376} = 0.2\%$

Vertical Analysis

	2010	2009
Stockholders' equity	$\frac{14,400}{26,275} = 54.8\%$	$\frac{14,376}{25,142} = 57.2\%$

The horizontal analysis reveals that total equity increased by \$24 million during 2010, which is an increase of only 0.2% from the prior year. This small percentage does not mean that all equity accounts were unchanged, though. Walgreens' stockholders' equity section, as shown on page 251, shows that the company generated a sizeable increase in retained earnings. This indicates that Walgreens increased its equity through profitable operations.

However, the company also increased its treasury stock significantly, which completely offset the increase to retained earnings. The vertical analysis shows that total equity as a percentage of total assets dropped from 57.2% in 2009 to 54.8% in 2010.

For comparison purposes, the 2010 horizontal and vertical analyses of **CVS Caremark** are listed below. CVS Caremark experienced greater growth in equity during the year and maintains a higher percentage of equity to assets.

Total Equity	Horizontal Analysis	Vertical Analysis
Walgreens	0.2%	54.8%
CVS Caremark	5.4%	60.6%

Earnings per Share

The preceding analysis shows that although **Walgreens'** total equity was basically unchanged in 2010, the company did experience an increase in equity due to profitable operations. This is what all stockholders want—greater claims on assets resulting from profitable operations. Another measure of the ability to generate equity through profitable operations is earnings per share. **Earnings per share** compares a company's net income to the number of shares of common stock outstanding. It is calculated as follows:

$$\text{Earnings per Share} = \frac{\text{Net Income}}{\text{Average Number of Common Shares Outstanding}}$$

where average common shares outstanding is:

$$\frac{\text{Beginning shares outstanding} + \text{Ending shares outstanding}}{2}$$

Earnings per share is a useful ratio because it "standardizes" earnings by a company's size. The ratio can therefore be used to compare the profitability of companies of vastly different sizes.

Earnings per share A comparison of a company's net income to the number of shares of common stock outstanding that measures the ability to generate equity through profitable operations.

Return on equity A comparison of a company's net income to total stockholders' equity that measures the ability to use existing equity to generate additional equity.

IFRS

Both GAAP and IFRS require the disclosure of earnings per share, but GAAP provides slightly more detail in how to make the calculation.

Walgreens' earnings per share is calculated as follows using the information in Exhibit 10-2:

$$\frac{2{,}091}{(939 + 989)/2} = 2.17$$

The 2.17 ratio reveals that Walgreens earned $2.17 in profit for every share of common stock outstanding during the year. This is an improvement over the last year, when the company earned only $2.03 of earnings per share. However, it is less than the $2.51 earnings per share of its competitor, CVS Caremark.

Accounting standards require that companies disclose their annual earnings per share in their financial statements. Like most companies, Walgreens reports its ratio at the bottom of its income statement.

Return on Equity

Another measure of a company's ability to generate equity is return on equity. **Return on equity** compares a company's net income to its total stockholders' equity and provides an indication of how well a company uses its existing equity to generate additional equity. Stockholders naturally want this ratio to be as high as possible. It is calculated as follows:

$$\text{Return on Equity} = \frac{\text{Net Income}}{\text{Average Stockholders' Equity}}$$

where average stockholders' equity is:

$$\frac{\text{Beginning equity} + \text{Ending equity}}{2}$$

Walgreens' return on equity is calculated as follows from the information in Exhibit 10-2:

$$\frac{2{,}091}{(14{,}400 + 14{,}376)/2} = 14.5\%$$

The 14.5% ratio indicates that for every dollar of equity held during 2010, Walgreens generated 14.5 cents of additional equity through profitable operations. This compares favorably to **CVS Caremark's** return on equity of 9.3% over the same period. Walgreens was successful in effectively using its existing equity to generate more equity for stockholders.

Dividend Payout Ratio

In addition to examining how well a company generates additional equity, stockholders often examine how a company pays out that equity through dividends. One ratio to do this is the dividend payout ratio.

The **dividend payout ratio** compares a company's dividends to its earnings. The ratio demonstrates the percentage of earnings a company has decided to distribute to owners through cash dividends. The ratio can be calculated in one of two ways, depending on how a company reports its dividend information. If a company reports only the dollar amount of annual dividends, the ratio is calculated by dividing total dividends by net income. If a company reports a dividend per share number, the ratio is calculated by dividing dividends per share by earnings per share. Either way, the result will be the same (except for small differences due to the rounding of per share values). Both calculations are as follows.

$$\text{Dividend Payout Ratio} = \frac{\text{Dividends}}{\text{Net Income}} \quad \text{or} \quad \frac{\text{Dividends per Share}}{\text{Earnings per Share}}$$

Walgreens reports both total and per share earnings on its income statement and total and per share dividends on its statement of stockholders' equity. These amounts are included in Exhibit 10-2 and are used to calculate Walgreens' dividend payout ratio as follows. Note that the resulting ratios differ slightly due to the rounding of the per share amounts.

<u>"Total" calculation</u>

$$\frac{570}{2{,}091} = 27.3\%$$

<u>"Per share" calculation</u>

$$\frac{0.5875}{2.13} = 27.6\%$$

A ratio of 27.3% indicates that for every dollar of earnings during 2010, Walgreens declared about 27 cents in cash dividends. This is greater than CVS Caremark' ratio of 14.0%. However, an 27.3% ratio is not necessarily better than an 14.0% ratio. The ratios simply reflect each company's dividend policy. For 2010, Walgreens paid out more of its earnings than did CVS Caremark. Thus, stockholders who want to receive more of the profits in dividends would prefer Walgreens. However, stockholders who want the company to plow more earnings back into operations instead of paying more dividends would prefer CVS Caremark.

Dividend Yield

In addition to knowing what percentage of earnings is paid in dividends, stockholders want to know how much their investment in a company's stock returns to them. Stockholders generate a return on their investment in two ways—an increase in the stock price and a receipt of dividends. The return from receiving dividends can be calculated with the dividend yield ratio. The **dividend yield ratio** divides dividends per share by the market price per share of stock as follows:

$$\text{Dividend Yield} = \frac{\text{Dividends per share}}{\text{Market Price per share}}$$

According to Exhibit 10-2, Walgreens reports dividends per share of $0.5875 on its 2010 statement of stockholders' equity. Market price information can be found on most any financial website. We will use the stock price of $34.04, which is the closing price on the first day of the 2010 fiscal year (September 1, 2009). As a result, the dividend yield reveals the return to a stockholder who bought the stock at the beginning of the fiscal year ending August 31, 2010.

$$\frac{0.5875}{34.04} = 1.7\%$$

The 1.7% ratio indicates that an investment in Walgreens stock on September 1, 2009, would yield a return from dividends close to two cents for each dollar invested. This compares to a dividend yield for CVS Caremark of 1.1%. Thus, the yield for Walgreens is higher.

Dividend payout ratio A comparison of a company's dividends to its earnings that measures the percentage of current earnings distributed to owners.

Dividend yield ratio A comparison of dividends per share to the market price per share of stock that measures the percentage return from dividends.

HOME DEPOT ANALYSIS

Using **Home Depot's** information in Appendix C, calculate and interpret (1) horizontal and vertical analyses of total equity, (2) earnings per share, (3) return on equity, (4) dividend payout ratio, and (5) dividend yield, assuming a market price of $45.

(1) *Horizontal Analysis*

$$(\$18,889 - \$19,393)/\$19,393 = 2.6\%$$

Vertical Analysis

$$\$18,889/\$40,125 = 47.1\%$$

The 2.6% horizontal analysis reflects a decrease in Home Depot's total equity. This decrease was due mainly to the large increase in Treasury Stock from the prior year. The 47.1% vertical analysis shows that a little less than half of the company's assets are generated through equity.

(2) *Earnings per Share*

$$\$3,338/[(1,623 + 1,698)/2] = \$2.01$$

The $2.01 earnings per share indicates that Home Depot earned two dollars in income for each share of stock outstanding. This ratio is higher than each of the previous two years, which reveals that the company has been more profitable this year, given its size.

(3) *Return on Equity*

$$\$3,338/[(\$18,889 + \$19,393)/2] = 17.4\%$$

The 17.4% return on equity ratio indicates that Home Depot earned over 17 cents in income for every $1 of equity. Such a return gives the company many options. One option is to pay dividends to the owners, while another is to retain the profits and grow the company. Home Depot pays dividends, so it is doing both—rewarding its stockholders through dividends and growing the company.

(4) *Dividend Payout Ratio*

$$\$1,569/\$3,338 = 47.0\% \quad \text{or} \quad \$0.945/\$2.01 = 47.0\%$$

The 47.0% dividend payout ratio indicates that Home Depot paid to owners approximately 47 cents for every dollar it earned during the year. In the two preceding years, the company's ratio was 57.3% and 67.3%. The predominant reason for the decrease is that Home Depot's income increased during that time while dividends remained stable, thereby decreasing the payout ratio.

(5) *Dividend Yield*

$$\$0.945/\$45 = 2.1\%$$

The 2.1% dividend yield indicates that Home Depot's dividend yield was two percent of the stock's value.

Stockholders' Equity and Cash Flows

When examining a company's equity, it is always important to analyze how equity has been used to generate or use cash. Equity can significantly affect a company's cash through the issuance of stock, the purchase of treasury stock, and the payment of cash dividends. Each of these activities is reported in the financing activities section of the statement of cash flows. The following is the financing activities of **Walgreens'** 2010 statement of cash flows.

Walgreens' activity affected cash flows in all three years presented. Over the three years, Walgreens has paid $2,329 million in cash to repurchase its stock ($1,756 + $279 + $294). It has also paid out $1,363 million in cash dividends ($541 + $446 + $376). This totals almost $3.6 billion that has been paid out to stockholders over three years. This is a significant amount of cash.

Financing Activities Section of Walgreens' 2010 Statement of Cash Flows

(In millions)	**2010**	**2009**	**2008**
Cash Flows from Financing Activities			
Net payment from short-term borrowings	$ —	$ (70)	$(802)
Net proceeds from issuance of long-term debt	—	987	1,286
Payments of long-term debt	(576)	—	(28)
Stock purchases	(1,756)	(279)	(294)
Proceeds related to employee stock plans	233	138	210
Cash dividends paid	(541)	(446)	(376)
Other	(37)	(21)	(29)
Net cash (used for) provided by financing activities	$(2,677)	$(309)	$ (33)

In addition to examining the statement of cash flows, it can be beneficial to examine the notes to the financial statements to find additional information with cash flow consequences. In **Walgreens'** capital stock note, it discloses the following information:

Excerpts from Walgreens' 2010 Capital Stock Note

In connection with the Company's capital policy, its Board of Directors authorized a share repurchase program (2009 repurchase program) and set a long-term dividend payout ratio target between 30 and 35 percent. The 2009 repurchase program, which was completed in September 2010, allowed for the repurchase of up to $2,000 million of the Company's common stock prior to its expiration on December 31, 2013. Shares totaling $1,640 million were purchased in conjunction with the 2009 repurchase program during fiscal 2010.

On October 13, 2010, the Board of Directors authorized a new share repurchase program (2011 repurchase program) which allows for the repurchase of up to $1,000 million of the Company's common stock prior to its expiration on December 31, 2012. In addition, the Company continues to repurchase shares to support the needs of the employee stock plans.

The note discloses details of Walgreens' stock repurchase program. The note states that the 2009 repurchase program has been fully executed but that the board of directors has approved another program to run through December of 2012. Therefore, it appears that Walgreens will continue its payments of cash to stockholders in the next few years.

HOME DEPOT ANALYSIS

Look at **Home Depot's** statement of cash flows in Appendix C. How much cash has the company paid in dividends and for the repurchase of stock over the past three years?

According to the financing activities section of its statement of cash flows, Home Depot has paid $2,891 million over the past three years to repurchase stock and $4,615 million in dividends, for a total cash outflow of $7,506 million.

STUDY TOOLS 10

Chapter review card

- Learning Objective and Key Concept Reviews
- Key Definitions and Formulas

Online (Located at www.cengagebrain.com)

- Flash Cards and Crossword Puzzles
- Games and Quizzes
- E-Lectures
- Homework Assignments (as directed by your instructor)

CONCEPT QUESTIONS

1. (LO1) What are the characteristics of a corporation that distinguish it from a sole proprietorship and a partnership?
2. (LO1) What is the difference in the liability exposure of the owner of a corporation compared to the owner in a sole proprietorship or a partnership?
3. (LO1) A corporation is subject to double taxation. In what ways is this true?
4. (LO2) What is the difference between shares of common stock that are authorized, issued, and outstanding?
5. (LO2) What are the four rights that an investor receives when purchasing common stock from a corporation?
6. (LO2) What is par value of common stock, and how is it determined?
7. (LO2) Where and how is common stock reported?
8. (LO3) Who decides whether or not a company will issue a dividend?
9. (LO3) What are the important dates associated with dividends?
10. (LO3) How is the declaration of a cash dividend recorded?
11. (LO3) Where and how are cash dividends reported?
12. (LO3) What is a stock dividend, and why do some argue that a stock dividend has very little value to stockholders?
13. (LO3) What are the differences between small and large stock dividends?
14. (LO3) What is a stock split, and how does it compare to a stock dividend?
15. (LO4) What is preferred stock?
16. (LO4) What is the difference between cumulative and noncumulative preferred stock?
17. (LO5) What is treasury stock, and how is it recorded and reported?
18. (LO5) Are shares of treasury stock considered outstanding shares? Explain.
19. (LO6) Describe four ratios used to evaluate a company's equity.
20. (LO6) In what section of the statement of cash flows are equity activities reported?

MULTIPLE CHOICE

1. (LO1) Which of the following is not a distinguishing characteristic of the corporation as a form of business?
   a. Separate legal entity
   b. Unlimited liability of owners
   c. Ability to raise capital
   d. Double taxation
2. (LO1) The income of the corporation is taxed:
   a. at the personal level when dividends are paid.
   b. at the corporate level.
   c. both a and b.
   d. neither a nor b.
3. (LO2) The number of shares that a company can issue according to its corporate charter is referred to as:
   a. issued shares.
   b. authorized shares.
   c. outstanding shares.
   d. none of the above.
4. (LO2) Which of the following rights are received by investors when they purchase common stock?
   a. The right to participate proportionally in dividends
   b. The right to vote
   c. The right of preemption
   d. All of the above
5. (LO2) What is the arbitrary value that determines an entity's legal capital?
   a. Issue value
   b. Face value
   c. Par value
   d. Stated value
6. (LO2) A company issues 200 shares of $2 par value common stock for $10 per share. What amount will be credited to the Common Stock account when recording this transaction?
   a. $400
   b. $2,000
   c. $1,600
   d. None of the above
7. (LO2) A company issues 200 shares of $2 par value common stock for $10 per share. What amount will be credited to the Additional Paid-In Capital account when recording this transaction?
   a. $400
   b. $1,600
   c. $2,000
   d. None of the above
8. (LO3) A distribution of profits to owners by a corporation is known as:
   a. a gift.
   b. a settlement.
   c. a payment.
   d. a dividend.

9. (LO3) Which of the following statements concerning dividends is true?
   a. The board of directors decides when to distribute dividends
   b. A corporation does not have to pay a dividend every year
   c. Dividends can be paid in methods other than cash
   d. All of the above are true
10. (LO3) On February 1, a company declares a cash dividend, payable on March 1, to stockholders of record on February 20. March 1 is the:
    a. payment date.
    b. date of declaration.
    c. date of record.
    d. dividend date.
11. (LO3) On the date that a dividend is declared, what account is debited for the total amount of the dividend?
    a. Cash
    b. Dividends Receivable
    c. Dividends Payable
    d. Retained Earnings
12. (LO3) A company declares a $.10 per share dividend when it has 100,000 shares authorized and 40,000 issued and outstanding. What is the amount of the dividend?
    a. $10,000
    b. $6,000
    c. $40,000
    d. $4,000
13. (LO3) On June 4, a company declares a $32,000 dividend to be paid on June 15 to stockholders of record on June 10. On June 15, the company would record:
    a. no entry.
    b. an entry that debits Dividends Payable for $32,000.
    c. an entry that credits Dividends Payable for $32,000.
    d. an entry that debits Common Stock for $32,000.
14. (LO3) If a company has 200,000 outstanding shares and issues a 10% stock dividend, how many outstanding shares will there be following this dividend?
    a. 200,000
    b. 180,000
    c. 202,000
    d. 220,000
15. (LO3) A company with 500,000 outstanding shares of $.25 par common stock issues a 50% stock dividend when the stock is selling for $30 per share. What is the value of this stock dividend?
    a. $7,500,000
    b. $125,000
    c. $62,500
    d. $1,875,000
16. (LO3) Which of the following is true concerning a stock dividend?
    a. A stock dividend is a distribution of assets
    b. A stock dividend does not change a stockholder's ownership percentage
    c. A stock dividend usually does not result in any change to the market price of individual shares
    d. A stock dividend is never stated in percentage terms
17. (LO3) Which of the following describes the nature of a stock split?
    a. A stock split is not considered to be an accounting transaction
    b. Stock splits apply to all authorized shares
    c. A stock split results in a proportional change in the per share par value of the stock
    d. All of the above describe the nature of stock splits
18. (LO4) Which of the following is true regarding preferred stock?
    a. Preferred stockholders are often given priority over common stockholders in the receipt of dividends
    b. When a company liquidates, preferred stockholders normally receive residual assets before common stockholders
    c. Both a and b
    d. Neither a nor b
19. (LO4) When recording the issuance of preferred stock, what amount is credited to the Preferred Stock account if 100 shares of $3 par value preferred stock are issued for $6 per share?
    a. $600
    b. $100
    c. $300
    d. None of the above
20. (LO4) A company with 4,000 shares of $1 par common stock and 3,000 shares of 10% $10 par preferred stock issues a $10,000 cash dividend. How is the dividend allocated to common and preferred stockholders if there was one year of dividends in arrears?
    a. $6,000 to common stockholders; $4,000 to preferred stockholders
    b. $4,000 to common stockholders; $6,000 to preferred stockholders
    c. $7,000 to common stockholders; $3,000 to preferred stockholders
    d. $3,000 to common stockholders; $7,000 to preferred stockholders

21. (LO5) Corporations sometimes purchase treasury stock because:
    a. they want to increase the number of shares held by stockholders.
    b. management believes that the stock price is overvalued.
    c. they need shares that can be issued to employees under the company's stock compensation plans.
    d. none of the above.
22. (LO5) What accounts are affected when recording the purchase of treasury stock?
    a. Debit Treasury Stock, Credit Cash
    b. Debit Cash, Credit Treasury Stock
    c. Debit Cash, Credit Common Stock
    d. Debit Treasury Stock, Credit Common Stock
23. (LO5) How is treasury stock reported on the financial statements of a corporation?
    a. As a liability on the balance sheet
    b. As a positive amount in the stockholders' equity section of the balance sheet
    c. As a negative amount in the stockholders' equity section of the balance sheet
    d. None of the above
24. (LO6) In performing a vertical analysis of total stockholders' equity, one would:
    a. divide current year equity by prior year equity.
    b. divide equity by liabilities.
    c. divide equity by total assets.
    d. divide common stock by total equity.
25. (LO6) Which of the following is true regarding Earnings per share?
    a. This is a good measure of liquidity for a corporation
    b. It is calculated by dividing net income by average shares of common stock outstanding
    c. This calculation is not a required disclosure
    d. It is calculated by dividing net income by total equity
26. (LO6) What ratio compares a company's dividends to its earnings to demonstrate the percentage of earnings a company has decided to distribute to owners through cash dividends?
    a. Earnings per share
    b. Dividend payout ratio
    c. Return on equity
    d. Dividend yield
27. (LO6) Equity activities such as the issuance of stock and the payment of cash dividends are reported in which section of the statement of cash flows?
    a. Investing
    b. Financing
    c. Operating
    d. None of the above

BRIEF EXERCISES

1. Corporate Characteristics LO1

Megan is a shareholder in Green Corporation. She mentions to you that any dividends that she receives from Green are taxed twice.

Required
Identify and describe the corporate characteristic to which Megan is referring.

2. Recording the Issuance of Common Stock LO2

A company issued 200 shares of $2 par value stock for $10 per share on January 14.

Required
Prepare the entry that the company would make to record the issuance. How would the entry change if the par value was $1?

3. Calculating Cash Dividends LO3

Jonathan owns 3% of the common stock of XYZ Corporation. On February 3, XYZ declares $3,000,000 in dividends, payable on February 22.

Required
What amount will Jonathan receive on February 22? What effect does the dividend have on XYZ's total stockholders' equity?

4. Recording Cash Dividends LO3

A company with 2,000,000 outstanding shares of stock declared a $0.10 per share dividend on July 10. The dividend is payable on July 31 to stockholders of record on July 17.

Required
Prepare the entries that the company would make on the date of declaration and payment date. What is the total effect of both entries on total stockholders' equity?

5. Recording Large and Small Stock Dividends LO3

Albertine Industries declared a 10% stock dividend on August 15 to be distributed on September 10 to stockholders of record on August 28. On August 15, Albertine had 3,000,000 shares of $1 par stock outstanding, and its stock was trading at $7 per share.

Required
Prepare the August 15 entry for Albertine. How would the entry change if the stock dividend was 50%?

6. Effect of a Stock Split LO3

A company has 100,000 shares of $2.25 par common stock outstanding when it decides to split its stock 3-for-1.

Required
How many shares of stock are outstanding after the split. What is the new par value of each share of stock?

7. Recording the Issuance of Preferred Stock LO4

A company issues 600 shares of $4 par value preferred stock for $12 per share on March 15.

Required
Prepare the entry that the company would make to record the issuance.

8. Cash Dividends LO3, 4

A company has common stock and cumulative preferred stock. The preferred stock is 4%, $10 par, and there are 25,000 shares outstanding. The company didn't pay dividends in the previous two years. In the current year, the company declares dividends of $37,000.

Required
Determine the amount of current year dividends allocated to common stockholders.

9. Recording the Purchase of Treasury Stock LO5

Russell Corporation uses the cost method to account for treasury stock. On February 3, Russell purchases 3,000 shares of its own $2 par value common stock when it is trading for $15 per share.

Required
Prepare the entry that Russell Corporation would make to record the purchase.

10. Calculate Stockholders' Equity LO2, 5

Jet Prep Company has a retained earnings balance of $150,000, a treasury stock balance of $30,000, and a common stock balance of $200,000. The market value of Jet Prep's common stock is $400,000.

Required
Calculate total stockholders' equity that would be reported on the balance sheet.

11. Effect of Equity Transactions LO2, 3, 4, 5

A company enters into the following independent transactions:

1. Issues common stock for cash
2. Declares and pays a cash dividend
3. Declares and distributes a stock dividend
4. Purchases treasury stock for cash
5. Declares a 2-for-1 stock split

Required
Describe whether each transaction would *increase*, *decrease*, or *not affect* total stockholders' equity, retained earnings, contributed capital, and cash flows from financing activities.

12. Reporting Stockholders' Equity LO2, 4, 5

The following December 31 balances are provided by Ellen Corporation:

Treasury stock (20,000 shares)	$ 100,000
Preferred stock (5%, $75 par, cumulative)	750,000
Additional paid-in capital	1,500,000
Retained earnings	2,224,000
Common stock ($4 par value, 500,000 shares authorized)	1,400,000

Required
Prepare the stockholders' equity section of Ellen's balance sheet.

13. Calculate Return on Equity LO6

During the year, a company generated $95,000 in net income. Also during the year, the company's stockholders' equity grew from $550,000 at the beginning of the year to $595,300 at the end of the year.

Required
Calculate the company's return on equity for the year. Round percentages to one decimal point (i.e., 9.4%).

14. Calculate the Dividend Payout Ratio LO6

During the past year, Beems Company paid dividends of $35,000, earned net income of $165,000, and ended the year with earnings per share of $2.24.

Required
Calculate Beems' dividend payout ratio. Round percentages to one decimal point (i.e., 9.4%).

15. Reporting Cash Flows Associated with Equity LO6

A company enters into the following transactions relating to its equity:

1. Issues preferred stock for cash
2. Converts preferred stock to common stock
3. Issues common stock for cash
4. Issues common stock for a building
5. Reissues for cash stock that was held as treasury stock
6. Purchases treasury stock for cash
7. Pays a cash dividend on common stock
8. Declares a 3-for-1 stock split
9. Distributes a 50% stock dividend

Required
Identify whether each transaction would be reported as a financing activity on the statement of cash flows or not reported on the statement of cash flows.

16. Evaluate Equity LO6

A company provides the following information:

	2012	2011
Return on equity	33.4%	32.1%
Earnings per share	$2.86	$2.43
Dividend payout ratio	1.0%	1.0%
Dividend yield	0.0004%	0.0003%

Required
Comment on the profitability of the company and its dividend policy.

EXERCISES

17. Corporate Form of Business LO1

The following characteristics were discussed in the text:

a. Separate legal entity
b. Liability of owners
c. Ability to raise capital
d. Transferability of ownership
e. Taxation
f. Regulation

Required
Describe how each characteristic relates to the corporate form of business.

18. Recording Stock Transactions LO2, 4, 5

Irons Incorporated entered into the following stock transactions:

Apr. 5	Issued 30,000 shares of $3 par value common stock for $180,000.
May 31	Purchased 1,000 shares of treasury stock for $50,000.
Oct. 1	Issued 3,000 shares of $40 par value preferred stock for $65 per share.

Required
Prepare the journal entries to record the transactions. Use the cost method to account for the purchase of treasury stock.

19. Stock Terminology LO2, 5

The stockholders' equity section of Lester Company's balance sheet follows:

Stockholders' equity	
Common stock, 500,000 shares authorized, 450,000 shares issued	$ 450,000
Additional paid-in capital	4,050,000
Retained earnings	1,425,000
Treasury stock, at cost, 16,000 shares	(480,000)
Total stockholders' equity	$5,445,000

Required

a. How many shares of common stock are authorized, issued, and outstanding?
b. What is the par value per share of the common stock?
c. How much in total capital has Lester received from the issuance of stock?
d. What is the average cost of a share of treasury stock?

20. Cash Dividends LO3

On December 15, Taylor Corporation declared a cash dividend of $0.77 per share to be paid on January 15 to stockholders of record on December 31. Taylor has 154 million shares of common stock outstanding.

Required
Identify the date of declaration, the date of record, and the payment date, and prepare all necessary journal entries on those dates.

21. Stock Dividends LO3

Hudson High Rises declared a 10% stock dividend on July 1 to be distributed on August 1 to stockholders of record on July 15. On July 1, Hudson has 1,000,000 authorized shares and 250,000 outstanding shares. Hudson's $2 par stock is trading at $15 per share on July 1.

Required

a. Prepare all necessary journal entries to record the stock dividend.
b. Prepare all necessary journal entries to record the stock dividend, assuming the percentage was 30% instead of 10%.

22. Recording Cash and Stock Dividends LO3

Kirk Corporation had the following amounts in equity before issuing its annual dividend:

Common stock (35,000 shares outstanding)	$105,000
Additional paid-in capital	285,000
Retained earnings	440,000

Kirk has decided to issue a 5% stock dividend simultaneously with a $1 per share cash dividend. The date of declaration is November 12, and the payment date is November 29.

Required
Prepare all journal entries necessary to record the declaration and payment of dividends. Assume that the stock was trading for $10 on the date of declaration and $12 on the date of payment. Also, assume the cash dividends were not paid on the additional shares of stock from the stock dividend.

23. Effect of Dividends LO3

Elam Enterprises is considering the following three actions regarding its equity:

Action 1: Declaring a 30% stock dividend.
Action 2: Declaring a $12,000 cash dividend.
Action 3: Declaring a 2-for-1 stock split.

Required
Describe whether each action would *increase, decrease,* or *not affect* the following: (1) Total Stockholders' Equity, (2) Retained Earnings, (3) Contributed Capital, (4) Par Value per Share, and (5) Price per Share.

24. Stock Dividends versus Stock Splits LO3

Morgan Incorporated is looking to increase its number of shares of outstanding common stock to bring down its stock price. The board of directors is trying to decide if a 2-for-1 stock split or a 100% stock dividend is more appropriate. Morgan's stockholders' equity follows:

Common stock, $2 par, 100,000 shares issued and outstanding	$ 200,000
Additional paid-in capital	660,000
Retained earnings	775,000
Total stockholders' equity	$1,635,000

Required

a. Assess the pros and cons of the stock split versus the stock dividend.
b. Create a new stockholders' equity section if Morgan chooses (1) a stock dividend or (2) a stock split.

25. Cash Dividends LO3, 4

Cope Company declares a $90,000 dividend. Cope's common stock has a $5 par value and 80,000 shares outstanding. Cope's preferred stock is 5%, $12 par, and there are 20,000 shares outstanding. Cope has not paid dividends in the past three years. Cope's preferred stock is cumulative.

Required

a. Determine how the $90,000 in dividends should be allocated to preferred and common stockholders.
b. Prepare the journal entry that would be recorded on the date of declaration.
c. Determine how the $90,000 in dividends should be allocated to preferred and common stockholders, assuming that the preferred stock is noncumulative.

26. Preferred Stock Cash Dividends LO3, 4, 5

The equity section of Jeans Incorporated is as follows:

Preferred stock, 5% cumulative, 6,000 shares issued and outstanding	$120,000
Common stock, $1 par value, 36,000 shares issued	180,000
Retained earnings	250,000
Treasury stock, 6,000 shares, at cost	(30,000)
Total stockholders' equity	$520,000

Required

Calculate the amount of dividends allocated to common and preferred stockholders under the following situations: (a) $18,000 of total dividends and no preferred dividends in arrears and (b) $24,000 of total dividends and two years of preferred dividends in arrears. How much did each common stockholder receive per share under each scenario?

27. Treasury Stock LO5

On January 15, Capital Corporation purchased 2,000 shares of its own common stock when the stock was trading at $45. On June 15, Capital Corporation reissued 500 of these same shares for $50 per share.

Required

Prepare the journal entries to record the purchase and reissuance of the treasury stock. Use the cost method.

28. Treasury Stock LO5

The equity section of Wilkins Homes' balance sheet at the beginning of the year is as follows:

Common stock, $1 par value, 100,000 shares issued	$ 100,000
Additional paid-in capital	700,000
Retained earnings	825,000
Treasury stock (2,000 shares)	(20,000)
Total stockholders' equity	$1,605,000

During the year, Wilkins reissues 1,000 shares of treasury stock for $15 per share and then purchases an additional 1,600 shares of treasury stock at $16 per share.

Required

a. Prepare the journal entries to record the treasury stock transactions.
b. Prepare the equity section of Wilkins' balance sheet after the treasury stock transactions.

29. Reporting Stockholders' Equity LO2, 5

A portion of the balance sheet of Amanda Airlines appears below:

Common stock, $5 par, 5,000 shares issued, 4,000 outstanding	$ (a)
Additional paid-in capital	(b)
Total contributed capital	170,000
Retained earnings	75,000
(d)	(8,000)
Total stockholders' equity	$ (c)

Required

Fill in missing values a–d and determine the cost per share of the treasury stock.

30. Evaluate Equity LO6

The following is selected financial information for Lee Incorporated:

(in millions)	2012	2011
Average common stockholders' equity	$3,430.5	$2,921.6
Dividends declared on common stock	125.5	104.3
Net income	775.9	691.4

Required

a. Calculate the return on equity for Lee Incorporated for 2012 and 2011. Round percentages to one decimal point (i.e., 9.4%).
b. Calculate the dividend payout ratio for 2012 and 2011. Round percentages to one decimal point (i.e., 9.4%).
c. Compare the financial performance for the two years and comment on which year was more successful, based on these measures, and possible reasons why.

31. Evaluate Equity LO6

Laura's Boutique is trying to calculate different financial measures to analyze its performance. Net income for the year was $80 million. There are 150 million shares issued and 125 million shares outstanding.

Required

a. Calculate earnings per share for the year.
b. Interpret the results of this calculation. What could the company possibly do to improve this financial measure?

32. Evaluate Equity LO6

Kristi's Kites provided the following information from its financial statements:

Net income	$164,500
Average number of common shares outstanding	235,000
Average stockholders' equity	$576,000

Required:

Calculate the earnings per share and return on equity for Kristi's Kites. Round percentages to one decimal point (i.e., 9.4%). How are the two profitability ratios different?

33. Evaluate Equity LO6

Kay Company's stock on the last day of the year was $39. Kay reported dividends per share of $0.49 and total dividends of $637,000 on its statement of stockholders' equity. Net income for the year was $4,000,000. The average number of common shares outstanding is 1,300,000.

Required:

a. Calculate the dividend payout ratio and the dividend yield for Kay Company. Round percentages to one decimal point (i.e., 9.4%).
b. Where do you find dividends paid in the statement of cash flows?

34. Accounting Terms LO1, 2

The following is a list of terms and definitions associated with equity:

1. Preemptive right
2. Sole proprietorship
3. Right to dividends
4. Public corporation
5. Right to residual assets
6. Par value
7. Right to vote
8. Contributed capital

a. Ensures that stockholders receive a proper portion of assets upon liquidation.
b. Ensures that stockholders can participate in the company they own.
c. Ensures that stockholders can maintain their ownership percentage when new shares are issued.
d. Ensures that stockholders receive a proper portion of dividends paid.
e. An arbitrary value that determines an entity's legal capital.
f. A corporation whose stock is available to the public at large.
g. A form of business with one owner.
h. The equity generated through the sale of capital stock.

Required

Match each term with the appropriate definition.

35. Accounting Terms LO3, 4, 5

The following is a list of terms and definitions associated with equity:

1. Treasury stock
2. Cumulative
3. Stock split
4. Dividend
5. Stock dividend
6. Non-cumulative
7. Authorized shares
8. Preferred stock

a. The number of shares the corporate charter allows a company to issue.
b. A form of capital stock that receives certain priorities over common stock.
c. A company's own common stock that has been issued to an investor, repurchased by the company, and is being held by the company for future use.
d. A distribution to owners.
e. A type of preferred stock that grants to stockholders preference for current-year dividends only.
f. A type of preferred stock that grants to stockholders preference to current-year dividends as well as all unpaid dividends from prior years.
g. A distribution of a company's own common stock to existing stockholders.
h. This increases a company's shares of stock according to some specified ratio.

Required

Match each term with the appropriate definition.

PROBLEMS

36. Recording and Reporting Equity LO2, 3, 5, 6

Camp Corporation had the following balances in its stockholders' equity at January 1:

Common stock, $2 par value, 450,000 shares issued	$ 900,000
Additional paid-in capital	1,200,000
Retained earnings	2,225,000
Treasury stock, at cost, 8,000 shares	(48,000)

During the year, Camp Corporation had the following transactions related to stockholders' equity:

Mar. 1 Issued 200,000 shares of common stock for cash at $8 per share.
July 1 Declared a 10% stock dividend, payable August 1. The stock was trading at $7 per share on July 1.
Aug. 15 Declared a $0.50 per share cash dividend to stockholders of record on September 1, payable September 15.
Oct. 1 Bought back 6,000 shares of common stock for $45,000.

In addition to the above transactions, assume that during the year Camp generated net income of $520,000.

Required

a. Prepare the journal entries to record the four transactions.
b. Post all necessary items to a Retained Earnings T-account to update the account. Hint: Do not forget the effect of net income.
c. Prepare Camp's December 31 stockholders' equity section.
d. Using end-of-year outstanding shares, calculate earnings per share for the year.

37. Errors in Equity Transactions LO2, 3, 5, 6

McLelland Industries had the following stockholders' equity balances:

	December 31	January 1
Preferred stock, $5 par value, 6,400 shares issued and outstanding	$ 38,400	$ 32,000
Common stock, $1 par value, 28,200 and 28,000 shares issued, respectively	35,000	28,000
Additional paid-in capital	678,000	700,000
Retained earnings	80,600	77,000
Treasury stock, at cost, 1,720 and 2,000 shares, respectively	(39,600)	(48,000)

When asked why the company's equity balances changed during the year, McLelland provided the following explanations:

Preferred stock—The market value of the shares rose during the year from $5 to $6. The increase was placed in an Investment in Preferred Stock account.

Common stock—The issuance of 200 shares for cash was recorded entirely in the account.

Additional paid-in capital—Cash dividends paid during the year were subtracted from this account.

Retained earnings—Net income of $12,000 was added to the account during the closing process. Also, the stock dividend taken from treasury stock (see below) was subtracted from the account.

Treasury stock—A 1% common stock dividend (280 shares when the market price was $30) was recorded using only the retained earnings and treasury stock accounts. The dividend was declared and distributed on the same day, so one entry was made.

Required

a. Identify all errors in McLelland's treatment and prepare the incorrect entries that McLelland most likely made.
b. Prepare, if necessary, the correct entries that McLelland should have made.
c. Prepare a corrected stockholders' equity section as of December 31.

38. Evaluating Equity LO6

The following are financial measures from the financial statements of Brown Buildings for the past two years:

	2012	2011
Total assets	$4,255,350	$3,895,700
Total liabilities	2,050,150	1,980,300
Total stockholders' equity	2,205,200	1,915,400

Required

a. Conduct a horizontal analysis of Brown Buildings. Comment on your findings and possible reasons for these findings.
b. Conduct a vertical analysis for both years for Brown Buildings. Compare and briefly interpret the results of the two years.

39. Evaluating Equity LO6

Olson Outlet Malls is trying to determine if its equity is comparable to other malls in the area.

	2012	2011
Total assets	$1,374,000	$1,506,000
Total liabilities	$ 588,000	$ 732,000
Total stockholders' equity	$ 786,000	$ 774,000
Net income	$ 198,500	
Average number of common shares outstanding	266,000	
Average stockholders' equity	$ 780,000	
Market price of stock	$ 21	
Total dividends	$ 59,000	
Dividends per share	$ 0.223	

Required

a. Conduct horizontal and vertical analyses for Olson. Round percentages to one decimal point (i.e., 9.4%).
b. Calculate the earnings per share and return on equity. Round percentages to one decimal point (i.e., 9.4%).
c. Calculate the dividend payout ratio and the dividend yield. Round percentages to one decimal point (i.e., 9.4%).
d. Interpret the results of your calculations.

CASES

40. Research and Analysis LO2, 3, 5, 6

Access the 2010 annual report for **Tootsie Roll Industries** by clicking on the *Company Information* and *Financial Information* links at www.tootsie.com.

Required

1. Examine the company's balance sheet and conduct horizontal and vertical analyses of the company's total shareholders' equity. Round percentages to one decimal point (i.e., 9.4%).
2. Calculate the company's 2010 return on equity ratio. Using the dividend and price data found on page 28 of the annual report, calculate the company's 2010 dividend yield from cash dividends assuming that an investor purchased the stock at the low price during the first quarter of 2010. Round percentages to one decimal point (i.e., 9.4%).
3. Examine the company's statement of retained earnings and determine the value of stock dividends declared during 2010.
4. Examine the financing activities section of the company's statement of cash flows. How would you characterize the company's activity over the past three years?
5. Based on your answers above, write a paragraph explaining your opinion of Tootsie Roll's 2010 equity position. Use your answers as supporting facts.

41. Research and Analysis LO2, 3, 6

Access the 2010 annual report for **Williams-Sonoma, Inc.** by clicking on the *INVESTOR INFORMATION, SEC FILINGS,* and *ANNUAL REPORTS* links at www.williams-sonomainc.com.

Required

a. Conduct horizontal and vertical analyses of the equity accounts of the company. Round percentages to one decimal point (i.e., 9.4%).
b. Calculate the following ratios for the company: return on equity; earnings per share; dividend payout ratio; and dividend yield. Use dividends paid for dividend ratios. Also, use the 2009 year ending stock price on page 65 of the report for the dividend yield calculation. Round percentages to one decimal point (i.e., 9.4%).
c. Evaluate the information in (a) and (b). Would this be a company in which you would want to invest?

42. Entrepreneurial Decision Making LO1, 2

Jeff Blake is an entrepreneur and owner of Wood Creations, a sole proprietorship. The business, which manufactures tables, chairs, cabinets, and other furniture, is growing, and Jeff is exploring the idea of purchasing a brand new manufacturing facility. Because he does not have the money to do so, he believes his options are to borrow the money or to convert the business to a corporation and sell stock.

Required

Describe the decision that you think Jeff should make. Make sure to explain the advantages and disadvantages of the course of action that you choose.

43. Written Communication LO4

A friend of yours has e-mailed you to ask for some investing advice. He is considering buying stock in a certain company and is trying to determine whether he wants to invest in the company's common or preferred stock.

Required

Draft an e-mail to your friend explaining to him the similarities and differences between common and preferred stock. Include reasons why you feel one might be more preferable over the other.

MAKING IT REAL!

ACCT2 will prepare you for the real world by showing you how accounting information is used to make business decisions.

Throughout the text, take a look at the **Making it Real** features that highlight everyday businesses!

Home Depot Analysis boxes found within each chapter give students experience with analyzing financial data found in Home Depot's 2010 Annual Report. The excerpted annual report is located in the back of the text.

IFRS "Sticky Notes" have been incorporated into the chapters to briefly highlight important differences between U.S. GAAP and international reporting standards.

Each chapter contains a wealth of recent financial statements from today's leading companies such as Wendy's; Bed, Bath, and Beyond; American Eagle Outfitters; Domino's Pizza; and many more.

Each chapter's final learning objective usually includes a discussion of analysis that includes both vertical and horizontal presentation as well as coverage of important rations that relate to the chapter topics.

GO ONLINE! Visit **CengageNOW™** for **ACCT2** at www.cengagebrain.com.

Rubberball/Mike Kemp/Getty Images

Statement of Cash Flows

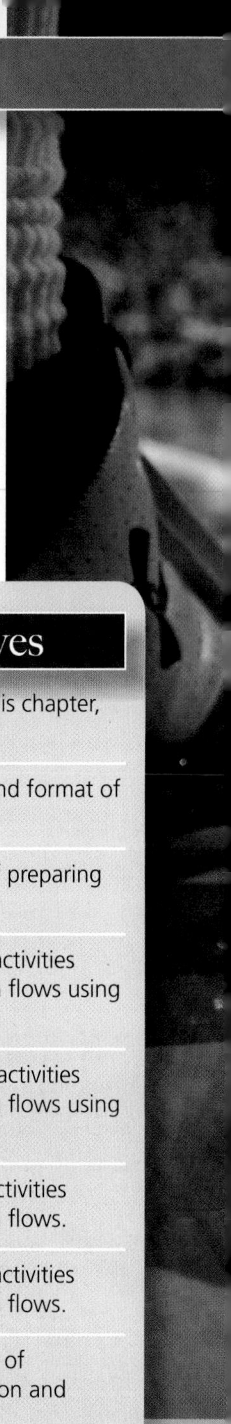

Learning Objectives

After studying the material in this chapter, you should be able to:

LO1 Describe the purpose and format of the statement of cash flows.

LO2 Describe the process of preparing the statement of cash flows.

LO3 Prepare the operating activities section of the statement of cash flows using the direct method.

LO4 Prepare the operating activities section of the statement of cash flows using the indirect method.

LO5 Prepare the investing activities section of the statement of cash flows.

LO6 Prepare the financing activities section of the statement of cash flows.

LO7 Evaluate the statement of cash flows through the calculation and interpretation of ratio analyses.

Introduction

As discussed in Chapter 1, the statement of cash flows provides information on how a company generates and distributes cash over a period of time. This chapter examines the purpose and format of the statement of cash flows and also demonstrates how the statement is prepared. The chapter concludes with an analysis of how to use the statement to generate useful information about a company and its cash.

LO1 The Statement of Cash Flows

One of the most important resources of any company is cash. If a company cannot generate sufficient cash, its ability to continue operations is significantly limited. As a result, management, investors, and creditors want to know how a company is managing its cash. How did the company use its cash? How did it generate cash? What are the prospects of the company paying a cash dividend? Will the company be able to satisfy its upcoming interest and loan obligations? Does the company have enough cash to expand its manufacturing facilities? Answers to these and other questions can be found through an examination of the statement of cash flows.

The **statement of cash flows** is a financial statement that summarizes a company's inflows and outflows of cash over a period of time. Its purpose is to inform users on how and why a company's cash changed during the period. So that it is as informative as possible, the statement groups and reports cash flows in three major categories: operating, investing, and financing. Cash flows from each of the three categories are then combined to determine the company's net change in cash and cash equivalents. This net change will be equal to the difference between

Statement of cash flows A financial statement that summarizes a company's inflows and outflows of cash over a period of time with a purpose to inform users on how and why a company's cash changed during the period.

One of the keys to success for a company like Under Armour is to convert its merchandise into cash.

Peyton Williams/UNC/Getty Images

the beginning and ending cash and cash equivalents balances from the balance sheet. Note that from this point forward, the term *cash* will be used to represent cash and cash equivalents.

The basic structure of the statement is as follows:

Cash Flows Provided (Used) by Operating Activities
+/− Cash Flows Provided (Used) by Investing Activities
+/− Cash Flows Provided (Used) by Financing Activities
Net Increase (Decrease) in Cash
+ Cash, Beginning of Year
Cash, End of Year

One of the most important resources of any company is cash. If a company cannot generate sufficient cash, its ability to continue operations is significantly limited.

The following sections discuss the three groupings of cash flows. For illustration purposes, Exhibit 11-1 on the next page contains **Under Armour, Inc.'s** statement of cash flows for the year ending December 31, 2010. All dollar amounts are in thousands.

Cash Flows from Operating Activities

Cash flows provided (used) by operating activities are those cash inflows and outflows arising from the company's operations. These inflows and outflows are sometimes called operating cash flows and would include the following:

- Cash inflows from sales or services
- Cash outflows for operating items such as inventory purchases, salaries, insurance, and supplies

Basically, any cash flow associated with a company's revenues or expenses should be considered an operating cash flow. Because of this, the net cash flow from operating activities can be thought of as net income on a cash basis.

Cash flows provided (used) by operating activities Cash inflows and outflows arising from the company's operations; often called operating cash flows.

Cash flows provided (used) by investing activities Cash inflows and outflows arising from the acquisition and disposal of non-current assets; often called investing cash flows.

Cash flows provided (used) by financing activities Cash inflows and outflows associated with the generation and return of capital; often called financing cash flows.

Operating cash flows are reported first on the statement of cash flows. Like most companies, Under Armour reports operating cash flows using the indirect method. The indirect method calculates operating cash flows by adjusting net income from an accrual basis to a cash basis. This calculation will be demonstrated in a later section. For now, you should simply note that many of the adjustments in Exhibit 11-1 involve accounts associated with operations—depreciation expense, accounts receivable, inventory, accounts payable, and income taxes. Under Armour generated over $50 million of cash from operations in 2010.

Cash Flows from Investing Activities

Cash flows provided (used) by investing activities are those cash inflows and outflows arising from the acquisition and disposal of non-current assets. They are often called investing cash flows and would include the following:

- Cash inflows from the sale of property, facilities, equipment, or investments
- Cash outflows for the purchase of property, facilities, equipment, or investments

Investing cash flows are reported after operating activities. Exhibit 11-1 reveals that Under Armour experienced net cash outflows of almost $42 million in 2010. The main contributor to that total was over $30 million for the purchase of property and equipment. In fact, in each of the years presented, the bulk of Under Armour's net investing cash outflows resulted from these purchases. This makes sense for a company that is growing.

Cash Flows from Financing Activities

Cash flows provided (used) by financing activities are those cash inflows and outflows associated with the generation and return of capital. These are often called financing cash flows and would include the following:

- Cash inflows from borrowings or stock issuances
- Cash outflows to satisfy debt obligations or to repurchase treasury stock
- Cash outflows for dividends to stockholders

Exhibit 11-1 Under Armour, Inc.'s 2010 Statement of Cash Flows

Under Armour, Inc. and Subsidiaries
Consolidated Statements of Cash Flows
(in thousands)

	Year Ended December 31, 2010	2009	2008
Cash flows from operating activities			
Net income	$ 68,477	$ 46,785	$ 38,229
Adjustments to reconcile net income to net cash provided by (used in) operating activities			
Depreciation and amortization	31,321	28,249	21,347
Unrealized foreign currency exchange rate (gains) losses	1,280	(5,222)	5,459
Loss on disposal of property and equipment	44	37	15
Stock-based compensation	16,227	12,910	8,466
Deferred income taxes	(10,337)	(5,212)	(2,818)
Changes in reserves and allowances	2,322	1,623	8,711
Changes in operating assets and liabilities:			
Accounts receivable	(32,320)	3,792	2,634
Inventories	(65,239)	32,998	(19,497)
Prepaid expenses and other assets	(4,099)	1,870	(7,187)
Accounts payable	16,158	(4,386)	16,957
Accrued expenses and other liabilities	21,330	11,656	(5,316)
Income taxes payable and receivable	4,950	(6,059)	2,516
Net cash provided by operating activities	50,114	119,041	69,516
Cash flows from investing activities			
Purchase of property and equipment	(30,182)	(19,845)	(38,594)
Purchase of intangible assets	—	—	(600)
Purchase of trust-owned life insurance policies	(478)	(35)	(2,893)
Deposit for purchase of long-term investment	(11,125)	—	—
Proceeds from sales of property and equipment	—	—	21
Net cash used in investing activities	(41,785)	(19,880)	(42,066)
Cash flows from financing activities			
Proceeds from revolving credit facility	—	—	40,000
Payments on revolving credit facility	—	(25,000)	(15,000)
Proceeds from long-term debt	5,262	7,649	13,214
Payments on long-term debt	(9,446)	(7,656)	(6,490)
Payments on capital lease obligations	(97)	(361)	(464)
Excess tax benefits from stock-based compensation arrangements	4,189	5,127	2,131
Proceeds from exercise of stock options and other stock issuances	7,335	5,128	1,990
Payments of debt financing costs	—	(1,354)	—
Net cash provided by (used in) financing activities	7,243	(16,467)	35,381
Effect of exchange rate changes on cash and cash equivalents	1,001	2,561	(1,377)
Net increase in cash and cash equivalents	16,573	85,255	61,454
Cash and cash equivalents			
Beginning of year	187,297	102,042	40,588
End of year	$203,870	$187,297	$102,042

Basically, any cash flows associated with debt or equity (other than interest payments) are considered to be financing cash flows.

Financing cash flows are reported after investing cash flows. Exhibit 11-1 reveals that **Under Armour** generated over $7 million in cash in 2010 from financing activities. This net cash flow resulted from several activities. According to the statement, Under Armour made over $9 million in payments on long-term debt, borrowed over $5 million in additional long-term debt, and generated over $11 million from stock-related activities. Note that in the prior year (2009), Under Armour experienced a $16 million outflow from financing activities, mainly due to the $25 million repayment of a credit facility.

Net Increase (Decrease) in Cash

After a company reports its operating, investing, and financing cash flows, it sums the three and reconciles the company's beginning and ending cash balances. The following is a condensed version of Under Armour's statement of cash flows, showing only the major subtotals:

Under Armour's 2010 Condensed Statement of Cash Flows

	2010	2009	2008
Net cash provided by (used in) operating activities	$ 50,114	$119,041	$69,516
Net cash used in investing activities	(41,785)	(19,880)	(42,066)
Net cash provided by financing activities	7,243	(16,467)	35,381
Effect of exchange rate changes	1,001	2,561	(1,377)
Net increase (decrease) in cash and cash equivalents	16,573	85,255	61,454
Cash, beginning of year	187,297	102,042	40,588
Cash, end of year	$203,870	$ 187,297	$102,042

Under Armour's net increase in cash during 2010 was over $16.5 million. This increase consisted of the sum of operating, investing, and financing cash flows as well as an additional adjustment for exchange rate changes. While exchange rate adjustments are not covered in this chapter, they are often necessary for companies such as Under Armour that conduct business in various currencies. Adding the 2010 increase of over $16.5 million to the beginning balance of cash of over $187 million yields the 2010 year-end balance in cash of nearly $204 million. Both the $187 million and $204 million can be found as the 2009 and 2010 cash balances in the first row of Under Armour's 2010 balance sheet.

Additional Disclosures

All publicly traded companies prepare the statement of cash flows using a format similar to what has been described. In some cases, companies must also make one or both of the following two disclosures:

- Significant non-cash investing or financing activities
- Cash paid for interest and taxes

The first disclosure relates to significant investing or financing transactions in which no cash is exchanged. Examples would include the purchase of property through the issuance of mortgage debt, the conversion of long-term debt into common stock, or the payment of dividends by the issuance of stock. Even though such transactions do not involve cash, they are important for properly understanding a company's cash flows and therefore must be disclosed either on the face of the statement or in the notes to the financial statements.

Although Exhibit 11-1 does not show it, Under Armour does make additional non-cash disclosures on its statement of cash flows. The only significant non-cash activity reported in 2010 is the purchase of property and equipment through certain obligations. While the schedule does not provide further explanation on the nature of the obligations, it does reveal that the company acquired almost $3 million in fixed assets by creating future obligations rather than paying cash.

Under Armour's 2010 Disclosures of Non-Cash Financing and Investing Activities

(in thousands)	2010	2009	2008
Purchase of property and equipment through certain obligations	$2,922	$4,784	$2,486
Purchase of intangible asset through certain obligations	—	2,105	—

The second disclosure relates to interest and taxes. When a company uses the indirect method to report operating cash flows, the amount of interest and taxes paid are not shown in the operating activities of the statement of cash flows. However, accounting standards require that companies disclose the amount of interest and taxes paid. Companies like **Under Armour** often disclose this information as an additional disclosure at the bottom of their statements of cash flows. Although Exhibit 11-1 does not show it, Under Armour does include the following additional disclosure at the bottom of its statement:

Under Armour's 2010 Disclosure of Interest and Taxes Paid

	2010	2009	2008
Cash paid for income taxes	$38,773	$40,834	$29,561
Cash paid for interest	992	1,273	1,444

LO2 Preparing the Statement of Cash Flows

Chapter 4 discussed the preparation of the income statement, the statement of retained earnings, and the balance sheet. Each of these statements is prepared

MAKING IT REAL

Having positive cash flows gives companies flexibility to do many different things. For one company, it recently resulted in a "first" in its history.

Cisco Systems Inc. was founded in 1984. Over the 25+ years of its existence, it had never paid a cash dividend to its stockholders, choosing instead to use its cash to grow its business. However, due in part to its solid cash position and healthy cash flows, that all changed in 2011. On March 18, 2011, Cisco's Board of Directors approved the initiation of quarterly cash dividends to its shareholders. The company further stated that the dividend would be the first to be paid to stockholders in the company's history. The dividend was set at $.06 per share.

Eimantas Buzas/Shutterstock

Source: http://newsroom.cisco.com/press-release-content?type=webcontent&articleId=5967558.

HOME DEPOT ANALYSIS

Look at **Home Depot's** statement of cash flows in Appendix C. In the most recent year, what were the company's net cash flows from operating, investing, and financing activities? Also, what amount of cash was paid for capital expenditures and dividends in the most recent year? Finally, how much did the company pay in income taxes in the most recent year?

In the most recent year, Home Depot generated (in thousands) net cash flows of $4,585 from operating activities and used net cash flows of $1,012 from investing activities and $4,451 from financing activities. During the most recent year, the company paid $1,096 for capital expenditures, $1,569 for dividends, and $2,067 for income taxes.

with numbers from an adjusted trial balance. That is, they are prepared by rearranging numbers already provided by the accounting system.

The preparation of the statement of cash flows is different. First, information is collected from a variety of sources. Second, preparing the statement requires an examination of the changes in all non-cash accounts. To understand why, consider the fundamental accounting equation:

$$\text{Assets} = \text{Liabilities} + \text{Equity}$$

Cash can be isolated by breaking it out from other assets to yield the following:

$$\text{Cash} + \text{Non-Cash Assets} = \text{Liabilities} + \text{Equity}$$

Moving non-cash assets from the left side of the equation to the right side then results in the following:

$$\text{Cash} = \text{Liabilities} + \text{Equity} - \text{Non-Cash Assets}$$

Using Δ to denote a change, this equation can also be rewritten to show that the change in cash for a given period is equal to the changes in all other non-cash accounts (liabilities, equity, and non-cash assets):

$$\Delta\,\text{Cash} = \Delta\,\text{Liabilities} + \Delta\,\text{Equity} - \Delta\,\text{Non-cash Assets}$$

As a result, to explain a company's change in cash, you must explain the changes in the company's non-cash accounts. And to do that, you need the following three items:

- A comparative balance sheet
- An income statement
- Additional information on changes in account balances

A comparative balance sheet provides the beginning and ending balances of all non-cash accounts, from which changes for the period are calculated.

Direct method Method of reporting cash flows from operating activities in which cash inflows and outflows from operations are reported separately on the statement of cash flows.

Indirect method Method of reporting cash flows from operating activities in which net income is adjusted from an accrual basis to a cash basis.

To explain a company's change in cash, you must explain the changes in the company's non-cash accounts.

An income statement provides a company's revenue and expense balances for the period. These balances are used to prepare the operating activities section of the statement of cash flows. Additional information on changes in account balances is needed to determine if a balance changed because of non-cash activity. For example, the issuance of stock to satisfy a debt obligation changes both equity and liability balances, but cash is not affected. Knowledge of such significant non-cash transactions keeps one from erroneously concluding that the company received cash for the issuance of stock and paid cash for the retirement of the debt.

Direct and Indirect Methods for Operating Cash Flows

When preparing the statement of cash flows, all companies report cash flows from operating, investing, and financing activities. The manner in which cash flows from investing and financing activities are reported is the same for all companies. However, companies can report their cash flows from operating activities using either the *direct method* or the *indirect method*. Both methods will yield the same net cash flows from operating activities. The only difference is the manner in which those cash flows are reported.

Under the **direct method**, a company reports its cash inflows from operations followed by its cash outflows for operations. Typically, cash outflows are broken out into a few categories including cash payments for inventory, operating expenses, interest, and taxes. The difference between inflows and outflows is the company's net cash flow from operating activities. The method is called "direct" because both inflows and outflows are shown directly on the statement.

Under the **indirect method**, a company reports its cash flows from operating activities by adjusting its net income from an accrual basis to a cash basis. The method is called "indirect" because it does not directly report cash inflows and cash outflows from operations. Rather, it reports the adjustments necessary to convert net income to the net cash flow from operating activities. Adjustments typically arise from non-cash revenues and expenses and/or changes in current assets and current liabilities.

A company is free to use either the direct or indirect method in its statement of cash flows. However, accounting standards require that if a company uses the direct method in its statement, it must disclose the indirect method as well. As a result, the vast majority of companies use the indirect method.

The vast majority of publicly traded companies use the indirect method to report cash flows from operating activities.

Exhibit 11-2 Hardin Supply Company Financial Statements

Hardin Supply Company
Income Statement
For the Year Ending December 31, 2012
(in thousands)

Sales		$432
Cost of goods sold		281
Gross profit		$151
Operating expenses:		
Depreciation expense	$25	
Insurance expense	14	
Salaries expense	63	
Utilities expense	28	130
Operating income		$ 21
Gain on sale of equipment		1
Income before taxes		$ 22
Income tax expense		8
Net income		$ 14

Hardin Supply Company
Comparative Balance Sheet
December 31, 2012

	2012	2011
Cash and cash equivalents	$ 18	$ 45
Accounts receivable	45	41
Inventory	101	92
Prepaid insurance	11	15
Total current assets	175	193
Long-term investments	22	0
Equipment, at cost	232	166
Less: Accumulated depreciation	(57)	(37)
Total assets	$372	$322
Accounts payable	$ 37	$ 29
Salaries payable	21	21
Utilities payable	27	22
Taxes payable	0	7
Total current liabilities	85	79
Long-term debt	45	0
Total liabilities	130	79
Common stock	165	165
Retained earnings	87	78
Treasury stock	(10)	0
Total stockholders' equity	242	243
Total liabilities and stockholders' equity	$372	$322

Example Data

To demonstrate how to prepare a statement of cash flows, the information for Hardin Supply Company in Exhibit 11-2 will be used. Note that Hardin provides both an income statement and a comparative balance sheet and that all numbers are in thousands. For simplicity, references to thousands will be omitted in the discussions. Additional information will be provided as needed.

LO3 Reporting Cash Flows from Operating Activities—Direct Method

This section demonstrates the calculation of cash flows from operating activities under the direct method.

When reporting operating cash flows under the direct method, companies report 1) cash receipts from operating activities and 2) cash payments for operating activities. Cash receipts are calculated by converting revenues from the income statement to cash collections. Cash payments are calculated by converting expenses from the income statement to cash payments.

The following sections demonstrate this conversion process. The first section considers cash receipts from customers. The next sections consider cash payments in three main groups: cash paid for inventory, for operating expenses, and for income taxes. For each calculation, two approaches are demonstrated—one focusing on the changes in account balances and another using a debit/credit approach.

Cash Received from Customers

Hardin's income statement shows that the company generated $432 in sales during the year. To determine cash receipts from those sales, the balance sheet account related to sales—accounts receivable—must be examined.

Hardin's balance sheet shows that accounts receivable increased $4 during the year. The accounts receivable account increases when sales are made but no cash is collected. Therefore, a $4 increase means that $4 of Hardin's $432 of sales were not collected during the year. Therefore, cash collections were $428.

Sales for the period	$432
Less: Increase in accounts receivable	4
Cash collected from sales	$428

Note that had Hardin's accounts receivable decreased during the year, the decrease would have been added to sales.

The conversion of sales to cash collections can be summarized as follows:

Balance from Income Statement	Adjustment	Balance for Statement of Cash Flows
Sales	− Increase in accounts receivable or + Decrease in accounts receivable	= Cash collected from sales

A second approach for calculating cash receipts from sales is to prepare the journal entry that Hardin would hypothetically make if it recorded its annual sales and the change in receivables in only one entry.

Given sales of $432, Hardin would credit Sales for $432. Hardin would also debit Accounts Receivable for $4 to reflect the increase in the account. To balance the entry, Hardin would debit Cash for $428. Thus, cash collections from sales are $428.

Hypothetical Entry	Accounts Receivable	4	
	Cash	428	
	Sales		432

Cash Paid for Inventory

Hardin's income statement shows that the company had $281 of cost of goods sold during the year. To convert this expense to cash paid for inventory, Hardin must first calculate total purchases for the period and then calculate the cash paid for those purchases.

To calculate purchases, Hardin must examine the inventory account. Inventory increased by $9 during the year. An increase in the inventory account means that Hardin bought more inventory than it sold. Therefore, Hardin must have purchased $290 of inventory during the year.

Inventory sold during the period	$281
Plus: Increase in inventory	9
Inventory purchased during the period	$290

Note that had Hardin's inventory decreased during the year, the decrease would have been subtracted from inventory to calculate purchases.

To calculate cash paid for these purchases, Hardin must examine accounts payable. Accounts payable increased $8 during the year. The accounts payable account increases when purchases are made but no cash is paid. Therefore, Hardin must have paid for only $282 of its $290 in purchases.

Inventory purchased during the period	$290
Less: Increase in accounts payable	8
Cash paid to suppliers for the period	$282

Note that had Hardin's accounts payable decreased during the year, the decrease would have been added to purchases to calculate cash paid.

The conversion of cost of goods sold to cash paid for inventory can be summarized as shown on the next page.

Cash paid for inventory can also be determined by preparing the entry that Hardin would hypothetically make to record the activity in the cost of goods sold, inventory, and accounts payable accounts.

Given cost of goods sold of $281, Hardin would debit Cost of Goods Sold for $281. Hardin would also debit Inventory $9 for its increase during the year and credit Accounts Payable $8 for its increase during the year. To balance the entry, Hardin would credit Cash for $282. Thus, cash paid for inventory is $282.

Balance from Income Statement	Adjustment		Adjustment	Balance for Statement of Cash Flows
	+ Increase in inventory		− Increase in accounts payable	
Cost of goods sold	or	= Purchases	or	= Cash paid for inventory
	− Decrease in inventory		+ Decrease in accounts payable	

Hypothetical Entry	Cost of Goods Sold	281	
	Inventory	9	
	Accounts Payable		8
	Cash		282

Cash Paid for Operating Expenses

Hardin's income statement shows several operating expenses. The following sections demonstrate how operating expenses are converted to cash paid. The first section illustrates an expense related to a current asset. The second section illustrates two expenses relating to current liabilities.

Insurance Expense Hardin's income statement shows $14 of insurance expense during the year. To determine the cash paid for insurance, the related balance sheet account—prepaid insurance—must be examined.

Prepaid insurance decreased $4, meaning that Hardin used $4 of insurance it had purchased in a previous period. As a result, cash paid for insurance in the current period was only $10.

Insurance expense for the period	$14
Less: Decrease in prepaid insurance	4
Cash paid for insurance	$10

Note that had Hardin's prepaid insurance increased during the year, the increase would have been added to insurance expense.

The conversion of insurance expense to cash paid for insurance is summarized at the bottom of this page.

Using the entry approach to calculate cash payments for insurance, Hardin would debit Insurance Expense for $14 and credit Prepaid Insurance for $4. Cash would then be credited to balance the entry, showing cash payments for insurance to be $10.

Hypothetical Entry	Insurance Expense	14	
	Prepaid Insurance		4
	Cash		10

Salaries Expense and Utilities Expense Hardin's income statement shows $63 of salaries expense and $28 of utilities expense during the year. To determine the cash paid for these operating expenses, the related balance sheet accounts—salaries payable and utilities payable—must be examined.

Salaries payable did not change during the year, so Hardin must have paid exactly $63 to employees.

Salaries expense for the period	$63
Change in salaries payable	0
Cash paid to employees	$63

Utilities payable increased $5 during the year, meaning that Hardin incurred utilities during the year for which it did not pay. Therefore, Hardin paid only $23 for utilities during the year.

Utilities expense for the period	$28
Less: Increase in utilities payable	5
Cash paid for utilities	$23

Balance from Income Statement	Adjustment	Balance for Statement of Cash Flows
	+ Increase in prepaid insurance	
Insurance expense	or	= Cash paid for insurance
	− Decrease in prepaid insurance	

Note that had Hardin's utilities payable decreased during the year, the decrease would have been added to utilities expense.

The conversion of these operating expenses to cash paid for salaries and utilities can be summarized as follows:

Balance from Income Statement	Adjustment	Balance for Statement of Cash Flows
Salaries expense	− Increase in salaries payable or + Decrease in salaries payable	= Cash paid for salaries
Utilities expense	− Increase in utilities payable or + Decrease in utilities payable	= Cash paid for utilities

Using the entry approach to calculate the cash payments for salaries, Hardin would debit Salaries Expense for $63. Nothing is recorded for Salaries Payable because the account balance was unchanged. Cash is then credited to balance the entry, showing cash payments to be $63.

Hypothetical Entry	Salaries Expense	63	
	Cash		63

For utilities, Hardin would debit Utilities Expense for $28 and credit Utilities Payable for $5. Cash would be credited to balance the entry, showing cash payments to be $23.

Hypothetical Entry	Utilities Expense	28	
	Utilities Payable		5
	Cash		23

Cash Paid for Taxes

Hardin's income statement shows $8 of income tax expense during the year. To determine the cash paid for taxes, the related balance sheet account—taxes payable—must be examined.

Taxes payable decreased $7 during the year, meaning that Hardin paid not only current-year taxes of $8, but also $7 of prior-year taxes. Thus, taxes paid in this period were $15.

Income tax expense for the period	$ 8
Plus: Decrease in taxes payable	7
Cash paid for taxes	$15

Note that had Hardin's taxes payable increased during the year, the increase would have been subtracted from income tax expense.

The conversion of income tax expense to cash paid for taxes is summarized at the bottom of this page.

To calculate cash payments using the entry method, Hardin would debit Income Tax Expense for $8 and debit Taxes Payable for $7. Cash would be credited to balance the entry, showing cash payments to be $15.

Hypothetical Entry	Income Tax Expense	8	
	Income Tax Payable	7	
	Cash		15

IFRS

Under GAAP, cash flows associated with taxes are classified as operating activities. Under IFRS, they are also classified as operating activities unless they can be specifically identified with investing or financing activities.

Other Revenues and Expenses

Hardin's income statement contains two additional items: depreciation expense and gain on sale of equipment. For the following reasons, these items are ignored under the direct method.

Balance from Income Statement	Adjustment	Balance for Statement of Cash Flows
Income tax expense	− Increase in taxes payable or + Decrease in taxes payable	= Cash paid for taxes

Recall from Chapter 8 that depreciation expense is a non-cash charge, meaning that cash is not affected when depreciation is recorded. As a result, depreciation expense is ignored when preparing the operating activities section under the direct method. This is always the case.

Recall also from Chapter 8 that a gain on the sale of equipment occurs when cash received from the sale exceeds the equipment's book value. Because the sale of equipment is an investing activity, all cash received from the sale will be reported as a cash inflow from investing activities. As a result, the gain on the sale is ignored when preparing the operating activities section under the direct method. The same would be true for a loss on the sale of equipment or any other gain or loss from an investing or financing activity.

Net Operating Cash Flows

Based on the previous calculations, Hardin's operating activities section of its statement of cash flows is shown in Exhibit 11-3. A summary of adjustments used to generate the numbers is found in Exhibit 11-4.

Exhibit 11-3 Hardin's Operating Cash Flows Using the Direct Method

Cash flows from operating activities

Cash receipts from customers		$428
Less cash payments:		
To suppliers	$282	
To employees	63	
For insurance	10	
For utilities	23	
For taxes	15	393
Net cash provided by operating activities		$ 35

The indirect method calculates and reports net cash flows from operating activities by adjusting net income from an accrual basis to a cash basis.

LO4 Reporting Cash Flows from Operating Activities—Indirect Method

This section demonstrates the calculation of cash flows from operating activities under the indirect method.

When reporting operating cash flows under the indirect method, companies report the adjustment of net income from an accrual basis to a cash basis. This usually requires many adjustments, but they can be grouped into three main types:

- Non-cash effects on net income
- Gains and losses from investing and/or financing activities
- Changes in current assets and liabilities

The following sections demonstrate these adjustments using the Hardin Supply Company information in Exhibit 11-2.

Exhibit 11-4 Summary of Adjustments Used in the Direct Method

Balance from Income Statement	Adjustment			Balance for Statement of Cash Flows
Sales	− Increase in accounts receivable	OR	+ Decrease in accounts receivable	= Cash collected from sales
Cost of goods sold	+ Increase in inventory	OR	− Decrease in inventory	= Cash paid for inventory
		and		
	− Increase in accounts payable	OR	+ Decrease in accounts payable	
Operating expenses	+ Increase in current asset	OR	− Decrease in current asset	= Cash paid for operations
		or		
	− Increase in current liability	OR	+ Decrease in current liability	
Income tax expense	− Increase in taxes payable	OR	+ Decrease in taxes payable	= Cash paid for taxes

Adjustments for Non-Cash Items

Accrual-based net income often includes expenses that have no related cash consequences. The most common example is depreciation expense, which is an allocation of the historical cost of a fixed asset. While depreciation reduces accrual-based net income, it does not result in any cash payment. Therefore, to adjust net income to a cash basis, the effect of depreciation must be removed from net income. This is accomplished by adding depreciation expense back to net income. Other examples of non-cash expenses are amortization expense, bad debt expense, and impairment losses.

The general adjustment for all non-cash expenses is therefore as follows:

Adjustment rule for non-cash expenses
Add back to net income all non-cash expenses

Hardin Supply Company's income statement in Exhibit 11-2 shows only one non-cash expense: depreciation expense of $25. Therefore, the $25 would be added back to net income.

Adjustments for Gains and Losses from Investing and Financing Activities

Sometimes, a company's net income will include a gain or loss arising from an investing or financing activity. For example, a company might generate a gain from the sale of equipment or a loss from the sale of an intangible asset. Another company might generate a gain from the early retirement of debt or a loss from a bond redemption.

When such activity occurs, the entire cash inflow associated with the transaction will be reported as either an investing or financing cash flow. As a result, the effect of the gain or loss must be removed from net income so that operating cash flows are not affected by the transaction. Gains must be subtracted from income, and losses must be added back to income.

Adjustment rules for gains and losses from investing and financing activities
Subtract from net income any gains arising from investing or financing activities
Add back to net income any losses arising from investing or financing activities

Hardin's income statement shows only one gain or loss from an investing or financing activity: a $1 gain on the sale of equipment. Because the cash received from the sale will be reported as an investing cash flow, the effect of the gain must be removed from income. Therefore, income is reduced by $1.

Adjustments for Current Assets and Current Liabilities

The third type of adjustment involves the changes in a company's current assets and current liabilities. Current assets and current liabilities change during a period because a company's revenues do not equal cash received and its expenses do not equal cash paid.

For example, a change in accounts receivable means that a company's cash collections do not equal its sales revenue. If accounts receivable increases, sales revenue is greater than cash collections. If accounts receivable decreases, cash collections are greater than sales revenue. Likewise, a change in salaries payable means that a company's cash payments do not equal its salaries expense. If salaries payable increases, salaries expense is greater than cash payments. If salaries payable decreases, cash payments are greater than salaries expense.

Because the indirect method adjusts accrual-based income to cash-based income, these differences must be removed from accrual-based net income. That is, the revenues and expenses of net income must be adjusted so that they reflect cash receipts and cash payments. This is accomplished with the following adjustments:

Adjustment rules for current assets and current liabilities
Add to net income a decrease in current assets
Subtract from net income an increase in current assets
Add to net income an increase in current liabilities
Subtract from net income a decrease in current liabilities

Hardin's balance sheet shows changes in several current assets and current liabilities. The following sections describe the adjustment that each change requires.

Change in Accounts Receivable Hardin's balance sheet shows a $4 increase in accounts receivable. Accounts receivable increases when sales are made without receiving cash. Therefore, $4 of Hardin's reported sales revenue was not collected in cash and must be removed from revenues. Removing $4 from revenue is accomplished by subtracting $4 from net income.

Change in Inventory Hardin's balance sheet shows that inventory increased by $9 during the year. Inventory increases when a company purchases more inventory that it sells. Therefore, Hardin must have purchased $9 more in inventory than it sold during the year. So that net income reflects all payments for purchases, the $9 must be added to cost of goods sold. This results in a reduction to net income of $9.

Change in Prepaid Insurance Hardin's balance sheet shows a decrease in prepaid insurance of $4. Prepaid insurance decreases when a company uses insurance that it has already purchased. Thus, a decrease of $4 means that Hardin used $4 of insurance that it purchased in a previous period. As a result, insurance expense is $4 greater than the cash paid for insurance and should be reduced to reflect the cash paid for insurance. Reducing expenses by $4 is accomplished by adding $4 to net income.

Change in Accounts Payable Hardin's balance sheet shows that accounts payable increased by $8 during the year. Accounts payable increases when inventory is purchased without paying cash, so an $8 increase means that Hardin did not pay for $8 of its purchases calculated previously. Therefore, the $8 must be removed from expenses. This is accomplished by adding $8 to net income.

Change in Utilities Payable Hardin's balance sheet shows an increase of $5 in utilities payable. Utilities payable increases when a company incurs utilities expense but does not pay cash. Thus, the $5 increase means that Hardin's expenses are $5 greater than the cash paid. As a result, the $5 of expenses must be removed from net income. This is accomplished by adding $5 to net income.

Change in Taxes Payable Hardin's balance sheet shows that taxes payable decreased $7 during the period to end at a zero balance. Taxes payable decreases when a company pays not only for current-period taxes but also prior-period taxes. The $7 decrease therefore means that Hardin paid $7 more than it expensed. As a result, the $7 should be added to expenses. This is accomplished by subtracting $7 from net income.

Net Operating Cash Flows

The six adjustments from changes in current assets and current liabilities, along with the two adjustments for non-cash items, are shown in Exhibit 11-5. The adjustments result in $35 in net cash provided by operating activities. If you are learning both the direct and indirect methods, you should note that the $35 is the same as calculated under the direct method.

Exhibit 11-5 Hardin's Operating Cash Flows Using the Indirect Method

Cash flows from operating activities		
Net income		$14
Adjustments to reconcile net income to net cash provided by operating activities		
Depreciation expense	$25	
Gain on sale of equipment	(1)	
Increase in accounts receivable	(4)	
Increase in inventory	(9)	
Decrease in prepaid insurance	4	
Increase in accounts payable	8	
Increase in utilities payable	5	
Decrease in taxes payable	(7)	21
Net cash provided by operating activities		$35

LO5 Computing Cash Flows from Investing Activities

This section demonstrates the calculation of cash flows from investing activities. Recall that investing activities include the purchase and sale of non-current assets such as fixed assets, intangible assets, and long-term investments.

To calculate cash flows from investing activities, all changes in non-current assets must be examined. In general, an increase in a non-current asset suggests a purchase and therefore a cash outflow. A decrease suggests a sale and therefore a cash inflow. However, to be sure, any available information on the changes must be examined to determine whether the change resulted from a non-cash transaction or whether the change was the net effect of both increases and decreases to the account.

To illustrate, consider again Hardin's balance sheet in Exhibit 11-2. It shows three non-current asset accounts: "Long-term investments, Equipment, and Accumulated depreciation." In the following sections, each account balance is examined to determine Hardin's cash flows from investing activities.

Kristian Sekulic/Shutterstock.com

Investing activities include the purchase and sale of non-current assets such as fixed assets, intangible assets, and long-term investments.

Investments

According to Hardin's balance sheet, investments increased $22. Without any information to the contrary, it is assumed that Hardin bought investments for $22 cash. Thus, a cash outflow of $22 from the purchase of investments is reported in investing activities.

Equipment

Hardin's balance sheet shows a $66 increase in equipment during the year. Thus, Hardin must have purchased equipment during the year. Hardin's income statement shows a $1 gain on the sale of equipment. Thus, Hardin must have sold equipment during the year. As a result, there are both cash inflows and outflows related to equipment. Each will be considered separately.

Cash Inflows To calculate cash inflows, Hardin must provide additional information on the sale. Assume that Hardin discloses that the $1 gain on the sale of equipment arose from selling equipment with a cost of $10 and accumulated depreciation of $5 for $6. Thus, a $6 inflow from the sale of equipment should be included in investing activities. Note here that the gain from the sale is ignored. Only the cash flow from the sale is of interest at this point. The gain is accounted for in operating activities.

Cash Outflows Hardin's equipment account increased $66 during the year. Absent any additional information, it would be assumed that Hardin purchased $66 in equipment for cash. However, Hardin's additional information discloses that equipment with a cost of $10 was sold during the year. Therefore, Hardin must have purchased $76 in equipment during the year. The calculation of purchases is shown as follows:

Beginning balance	$166		
Plus: Purchases	??	⟶	?? = $76
Less: Sales	10		
Ending balance	$232		

Accumulated Depreciation

Recall from Chapter 8 that accumulated depreciation is the account that collects depreciation expense. Therefore it changes when either depreciation expense is recorded or fixed assets are sold. Depreciation expense does not affect cash, and any sale of equipment is already considered when examining the equipment account. Therefore, the change in the accumulated depreciation account can be ignored.

Summary of Investing Cash Flows

The three cash flows from investing activities are shown in Exhibit 11-6. The three items resulted in a net cash outflow from investing activities of $(92). Hardin was using its cash to invest in additional non-current assets.

Exhibit 11-6 Hardin's Investing Cash Flows

Cash flows from investing activities	
Purchase of equipment	$(76)
Sale of equipment	6
Purchase of investments	(22)
Net cash used in investing activities	$(92)

LO6 Computing Cash Flows from Financing Activities

This section demonstrates the calculation of cash flows from financing activities. Recall that financing activities include generating and repaying capital to investors and creditors. Common financing activities include the issuance of stock or debt and the repurchase of stock, the payment of dividends, and the repayment of debt. Note that although payments of dividends to stockholders are considered a financing activity, payments of interest to creditors are not. Because interest is an expense that is reported on the income statement, payments for interest are reported as operating activities rather than financing activities.

To calculate cash flows from financing activities, the balances for long-term liabilities, equity accounts, and dividends must be examined. In general, an increase in a liability or an equity account such as common stock suggests a cash inflow from either borrowing or selling stock. A decrease in a liability or an increase in treasury stock or dividends suggests a cash outflow from payments to creditors or investors. However, to be sure, any available information on the changes must be examined to determine whether the change resulted from a non-cash transaction or whether the change was the net effect of both increases and decreases to the account.

To illustrate, consider again Hardin's balance sheet in Exhibit 11-2. It shows one long-term liability and three equity accounts. Hardin provides no additional information regarding the accounts. In the following sections, each account balance is examined to determine Hardin's cash flows from financing activities.

Long-Term Debt

According to Hardin's balance sheet, long-term debt increased \$45 during the year. Absent any information to the contrary, it is assumed that Hardin borrowed \$45 in cash. Thus, a cash inflow of \$45 from the issuance of debt is reported in financing activities.

Common Stock

Hardin's balance sheet shows no change in the common stock account. Thus, absent any additional information, it is assumed there was no effect on cash from the common stock account.

Treasury Stock

Hardin's balance sheet shows a \$10 increase in treasury stock. Recall from Chapter 10 that the treasury stock account records the cost of a company's own stock that has been repurchased. Absent any additional information telling us otherwise, it is assumed that Hardin purchased the stock for \$10 cash. Thus, a cash outflow of \$10 from the purchase of treasury stock is reported in financing activities.

Common financing activities include the issuance of stock or debt and the repurchase of stock, the payment of dividends, and the repayment of debt.

Retained Earnings

The fourth and final account is retained earnings. Recall from earlier chapters that the retained earnings balance is affected by two things—net income and dividends declared. Net income increases the balance while dividends decrease the balance. Hardin's balance sheet shows that retained earnings increased \$9 during the year, from \$78 to \$87. Hardin's income statement shows that net income was \$14. Therefore dividends declared can be calculated as follows:

Retained earnings, beginning balance	\$78	
Plus: Net income	14	
Less: Dividends declared	??	→ ?? = \$5
Retained earnings, ending balance	\$87	

Now that dividends declared are known, the amount paid can be calculated. If dividends were declared but not paid, the balance sheet would show a balance in dividends payable in current liabilities. Neither year shows a balance, so all \$5 of the dividends must have been paid. Thus, a cash outflow of \$5 from the payment of dividends is reported in financing activities.

Net Financing Cash Flows

The three cash flows from financing activities are shown in Exhibit 11-7. The three items resulted in a net cash inflow from financing activities of \$30. Hardin generated \$30 more from financing activities than it paid.

Exhibit 11-7 Hardin's Financing Cash Flows

Cash flows from financing activities	
Issuance of long-term debt	\$45
Payment of dividends	(5)
Purchase of treasury stock	(10)
Net cash provided by financing activities	\$30

The statement of cash flows reports how a company generated and used its cash during the year.

Complete Statement of Cash Flows—Indirect Method

Hardin's final statement of cash flows, using the indirect method, is shown in Exhibit 11-8. The net decrease in cash of $27 corresponds to the change in the cash account from Hardin's balance sheet. Note that the full statement under the direct method would result in the same net decrease in cash.

Exhibit 11-8 Hardin Supply Company Statement of Cash Flows

Hardin Supply Company
Statement of Cash Flows
For the Year Ending December 31, 2012

Cash flows from operating activities		
Net income		$ 14
Adjustments to reconcile net income to net cash provided by operating activities		
Depreciation expense	$ 25	
Gain on sale of equipment	(1)	
Increase in accounts receivable	(4)	
Increase in inventory	(9)	
Decrease in prepaid insurance	4	
Increase in accounts payable	8	
Increase in utilities payable	5	
Decrease in taxes payable	(7)	21
Net cash provided by operating activities		$ 35
Cash flows from investing activities		
Purchases of equipment	$(76)	
Sale of equipment	6	
Purchases of investments	(22)	
Net cash used in investing activities		(92)
Cash flows from financing activities		
Issuance of long-term debt	$ 45	
Payment of dividends	(5)	
Purchase of treasury stock	(10)	
Net cash provided by financing activities		30
Net decrease in cash		$(27)
Cash, beginning of the year		45
Cash, end of the year		$ 18

Free cash flow The excess cash a company generates beyond what it needs to invest in productive capacity and pay dividends to stockholders.

LO7 Analyzing a Company's Statement of Cash Flows

The statement of cash flows reports how a company generated and used its cash during the year. As a result, the statement can be used to answer many question about a company's cash. Two of the broader questions that can be addressed are as follows:

- Is the company able to generate enough cash to grow?
- Is the company able to generate enough cash to satisfy its obligations?

The following sections examine these questions for **Under Armour**. The examination will require the information from the company's statement of cash flows and notes to the financial statements. The required information is found in Exhibit 11-9, which is excerpted from Under Armour's 2010 Annual Report.

Exhibit 11-9 Account Balances from Under Armour's 2010 Annual Report

Source	Accounts	2010	2009
Statement of Cash Flows	Cash flows from operating activities	$50,114	$119,041
	Capital expenditures	30,182	19,845
	Dividends	0	0
Notes to Financial Statements	Average debt maturing in next five years	$ 3,188	

Free Cash Flow

When assessing a company's cash flows, a commonly used calculation is free cash flow. **Free cash flow** is the cash a company generates in excess of its investments in productive capacity and payments to stockholders in the form of dividends. Free cash flow is a measure of a company's ability to generate cash for expansion, for other forms of improved operations, for the repayment of debt, or for increased returns to stockholders. While free cash flow can be defined in many ways, the most straightforward definition is as follows:

Cash flows from operating activities
Less: Capital expenditures
Less: Dividends
Free cash flow

HOME DEPOT ANALYSIS

Look at **Home Depot's** statement of cash flows and the last sentence in Note 5 in Appendix C. Calculate and interpret (1) free cash flow and (2) cash flow adequacy ratio.

(1) Free cash flow:

$4,585 − $1,096 − $1,569 = $1,920

Home Depot generated $1,920 million in free cash flow in the most recent year. This cash could be used for further expansion, to pay down debt balances, or for other purposes determined by company management.

(2) Cash flow adequacy ratio:

$1,920/$476.6 = 4.1

The 4.1 cash flow adequacy ratio indicates that Home Depot can pay four times as much as the average debt coming due in the next five years. Thus, the company currently has adequate cash flow to service its maturing debt. [Note: The $476.6 balance is determined by taking the average debt maturing in the next five years: ($1,000 + $29 + $1,300 + $28 + $26)/5.]

The calculation starts with cash flows from operating activities, which is a measure of a company's ability to generate cash from its current operations. It then subtracts capital expenditures, which refers to the cash that a company spends on fixed assets during the year, and dividends, which are payments to stockholders during the year. The cash that remains is "free" to be used as the company chooses.

Under Armour's 2010 free cash flow is calculated as follows from the information in Exhibit 11-9:

	2010	2009
Cash flows from operating activities	50,114	119,041
– Capital expenditures	30,182	19,845
– Dividends	0	0
Free cash flow	19,932	99,196

In both 2010 and 2009, Under Armour generated positive free cash flow. That is, it generated more cash from operations than it paid for property and equipment and dividends. As a result, the company generated cash that was free to be used for other purposes. Note however that Under Armour experienced a significant decrease in its free cash flow from 2009 to 2010. This was a function of both a decrease in cash generated from operations and an increase in capital expenditures.

Cash Flow Adequacy Ratio

A second ratio that is commonly used to assess a company's cash is the cash flow adequacy ratio. The **cash flow adequacy ratio** compares free cash flow to the average amount of debt maturing in the next five years. It is calculated as follows:

Terri Miller/E-Visual Communications, Inc.

$$\text{Cash flow adequacy ratio} = \frac{\text{Free cash flow}}{\text{Average amount of debt maturing in five years}}$$

Because this ratio compares free cash flow to maturing debt, it represents a company's ability to generate enough cash to pay its debt. In general, companies would like this ratio to be higher rather than lower. All

Cash flow adequacy ratio Compares free cash flow to the average amount of debt maturing in the next five years and measures the ability to pay maturing debt.

other things equal, a higher ratio indicates a greater ability to generate sufficient cash from operations to pay upcoming debt.

Under Armour's 2010 cash flow adequacy ratio is calculated as follows:

$$\frac{19,932}{3,188} = 6.3$$

The 6.3 ratio indicates that Under Armour generated over $6.30 in free cash flow for every $1 of debt maturing in each of the next five years. Thus, it appears that Under Armour is generating sufficient cash to service its upcoming debt payments.

STUDY TOOLS 11

Chapter review card

- Learning Objective and Key Concept Reviews
- Key Definitions and Formulas

Online (Located at www.cengagebrain.com)

- Flash Cards and Crossword Puzzles
- Games and Quizzes
- E-Lectures
- Homework Assignments (as directed by your instructor)

CONCEPT QUESTIONS

1. (LO1) What are the three sections found on the statement of cash flows?
2. (LO1) Give an example of a transaction that would be classified under each of the three sections on the statement of cash flows.
3. (LO1) What two additional disclosures are made on the statement of cash flows?
4. (LO2) What three pieces of information are needed to prepare a statement of cash flows?
5. (LO2) Describe the two methods for reporting operating cash flows. Do they result in the same amount? Which one is used by most companies?
6. (LO3) Computing operating cash flows under the direct method requires the conversion of certain balances into cash receipts and cash payments. What are those balances?
7. (LO3) Describe the following conversions under the direct method: sales to cash receipts; cost of goods sold to cash paid for inventory; and salaries expense to cash payments for salaries.
8. (LO4) What are the three main types of adjustments used when computing operating cash flows under the indirect method?
9. (LO4) Under the indirect method, what adjustments to net income are required for the following: non-cash expenses; gains and losses from non-operating activities; and changes in current assets and current liabilities?
10. (LO5) Changes in what accounts must be examined to calculate investing cash flows? What does an increase in those accounts suggest? What does a decrease suggest?
11. (LO6) Changes in what accounts must be examined to calculate financing cash flows? What does an increase in those accounts suggest? What does a decrease suggest?
12. (LO6) Are interest payments to creditors considered a financing activity? What about dividend payments to stockholders?
13. (LO7) What is free cash flow and how is it calculated?
14. (LO7) What does the cash flow adequacy ratio show and how is it calculated?

MULTIPLE CHOICE

1. (LO1) Which of the following regarding the statement of cash flows is *incorrect*?
   a. It is one of the four basic financial statements.
   b. Information about a company's cash payments and receipts is provided.
   c. It is a reconciliation of the cash in the company's bank accounts to the balance sheet.
   d. It is divided into three main sections.
2. (LO1) Which of the following is an example of a cash flow resulting from an operating activity?
   a. Cash received from the sale of inventory.
   b. Cash received from the sale of common stock.
   c. A cash dividend payment.
   d. Cash paid for equipment
3. (LO1) The statement of cash flows presents a company's cash flows for a period of time divided into what three sections?
   a. Operating, Investing, and Non-Operating.
   b. Operating, Financing, and Non-Operating.
   c. Operating, Investing, and Financing.
   d. Investing, Financing, and Non-Operating.
4. (LO1) Which of the following cash flows is an example of a financing activity?
   a. Cash payments for inventory.
   b. Cash paid to acquire new manufacturing equipment.
   c. Cash received from the issuance of common stock.
   d. A stock dividend issued to the stockholders of a company.
5. (LO1) Which of the following is an example of an investing cash flow?
   a. Cash received from sale of long-term investment.
   b. Cash paid for equipment.
   c. Cash received from sale of building.
   d. All of the above.
6. (LO1) Which of the following is an additional disclosure often included on the statement of cash flows?
   a. Significant non-cash investing and financing activities.
   b. Cash paid for interest and taxes.
   c. Neither a nor b.
   d. Both a and b.
7. (LO1) A company recently purchased new land by issuing bonds payable. Under which section of the statement of cash flows would this transaction appear?
   a. Operating activities
   b. Investing activities
   c. Financing activities
   d. Additional disclosure of non-cash transactions
8. (LO1, 2) Which of the following is *correct* about the statement of cash flows?
   a. Operating cash flows can be calculated with either the direct method or the income method.
   b. Financing cash flows are normally shown as the last section on the statement.
   c. The statement shows the cash subtotals associated with four types of activities.
   d. Investing cash flows only relate to stocks and bonds.
9. (LO3) A company shows sales of $100,000 during the year. The company's balance in accounts receivable decreased $6,000 during the year. How much cash was received from customers during the year?
   a. $98,000
   b. $94,000
   c. $100,000
   d. $106,000
10. (LO3) A company's balance in inventory is $53,000 at the beginning and end of the year. Its beginning balance in accounts payable is $30,000, and its ending balance is $35,000. Cost of goods sold for the year is $78,000. How much cash was paid for inventory during the current year?
    a. $73,000
    b. $83,000
    c. $78,000
    d. $88,000
11. (LO3) A company's income statement shows insurance expense of $6,000 for the current period. The balance sheet shows that the balance in prepaid insurance increased from $9,000 to $11,000 during the year. How much cash was paid for insurance during the year?
    a. $8,000
    b. $11,000
    c. $9,000
    d. $6,000
12. (LO3) A company's income statement shows salaries expense of $22,000 for the current year. The balance in salaries payable increased $3,000 during the year. How much cash was paid for salaries during the year?
    a. $22,000
    b. $19,000
    c. $25,000
    d. $3,000
13. (LO3) Which of the following would not be reported on a statement of cash flows prepared under the direct method?
    a. Cash receipts from customers.
    b. Gain on sale of equipment.
    c. Cash paid to suppliers.
    d. Cash paid for taxes.

14. (LO4) A company generates net income of $75,000 during the year. In that same year, accounts payable decreased $5,000, inventory decreased by $2,000, and accounts receivable increased by $4,000. Using the indirect method, calculate operating cash flows.
    a. $66,000
    b. $76,000
    c. $68,000
    d. $74,000
15. (LO4) Which of the following would not be an adjustment to net income under the indirect method of calculating operating cash flows?
    a. Gain on the sale of equipment
    b. An increase in prepaid insurance
    c. Depreciation expense
    d. Each of the above would be an adjustment under the indirect method
16. (LO4) When calculating operating cash flows under the indirect method, an increase in a current asset should be _______ to net income and a decrease in a current liability should be ________ to net income?
    a. subtracted, added
    b. added, subtracted
    c. subtracted, subtracted
    d. added, added
17. (LO4) Under the indirect method of calculating operating cash flows, which of the following would be added to net income?
    a. Increase in current assets
    b. Non-cash expenses
    c. Gain on sale of equipment
    d. Decrease in current liabilities
18. (LO5) Which of the following activities would *not* be classified under the investing activities section on the statement of cash flows?
    a. Cash paid for the stock of another company
    b. The purchase of new equipment
    c. Cash paid to purchase treasury stock
    d. Buying a patent from a competitor
19. (LO5) A review of Smith Inc.'s balance sheet shows that the balance in long-term investments increased $12,000 during the year while the balance in the equipment account increased $55,000. Additional information shows that the company sold for $5,000 cash some equipment with a cost of $15,000. What is the net cash used in investing activities for the prior year?
    a. $77,000
    b. $67,000
    c. $72,000
    d. None of the above
20. (LO6) Which of the following activities would *not* be classified under the financing activities section of the statement of cash flows?
    a. Issuance of common stock for cash.
    b. Payment of principal on bonds.
    c. Cash received from a note issued to a creditor.
    d. Dividends declared but not yet paid.
21. (LO6) If a company issues long-term debt for $50,000 in cash, declares and pays dividends of $15,000, and announces plans to repurchase $25,000 worth of treasury stock, what is the net cash provided (used) by financing activities?
    a. $10,000 provided
    b. $10,000 used
    c. $40,000 provided
    d. $35,000 provided
22. (LO7) The cash flow adequacy ratio:
    a. Compares free cash flow to the average amount of debt maturing in five years.
    b. Provides an indication of a company's ability to generate enough cash to pay its debts.
    c. Both a and b
    d. Neither a nor b
23. (LO7) Free cash flow is calculated as:
    a. Net income less capital expenditures and dividends
    b. Cash from operating activities less capital expenditures
    c. Cash from operating activities less net income
    d. Cash from operating activities less capital expenditures and dividends

BRIEF EXERCISES

1. Classify Cash Flows LO1

A company has the following cash transactions during the year:

a. Purchases inventory
b. Issues long-term debt
c. Purchases a building
d. Sells common stock to investors
e. Pays an account payable

Required

Identify whether each item a) is a cash inflow or outflow and b) should be reported as an operating, investing, or financing cash flow.

2. Calculate Cash Paid for Salaries LO3

A company has salaries expense of $250,000 for the year. During the year salaries payable increased $25,000. Cash also decreased $40,000.

Required

Determine the amount of cash paid for salaries during the year.

3. Calculate Cash Collections LO3

McDoogle Company's balance sheet showed an accounts receivable balance of $75,000 at the beginning of the year and $97,000 at the end of the year. McDoogle reported sales of $1,150,000 on its income statement.

Required
Using the direct method, determine the amount that McDoogle will report as cash collections in the operating activities section of the statement of cash flows.

4. Calculate Cash Paid for Taxes LO3

Brandon Manufacturing uses the direct method for its statement of cash flows and provides the following account balances:

Taxes payable, beginning of year	$14,000
Taxes payable, end of year	8,000
Tax expense during the year	32,000

Required
Calculate cash paid for taxes.

5. Identify Indirect Method Adjustments LO4

A company experiences the following items during the year:

a. Depreciation expense
b. Increase in income taxes payable
c. Decrease in accounts receivable
d. Increase in prepaid expenses
e. Gain on sale of investments

Required
Identify whether each item would be an addition to or subtraction from net income when calculating operating cash flows using the indirect method.

6. Calculate Operating Cash Flows Using the Indirect Method LO4

A company generated $124,200 in net income during the year. Also during the year, the company recorded $12,800 in depreciation expense and experienced a $2,300 decrease in accounts receivable and a $4,760 increase in accounts payable.

Required
Calculate the company's operating cash flows using the indirect method.

7. Reporting Cash Flows from Sale of Equipment LO3, 4, 5

A company sells equipment with a book value of $23,000 for $25,000 cash.

Required
How would the sale of equipment be reported on the statement of cash flows under the a) indirect method and b) the direct method?

8. Calculate Investing and Financing Cash Flows LO5, 6

Scott Inc. had the following activities during the year:

- Purchased a building by paying $40,000 down and financing the remaining $100,000 on a 5-year note.
- Reissued 1,000 shares of treasury stock with a cost of $5 per share for $8 per share.
- Issued a $20,000 dividend to stockholders, half of which was paid in common stock.
- Sold equipment for cash. The equipment had a book value of $28,500, and Scott recognized a gain of $2,000 on the sale.
- Sold investments for $37,200 cash, recognizing a loss of $1,100.

Required
For each item, calculate Scott's net cash flow and identify whether the cash flow is an investing activity or a financing activity. Ignore any effects on operating cash flows.

9. Calculate Free Cash Flow and Cash Flow Adequacy Ratio LO7

During the year, Lewis Jewellers generated net income of $303,000 and cash flow from operations of $340,000. Lewis also bought a building for $265,000 to open a new store and paid $22,000 in dividends. Lewis calculates that over the next five years, the company will have $10,000 of debt maturing annually.

Required
Calculate Lewis' free cash flow and cash flow adequacy ratio.

EXERCISES

10. Classify Cash Flows LO1

A company enters into the following transactions:

a. Issued $25,000 of common stock for cash.
b. Issued a long-term note in exchange for a machine worth $45,000.
c. Received $21,000 in cash from collecting accounts receivable.
d. Paid $7,500 on accounts payable.
e. Issued $50,000 of common stock to satisfy a $50,000 note payable.
f. Declared and paid a cash dividend of $78,000.
g. Sold an investment costing $10,000 for $10,000 in cash.

Required
Classify each transaction as a cash inflow or a cash outflow from operating activities, investing activities, or financing activities, or as a non-cash transaction.

11. Classify Cash Flows LO1

A company enters into the following transactions:

a. Interest is paid on a note payable.
b. Salaries are paid to the company's employees.
c. Bonds are issued in exchange for cash.
d. Income taxes are paid by the company.
e. New heavy machinery is purchased with cash.
f. Convertible bonds are issued in exchange for land.
g. Cash dividends are paid to stockholders.
h. The common stock of another company is purchased as an investment.
i. The company purchases its own common stock.

j. Common stock is given to the bank in return for cancellation of a note.
k. An amount due from a customer is collected.
l. Intangible assets are purchased from another company for cash.

Required
Indicate whether each transaction would appear under operating activities, investing activities, or financing activities. Also note if a transaction is a significant non-cash transaction that would require additional disclosure.

12. Classify Cash Flows LO1

A company entered into the following transactions:

a. Purchased new machinery for $24,000 cash.
b. Paid a $2,500 account payable relating to inventory.
c. Recorded cash sales of $52,000.
d. Purchased a new warehouse for $275,000. The seller of the building accepted 10,000 shares of common stock as payment.
e. Issued bonds at face value for $25,000.
f. Purchased 200 shares of treasury stock for $7,000.
g. Purchased a new light truck for $18,000 by signing a 180-day note payable.
h. Collected a $3,000 receivable from a customer.
i. Sold 250 shares of Microsoft stock for its book value of $25,000.
j. Paid $2,000 for renewal of an insurance policy.
k. Paid dividends of $5,000 in cash.

Required
Classify each transaction as a cash inflow or outflow from operating activities, investing activities, or financing activities, or as an item reported in a supplemental schedule of the statement of cash flows.

13. Calculate Cash Received from Sales LO3

Mueller Industries uses the direct method for its statement of cash flows and provides the following account balances:

Accounts receivable, beginning of year	$ 125,000
Accounts receivable, end of year	85,000
Credit sales during the year	225,000
Cash sales during the year	35,000

Required
Calculate cash received from customers.

14. Calculate Cash Paid for Inventory LO3

Key Locks Group uses the direct method for its statement of cash flows and provides the following account balances:

Inventory, beginning of year	$ 55,000
Inventory, end of year	40,000
Accounts payable, beginning of year	15,000
Accounts payable, end of year	10,000
Cost of goods sold during the year	175,000

Required
Calculate cash paid to suppliers for inventory.

15. Calculate Cash Paid for Operating Expenses LO3

The following information is available for a company's rent and income taxes:

Prepaid rent, beginning of year	$25,000
Prepaid rent, end of year	31,000
Rent expense	40,000
Cash paid for rent during the year	??

Income taxes payable, beginning of year	$25,000
Income taxes payable, end of year	31,000
Income tax expense	40,000
Cash payments for income taxes during the year	??

Required
Calculate the missing information.

16. Prepare Operating Cash Flows Under the Direct Method LO3

Searcy Enterprises provides the following information at year end:

Sales	$ 320,000
Cost of goods sold	180,000
Salaries expense	45,000
Income tax expense	12,000
Increase in accounts receivable	2,000
Decrease in inventory	4,000
Increase in accounts payable	6,000
Increase in salaries payable	5,000
Decrease in taxes payable	1,000

Required
Prepare the operating activities section of the statement of cash flows using the direct method.

17. Classify Adjustments Under the Indirect Method LO4

A company that uses the indirect method to report operating activities experiences the following events:

a. Decrease in accounts payable.
b. Increase in accounts receivable.
c. Purchase of a new conveyer belt system.
d. Purchase of company's own common stock.
e. Gain on the sale of old conveyer belt system.
f. Depreciation expense.
g. Increase in inventory.
h. Increase in bonds payable.
i. Bad debt expense.

Required
Indicate whether each item should be added to net income, deducted from net income, or not reported in the operating activities section of the statement of cash flows.

18. Prepare Operating Cash Flows Under the Indirect Method LO4

The following information was reported by Shady Imports Company:

	2012	2011
Accounts receivable	$55,000	$47,000
Inventory	35,000	45,000
Prepaid insurance	12,000	10,000
Accounts payable	22,000	15,000
Income taxes payable	10,000	14,000
Interest payable	12,000	9,000
Net income	45,000	
Depreciation expense	25,000	

Required

Prepare the operating activities section of the statement of cash flows using the indirect method and explain why cash flows from operating activities is more or less than net income.

19. Calculating Operating Cash Flows Using the Indirect Method LO4

Cornett Systems provides the following information from the most recent year:

Net income	$744,000
Increase in net current assets	27,000
Increase in net current liabilities	31,000
Gain on sale of investments	3,500
Depreciation expense	86,000
Loss on bond redemption	5,600
Purchase of equipment	62,300

Required

Prepare the operating activities section of Cornett's statement of cash flows using the indirect method.

20. Adjustments to Net Income Under the Indirect Method LO4

A company reports the following operating cash flows on its statement of cash flows (in millions):

Net income		$98
Adjustments to reconcile net income to net cash		
provided by operating activities		
Accounts receivable	$(32)	
Inventory	12	
Prepaid insurance	(5)	
Accounts payable	(13)	
Salaries payable	0	
Taxes payable	2	(36)
Net cash provided by operating activities		$62

Required

Identify whether the following account balances increased or decreased during the year: (a) accounts receivable, (b) inventory, (c) prepaid insurance, (d) accounts payable, (e) salaries payable, and (f) taxes payable.

21. Interpreting Operating Cash Flows LO4

The CEO of Cassette Tape Manufacturers is pleased because the company's cash flows from operations exceed net income. He considers this a sign of success. Cassette Tape's statement of cash flows shows the following operating cash flows:

Net income		$ 94,350
Adjustments to reconcile net income to net		
cash provided by operating activities		
Increase in accounts receivable	$(32,284)	
Increase in inventory	(8,590)	
Increase in accounts payable	48,300	7,426
Net cash provided by operating activities		$101,776

Required

Discuss whether the CEO should be pleased with the operating cash flows. Specifically, what items may indicate that Cassette Tape has a potential problem?

22. Understanding Adjustments Under the Indirect Method LO4

A company reports the following adjustments to net income under the indirect method of calculating operating cash flows:

Increases to net income	Decreases to net income
Decrease in accounts receivable	Decrease in accounts payable
Decrease in prepaid insurance	Decrease in salaries payable
Increase in taxes payable	Gain on sale of equipment
Depreciation expense	

Required

For each item, explain the circumstances that would require the adjustment. For example, a *decrease in accounts receivable* means that cash collections for the year are greater than sales. Therefore, a decrease in accounts receivable is added to net income.

23. Compare Direct and Indirect Methods LO2, 3, 4

The following items may or may not appear on the statement of cash flows:

a. Net income
b. Cash paid for equipment
c. Cash received from customers
d. Increase in accounts receivable
e. Gain on sale of investment
f. Cash received from issuing bonds
g. Decrease in prepaid insurance
h. Cash paid for insurance
i. Convert bonds into common stock
j. Dividends paid
k. Depreciation expense
l. Cash paid for salaries

Required
Identify whether each item (1) would not appear on the statement of cash flows, (2) would appear on the statement if the direct method is used, (3) would appear on the statement if the indirect method is used, or (4) would appear on a statement if either the direct or indirect method is used.

24. Classifying Transactions Under the Indirect Method LO4, 5, 6

The following is a list of transactions and changes in account balances that occurred during the year:

a. Income taxes payable decreased.
b. Paid cash in satisfaction of a matured bond payable.
c. Paid a cash dividend.
d. Accounts payable increased.
e. Accounts receivable doubled before returning to the beginning balance by year end.
f. Sold equipment for cash at a gain.
g. Purchased a new warehouse by issuing bonds.
h. Purchased inventory for cash.
i. Purchased treasury stock.

Required
Assuming the indirect method for operating activities, indicate whether each transaction would be included in operating activities, investing activities, financing activities, non-cash disclosures, or not reported. Note that some transactions may impact multiple sections.

25. Calculate Cash Flows from Investing Activities LO5

The following information is taken from the balance sheet of Cheese Wheel Company:

	2012	2011
Equipment	$85,000	$120,000
Accumulated depreciation	50,000	55,000

Depreciation expense of $15,000 was reported on the 2012 income statement. Equipment with an original cost of $35,000 was sold for its book value.

Required
Compute the amount of cash received from the sale of the equipment.

26. Calculate Cash Flows from Investing Activities LO5

The following transactions occurred during the year:

a. A new warehouse was purchased for $110,000 cash.
b. The company's own common stock was purchased for $22,000.
c. An old warehouse costing $80,000 was sold for $45,000, resulting in a gain of $5,000.
d. The company purchased stock in Boston Beer Inc. for $7,500 cash.
e. Stock of Tazer Inc. was sold for $12,500, resulting in a gain of $7,500.

Required
Use this information to compute cash flows from investing activities.

27. Calculate Cash Flows from Financing Activities LO6

The following transactions occurred during the year:

a. Common stock was issued in exchange for a new heavy truck.
b. A cash dividend of $20,000 was paid.
c. A 90-day note payable was issued for $5,000 cash.
d. $25,000 was paid to acquire the company's own common stock.
e. Depreciation expense for the year was $30,000.
f. Bonds with a face value of $25,000 were issued at par.

Required
Use this information to compute cash flows from financing activities.

28. Interpreting Investing and Financing Cash Flows LO5, 6

Jones Corp. reports the following cash flows from investing and financing activities over the past three years (in thousands):

	2012	2011	2010
Cash flows from investing activities			
Capital expenditures	$(803)	$(2,768)	$ (752)
Sale of investments	—	1,204	—
Purchase of investments	—	(1,204)	—
Net cash used by investing activities	$(803)	$(2,768)	$ (752)
Cash flows from financing activities			
Issuance of long-term debt	—	—	$3,200
Payment of dividends	$(50)	$ (50)	(66)
Purchase of treasury stock	—	(1,200)	—
Net cash used/provided by financing activities	$(50)	$(1,250)	$3,134

Required
From the information above, describe the major ways in which Jones used investing and financing cash flows over the last three years.

29. Errors in Statement of Cash Flows LO3, 5, 6

Waggoner Company prepares the following statement of cash flows under the direct method:

Waggoner Company Statement of Cash Flows December 31, 2012		
Cash flows from operating activities		
Cash receipts from customers		$423
Less cash payments		
To suppliers	$ 91	
For equipment	44	
To employees	58	
For taxes	12	205
Net cash used by operating activities		$218
Cash flows from investing activities		
Depreciation expense	$ 14	
Purchase of short-term investments	(28)	
Net cash used by investing activities		(14)
Cash flows from financing activities		
Payment of dividends	$ 7	
Repayment of bonds	(105)	
Net cash used by financing activities		(98)
Net increase in cash		$106
Cash, beginning of the year		10
Cash, end of the year		$ 88

Required

Identify the errors Waggoner has made in its statement and prepare a corrected statement. Assume that the beginning and ending cash balances are correct.

30. Analyzing Cash Flows LO7

Lowball Ltd. and Cheapskate Inc. are both no-frills, discount distribution companies. The following financial information regarding each company is available:

	Lowball	Cheapskate
Cash flows from operating activities	$225,000	$225,000
Net income	125,000	125,000
Capital expenditures	50,000	65,000
Dividends declared and paid	30,000	10,000
Average amount of debt maturing in 5 years	20,000	30,000

Required

a. Indicate which company generated more free cash flow.
b. Indicate which company has the better cash flow adequacy ratio.
c. Does one company have a better cash position? If so, explain why.

31. Evaluate Cash Flows LO7

Newberry Company provides the following information from the past three years:

	2012	2011	2010
Capital expenditures	$ 72,185	$ 47,246	$ 32,180
Dividends	5,800	5,350	5,015
Operating cash flows	111,408	130,230	127,560
Average debt maturing in five years	64,257	50,937	45,780

Required

For each year, calculate Newberry's free cash flow and cash flow adequacy ratio. What can you conclude about Newberry's financial condition?

PROBLEMS

32. Prepare Operating Cash Flows LO3, 4

The following information is provided for HMG Company:

Balances at 12/31	**2012**	**2011**
Accounts receivable	$ 2,500	$ 1,500
Inventory	26,000	32,000
Supplies	2,000	1,000
Accounts payable	4,000	3,000
Taxes payable	2,000	3,500
Interest payable	1,500	2,500
2012 Income Statement		
Sales		$80,000
Cost of goods sold		55,000
Gross profit		$25,000
Supplies expense		6,000
Depreciation expense		2,000
Total operating expenses		$ 2,000
Income before interest and taxes		$17,000
Interest expense		4,000
Income before taxes		$13,000
Income tax expense		4,000
Net Income		$ 9,000

Required

Prepare the operating activities section of the statement of cash flows using the a) direct method and b) indirect method.

33. Comparing Net Income and Cash Flows LO1, 2, 3, 5, 6

The following events occurred at Clark Corp. during its first year of business ending on December 31:

- Clark sold $78,000 of common stock for cash.
- Clark paid $7,500 at the beginning of the year to rent office space for the year.

- Computer equipment was purchased for $25,000 cash at the beginning of the year. The equipment is expected to be useful for 5 years with no salvage value. Clark uses straight-line depreciation.
- Service revenue in the first year amounted to $120,000, $25,000 of which was on account.
- Accounts receivable from customers at the end of the year totaled $5,000.
- Salaries expense amounted to $62,500 for the year. Salaries payable at the end of the year was $3,000.
- Clark declared and paid a $5,000 cash dividend to stockholders at the end of the first year.

Required

a. Prepare Clark's income statement for the year.
b. Prepare Clark's complete statement of cash flows for the year using the direct method.
c. Explain why Clark generated more or less operating cash flows than net income.

34. Prepare a Statement of Cash Flows Using the Indirect Method LO1, 2, 4, 5, 6

The comparative balance sheet for Two Kicks Company is as follows:

Comparative Balance Sheets at 12/31

	2012	2011
Cash and cash equivalents	$ 65,000	$ 45,000
Accounts receivable	50,000	55,000
Inventory	125,000	175,000
Property and equipment	930,000	745,000
Accumulated depreciation	(270,000)	(200,000)
Total assets	$ 900,000	$ 820,000
Accounts payable	$ 110,000	$ 105,000
Bonds payable (long-term)	180,000	200,000
Total liabilities	290,000	305,000
Common stock	350,000	280,000
Retained earnings	260,000	235,000
Total stockholders' equity	610,000	515,000
Total liabilities and stockholders' equity	$ 900,000	$ 820,000

The following additional information is available:

a. Net income for 2012 was $50,000.
b. Cash dividends of $25,000 were paid during the year.
c. A portion of outstanding bonds matured and were redeemed for cash by the bondholders. No new bonds were issued during the year.
d. Common stock was issued for cash.
e. Property and equipment were purchased for cash. No long-term assets were sold during the year.
f. The change in accumulated depreciation is a result of depreciation expense.

Required

Prepare a complete statement of cash flows for the year using the indirect method for the operating activities section.

35. Prepare a Statement of Cash Flows LO1, 2, 3, 4, 5, 6

Available financial information for Blue Bomber Company is as follows:

Comparative Balance Sheets at 12/31

	2012	2011
Cash and cash equivalents	$ 75,000	$ 45,000
Accounts receivable	45,000	55,000
Inventory	200,000	175,000
Prepaid insurance	30,000	35,000
Total current assets	350,000	310,000
Equipment	800,000	720,000
Accumulated depreciation	(240,000)	(170,000)
Total equipment	560,000	550,000
Total assets	$ 910,000	$ 860,000
Accounts payable	$110,000	$115,000
Accrued salaries	10,000	35,000
Total current liabilities	120,000	150,000
Bonds payable	180,000	230,000
Total liabilities	300,000	380,000
Common stock	350,000	250,000
Retained earnings	260,000	230,000
Total stockholders' equity	610,000	480,000
Total liabilities and stockholders' equity	$910,000	$860,000

Income Statement
For the Year Ending 12/31/12

Sales	$450,000
Cost of goods sold	225,000
Gross profit	$225,000
Depreciation expense	70,000
Other operating expenses	30,000
Income before interest and taxes	$125,000
Interest expense	20,000
Income before taxes	$105,000
Income tax expense	30,000
Net Income	$ 75,000

The following additional information is available:

a. Cash dividends of $45,000 were declared and paid during the year.
b. Equipment was purchased for cash.
c. A portion of bonds payable matured and was paid with cash.
d. Common stock was issued for cash.

Required
Prepare a complete statement of cash flows for Blue Bomber for 2012 using the direct method for the operating activities section. In a separate schedule, show the operating activities section using the indirect method.

36. Prepare a Statement of Cash Flows
LO1, 2, 3, 4, 5, 6

The following is Folex Company's income statement and balance sheet (in millions):

Income Statement For the Year Ending 12/31/12	
Sales	$750
Cost of goods sold	450
Gross profit	$300
Operating expenses	100
Income before interest and taxes	$200
Interest expense	15
Income before taxes	$185
Income tax expense	75
Net income	$110

Balance Sheet December 31	2012	2011
Cash	$ 45	$ 80
Accounts receivable	155	115
Inventory	225	190
Prepaid insurance	22	32
Total current assets	447	417
Property and equipment	1,250	1,050
Accumulated depreciation	(175)	(140)
Total property and equipment	1,075	910
Total assets	$1,522	$1,327
Accounts payable	$ 120	$ 135
Income taxes payable	155	175
Total current liabilities	275	310
Bonds payable	400	325
Total liabilities	675	635
Common stock	525	475
Retained earnings	322	217
Total stockholders' equity	847	692
Total liabilities and stockholders' equity	$1,522	$1,327

The following additional information is available:

i) Operating expenses include $35 million of depreciation.
ii) Property and equipment were acquired for cash.
iii) Additional common stock was issued for cash.
iv) Additional cash was obtained by issuing bonds.
v) Dividends were paid.

The CEO has posed some questions regarding this year's results. She is pleased that the profit margin is approaching 15 percent. However, the decrease in the cash balance during such a profitable year troubles her.

Required

a. Prepare a complete statement of cash flows for Folex using the direct method for operating cash flows. Prepare a separate schedule showing operating cash flows using the indirect method.
b. Based on the statement you prepare, explain to the CEO why cash decreased during a profitable year.

CASE

37. Research and Analysis LO1, 7

Access the 2010 annual report for **Callaway Golf Company** by clicking on the *Investor Relations* and *Annual Reports* links at www.callawaygolf.com.

a. Examine the company's statement of cash flows and calculate the company's free cash flows in each of the last three years.
b. Identify the year in which the change in cash was positive and identify the company action that enabled it to increase its cash position.
c. Based on your answers above, write a paragraph describing Callaway's cash position over the past three years.

38. Ethics in Accounting LO2, 3, 7

You are the accountant of a small company that wants to expand. The CEO is negotiating a loan with the bank, and the bank requires a statement of cash flows. The CEO is concerned because operating cash flows are down compared to prior years. The main reason is deteriorating collections from accounts receivables. The CEO presents three options to address the situation prior to year end and the preparation of the statement of cash flows:

Option 1: Convert some of the oldest receivables to long-term notes receivable
Option 2: Sell some receivables to a collector for $0.65 per $1 of receivables
Option 3: Delay payment of all outstanding accounts payable until the next year

Required

a. Comment on the appropriateness of each option.
b. Is there an ethical dilemma involved?
c. How would you respond to the CEO?

39. Research and Analysis LO7

Access the 2010 annual report of **Waste Management** by clicking on the *Investor Relations, Financial Reporting*, and *Annual Reports* links at www.wm.com.

Required

a. Review the company's statement of cash flows and calculate free cash flow for each of the three years presented.
b. According to the statement, in what major way did the company use its free cash flow over the three-year period?
c. What is the major difference between net income and operating cash flows? Does that make sense for a company like Waste Management?
d. What is your overall impression of the company's statement of cash flows?

40. Entrepreneurial Decision Making LO1, 7

James M. Jones Jr. is an entrepreneur and the founder of Tasty Cakes Bakery. During the last year, Tasty Cakes generated $40,000 in operating cash flows, paid $10,000 in capital expenditures (as he does almost every year), and paid $5,000 in dividends. Jones is interested in significantly expanding this year. To do so, he needs to spend $100,000 on equipment in addition to his normal capital expenditures. He believes that if he buys the equipment, his operating cash flows will surely increase by 25% and possibly could double. He has spoken with the bank, which has offered the following two installment note options where an equal amount of principal is due each year:

Option 1: Two-year, 5%, $100,000 installment note

Option 2: Six-year, 10%, $100,000 installment note

Required

a. Calculate Tasty Cake's free cash flow.
b. Identify the advantages and disadvantages of each option the bank provides.
c. Which option should Jones choose and why?

Hill Street Studios/Getty Images

ACCT

Financial Statement Analysis

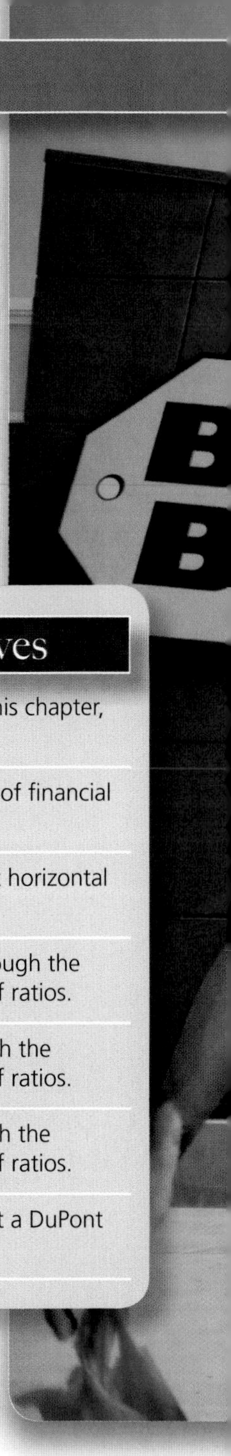

Learning Objectives

After studying the material in this chapter, you should be able to:

LO1 Understand the nature of financial statement analysis.

LO2 Calculate and interpret horizontal and vertical analyses.

LO3 Assess profitability through the calculation and interpretation of ratios.

LO4 Assess liquidity through the calculation and interpretation of ratios.

LO5 Assess solvency through the calculation and interpretation of ratios.

LO6 Calculate and interpret a DuPont analysis.

Introduction

The first eleven chapters of this book examined the various aspects of financial accounting, which is the process of identifying, measuring, and communicating economic information to permit informed decisions. This chapter demonstrates how to analyze the products of this process—the income statement, the balance sheet, the statement of stockholders' equity, and the statement of cash flows—to make informed decisions about a company. That is, the chapter focuses on financial statement analysis. It will use the financial statements of **Best Buy** as an example.

LO1 Financial Statement Analysis

Financial statement analysis is the process of applying analytical tools to a company's financial statements to understand the company's financial health. The goal of such an analysis is to provide some context for understanding the accounting numbers on the financial statements. Ultimately, financial analysis should help an investor, creditor, or any other interested party better understand a company's financial position and therefore make better decisions about the company. Enabling good decisions is one goal of financial accounting, and it should be the product of financial statement analysis.

Financial analysis requires the following:

- Financial information
- Standards of comparison
- Analysis tools

Financial statement analysis The process of applying analytical tools to a company's financial statements to understand the company's financial health.

Financial Information

All publicly traded companies must prepare audited financial statements each year and file them with the Securities and Exchange Commission. These statements include the income statement, the balance sheet, the statement of stockholders'

Financial statement analysis can help investors understand how effectively and efficiently a company like Best Buy is profiting from its customers.

© Chris Rank/Bloomberg via Getty Images

equity, and the statement of cash flows. Financial statements contain multiple years of data for comparative purposes and are the starting point for any analysis.

In addition to financial statements, companies provide other information that should be consulted to augment a financial analysis. For example, a company's notes to its financial statements will provide further explanation of items on the financial statements and additional disclosures not included on the statements. A company's Management's Discussion and Analysis (MD&A) will contain management's commentary on many aspects of company operations and future plans. Even company press releases, earnings conference calls, and notifications of stockholder meetings can contain helpful information. Finally, it is always a good idea to consult independent, third-party analysis.

In this chapter, the financial information provided by **Best Buy Co., Inc.** will be used to illustrate the process of financial analysis. Our focus will be predominantly on information from

Enabling good decisions is one goal of financial accounting, and it should be the product of financial statement analysis.

the income statement and the balance sheet. As a result, only those two statements are shown in the text. However, when information beyond those statements is required, it will be provided in the text.

Standards of Comparison

When conducting a financial analysis, there should be some benchmarks for comparison. The most common benchmark is the prior year(s) of the same company. This is often called an intracompany comparison because it is a comparison within a company. Horizontal analysis is an excellent example of an intracompany analysis.

Another common benchmark is competitors. Comparisons among competitors are often called intercompany comparisons because they are between companies. Vertical analysis is an excellent tool for intercompany analysis because it removes the effect of company size.

A final benchmark is industry standards. Often, industry benchmarks can be obtained from financial websites.

The analysis in this text will use both intracompany and intercompany comparisons. For intercompany comparisons, the text will use **Best Buy's** smaller competitor, **hhgregg**.

Analysis Tools

There are many analysis tools used to conduct a financial analysis. Three of the more common are the following: horizontal analysis, vertical analysis, and ratio analysis. Horizontal analysis is a comparison of a company's financial results across time. Vertical analysis is a comparison of financial balances to a base account from the same company. Ratio analysis is a comparison of different balances from the financial statements to provide the context to understand the financial results. Typically, multiple individual ratios are grouped together to assess a company's profitability, its ability to satisfy its debts, and its ability to survive in the long term.

Horizontal analysis An analysis technique that calculates the change in an account balance from one period to the next and expresses that change in both dollar and percentage terms.

The remainder of this text demonstrates and discusses horizontal, vertical, and ratio analyses of Best Buy's 2010 financial statements.

LO2 Horizontal and Vertical Analyses

Horizontal Analysis

Horizontal analysis was first introduced in Chapter 2. Recall that horizontal analysis is a technique that compares account balances over time. Formally, **horizontal analysis** is an analysis technique that calculates the change in an account balance from one period to the next and expresses that change in both dollar and percentage terms. The actual calculations are as follows.

$$\text{Dollar change in account balance} = \text{Current-year balance} - \text{Prior-year balance}$$

$$\text{Percentage change in account balance} = \frac{\text{Dollar change}}{\text{Prior-year balance}}$$

Horizontal analysis is a simple but powerful analysis tool. It reveals significant changes in account balances and therefore identifies items for further investigation. For example, if a horizontal analysis reveals an unusually large increase in operating expenses, the user will likely focus attention on why those expenses increased so much. That is the nature of horizontal analysis—it often provides the right questions to ask.

Horizontal analysis is calculated for both the balance sheet and the income statement. Changes in critical account balances—such as inventory for a retailer or liabilities for a company in financial trouble—are usually examined first. Also examined are any significant changes in other account balances. Insignificant changes are often ignored because they would not affect decision making.

As you consider the results of a horizontal analysis, keep in mind that a large percentage change may not be as significant as it seems. For example, an account that grows from \$1 million to \$3 million experiences a 200% increase, but such an increase is immaterial to a \$50 billion company. Therefore, the review of a horizontal analysis should consider both the dollar and percentage changes.

Balance Sheet Analysis Exhibit 12-1 contains a horizontal analysis of a condensed version of Best Buy's 2010 balance sheet.

Horizontal analysis is a simple but powerful analysis tool. It often provides the right question to ask.

The analysis shows a small reduction in overall assets of 2.5%. The company experienced significant decreases in cash (down 39.6%) and property and equipment (down 6.1%). According to the company's statement of cash flows, a significant part of the decrease in cash was the repurchase and retirement of the company's common stock. In contrast, both receivables and merchandise inventory increased during the year. For an electronics retailer operating in difficult economic conditions, increasing inventory and receivables when all other assets are decreasing can be a troubling sign and should be monitored.

The analysis also shows decreases in most liability accounts. The only exceptions are unredeemed gift card liabilities and current portion of long-term debt. But, notice that the latter increased about as much as the company's long-term debt balance decreased. This suggests that the company reclassified some long-term debt as current liabilities in 2010. As a result, total liabilities decreased 6.9%, which appears reasonable given the decrease in total assets.

An examination of stockholders' equity shows a large increase in the company's largest equity account, retained earnings. Such an increase is the result of profitable operations and is a sign of strong financial performance. There is also a significant decrease in the company's additional paid-in capital account. According to the company's statement of stockholders' equity, this decrease was the result of the repurchase and retirement of common stock.

Overall, the horizontal analysis shows a slightly contracting company with some potential concerns regarding receivables and inventory.

Exhibit 12-1 Horizontal Analysis of Best Buy's 2010 Condensed Balance Sheet

$ in millions	2010	2009	$ Change	% Change
Assets				
Current Assets				
Cash and cash equivalents	$ 1,103	$ 1,826	$(723)	(39.6%)
Receivables	2,348	2,020	328	16.2%
Merchandise inventories	5,897	5,486	411	7.5%
Other current assets	1,125	1,234	(109)	(8.8%)
Total current assets	10,473	10,566	(93)	(0.9%)
Property and Equipment, net	3,823	4,070	(247)	(6.1%)
Goodwill	2,454	2,452	2	0.1%
Other Assets	1,099	1,214	(115)	(9.5%)
Total Assets	$17,849	$18,302	$(453)	(2.5%)
Liabilities and Stockholders' Equity				
Current Liabilities				
Accounts payable	$ 4,894	$ 5,276	$(382)	(7.2%)
Unredeemed gift card liabilities	474	463	11	2.4%
Accrued liabilities	2,297	2,541	(244)	(9.6%)
Short-term debt	557	663	(106)	(16.0%)
Current portion of long-term debt	441	35	406	1160.0%
Total current liabilities	8,663	8,978	(315)	(3.5%)
Long-Term Liabilities	1,183	1,256	(73)	(5.8%)
Long-Term Debt	711	1,104	(393)	(35.6%)
Total liabilities	10,557	11,338	(781)	(6.9%)
Stockholders' Equity				
Common stock	39	42	(3)	(7.1%)
Additional paid-in capital	18	441	(423)	(95.9%)
Retained earnings	6,372	5,797	575	9.9%
Other equity	863	684	179	26.2%
Total stockholders' equity	7,292	6,964	328	4.7%
Total Liabilities and Stockholders' Equity	$17,849	$18,302	$(453)	(2.5%)

Exhibit 12-2 Horizontal Analysis of Best Buy's 2010 Condensed Income Statement

$ in millions For the Fiscal Years Ending	2010	2009	$ Change	% Change
Revenue	$50,272	$49,694	$ 578	1.2%
Cost of goods sold	37,635	37,534	101	0.3%
Gross profit	12,637	12,160	477	3.9%
Selling, general and administrative expenses	10,325	9,873	452	4.6%
Restructuring charges and impairments	198	52	146	280.8%
Operating income	2,114	2,235	(121)	(5.4%)
Other income (expense)			—	
Investment income and other	51	54	(3)	(5.6%)
Interest expense	(87)	(94)	7	(7.4%)
Other	(87)	(76)	(11)	14.5%
Earnings before income tax expense	1,991	2,119	(128)	(6.0%)
Income tax expense	714	802	(88)	(11.0%)
Net earnings	$ 1,277	$ 1,317	$ (40)	(3.0%)

Income Statement Analysis Exhibit 12-2 contains a horizontal analysis of a condensed version of **Best Buy's** 2010 income statement.

The analysis shows that revenue increased 1.2% while cost of goods sold increased 0.3%. The good news is that the company increased its sales faster than its cost of sales. Any time a company can do that, it can increase profitability for its owners.

However, the bad news is that the rate of growth in sales was only 1.2%. Furthermore, operating expenses increased 4.6% during the year, resulting in a 5.4% decrease in operating profit and a 3.0% decrease in net earnings.

Overall, Best Buy was profitable in 2010, but the trend is not positive.

Vertical Analysis

Vertical analysis was also introduced in Chapter 2. Recall that vertical analysis is a technique that compares

MAKING IT REAL

A retailer can grow sales by adding new stores and/or increasing sales in existing stores. A horizontal analysis does not distinguish between those two sources of sales growth. It only shows total sales growth. Because investors want to know how much of the growth is attributable to each source, companies disclose "same-store" or "comparable-store" sales in their Management's Discussion and Analysis (MD&A). Same-store sales represent the growth in sales for stores that were open all year in both years presented. In its 2010 MD&A, Best Buy reports that the 1.2% increase in sales revenue "resulted primarily from the net addition of 147 new stores . . . and the positive impact of foreign currency exchange rate fluctuations . . ." but was "partially offset by a (1.8%) comparable store sales decline." This shows that had Best Buy not opened stores during the year, it likely would have seen a decline in overall sales revenue. The company acknowledged in its discussion that "customer appetite for certain product categories was below industry expectations."

Richard Levine/Alamy

account balances within one year. Formally, **vertical analysis** is an analysis technique that states each account balance on a financial statement as a percentage of a base amount on the statement. The base account is total assets for the balance sheet and either sales or revenues for the income statement. The actual calculation is as follows.

	For the Balance Sheet		For the Income Statement
Percentage =	$\frac{\text{Account balance}}{\text{Total Assets}}$	or	$\frac{\text{Account balance}}{\text{Net Sales or Revenue}}$

Like horizontal analysis, vertical analysis is a simple but powerful tool. The dividing of each account balance by either assets or revenues accomplishes two purposes. First, it shows the relative importance of each account to the company. Second, it standardizes the account balances by firm size so that companies of different sizes can be compared.

To illustrate, suppose a company with $10 million in total assets has $1 million in cash while another company with $100 billion in assets has $10 billion in cash. The $100 billion company has more cash, but it is also a much bigger company. A vertical analysis would show that each company has 10% of its assets in cash ($1/$10 = $10/$100 = 10%). By dividing by total assets, the analysis makes possible a meaningful comparison of two companies of vastly different sizes. Because vertical analysis removes the effect of size, an analysis prepared on a financial statement is appropriately called a common-size financial statement.

Balance Sheet Analysis Exhibit 12-3 contains a vertical analysis of **Best Buy's** condensed 2010 balance sheet.

Vertical analysis An analysis technique that states each account balance on a financial statement as a percentage of a base amount on the statement.

Exhibit 12-3 Vertical Analysis of Best Buy's 2010 Condensed Balance Sheet

$ in millions	2010		2009	
Assets				
Current Assets				
Cash and cash equivalents	$ 1,103	6.2%	$ 1,826	10.0%
Receivables	2,348	13.2%	2,020	11.0%
Merchandise inventories	5,897	33.0%	5,486	30.0%
Other current assets	1,125	6.3%	1,234	6.7%
Total current assets	10,473	58.7%	10,566	57.7%
Property and Equipment, net	3,823	21.4%	4,070	22.2%
Goodwill	2,454	13.7%	2,452	13.4%
Other Assets	1,099	6.2%	1,214	6.6%
Total Assets	$17,849	100.0%	$18,302	100.0%
Liabilities and Stockholders' Equity				
Current Liabilities				
Accounts payable	$ 4,894	27.4%	$ 5,276	28.8%
Unredeemed gift card liabilities	474	2.7%	463	2.5%
Accrued liabilities	2,297	12.9%	2,541	13.9%
Short-term debt	557	3.1%	663	3.6%
Current portion of long-term debt	441	2.5%	35	0.2%
Total current liabilities	8,663	48.5%	8,978	49.1%
Long-Term Liabilities	1,183	6.6%	1,256	6.9%
Long-Term Debt	711	4.0%	1,104	6.0%
Total liabilities	10,557	59.1%	11,338	61.9%
Stockholders' Equity				
Common stock	39	0.2%	42	0.2%
Additional paid-in capital	18	0.1%	441	2.4%
Retained earnings	6,372	35.7%	5,797	31.7%
Other equity	863	4.8%	684	3.7%
Total stockholders' equity	7,292	40.9%	6,964	38.1%
Total Liabilities and Stockholders' Equity	$17,849	100.0%	$18,302	100.0%

The analysis shows large percentages of assets in both inventory and property and equipment. Such percentages are not surprising given that **Best Buy** is a retailer. Of some concern is the increased percentage associated with receivables (13.2% in 2010 versus 11.0% in 2009) and the decreased percentage associated with cash (6.2% in 2010 versus 10.0% in 2009). The ability of Best Buy to collect cash from its receivables should be monitored.

The analysis of liabilities and stockholders' equity shows that about half of the company's assets are generated by current liabilities, with the majority of those liabilities in accounts payable. In total, 59.1% of Best Buy's assets are generated by liabilities. This is a slight decrease from 2009, when 61.9% of assets were generated by liabilities. In 2010, about 36% of assets were generated through profitable operations that were retained in the business.

Overall, the vertical analysis shows a reasonably healthy balance sheet, with the possible exception of the growing receivables.

Income Statement Analysis Exhibit 12-4 contains a vertical analysis of Best Buy's condensed 2010 income statement.

Exhibit 12-4 Vertical Analysis of Best Buy's 2010 Condensed Income Statement

$ in millions **For the Fiscal Years Ending**	**2010**		**2009**	
Revenue	$50,272	100.0%	$49,694	100.0%
Cost of goods sold	37,635	74.9%	37,534	75.5%
Gross profit	12,637	25.1%	12,160	24.5%
Selling, general and administrative expenses	10,325	20.5%	9,873	19.9%
Restructuring charges and impairments	198	0.4%	52	0.1%
Operating income	2,114	4.2%	2,235	4.5%
Other income (expense)				
Investment income and other	51	0.1%	54	0.1%
Interest expense	(87)	(0.2%)	(94)	(0.2%)
Other	(87)	(0.2%)	(76)	(0.2%)
Earnings before income tax expense	1,991	4.0%	2,119	4.3%
Income tax expense	714	1.4%	802	1.6%
Net earnings	$ 1,277	2.5%	$ 1,317	2.7%

The analysis shows that cost of goods sold is approximately 74.9% of sales revenue, leaving a 2010 gross profit of 25.1%, or about a quarter for each dollar of sales. This is a slight improvement over 2009, when the company generated gross profit of 24.5%. However, the improvement in gross profit is offset by increases in operating expenses. Operating expenses were 20.5% of revenue in 2010 and 19.9% in 2009. It cost Best Buy more to operate its business in 2010. Overall, Best Buy was profitable during 2010, but it was less profitable than in 2009 (2.5% in 2010 versus 2.7% in 2009).

Now that horizontal and vertical analyses have been conducted on both the income statement and the balance sheet, attention can be shifted to ratio analyses, starting with an analysis of Best Buy's profitability.

Everyone associated with a company—stockholders, creditors, employees, suppliers—wants the company to generate profits.

LO3 Profitability Analysis

One of the most important aspects of any financial analysis is profitability. Everyone associated with a company—stockholders, creditors, employees, suppliers—wants the company to generate profits. To determine a company's profitability, one can look at net income, but that tells only a portion of the story. It does not reveal how efficiently and effectively those profits were generated. To find out, one must compare net income to other company values such as sales, assets, equity, outstanding shares, and market prices.

The following ratios are commonly used to analyze profitability. Note that each ratio compares net income to some other financial aspect of the company. Because each ratio reveals something different about a company's income, they are best used in tandem so that a broad understanding of a company's profitability can be obtained.

Profitability Ratio	Relationship
Profit Margin	Income to Sales
Return on Equity	Income to Stockholders' Equity
Return on Assets	Income to Total Assets
Earnings per Share	Income to Shares Outstanding
Price to Earnings	Stock Price to Income

In the following sections, the text will explain each ratio and show the calculation for **Best Buy's** most recent year. Unless otherwise noted, data for each calculation is obtained from Exhibits 12-1 or 12-2. Immediately after the calculation, Best Buy's ratios for the current and prior two years and **hhgregg's** current- and prior-year ratios will be provided for comparison purposes. After all ratios are presented, a summary of what was learned from the ratios about Best Buy's profitability will be provided.

Profit Margin

The **profit margin ratio** compares net income to net sales and measures the ability of a company to generate profits from sales. A higher ratio indicates a greater ability to generate profits from sales.

$$\text{Profit Margin} = \frac{\text{Net Income}}{\text{Net Sales}}$$

$$\frac{1{,}277}{50{,}272} = 2.5\%$$

	2010	2009	2008
Best Buy	2.5%	2.7%	2.2%
hhgregg	2.2%	2.6%	2.6%

Best Buy's 2010 profit margin is 2.5%, meaning that the company generated two and a half cents of profit for every dollar of sales in 2010. This is similar to both prior years and hhgregg. Over the past three years, both companies have struggled to make just over a couple of cents per dollar in profits.

Return on Equity

The **return on equity ratio** compares net income to the average balance in stockholders' equity during the year. The ratio represents how effectively a company uses the equity provided by stockholders during the year to generate additional equity for its owners. Stockholders naturally want this ratio to be as high as possible.

$$\text{Return on Equity} = \frac{\text{Net Income}}{\text{Average Stockholders' Equity}}$$

where average equity is as follows:

$$\frac{\text{Beginning equity} + \text{Ending equity}}{2}$$

$$\frac{1{,}277}{(7{,}292 + 6{,}964)/2} = 17.9\%$$

	2010	2009	2008
Best Buy	17.9%	22.7%	22.0%
hhgregg	16.9%	20.7%	35.3%

The 2010 ratio of 17.9% shows that Best Buy generated less than twenty cents in profits for every dollar of resources provided by stockholders. This is slightly lower than the ratios in the prior two years but is slightly ahead of hhgregg's. Such an annual return will result in a doubling of equity in approximately five years.

Return on Assets

The **return on assets ratio** compares net income to average total assets during the year. It represents a company's ability to generate profits from its entire resource base, not just those resources provided by owners. Like the return on equity, investors would like the ratio as high as possible.

Profit margin ratio Compares net income to net sales and measures the ability to generate profits from sales.

Return on equity ratio Compares net income to average stockholders' equity and measures the ability to generate profits from equity.

Return on assets ratio Compares net income to average total assets and measures the ability to generate profits from assets.

Yuri Arcurs/Shutterstock.com

$$\text{Return on Assets} = \frac{\text{Net Income}}{\text{Average Total Assets}}$$

where average assets is as follows:

$$\frac{\text{Beginning total assets} + \text{Ending total assets}}{2}$$

$$\frac{1{,}277}{(17{,}849 + 18{,}302)/2} = 7.1\%$$

	2010	2009	2008
Best Buy	7.1%	7.7%	7.0%
hhgregg	8.3%	8.2%	12.8%

The 2010 ratio of 7.1% shows that **Best Buy** generated about seven cents in profits for every dollar of assets it possessed during the year. This was similar to the prior two years and slightly lower than **hhgregg's** ratio. Best Buy was not as effective as its competitor at using its existing resources to generate profits.

Earnings per Share

Earnings per share compares a company's net income to the average number of shares of common stock outstanding during the year. The ratio represents the return on each share of stock owned by an investor. Although companies normally disclose earnings per share on their income statements, the calculation will be demonstrated nonetheless.

Earnings per share Compares net income to common stock outstanding and represents profits generated per share of stock.

Price to earnings ratio Compares net income to a company's stock price and provides an indication of investor perceptions of the company.

The price to earnings ratio provides an indication of current investor perceptions of the company.

$$\text{Earnings per Share} = \frac{\text{Net Income}}{\text{Average Number of Common Shares Outstanding}}$$

where average outstanding shares is as follows:

$$\frac{\text{Beginning outstanding shares} + \text{Ending outstanding shares}}{2}$$

The beginning and ending outstanding shares are collected from the textual information on the balance sheet (not shown in the text). Shares outstanding were 392.6 million in 2010 and 418.8 million in 2009.

$$\frac{1{,}277}{(392.6 + 418.8)/2} = \$3.15$$

	2010	2009	2008
Best Buy	$3.15	$3.16	$2.43
hhgregg	$1.23	$1.10	$1.12

The $3.15 value shows that Best Buy earned $3.15 in profits for every share of common stock outstanding during the year. This is very similar to the prior year and well above the $1.23 earned by hhgregg in 2010.

Notice that part of the reason that Best Buy was able to maintain a similar 2010 earning per share is because it reduced the number of shares of stock outstanding, from 418.8 million to 392.6 million. This shows that a company can boost its earnings per share in one of two ways—increased profitability and/or reduced outstanding shares.

Price to Earnings Ratio

The **price to earnings ratio** compares net income to the current market price of the company's common stock. Because a company's stock price represents the value of the company per share of stock, the ratio uses earnings per share rather than net income. It is also the first ratio in which income is in the denominator rather than the numerator. That is why the ratio is called price to earnings rather than earnings to price.

$$\text{Price to Earnings Ratio} = \frac{\text{Current Stock Price per Share}}{\text{Earnings per Share}}$$

Because the price to earnings ratio uses stock prices, it provides an indication of current investor perceptions of the company. For example, a price to earnings ratio of 10 means that investors are willing to pay ten times current earnings per share to buy one share of stock. A ratio of 15 means that investors will pay fifteen times current earnings. A higher price to earnings ratio generally indicates that investors are more optimistic about the future prospects of a company. A lower ratio generally indicates that investors are less optimistic about the company's future.

The following calculation of **Best Buy's** 2010 price to earnings ratio uses the $32.21 stock price at the close of business on February 26, 2011, the end of the company's 2010 fiscal year.

$$\frac{32.21}{3.15} = 10.2$$

	2010	2009	2008
Best Buy	10.2	11.3	11.8
hhgregg	10.9	22.9	13.5

Best Buy's ratio of 10.2 shows that a share of Best Buy's stock was selling for about 10 times earnings per share at the close of its most recent fiscal year. This is a decrease from the prior two years. Thus, while investors are still willing to pay a premium for current earnings, they are willing to pay less of a premium than before. This indicates a slight decrease in perceptions about the future prospects of the company. Note that **hhgregg** has seen an even more dramatic decrease from 2009 to 2010, falling from 22.9 to 10.9.

A company must maintain the ability to pay its liabilities as they come due.

Summary of Profitability

Based on the five ratios examined, it is clear that Best Buy is profitable. However, its profitability has either stayed the same or declined from the prior year. This is a trend to watch closely, especially in an industry that depends on consumer spending.

LO4 Liquidity Analysis

A major concern in any financial analysis is an assessment of a company's liquidity. **Liquidity** refers to the ability of a company to satisfy its short-term obligations. A company must maintain the ability to pay its liabilities as they come due. Failing to do so can result in additional expenses and, ultimately, bankruptcy. As a result, everyone associated with a company—stockholders, creditors, employees, suppliers—wants to see adequate liquidity.

The following ratios are commonly used to assess a company's liquidity. While each ratio reveals information

Liquidity The ability of a company to satisfy its short-term obligations.

HOME DEPOT ANALYSIS

Using **Home Depot's** information in Appendix C, calculate Home Depot's profitability ratios and make a general assessment about the company's profitability. Home Depot's stock price on January 30, 2011 was $36.25.

Profit Margin: Net Income/Sales = $3,338/$67,997 = 4.91%

Return on Equity: Net Income/Average Stockholders' Equity = $3,338/[($18,889 + $19,393)/2] = 17.44%

Return on Assets: Net Income/Average Total Assets = $3,338/[($40,125 + $40,877)/2] = 8.24%

Earnings per Share: Net Income/Average Outstanding Shares = $3,338/[(1,623 + 1,698)/2] = $2.01

Price to Earnings Ratio: Stock Price/Earnings per Share = $36.25/$2.01 = 18.0

Home Depot shows many positive signs of profitability. It earns almost five cents for every dollar of sales, over seventeen cents for every dollar provided by stockholders, and $2.01 for every outstanding share of common stock. With a 18.0 price to earnings ratio, stockholders appear optimistic about Home Depot's future prospects.

on its own, using the ratios in tandem provides a much richer understanding of liquidity. Note that each ratio focuses on some aspect of either current liabilities or current assets.

Liquidity Ratios	Relationship
Current Ratio	Current Assets to Current Liabilities
Quick Ratio	Cash-like Assets to Current Liabilities
Receivables Turnover Ratio	Sales to Accounts Receivable
Inventory Turnover Ratio	Cost of Goods Sold to Inventory

As in the previous section on profitability, the following sections will explain and calculate each ratio for **Best Buy** using data from Exhibits 12-1 and 12-2. A comparison of Best Buy's and **hhgregg's** ratios will follow each calculation. After all ratios are presented, a summary of what was learned about Best Buy's liquidity will be provided.

Current Ratio

The **current ratio** is one of the most frequently used ratios in financial analysis. It compares current assets to current liabilities. It therefore compares assets that should be turned into cash within one year to liabilities that should be paid within one year. A higher ratio indicates more assets available to satisfy current obligations and therefore greater liquidity.

$$\text{Current Ratio} = \frac{\text{Current Assets}}{\text{Current Liabilities}}$$

$$\frac{10{,}473}{8{,}663} = 1.21$$

	2010	2009	2008
Best Buy	1.21	1.18	0.97
hhgregg	2.00	1.88	1.68

Best Buy's ratio of 1.21 shows that it had $1.21 in current assets for every dollar of current liabilities. This is higher than both prior years, meaning that Best Buy is becoming more liquid over time. The same is happening at hhgregg, where the current ratio has risen to 2.00 in 2010.

While you might think that hhgregg's 2.0 ratio is much better than Best Buy's 1.21 ratio, a lower ratio is not necessarily bad. In fact, many investors would be critical of maintaining a current ratio that is too high. They would rather the company keep only an adequate amount of assets in current assets and invest the rest in more productive and higher-yielding assets such as property, equipment, or investments. Thus, some investors would be more pleased with Best Buy's ratio of 1.21 than hhgregg's ratio of 2.00.

Current ratio Compares current assets to current liabilities and measures the ability to pay current obligations.

Quick ratio Compares cash and near-cash assets to current liabilities and measures the ability to pay current liabilities immediately.

Quick Ratio

While the current ratio is an excellent measure of liquidity, it does have some limitations. In particular, current assets often include inventory that must be sold before cash can be generated to pay off current liabilities. Because of this, several additional ratios are used to provide more detail regarding a company's liquidity. One is the quick ratio.

The **quick ratio** compares a company's cash and near-cash assets, called *quick assets*, to its current liabilities. Quick assets include cash, short-term investments, and accounts receivable. Sometimes called the *acid-test ratio*, the quick ratio measures the degree to which a company could pay off its current liabilities immediately. Like the current ratio, a higher quick ratio indicates greater liquidity.

$$\text{Quick Ratio} = \frac{\text{Cash} + \text{Short-term Investments} + \text{Accounts Receivable}}{\text{Current Liabilities}}$$

$$\frac{1{,}103 + 22 + 2{,}348}{8{,}663} = 0.40$$

	2010	2009	2008
Best Buy	0.40	0.44	0.28
hhgregg	0.61	0.87	0.32

Best Buy's balance sheet in Exhibit 12-1 does not show a balance in short-term investments. However, the ratio calculation includes $22 million in short-term investments. This is because in Best Buy's notes to the financial statements, the company discloses that $22 million in short-term investments are included on the balance sheet within other assets. The company does not separately report the $22 millions balance. This is an application of materiality.

Best Buy's ratio of 0.40 shows that at the end of its fiscal year, the company had 40 cents in cash and near-cash assets for every dollar of current liabilities. This indicates that Best Buy could pay 40% of its current liabilities if they came due immediately. This is similar to the prior year and slightly lower than hhgregg.

Receivables Turnover Ratio

The **receivables turnover ratio** compares a company's credit sales during a period to its average accounts receivable balance during that period. It measures a company's ability to make and collect sales. A higher turnover ratio means that the company is better able to generate and collect sales. Therefore, a higher ratio generally leads to better liquidity. Because credit sales are not usually reported by companies, the ratio uses net sales as a substitute.

$$\text{Receivables Turnover Ratio} = \frac{\text{Net Sales}}{\text{Average Accounts Receivables}}$$

where average accounts receivable is as follows:

$$\frac{\text{Beginning accounts receivable} + \text{Ending accounts receivable}}{2}$$

$$\frac{50{,}272}{(2{,}348 + 2{,}020)/2} = 23.0$$

	2010	2009	2008
Best Buy	23.0	25.6	37.2
hhgregg	69.9	68.1	76.0

Best Buy's ratio of 23.0 is lower than its previous two ratios and three times lower than **hhgregg's** current-year ratio. This could be a cause of concern. The horizontal analyses of receivables in Exhibit 12-1 (16.2%) and sales revenue in Exhibit 12-2 (1.2%) show that receivables are increasing at a much faster rate than sales. Such a trend should be monitored closely.

Inventory Turnover Ratio

The **inventory turnover ratio** compares a company's cost of goods sold during a period to its average inventory balance during that period. It reveals how many times a company is able to sell its inventory balance in a period. In general, companies want this ratio to be higher because it indicates that the company sold more inventory while maintaining less inventory on hand. This means that the company generated more sales revenue while reducing the costs of stocking inventory on the shelves.

$$\text{Inventory Turnover Ratio} = \frac{\text{Cost of Goods Sold}}{\text{Average Inventory}}$$

where average inventory is as follows:

$$\frac{\text{Beginning inventory} + \text{Ending inventory}}{2}$$

$$\frac{37{,}635}{(5{,}897 + 5{,}486)/2} = 6.6$$

	2010	2009	2008
Best Buy	6.6	7.3	7.2
hhgregg	7.0	6.2	7.0

Receivables turnover ratio Compares credit sales to average accounts receivable and measures the ability to make and collect sales.

Inventory turnover ratio Compares cost of goods sold to average inventory and measures the ability to sell inventory.

HOME DEPOT ANALYSIS

Using Home Depot's information in Appendix C, calculate Home Depot's liquidity ratios and make a general assessment about the company's liquidity.

Current Ratio: Current Assets/Current Liabilities = $13,479/$10,122 = 1.33

Quick Ratio: (Cash + Short-term Investments + Accounts Receivable)/Current Liabilities = ($545 + $0 + $1,085)/$10,122 = 0.16

Receivables Turnover: Net Sales/Average Accounts Receivable = $67,997/[($1,085 + $964)/2] = 66.4

Inventory Turnover: Cost of Goods Sold/Average Inventory = $44,693/[($10,625 + $10,188)/2] = 4.29

While Home Depot carries more in current assets than current liabilities, the quick ratio shows that the company does not maintain very high levels of quick assets given current liabilities. However, the inventory turnover ratio indicates that the company is successful in selling its inventory. Therefore, Home Depot appears to have adequate liquidity.

If a company cannot satisfy its obligations and becomes insolvent, it can fall into bankruptcy, which can result in significant losses to investors and creditors.

A 6.6 ratio shows that during 2010 **Best Buy** sold more than six and a half dollars of inventory for every dollar of inventory it had on its shelves. Although Best Buy's ratio is slightly lower than both the prior year and **hhgregg**, it shows that Best Buy's ability to sell inventory is relatively stable.

Summary of Liquidity Analysis

Based on the four ratios examined, it appears that Best Buy has sufficient liquidity. The majority of its current assets are tied up in inventory, but it appears that the company is selling through its inventory adequately. Of potential concern is the increase in accounts receivable. While not yet a threat to liquidity, it is a trend to watch closely.

LO5 Solvency Analysis

A third component of any financial analysis is an examination of solvency. **Solvency** refers to a company's ability to satisfy its long-term obligations. If a company cannot satisfy its obligations and becomes *insolvent*, it can fall into bankruptcy, which can result in significant losses to investors and creditors. Therefore, both investors and creditors are interested in assessing solvency.

A company's solvency is related to its use of financial leverage. **Financial leverage** refers to the degree to which a company obtains capital through debt rather than equity in an attempt to increase returns to stockholders. Leverage is beneficial to stockholders when the return on borrowed funds exceeds the cost of borrowing those funds. In that case, leverage is positive. It is harmful, or negative, when the cost of borrowing the funds exceeds the return on those borrowed funds. As a company uses more financial leverage, it creates an opportunity for greater returns to stockholders, but it also creates greater solvency risk.

Financial leverage The degree to which a company obtains capital through debt rather than equity in an attempt to increase returns to stockholders.

Debt to assets ratio Compares total liabilities to total assets and measures the percentage of assets provided by creditors.

AP Images/PRNewsFoto/Mitsubishi Digital Electronics America, Inc.

Although it is impossible to know whether a company will or will not be able to pay future obligations and remain solvent, the following three ratios can provide some indication of a company's general solvency.

Solvency Ratios	Relationship
Debt to Assets	Total Liabilities to Total Assets
Debt to Equity	Total Liabilities to Total Equity
Times Interest Earned	Net Income to Interest Expense

As in the previous sections, the following sections will explain and calculate each ratio for Best Buy using data from Exhibits 12-1 and 12-2. A comparison of Best Buy's and hhgregg's ratios will follow each calculation. After all ratios are presented, a summary of what was learned about Best Buy's solvency will be provided.

Debt to Assets Ratio

The **debt to assets ratio** compares a company's total liabilities to its total assets and yields the percentage of assets provided by creditors. As such, the ratio provides a measure of a company's capital structure. Capital structure refers to the manner in which a company has financed its assets—either through debt or equity—and is also an indication of how much financial leverage a company is using. Since debt and any related interest must be repaid, companies with a higher percentage of assets provided by creditors have a riskier capital structure. In other words, they are using more financial leverage, and they therefore have a greater risk of insolvency.

$$\text{Debt to Assets Ratio} = \frac{\text{Total Liabilities}}{\text{Total Assets}}$$

$$\frac{10{,}557}{17{,}849} = 0.59$$

	2010	2009	2008
Best Buy	0.59	0.62	0.71
hhgregg	0.42	0.58	0.64

Best Buy's ratio of 0.59 shows that a little over half of every dollar of assets is generated through liabilities. This ratio is lower than in both prior years, indicating a decreasingly risky capital structure and a smaller use of financial leverage. However, it is higher than **hhgregg's** ratio of 0.42, showing that Best Buy has a somewhat riskier capital structure.

Debt to Equity Ratio

The **debt to equity ratio** compares a company's total liabilities to its total equity. Like the debt to assets ratio, this ratio provides a measure of a company's capital structure and financial leverage by directly comparing the two aspects of capital structure—liabilities and equity. Higher debt to equity ratios indicate a riskier capital structure and therefore greater risk of insolvency. Companies with higher debt to equity ratios are also said to be highly leveraged.

$$\text{Debt to Equity Ratio} = \frac{\text{Total Liabilities}}{\text{Total Equity}}$$

$$\frac{10{,}557}{7{,}292} = 1.45$$

	2010	2009	2008
Best Buy	1.45	1.63	2.41
hhgregg	0.74	1.39	1.80

Best Buy's ratio of 1.45 shows that it had about one and a half dollars of liabilities for every dollar of equity at the end of the most recent year. This is lower than in the previous two years, indicating that its capital structure is becoming less dependent on liabilities and therefore less risky. The same is happening with hhgregg. Its ratio declined over the three years presented. As you can see, the interpretation of the debt to equity ratio is the same as the debt to assets ratio.

Debt to equity ratio Compares total liabilities to total equity and measures a company's capital structure and financial leverage.

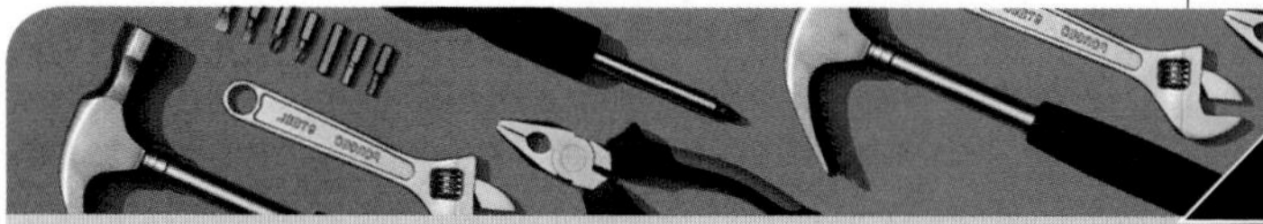

HOME DEPOT ANALYSIS

Using **Home Depot's** information in Appendix C, calculate Home Depot's solvency ratios and make a general assessment about the company's solvency.

Debt to Assets Ratio:	**Total Liabilities / Total Assets = \$21,236/\$40,125 = 0.53**
Debt to Equity Ratio:	**Total Liabilities / Total Equity = \$21,236/\$18,889 = 1.12**
Times Interest Earned:	**Net Income + Interest Expense + Income Tax Expense / Interest Expense = (\$3,338 + \$530 + \$1,935)/\$530 = 10.95**

According to these ratios, Home Depot finances its assets with more liabilities than equity. However, the times interest earned ratio shows that the company can comfortably pay interest expense with current-year earnings. Thus, Home Depot's solvency appears secure.

Times Interest Earned

In addition to examining a company's capital structure, it is wise to assess whether a company can pay the interest on its debt. To answer this question, many use the times interest earned ratio.

The **times interest earned ratio** compares a company's net income to its interest expense. It shows how well a company can pay interest out of current-year earnings. As such, it helps creditors and investors determine whether a company can service its current debt by making its required interest payments.

$$\text{Times Interest Earned Ratio} = \frac{\text{Net Income} + \text{Interest Expense} + \text{Income Tax Expense}}{\text{Interest Expense}}$$

Note that the ratio adjusts net income by adding back interest expense and income tax expense. These are added back to "gross up" income to the amount of earnings that were available to make interest payments. Once this adjustment is made, the ratio yields the number of times that current interest payments could be made out of current earnings. A higher ratio indicates a greater ability to make payments, and therefore less risk of insolvency.

$$\frac{1{,}277 + 87 + 714}{87} = 23.9$$

	2010	2009	2008
Best Buy	23.9	23.5	18.8
hhgregg	16.9	13.3	9.8

Best Buy's ratio of 23.9 indicates that the company earned many times more than its interest expense. Specifically, for every dollar of interest expense, the company earned almost twenty-four dollars in profits. Best Buy should have no problem paying its interest as it comes due.

Times interest earned ratio Compares net income to interest expense and measures the ability to pay interest out of current earnings.

DuPont analysis Decomposes a company's return on equity into measures of operating efficiency, asset effectiveness, and capital structure.

Summary of Solvency

Based on the three ratios examined, it appears that Best Buy's capital structure is trending toward less debt. Thus, its solvency risk has decreased.

LO6 DuPont Analysis

All investors want to maximize the returns on their investments in a company. An investor's return is measured by the return on equity. To better understand how the return was generated, investors often conduct a DuPont analysis.

A **DuPont analysis** provides insight into how a company's return on equity was generated by decomposing the return into three components: operating efficiency, asset effectiveness, and capital structure. The actual calculations of the analysis are as follows:

DuPont Analysis

Operating Efficiency		*Asset Effectiveness*		*Capital Structure*		*Return on Equity*
$\frac{\text{Net Income}}{\text{Sales}}$	×	$\frac{\text{Sales}}{\text{Assets}}$	×	$\frac{\text{Assets}}{\text{Equity}}$	=	$\frac{\text{Net Income}}{\text{Equity}}$

The first component is a company's operating efficiency. It is calculated as net income divided by sales, which is also known as the profit margin ratio. This component reveals a company's ability to turn sales into profits. The higher the ratio, the more efficient a company is in turning sales into profits.

The second component is a company's effectiveness at using its assets. It is calculated as sales divided by assets. This ratio is commonly known as the asset turnover ratio. It measures the ability of a company to generate sales from its asset base. The higher the ratio, the more effective a company is in generating sales given its assets.

The third component is a company's capital structure. For this analysis, it is calculated as assets divided by equity. This ratio is similar to the debt to assets and debt to equity ratios in that it measures how a company has generated its assets. The higher the ratio, the more a company is financing its assets with debt rather than equity. So, a higher ratio means more financial leverage and a riskier capital structure. Sometimes, this ratio is called the leverage multiplier.

Best Buy's most recent DuPont analysis is shown as follows. Also shown are the results of the same analysis for the prior year. Note that the return on equity numbers are slightly different than those calculated previously in the text because a DuPont analysis does not use average equity in the calculation of return on equity.

Best Buy
DuPont Analysis
2010

Net Income / Sales	×	Sales / Assets	×	Assets / Equity	=	Net Income / Equity
1,277 / 50,272	×	50,272 / 17,849	×	17,849 / 7,292	=	1,277 / 7,292
0.025	×	2.82	×	2.45	=	0.175

2009

0.027	×	2.72	×	2.63	=	0.189

The analysis shows why Best Buy's return to its owners was down in 2010 compared to 2009. The company was more effective at generating sales from its asset base (2.82 versus 2.72), but it was not able to increase profits from those sales (0.025 versus 0.027). This translated into somewhat stagnant profits. But, the company moved to a capital structure with less debt and more equity (2.45 versus 2.63). As a result, the company's profits were spread over a greater amount of equity, thereby decreasing the return on that equity.

One of the main benefits of a DuPont analysis is the ability to ask what-if questions. For example, what if Best Buy was able to squeeze out another $0.02 of profit on each dollar of sales? How would that affect the return to owners? The analysis shows that the 2010 return would increase to 0.310 (0.045 × 2.82 × 2.45).

Alternatively, what if Best Buy took a riskier leverage position by increasing its assets to equity ratio from 2.45 to 4.00? Is that in the best interests of owners? Assuming nothing else changes, the answer is yes. The return on equity would rise to 0.286 (0.025 × 2.82 × 4.00).

Finally, what if the market for electronics took a significant downturn and Best Buy was only able to generate sales of 1.5 times assets on hand? Would that significantly affect the return to investors? The analysis shows that it would. The return would fall to 0.093 (0.025 × 1.50 × 2.45).

Like all ratio analyses, the DuPont analysis is a helpful tool for providing feedback on past performance and expectations for future performance. As such, it is relevant information that can affect the decision making of managers, investors, and creditors.

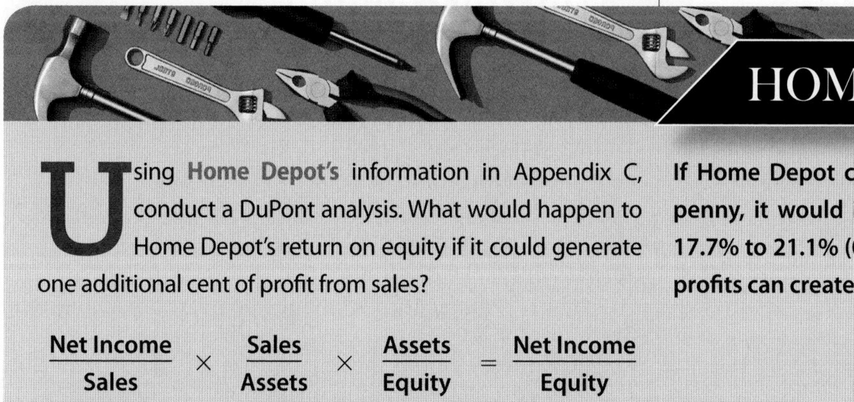

HOME DEPOT ANALYSIS

Using **Home Depot's** information in Appendix C, conduct a DuPont analysis. What would happen to Home Depot's return on equity if it could generate one additional cent of profit from sales?

Net Income / Sales	×	Sales / Assets	×	Assets / Equity	=	Net Income / Equity
$3,338 / $67,997	×	$67,997 / $40,125	×	$40,125 / $18,889	=	$3,338 / $18,889
0.049	×	1.69	×	2.12	=	0.177

If Home Depot could increase its profit margin by one penny, it would increase the return to its owners from 17.7% to 21.1% (0.059 × 1.69 × 2.12). A small change in profits can create large changes in stockholder returns.

STUDY TOOLS 12

Chapter review card

- Learning Objective and Key Concept Reviews
- Key Definitions and Formulas

Online (Located at www.cengagebrain.com)

- Flash Cards and Crossword Puzzles
- Games and Quizzes
- E-Lectures
- Homework Assignments (as directed by your instructor)

CONCEPT QUESTIONS

1. (LO1) What three items does a financial analysis require?
2. (LO1) What are some common standards of comparison in a financial analysis?
3. (LO2) Which type of analysis compares account balances over time?
4. (LO2) Describe the calculations associated with a horizontal analysis.
5. (LO2) What type of analysis compares each account on a statement to a base amount?
6. (LO2) What base amounts are used in vertical analyses of the income statement and the balance sheet?
7. (LO3) Identify five ratios commonly used to analyze a company's profitability.
8. (LO3) Show the calculation of each of the five profitability ratios and describe what each ratio reveals.
9. (LO4) What does liquidity refer to?
10. (LO4) Identify four ratios commonly used to analyze a company's liquidity.
11. (LO4) Show the calculation of each of the four liquidity ratios and describe what each ratio reveals.
12. (LO5) What does solvency refer to?
13. (LO5) Identify three ratios commonly used to analyze a company's solvency.
14. (LO5) Show the calculation of each of the three solvency ratios and describe what each ratio reveals.
15. (LO6) A DuPont analysis breaks a company's return on equity into three components. Describe those components.
16. (LO6) Why is a DuPont analysis valuable?

MULTIPLE CHOICE

1. (LO2) In a horizontal analysis, the change in an account balance is expressed as a percentage change compared to:
   a. net income.
   b. total assets.
   c. prior-year account balance.
   d. both A and B.
2. (LO2) Pauley Corp.'s balance in inventory increased from $50,000 to $60,000. A horizontal analysis of inventory would show:
   a. a 20.0% increase in inventory.
   b. a 12.5% decrease in inventory.
   c. a 12.5% increase in inventory.
   d. none of the above.
3. (LO2) A horizontal analysis of sales and cost of goods sold yields the following:

Sales	15.8%
Cost of Goods Sold	18.9%

Which of the following best describes these results?

a. The company's cost of sales grew faster than its sales
b. The company's cost of sales fell faster than its sales
c. The company's sales fell slower than its cost of sales
d. None of the above

4. (LO2) When performing a vertical analysis, which of the following is usually the base amount for accounts payable?
   a. Net income
   b. Total liabilities
   c. Total assets
   d. Common stock
5. (LO2) The following example shows what type of analysis?

	Account Balance	Percentage
Cash	$ 150,000	15%
Equipment	350,000	35%
Property	500,000	50%
Total Assets	$1,000,000	100%

   a. Horizontal analysis
   b. Ratio analysis
   c. Vertical analysis
   d. Fundamental analysis
6. (LO2) A financial statement on which a vertical analysis is conducted is often called:
   a. a standardized statement.
   b. a common-size statement.
   c. a same-size statement.
   d. none of the above.
7. (LO2) A vertical analysis can be used to compare different companies because it removes the effects of:
   a. accounting techniques.
   b. company profitability.
   c. company size.
   d. none of the above.
8. (LO3) Profitability ratios usually compare some financial aspect of a company to:
   a. current assets.
   b. total assets.
   c. net income.
   d. stock price.
9. (LO3) Which of the following is not a profitability ratio?
   a. Inventory turnover
   b. Earnings per share
   c. Profit margin
   d. Price to earnings
10. (LO3) Dividing net income by average total assets yields:
    a. return on equity.
    b. return on assets.
    c. profit margin.
    d. price to earnings.
11. (LO3) Which of the following would be considered good news for a company?
    a. Its return on assets decreases
    b. Its return on equity stays the same
    c. Its profit margin increases
    d. Its earnings per share decreases
12. (LO3) A company reports net income of $45,000 when the balance in stockholder's equity increased from $200,000 to $300,000. What is the company's return on equity?
    a. 22.5%
    b. 15.0%
    c. 18.0%
    d. 9.6%
13. (LO4) Which of the following ratios assists in evaluating a company's ability to pay its short-term obligations?
    a. Current ratio
    b. Debt to equity ratio
    c. Debt to assets ratio
    d. Return on assets
14. (LO4) Liquidity refers to:
    a. the ability to be profitable.
    b. the ability to pay short-term obligations.
    c. the ability to generate cash from receivables.
    d. the ability to profit from sales.
15. (LO4) Which of the following would likely be considered bad news for a company?
    a. Its inventory turnover ratio decreased dramatically
    b. Its quick ratio increased significantly
    c. Its receivables turnover ratio increased slightly
    d. Its current ratio was unchanged
16. (LO4) A company has a current ratio of 1.5. This means that:
    a. the company has $1.50 in current assets for every $1.00 in current liabilities.
    b. the company earned $1.50 per share of stock.
    c. the company has more current liabilities than current assets.
    d. none of the above.
17. (LO4) A company reports $45,600 in cost of goods sold in a year when its inventory increased from $6,000 to $8,600. What was the company's inventory turnover ratio?
    a. 5.3
    b. 7.6
    c. 6.2
    d. 8.1
18. (LO5) Solvency refers to:
    a. the ability to sell inventory.
    b. the ability to pay short-term obligations.
    c. the ability to generate cash from receivables.
    d. the ability to pay long-term obligations.

19. (LO5) Which of the following ratios is not a solvency ratio?
    a. Debt to assets ratio
    b. Debt to equity ratio
    c. Times interest earned ratio
    d. Inventory turnover ratio
20. (LO5) The debt to assets ratio can be viewed as a good indicator of a company's:
    a. stock price.
    b. capital structure.
    c. liquidity.
    d. profitability.
21. (LO6) Which of the following is not one of the three components in a DuPont analysis?
    a. Operating efficiency
    b. Asset effectiveness
    c. Capital structure
    d. All of the above are components of a DuPont analysis

BRIEF EXERCISES

1. Financial Statement Analysis LO1

Financial statement analysis is defined as the process of applying analytical tools to a company's financial statements to understand the company's financial health.

Required

Identify and briefly describe the three items required to conduct successful financial statement analysis.

2. Calculate Horizontal Analysis LO2

At the end of 2012, a company has a balance of $1,755,000 in cash and cash equivalents. At the beginning of the year, the company had a $1,560,000 balance.

Required

Perform a horizontal analysis of cash and briefly explain the result. Round percentages to one decimal point (i.e., 12.8%).

3. Calculate Vertical Analysis LO2

Alyssa's Sporting Goods generated gross profit of $2,550,000 and net sales of $4,090,000 during the year. Operating expenses were $655,000.

Required

Perform a vertical analysis of operating expenses and briefly explain the result. Round percentages to one decimal point (i.e., 12.8%).

4. Calculate Profit Margin LO3

Jim's Computer Warehouse produced net income of $150,000 and cost of goods sold of $400,000 for the year. Net sales were $980,000.

Required

Calculate Jim's profit margin for the year and briefly explain the result. Round percentages to one decimal point (i.e., 12.8%).

5. Calculate Return on Assets LO3

During 2012, a company generated net income of $158,000. Total assets at the beginning of the year were $1,480,000 while they were $1,515,000 at the end of the year.

Required

Calculate the company's return on assets and briefly explain the result. Round percentages to one decimal point (i.e., 12.8%).

6. Calculate Earnings Per Share LO3

During 2012, Blue Corporation produced net income of $1,550,000. The average number of shares of common stock outstanding for the year was 498,000.

Required

Calculate Blue's earnings per share for the year and briefly explain the result.

7. Calculate Current Ratio LO4

A company has current assets of $155,900 and total assets of $378,000. Current liabilities are $121,500, and total liabilities are $265,350.

Required

Calculate the company's current ratio and briefly explain the result.

8. Calculate Inventory Turnover Ratio LO4

In 2012, Ralph's Rug Outlet generated net sales of $1,250,000 and cost of goods sold of $723,000. Ralph's average inventory of rugs during the year was $95,300.

Required

Calculate Ralph's inventory turnover ratio for the year and briefly explain the result.

9. Calculate Debt to Assets Ratio LO5

A company has current assets of $155,900 and total assets of $378,000. Current liabilities are $121,500 and total liabilities are $265,350.

Required

Calculate the company's debt to assets ratio and briefly explain the result.

10. Calculate Times Interest Earned Ratio LO5

Stinky Carpet Cleaning Service produced net income of $125,600 in 2012. Interest expense was $12,550 during the year, and income tax expense was $42,000.

Required

Calculate Stinky's times interest earned ratio and briefly explain the result.

11. DuPont Analysis LO6

After conducting a DuPont analysis, it is determined that a company's operating efficiency is 0.035. Asset effectiveness is 3.08, and capital structure is 2.65.

Required
Calculate the company's return on equity.

EXERCISES

12. Horizontal Analysis LO2

The following asset information is available for BSI Inc.:

	2012	2011
Cash	$ 35,000	$ 60,000
Accounts receivable	60,000	55,000
Inventory	125,000	175,000
Total current assets	220,000	290,000
Property and equipment	175,000	150,000
Total assets	$395,000	$440,000

Required
Prepare a horizontal analysis of BSI's assets. Round percentages to one decimal point (i.e., 12.8%).

13. Horizontal Analysis LO2

The income statements of Crisp Corp. for the past two years are as follows:

Income Statements For the Years Ending December 31	2012	2011
Sales	$300,000	$250,000
Cost of goods sold	125,000	100,000
Gross profit	$175,000	$150,000
Operating expenses	75,000	50,000
Operating income	$100,000	$100,000
Interest expense	35,000	15,000
Income before taxes	$ 65,000	$ 85,000
Income tax expense	25,000	30,000
Net income	$ 40,000	$ 55,000

Required
Prepare and interpret a horizontal analysis of Crisp's income statements. Round percentages to one decimal point (i.e., 12.8%).

14. Vertical Analysis LO2

The following asset information is available for LOC Inc.:

	2012
Cash	$ 15,000
Accounts receivable	30,000
Inventory	75,000
Total current assets	120,000
Property and equipment	205,000
Total assets	$325,000

Required
Prepare a vertical analysis of assets. Round percentages to one decimal point (i.e., 12.8%).

15. Vertical Analysis LO2

The income statements of High Noon Corp. for the past two years are as follows:

Income Statements For the Years Ending December 31	2012	2011
Sales	$725,000	$700,000
Cost of goods sold	345,000	385,000
Gross profit	$380,000	$315,000
Operating expenses	175,000	180,000
Operating income	$205,000	$135,000
Interest expense	45,000	40,000
Income before taxes	$160,000	$ 95,000
Income tax expense	55,000	30,000
Net income	$105,000	$ 65,000

Required
Prepare and interpret a vertical analysis of High Noon's income statements. Round percentages to one decimal point (i.e., 12.8%). What was the most significant reason for the change in profitability?

16. Interpret Horizontal Analysis LO2

Three companies report the following horizontal analyses:

	Company A	Company B	Company C
Accounts receivable	1.1%	14.1%	2.1%
Inventory	10.4	(1.7)	6.4
Sales	(3.2)	1.6	8.6
Total assets	1.4	(2.5)	7.0

Required
For each company, describe what the percentages reveal about the company. Which of the companies would you be most concerned about?

17. Interpret Vertical Analysis LO2

A grocery store and a jewelry store provide the following vertical analyses of certain accounts:

	Company A	Company B
Gross profit	26.0%	55.2%
Operating expenses	22.2	48.0
Net income	3.8	7.2
Inventory	30.4	68.2
Property and equipment	57.8	32.5

Required
Identify which company is likely the grocer and which is likely the jewelry store. Explain the reasons for your conclusions.

18. Identify Ratios LO3, 4, 5

The following ratios are often used in financial statement analysis:

________ Return on equity
________ Debt to assets ratio
________ Times interest earned
________ Quick ratio
________ Inventory turnover ratio
________ Price to earnings ratio
________ Profit margin
________ Current ratio
________ Debt to equity ratio

Required

Identify each ratio as a profitability, liquidity, or solvency ratio.

19. Interpret Ratios LO3, 4, 5

The following information is available for Warmouth Enterprises:

	2012	2011
Profit margin	8.7	8.3
Return on assets	10.2	10.4
Price to earnings ratio	13.5	12.0
Quick ratio	0.8	0.9
Inventory turnover ratio	5.5	7.2
Receivables turnover ratio	11.3	15.5
Times interest earned	7.2	6.4

Required

For each ratio, indicate whether the change in the ratio is favorable or unfavorable and why.

20. Define Ratios LO3, 4, 5

The following statements describe various financial statement analysis ratios:

a. Shows the return to each share of stock owned by an investor
b. Measures the difference between quick assets and current liabilities
c. Measures the ability of a company to generate profits from sales
d. Provides a measure of a company's capital structure
e. Shows a company's ability to generate profits from its entire resource base
f. Gives information as to how a company manages its inventory
g. Measures a company's capital structure using liabilities and equity
h. Shows how effectively a company uses its current equity to generate additional equity
i. Gives a less strict measure of a company's ability to meet its short-term obligations
j. Shows how well a company can pay interest on debt out of current-year earnings
k. Measures a company's ability to make and collect sales
l. Provides an indication of current investor perceptions of the company

Required

Identify the appropriate ratio for each of the descriptions.

21. Profitability Ratios LO3

The following financial information about Cloudburst Co. is available:

Sales	$600,000
Net income	130,000
Average total assets	900,000
Average stockholders' equity	440,000

The following additional information is available:

- 500,000 shares of common stock were outstanding during the year.
- The stock was recently trading for $5.00 per share.

Required

Compute the following ratios: profit margin, return on equity, return on assets, earnings per share, and price to earnings. Round percentages to one decimal point (i.e., 12.8%).

22. Profitability Ratios LO3

The following financial information about NGC Company is available:

Net income	$ 150,000
Common shares outstanding, January 1	400,000
Common shares outstanding, December 31	500,000
Market price at December 31	$ 10.00
Sales	$ 945,000
Total assets, January 1	$ 800,000
Total assets, December 31	$1,000,000
Stockholders' equity, January 1	$ 450,000
Stockholders' equity, December 31	$ 475,000

Required

Compute and interpret the following ratios: profit margin, return on equity, return on assets, earnings per share, and price to earnings. Round percentages to one decimal point (i.e., 12.8%).

23. Profitability Ratios and Leverage LO3

The following financial information about Stephens Company is available:

Net income	$ 450,000
Sales	$4,805,000
Average assets	$2,930,000
Average equity	$ 730,000
Common shares outstanding January 1	500,000
Common shares outstanding December 31	750,000
Market price at December 31	$ 9.35

Required
Calculate all profitability ratios for Stephens. Round percentages to one decimal point (i.e., 12.8%). Does it appear that the company is using financial leverage effectively or ineffectively? Why?

24. Liquidity Ratios LO4

The following information was taken from the financial statements of Connor Cookers and Olson Ovens:

(in millions)	2012	2011
Total current assets		
Connor Cookers	$ 46,448	$249,664
Olson Ovens	155,117	153,188
Cash		
Connor Cookers	24,311	48,936
Olson Ovens	28,894	28,406
Accounts receivable		
Connor Cookers	8,216	186,766
Olson Ovens	114,645	114,511
Inventory		
Connor Cookers	13,921	13,962
Olson Ovens	11,578	10,271
Current liabilities		
Connor Cookers	69,036	74,457
Olson Ovens	80,220	85,037
Sales		
Connor Cookers	207,349	194,655
Olson Ovens	160,123	176,896
Cost of goods sold		
Connor Cookers	80,153	79,411
Olson Ovens	76,740	71,561

Required
For each company, compute the following 2012 ratios: receivables turnover ratio, inventory turnover ratio, current ratio, and quick ratio. Based in your calculations, discuss the liquidity of each company.

25. Transactions Affecting Liquidity Ratios LO4

Robinson Tools has $50,000 of quick assets, $135,000 of total current assets, and $100,000 of total current liabilities prior to the following transactions.

1. Made sales on account of $10,000
2. Paid cash for accounts due to suppliers, $15,000
3. Received cash for accounts receivable of $15,000
4. Prepaid expenses of $7,500 with cash
5. Purchased inventory of $20,000 on account
6. Paid a $5,000 cash dividend
7. Repaid short-term loans of $10,000 with cash
8. Purchased short-term investments of $15,000 with cash
9. Borrowed $25,000 from the bank by signing a 90-day note
10. Sold inventory of $30,000 for cash

Required
Indicate whether each transaction would increase, decrease, or have no effect on Robinson's current and quick ratios. Treat each transaction independently.

26. Solvency Ratios LO5

The following information was taken from the financial statements of TKO Company:

	2012	2011
Total assets	$200,000	$125,000
Total liabilities	75,000	75,000
Total equity	125,000	50,000
Operating income	35,000	30,000
Interest expense	7,000	7,500

Required
Compute the debt to assets ratio, the debt to equity ratio, and times interest earned for both years.

27. Solvency Ratios LO5

The following financial information regarding Foshee Flapjacks is available:

2012 Balance Sheet	
Total assets	$530,000
Total liabilities	140,000
Total stockholders' equity	390,000

2012 Income Statement	
Sales	$250,000
Cost of goods sold	125,000
Gross profit	$125,000
Operating expenses	40,000
Operating income	$ 85,000
Interest expense	10,000
Income before taxes	$ 75,000
Income tax expense	25,000
Net income	$ 50,000

Required
Compute the following ratios: debt to assets, debt to equity, and times interest earned. Discuss the solvency of Foshee Flapjacks. Does the company rely more on equity or debt to finance its operations?

28. Sensitivity of Solvency Ratios LO5

The following financial information regarding Wick Industries is available:

Total liabilities	$150,000
Total equity	400,000
Total assets	550,000
Income tax expense	20,000
Net income	35,000
Operating cash flows	125,000
Interest expense	15,000

Wick would like to increase its return to stockholders. To do so, it wants to increase its debt to assets ratio to 0.70 by issuing debt and buying back common stock.

Required

a. Calculate Wick's current debt to equity, debt to assets, and times interest earned ratios.
b. How much debt would Wick have to issue to buy enough common stock to raise its debt to assets ratio to 0.70?
c. What would concern you about Wick's plan?

29. DuPont Analysis LO6

The following financial information about Carbon Company is available:

	2012
Total average assets	$200,000
Total average equity	125,000
Sales	35,000
Net income	7,000

Required

Prepare a DuPont analysis for Carbon Company.

30. DuPont Analysis LO6

The following financial information about Cole's Colas, Inc., is available:

	2012
Total average assets	$350,000
Total average equity	190,000
Sales	55,000
Net income	9,000

Required

Prepare a DuPont analysis for Cole's Colas and interpret each component of the analysis.

31. DuPont Analysis LO6

During the year, Shields Corp. generated net income of $123,547 on sales of $1,540,005. At the end of the year, Shields had total assets of $920,558 and total equity of $403,346.

Required

a. Conduct a DuPont analysis to identify Shields' return on equity and the return's three components.
b. Shields is considering plans that would either (1) double its operating efficiency or (2) increase its capital structure by half of its current value. Which plan would provide the greatest increase to return on equity?

32. Financial Analysis Terms LO2, 3, 4, 5, 6

The following is a list of terms and definitions associated with financial statement analysis tools:

1. Horizontal analysis
2. Current ratio
3. Vertical analysis
4. Quick ratio
5. Profit margin
6. Inventory turnover ratio
7. Return on equity
8. Price to earnings ratio
9. Capital structure
10. Dividend payout ratio

a. A comparison of net income to sales that measures a company's ability to generate profits
b. A liquidity ratio that compares cash and near cash assets to current liabilities
c. The mix of debt and equity that a company uses to generate its assets
d. Compares the income of a company in terms of earnings per share with the price of one share of stock
e. A technique that calculates both the dollar and percentage change in account balances from one term to the next
f. A measure of how many times a company is able to sell its inventory balance in a period
g. A technique that compares account balances within one year
h. A measure of the percentage of earnings that a company pays out as dividends
i. A ratio comparing a company's current liabilities to current assets
j. A comparison of net income to the average balance in stockholders' equity during the year

Required

Match each term with the appropriate definition.

33. Financial Analysis Terms LO2, 3, 4, 5, 6
The following is a list of terms and definitions associated with financial statement analysis tools:

1. Return on assets
2. Debt to equity ratio
3. Earnings per share
4. Times interest earned
5. Financial leverage
6. Receivables turnover ratio
7. Debt to assets ratio
8. Solvency
9. Liquidity
10. DuPont analysis

a. A company's ability to continue in business in the long term by satisfying long-term obligations
b. A technique that breaks return on equity into three components
c. A comparison of net income to average total assets during the period
d. Refers to a company's ability to meet its short-term obligations
e. The practice of obtaining capital through debt rather than equity to increase returns for the stockholders
f. A comparison of total liabilities to total stockholders' equity
g. A measure of how often a company turns over its receivables balance during the year
h. A comparison of net income before interest and taxes to interest expense
i. Net income presented on a per share basis
j. A comparison of total liabilities to total assets

Required
Match each term with the appropriate definition.

PROBLEMS

34. Analyzing Financial Statements LO2, 3, 4, 5
The following financial information is available for Last Chance Repossessions Company as of December 31, 2012:

Comparative Balance Sheet	2012	2011
Cash	$ 15,000	$ 10,000
Accounts receivable	30,000	25,000
Inventory	75,000	75,000
Prepaid insurance	10,000	15,000
Total current assets	130,000	125,000
Property and equipment	500,000	400,000
Accumulated depreciation	100,000	85,000
Total property and equipment	400,000	315,000
Total assets	$530,000	$440,000
Accounts payable	$ 40,000	$ 50,000
Other current liabilities	25,000	40,000
Total current liabilities	65,000	90,000
Bonds payable	75,000	150,000
Total liabilities	140,000	240,000
Common stock	290,000	150,000
Retained earnings	100,000	50,000
Total stockholders' equity	390,000	200,000
Total liabilities and stockholders' equity	$530 000	$440,000

Income Statement	2012
Sales	$400,000
Cost of goods sold	210,000
Gross profit	$190,000
Operating expenses	55,000
Operating income	$135,000
Interest expense	15,000
Income before taxes	$120,000
Income tax expense	50,000
Net income	$ 70,000

Required
Calculate all profitability, liquidity, and solvency ratios (except earnings per share, price to earnings, and debt to equity) and comment on Last Chance's overall profitability, liquidity, and solvency. Round percentages to one decimal point (i.e., 12.8%).

35. Analyzing Financial Statements LO2, 3, 4, 5
Amanda's Anchors has applied for a loan from a local bank. The bank is basing its decision on the following information:

Ratio	Industry Average
Current ratio	1.50
Quick ratio	0.80
Receivables turnover ratio	18.00
Inventory turnover ratio	20.00
Debt to assets ratio	0.56
Times interest earned	6.52
Profit margin	10.25%
Return on assets	11.50%
Return on equity	20.30%

Amanda's Anchors Income Statement For the Year Ending December 31, 2012	
Sales	$600,000
Cost of goods sold	350,000
Gross profit	$250,000
Operating expenses	100,000
Operating income	$150,000
Interest expense	25,000
Income before taxes	$125,000
Income tax expense	65,000
Net income	$ 60,000

Amanda's Anchors Balance Sheet	December 31, 2012	December 31, 2011
Cash	$ 75,000	$ 60,000
Accounts receivable	30,000	20,000
Inventory	30,000	20,000
Prepaid insurance	5,000	5,000
Total current assets	140,000	105,000
Property and equipment	600,000	550,000
Accumulated depreciation	140,000	110,000
Total property and equipment	460,000	440,000
Total assets	$600,000	$545,000
Accounts payable	$ 60,000	$ 60,000
Other current liabilities	40,000	45,000
Total current liabilities	100,000	105,000
Bonds payable	150,000	150,000
Total liabilities	250,000	255,000
Common stock	250,000	250,000
Retained earnings	100,000	40,000
Total stockholders' equity	350,000	290,000
Total liabilities and stockholders' equity	$600,000	$545,000

Required

For Amanda's Anchors, calculate the ratios for which the bank has an industry average. After comparing Amanda's ratios to the industry averages, should the bank approve the loan? Why or why not?

36. Using Ratios to Evaluate a Business Purchase LO3, 4, 5

Overtake Financial Group is a large corporation whose sole activity is the acquisition of quality subsidiary companies. You are a senior analyst for Overtake, and your manager has just come to you with the following financial statements for Burning Corn Company, an ethanol producing firm based in Nebraska, which is currently trading at $5 per share. He wants you to analyze the company and give a recommendation on whether or not to submit a bid for Burning Corn.

Burning Corn Company Comparative Balance Sheet at December 31	2012	2011
Cash	$ 10,000	$ 20,000
Accounts receivable	30,000	45,000
Inventory	105,000	75,000
Prepaid insurance	5,000	15,000
Total current assets	150,000	155,000
Property and equipment	375,000	325,000
Accumulated depreciation	55,000	40,000
Total property and equipment	320,000	285,000
Total assets	$470,000	$440,000
Accounts payable	$ 60,000	$ 50,000
Notes payable	25,000	25,000
Total current liabilities	85,000	5,000
Bonds payable	280,000	280,000
Total liabilities	365,000	355,000
Common stock (Avg. 100,000 shares outstanding)	75,000	75,000
Retained earnings	30,000	10,000
Total stockholders' equity	105,000	85,000
Total liabilities and stockholders' equity	$470,000	$440,000

Burning Corn Company 2012 Income Statement	
Sales	$250,000
Cost of goods sold	150,000
Gross profit	$100,000
Administrative expenses	25,000
Depreciation expense	15,000
Total operating expenses	40,000
Operating income	$ 60,000
Interest expense	10,000
Income before taxes	$ 50,000
Income tax expense	25,000
Net income	$ 25,000

Required

Prepare a brief written analysis of Burning Corn's profitability, liquidity, and solvency. Include a table of calculated ratios and your recommendation on whether Overtake should bid on the company. Round percentages to one decimal point (i.e., 12.8%).

CASES

37. Research and Analysis LO1, 3, 4, 5, 6

Access the 2010 annual report for **Dick's Sporting Goods** by clicking on the *About Us, Investor Relations,* and *Annual Reports* links at www.dickssportinggoods.com.

Required

a. Examine the company's income statement and balance sheet and calculate all profitability, liquidity, and solvency ratios for 2010. To calculate the price to earnings ratio, use the high stock price for the fiscal quarter ended January 29, 2011 (found on page 82).
b. Based on your answers above, write a paragraph explaining your opinion of the financial health of Dick's Sporting Goods.
c. Calculate a DuPont analysis and explain what would happen to the company's return on equity if it was able to improve its operating efficiency by one penny.

38. Research and Analysis LO3, 4, 5

Access the 2010 annual report of **American Eagle Outfitters** by clicking on the *About AEO Inc., AE Investment Info*, and *Historical Annual Reports* links at www.ae.com. Also, access the 2010 annual report of **Gap Inc.** by clicking on the *Investors, Financials,* and *Annual Reports & Proxy* links at www.gapinc.com.

Required

a. Conduct horizontal and vertical analyses on each company's income statement.
b. Compute all profitability ratios (except price to earnings) for each company for the most recent year.
c. Compare the profitability of each company.
d. Conduct a DuPont analysis.
e. Which company's stockholders would benefit the most from a $0.01 increase in profits per dollar of sales?

39. Ethics in Accounting LO4

Retraction Company currently has a line of credit with HSC Bank. The interest rate on the line of credit increases from 7.25% to 10.25% if the following terms of the credit agreement are not met:

a) Retraction's current ratio must remain above 1.2 at all times.
b) Retraction's times interest earned must be 3.0 or greater at all times.

The following preliminary financial information has been prepared by the accountants of Retraction Company:

Current assets	$100,000
Current liabilities	75,000
Income before interest and taxes	25,000
Interest expense	7,000

Your senior accounting manager calls to your attention that current assets include $10,000 worth of an investment in callable bonds, which do not mature for 5 years but will be callable if the company so desires in 10 months. He also notes $12,000 worth of revenue, which is attributed to a service contract for which Retraction has received payment but has not yet performed the services. There should be no reasonable reason why the contract will not be fulfilled.

Required

a. Based on the financial information presented above, is Retraction within the guidelines set forth in its credit agreement?
b. Would you change the treatment of the two items your senior manager brought to your attention? Do you see any problem with the way these items are classified? Explain your answer.
c. Based on your response to part (b), prepare revised financial information if it is necessary. If you revised the information, is Retraction still compliant with its loan agreement?

40. Written Communication LO3, 4, 5

The following financial ratios have been provided to you by your company:

	2012	2011	2010
Horizontal analysis of sales	47.0%	26.0%	15.0%
Profit margin	8.2%	7.5%	6.8%
Return on equity	13.1%	12.3%	11.1%
Current ratio	2.4	2.1	1.8
Quick ratio	0.9	1.1	1.2
Inventory turnover ratio	4.4	4.6	4.7
Debt to assets ratio	0.8	0.7	0.6

Your boss has asked you to prepare a press release to highlight the company's financial results. Analysts have been predicting a strong year, and the CEO wants these highlights to reflect that.

Required

Prepare a brief press release describing the general performance of the company. Use the ratios as supporting evidence.

ACCT

Appendix A
Investments

Learning Objectives

After studying the material in this chapter, you should be able to:

LO1 Identify and understand the accounting for different types and classifications of investments.

Investments

Companies commonly invest in other entities by purchasing debt securities or equity securities issued by those entities.

A *debt security* is a financial instrument issued by an entity (such as a corporation, a municipality, or a university) to borrow cash from another entity. A common example of a debt security is a bond. When a company invests in a debt security, it is in effect loaning cash to the borrowing entity. In return, the investing company usually receives periodic interest payments from the borrowing entity. In most cases, the investing company can sell the debt security at any time or hold it until it matures.

An *equity security* is a financial instrument issued by an entity to raise capital in exchange for an ownership interest in the entity. A common example of an equity security is common stock issued by a corporation. When a company invests in an equity security, it is entitled to any dividends paid by the issuing entity. Most equity securities can be sold at almost any time.

This appendix focuses on how to account for investments in debt securities and investments in equity securities in which the investor does not have a significant influence over the target company. Usually, investments of less than 20% of the target company's common stock meet this criteria. The accounting for investments that are greater than 20% is left to more advanced textbooks.

To illustrate the accounting for investments, the following four events associated with investments will be considered:

- Purchasing the investment
- Recording periodic investment income
- Reporting the investment on the balance sheet
- Selling the investment

Recording the Purchase of Investments

Like other assets, investments are recorded at the cost of acquisition. To illustrate, suppose that on January 1, 2012, Abernathy Inc. purchases the following investments: a $100,000 20-year bond issued by the city of Decatur, 6,000 shares of Eagle Company common stock for $60,000, and 500 shares of C & L Inc. common stock for $10,000. Abernathy would record the purchases as follows:

Jan. 1	Investment in Decatur Bonds	100,000	
	Investment in Eagle Company	60,000	
	Investment in C & L Inc.	10,000	
	Cash		170,000
	(To record purchase of investments)		

Assets	=	Liabilities	+	Equity
+100,000				
+60,000				
+10,000				
−170,000				

The entry increases each investment account for the cost of each security and reduces Abernathy's Cash account for the total cost of the purchase. Because Abernathy has simply exchanged cash for other assets, total assets remain unchanged.

Recording Investment Income

Investment income from debt or equity securities is recorded when earned. Because debt securities pay interest and equity securities distribute dividends, periodic investment income will be recorded as either interest revenue or dividend revenue. Both interest revenue and dividend revenue are reported on the income statement, usually as part of other revenues and expenses.

To illustrate, suppose that Abernathy receives $5,000 of interest on the Decatur bonds on June 30 and $3,000 of cash dividends from Eagle Company on September 15. Abernathy would record the receipts as follows:

June 30	Cash	5,000	
	Interest Revenue		5,000
	(To record receipt of interest)		

Assets	=	Liabilities	+	Equity
+5,000				+5,000

Sept. 15	Cash	3,000	
	Dividend Revenue		3,000
	(To record receipt of dividends)		

Assets	=	Liabilities	+	Equity
+3,000				+3,000

In both entries, Abernathy increases Cash to reflect the cash that is flowing into the company from its investments. The first entry increases Interest Revenue while the second increases Dividend Revenue. In both entries, assets and equity increase. Similar entries would be made each time interest or dividends are received.

Reporting Investments on the Balance Sheet

Like other assets, investments are reported on the balance sheet. However, the manner in which they are reported depends on how they are classified. Accounting rules require that investments in debt securities and equity securities without significant influence be classified into one of the following three categories. Each category is based on what management intends to do with the investments:

- Held-to-maturity securities
- Trading securities
- Available-for-sale securities

Held-to-maturity securities are those securities that an investor has the positive intent and ability to hold until they mature. Since equity securities such as common stock do not mature, only debt securities can be classified as held-to-maturity securities. Investments in held-to-maturity securities are reported on the balance sheet at their historical costs. They are reported as non-current assets.

Trading securities are those securities that an investor intends to sell in the near term. Either debt or equity securities can be classified as trading securities. However, common stock is the most common type of trading security. Trading securities are reported on the balance sheet at their market values. This is an exception to the cost principle, but it is allowed because market values of most equity securities are objectively measured and easily known. Trading securities are included in current assets.

Available-for-sale securities are those securities that a company does not intend to hold to maturity but also does not intend to sell in the near term. In other words, an available-for-sale security is any security that is neither a held-to-maturity security nor a trading security. Either debt or equity securities can be classified as available-for-sale securities. Like trading securities, available-for-sale securities are reported on the balance sheet at their market values. Available-for-sale securities are usually reported as non-current assets.

Because trading and available-for-sale securities are reported at their market values, adjustments may be necessary at the balance sheet date. For example, if the market value of a trading security is greater than its cost, the investment account must be increased. If the market value of an available-for-sale security is less than its cost, the investment account must be decreased.

To illustrate, suppose that Abernathy is preparing its balance sheet on December 31, 2012. It has decided to hold the Decatur bonds for the full 20 years, to sell the Eagle investment within 90 days, and to hold the C & L investment indefinitely. The following table contains each investment, its classification, its cost and market value as of December 31, and any resulting unrealized gain or loss.

Investment	Classification	Original cost	Market value	Unrealized gain or (loss)
Decatur	Held-to-maturity	$100,000	$99,000	$ (1,000)
Eagle	Trading	60,000	64,300	4,300
C & L	Available-for-sale	10,000	9,800	(200)

The unrealized gain or loss is the difference between an investment's cost and its market value. When the market value exceeds the cost, Abernathy has an unrealized gain. When the cost exceeds the market value, Abernathy has an unrealized loss. The term *unrealized* is used because Abernathy still owns the investments. A gain or loss is *realized* only when an investment is sold and cash is received.

Because the Decatur bonds are classified as held-to-maturity, they are reported at their cost of $100,000. The market value and the unrealized loss are ignored, and no adjustment is needed.

Because the Eagle investment is classified as trading, it must be reported at its market value of $64,300. Therefore, Abernathy must adjust the investment account with the following entry.

Dec. 31	Investment in Eagle Company	4,300	
	Unrealized Gain on Trading Securities		4,300
	(To adjust investment to market value)		

Assets	=	Liabilities	+	Equity
+4,300				+4,300

In this entry, Abernathy first increases the investment account by $4,300 so that the balance in the account rises from $60,000 to $64,300. Abernathy then increases Unrealized Gain on Trading Securities to reflect the increase in the value of Abernathy's investment. Unrealized gains or losses on trading securities are treated like any other revenue or expense—they are included in the calculation of net income. In this case, the gain would be reported in other revenues on the income statement, which results in an increase to equity.

Because the C & L investment is classified as available-for-sale, it too must be reported at its market value. However, the adjustment is a little different from the Eagle example.

Dec. 31	Unrealized Gain/Loss on Available-for-Sale Securities	200	
	Investment in C & L Inc.		200
	(To adjust investment to market value)		

Assets	=	Liabilities	+	Equity
−200				−200

In this entry, Abernathy decreases the investment account by $200 so that the balance in the account decreases from $10,000 to $9,800, the market value. Abernathy then debits Unrealized Gain/Loss on Available-for-Sale Securities to reflect the decrease in the value of Abernathy's investment. Unlike the unrealized gain account used for the trading security, this unrealized gain/loss account for available-for-sale securities is not included in the calculation of net income. Rather, it is reported on the balance sheet as an increase or decrease to equity. Specifically, it is reported as a component of Accumulated Other Comprehensive Income, a line item within the stockholders' equity section of the balance sheet. Note that the account can have either a debit or credit balance. A debit balance represents unrealized losses to date while a credit balance represents unrealized gains to date.

After both adjustments are made, the investment balances on the December 31 balance sheet would appear as follows:

Investments on December 31 Balance Sheet	
Current assets	
Trading securities	$ 64,300
Noncurrent assets	
Held-to-maturity securities	100,000
Available-for-sale securities	9,800

Recording the Sale or Maturity

The recording of the maturity or sale of an investment also depends on how the investment is classified. The following sections demonstrate how each classification is handled.

Held-to-Maturity Securities When a held-to-maturity security *matures*, a company must record the cash that is received at maturity and eliminate the investment account. When a held-to-maturity security is *sold*, a company must record the cash from the sale, eliminate the investment account, and record any difference as a gain or loss from the sale.

To illustrate a maturity, suppose that Abernathy holds the Decatur bonds until they mature. Abernathy will record the receipt of $100,000 as follows:

At maturity	Cash	100,000	
	Investment in Decatur Bonds		100,000
	(To record maturity of bonds)		

Assets	=	Liabilities	+	Equity
+100,000				
−100,000				

In this entry, Abernathy is simply increasing Cash and decreasing the investment account. Because Abernathy is exchanging one asset for another, total assets remain unchanged.

To illustrate a sale, suppose that Abernathy sells the Decatur bonds for $101,000 immediately after an interest payment. Abernathy will record the sale as follows:

At sale	Cash	101,000	
	Gain on Sale of Investment		1,000
	Investment in Decatur Bonds		100,000
	(To record sale of bonds)		

Assets	=	Liabilities	+	Equity
+101,000				+1,000
−100,000				

In this entry, Abernathy increases Cash for the amount received, eliminates the investment account, and increases Gain on Sale of Investment for the difference of $1,000.

Trading Securities When a trading security is sold, any cash received is recorded, the investment account is eliminated, and any gain or loss on the sale is recorded.

To illustrate, suppose that on February 15, 2013, Abernathy sells its investment in Eagle Company when the market value of the investment is $65,200. Abernathy would make the following entry to record the sale:

Feb. 15 2013	Cash	65,200	
	Investment in Eagle Company		64,300
	Gain on Sale of Investment		900
	(To record sale of investment at a gain)		

Assets	=	Liabilities	+	Equity
+65,200				+900
−64,300				

In this entry, Abernathy first increases Cash for the amount received from the sale. It then decreases Investment in Eagle Company by $64,300 since that was its balance on December 31. The difference between the cash received and the current account balance is the amount of gain realized on the sale. Therefore, Gain on Sale of Investment is increased by $900. As a result of this sale, both assets and equity increased $900.

Note in this example that Abernathy's total gain on the value of the investment was $5,200 (sales price – cost = $65,200 – $60,000 = $5,200). A portion of that gain ($4,300) was included in net income in the prior period when the investment was adjusted to its market value. The remainder of the gain ($900) was included in net income when the investment was sold. So, the $5,200 total gain was spread across two accounting periods.

Available-for-Sale Securities When an available-for-sale security is sold, any cash received is recorded, the investment and any existing unrealized gain or loss are eliminated, and any realized gain or loss on the sale is recorded.

To illustrate, suppose that Abernathy sells its investment in C & L Inc. for $9,700 on March 8, 2013. At the time of the sale, Abernathy would make the following entry:

Mar. 8 2013	Cash	9,700	
	Loss on Sale of Investment	300	
	Unrealized Gain/Loss on Available-for-Sale Securities		200
	Investment in C & L Inc.		9,800
	(To record sale of investment at a loss)		

Assets	=	Liabilities	+	Equity
+9,700				−300
−9,800				+200

In this entry, Abernathy increases Cash for the amount of cash received. Because the Investment in C & L Inc. account was adjusted to $9,800 on December 31, Abernathy decreases the account by $9,800 to eliminate it. Furthermore, the Unrealized Gain/Loss balance of $200 that was created on December 31 is also eliminated since Abernathy no longer has that unrealized loss. Finally, Abernathy records a realized loss on the investment of $300. This is the difference between the amount received from the sale and the original cost of the investment. This $300 loss is included in the calculation of net income along with other expenses and revenues.

HOME DEPOT ANALYSIS

Look at the Short-Term Investments paragraph in Home Depot's first note in Appendix C. How does Home Depot classify and report its investments?

Home Depot states that short-term investments are classified as available-for-sale securities. Therefore, they are reported at fair (or market) values.

EXERCISES

1. Investment Classifications LO1

Below is a list of the various investments of Baldy Corporation:

1. Shares of GM stock to be held indefinitely
2. State bonds that will be held until they mature
3. Corporate bonds that the company might or might not sell
4. 15-year Nike bonds that the company plans to sell quickly
5. Target common stock, which the company is actively trying to sell

Required

Identify each of the investments as held-to-maturity, available-for-sale, or trading securities.

2. Debt Security Investment LO1

On January 1, 2012, the Hackman Company purchases $300,000 of 8% bonds for face value. Hackman plans to hold the bonds until they mature on January 1, 2019. Interest is paid semiannually on June 30 and December 31. Hackman's year-end is December 31.

Required

a. How should Hackman classify its investment? Explain your answer.
b. Prepare all appropriate journal entries for 2012. Be sure to include any necessary adjusting entry at year-end.

3. Equity Security Investment LO1

On December 1, 2012, Wallace, Inc., purchases 500 shares of King Corporation common stock at $30 per share. Wallace plans to sell it at a profit as soon as it rises in value. On December 22, King declares a dividend of $1 per share to be paid on January 5, 2010. At December 31, 2012, King's stock was trading at $35 per share. Wallace sells the stock at $34 per share on January 15, 2013.

Required

a. How should Wallace classify its investment? Explain your answer.
b. Prepare all necessary journal entries from the purchase of the stock to its sale.
c. What is the effect of these transactions on the 2012 and 2013 income statements?

4. Equity Security Investment LO1

On January 31, 2012, the Coburn Company purchases 10,000 shares of Hughes Corporation common stock at $10 per share. Coburn plans to hold the stock for an extended period of time rather than place it in its active trading portfolio. At December 31, 2012, Hughes common stock is trading at $8 per share. On March 31, 2013, Coburn sells the stock for $90,000.

Required

a. How should Coburn classify its investment? Explain your answer.
b. Prepare all necessary journal entries from the purchase of the stock through to its sale.
c. What is the effect of these transactions on the 2012 and 2013 income statements?

5. Effect on Net Income LO1

The following is a list of possible events:

1. Trading securities appreciate in value over the course of the year.
2. Held-to-maturity securities are redeemed at maturity.
3. Available-for-sale securities are sold for less than their market value.
4. Available-for-sale securities appreciate in value during the current period.
5. Interest payments are received in the current year.
6. Trading securities are sold at a value greater than market value.

Required

Identify whether each item increases, decreases, or has no effect on net income for the current period.

PROBLEMS

6. Investment Entries LO1

Huang, Inc., enters into the following transactions during 2012:

Jan. 1	Purchased $100,000, 6%, 10-year corporate bonds at face value. The bonds pay interest annually on December 31. Huang plans to hold the bonds to maturity.
Mar. 31	Purchased 500 shares of Bubbles, Inc., common stock at $30 per share. Huang plans to hold the shares indefinitely.
Nov. 15	Purchased 300 shares of Libor, Inc., common stock at $45 per share. Huang plans to sell these shares in January.
Dec. 8	Received a dividend of $1 per share on the Libor, Inc., stock.
Dec. 31	Received interest payment on the corporate bonds purchased on January 1.
Dec. 31	Noted the following market values: Bubbles stock—$40 per share; Libor stock—$44 per share; corporate bonds—$98,000.

Required

a. Prepare all appropriate journal entries associated with Huang's investments during 2012, including any necessary adjustments at year-end.
b. Determine the net effect on 2012 net income of all investment activity.

ACCT

Appendix B

Time Value of Money

Introduction

When decisions are affected by cash flows that are paid or received in different time periods, it is necessary to adjust those cash flows for the time value of money (TVM). Because of our ability to earn interest on money invested, we would prefer to receive \$1 today rather than a year from now. Likewise, we would prefer to pay \$1 a year from now rather than today. A common technique used to adjust cash flows received or paid in different time periods is to discount those cash flows by finding their present value. The **present value (PV)** of cash flows is the amount of future cash flows discounted to their equivalent worth today. To fully understand the calculations involved in finding the present value of future cash flows, it is necessary to step back and examine the nature of interest and the calculation of interest received and paid. Interest is simply a payment made to use someone else's money. When you invest money in a bank account, the bank pays you interest for the use of your money for a period of time. If you invest \$100 and the bank pays you \$106 at the end of the year, it is clear that you earned \$6 of interest on your money (and 6 percent interest for the year).

Future Value

Mathematically, the relationship between your initial investment (present value), the amount in the bank at the end of the year (future value), and the interest rate (r) is as follows:

$$FV_{(\text{Year 1})} = PV(1 + r)$$

In our example, $FV_{(\text{Year 1})} = 100(1 + 0.06) = \$106$. If you leave your money in the bank for a second year, what happens? Will you earn an additional \$6 of interest? It depends on whether the bank pays you simple interest or compound interest. **Simple interest** is interest on the invested amount only, whereas **compound interest** is interest on the invested amount plus interest on previous interest earned but not withdrawn. Simple interest is sometimes computed on short-term investments and debts (that is, those that are shorter than six months to a year). Compound interest is typically computed for financial arrangements longer than one year. We will assume that interest is compounded in all examples in this book. Extending the future-value formula to find the amount we have in the bank in two years gives us the following formula:

$$FV_{(\text{Year 2})} = PV(1 + r)(1 + r)$$

or

$$FV_{(\text{Year 2})} = PV(1 + r)^2$$

In our example, $FV_{(\text{Year 2})} = 100(1 + 0.06)^2$, or \$112.36. We earned \$6.36 of interest in Year 2—\$6 on our original \$100 investment and \$0.36 on the \$6 of interest earned but not withdrawn in Year 1 (\$6 × 0.06).

In this example, we have assumed that compounding is on an annual basis. Compounding can also be calculated semiannually, quarterly, monthly, daily, or even continually. Go back to our original \$100 investment in the bank. If the bank pays 6 percent interest compounded semiannually instead of annually, we would have \$106.09 after one year. Note that the interest rate is typically expressed as a percentage rate per year. We are

Present value (PV) The amount of future cash flows discounted to their equivalent worth today.

Simple interest Interest on the invested amount only.

Compound interest Interest on the invested amount plus interest on previous interest earned but not withdrawn.

Exhibit B-1 The Impact of More Frequent Compounding on the Future Value of $100

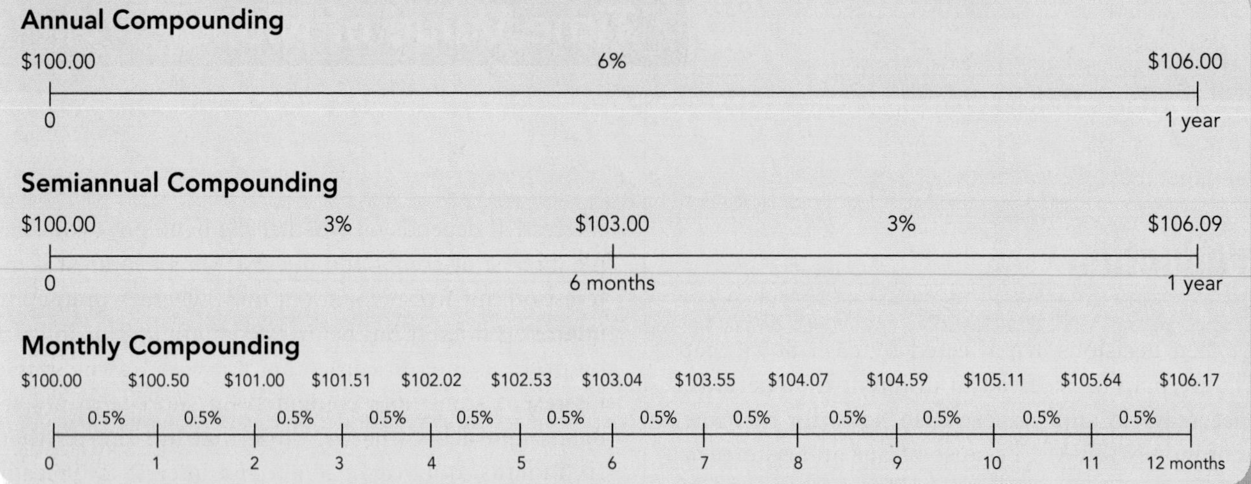

really earning 3 percent for each semiannual period, not 6 percent. It is usually easier to visualize the concept of interest rate compounding graphically, with the help of time lines. Exhibit B-1 graphically demonstrates the impact of annual, semiannual, and monthly compounding of the 6 percent annual rate on our original $100 investment.

Mathematically, our formula for future value can once again be modified slightly to account for interest rates compounded at different intervals. $FV_{(n \text{ periods in the future})} = PV(1 + r)^n$, where n is the number of compounding periods per year multiplied by the number of years, and r is the annual interest rate divided by the number of compounding periods per year. Before the advent of handheld calculators and computers, tables were developed to simplify the calculation of FV by providing values for $(1 + r)^n$ for several combinations of n and r. These tables are still commonly used, and an example is provided in Exhibit B-2. The factors in Exhibit B-2 are commonly referred to as cumulative factors (CF) and are simply calculations of $(1 + r)^n$ for various values of n and r.

Using this new terminology, the future value formula is simply

$$FV_{(n \text{ periods in the future})} = PV(CF_{n,r})$$

Exhibit B-2 Future Value of $1

n/r	0.5%	1%	2%	3%	4%	5%	6%	7%	8%	10%	12%
1	1.0050	1.0100	1.0200	1.0300	1.0400	1.0500	1.0600	1.0700	1.0800	1.1000	1.1200
2	1.0100	1.0201	1.0404	1.0609	1.0816	1.1025	1.1236	1.1449	1.1664	1.2100	1.2544
3	1.0151	1.0303	1.0612	1.0927	1.1249	1.1576	1.1910	1.2250	1.2597	1.3310	1.4049
4	1.0202	1.0406	1.0824	1.1255	1.1699	1.2155	1.2625	1.3108	1.3605	1.4641	1.5735
5	1.0253	1.0510	1.1041	1.1593	1.2167	1.2763	1.3382	1.4026	1.4693	1.6105	1.7623
6	1.0304	1.0615	1.1262	1.1941	1.2653	1.3401	1.4185	1.5007	1.5869	1.7716	1.9738
7	1.0355	1.0721	1.1487	1.2299	1.3159	1.4071	1.5036	1.6058	1.7138	1.9487	2.2107
8	1.0407	1.0829	1.1717	1.2668	1.3686	1.4775	1.5938	1.7182	1.8509	2.1436	2.4760
9	1.0459	1.0937	1.1951	1.3048	1.4233	1.5513	1.6895	1.8385	1.9990	2.3579	2.7731
10	1.0511	1.1046	1.2190	1.3439	1.4802	1.6289	1.7908	1.9672	2.1589	2.5937	3.1058
11	1.0564	1.1157	1.2434	1.3842	1.5395	1.7103	1.8983	2.1049	2.3316	2.8531	3.4785
12	1.0617	1.1268	1.2682	1.4258	1.6010	1.7959	2.0122	2.2522	2.5182	3.1384	3.8960
24	1.1272	1.2697	1.6084	2.0328	2.5633	3.2251	4.0489	5.0724	6.3412	9.8497	15.1786
36	1.1967	1.4308	2.0399	2.8983	4.1039	5.7918	8.1473	11.4239	15.9682	30.9127	59.1356
48	1.2705	1.6122	2.5871	4.1323	6.5705	10.4013	16.3939	25.7289	40.2106	97.0172	230.3908

With 6 percent annual compounding, our \$100 investment grows to

$$\$100(CF_{1,6\%}) = \$100(1.060) = \$106.00$$

With 6 percent semiannual compounding,

$$\$100(CF_{2,3\%}) = \$100(1.0609) = \$106.09$$

With 6 percent monthly compounding,

$$\$100(CF_{12,.5\%}) = \$100(1.0617) = \$106.17$$

Most financial calculators will compute future value after the user inputs data for present value, the annual interest rate, the number of compounding periods per year, and the number of years. For example, using a business calculator to compute the future value of \$100.00 with 6 percent annual compounding requires the following steps:

Keys	Display	Description
1 [P/YR]	1.00	Sets compounding periods per year to 1 because interest is compounded annually
100 [±] [PV]	−100.00	Stores the present value as a negative number
6.0 [I/YR]	6.0	Stores the annual interest rate
1 [N]	1	Sets the number of years or compounding periods to 1
[FV]	106.00	Calculates the future value

Calculating the future value of \$100 with 6 percent monthly compounding simply requires changing both the compounding periods per year (*P/YR*) and number of compounding periods (*N*) to 12.

Keys	Display	Description
12 [P/YR]	12	Sets compounding periods per year to 12
12 [N]	12	Sets the number of compounding periods to 12
[FV]	106.17	Calculates the future value

Exhibit B-3 Finding the Future Value Using the FV Function in Excel

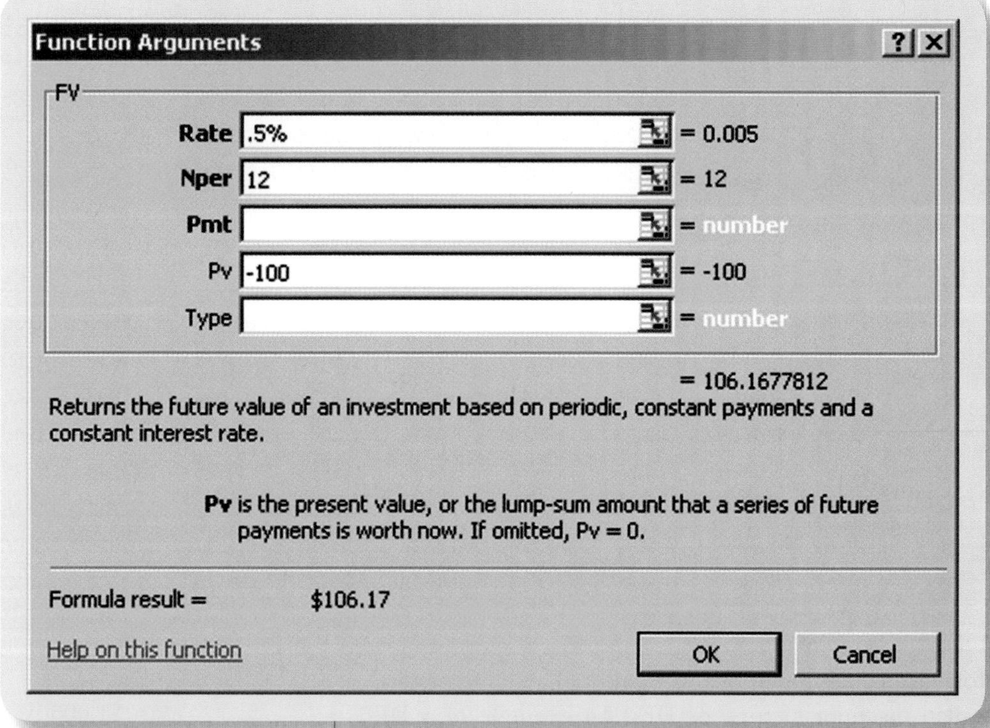

Likewise, many spreadsheet programs have built-in functions (formulas) that calculate future value. The Excel function called FV simply requires input of an interest rate (Rate), number of compounding periods (Nper), and present value (Pv) in the following format: =FV(Rate, Nper, Pmt, Pv, Type).[1] Entries for Pmt and Type are not applicable to simple future-value problems. To calculate the future value of \$100 in one year at 6 percent interest compounded monthly, enter =FV(.5%,12,−100). Excel returns a value of \$106.17 (see Exhibit B-3).

Present Value

A present value formula can be derived directly from the future value formula. If

$$FV_{(n \text{ periods in the future})} = PV(1 + r)^n$$

then

$$PV = \frac{FV}{(1 + r)^n} \quad \text{or} \quad PV = FV\left(\frac{1}{(1 + r)^n}\right)$$

Just as a cumulative factor table was developed to calculate $(1 + r)^n$, present value tables calculate $1 \div (1 + r)^n$

[1]Built-in functions can be accessed in Microsoft Excel by clicking on the Paste function icon, clicking on *financial*, and then scrolling down to the desired function.

Exhibit B-4 Present Value of $1

n/r	0.5%	1%	2%	3%	4%	5%	6%	7%	8%	10%	12%
1	0.9950	0.9901	0.9804	0.9709	0.9615	0.9524	0.9434	0.9346	0.9259	0.9091	0.8929
2	0.9901	0.9803	0.9612	0.9426	0.9246	0.9070	0.8900	0.8734	0.8573	0.8264	0.7972
3	0.9851	0.9706	0.9423	0.9151	0.8890	0.8638	0.8396	0.8163	0.7938	0.7513	0.7118
4	0.9802	0.9610	0.9238	0.8885	0.8548	0.8227	0.7921	0.7629	0.7350	0.6830	0.6355
5	0.9754	0.9515	0.9057	0.8626	0.8219	0.7835	0.7473	0.7130	0.6806	0.6209	0.5674
6	0.9705	0.9420	0.8880	0.8375	0.7903	0.7462	0.7050	0.6663	0.6302	0.5645	0.5066
7	0.9657	0.9327	0.8706	0.8131	0.7599	0.7107	0.6651	0.6227	0.5835	0.5132	0.4523
8	0.9609	0.9235	0.8535	0.7894	0.7307	0.6768	0.6274	0.5820	0.5403	0.4665	0.4039
9	0.9561	0.9143	0.8368	0.7664	0.7026	0.6446	0.5919	0.5439	0.5002	0.4241	0.3606
10	0.9513	0.9053	0.8203	0.7441	0.6756	0.6139	0.5584	0.5083	0.4632	0.3855	0.3220
11	0.9466	0.8963	0.8043	0.7224	0.6496	0.5847	0.5268	0.4751	0.4289	0.3505	0.2875
12	0.9419	0.8874	0.7885	0.7014	0.6246	0.5568	0.4970	0.4440	0.3971	0.3186	0.2567
24	0.8872	0.7876	0.6217	0.4919	0.3901	0.3101	0.2470	0.1971	0.1577	0.1015	0.0659
36	0.8356	0.6989	0.4902	0.3450	0.2437	0.1727	0.1227	0.0875	0.0626	0.0323	0.0169
48	0.7871	0.6203	0.3865	0.2420	0.1522	0.0961	0.0610	0.0389	0.0249	0.0103	0.0043

for various combinations of *n* and *r*. These factors are called discount factors, or DFs. An example of a DF table is provided in Exhibit B-4. Our PV formula can now be rewritten as follows:

$$PV = FV(DF_{n,r})$$

Now we are ready to calculate the present value of a future cash flow. For example, how much must be invested today at 8 percent compounded annually to have $1,000 in two years? Mathematically,

$$PV = \$1{,}000\left(\frac{1}{(1 \times 0.08)^2}\right) = \$857.34$$

or using the DF table,

$$PV = \$1{,}000(DF_{2,.08}) = \$1{,}000(0.8573) = \$857.30 \text{ (rounded)}$$

Once again, the frequency of compounding affects our calculation. Just as more frequent compounding *increases* future values, increasing the frequency of compounding decreases present values. This is demonstrated in Exhibit B-5 for annual, semiannual, and quarterly compounding.

Exhibit B-5 The Impact of More Frequent Compounding on the Present Value of $1,000

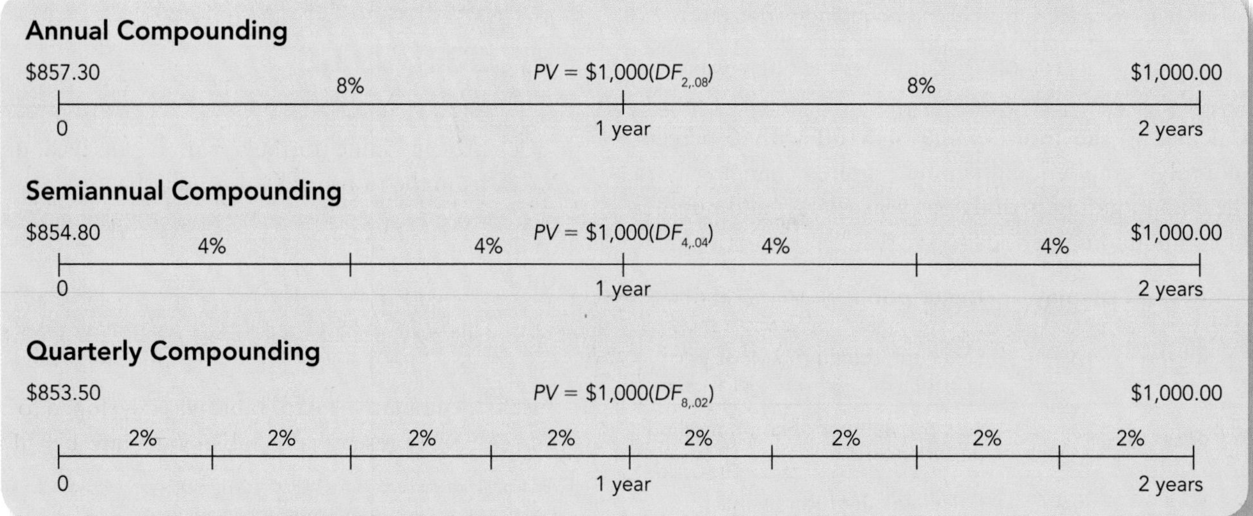

Using a business calculator to compute present value is similar to computing future value. For example, the present value of $1,000 received or paid in two years at 8 percent compounded quarterly requires the following steps:

Keys	Display	Description
4 [P/YR]	4.00	Sets the compounding periods per year to 4
1,000 [FV]	1000.00	Stores the future value as a positive number
8.0 [I/YR]	8.0	Stores the annual interest rate
8 [N]	8.0	Sets the number of compounding periods to 8
[PV]	-853.49	Calculates the present value

In Microsoft Excel, the built-in function is called PV and requires input of the applicable interest rate (Rate), number of compounding periods (Nper), and future value (Fv) in the following format: =PV(Rate, Nper, Pmt, Fv, Type). In the previous example, entering =PV(2%,8,−1000) returns a value of $853.49. Note once again that Pmt and Type are left blank in simple present value problems, as they were in future value calculations (see Exhibit B-6).

When *FV* and *PV* are known, either formula can be used to calculate one of the other variables in the equations (n or r). For example, if you know that your $100 bank deposit is worth $200 in six years, what rate of interest compounded annually did you earn? Using the mathematical present value formula,

$$PV = FV\left(\frac{1}{(1 + r)^n}\right) \quad \text{or} \quad \$100 = \$200\left(\frac{1}{(1 + r)^6}\right)$$

Simplifying by dividing each side by $100, $1 = 2 \div (1 + r)^6$, and multiplying each side by $(1 + r)^6$, the equation is simplified to $(1 + r)^6 = 2$. The value of r can be calculated by using a financial calculator or mathematically by using logarithmic functions.[2] When using a business calculator, the following steps are typical:

Keys	Display	Description
1 [P/YR]	1.00	Sets compounding periods per year to 1
200 [FV]	200	Stores the future value
100 [±] [PV]	-100	Stores the present value as a negative number
2 [N]	2.0	Sets the number of compounding periods to 2
[I/YR]	0.122462	Calculates the annual interest rate

The tables can also be used to solve for n and r. Using our table formula, $PV = FV(DF_{n,r})$, if $PV = 100$ and $FV = 200$, DF must be equal to 0.5. If we know that n is equal to 6, we can simply move across the table until we find a factor close to 0.5. The factor at 12 percent is 0.5066. If we examine the factors at both 10 percent (0.5645) and 14 percent (0.456), we can infer that the actual interest rate will be slightly higher than 12 percent. Our logarithmic calculation is 12.2462 percent. In Microsoft Excel, the RATE function requires input of Nper, Pv, and Fv in the following format:

Exhibit B-6 Finding the Present Value Using the PV Function in Excel

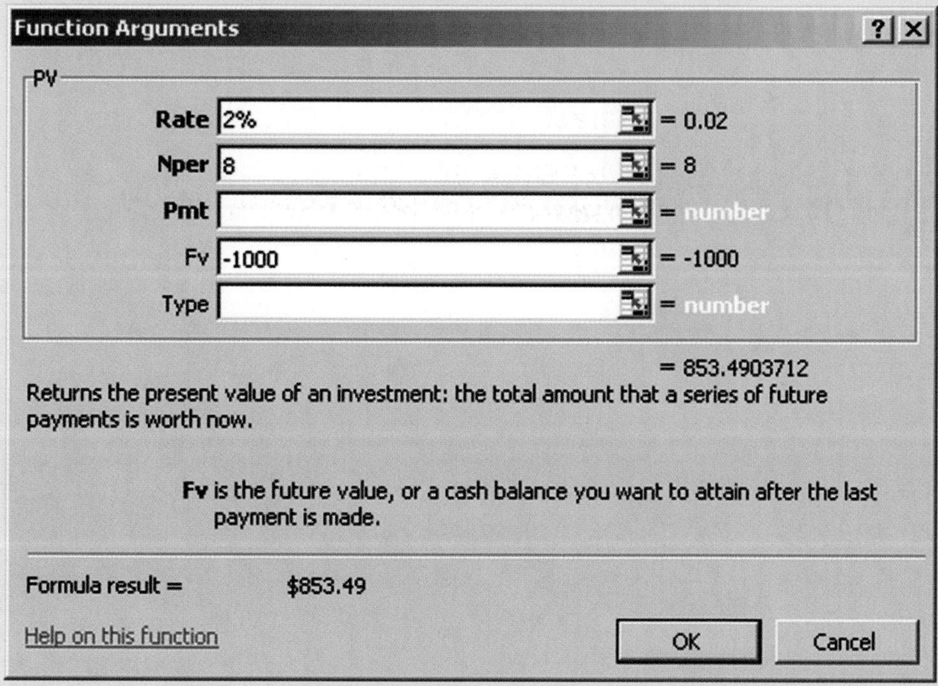

[2]In logarithmic form, $(1 + r)^6 = 2$ can be rewritten as $\log(1 + r)^6 = \log 2$, or $6 \log(1 + r) = \log 2$. Therefore, $\log(1 + r) = \log 2 \div 6$, which simplifies to $\log(1 + r) = 0.1155245$. Switching back to the equivalent exponential form, $e0.1155245 = (1 + r)$, $(1 + r) = 1.122462$, and $r = 0.122462$ (12.2462%).

Exhibit B-7 Finding the Interest Rate Using the RATE Function in Excel

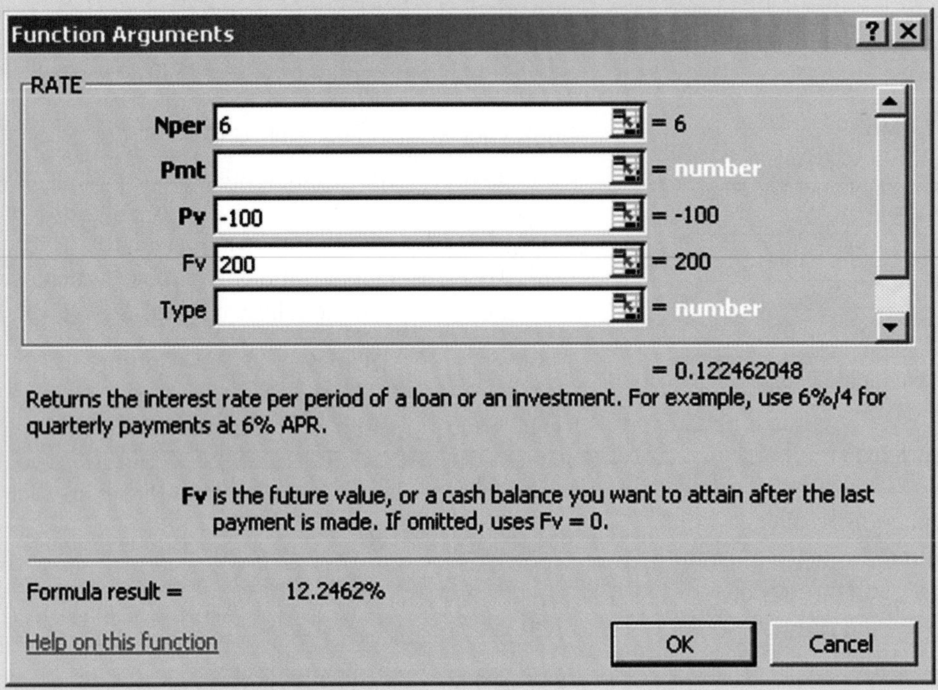

=RATE(Nper, Pmt, Pv, Fv, Type, Guess). Because Excel uses an iterative trial-and-error method to calculate the interest rate, Guess provides a starting point. It is generally not necessary but may be required in complicated problems. Entering =RATE(6,−100,200) returns an interest rate of 12.2462 percent (see Exhibit B-7).

The calculation of n is done in a similar fashion. If we know that our investment earns 12 percent but do not know how long it will take for our \$100 to grow to \$200, mathematically, we have the following:

$$PV = FV\left(\frac{1}{(1 + r)^n}\right)$$

or

$$\$100 = \$200\left(\frac{1}{(1 + 0.12)^n}\right)$$

Solving the equation by using logarithms or a financial calculator gives us an n of 6.116 years.[3] Using the DF formula, DF must again be equal to 0.5. If r is known to be 12 percent, we simply move down the 12 percent column until we find a DF close to 0.5. Not surprisingly, we find a factor of 0.5066 for an n of 6. Examining the factors for an n of 5(0.5674) and 7(0.4523), we can infer that the actual time will be something slightly greater than 6 years. The NPER function in Microsoft Excel requires input of Rate, Pmt, Pv, Fv, and Type in the following format: =NPER(12%,−100, 200), and returns a value of 6.116 years. Note that Pv is entered as a negative amount and that Pmt and Type are not necessary, as this is essentially a present value problem (see Exhibit B-8).

Exhibit B-8 Finding the Number of Periods Using the NPER Function in Excel

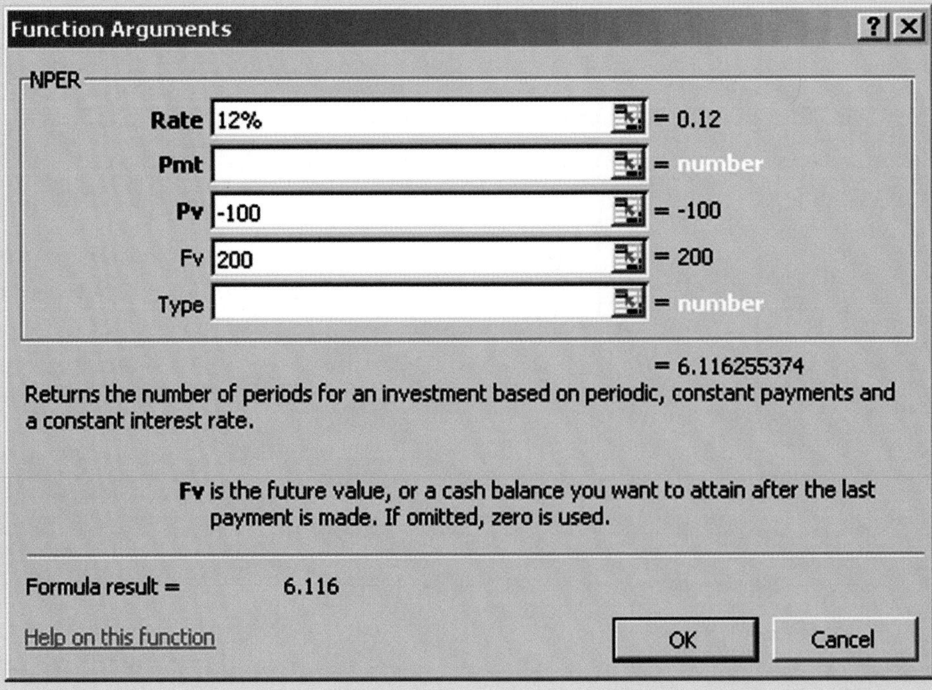

[3]Using a business calculator, simply input 1 P/YR, 200 FV, 100 PV, and 12 I/YR and solve for n. In logarithmic form, $(1 + 0.12)^n = 2$ can be rewritten as $\log(1 + 0.12)^n = \log 2$, or $n \log 1.12 = \log 2$. Therefore, $n = (\log 2) \div (\log 1.12) = 6.116$.

Annuities

An **annuity** is a series of cash flows of equal amount paid or received at regular intervals.[4] Common examples include mortgage and loan payments. The present value of an ordinary annuity (PVA) is the amount invested or borrowed today that will provide for a series of withdrawals or payments of equal amount for a set number of periods. Conceptually, the present value of an annuity is simply the sum of the present values of each withdrawal or payment. For example, the present value of an annuity of \$100 paid at the end of each of the next four years at an interest rate of 10 percent looks like this:

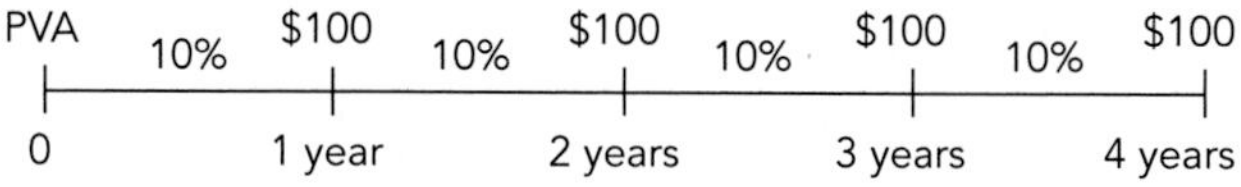

Although cumbersome, the present value of an annuity can be calculated by finding the present value of each \$100 payment, using the present value table on page B-4 (see Exhibit B-4).

$$PVA = \$100(DF_{1,.10}) + \$100(DF_{2,.10}) + \$100(DF_{3,.10}) + \$100(DF_{4,.10})$$

$$= \$100(0.9091) + \$100(0.8264) + \$100(0.7513) + \$100(0.6830)$$

$$= \$316.98$$

[4]An ordinary annuity is paid or received at the end of each period, whereas an annuity due is paid or received at the beginning of each period. In examples throughout this book, we will assume the annuity is ordinary.

The mathematical formula for PVA can be derived from the formula for PV and is equal to:

$$PVA_{n,r} = R\left(\frac{1 - \dfrac{1}{(1+r)^n}}{r}\right)$$

where R refers to the periodic payment or withdrawal (commonly called a rent). Calculated values for various combinations of n and r are provided in Exhibit B-9.

Exhibit B-9 Present Value of an Ordinary Annuity

n/r	0.50%	1%	2%	3%	4%	5%	6%	7%	8%	10%	12%
1	0.9950	0.9901	0.9804	0.9709	0.9615	0.9524	0.9434	0.9346	0.9259	0.9091	0.8929
2	1.9851	1.9704	1.9416	1.9135	1.8861	1.8594	1.8334	1.8080	1.7833	1.7355	1.6901
3	2.9702	2.9410	2.8839	2.8286	2.7751	2.7232	2.6730	2.6243	2.5771	2.4869	2.4018
4	3.9505	3.9020	3.8077	3.7171	3.6299	3.5460	3.4651	3.3872	3.3121	3.1699	3.0373
5	4.9259	4.8534	4.7135	4.5797	4.4518	4.3295	4.2124	4.1002	3.9927	3.7908	3.6048
6	5.8964	5.7955	5.6014	5.4172	5.2421	5.0757	4.9173	4.7665	4.6229	4.3553	4.1114
7	6.8621	6.7282	6.4720	6.2303	6.0021	5.7864	5.5824	5.3893	5.2064	4.8684	4.5638
8	7.8230	7.6517	7.3255	7.0197	6.7327	6.4632	6.2098	5.9713	5.7466	5.3349	4.9676
9	8.7791	8.5660	8.1622	7.7861	7.4353	7.1078	6.8017	6.5152	6.2469	5.7590	5.3282
10	9.7304	9.4713	8.9826	8.5302	8.1109	7.7217	7.3601	7.0236	6.7101	6.1446	5.6502
11	10.6770	10.3676	9.7868	9.2526	8.7605	8.3064	7.8869	7.4987	7.1390	6.4951	5.9377
12	11.6189	11.2551	10.5753	9.9540	9.3851	8.8633	8.3838	7.9427	7.5361	6.8137	6.1944
24	22.5629	21.2434	18.9139	16.9355	15.2470	13.7986	12.5504	11.4693	10.5288	8.9847	7.7843
36	32.8710	30.1075	25.4888	21.8323	18.9083	16.5469	14.6210	13.0352	11.7172	9.6765	8.1924
48	42.5803	37.9740	30.6731	25.2667	21.1951	18.0772	15.6500	13.7305	12.1891	9.8969	8.2972

The PVA formula can therefore be rewritten as follows:

$$PVA = R(DFA_{n,r})$$

As previously discussed, common examples of annuities are mortgages and loans. For example, say you are thinking about buying a new car. Your bank offers to loan you money at a special 6 percent rate compounded monthly for a 24-month term. If the maximum monthly payment you can afford is \$399, how large a car loan can you get? In other words, what is the present value of a \$399 annuity paid at the end of each of the next 24 months, assuming an interest rate of 6 percent compounded monthly?

Annuity A series of cash flows of equal amount paid or received at regular intervals.

Using a time line, the problem looks like this:

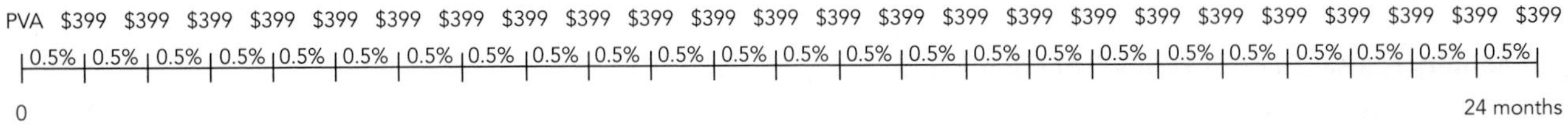

Mathematically,

$$PVA_{24,.005} = 399\left(\frac{1 - \dfrac{1}{(1 + 0.5)^{24}}}{0.005}\right)$$

Using the DFA table,

$$PVA_{24,.005} = \$399(DFA_{24,.005}) = \$399(22.5629) = \$9{,}002.60 \text{ (rounded)}$$

The following steps are common when using a business calculator:

Keys	Display	Description
12 [P/YR]	12.00	Set periods per year
2×12 [N]	24.00	Stores number of periods in loan
0 [FV]	0	Stores the amount left to pay after 2 years
6 [I/YR]	6	Stores interest rate
399 [±] [PMT]	-399.00	Stores desired payment as a negative number
[PV]	9,002.58	Calculates the loan you can afford with a $399 per month payment

In Microsoft Excel, the PV function is used to calculate the present value of an annuity, with additional entries for the payment amount (Pmt) and type of annuity (Type). The payment is entered as a negative number, and the annuity type is 0 for ordinary and 1 for an annuity due. The format is therefore PV(Rate, Nper, Pmt, Fv, Type). Entering =PV(.5%,24,−399,0,0) returns a value of $9,002.58 (see Exhibit B-10).

The PVA formula can also be used to calculate *R*, *r*, and *n* if the other variables are known. This is most easily accomplished using the DFA table or using a financial calculator. If the car you want to buy costs $20,000 and you can afford a $3,000 down payment (your loan balance is $17,000), how much will your 36 monthly payments be, assuming that the bank charges you 6 percent interest compounded monthly?

Using the DFA table,

$$PVA_{36,.005} = R(DFA_{36,.005})$$
$$\$17{,}000 = R(32.871)$$
$$R = \$517.17$$

The following steps are common when using a business calculator:

Keys	Display	Description
12 [P/YR]	12.00	Set periods per year
3×12 [N]	36.00	Stores number of periods in loan
0 [FV]	0	Stores the amount left to pay after 3 years
6 [I/YR]	6	Stores interest rate
17,000 [PV]	17,000	Stores amount borrowed
[PMT]	-517.17	Calculates the monthly payment

In Microsoft Excel, the calculation is simply =PMT (.005,36,−17000,0,0) (see Exhibit B-11).

In a similar fashion, assume that a used-car dealer offers you a "special deal" in which you can borrow $12,000 with low monthly payments of $350 per month for 48 months. What rate of interest are you being charged in this case? Using the DFA table,

$$PVA_{48,.??} = \$350(DFA_{48,.??})$$
$$\$12{,}000 = 350(DFA_{48,.??})$$
$$DFA_{48,.??} = 34.2857$$

Looking at the row for an *n* of 48, we see that a DFA of 34.2857 is about halfway between an *r* of 1 percent and *r* of 2 percent (closer to 1 percent), which means that you are being charged an annual rate of almost 18 percent (1.5% × 12)—not such a good deal after all! Using a business calculator, observe the following:

Keys	Display	Description
12 [P/YR]	12.00	Set periods per year
4×12 [N]	48.00	Stores number of periods in loan
0 [FV]	0	Stores the amount left to pay after 4 years
12,000 [PV]	12,000	Stores amount borrowed
350 [±] [PMT]	-350	Stores the monthly payment
[I/YR]	17.60	Calculates the annual interest rate

Exhibit B-10 Finding the Present Value of an Annuity Using the PV Function in Excel

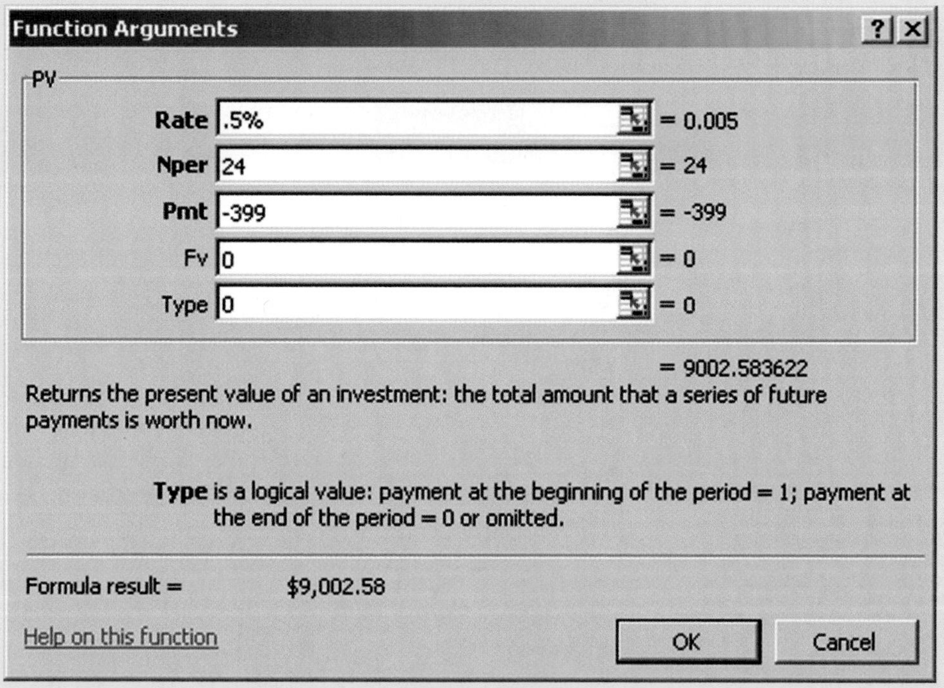

Exhibit B-11 Finding the Payment Using the PMT Function in Excel

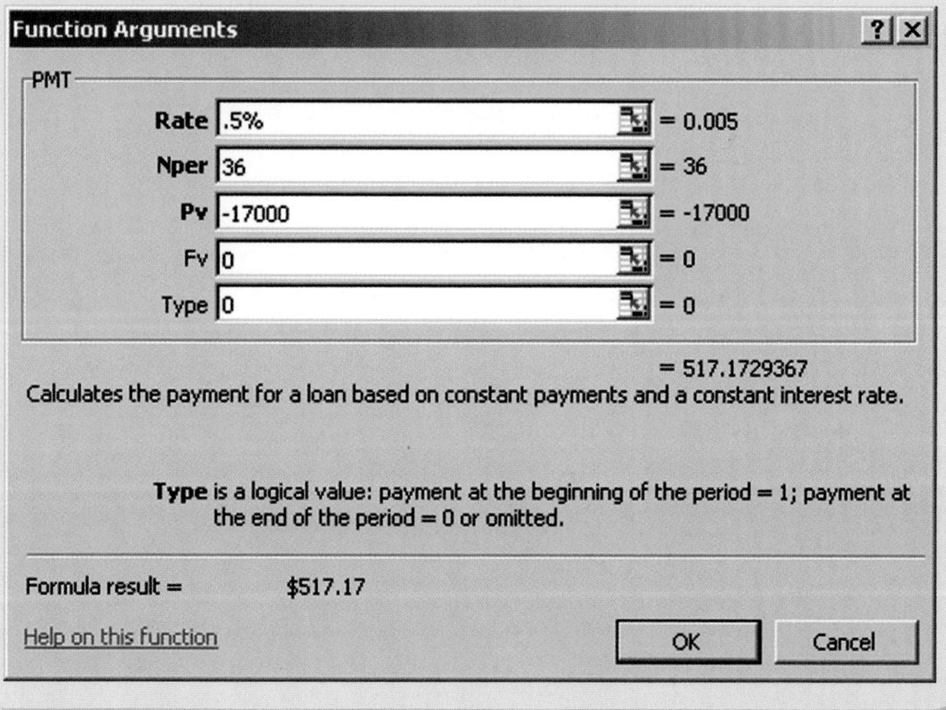

In Excel, =RATE(48, −350,12,000,0) generates a monthly rate of 1.4667 percent and an annual rate of 17.60 percent. The use of the RATE function requires that the payments are the same each period. Excel's IRR function is more flexible, allowing different payments. However, each payment has to be entered separately. For example, if the car is purchased for $17,000 with annual payments of $4,000, $5,000, $6,000, and $7,000 at the end of each of the next four years, the interest rate charged on the car loan can be calculated by using the IRR function (see Exhibit B-12).

Exhibit B-12 Finding the Interest Rate Using the IRR

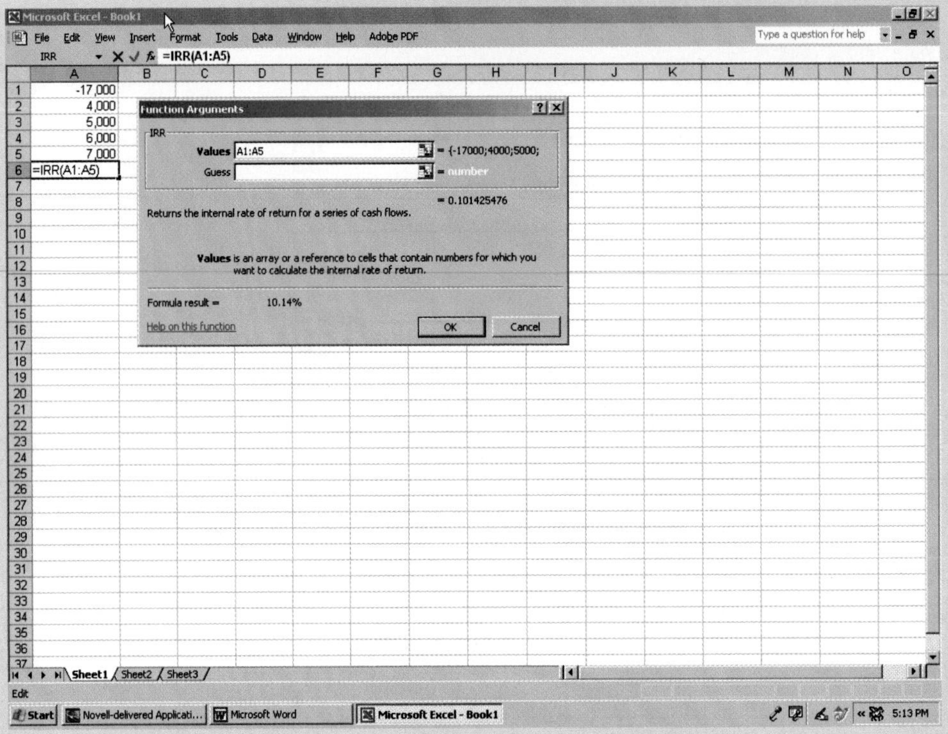

ACCT

Appendix C

Home Depot 2010 Annual Report (Excerpted)

Item 8. Financial Statements and Supplementary Data.

Management's Responsibility for Financial Statements

The financial statements presented in this Annual Report have been prepared with integrity and objectivity and are the responsibility of the management of The Home Depot, Inc. These financial statements have been prepared in conformity with U.S. generally accepted accounting principles and properly reflect certain estimates and judgments based upon the best available information.

The financial statements of the Company have been audited by KPMG LLP, an independent registered public accounting firm. Their accompanying report is based upon an audit conducted in accordance with the standards of the Public Company Accounting Oversight Board (United States).

The Audit Committee of the Board of Directors, consisting solely of independent directors, meets five times a year with the independent registered public accounting firm, the internal auditors and representatives of management to discuss auditing and financial reporting matters. In addition, a telephonic meeting is held prior to each quarterly earnings release. The Audit Committee retains the independent registered public accounting firm and regularly reviews the internal accounting controls, the activities of the independent registered public accounting firm and internal auditors and the financial condition of the Company. Both the Company's independent registered public accounting firm and the internal auditors have free access to the Audit Committee.

Management's Report on Internal Control over Financial Reporting

Our management is responsible for establishing and maintaining adequate internal control over financial reporting, as such term is defined in Rule 13a-15(f) promulgated under the Securities Exchange Act of 1934, as amended (the "Exchange Act"). Under the supervision and with the participation of our management, including our Chief Executive Officer and Chief Financial Officer, we conducted an evaluation of the effectiveness of our internal control over financial reporting as of January 30, 2011 based on the framework in *Internal Control – Integrated Framework* issued by the Committee of Sponsoring Organizations of the Treadway Commission (COSO). Based on our evaluation, our management concluded that our internal control over financial reporting was effective as of January 30, 2011 in providing reasonable assurance regarding the reliability of financial reporting and the preparation of financial statements for external purposes in accordance with U.S. generally accepted accounting principles. The effectiveness of our internal control over financial reporting as of January 30, 2011 has been audited by KPMG LLP, an independent registered public accounting firm, as stated in their report which is included on page 30 in this Form 10-K.

/s/ FRANCIS S. BLAKE

Francis S. Blake
Chairman &
Chief Executive Officer

/s/ CAROL B. TOMÉ

Carol B. Tomé
Chief Financial Officer &
Executive Vice President – Corporate Services

Report of Independent Registered Public Accounting Firm

The Board of Directors and Stockholders
The Home Depot, Inc.:

We have audited The Home Depot Inc.'s internal control over financial reporting as of January 30, 2011, based on criteria established in *Internal Control – Integrated Framework* issued by the Committee of Sponsoring Organizations of the Treadway Commission (COSO). The Home Depot Inc.'s management is responsible for maintaining effective internal control over financial reporting and for its assessment of the effectiveness of internal control over financial reporting, included in the accompanying Management's Report on Internal Control Over Financial Reporting. Our responsibility is to express an opinion on the Company's internal control over financial reporting based on our audit.

We conducted our audit in accordance with the standards of the Public Company Accounting Oversight Board (United States). Those standards require that we plan and perform the audit to obtain reasonable assurance about whether effective internal control over financial reporting was maintained in all material respects. Our audit included obtaining an understanding of internal control over financial reporting, assessing the risk that a material weakness exists, and testing and evaluating the design and operating effectiveness of internal control based on the assessed risk. Our audit also included performing such other procedures as we considered necessary in the circumstances. We believe that our audit provides a reasonable basis for our opinion.

A company's internal control over financial reporting is a process designed to provide reasonable assurance regarding the reliability of financial reporting and the preparation of financial statements for external purposes in accordance with generally accepted accounting principles. A company's internal control over financial reporting includes those policies and procedures that (1) pertain to the maintenance of records that, in reasonable detail, accurately and fairly reflect the transactions and dispositions of the assets of the company; (2) provide reasonable assurance that transactions are recorded as necessary to permit preparation of financial statements in accordance with generally accepted accounting principles, and that receipts and expenditures of the company are being made only in accordance with authorizations of management and directors of the company; and (3) provide reasonable assurance regarding prevention or timely detection of unauthorized acquisition, use, or disposition of the company's assets that could have a material effect on the financial statements.

Because of its inherent limitations, internal control over financial reporting may not prevent or detect misstatements. Also, projections of any evaluation of effectiveness to future periods are subject to the risk that controls may become inadequate because of changes in conditions, or that the degree of compliance with the policies or procedures may deteriorate.

In our opinion, The Home Depot, Inc. maintained, in all material respects, effective internal control over financial reporting as of January 30, 2011, based on criteria established in *Internal Control – Integrated Framework* issued by the Committee of Sponsoring Organizations of the Treadway Commission.

We also have audited, in accordance with the standards of the Public Company Accounting Oversight Board (United States), the Consolidated Balance Sheets of The Home Depot, Inc. and subsidiaries as of January 30, 2011 and January 31, 2010, and the related Consolidated Statements of Earnings, Stockholders' Equity and Comprehensive Income, and Cash Flows for each of the fiscal years in the three-year period ended January 30, 2011, and our report dated March 24, 2011 expressed an unqualified opinion on those consolidated financial statements.

/s/ KPMG LLP

Atlanta, Georgia
March 24, 2011

Report of Independent Registered Public Accounting Firm

The Board of Directors and Stockholders
The Home Depot, Inc.:

We have audited the accompanying Consolidated Balance Sheets of The Home Depot, Inc. and subsidiaries as of January 30, 2011 and January 31, 2010, and the related Consolidated Statements of Earnings, Stockholders' Equity and Comprehensive Income, and Cash Flows for each of the fiscal years in the three-year period ended January 30, 2011. These Consolidated Financial Statements are the responsibility of the Company's management. Our responsibility is to express an opinion on these Consolidated Financial Statements based on our audits.

We conducted our audits in accordance with the standards of the Public Company Accounting Oversight Board (United States). Those standards require that we plan and perform the audit to obtain reasonable assurance about whether the financial statements are free of material misstatement. An audit includes examining, on a test basis, evidence supporting the amounts and disclosures in the financial statements. An audit also includes assessing the accounting principles used and significant estimates made by management, as well as evaluating the overall financial statement presentation. We believe that our audits provide a reasonable basis for our opinion.

In our opinion, the Consolidated Financial Statements referred to above present fairly, in all material respects, the financial position of The Home Depot, Inc. and subsidiaries as of January 30, 2011 and January 31, 2010, and the results of their operations and their cash flows for each of the fiscal years in the three-year period ended January 30, 2011, in conformity with U.S. generally accepted accounting principles.

We also have audited, in accordance with the standards of the Public Company Accounting Oversight Board (United States), The Home Depot, Inc.'s internal control over financial reporting as of January 30, 2011, based on criteria established in *Internal Control – Integrated Framework* issued by the Committee of Sponsoring Organizations of the Treadway Commission (COSO), and our report dated March 24, 2011 expressed an unqualified opinion on the effectiveness of the Company's internal control over financial reporting.

/s/ KPMG LLP

Atlanta, Georgia
March 24, 2011

THE HOME DEPOT, INC. AND SUBSIDIARIES
CONSOLIDATED STATEMENTS OF EARNINGS

amounts in millions, except per share data	Fiscal Year Ended[1] January 30, 2011	January 31, 2010	February 1, 2009
NET SALES	**$67,997**	$66,176	$71,288
Cost of Sales	**44,693**	43,764	47,298
GROSS PROFIT	**23,304**	22,412	23,990
Operating Expenses:			
Selling, General and Administrative	**15,849**	15,902	17,846
Depreciation and Amortization	**1,616**	1,707	1,785
Total Operating Expenses	**17,465**	17,609	19,631
OPERATING INCOME	**5,839**	4,803	4,359
Interest and Other (Income) Expense:			
Interest and Investment Income	**(15)**	(18)	(18)
Interest Expense	**530**	676	624
Other	**51**	163	163
Interest and Other, net	**566**	821	769
EARNINGS FROM CONTINUING OPERATIONS BEFORE PROVISION FOR INCOME TAXES	**5,273**	3,982	3,590
Provision for Income Taxes	**1,935**	1,362	1,278
EARNINGS FROM CONTINUING OPERATIONS	**3,338**	2,620	2,312
EARNINGS (LOSS) FROM DISCONTINUED OPERATIONS, NET OF TAX	**-**	41	(52)
NET EARNINGS	**$ 3,338**	$ 2,661	$ 2,260
Weighted Average Common Shares	**1,648**	1,683	1,682
BASIC EARNINGS PER SHARE FROM CONTINUING OPERATIONS	**$ 2.03**	$ 1.56	$ 1.37
BASIC EARNINGS (LOSS) PER SHARE FROM DISCONTINUED OPERATIONS	**$ -**	$ 0.02	$ (0.03)
BASIC EARNINGS PER SHARE	**$ 2.03**	$ 1.58	$ 1.34
Diluted Weighted Average Common Shares	**1,658**	1,692	1,686
DILUTED EARNINGS PER SHARE FROM CONTINUING OPERATIONS	**$ 2.01**	$ 1.55	$ 1.37
DILUTED EARNINGS (LOSS) PER SHARE FROM DISCONTINUED OPERATIONS	**$ -**	$ 0.02	$ (0.03)
DILUTED EARNINGS PER SHARE	**$ 2.01**	$ 1.57	$ 1.34

(1) Fiscal years ended January 30, 2011, January 31, 2010 and February 1, 2009 include 52 weeks.

See accompanying Notes to Consolidated Financial Statements.

THE HOME DEPOT, INC. AND SUBSIDIARIES

CONSOLIDATED BALANCE SHEETS

amounts in millions, except share and per share data	January 30, 2011	January 31, 2010
ASSETS		
Current Assets:		
Cash and Cash Equivalents	**$ 545**	$ 1,421
Receivables, net	**1,085**	964
Merchandise Inventories	**10,625**	10,188
Other Current Assets	**1,224**	1,327
Total Current Assets	**13,479**	13,900
Property and Equipment, at cost:		
Land	**8,497**	8,451
Buildings	**17,606**	17,391
Furniture, Fixtures and Equipment	**9,687**	9,091
Leasehold Improvements	**1,373**	1,383
Construction in Progress	**654**	525
Capital Leases	**568**	504
	38,385	37,345
Less Accumulated Depreciation and Amortization	**13,325**	11,795
Net Property and Equipment	**25,060**	25,550
Notes Receivable	**139**	33
Goodwill	**1,187**	1,171
Other Assets	**260**	223
Total Assets	**$40,125**	$40,877
LIABILITIES AND STOCKHOLDERS' EQUITY		
Current Liabilities:		
Accounts Payable	**$ 4,717**	$ 4,863
Accrued Salaries and Related Expenses	**1,290**	1,263
Sales Taxes Payable	**368**	362
Deferred Revenue	**1,177**	1,158
Income Taxes Payable	**13**	108
Current Installments of Long-Term Debt	**1,042**	1,020
Other Accrued Expenses	**1,515**	1,589
Total Current Liabilities	**10,122**	10,363
Long-Term Debt, excluding current installments	**8,707**	8,662
Other Long-Term Liabilities	**2,135**	2,140
Deferred Income Taxes	**272**	319
Total Liabilities	**21,236**	21,484
STOCKHOLDERS' EQUITY		
Common Stock, par value $0.05; authorized: 10 billion shares; issued: 1.722 billion shares at January 30, 2011 and 1.716 billion shares at January 31, 2010; outstanding: 1.623 billion shares at January 30, 2011 and 1.698 billion shares at January 31, 2010	**86**	86
Paid-In Capital	**6,556**	6,304
Retained Earnings	**14,995**	13,226
Accumulated Other Comprehensive Income	**445**	362
Treasury Stock, at cost, 99 million shares at January 30, 2011 and 18 million shares at January 31, 2010	**(3,193)**	(585)
Total Stockholders' Equity	**18,889**	19,393
Total Liabilities and Stockholders' Equity	**$40,125**	$40,877

See accompanying Notes to Consolidated Financial Statements.

THE HOME DEPOT, INC. AND SUBSIDIARIES

CONSOLIDATED STATEMENTS OF STOCKHOLDERS' EQUITY AND COMPREHENSIVE INCOME

amounts in millions, except per share data	Common Stock Shares	Common Stock Amount	Paid-In Capital	Retained Earnings	Accumulated Other Comprehensive Income (Loss)	Treasury Stock Shares	Treasury Stock Amount	Stockholders' Equity	Total Comprehensive Income
BALANCE, FEBRUARY 3, 2008	**1,698**	**$ 85**	**$5,800**	**$11,388**	**$ 755**	**(8)**	**$ (314)**	**$17,714**	
Net Earnings	—	—	—	2,260	—	—	—	2,260	$2,260
Shares Issued Under Employee Stock Plans	9	—	68	—	—	—	—	68	
Tax Effect of Sale of Option Shares by Employees	—	—	7	—	—	—	—	7	
Translation Adjustments	—	—	—	—	(831)	—	—	(831)	(831)
Cash Flow Hedges, net of tax	—	—	—	—	(1)	—	—	(1)	(1)
Stock Options, Awards and Amortization of Restricted Stock	—	—	176	—	—	—	—	176	
Repurchases of Common Stock	—	—	—	—	—	(3)	(70)	(70)	
Cash Dividends ($0.90 per share)	—	—	—	(1,521)	—	—	—	(1,521)	
Other	—	—	(3)	(34)	—	—	12	(25)	
Comprehensive Income									$1,428
BALANCE, FEBRUARY 1, 2009	**1,707**	**$ 85**	**$6,048**	**$12,093**	**$ (77)**	**(11)**	**$ (372)**	**$17,777**	
Net Earnings	—	—	—	2,661	—	—	—	2,661	$2,661
Shares Issued Under Employee Stock Plans	9	1	57	—	—	—	—	58	
Tax Effect of Sale of Option Shares by Employees	—	—	(2)	—	—	—	—	(2)	
Translation Adjustments	—	—	—	—	426	—	—	426	426
Cash Flow Hedges, net of tax	—	—	—	—	11	—	—	11	11
Stock Options, Awards and Amortization of Restricted Stock	—	—	201	—	—	—	—	201	
Repurchases of Common Stock	—	—	—	—	—	(7)	(213)	(213)	
Cash Dividends ($0.90 per share)	—	—	—	(1,525)	—	—	—	(1,525)	
Other	—	—	—	(3)	2	—	—	(1)	2
Comprehensive Income									$3,100
BALANCE, JANUARY 31, 2010	**1,716**	**$ 86**	**$6,304**	**$13,226**	**$ 362**	**(18)**	**$ (585)**	**$19,393**	
Net Earnings	—	—	—	3,338	—	—	—	3,338	$3,338
Shares Issued Under Employee Stock Plans	6	—	42	—	—	—	—	42	
Tax Effect of Sale of Option Shares by Employees	—	—	2	—	—	—	—	2	
Translation Adjustments	—	—	—	—	206	—	—	206	206
Cash Flow Hedges, net of tax	—	—	—	—	(116)	—	—	(116)	(116)
Stock Options, Awards and Amortization of Restricted Stock	—	—	214	—	—	—	—	214	
Repurchases of Common Stock	—	—	—	—	—	(81)	(2,608)	(2,608)	
Cash Dividends ($0.945 per share)	—	—	—	(1,569)	—	—	—	(1,569)	
Other	—	—	(6)	—	(7)	—	—	(13)	(7)
Comprehensive Income									$3,421
BALANCE, JANUARY 30, 2011	**1,722**	**$ 86**	**$6,556**	**$14,995**	**$ 445**	**(99)**	**$(3,193)**	**$18,889**	

See accompanying Notes to Consolidated Financial Statements.

THE HOME DEPOT, INC. AND SUBSIDIARIES
CONSOLIDATED STATEMENTS OF CASH FLOWS

amounts in millions	Fiscal Year Ended[1] January 30, 2011	January 31, 2010	February 1, 2009
CASH FLOWS FROM OPERATING ACTIVITIES:			
Net Earnings	**$ 3,338**	$ 2,661	$ 2,260
Reconciliation of Net Earnings to Net Cash Provided by Operating Activities:			
Depreciation and Amortization	**1,718**	1,806	1,902
Impairment Related to Rationalization Charges	**—**	—	580
Impairment of Investment	**—**	163	163
Stock-Based Compensation Expense	**214**	201	176
Changes in Assets and Liabilities:			
(Increase) Decrease in Receivables, net	**(102)**	(23)	121
(Increase) Decrease in Merchandise Inventories	**(355)**	625	743
Decrease (Increase) in Other Current Assets	**12**	4	(7)
(Decrease) Increase in Accounts Payable and Accrued Expenses	**(133)**	59	(646)
Increase (Decrease) in Deferred Revenue	**10**	(21)	(292)
(Decrease) Increase in Income Taxes Payable	**(85)**	(174)	262
Increase (Decrease) in Deferred Income Taxes	**104**	(227)	(282)
(Decrease) Increase in Other Long-Term Liabilities	**(61)**	(19)	306
Other	**(75)**	70	242
Net Cash Provided by Operating Activities	**4,585**	5,125	5,528
CASH FLOWS FROM INVESTING ACTIVITIES:			
Capital Expenditures, net of $62, $10 and $37 of non-cash capital expenditures in fiscal 2010, 2009 and 2008, respectively	**(1,096)**	(966)	(1,847)
Proceeds from Sales of Property and Equipment	**84**	178	147
Purchases of Investments	**—**	—	(168)
Proceeds from Sales and Maturities of Investments	**—**	33	139
Net Cash Used in Investing Activities	**(1,012)**	(755)	(1,729)
CASH FLOWS FROM FINANCING ACTIVITIES:			
Repayments of Short-Term Borrowings, net	**—**	—	(1,732)
Proceeds from Long-Term Borrowings, net of discount	**998**	—	—
Repayments of Long-Term Debt	**(1,029)**	(1,774)	(313)
Repurchases of Common Stock	**(2,608)**	(213)	(70)
Proceeds from Sales of Common Stock	**104**	73	84
Cash Dividends Paid to Stockholders	**(1,569)**	(1,525)	(1,521)
Other Financing Activities	**(347)**	(64)	(128)
Net Cash Used in Financing Activities	**(4,451)**	(3,503)	(3,680)
(Decrease) Increase in Cash and Cash Equivalents	**(878)**	867	119
Effect of Exchange Rate Changes on Cash and Cash Equivalents	**2**	35	(45)
Cash and Cash Equivalents at Beginning of Year	**1,421**	519	445
Cash and Cash Equivalents at End of Year	**$ 545**	$ 1,421	$ 519
SUPPLEMENTAL DISCLOSURE OF CASH PAYMENTS MADE FOR:			
Interest, net of interest capitalized	**$ 579**	$ 664	$ 622
Income Taxes	**$ 2,067**	$ 2,082	$ 1,265

(1) Fiscal years ended January 30, 2011, January 31, 2010 and February 1, 2009 include 52 weeks.

See accompanying Notes to Consolidated Financial Statements.

NOTES TO CONSOLIDATED FINANCIAL STATEMENTS

1. SUMMARY OF SIGNIFICANT ACCOUNTING POLICIES

Business, Consolidation and Presentation

The Home Depot, Inc. and its subsidiaries (the "Company") operate The Home Depot stores, which are full-service, warehouse-style stores averaging approximately 105,000 square feet in size. The stores stock approximately 30,000 to 40,000 different kinds of building materials, home improvement supplies and lawn and garden products that are sold to do-it-yourself customers, do-it-for-me customers and professional customers. At the end of fiscal 2010, the Company was operating 2,248 stores, which included 1,976 The Home Depot stores in the United States, including the Commonwealth of Puerto Rico and the territories of the U.S. Virgin Islands and Guam ("U.S."), 179 The Home Depot stores in Canada, 85 The Home Depot stores in Mexico and 8 The Home Depot stores in China. The Consolidated Financial Statements include the accounts of the Company and its wholly-owned subsidiaries. All significant intercompany transactions have been eliminated in consolidation.

Fiscal Year

The Company's fiscal year is a 52- or 53-week period ending on the Sunday nearest to January 31. Fiscal years ended January 30, 2011 ("fiscal 2010"), January 31, 2010 ("fiscal 2009") and February 1, 2009 ("fiscal 2008") include 52 weeks.

Use of Estimates

Management of the Company has made a number of estimates and assumptions relating to the reporting of assets and liabilities, the disclosure of contingent assets and liabilities, and reported amounts of revenues and expenses in preparing these financial statements in conformity with U.S. generally accepted accounting principles. Actual results could differ from these estimates.

Fair Value of Financial Instruments

The carrying amounts of Cash and Cash Equivalents, Receivables and Accounts Payable approximate fair value due to the short-term maturities of these financial instruments. The fair value of the Company's investments is discussed under the caption "Short-Term Investments" in this Note 1. The fair value of the Company's Long-Term Debt is discussed in Note 11.

Cash Equivalents

The Company considers all highly liquid investments purchased with original maturities of three months or less to be cash equivalents. The Company's cash equivalents are carried at fair market value and consist primarily of high-grade commercial paper, money market funds and U.S. government agency securities.

Short-Term Investments

Short-term investments are recorded at fair value based on current market rates and are classified as available-for-sale. The Company's short-term investments are included in Other Current Assets in the accompanying Consolidated Balance Sheets.

Accounts Receivable

The Company has an agreement with a third-party service provider who directly extends credit to customers, manages the Company's private label credit card program and owns the related receivables. The Company evaluated the third-party entities holding the receivables under the program and concluded that they should not be consolidated by the Company. The agreement with the third-party service provider expires in 2018, with the Company having the option, but no obligation, to purchase the receivables at the end of the agreement. The deferred interest charges incurred by the Company for its deferred financing programs offered to its customers are included in Cost of Sales. The interchange fees charged to the Company for the customers' use of the cards and the profit sharing with the third-party administrator are included in Selling, General and Administrative expenses ("SG&A"). The sum of the three is referred to by the Company as "the cost of credit" of the private label credit card program.

In addition, certain subsidiaries of the Company extend credit directly to customers in the ordinary course of business. The receivables due from customers were $42 million and $38 million as of January 30, 2011 and January 31, 2010, respectively. The Company's valuation reserve related to accounts receivable was not material to the Consolidated Financial Statements of the Company as of the end of fiscal 2010 or 2009.

Merchandise Inventories

The majority of the Company's Merchandise Inventories are stated at the lower of cost (first-in, first-out) or market, as determined by the retail inventory method. As the inventory retail value is adjusted regularly to reflect market conditions, the inventory valued using the retail method approximates the lower of cost or market. Certain subsidiaries, including retail operations in Canada, Mexico and China, and distribution centers, record Merchandise Inventories at the lower of cost or market, as determined by a cost method. These Merchandise Inventories represent approximately 20% of the total Merchandise Inventories balance. The Company evaluates the inventory valued using a cost method at the end of each quarter to ensure that it is carried at the lower of cost or market. The valuation allowance for Merchandise Inventories valued under a cost method was not material to the Consolidated Financial Statements of the Company as of the end of fiscal 2010 or 2009.

Independent physical inventory counts or cycle counts are taken on a regular basis in each store and distribution center to ensure that amounts reflected in the accompanying Consolidated Financial Statements for Merchandise Inventories are properly stated. During the period between physical inventory counts in stores, the Company accrues for estimated losses related to shrink on a store-by-store basis based on historical shrink results and current trends in the business. Shrink (or in the case of excess inventory, "swell") is the difference between the recorded amount of inventory and the physical inventory. Shrink may occur due to theft, loss, inaccurate records for the receipt of inventory or deterioration of goods, among other things.

Income Taxes

Income taxes are accounted for under the asset and liability method. The Company provides for federal, state and foreign income taxes currently payable, as well as for those deferred due to timing differences between reporting income and expenses for financial statement purposes versus tax purposes. Deferred tax assets and liabilities are recognized for the future tax consequences attributable to temporary differences between the financial statement carrying amounts of existing assets and liabilities and their respective tax bases. Deferred tax assets and liabilities are measured using enacted income tax rates expected to apply to taxable income in the years in which those temporary differences are expected to be recovered or settled. The effect of a change in income tax rates is recognized as income or expense in the period that includes the enactment date.

The Company recognizes the effect of income tax positions only if those positions are more likely than not of being sustained. Recognized income tax positions are measured at the largest amount that is greater than 50% likely of being realized. Changes in recognition or measurement are reflected in the period in which the change in judgment occurs.

The Company and its eligible subsidiaries file a consolidated U.S. federal income tax return. Non-U.S. subsidiaries and certain U.S. subsidiaries, which are consolidated for financial reporting purposes, are not eligible to be included in the Company's consolidated U.S. federal income tax return. Separate provisions for income taxes have been determined for these entities. The Company intends to reinvest substantially all of the unremitted earnings of its non-U.S. subsidiaries and postpone their remittance indefinitely. Accordingly, no provision for U.S. income taxes for these non-U.S. subsidiaries was recorded in the accompanying Consolidated Statements of Earnings.

Depreciation and Amortization

The Company's Buildings, Furniture, Fixtures and Equipment are recorded at cost and depreciated using the straight-line method over the estimated useful lives of the assets. Leasehold Improvements are amortized using the straight-line method over the original term of the lease or the useful life of the improvement, whichever is shorter. The Company's Property and Equipment is depreciated using the following estimated useful lives:

	Life
Buildings	5 – 45 years
Furniture, Fixtures and Equipment	2 – 20 years
Leasehold Improvements	5 – 45 years

Capitalized Software Costs

The Company capitalizes certain costs related to the acquisition and development of software and amortizes these costs using the straight-line method over the estimated useful life of the software, which is three to six years. These costs are included in Furniture, Fixtures and Equipment in the accompanying Consolidated Balance Sheets. Certain development costs not meeting the criteria for capitalization are expensed as incurred.

Revenues

The Company recognizes revenue, net of estimated returns and sales tax, at the time the customer takes possession of merchandise or receives services. The liability for sales returns is estimated based on historical return levels. When the Company receives payment from customers before the customer has taken possession of the merchandise or the service has been performed, the amount received is recorded as Deferred Revenue in the accompanying Consolidated Balance Sheets until the sale or service is complete. The Company also records Deferred Revenue for the sale of gift cards and recognizes this revenue upon the redemption of gift cards in Net Sales. Gift card breakage income is recognized based upon historical redemption patterns and represents the balance of gift cards for which the Company believes the likelihood of redemption by the customer is remote. During fiscal 2010, 2009 and 2008, the Company recognized $46 million, $40 million and $37 million, respectively, of gift card breakage income. This income is included in the accompanying Consolidated Statements of Earnings as a reduction in SG&A.

Services Revenue

Net Sales include services revenue generated through a variety of installation, home maintenance and professional service programs. In these programs, the customer selects and purchases material for a project and the Company provides or arranges professional installation. These programs are offered through the Company's stores. Under certain programs, when the Company provides or arranges the installation of a project and the subcontractor provides material as part of the installation, both the material and labor are included in services revenue. The Company recognizes this revenue when the service for the customer is complete.

All payments received prior to the completion of services are recorded in Deferred Revenue in the accompanying Consolidated Balance Sheets. Services revenue was $2.7 billion, $2.6 billion and $3.1 billion for fiscal 2010, 2009 and 2008, respectively.

Self-Insurance

The Company is self-insured for certain losses related to general liability, workers' compensation, medical, product liability and automobile claims. The expected ultimate cost for claims incurred as of the balance sheet date is not discounted and is recognized as a liability. The expected ultimate cost of claims is estimated based upon analysis of historical data and actuarial estimates.

Prepaid Advertising

Television and radio advertising production costs, along with media placement costs, are expensed when the advertisement first appears. Amounts included in Other Current Assets in the accompanying Consolidated Balance Sheets relating to prepayments of production costs for print and broadcast advertising as well as sponsorship promotions were not material at the end of fiscal 2010 and 2009.

Vendor Allowances

Vendor allowances primarily consist of volume rebates that are earned as a result of attaining certain purchase levels and advertising co-op allowances for the promotion of vendors' products that are typically based on guaranteed minimum amounts with additional amounts being earned for attaining certain purchase levels. These vendor allowances are accrued as earned, with those allowances received as a result of attaining certain purchase levels accrued over the incentive period based on estimates of purchases.

Volume rebates and certain advertising co-op allowances earned are initially recorded as a reduction in Merchandise Inventories and a subsequent reduction in Cost of Sales when the related product is sold. Certain advertising co-op allowances that are reimbursements of specific, incremental and identifiable costs incurred to promote vendors' products are recorded as an offset against advertising expense. In fiscal 2010, 2009 and 2008, gross advertising expense was $864 million, $897 million and $1.0 billion, respectively, and is included in SG&A. Specific, incremental and identifiable advertising co-op allowances were $90 million, $105 million and $107 million for fiscal 2010, 2009 and 2008, respectively, and are recorded as an offset to advertising expense in SG&A.

Cost of Sales

Cost of Sales includes the actual cost of merchandise sold and services performed, the cost of transportation of merchandise from vendors to the Company's stores, locations or customers, the operating cost of the Company's sourcing and distribution network and the cost of deferred interest programs offered through the Company's private label credit card program.

The cost of handling and shipping merchandise from the Company's stores, locations or distribution centers to the customer is classified as SG&A. The cost of shipping and handling, including internal costs and payments to third parties, classified as SG&A was $438 million, $426 million and $501 million in fiscal 2010, 2009 and 2008, respectively.

Impairment of Long-Lived Assets

The Company evaluates its long-lived assets each quarter for indicators of potential impairment. Indicators of impairment include current period losses combined with a history of losses, management's decision to relocate or close a store or other location before the end of its previously estimated useful life, or when changes in other circumstances indicate the carrying amount of an asset may not be recoverable. The evaluation for long-lived assets is performed at the lowest level of identifiable cash flows, which is generally the individual store level.

The assets of a store with indicators of impairment are evaluated by comparing its undiscounted cash flows with its carrying value. The estimate of cash flows includes management's assumptions of cash inflows and outflows directly resulting from the use of those assets in operations, including gross margin on Net Sales, payroll and related items, occupancy costs, insurance allocations and other costs to operate a store. If the carrying value is greater than the undiscounted cash flows, an impairment loss is recognized for the difference between the carrying value and the estimated fair market value. Impairment losses are recorded as a component of SG&A in the accompanying Consolidated Statements of Earnings. When a leased location closes, the Company also recognizes in SG&A the net present value of future lease obligations less estimated sublease income.

As part of its Rationalization Charges, the Company recorded no asset impairments in fiscal 2010 and 2009 and recorded $580 million of asset impairments in fiscal 2008. Also as part of its Rationalization Charges, the Company recorded no lease obligation costs in fiscal 2010 and recorded $84 million and $252 million of lease obligation costs in fiscal 2009 and 2008, respectively. See Note 2 for more details on the Rationalization Charges. The Company also recorded impairments and other lease obligation costs on other closings and relocations in the ordinary course of business, which were not material to the Consolidated Financial Statements in fiscal 2010, 2009 and 2008.

Goodwill and Other Intangible Assets

Goodwill represents the excess of purchase price over the fair value of net assets acquired. The Company does not amortize goodwill, but does assess the recoverability of goodwill in the third quarter of each fiscal year, or more often if indicators warrant, by determining whether the fair value of each reporting unit supports its carrying value. The fair values of the Company's identified reporting units were estimated using the present value of expected future discounted cash flows.

The Company amortizes the cost of other intangible assets over their estimated useful lives, which range up to 20 years, unless such lives are deemed indefinite. Intangible assets with indefinite lives are tested in the third quarter of each fiscal year for impairment, or more often if indicators warrant. Impairment charges related to goodwill and other intangible assets were not material for fiscal 2010, 2009 or 2008.

Stock-Based Compensation

The per share weighted average fair value of stock options granted during fiscal 2010, 2009 and 2008 was $6.70, $6.61 and $6.46, respectively. The fair value of these options was determined at the date of grant using the Black-Scholes option-pricing model with the following assumptions:

	Fiscal Year Ended		
	January 30, 2011	**January 31, 2010**	**February 1, 2009**
Risk-free interest rate	**3.1%**	2.3%	2.9%
Assumed volatility	**26.4%**	41.5%	33.8%
Assumed dividend yield	**2.9%**	3.9%	3.5%
Assumed lives of option	**5 years**	6 years	6 years

Derivatives

The Company uses derivative financial instruments from time to time in the management of its interest rate exposure on long-term debt and its exposure on foreign currency fluctuations. The Company accounts for its derivative financial instruments in accordance with the Financial Accounting Standards Board Accounting Standards Codification ("FASB ASC") 815-10. The fair value of the Company's derivative financial instruments is discussed in Note 11.

Comprehensive Income

Comprehensive Income includes Net Earnings adjusted for certain revenues, expenses, gains and losses that are excluded from Net Earnings under U.S. generally accepted accounting principles. Adjustments to Net Earnings and Accumulated Other Comprehensive Income consist primarily of foreign currency translation adjustments.

Foreign Currency Translation

Assets and liabilities denominated in a foreign currency are translated into U.S. dollars at the current rate of exchange on the last day of the reporting period. Revenues and expenses are generally translated using average exchange rates for the period and equity transactions are translated using the actual rate on the day of the transaction.

Segment Information

The Company operates within a single reportable segment primarily within North America. Net Sales for the Company outside of the U.S. were $7.5 billion, $7.0 billion and $7.4 billion for fiscal 2010, 2009 and 2008, respectively. Long-lived assets outside of the U.S. totaled $3.2 billion and $3.0 billion as of January 30, 2011 and January 31, 2010, respectively.

Reclassifications

Certain amounts in prior fiscal years have been reclassified to conform with the presentation adopted in the current fiscal year.

2. RATIONALIZATION CHARGES

In fiscal 2008, the Company reduced its square footage growth plans to improve free cash flow, provide stronger returns for the Company and invest in its existing stores to continue improving the customer experience. As a result of this store rationalization plan, the Company determined that it would no longer pursue the opening of approximately 50 U.S. stores that had been in its new store pipeline. The Company expects to dispose of or sublet any remaining pipeline locations over varying periods. The Company also closed 15 underperforming U.S. stores in the second quarter of fiscal 2008, and the Company expects to dispose of or sublet any remaining locations over varying periods.

Also in fiscal 2008, the Company announced that it would exit its EXPO, THD Design Center, Yardbirds and HD Bath businesses (the "Exited Businesses") in order to focus on its core The Home Depot stores. The Company closed the Exited Businesses in the first quarter of fiscal 2009 and expects to dispose of or sublet any remaining locations over varying periods. These steps impacted approximately 5,000 associates in those locations, their support functions and their distribution centers.

Finally, in January 2009 the Company also restructured its support functions to better align the Company's cost structure. These actions impacted approximately 2,000 associates.

The Company did not incur any material charges related to these actions (collectively, the "Rationalization Charges") in fiscal 2010 and recognized $146 million and $951 million in total pretax charges for fiscal 2009 and 2008, respectively. The Company does not expect any further material charges related to these actions.

Activity related to Rationalization Charges for fiscal 2010, 2009 and 2008 was as follows (amounts in millions):

	Asset Impairments	Lease Obligation Costs, net	Severance	Other	Total
Fiscal 2008 Charges	$580	$252	$ 78	$ 41	$951
Cash Uses	—	39	6	18	63
Non-cash Activity	542	—	—	3	545
Accrued Balance at February 1, 2009	38	213	72	20	343
Fiscal 2009 Charges	—	84	8	54	146
Cash Uses	—	106	80	71	257
Non-cash Activity	15	—	—	3	18
Accrued Balance at January 31, 2010	23	191	—	—	214
Cash Uses	—	**42**	—	—	**42**
Non-cash Activity	**19**	**(9)**	—	—	**10**
Accrued Balance at January 30, 2011	**$ 4**	**$158**	**$—**	**$—**	**$162**

Inventory markdown costs reflected in Other are included in Cost of Sales in the accompanying Consolidated Statements of Earnings, and costs related to asset impairments, lease obligations, severance and other miscellaneous costs are included in SG&A expenses. Asset impairment charges, including contractual costs to complete certain assets, were determined based on fair market value using market data for each individual property. Lease obligation costs represent the present value of contractually obligated rental payments offset by estimated sublet income, including estimates of the time required to sublease the locations. The payments related to the leased locations therefore are not generally incremental uses of cash.

3. CHANGE IN ACCOUNTING PRINCIPLE

During fiscal 2008, the Company implemented a new enterprise resource planning ("ERP") system, including a new inventory system, for its retail operations in Canada. Along with this implementation, the Company changed its method of accounting for Merchandise Inventories for its retail operations in Canada from the lower of cost (first-in, first-out) or market, as determined by the retail inventory method, to the lower of cost or market using a weighted-average cost method. As of the end of fiscal 2008, the implementation of the new inventory system and related conversion to the weighted-average cost method for Canadian retail operations was complete.

The new ERP system allows the Company to utilize the weighted-average cost method, which the Company believes will result in greater precision in the costing of inventories and a better matching of cost of sales with revenue generated. The effect of the change on the Merchandise Inventories and Retained Earnings balances was not material. Prior to the inventory system conversion, the Company could not determine the impact of the change to the weighted-average cost method, and therefore, could not retroactively apply the change to periods prior to fiscal 2008.

4. HD SUPPLY DISPOSITION

On August 30, 2007, the Company closed the sale of HD Supply, Inc. In accordance with FASB ASC 360-10, the Company reclassified the results of HD Supply as discontinued operations in its Consolidated Statements of Earnings for all periods presented. Settlement of working capital matters arising from the sale of HD Supply resulted in earnings from discontinued operations of $41 million, net of tax, in fiscal 2009 and a loss from discontinued operations of $52 million, net of tax, in fiscal 2008.

In connection with the sale, the Company purchased a 12.5% equity interest in the newly formed HD Supply for $325 million. In fiscal 2008, the Company determined its 12.5% equity interest in HD Supply was impaired and recorded a $163 million charge to write-down the investment. In fiscal 2009, the Company determined its equity interest in HD Supply was further impaired and recorded an additional charge of $163 million to write-down the remaining investment. These charges are included in Interest and Other, net, in the accompanying Consolidated Statements of Earnings.

Also in connection with the sale, the Company guaranteed a $1.0 billion senior secured amortizing term loan of HD Supply. The Company is responsible for up to $1.0 billion and any unpaid interest in the event of nonpayment by HD Supply. As reported in the quarterly report on Form 10-Q of HD Supply for the period ended October 31, 2010, the outstanding balance of this term loan as of October 31, 2010 was $940 million. The guaranteed loan is collateralized by certain assets of HD Supply. The original expiration date of the guarantee was August 30, 2012. On March 19, 2010, the Company amended the guarantee to extend the expiration date to April 1, 2014. The fair value of the guarantee at August 30, 2007 was $16 million and was recorded as a liability of the Company in Other Long-Term Liabilities. The extension of the guarantee increased the fair value of the guarantee to $67 million, resulting in a $51 million charge to Interest and Other, net, for fiscal 2010.

5. DEBT

The Company has commercial paper programs that allow for borrowings up to $2.0 billion. All of the Company's short-term borrowings in fiscal 2010 and 2009 were under these commercial paper programs. In connection with the commercial paper programs, the Company has a back-up credit facility with a consortium of banks for borrowings up to $2.0 billion. The credit facility expires in July 2013 and contains various restrictive covenants. At January 30, 2011, the Company was in compliance with all of the covenants, and they are not expected to impact the Company's liquidity or capital resources.

Short-Term Debt under the commercial paper programs was as follows (amounts in millions):

	January 30, 2011	January 31, 2010
Balance outstanding at fiscal year-end	**$—**	$ —
Maximum amount outstanding at any month-end	**$—**	$190
Average daily short-term borrowings	**$ 5**	$ 55
Weighted average interest rate	**0.4%**	1.1%

The Company's Long-Term Debt at the end of fiscal 2010 and 2009 consisted of the following (amounts in millions):

	January 30, 2011	January 31, 2010
4.625% Senior Notes; due August 15, 2010; interest payable semi-annually on February 15 and August 15	**$ —**	$ 999
5.20% Senior Notes; due March 1, 2011; interest payable semi-annually on March 1 and September 1	**1,000**	1,000
5.25% Senior Notes; due December 16, 2013; interest payable semi-annually on June 16 and December 16	**1,297**	1,258
5.40% Senior Notes; due March 1, 2016; interest payable semi-annually on March 1 and September 1	**3,033**	3,040
3.95% Senior Notes; due September 15, 2020; interest payable semi-annually on March 15 and September 15	**499**	—
5.875% Senior Notes; due December 16, 2036; interest payable semi-annually on June 16 and December 16	**2,960**	2,960
5.40% Senior Notes; due September 15, 2040; interest payable semi-annually on March 15 and September 15	**499**	—
Capital Lease Obligations; payable in varying installments through January 31, 2055	**452**	408
Other	**9**	17
Total debt	**9,749**	9,682
Less current installments	**1,042**	1,020
Long-Term Debt, excluding current installments	**$8,707**	$8,662

At January 30, 2011, the Company had outstanding interest rate swaps, accounted for as fair value hedges, that expire on December 16, 2013 with a notional amount of $1.25 billion that swap fixed rate interest on the Company's $1.25 billion 5.25% Senior Notes for variable interest equal to LIBOR plus 259 basis points. At January 30, 2011, the approximate fair value of these agreements was an asset of $47 million, which is the estimated amount the Company would have received to settle the agreements and is included in Other Assets in the accompanying Consolidated Balance Sheets.

In May 2010, the Company entered into a forward starting interest rate swap agreement with a notional amount of $500 million, accounted for as a cash flow hedge, to hedge interest rate fluctuations in anticipation of issuing long-term debt to refinance debt maturing in fiscal 2011. At January 30, 2011, the approximate fair market value of this agreement was a liability of $2 million, which is the estimated amount the Company would have paid to settle the agreement and is included in Other Long-Term Liabilities in the accompanying Consolidated Balance Sheets.

In September 2010, the Company issued $500 million of 3.95% Senior Notes due September 15, 2020 at a discount of $1 million and $500 million of 5.40% Senior Notes due September 15, 2040 at a discount of $1 million (together, the "September 2010 issuance"). Interest on these Senior Notes is due semi-annually on March 15 and September 15 of each year. The net proceeds of the September 2010 issuance were used to refinance the Company's 4.625% Senior Notes that matured August 15, 2010 in the aggregate principal amount of $1.0 billion. The $2 million discount associated with the September 2010 issuance is being amortized over the term of the Senior Notes using the effective interest rate method. Issuance costs were $8 million and are being amortized over the term of the Senior Notes.

In fiscal 2009 and 2010, the Company entered into forward starting interest rate swap agreements with a combined notional amount of $1.0 billion to hedge interest rate fluctuations in anticipation of the September 2010 issuance, which were accounted for as cash flow hedges. Upon the September 2010 issuance, the Company paid $193 million to settle these forward starting interest rate swap agreements. This amount, net of income taxes, is included in Accumulated Other Comprehensive Income and is being amortized to Interest Expense over the lives of the Senior Notes issued in September 2010.

During fiscal 2007 and 2008, the Company entered into interest rate swaps, accounted for as fair value hedges, with notional amounts of $3.0 billion, that swapped fixed rate interest on the Company's $3.0 billion 5.40% Senior Notes due March 1, 2016 for variable rate interest equal to LIBOR plus 60 to 149 basis points. In fiscal 2008, the Company received $56 million to settle these swaps, which is being amortized to reduce net Interest Expense over the remaining term of the debt.

The Senior Notes may be redeemed by the Company at any time, in whole or in part, at a redemption price plus accrued interest up to the redemption date. The redemption price is equal to the greater of (1) 100% of the principal amount of the Senior Notes to be redeemed, or (2) the sum of the present values of the remaining scheduled payments of principal and interest to maturity.

Additionally, if a Change in Control Triggering Event occurs, as defined by the terms of the September 2010 Issuance and the 5.25% Senior Notes and the 5.875% Senior Notes issuance (together, the "December 2006 Issuance"), holders of the September 2010 Issuance and the December 2006 Issuance have the right to require the Company to redeem those notes at 101% of the aggregate principal amount of the notes plus accrued interest up to the redemption date.

The Company is generally not limited under the indenture governing the Senior Notes in its ability to incur additional indebtedness or required to maintain financial ratios or specified levels of net worth or liquidity. Further, while the indenture governing the Senior Notes contains various restrictive covenants, none is expected to impact the Company's liquidity or capital resources.

At January 30, 2011, the Company had outstanding cross currency swap agreements with a notional amount of $590 million, accounted for as cash flow hedges, to hedge foreign currency fluctuations on certain intercompany debt. At January 30, 2011, the approximate fair value of these agreements was a liability of $38 million, which is the estimated amount the Company would have paid to settle the agreements and is included in Other Long-Term Liabilities in the accompanying Consolidated Balance Sheets.

Interest Expense in the accompanying Consolidated Statements of Earnings is net of interest capitalized of $3 million, $4 million and $20 million in fiscal 2010, 2009 and 2008, respectively. Maturities of Long-Term Debt are $1.0 billion for fiscal 2011, $29 million for fiscal 2012, $1.3 billion for fiscal 2013, $28 million for fiscal 2014, $26 million for fiscal 2015 and $7.3 billion thereafter.

6. INCOME TAXES

The components of Earnings from Continuing Operations before Provision for Income Taxes for fiscal 2010, 2009 and 2008 were as follows (amounts in millions):

	Fiscal Year Ended		
	January 30, 2011	January 31, 2010	February 1, 2009
United States	**$4,854**	$3,586	$3,136
Foreign	**419**	396	454
Total	**$5,273**	$3,982	$3,590

The Provision for Income Taxes consisted of the following (amounts in millions):

	Fiscal Year Ended		
	January 30, 2011	January 31, 2010	February 1, 2009
Current:			
Federal	**$1,478**	$1,157	$1,283
State	**181**	184	198
Foreign	**151**	195	85
	1,810	1,536	1,566
Deferred:			
Federal	**79**	(121)	(209)
State	**21**	(24)	(56)
Foreign	**25**	(29)	(23)
	125	(174)	(288)
Total	**$1,935**	$1,362	$1,278

The Company's combined federal, state and foreign effective tax rates for fiscal 2010, 2009 and 2008, net of offsets generated by federal, state and foreign tax benefits, were approximately 36.7%, 34.2% and 35.6%, respectively.

The reconciliation of the Provision for Income Taxes at the federal statutory rate of 35% to the actual tax expense for the applicable fiscal years was as follows (amounts in millions):

	Fiscal Year Ended		
	January 30, 2011	January 31, 2010	February 1, 2009
Income taxes at federal statutory rate	**$1,846**	$1,394	$1,257
State income taxes, net of federal income tax benefit	**131**	104	92
Other, net	**(42)**	(136)	(71)
Total	**$1,935**	$1,362	$1,278

The tax effects of temporary differences that give rise to significant portions of the deferred tax assets and deferred tax liabilities as of January 30, 2011 and January 31, 2010 were as follows (amounts in millions):

	January 30, 2011	January 31, 2010
Current:		
Deferred Tax Assets:		
Property and equipment	**$ 64**	$ 85
Accrued self-insurance liabilities	**115**	109
Other accrued liabilities	**196**	303
Deferred compensation	**393**	372
Current Deferred Tax Assets	**768**	869
Deferred Tax Liabilities:		
Accelerated inventory deduction	**(106)**	(114)
Other	**(114)**	(111)
Current Deferred Tax Liabilities	**(220)**	(225)
Current Deferred Tax Assets, net	**548**	644
Noncurrent:		
Deferred Tax Assets:		
Accrued self-insurance liabilities	**345**	338
State income taxes	**69**	123
Capital loss carryover	**141**	86
Net operating losses	**66**	74
Foreign tax credit carry forward	**30**	65
Impairment of investment	**120**	114
Other	**212**	174
Valuation allowance	**(66)**	(15)
Noncurrent Deferred Tax Assets	**917**	959
Deferred Tax Liabilities:		
Property and equipment	**(1,073)**	(1,178)
Goodwill and other intangibles	**(95)**	(88)
Noncurrent Deferred Tax Liabilities	**(1,168)**	(1,266)
Noncurrent Deferred Tax Liabilities, net	**(251)**	(307)
Net Deferred Tax Assets	**$ 297**	$ 337

Current deferred tax assets and current deferred tax liabilities are netted by tax jurisdiction and noncurrent deferred tax assets and noncurrent deferred tax liabilities are netted by tax jurisdiction, and are included in the accompanying Consolidated Balance Sheets as follows (amounts in millions):

	January 30, 2011	January 31, 2010
Other Current Assets	**$ 553**	$ 650
Other Assets	**21**	12
Other Accrued Expenses	**(5)**	(6)
Deferred Income Taxes	**(272)**	(319)
Net Deferred Tax Assets	**$ 297**	$ 337

The Company believes that the realization of the deferred tax assets is more likely than not, based upon the expectation that it will generate the necessary taxable income in future periods, and except for certain net operating and capital losses discussed below, no valuation reserves have been provided.

At January 30, 2011, the Company had state and foreign net operating loss carryforwards available to reduce future taxable income, expiring at various dates from 2011 to 2028. Management has concluded that it is more likely than not that the tax benefits related to the net operating losses will be realized. However, certain foreign net operating losses are in jurisdictions where the expiration period is too short to be assured of utilization. Therefore, a valuation allowance has been provided to reduce the deferred tax asset related to net operating losses to an amount that is more likely than not to be realized. Total valuation allowances related to net operating losses at January 30, 2011 and January 31, 2010 were $21 million and $15 million, respectively.

As a result of its sale of HD Supply, the Company incurred a tax loss, resulting in a net capital loss carryover of approximately $397 million as of January 30, 2011. Portions of the net capital loss carryover will expire in fiscal years 2013 through 2015 if not used. The Company has concluded that it is not more likely than not that all of the tax benefits related to the capital loss carryover will be realized based on its ability to generate adequate capital gain income during the carryover period. Therefore, a valuation allowance of $45 million has been provided.

The Company had foreign tax credit carryforwards of $30 million and $65 million as of January 30, 2011 and January 31, 2010, respectively. The foreign tax credit carryforwards will expire in 2020. Management has concluded that it is more likely than not that the tax benefits related to the foreign tax credit carryforwards will be realized based on the Company's ability to generate foreign source income during the carryforward period. Therefore, no valuation allowance has been provided.

The Company has not provided for U.S. deferred income taxes on approximately $2.0 billion of undistributed earnings of international subsidiaries because of its intention to indefinitely reinvest these earnings outside the U.S. The determination of the amount of the unrecognized deferred U.S. income tax liability related to the undistributed earnings is not practicable; however, unrecognized foreign income tax credits would be available to reduce a portion of this liability.

The Company's income tax returns are routinely examined by domestic and foreign tax authorities. The Company's U.S. federal and Canadian tax returns for fiscal years 2005 through 2007 are currently under audit by the IRS and the Canadian tax authorities. There are also ongoing U.S. state and local and other foreign audits covering tax years 2003 to 2009. The Company does not expect the results from any income tax audit to have a material impact on the Company's financial statements.

The Company believes that certain adjustments under examination by the IRS and in certain states will be agreed upon within the next twelve months. The Company has classified approximately $63 million of the reserve for unrecognized tax benefits as a short-term liability in the accompanying Consolidated Balance Sheets. Final settlement of these audit issues may result in payments that are more or less than these amounts, but the Company does not anticipate the resolution of these matters will result in a material change to its consolidated financial position or results of operations.

Reconciliations of the beginning and ending amount of gross unrecognized tax benefits for continuing operations for fiscal 2010, 2009 and 2008 were as follows (amounts in millions):

	January 30, 2011	**January 31, 2010**	**February 1, 2009**
Unrecognized tax benefits balance at beginning of fiscal year	**$ 659**	$695	$ 608
Additions based on tax positions related to the current year	**174**	55	67
Additions for tax positions of prior years	**84**	33	231
Reductions for tax positions of prior years	**(181)**	(28)	(142)
Reductions due to settlements	**(65)**	(94)	(65)
Reductions due to lapse of statute of limitations	**(9)**	(2)	(4)
Unrecognized tax benefits balance at end of fiscal year	**$ 662**	$659	$ 695

The amount of unrecognized tax benefits was $298 million, $386 million and $401 million as of January 30, 2011, January 31, 2010 and February 1, 2009, respectively, that if recognized would affect the annual effective income tax rate.

Interest and penalties associated with uncertain tax positions provided income of $32 million in fiscal 2010, expense of $41 million in fiscal 2009 and income of $19 million in fiscal 2008. Total accrued interest and penalties as of January 30, 2011 and January 31, 2010 are $84 million and $138 million, respectively. Interest and penalties are included in Interest Expense and SG&A, respectively, in the accompanying Consolidated Statements of Earnings.

7. EMPLOYEE STOCK PLANS

The Home Depot, Inc. 2005 Omnibus Stock Incentive Plan ("2005 Plan") and The Home Depot, Inc. 1997 Omnibus Stock Incentive Plan ("1997 Plan" and collectively with the 2005 Plan, the "Plans") provide that incentive and non-qualified stock options, stock appreciation rights, restricted shares, performance shares, performance units and deferred shares may be issued to selected associates, officers and directors of the Company. Under the 2005 Plan, the maximum number of shares of the Company's common stock authorized for issuance is 255 million shares, with any award other than a stock option reducing the number of shares available for issuance by 2.11 shares. As of January 30, 2011, there were 175 million shares available for future grants under the 2005 Plan. No additional equity awards could be issued from the 1997 Plan after the adoption of the 2005 Plan on May 26, 2005.

Under the terms of the Plans, incentive stock options and non-qualified stock options must have an exercise price at or above the fair market value of the Company's stock on the date of the grant. Typically, incentive stock options and non-qualified stock options vest at the rate of 25% per year commencing on the first or second anniversary date of the grant and expire on the tenth anniversary date of the grant. Certain of the non-qualified stock options also include performance options which vest on the later of the first anniversary date of the grant and the date the closing price of the Company's common stock has been 25% greater than the exercise price of the options for 30 consecutive trading days. Additionally, certain stock options may become non-forfeitable upon age 60, provided the associate has had five years of continuous service. The Company recognized $20 million, $19 million and $47 million of stock-based compensation expense in fiscal 2010, 2009 and 2008, respectively, related to stock options.

Restrictions on the restricted stock issued under the Plans generally lapse according to one of the following schedules: (1) the restrictions on the restricted stock lapse over various periods up to five years, (2) the restrictions on 25% of the restricted stock lapse upon the third and sixth anniversaries of the date of issuance with the remaining 50% of the restricted stock lapsing upon the associate's attainment of age 62, or (3) the restrictions on 25% of the restricted stock lapse upon the third and sixth anniversaries of the date of issuance with the remaining 50% of the restricted stock lapsing upon the earlier of the associate's attainment of age 60 or the tenth anniversary date. The Company has also granted performance shares under the Plans, the payout of which is dependent on either (1) the Company's total shareholder return percentile ranking compared to the performance of individual companies included in the S&P 500 index at the end of the three-year performance cycle, or (2) the Company's performance against target average return on invested capital and operating profit over a three-year performance cycle. Additionally, certain awards may become non-forfeitable upon the attainment of age 60, provided the associate has had five years of continuous service. The fair value of the restricted stock and performance shares is expensed over the period during which the restrictions lapse. The Company recorded stock-based compensation expense related to restricted stock and performance shares of $167 million, $158 million and $109 million in fiscal 2010, 2009 and 2008, respectively.

In fiscal 2010, 2009 and 2008, there were an aggregate of 479 thousand, 666 thousand and 641 thousand deferred shares, respectively, granted under the Plans. For associates, each deferred share entitles the individual to one share of common stock to be received up to five years after the grant date of the deferred shares, subject to certain deferral rights of the associate. Additionally, certain awards may become non-forfeitable upon age 60, provided the associate has had five years of continuous service. The Company recorded stock-based compensation expense related to deferred shares of $14 million, $14 million and $9 million in fiscal 2010, 2009 and 2008, respectively.

As of January 30, 2011, there were 2 million non-qualified stock options outstanding under non-qualified stock option plans that are not part of the Plans.

The Company maintains two Employee Stock Purchase Plans ("ESPPs") (U.S. and non-U.S. plans). The plan for U.S. associates is a tax-qualified plan under Section 423 of the Internal Revenue Code. The non-U.S. plan is not a Section 423 plan. As of January 30, 2011, there were 11 million shares available under the plan for U.S associates and 20 million shares available under the non-U.S. plan. The purchase price of shares under the ESPPs is equal to 85% of the stock's fair market value on the last day of the purchase period, which is a six-month period ending on December 31 and June 30 of each year. During fiscal 2010, there were 3 million shares purchased under the ESPPs at an average price of $26.50. Under the outstanding ESPPs as of January 30, 2011, employees have contributed $7 million to purchase shares at 85% of the stock's fair market value on the last day (June 30, 2011) of the purchase period. The Company recognized $13 million, $10 million and $11 million of stock-based compensation expense in fiscal 2010, 2009 and 2008, respectively, related to the ESPPs.

In total, the Company recorded stock-based compensation expense, including the expense of stock options, ESPPs, restricted stock, performance shares and deferred shares, of $214 million, $201 million and $176 million, in fiscal 2010, 2009 and 2008, respectively.

The following table summarizes stock options outstanding at January 30, 2011, January 31, 2010 and February 1, 2009, and changes during the fiscal years ended on these dates (shares in thousands):

	Number of Shares	Weighted Average Exercise Price
Outstanding at February 3, 2008	52,365	$38.98
Granted	5,226	26.09
Exercised	(777)	22.55
Canceled	(4,800)	39.14
Outstanding at February 1, 2009	52,014	$37.91
Granted	4,174	23.29
Exercised	(374)	24.50
Canceled	(6,505)	37.65
Outstanding at January 31, 2010	49,309	$36.81
Granted	**3,723**	**32.24**
Exercised	**(1,294)**	**26.63**
Canceled	**(7,271)**	**43.95**
Outstanding at January 30, 2011	**44,467**	**$35.56**

The total intrinsic value of stock options exercised was $9 million, $1 million and $4 million in fiscal 2010, 2009 and 2008, respectively. As of January 30, 2011, there were approximately 44 million stock options outstanding with a weighted average remaining life of four years and an intrinsic value of $51 million. As of January 30, 2011, there were approximately 33 million stock options exercisable with a weighted average exercise price of $38.21, a weighted average remaining life of two years, and an intrinsic value of $49 million. As of January 30, 2011, there were approximately 41 million stock options vested or expected to ultimately vest. As of January 30, 2011, there was $45 million of unamortized stock-based compensation expense related to stock options, which is expected to be recognized over a weighted average period of two years.

The following table summarizes restricted stock and performance shares outstanding at January 30, 2011 (shares in thousands):

	Number of Shares	Weighted Average Grant Date Fair Value
Outstanding at February 3, 2008	11,715	$39.14
Granted	7,938	27.14
Restrictions lapsed	(1,251)	34.37
Canceled	(2,115)	34.86
Outstanding at February 1, 2009	16,287	$34.22
Granted	8,257	23.41
Restrictions lapsed	(1,686)	34.65
Canceled	(2,195)	31.84
Outstanding at January 31, 2010	20,663	$30.11
Granted	**5,799**	**32.31**
Restrictions lapsed	**(5,276)**	**32.28**
Canceled	**(1,747)**	**30.11**
Outstanding at January 30, 2011	**19,439**	**$30.18**

As of January 30, 2011, there was $259 million of unamortized stock-based compensation expense related to restricted stock and performance shares, which is expected to be recognized over a weighted average period of two years. The total fair value of restricted stock and performance shares vesting during fiscal 2010, 2009 and 2008 was $168 million, $41 million and $33 million, respectively.

8. LEASES

The Company leases certain retail locations, office space, warehouse and distribution space, equipment and vehicles. While most of the leases are operating leases, certain locations and equipment are leased under capital leases. As leases expire, it can be expected that, in the normal course of business, certain leases will be renewed or replaced.

Certain lease agreements include escalating rents over the lease terms. The Company expenses rent on a straight-line basis over the lease term which commences on the date the Company has the right to control the property. The cumulative expense recognized on a straight-line basis in excess of the cumulative payments is included in Other Accrued Expenses and Other Long-Term Liabilities in the accompanying Consolidated Balance Sheets.

Total rent expense, net of minor sublease income for fiscal 2010, 2009 and 2008 was $821 million, $823 million and $846 million, respectively. Certain store leases also provide for contingent rent payments based on percentages of sales in excess of specified minimums. Contingent rent expense for fiscal 2010, 2009 and 2008 was approximately $3 million, $4 million and $5 million, respectively. Real estate taxes, insurance, maintenance and operating expenses applicable to the leased property are obligations of the Company under the lease agreements.

The approximate future minimum lease payments under capital and all other leases at January 30, 2011 were as follows (amounts in millions):

Fiscal Year	Capital Leases	Operating Leases
2011	$ 114	$ 783
2012	96	699
2013	96	639
2014	92	582
2015	87	543
Thereafter through 2097	774	4,935
	1,259	$8,181
Less imputed interest	807	
Net present value of capital lease obligations	452	
Less current installments	41	
Long-term capital lease obligations, excluding current installments	$ 411	

Short-term and long-term obligations for capital leases are included in the accompanying Consolidated Balance Sheets in Current Installments of Long-Term Debt and Long-Term Debt, respectively. The assets under capital leases recorded in Property and Equipment, net of amortization, totaled $336 million and $299 million at January 30, 2011 and January 31, 2010, respectively.

9. EMPLOYEE BENEFIT PLANS

The Company maintains active defined contribution retirement plans for its employees (the "Benefit Plans"). All associates satisfying certain service requirements are eligible to participate in the Benefit Plans. The Company makes cash contributions each payroll period up to specified percentages of associates' contributions as approved by the Board of Directors.

The Company also maintains a restoration plan to provide certain associates deferred compensation that they would have received under the Benefit Plans as a matching contribution if not for the maximum compensation limits under the Internal Revenue Code. The Company funds the restoration plan through contributions made to a grantor trust, which are then used to purchase shares of the Company's common stock in the open market.

The Company's contributions to the Benefit Plans and the restoration plan were $171 million, $161 million and $158 million for fiscal 2010, 2009 and 2008, respectively. At January 30, 2011, the Benefit Plans and the restoration plan held a total of 16 million shares of the Company's common stock in trust for plan participants.

10. BASIC AND DILUTED WEIGHTED AVERAGE COMMON SHARES

The reconciliation of basic to diluted weighted average common shares for fiscal 2010, 2009 and 2008 was as follows (amounts in millions):

	Fiscal Year Ended		
	January 30, 2011	January 31, 2010	February 1, 2009
Weighted average common shares	**1,648**	1,683	1,682
Effect of potentially dilutive securities:			
Stock Plans	**10**	9	4
Diluted weighted average common shares	**1,658**	1,692	1,686

Stock plans consist of shares granted under the Company's employee stock plans as described in Note 7 to the Consolidated Financial Statements. Options to purchase 39 million, 48 million and 52 million shares of common stock at January 30, 2011, January 31, 2010 and February 1, 2009, respectively, were excluded from the computation of Diluted Earnings per Share because their effect would have been anti-dilutive.

11. FAIR VALUE MEASUREMENTS

The fair value of an asset is considered to be the price at which the asset could be sold in an orderly transaction between unrelated knowledgeable and willing parties. A liability's fair value is defined as the amount that would be paid to transfer the liability to a new obligor, not the amount that would be paid to settle the liability with the creditor. Assets and liabilities recorded at fair value are measured using a three-tier fair value hierarchy, which prioritizes the inputs used in measuring fair value. These tiers include:

- Level 1 – Observable inputs that reflect quoted prices in active markets
- Level 2 – Inputs other than quoted prices in active markets that are either directly or indirectly observable
- Level 3 – Unobservable inputs in which little or no market data exists, therefore requiring the Company to develop its own assumptions

Assets and Liabilities Measured at Fair Value on a Recurring Basis

The assets and liabilities of the Company that are measured at fair value on a recurring basis as of January 30, 2011 and January 31, 2010 were as follows (amounts in millions):

	Fair Value at January 30, 2011 Using			Fair Value at January 31, 2010 Using		
	Level 1	**Level 2**	**Level 3**	**Level 1**	**Level 2**	**Level 3**
Derivative agreements - assets	$ –	$ 47	$ –	$ –	$15	$ –
Derivative agreements - liabilities	–	(40)	–	–	(4)	–
Total	$ –	$ 7	$ –	$ –	$11	$ –

The Company uses derivative financial instruments from time to time in the management of its interest rate exposure on long-term debt and its exposure on foreign currency fluctuations. The fair value of the Company's derivative financial instruments was measured using level 2 inputs. The Company's derivative agreements are discussed further in Note 5.

Assets and Liabilities Measured at Fair Value on a Nonrecurring Basis

The assets and liabilities of the Company that were measured at fair value on a nonrecurring basis during fiscal 2010 and fiscal 2009 were as follows (amounts in millions):

	Fair Value Measured During Fiscal 2010 Level 3	**Gains (Losses)**
Store Rationalization - lease obligation costs, net	**$(158)**	**$ (9)**
Guarantee of HD Supply loan	**$ (67)**	**(51)**
Total for fiscal 2010		**$ (60)**

	Fair Value Measured During Fiscal 2009 Level 3	**Gains (Losses)**
HD Supply investment	$ —	$(163)
Store Rationalization - lease obligation costs, net	$(191)	(84)
Total for fiscal 2009		$(247)

During fiscal 2009, the Company impaired the remaining value of its investment in HD Supply using fair value measurements with unobservable inputs (level 3), as further discussed in Note 4. Lease obligation costs included in the Company's Rationalization Charges were measured on a nonrecurring basis using fair value measurements with unobservable inputs (level 3), as further discussed in Note 2. Additionally, the guarantee of the HD Supply loan was measured on a nonrecurring basis using fair value measurements with unobservable inputs (level 3), as further discussed in Note 4.

Long-lived assets and goodwill and other intangible assets were also analyzed for impairment on a nonrecurring basis using fair value measurements with unobservable inputs (level 3). Impairment charges related to goodwill and other intangible assets and long-lived assets in fiscal 2010 and 2009 were not material, as further discussed in Note 1 under the captions "Goodwill and Other Intangible Assets" and "Impairment of Long-Lived Assets," respectively.

The aggregate fair value of the Company's Senior Notes, based on quoted market prices (level 1), was $9.8 billion and $9.5 billion at January 30, 2011 and January 31, 2010, respectively, compared to a carrying value of $9.3 billion at both January 30, 2011 and January 31, 2010.

12. COMMITMENTS AND CONTINGENCIES

At January 30, 2011, the Company was contingently liable for approximately $606 million under outstanding letters of credit and open accounts issued for certain business transactions, including insurance programs, trade contracts and construction contracts. The Company's letters of credit are primarily performance-based and are not based on changes in variable components, a liability or an equity security of the other party.

The Company is involved in litigation arising from the normal course of business. In management's opinion, this litigation is not expected to have a material adverse effect on the Company's consolidated financial condition or results of operations.

13. QUARTERLY FINANCIAL DATA (UNAUDITED)

The following is a summary of the quarterly consolidated results of operations from continuing operations for the fiscal years ended January 30, 2011 and January 31, 2010 (amounts in millions, except per share data):

	Net Sales	Gross Profit	Earnings from Continuing Operations	Basic Earnings per Share from Continuing Operations	Diluted Earnings per Share from Continuing Operations
Fiscal Year Ended January 30, 2011:					
First Quarter	**$16,863**	**$ 5,794**	**$ 725**	**$ 0.43**	**$ 0.43**
Second Quarter	**19,410**	**6,582**	**1,192**	**0.72**	**0.72**
Third Quarter	**16,598**	**5,685**	**834**	**0.51**	**0.51**
Fourth Quarter	**15,126**	**5,243**	**587**	**0.36**	**0.36**
Fiscal Year	**$67,997**	**$23,304**	**$3,338**	**$ 2.03**	**$ 2.01**
Fiscal Year Ended January 31, 2010:					
First Quarter	$16,175	$ 5,450	$ 514	$ 0.31	$ 0.30
Second Quarter	19,071	6,388	1,116	0.66	0.66
Third Quarter	16,361	5,561	689	0.41	0.41
Fourth Quarter	14,569	5,013	301	0.18	0.18
Fiscal Year	$66,176	$22,412	$2,620	$ 1.56	$ 1.55

Note: The quarterly data may not sum to fiscal year totals.

Index

A

B

C

F

G

H

I

J

K

L

M

N

O

P

S

T

U

V

W

comprehensive chart of accounts

Assets

- Cash
- Petty cash
- Accounts receivable
- Allowance for bad debts
- Fuel
- Interest receivable
- Inventory
- Notes receivable
- Office supplies
- Prepaid insurance
- Prepaid rent
- Short-term investments
- Supplies
- Long-term investments
- Buildings
- Equipment
- Land
- Accumulated depreciation
- Copyrights
- Goodwill
- Patents

Liabilities

- Accounts payable
- Dividends payable
- Dividends payable—common
- Dividends payable—preferred
- Federal tax withholdings payable
- FICA taxes payable
- Income tax payable
- Interest payable
- Notes payable
- Salaries payable
- Sales tax payable
- State tax withholdings payable
- Unearned revenue
- Utilities Payable
- Bonds payable
- Discount on bonds payable
- Premium on bonds payable
- Mortgage payable

Equity

- Additional paid in capital
- Capital stock
- Common stock
- Common Stock to be Distributed
- Contributed capital
- Dividends
- Preferred stock
- Retained earnings
- Treasury stock

Revenues

- Sales
- Sales discounts
- Sales returns and allowances
- Service revenue
- Interest revenue
- Gain on disposal
- Gain on redemption

Expenses

- Administrative expense
- Advertising expense
- Amortization expense
- Bad debt expense
- Cash over and short
- Cost of goods sold
- Depreciation expense
- Fuel expense
- Income tax expense
- Insurance expense
- Interest expense
- Loss on disposal
- Loss on impairment
- Loss on redemption
- Maintenance expense
- Miscellaneous expense
- Payroll tax expense
- Postage expense
- Purchases
- Purchase discounts
- Purchase returns and allowances
- Rent expense
- Salaries expense
- Service charge expense
- Supplies expense
- Transportation-in
- Utilities expense

prepcard CHAPTER 1 Financial Accounting

What's Inside

Key topics in this chapter: Define what accounting is and summarize the four basic accounting assumptions; describe and explain the basic financial statements: income statement, balance sheet, statement of retained earnings, and statement of cash flows; describe the qualitative characteristics of an accounting information system; describe the conceptual framework of accounting.

Learning Objectives

LO1	Describe the four assumptions made when communicating accounting information.
LO2	Describe the purpose and structure of an income statement and the terms and principles used to create it.
LO3	Describe the purpose and structure of a balance sheet and the terms and principles used to create it.
LO4	Describe the purpose and structure of a statement of retained earnings and how it links the income statement and the balance sheet.
LO5	Describe the purpose and structure of a statement of cash flows and the terms and principles used to create it.
LO6	Describe the qualitative characteristics that make accounting information useful.
LO7	Describe the conceptual framework of accounting.

Chapter Outline

Lecture Example

My Box Inc. began operations on December 1, 2011. The financial statements for My Box Inc. are shown below for the month ended December 31, 2009 (the first month of operations). Determine the missing amounts for letters (a) through (n).

My Box Inc.
Income Statement
For the Month Ending Dec. 31, 2011

Service Revenue		$6,760
Operating expenses:		
Advertising expense	$ 250	
Rent expense	(a)	
Salaries expense	1,000	
Supplies expense	400	
Utilities expense	500	
Total operating expenses		(b)
Net income		$ (c)

My Box Inc.
Statement of Retained Earnings
For the Month Ending Dec. 31, 2011

Retained earnings, December 1	$ 0
+ Net income	(d)
− Dividends	400
Retained earnings, December 31	$3,210

My Box Inc.
Balance Sheet
Dec. 31, 2011

Assets	
Cash	$ (f)
Supplies	110
Land	(g)
Total assets	$4,590
Liabilities	
Accounts payable	$ (h)
Stockholders' Equity	
Capital stock	500
Retained earnings	(i)
Total liabilities & stockholders' equity	$ (j)

My Box Inc.
Statement of Cash Flows
For the Month Ending Dec. 31, 2011

Cash flows from operating activities:		
Net cash flow from operating activities		$4,380
Cash flows from investing activities:		
Cash payments for acquisition of land		(2,000)
Cash flows from financing activities:		
Cash received from issuing capital stock	$ (k)	
Cash payments for dividends	(l)	
Net cash flow from financing activities		(m)
Net cash flow and Dec. 31, 2011 cash balance		$ (n)

Lecture Example Solution

(a) 1,000	(b) 3,150	(c) 3,610	(d) 3,610	(e) 3,210	(f) 2,480	(g) 2,000
(h) 880	(i) 3,210	(j) 4,590	(k) 500	(l) 400	(m) 100	(n) 2,480

Visit **www.cengage.com/login** for additional materials to enhance your lectures!

Chapter Outline (continued)

Term	Definition	Reported on the
Asset	A resource of a business	Balance sheet
Liability	An obligation of a business	Balance sheet
Equity	The difference between assets and liabilities	Balance sheet
Contributed Capital	Equity resulting from contributions from owners	Balance sheet
Retained Earnings	Equity resulting from profitable operations	Balance sheet and statement of retained earnings
Revenue	An increase in assets resulting from selling a good or providing a service	Income statement
Expense	A decrease in assets resulting from selling a good or providing a service	Income statement
Dividend	A distribution to owners	Statement of retained earnings

Chapter Updates

- Revised Making It Real Box discusses General Motors' bankruptcy
- Removed simple depreciation expense from one of the chapter examples
- Streamlined some of the accounts used to improve student comprehension
- Added IFRS Post-it notes that briefly mention conceptual framework differences from U.S. GAAP
- Added Concept Questions, Multiple-Choice, and Brief Exercises
- Increased the number of assignable Exercises, Problems, and Cases

Your Students Will Ask About...

What is accounting? Who uses it? Why is it important?

Accounting is the language of business. Accounting is the 3 R's:

1st R = Record	2nd R = Report	3rd R = Review
Record: all business transactions (ex. receiving cash from customer, sales on account, buying supplies, paying salaries, etc.).	Once all transactions are reported, then the business prepares **R**eports: Income Statement, Retained Earnings, Balance Sheet, and Statement of Cash Flows.	Once the reports are prepared accurately, the owner/manager can **R**eview the financial results to be able to make sound business decisions.

Describe the accounting cycle and the concept of limited resources.

Accounting will help the business use the available resources effectively and efficiently to be able to meet the goals and objectives of the company.

What are the different account classifications and which financial statement do I use?

Statement	Purpose	Accounts	Time
Income Statement	Is the company profitable?	Revenues vs. Expenses	Over a specific period of time
Statement of Retained Earnings	How much does the company owe the owners as the result of operations?	BOY R/E + NI or − NL − Dividends = EOY R/E	Over a specific period of time
Balance Sheet	Snapshot picture of a business as of a specific period of time	Assets = Liabilities + Equity	At a specific point in time
Statement of Cash Flows	What were the company's sources and uses of cash?	Cash from operating, investment, and financing activities	Over a specific period of time

Comparative Analysis

Visit http://investor.shareholder.com/lowes/:

1. Look at Lowe's 2010 annual report. On the income statement, you can find the following three descriptions: 1) Lowe's Companies, Inc., 2) amounts in millions, 3) Fiscal Year Ended January 28, 2011. To which assumption does each description best relate?
2. Look at Lowe's consolidated statement of earnings. The statement contains one major source of revenues and five expenses. A) Can you identify them? B) What were the company's net earnings for 2010?
3. Look at Lowe's 2010 balance sheet. A) Write out in numbers the company's accounting equation (A = L + E) for 2010. B) How many different assets does the company disclose on the balance sheet?
4. Look at Lowe's 2010 statement of shareholders' equity. A) Which column of the statement contains the statement of retained earnings? B) How much is the beginning and ending balance of the statement of retained earnings? C) For the most recent year presented, is the amount for net income on the retained earnings the same as net income on the statement of earnings?
   D) Is the balance in retained earnings the same as the balance on the balance sheet?
5. Look at Lowe's 2010 statement of cash flows. How much cash did Lowe's generate or use for operating, investing, and financing activities during the most recent year?

Visit **www.cengage.com/login** for additional materials to enhance your lectures!

prepcard CHAPTER 2 Corporate Financial Statements

What's Inside

Key topics in this chapter: Define the three major forms of business; explain what Generally Accepted Accounting Principles are; list the main sections of a classified balance sheet and a multi-step income statement; prepare horizontal and vertical analyses of financial statements; explain what information is provided by the statement of stockholders' equity and what other information is presented in a company's annual report besides the financial statements.

Learning Objectives

LO1	Describe the three major forms of business.
LO2	Define generally accepted accounting principles and their origins.
LO3	Describe the main classifications of assets, liabilities, and equity in a classified balance sheet.
LO4	Describe the main subtotals of income on a multi-step income statement.
LO5	Analyze the balance sheet and the income statement using horizontal and vertical analyses.
LO6	Describe the purpose of a statement of stockholders' equity.
LO7	Describe the types of information usually disclosed along with financial statements.

Chapter Outline

Lecture Example

Statement of Stockholders' Equity:

1. What is total stockholders' equity based on the following account balances?

Common stock	$300,000
Retained earnings	100,000
Treasury stock	50,000

2. Prepare a comparative income statement, with vertical analysis for both 2012 and 2011 as a percent of sales, and comment upon significant changes.

Troy Company	2012	2011
Income tax expense	$ 4,000	$ 3,200
Administrative expenses	3,700	2,000
Net sales	80,000	60,000
Selling expenses	19,000	11,000
Cost of goods sold	40,000	32,000

Lecture Example Solution

1. **Answer: $350,000.** Treasury stock is common stock that the company has purchased back from stockholders. Since the purchase of treasury stock is effectively a return of capital to owners, the balance in Treasury Stock is subtracted from stockholders' equity. Treasury stock is a contra-equity account.

2. Troy Company
Comparative Income Statement
For Years Ending December 31, 2012 and 2011

	2012		2011	
Net sales	$80,000	100.0%	$60,000	100.0%
Cost of goods sold	40,000	50.0%	32,000	53.3%
Gross profit	$40,000	50.0%	$28,000	46.7%
Selling expenses	19,000	23.8%	11,000	18.3%
Administrative expense	3,700	4.6%	2,000	3.3%
Total operating expense	$22,700	28.4%	$13,000	21.7%
Operating profit	$17,300	21.6%	$15,000	25.0%
Income tax expense	4,000	5.0%	3,200	5.3%
Net income	$13,300	16.6%	$11,800	19.7%

Net income as a percentage of net sales was lower in 2012 than 2011 indicating lower profitability. The higher gross profit in 2012 (50.0% versus 46.7% in 2011) was more than offset by the higher operating expenses (28.4 in 2012 versus 21.7% in 2011).

Your Students Will Ask About...

What are the differences among the three types of business forms?

Characteristic	Proprietorship	Partnership	Corporation
Legal entity	No	No	Yes
Limited liability	No	No	Yes
Unlimited life	No	No	Yes
One owner allowed	Yes	No	Yes
Business taxed	No	No	Yes

What are the main advantages and disadvantages of forming a corporation?

Advantages	Disadvantages
Separate legal liability (explain limited liability)	Double tax (explain)
Ability to sell stock and raise capital	More regulation (paperwork)
Extra: You might want to briefly explain the requirements to apply for an S-corporation and the benefits of qualifying for an S-corporation (no double tax and limited liability).	

What is the difference between a private corporation and a public corporation?
Students get confused with the term "public corporation"; they think it must have something to do with public entity (government), etc. Explain that the term "public" stands for publicly traded, which means the ownership of the company is available to the public at large.

What are Generally Accepted Accounting Principles and what do they do?
Financial accounting practice is governed by concepts and rules known as generally accepted accounting principles (GAAP). You might want to give an example of how in every sport there is a regulatory body and without it no two teams could compete fairly with one another. Just like in sports, businesses have to follow business concepts such as consistency, objectivity, business entity, etc.

What can we do with a company's annual report?
Show the students several annual reports. You might want to use Home Depot's or Lowe's. Explain the main sections and provide examples of how the reports are used by external users.

Comparative Analysis

Visit http://investor.shareholder.com/lowes/:

1. Look at the full company name at the top of any of Lowe's financial statements. Can you tell from the name what form of business Lowe's uses?
2. Look at the third paragraph in Lowe's Report of Independent Registered Public Accounting Firm. According to the auditor, are Lowe's financial statements prepared in accordance with GAAP?
3. Look at Lowe's income statement. What form of income statement does the company use?
4. Conduct and interpret horizontal and vertical analyses of Lowe's inventory and cost of goods sold for 2011.

Chapter Updates

- Current year financial statements provided for Bed, Bath, and Beyond throughout the chapter
- IFRS Post-it included that discusses differences in reporting of extraordinary items from GAAP
- Revised Making It Real box with current year financials for both Wal-Mart and Target
- Home Depot Analysis feature has been updated to 2010 financials
- Added Concept Questions, Multiple-Choice, and Brief Exercises
- Increased the number of assignable Exercises, Problems, and Cases

prepcard CHAPTER 3 Recording Accounting Transactions

What's Inside

Key topics in this chapter: Explain why companies need accounting information systems; explain how different transactions affect the accounting equation; understand debits and credits in a double entry accounting system and how we use T-accounts; illustrate the process of journalizing, posting to the ledger, and preparing a trial balance.

Learning Objectives

LO1	Describe the purpose of an accounting information system.
LO2	Analyze the effect of accounting transactions on the accounting equation.
LO3	Understand how T-accounts and debits and credits are used in a double entry accounting system.
LO4	Describe the purpose of the journal, ledger, and trial balance.
LO5	Record and post accounting transactions and prepare a trial balance and financial statements.

Chapter Outline

Lecture Example

X Inc. entered into the following transactions in July, its first month of operations.

1) Sold common stock for $2,000 cash
2) Bought $450 of equipment on account
3) Bought $750 of supplies for cash
4) Provided services on account for $490
5) Paid $260 of the $450 payable created in (2)
6) Paid $550 cash for salaries
7) Provided services for $690 cash
8) Paid $200 in dividends
9) Collected $470 of the $490 receivable created in (4)

Journalize the transactions, post to the ledger, and prepare a trial balance.

Lecture Example Solution

1) Cash	2,000	
Common Stock		2,000
2) Equipment	450	
Accounts Payable		450
3) Supplies	750	
Cash		750
4) Accounts Receivable	490	
Service Revenue		490
5) Accounts Payable	260	
Cash		260
6) Salaries Expense	550	
Cash		550
7) Cash	690	
Service Revenue		690
8) Dividends	200	
Cash		200
9) Cash	470	
Accounts Receivable		470

Your Students Will Ask About...

Why do we need an accounting system? Why do we need to journalize and post manually when we have computers that can do it for us?

Explain that although many automated accounting programs can successfully do the work, accountants need to understand how an accounting system works. Give examples.

What is a debit and what is a credit?

T-accounts	
Debit is the **left** side of the T-account	**Credit** is the **right** side of the T-account
Asset, Expense, and Dividend accounts increase with debits	Liability, Equity, and Revenue accounts increase with credits
Asset, Expense, and Dividend accounts have a normal balance on the debit side	Liability, Equity, and Revenue accounts have a normal balance on the credit side

Some students have a hard time with debits and credits, especially if they have worked in banking or try to associate debits with a debit card. They may say: "Why does cash increase with debits? Every time that I use my debit card at the store, my cash goes down."

Tell your students that when a bank customer uses a debit card, the bank's liability to the customer is decreasing. The bank decreases its liability with a debit—thus, the term "debit card."

Why is cash received sometimes a revenue and sometimes a liability?

Explain the difference between the following two entries.

Received $1,000 cash from customers for services earned	Increase Cash Increase Service Revenue Cash 1,000 Service Revenue 1,000
Received $1,000 cash for services to be performed at a later date	Increase Cash Increase Liability Cash 1,000 Unearned Revenue 1,000

Lecture Example Solution (continued)

Cash

	Debit	Credit	
(1)	2,000	750	(3)
(7)	690	260	(5)
(9)	470	550	(6)
		200	(8)

Common Stock

	Debit	Credit	
		2,000	(1)

Accounts Receivable

	Debit	Credit	
(4)	490	470	(9)

Dividends

	Debit	Credit	
(8)	200		

Supplies

	Debit	Credit	
(3)	750		

Service Revenue

	Debit	Credit	
		490	(4)
		690	(7)

Equipment

	Debit	Credit	
(2)	450		

Salaries Expense

	Debit	Credit	
(6)	550		

Accounts Payable

	Debit	Credit	
(5)	260	450	(2)

X Inc. Trial Balance
July 31

	Debit	Credit
Cash	$1,400	
Accounts Receivable	20	
Supplies	750	
Equipment	450	
Accounts Payable		$ 190
Capital Stock		2,000
Service Revenue		1,180
Salaries Expense	550	
Dividends	200	
	$3,370	$3,370

Comparative Analysis

Visit http://investor.shareholder.com/lowes/:

1. Look at Lowe's balance sheet. How many accounts are listed?
2. Consider a scenario in which one stockholder of Lowe's sells his or her stock to another stockholder. Is this an economic event relating to Lowe's? Is it an accounting transaction?
3. Look at Lowe's income statement. Which accounts would be increased with a credit entry? Would the remaining accounts be increased with a debit entry?
4. Look at Lowe's balance sheet. Provide examples of accounts on the balance sheet that would be increased with a debit entry. Which of the accounts would be increased with a credit entry?

Chapter Updates

- Improved screening of financial statements to better differentiate between real-world statements and fictional statements
- Added Concept Questions, Multiple-Choice, and Brief Exercises
- Increased the number of assignable Exercises, Problems, and Cases

prepcard

CHAPTER 4
Accrual Accounting and Adjusting Entries

What's Inside

Key topics in this chapter: Define the accrual basis of accounting; explain and provide examples of the four major adjusting entries; explain the closing process and journalize the four basic closing entries; describe the steps of the accounting cycle.

Learning Objectives

LO1	Describe how income is measured and reported under the accrual and cash bases of accounting.
LO2	Identify the four major circumstances in which adjusting journal entries are necessary.
LO3	Record and post adjusting journal entries, and prepare an adjusted trial balance and financial statements.
LO4	Describe the purpose of the closing process and prepare closing entries.
LO5	Describe the steps of the accounting cycle.

Lecture Example Solution

Use this example to explain the consequences of not recording adjusting entries on the financial statements:

At the end of the fiscal year (December 31), the following adjusting entries were omitted:	(a) No adjusting entry was made to transfer the $1,000 of prepaid rent from the asset account to the expense account.	(b) No adjusting entry was made to record accrued fees of $500 for services provided to customers.

Assuming that financial statements are prepared before the errors are discovered, indicate the effect of each error, considered individually, by inserting the dollar amount in the appropriate spaces. Insert 0 if the error does not affect the item.

	Error (a)		Error (b)	
	Overstated	Understated	Overstated	Understated
(1) Assets at December 31 would be	$1,000	$ -0-	$ -0-	$ 500
(2) Liabilities at December 31 would be	$ -0-	$ -0-	$ -0-	$-0-
(3) Net income for the year would be	$1,000	$ -0-	$ -0-	$ 500
(4) Stockholders' equity at Dec. 31 would be	$1,000	$ -0-	$ -0-	$ 500

Chapter Outline

Your Students Will Ask About...

I don't understand adjusting entries! Why do we need to record adjusting entries?

Explain how the accrual basis of accounting requires companies to record revenues when earned and expenses when incurred regardless of when cash is received or paid. Show this example to explain this concept:
On 12/1/XX a doctor received $5,000 in advance from a patient for a procedure that will take place next year. Is the $5,000 payment a revenue for this year? Record the entries:

12/1/ XX	Cash	5,000	
	Unearned Revenue		5,000
	(To record 5,000 as a current liability as of December of current year)		
Adjusting entry after procedure is performed in January			
1/31/ XX	Unearned Revenue	5,000	
	Service Revenue		5,000
	(To record $5,000 of revenue earned in January)		

What financial statements are affected when recording adjusting entries? What are the consequences of not recording them?

All adjusting entries always affect the income statement and the balance sheet.

Adjusting entry for $1,200 supplies used during the period:

12/31/ XX	Supplies Expense	1,200	
	Supplies		1,200
	(To record 1,200 of supplies used during the period)		

Account	Financial Statement	Effect of not recording the adjusting entry
Supplies Expense	Income Statement	Understated
Supplies	Balance Sheet	Overstated

What is the difference between accruals and deferrals?

Provide one example of each.

Deferrals: Cash is received or paid now, but revenue or expense recognition will take place later. Use auto insurance as an example. From the insurer's perspective, it is an unearned revenue. From the student's perspective, it is a prepaid expense.

Accruals: Revenue or expense recognition takes place now, but cash will be received or paid later. Use utilities as an example. From the company's perspective, a bill is an account receivable. From the student's perspective, it is an account payable.

Comparative Analysis

Visit http://investor.shareholder.com/lowes/:

1. Look at the Revenue Recognition paragraph in Lowe's Note 1: Summary of Significant Accounting Policies. How can you tell from that paragraph that Lowe's uses the accrual basis of accounting?
2. Look at Lowe's statement of cash flows. Over the three years presented, what was the total net income on a cash basis and how does that compare to total net income on an accrual basis?
3. Look at the Revenue Recognition and Self-Insurance paragraphs in Lowe's Note 1: Summary of Significant Accounting Policies. Do these paragraphs represent examples of deferred revenues, accrued revenues, deferred expenses, or accrued expenses?

Chapter Updates

- Updated American Eagle financial statement data throughout the chapter to current year
- Revised Making It Real box on American Eagle Outfitters
- Added new infographic art for exhibits 4-2, 4-3, 4-4, and 4-5 to help better illustrate adjusting journal entry scenarios
- Added Concept Questions, Multiple-Choice, and Brief Exercises
- Increased the number of assignable Exercises, Problems, and Cases

prepcard CHAPTER 5 Internal Control and Cash

What's Inside

Key topics in this chapter: Describe the role, objectives, and the five components of internal controls; explain how to prepare a bank reconciliation and how it can help control cash; understand how to establish and how to replenish a petty cash fund; describe and illustrate the reporting of cash in the financial statements; and evaluate cash through horizontal, vertical, and ratio analyses.

Learning Objectives

LO1	Describe the role of internal control in a business.
LO2	Describe the five components of internal control.
LO3	Understand two methods of internal control over cash—bank reconciliations and petty cash funds.
LO4	Describe the reporting of cash.
LO5	Evaluate cash through the calculation and interpretation of horizontal, vertical, and ratio analyses.

Chapter Outline

Lecture Examples and Solutions

Instructions: Indicate the proper place for each of the following reconciling items by inserting the correct *letter* in the bank reconciliation form below in the Answers column.

ABC Co., Bank Reconciliation

Cash balance per bank statement	$ XX	Cash balance per ABC's records	$ XX
Additions	A	Additions	C
Deductions	B	Deductions	D
Adjusted balance	$ XX	Adjusted balance	$ XX

		Answers
1.	Bank debit memorandum for service charges, $35	*D*
2.	Bank credit memorandum for collection of loan, $5,000	*C*
3.	Canceled check for $135 erroneously listed on bank statement as $153	*A*
4.	Canceled check omitted from the journal, $45	*D*
5.	Deposit in transit, $3,000	*A*
6.	Checks outstanding, $16,200	*B*
7.	Bank debit memorandum for check returned for insufficient funds, $55	*D*
8.	Deposit of $950 recorded in journal as $590	*C*

Instructions: ABC decides to establish a petty cash fund of $200 on Jan. 1. On Feb. 15, the fund is replenished and the following receipts for items paid out of petty cash are recorded: office supplies, $40; postage, $35; miscellaneous, $55; repairs, $60. On Feb. 15, petty cash has a balance of $8. (Note: Explain that $2 is missing.)

Entry to establish petty cash fund:			
Jan. 1	Petty Cash	200	
	Cash		200
Entry to replenish the petty cash fund:			
Feb. 15	Supplies Expense	40	
	Postage Expense	35	
	Miscellaneous Expense	55	
	Repairs Expense	60	
	Cash Over and Short	2	
	Cash		192

Your Students Will Ask About...

What is so important about internal controls?
Explain to your students that companies have to establish a control framework to make sure the business objectives are achieved, assets are protected from theft and misuse, and financial data are recorded correctly.

Why do we need to record adjusting entries to adjust the company's cash after completing a bank reconciliation?
Remind your students that the adjustments made to the company's book balance must be journalized in order to adjust the company's cash balance to the actual cash balance.

Why is a new account needed for Petty Cash? Isn't cash the same thing?
Show your students the entry to set up petty cash and let them know that the set up of petty cash takes place usually only once, and petty cash from that day on will always show the same balance. For example, set up petty cash of $200.

Set up petty cash: Jan. 2011			Balance Sheet As of any time after Jan. 2011	
Petty Cash	200		Assets:	
Cash		200 →	Petty Cash	200

Why doesn't the replenishment of petty cash include a credit to petty cash?
Students have a hard time with this concept. They tend to credit petty cash instead of cash. Show them the replenishment entry and explain that cash is always credited for the total amount needed to bring the account up to date (original petty cash amount). (See lecture example.) Emphasize that expenses paid from a petty cash fund are recorded when the fund is replenished, not when the cash is disbursed.

What type of account is "cash over and short"?
"Cash over and short" is a temporary account (income statement account) and is not an asset (balance sheet account). It is credited when cash is over and debited when cash is short. Explain that the account will have credits and debits depending on if cash is over or short.

Comparative Analysis

Visit http://investor.shareholder.com/lowes/:

1. Look at the Report of Independent Registered Public Accounting Firm accompanying Lowe's financial statements. What was the auditor's opinion regarding the effectiveness of Lowe's internal control?
2. Look at Lowe's balance sheet account: cash and cash equivalents equal $652 million. Looking at the Cash and Cash Equivalents paragraph in Lowe's first note, what types of investments does the company include in cash equivalents?
3. Using Lowe's financial statements, calculate and interpret (1) horizontal and vertical analyses of cash and (2) free cash flow.

Chapter Updates

- Revised internal control report from Domino's Pizza as well as all financial data throughout
- New Making It Real box on Weatherford International discusses internal control monitoring issues
- Added Concept Questions, Multiple-Choice, and Brief Exercises
- Increased the number of assignable Exercises, Problems, and Cases

prepcard CHAPTER 6 Receivables

What's Inside

Key topics in this chapter: Describe the common classifications of receivables; explain the differences between the methods used to account for uncollectible receivables; demonstrate how to estimate bad debt expense; and understand the accounting for notes receivable.

Learning Objectives

LO1	Describe the recording and reporting of accounts receivable.
LO2	Understand the methods used to account for uncollectible receivables.
LO3	Understand the methods for estimating bad debt expense.
LO4	Evaluate accounts receivable through the calculation and interpretation of horizontal, vertical, and ratio analyses.
LO5	Understand the accounting for notes receivable.

Chapter Outline

Lecture Example

(a) Using the allowance method, prepare entries for the following:

(1) Record bad debt expense at December 31, the end of the fiscal year. The accounts receivable account has a balance of $500,000, and the allowance for bad debts account before adjustment has a credit balance of $1,000. Analysis of the receivables indicates that the allowance account should be $21,000.

(2) In March of the following fiscal year, $500 owed by S. Co. is written off as uncollectible.

(3) Eight months later, $250 of the S. Co. account is reinstated and payment of that amount is received.

(4) In October, $500 is received on $1,500 owed by C. Co., and the remainder is written off as uncollectible.

(b) Based on the data in (a) (1) above, what is the net realizable value of the accounts receivable as reported on the balance sheet as of December 31?

(c) Prepare entries to record transactions (1), (2), and (3) in (a) above assuming that the business uses the direct write-off method.

Lecture Example Solution

(a)	**(1)**	Bad Debt Expense	20,000	
		Allowance for Bad Debts		20,000
	(2)	Allowance for Bad Debts	500	
		Accounts Receivable—S. Co.		500
	(3)	Accounts Receivable—S. Co.	250	
		Allowance for Bad Debts		250
		Cash	250	
		Accounts Receivable—S. Co.		250
	(4)	Cash	500	
		Allowance for Bad Debts	1,000	
		Accounts Receivable—C. Co.		1,500
(b)		$479,000 ($500,000 − $21,000)		
(c)	**(1)**	Bad Debt Expense	500	
		Accounts Receivable—S. Co.		500
	(2)	Accounts Receivable—S. Co.	250	
		Bad Debt Expense		250
		Cash	250	
		Accounts Receivable—S. Co.		250
	(3)	Cash	500	
		Bad Debt Expense	1,000	
		Accounts Receivable—C. Co.		1,500

Your Students Will Ask About...

What are the differences between accounts receivable and notes receivable?

Explain and provide examples:

Accounts Receivable	Credit granted to customers for sales of merchandise or services on account. These receivables are usually collected within 30 to 60 days.	More informal. Usually no interest.
Notes Receivable	Credit granted through a formal credit instrument "promissory note." Notes are often used for credit periods of more than 60 days.	Formal, written promise to pay a specified amount. It includes date when payment is due, to whom payment will be made, and usually interest.

What are the differences between the direct write-off method and allowance method?

Explain "matching."

Direct Write-off Method	Allowance Method
When is the expense recorded:	
Under the direct write-off method, the expense of an uncollectible receivable is recognized when the company decides the account is uncollectible (throughout the year). This method should be used only when: • It is impossible to estimate uncollectible accounts with any reasonable accuracy OR • The amount of the uncollectible accounts is immaterial **No adjusting entry; therefore, it can violate the matching principle.** **Advantage:** Simplicity	Under the allowance method, the expense of uncollectible receivables is estimated and recorded at the end of the year (before the customers actually fail to pay). This method adheres to the matching principle by recognizing the expense of uncollectible accounts in the same period that the sales revenue is recorded. **It requires an adjusting entry:** Bad Debt Expense xxx Allowance for Bad Debts xxx
Write-off entry: Throughout the year as accounts default: Bad Debt Expense xxx Accounts Receivable xxx	**Write-off entry:** Throughout the year as accounts default: Allowance for Bad Debts xxx Accounts Receivable xxx
Very important: Explain that with the direct write-off method the write-off entry (see above) affects expenses and therefore the income statement.	Very important: Explain that with the allowance method, the write-off entry (see above) does NOT affect expenses or the income statement. Both accounts are balance sheet accounts.

When using the allowance method and estimating "bad debt expense" at end of year, how do we determine the amount of bad debt expense?

Show examples and explain in detail all three approaches: the percentage-of-sales approach, the percentage-of-receivables approach, and the aging of accounts receivable approach.

Comparative Analysis

Visit http://investor.shareholder.com/lowes/:

1. Look at Lowe's balance sheet. How can you tell how Lowe's accounts for the company's receivables?

Chapter Updates

- Revised financials for Colgate-Palmolive and Clorox chapter examples
- New IFRS note on wording differences between US GAAP and IFRS on requirements that must be met to record a credit sale
- Added Concept Questions, Multiple-Choice, and Brief Exercises
- Increased the number of assignable Exercises, Problems, and Cases

prepcard CHAPTER 7 Inventory

What's Inside

Key topics in this chapter: Describe the importance of inventory and illustrate the reporting of merchandise inventory in the financial statements; calculate cost of goods sold under the different costing methods; understand the income and tax effects of inventory cost flow assumptions; evaluate the effects of inventory errors; illustrate how inventory is estimated; explain how to apply the lower-of-cost-or-market rule to inventory.

Learning Objectives

LO1	Describe inventory and how it is recorded, expensed, and reported.
LO2	Calculate the cost of goods sold using different inventory costing methods.
LO3	Understand the income and tax effects of inventory cost flow assumptions.
LO4	Analyze the effects of inventory errors.
LO5	Demonstrate how inventory is estimated.
LO6	Apply the lower-of-cost-or-market rule to inventory.
LO7	Evaluate inventory through the calculation of horizontal, vertical, and ratio analyses.
LO8	Appendix: Record purchases and calculate the cost of goods sold under a periodic system.

Chapter Outline

Lecture Example

Beginning inventory, purchases, and sales data for July:

July 1	Inventory	10 units at $4
7	Sale	5 units
12	Purchase	15 units at $5
20	Sale	10 units

The business maintains a perpetual inventory system. Determine the (1) ending inventory and (2) cost of goods sold assuming the company uses (a) FIFO (first-in, first-out), (b) LIFO (last-in, first-out), or (c) moving average.

Lecture Example Solution

(a) FIFO

Date	Inventory Purchased	Inventory Sold	Inventory on Hand
July 1			10 × $4 = $40
July 7		5 × $4 = $20	5 × $4 = $20
July 12	15 × $5 = $75		5 × $4 = $20 15 × $5 = $75
July 20		5 × $4 = $20 5 × $5 = $25	10 × $5 = $50

(a) FIFO: (1) Ending inventory = $50 (2) Cost of goods sold = $65

(b) LIFO

Date	Inventory Purchased	Inventory Sold	Inventory on Hand
July 1			10 × $4 = $40
July 7		5 × $4 = $20	5 × $4 = $20
July 12	15 × $5 = $75		5 × $4 = $20 15 × $5 = $75
July 20		10 × $5 = $50	5 × $4 = $20 5 × $5 = $25

(b) LIFO: (1) Ending inventory = $45 (2) Cost of goods sold = $70

(c) Moving Average

Date	Inventory Purchased	Inventory Sold	Inventory on Hand
July 1			10 × $4 = $40
July 7		5 × $4 = $20	5 × $4 = $20
July 12	15 × $5 = $75		5 × $4 = $20 15 × $5 = $75 20 units = $95
July 20		10 × $4.75 = $47.50	10 × $4.75 = $47.50

Visit **www.cengage.com/login** for additional materials to enhance your lectures!

Chapter Outline (continued)

Your Students Will Ask About...

Why do we need so many different inventory methods? It just makes it more confusing.

Remind your students that the value of your inventory left at end of period is shown on the balance sheet and the value of the merchandise sold is shown on the income statement (cost of goods sold = COGS). Explain that most likely the cost of the merchandise changes throughout the year. When the pricing changes, it creates an issue: which units do you use for inventory and which ones for (COGS)? Explain:

Remind that FIFO and LIFO apply to COGS		
	COGS on the Income Statement	**Ending Inventory on the Balance Sheet**
First-in, first-out **FIFO**	First items purchased	Last items purchased
Last-in, first-out **LIFO**	Last items purchased	First items purchased

Do you mean that using different inventory methods will result in different amounts of net income?

Yes. Show an example like the lecture example (cost is increasing) and explain that you must make an assumption about which units are used for ending inventory and which units are used for inventory sold. Explain that depending on the method used—FIFO, LIFO, or moving average—it will have an impact on the financial statements. Show this:

During periods of rising prices (inflation)					
If using:	COGS	NI	RE	Tax	Balance Sheet (Asset)
FIFO	Low	High	High	High	High
LIFO	High	Low	Low	Low	Low

Lecture Example Solution (continued)

(c) Moving Average: (1) Ending inventory = \$47.50 (2) Cost of goods sold = \$67.50

Note: Explain that the total cost of inventory available for sale in all three methods is \$115 (\$40 + \$75). The difference is the allocation of the \$115 between COGS (income statement) and ending inventory (balance sheet). FIFO = \$50 + \$65 = \$115; LIFO = \$45 + \$70 = \$115; and Moving Average = \$47.50 + \$67.50 = \$115

Your Students Will Ask About... (continued)

What are the effects of errors on inventory?

If inventory is understated		
	Current Period	Next Period
Inventory	Understated	Correct
COGS	Overstated	Understated
Net Income	Understated	Overstated
Total Assets	Understated	Correct

Note: You can also use the same table to explain what happens if inventory is overstated.

Chapter Updates

- Revised real-world data for Wal-Mart and Safeway
- Added IFRS notes on differences in inventory treatments from US GAAP
- Significantly revised section on evaluating a company's management of inventory to include a recent example using SuperValu, Inc.
- Added Concept Questions, Multiple-Choice, and Brief Exercises
- Increased the number of assignable Exercises, Problems, and Cases

Comparative Analysis

Visit http://investor.shareholder.com/lowes/:

1. Look at Lowe's balance sheet and income statement. What name does the company use for its inventory and the cost of goods sold? Is inventory the company's largest current asset? What is its cost? Is the cost of goods sold the company's largest expense?
2. Look at the Merchandise Inventory paragraph of Lowe's first note. What cost flow assumption does the company use? As a result, which inventory units are represented by the \$8,321 million balance on the company's balance sheet, and which units are represented by the \$31,663 million cost of goods sold on the company's income statement?
3. Look at Lowe's Merchandise Inventory paragraph in its first note. Does it follow the lower-of-cost-or-market rule?
4. Using Lowe's financial information, calculate and interpret (1) horizontal and vertical analyses of inventory and cost of goods sold, (2) inventory turnover ratio, and (3) days in inventory ratio.

prepcard

CHAPTER 8 Fixed Assets and Intangible Assets

What's Inside

Key topics in this chapter: Define, classify, and account for fixed assets; compute depreciation expense using the following three methods: straight-line, double-declining-balance, and units-of-activity; revise depreciation estimates; classify expenditures after acquisition; journalize entries for disposal of fixed assets; evaluate a company's fixed assets; define and account for intangible assets.

Learning Objectives

LO1	Describe fixed assets and how they are recorded, expensed, and reported.
LO2	Calculate and compare depreciation expense using straight-line, double-declining-balance, and units-of-activity methods.
LO3	Understand the effects of adjustments that may be made during a fixed asset's useful life.
LO4	Record the disposal of fixed assets.
LO5	Evaluate fixed assets through the calculation and interpretation of horizontal, vertical, and ratio analyses.
LO6	Describe the cash flow effect of acquiring fixed assets.
LO7	Describe intangible assets and how they are recorded, expensed, and reported.

Chapter Updates

- Revised real-world data for McDonald's and Wendy's/Arby's
- Revised discussion of capital and revenue expeditures
- Improved screening and descriptions of the key formulas for the three depreciation methods
- Added Concept Questions, Multiple-Choice, and Brief Exercises
- Increased the number of assignable Exercises, Problems, and Cases

Lecture Example

Recording Fixed Assets: Cost Principle

1. What is the cost of the truck, based on the following data?

Truck purchase price	$55,000
Sales tax	3,300
Delivery and insurance cost during transit	500
Insurance (1-year policy after purchase)	1,500

2. Assuming the company paid cash, how do you record the entry to show the purchase of the truck?

   Assume the truck will have a 4-year useful life (90,000 miles) and $15,000 salvage value. It was purchased January 1, 2009. Compute depreciation expense for year one using the straight-line method (SLM), the double-declining-balance method (DDB), and the units-of-activity method (25,000 miles for year one).

Lecture Example Solution

1. $58,800. Following the cost principle, fixed assets should be recorded at the cost of acquiring them. This includes all costs incurred to get the asset delivered, installed, and ready to use. All the above costs (except for the one-year insurance policy) are necessary to get the asset into its condition and location for intended use and are therefore included in the cost of the truck.

2.

Equipment	58,800	
Cash		58,800
(To record the purchase of truck)		

Assets	=	Liabilities	+	Equity
+58,800				
−58,800				

SLM = (Cost − Salvage Value)/Useful Life = ($58,800 − $15,000)/4 = $10,950

DDB = Depreciation Rate × Net Book Value
DDB = (SLM × 2) × (Cost − Accumulated Depreciation)
DDB = (25% × 2) × ($58,800 − $0) = $29,400

Units-of-Activity Method:
Depreciation Exp. per unit: (Cost − Salvage Value)/Useful life units
= ($58,800 − $15,000)/90,000 = $0.487 per mile (rounded)

Depreciation Exp. = Depreciation Exp. per unit × Actual units of activity
= $0.487 × 25,000 miles = $12,175

Visit **www.cengage.com/login** for additional materials to enhance your lectures!

Your Students Will Ask About...

What is depreciation?

Explain how the matching principle plays a major role in how we record transactions and report the financial statements. Provide an example.

Machinery	Depreciation Expense
Recorded as an ASSET when purchased	Transferred to an EXPENSE account as used

This is what we called depreciation expense, which is the process of recording an estimated amount of the portion of the asset that was "used up" during each year. Since depreciation is only an estimate of the usefulness of a long-term asset that has expired, the asset account is not reduced directly. Rather, a contra-account called Accumulated Depreciation is used to reduce the asset. For example, the adjusting entry to record depreciation on a piece of machinery would be:

Depreciation Expense—Machinery . . . XXX
    Accumulated Depreciation—Machinery . . . XXX

Which depreciation method is the best to use?

Explain the advantages and disadvantages of the three methods illustrated within the chapter. For instance, straight-line method (ease of use), units-of-activity method (better matching), and double-declining-balance method (tax deferral).

Does it really matter if you classify an item as capital or revenue expenditure?

After reading the textbook, discuss how WorldCom treated operating expenses as capital expenditures. What were the consequences on WorldCom's income statement and balance sheet?

Chapter Outline

Comparative Analysis

Visit http://investor.shareholder.com/lowes/ and answer the following questions:

1. Look at Lowe's balance sheet. What name does the company use for its fixed assets, and what specific fixed asset accounts does it list? According to Lowe's notes, what is the historical cost of its fixed assets, how much depreciation expense has been accumulated to date, and what is the net book value of those fixed assets? According to Lowe's income statement, what depreciation expense does Lowe's report for the current year?
2. Calculate and interpret horizontal and vertical analyses of fixed assets and depreciation expense.
3. Look at Lowe's statement of cash flows. How much total cash has the company spent to acquire fixed assets over the past three years? Compare Lowe's capital expenditures in the most recent year to its cash from operations.

prepcard CHAPTER 9 Liabilities

What's Inside

Key topics in this chapter: Describe the importance of recording and reporting current liabilities and long-term liabilities; illustrate how bonds work and the corresponding journal entries for bond issuance, interest payments, and maturity; explain leases and contingent liabilities.

Learning Objectives

LO1	Describe the recording and reporting of various current liabilities.
LO2	Describe the reporting of long-term liabilities and the cash flows associated with those liabilities.
LO3	Understand the nature of bonds and record a bond's issuance, interest payments, and maturity.
LO4	Account for a bond that is redeemed prior to maturity.
LO5	Understand additional liabilities such as leases and contingent liabilities.
LO6	Evaluate liabilities through the calculation and interpretation of horizontal, vertical, and ratio analyses.
LO7	Appendix: Determine a bond's issuance price.
LO8	Appendix: Record bond interest payments under the effective interest method.

Chapter Outline

Lecture Example and Solution

Use this example to illustrate short-term note payable:

Note Payable: Journalize the following:

4/30 Issued a $5,000, 1-month, 6% note to AZ Co. for $5,000 cash.

5/31 Paid AZ Co. the amount owed on note dated April 30.

4/30	Cash	5,000	
	Notes Payable		5,000
5/31	Notes Payable	5,000	
	Interest Expense	25	
	Cash		5,025

Interest Expense = $5,000 × 6% × 1/12 = $25

Use this example to illustrate long-term bonds payable:

Bonds Payable: On the first day of the current fiscal year, $500,000 of 5-year, 5% bonds, with interest payable semiannually, were sold for $450,000. Prepare entries to record the following transactions for the current fiscal year:

(a) Issuance of the bonds
(b) First semiannual interest payment using the straight-line method

(a) Cash	450,000	
Discount on Bonds Payable	50,000	
Bonds Payable		500,000
(b) Interest Expense	17,500	
Discount on Bonds Payable		5,000
Cash		12,500

Use this example to explain the effect of amortizing the discount or premium on bonds payable:

True or False: The amount of interest expense reported on the income statement will be more than the interest paid to bondholders if the bonds were originally sold at a discount. **Explain that amortization of discount on bonds payable increases interest expense and amortization of premium decreases interest expense.**

Chapter Outline (continued)

Chapter Updates

- Added additional discussion on unearned revenues
- Revised real-world data for Advance Auto Parts
- New Making It Real box discusses Google's recent issuance of bonds
- Added Concept Questions, Multiple-Choice, and Brief Exercises
- Increased the number of assignable Exercises, Problems, and Cases

Your Students Will Ask About...

Why does it make a difference if liabilities are divided properly between current and long-term liabilities?
Explain the difference between short-term and long-term liabilities. Provide examples of annual reports and show the balance sheet and financial statement analysis.

What makes a current liability?
Explain that a current liability is an obligation that is expected to be satisfied or paid within one year or less. Examples of typical current liabilities are: purchases of inventory on account, compensation of employees (accrued wages), repayment of debt, and the incurrence of taxes.

I don't understand discounts and premiums on bonds payable. What type of account is a discount and a premium?
Explain why bonds are sold at a discount or at a premium. Provide examples of issuing bonds at a discount and at a premium. Explain what happens:

If stated rate equal to market rate	No discount	Interest payment **equals** interest expense
If stated rate less than market rate	Discount	Interest expense **greater than** the interest payment
If stated rate greater than market rate	Premium	Interest expense **less than** the interest payment

When do we report contingent liabilities?

	Circumstances	Treatment
If contingent liability is	Probable and can be estimated	Report on balance sheet
	Reasonably possible or cannot be estimated	Disclose in notes
	Remote	Ignore

Comparative Analysis

Visit http://investor.shareholder.com/lowes/.

1. Look at Lowe's balance sheet and statement of cash flows. What happened to the prior-year balance in Current maturities of long-term debt? Did Lowe's pay off the entire balance?
2. Look at Lowe's note on Leases. What is the amount of total minimum lease payments under operating leases and capitalized lease obligations? Which of the two amounts would be reported on the balance sheet?
3. Using Lowe's information, calculate and interpret (1) horizontal and vertical analyses of liabilities, (2) the current ratio, and (3) the debt to assets ratio.

prepcard CHAPTER 10 Stockholders' Equity

What's Inside

Key topics in this chapter: Describe the nature of the corporate form of business; describe and illustrate the characteristics of stock, classes of stock, and entries for issuing stock; illustrate the differences between cash dividends, stock dividends, and stock splits; understand treasury stock and how treasury stock is recorded and reported.

Learning Objectives

LO1	Describe the characteristics of the corporate form of business.
LO2	Describe the characteristics of common stock and how it is recorded and reported.
LO3	Understand cash dividends, stock dividends, and stock splits.
LO4	Describe the characteristics of preferred stock and how it receives preference in dividends.
LO5	Describe the characteristics of treasury stock and how it is recorded and reported.
LO6	Evaluate equity through the calculation of horizontal, vertical, and ratio analyses.

Chapter Outline

Lecture Examples and Solutions

1. Present entries to record the following:

(a) Issued 1,000 shares of $25 par common stock at $26.
(b) Issued 1,500 shares of no-par common stock in exchange for equipment with a fair market price of $50,000.
(c) Purchased 100 shares of treasury stock at $28.
(d) Sold 100 shares of treasury stock at $32.

(a)	Cash	26,000	
	Common Stock		25,000
	Additional Paid-In Capital		1,000
(b)	Equipment	50,000	
	Common Stock		50,000
(c)	Treasury Stock	2,800	
	Cash		2,800
(d)	Cash	3,200	
	Treasury Stock		2,800
	Additional Paid-In Capital		400

2. A company had stock outstanding as follows during each of its first three years of operations: 2,000 shares of 10%, $100 par, cumulative preferred stock; and 50,000 shares of $10 par common stock. The amounts distributed as dividends are presented below. Determine the total and per share dividends for each class of stock for each year by completing the schedule.

		Preferred		Common	
Year	Dividends	Total	Per Share	Total	Per Share
1	$10,000	(a)	(b)	(g)	(j)
2	25,000	(c)	(d)	(h)	(k)
3	60,000	(e)	(f)	(i)	(l)

(a) $10,000	(b) $5	(g) 0	(j) 0
(c) $25,000	(d) $12.5	(h) 0	(k) 0
(e) $25,000	(f) $12.5	(i) $35,000	(l) $0.70

Chapter Outline (continued)

Your Students Will Ask About...

What is a corporation? Are all privately held corporations small?
Review the characteristics of a corporation, including advantages like the limited liability of owners and the main disadvantage like the double taxation of corporate earnings. Give examples and explain the differences of privately held corporations and well-known publicly traded corporations.

What is the difference between stock issued and stock outstanding?
Explain that stock is issued once it has been sold to stockholders. Stock is "outstanding" if it is still owned by stockholders. Stock that has been reacquired by a corporation is considered issued but not outstanding. Illustrate this by using this equation:

Issued stock − Stock Reacquired = Outstanding Stock

Ask your students to solve the following problem: Company X is authorized to sell 100,000 shares of common stock; 75,000 shares have been issued, and 25,000 have been reacquired by X. How many shares are outstanding? (Answer = 50,000)

Is treasury stock an asset? Does it have a debit balance?
Reinforce the following concept: treasury stock is a contra-equity account, reducing shareholders' equity for the amount returned to shareholders through the purchase of treasury stock. Many students tend to assume that treasury stock is an asset because it has a debit balance.

Are companies supposed to pay dividends on treasury stock?
No, point out that a corporation does not pay dividends on treasury stock, vote on treasury stock, or recognize gains or losses if the treasury stock is reissued.

Your Students Will Ask About... (continued)

What is par value and why do we use it?
Point out that a corporation normally assigns to its common stock a value known as a par value. It is an arbitrary value, and it has lost much of its legal significance over time. Show a few examples of how par value is used when recording and reporting common stock.

Comparative Analysis

Visit http://investor.shareholder.com/lowes/.

1. Look at Lowe's balance sheet. What tells you that Lowe's is a corporation?
2. Look at Lowe's balance sheet. How many shares of common stock did Lowe's have issued and outstanding at the end of 2010? What was the stock's par value? Has the company properly recorded the par value of common stock?
3. Look at Lowe's statement of stockholders' equity and statement of cash flows. What was the total amount of dividends declared in the most recent year? What was the total amount of dividends paid during the year?
4. Look at Lowe's statement of stockholders' equity. Did the company issue any stock during the years presented? Was the issuance a stock dividend?
5. Using Lowe's information, calculate and interpret (1) horizontal and vertical analyses of total equity, (2) earnings per share, (3) return on equity, and (4) dividend payout ratio.
6. Look at Lowe's statement of cash flows. How much cash has the company paid in dividends and for the repurchase of stock over the past three years?

Chapter Updates

- Updated real-world data for Walgreen's
- Added Concept Questions, Multiple-Choice, and Brief Exercises
- Increased the number of assignable Exercises, Problems, and Cases

prepcard **CHAPTER 11**
Statement of Cash Flows

What's Inside

Key topics in this chapter: Describe the purpose of the statement of cash flows; illustrate how to prepare the statement of cash flows; compare the differences between the direct and indirect method when preparing the operating section of a statement of cash flows; illustrate how to prepare the investing and the financing activities section of the statement of cash flows; calculate ratio analysis of the statement of cash flows and interpret the results.

Learning Objectives

LO1	Describe the purpose and format of the statement of cash flows.
LO2	Describe the process of preparing the statement of cash flows.
LO3	Prepare the operating activities section of the statement of cash flows using the direct method.
LO4	Prepare the operating activities section of the statement of cash flows using the indirect method.
LO5	Prepare the investing activities section of the statement of cash flows.
LO6	Prepare the financing activities section of the statement of cash flows.
LO7	Calculate ratio analysis of the statement of cash flows and interpret the results.

Lecture Example

Using the indirect method, prepare a statement of cash flows for X Co. for year ended December 31, 20—. Assume that equipment costing $100,000 was purchased for cash, and equipment costing $60,000 with accumulated depreciation of $40,000 was sold for $15,000; that the stock was issued for cash; and that the only entries in the retained earnings account were net income of $49,000 and cash dividends declared of $11,000.

	Current Year	Preceding Year
Cash	$ 100,000	$ 78,000
Accounts receivable (net)	78,000	85,000
Inventories	101,500	90,000
Equipment	410,000	370,000
Accumulated depreciation	(150,000)	(158,000)
	$ 539,500	$ 465,000
Accounts payable	$ 58,500	$ 55,000
Cash dividends payable	5,000	4,000
Common stock, $10 par	262,000	230,000
Retained earnings	214,000	176,000
	$ 539,500	$ 465,000

Chapter Outline

Chapter Outline (continued)

Your Students Will Ask About...

If we already have the income statement, statement of retained earnings, and the balance sheet, why do we need an additional statement?
You can use the following example:

Income statements:

	Company A	Company B
Sales	100,000	100,000
Expenses	45,000	45,000
Net income	55,000	55,000
Cash held:		
Beginning of year	15,000	15,000
End of year	15,000	15,000
Increase in cash	0	0
Cash received:		
from customers	90,000	70,000
from sale of fixed assets	2,000	15,000
Total cash received	92,000	85,000
Cash paid:		
to suppliers	40,000	44,000
for purchase of fixed assets	50,000	31,000
for purchase of investments	2,000	0
Total cash paid	92,000	85,000
Increase in cash	0	0

Use this example to show how two companies can have the same amount of net income, but very different cash flows. For instance, explain how Company A not only is collecting sales on account faster, but also investing cash in fixed assets. This will help students realize that a statement of cash flows is necessary for a complete picture of a company's financial condition.

How can I know when the transaction is financing and when it is investing?

Cash Flows from Investing Activities:
Investments in yourself like:
Purchase of fixed assets
Sale of fixed assets
Investments in OTHERS like:
Purchase of equity or debt of another corporation
Sale of equity or debt of another corporation
Making a loan to another corporation

Your Students Will Ask About... (continued)

Cash Flows from Financing Activities:
Cash received/paid to obtain/repay funds to finance operations
Equity financing:
Purchasing/selling shares of treasury stock
Issuing or retiring shares of stock
Debt financing:
Borrowing cash
Repaying principal on a loan

Chapter Updates

- Updated real-world data for Under Armour, Inc.
- New Making It Real Box on cash flows at Cisco Systems
- Added Concept Questions, Multiple-Choice, and Brief Exercises
- Increased the number of assignable Exercises, Problems, and Cases

Lecture Example Solution

X Co.
Statement of Cash Flows
For Year Ending December 31, 20–

Cash flows from operating activities:		
Net income, per income statement		$ 49,000
Add: Depreciation	$ 32,000**	
Decrease in accounts receivable	7,000	
Increase in accounts payable	3,500	
Loss on sale of equipment	5,000	47,500
		$ 96,500
Deduct: Increase in inventories		11,500
Net cash flow from operating activities		$ 85,000
Cash flows from investing activities:		
Cash from sale of equipment	$ 15,000	
Less: Cash paid for purchase of equipment	100,000	
Net cash flow used for investing activities		(85,000)
Cash flows from financing activities:		
Cash received from sale of common stock	$ 32,000	
Less: Cash paid for dividends	10,000*	
Net cash flow provided by financing activities		22,000
Increase in cash		$ 22,000
Cash at the beginning of the year		78,000
Cash at the end of the year		$100,000

*$4,000 + $11,000 − $5,000 = $10,000
** $158,000 − $40,000 + ?? = $150,000 ?? = $32,000

Comparative Analysis

Visit http://investor.shareholder.com/lowes/.

1. Look at Lowe's statement of cash flows. In the most recent year, what were the company's net cash flows from operating, investing, and financing activities? Also, what amount of cash was paid for investments and dividends in the most recent year?
2. Look at Lowe's statement of cash flows. Calculate and interpret (1) free cash flow and (2) cash flow adequacy ratio.

Visit **www.cengage.com/login** for additional materials to enhance your lectures!

prepcard CHAPTER 12 Financial Statement Analysis

What's Inside

Key topics in this chapter: List and understand basic financial statement analytical procedures, calculate and interpret horizontal and vertical analyses, apply financial statement analysis to assess the solvency, liquidity, and profitability of a business.

Learning Objectives

LO1	Understand the nature of financial statement analysis.
LO2	Calculate and interpret horizontal and vertical analyses.
LO3	Assess profitability through the calculation and interpretation of ratios.
LO4	Assess liquidity through the calculation and interpretation of ratios.
LO5	Assess solvency through the calculation and interpretation of ratios.
LO6	Calculate and interpret a DuPont analysis.

Chapter Outline

Lecture Example

Revenue and expense data for X Co. are as follows:

	2011	2010
Administrative expenses	$ 37,000	$ 20,000
Cost of goods sold	400,000	320,000
Income tax	40,000	32,000
Net sales	800,000	600,000
Selling expenses	190,000	110,000

(a) Prepare a comparative income statement, with vertical analysis, stating each item for both 2011 and 2010 as a percent of sales.

(b) Comment upon significant changes disclosed by the comparative income statement.

Lecture Example Solution

(a)

X Co.
Comparative Income Statement
For Years Ending December 31, 2011 and 2010

	2011		2010	
	Amount	Percent	Amount	Percent
Net sales	$800,000	100.0%	$600,000	100.0%
Cost of goods sold	400,000	50.0%	320,000	53.3%
Gross profit	$400,000	50.0%	$280,000	46.7%
Selling expenses	$190,000	23.8%	$110,000	18.3%
Administrative exp.	37,000	4.6%	20,000	3.3%
Total operating exp.	$227,000	28.4%	$130,000	21.7%
Operating profit	$173,000	21.6%	$150,000	25.0%
Income tax	40,000	5.0%	32,000	5.3%
Net income	$133,000	16.6%	$118,000	19.7%

(b) There was a 3.3% decrease in the cost of goods sold, and a 1.3% increase in administrative expenses. However, the more significant increase of 5.5% in selling expenses offset the 3.3% decrease in cost of goods sold and contributed greatly to the 3.1% decrease in net income.

Chapter Outline (continued)

Your Students Will Ask About...

What do you mean by financial statement analysis?
Financial statement analysis is the process of applying analytical tools to a company's financial statements to understand the company's financial health. The goal is to enable stakeholders to better understand a company's financial position and therefore make better decisions about the company. The basic financial statement analytical procedures are horizontal analysis, vertical analysis, and ratio analysis.

Is horizontal analysis better than vertical analysis?
No. Explain that it depends. Horizontal analysis is a comparison of a company's financial results across time.

Dollar change in account balance	Current-yr. balance − Prior-yr. balance
Percentage change in account balance	$\frac{\text{Dollar Change}}{\text{Prior-year balance}}$

Vertical analysis is a comparison of financial statements to a base account from the same company.

	For the Balance Sheet	For the Income Statement
Percentage	$\frac{\text{Account balance}}{\text{Total assets}}$	$\frac{\text{Account balance}}{\text{Net sales or Revenue}}$

Ratio analysis is a comparison of different balances from the financial statements to provide the context to understand the financial results.

Do we have to memorize all these formulas?
Not really, just learn the basic ratios and understand their applications/usefulness.

Comparative Analysis

Visit http://investor.shareholder.com/lowes/.

1. Using Lowe's information, calculate Lowe's profitability ratios and make a general assessment about the company's profitability. Assume Lowe's stock price is $23.62.
2. Using Lowe's information, calculate Lowe's liquidity ratios and make a general assessment about the company's liquidity.
3. Using Lowe's information, calculate Lowe's solvency ratios and make a general assessment about the company's solvency.
4. Using Lowe's information, conduct a DuPont analysis. What would happen to Lowe's return on equity if it could generate one additional cent of profit from sales?

Chapter Updates

- Updated real-world data for Best Buy, Inc. throughout the chapter
- Added Concept Questions, Multiple-Choice, and Brief Exercises
- Increased the number of assignable Exercises, Problems, and Cases

reviewcard CHAPTER 8 Fixed Assets and Intangib…

Review Cards are provided for each chapter of the text in the student editions of ACCT. This sample review card is provided so that you can review the key elements contained within each card.

	Learning Objectives	Key Concepts
LO1	Describe fixed assets and how they are recorded, expensed, and reported.	Fixed assets are recorded at cost, expensed over their useful lives by depreciation, and reported on the balance sheet at net book value, which is the asset's cost less its accumulated depreciation.
	…are depreciation …ght-line, double- …nd units-of-activity	Double-declining-balance accelerates the expense to early years. Units-of-activity bases the expense on asset usage.
LO3	Understand the effects of adjustments that may be made during a fixed asset's useful life.	When an estimate on an existing fixed asset is changed, depreciation expense from that point forward is based on the new estimate. Expenditures that significantly increase a fixed asset's useful life or productive capacity are added to the asset's cost. When a fixed asset's market value falls permanently below its net book value, the asset is impaired and must be written down to market value.
LO4	Record the disposal of fixed assets.	When disposing of fixed assets, companies record a gain on disposal when the asset is sold for more than its net book value. A loss is recorded when it is sold for less than net book value.
LO5	Evaluate fixed assets through the calculation and interpretation of horizontal, vertical, and ratio analyses.	The fixed asset turnover ratio shows how effective a company is at using its fixed assets to produce revenues. The average age and average useful life ratios provide an indication of the remaining life of a company's fixed assets.
LO6	Describe the cash flow effect of acquiring fixed assets.	Cash paid for fixed assets is reported as a separate line item in the investing activities section of the statement of cash flows. A negative number indicates that a …y is buying fixed assets.
LO7	De… ar…	…le assets are recorded at their cost …rtized over their useful lives. An …y developed intangible asset is recorded only for those costs necessary to register it.

Learning Objectives remind students of the topics covered within the chapter and also provide a brief outline of the learning goals.

Key Concepts correlate to each of the chapter learning objectives and briefly summarize important concepts to promote better understanding of the broader subjects.

Cengagebrain.com is the website url where students go to access the study resources that comes with their book.

Ke…

Acc… cum… recognized to date on a fixed asset. (p. 184)

Amortization The process of spreading out the cost of an intangible asset over its useful life. (p. 204)

Average age of fixed assets A comparison of accumulated depreciation to depreciation expense that estimates the number of years, on average, that the company has used its fixed assets. (p. 200)

Average useful life of fixed assets A comparison of the cost of fixed assets to d…

Key Definitions are provided for quick review and study of important terminology from the chapter. Page references are included for easy reference back to the point of the chapter when the key term is first introduced.

Cost …e historical cost of a fixed asset being depre…ated. (p. 187)

Dep…eciable cost The difference between an asset's cost and its salvage value. (p. 187)

Depreciation The process of systematically and rationally allocating the cost of a fixed asset over its useful life. (p. 184)

Depreciation expense The portion of a fixed asset's cost that is recognized as an expense in the current period. (p. 184)

Depreciation method The method used to calculate depreciation expense, such as the straight-line method, the double-declining-balance method, and the units-of-activity method. (p. 187)

Double-declining-balance method A depreciation method that accelerates depreciation expense into the early years of an asset's life. (p. 188)

Fixed asset A tangible resource that is expected to be used in operations for more than one year and is not intended for resale. (p. 182)

Fixed asset turnover ratio A comparison of total revenues to the average net book value of fixed assets that measures the productivity of fixed assets. (p. 199)

Key Definitions (continued)

Franchise The right to operate a business under the trade name of the franchisor. (p. 202)

Goodwill An intangible asset equal to the excess that one company pays to acquire the net assets of another company. (p. 203)

Intangible asset A resource that is used in operations for more than one year but that has no physical substance. (p. 202)

Net book value The unexpired cost of a fixed asset, calculated by subtracting depreciation expense to date from the cost of the fixed asset. (p. 186)

Patent The right to manufacture, sell, or use a particular product or process exclusively for a limited period of time. (p. 202)

Revenue expenditure An expenditure that maintains the expected useful life or the productivity of a fixed asset. (p. 193)

Salvage value An estimate of the value of a fixed asset at the end of its useful life. (p. 187)

Straight-line method A depreciation method that results in the same amount of depreciation expense each year of the asset's useful life. (p. 187)

Trademark (trade name) The right to use exclusively a name, symbol, or phrase to identify a company. (p. 202)

Units-o
which dep
of the ass

Useful l
be used in

Demonstration Problems provide a worked-out solution so that students can review the answers to a problem they may encounter in the homework or on a test.

Demonstration Problem

Rooney Inc. purchases a new machine for $37,750. The machine has a useful life of 10 years and a salvage value of $2,750. Rooney estimates that the machine will be used for 17,500 hours.

a. Calculate the machine's annual depreciation expense using the straight-line method.

b. Calculate depreciation expense for the first three years of the asset's life using the double-declining-balance method.

c. Assuming that the machine is used for 3,000 hours one year, calculate depreciation expense for that year using the units-of-activity method.

d. Suppose that after five years of straight-line depreciation, Rooney increases the machine's useful life an additional two years. Calculate depreciation expense for year six.

e. Suppose instead that after six years of straight-line depreciation, Rooney sells the machine for $16,300. Calculate the gain or loss on the sale.

Key Formulas

Key Formulas provide a quick summary of the chapter's important formulas and equations when studying for quizzes or exams.

Straight-Line Method	Depreciation Expense
Double-Declining-Balance Method	Depreciation Expense = (Straight-Line Rate × 2) × (Cost – Accumulated Depreciation)
Units-of-Activity Method	$\text{Depreciation Expense per Unit} = \frac{\text{Cost} - \text{Salvage Value}}{\text{Useful Life in Units}}$
	Depreciation Expense = Depreciation Expense per Unit × Actual Units of Activity
Net Book Value	Cost − Accumulated Depreciation

Disposals	Gain on Disposal: Proceeds from Sale > Net Book Value
	Loss on Disposal: Proceeds from Sale < Net Book Value

Fixed Asset Turnover Ratio	$\frac{\text{Total Revenues}}{\text{Average Net Book Value of Fixed Assets}}$ where average net book value is: $\frac{\text{Beginning Net Book Value} + \text{Ending Net Book Value}}{2}$
Average Useful Life Ratio	$\text{Average Useful Life} = \frac{\text{Cost of Fixed Assets}}{\text{Depreciation Expense}}$
Average Age Ratio	$\text{Average Age} = \frac{\text{Accumulated Depreciation}}{\text{Depreciation Expense}}$

Demonstration Problem Solution

a. ($37,750 − $2,750) / 10 = $3,500 depreciation expense per year

b. Double-declining rate = (100% ÷ 10) × 2 = 20%
Year 1: 20% × $37,750 = $7,550 depreciation expense
Year 2: 20% × ($37,750 − $7,550) = $6,040 depreciation expense
Year 3: 20% × ($37,750 − $7,550 − $6,040) = $4,832 depreciation expense

c. ($37,750 − $2,750) / $17,500 = $2 depreciation expense per hour
3,000 hours × 2 = $6,000 depreciation expense

d.

Cost of the asset	$37,750
Less: Accumulated depreciation for five years ($3,500 × 5)	17,500
Net book value at time of revision	$20,250
Less: Salvage value	2,750
Remaining depreciable cost	$17,500
Divided by remaining useful life (5 years + 2 more years)	÷ 7
Depreciation expense for year 6	$ 2,500

e.

Cost of the asset	$37,750
Less: Accumulated depreciation for six years ($3,500 × 6)	21,000
Net book value at time of revision	$16,750
Sales price	16,000
Loss on sale	$ 750

CengageNOW Instructor Guide

What's Inside

The content on this card is designed to provide you with tips to best utilize what CengageNOW has to offer you and your students to improve outcomes and drive better results.

Setting Prerequisites to Drive Student Accountability

Assigning prerequisites offers you a way to make sure students are learning the material sequentially or to ensure they are achieving a certain level of proficiency before continuing their assignments.

- Set up a learning path that requires students to take assignments in a sequential order to build on what they know.
- Require students to get a certain grade on a pre-test before coming to lecture.
- Require students to get a certain grade on an assignment of brief exercises before moving on to longer problems or before coming to lecture.
- Have students complete a review assignment or a Blueprint Problem before a test or quiz is made available to them.

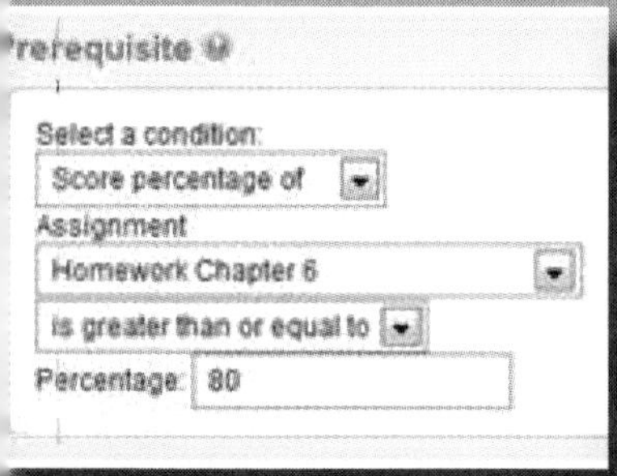

Note: You will actually be choosing the pre-requisite option on the second assignment you create, saying that this second assignment will only be available to students IF (for example) they receive an 85% on the first assignment in the series.

Providing the Right Amount of Help to Students:

"Assignment Takes" vs. "Check My Work"

Determining the right set of options depends on your pedagogical philosophy. The information below will help you determine how much feedback and how many chances you give students to complete their homework.

"Assignment Takes"

Number of times the student can take whole assignment and submit for grading.

Feedback setting: You can enable the setting that shows students the correct answers immediately after an assignment take is submitted or at a specified date in the future (such as the due date).

"Check My Work"

Number of times students can check what they got right or wrong on each question before submitting for grading.

Feedback setting: For students to receive additional guidance within assignment takes when they click on "Check My Work," select the feedback check box underneath where you select how many times you are allowing students to "Check their Work".

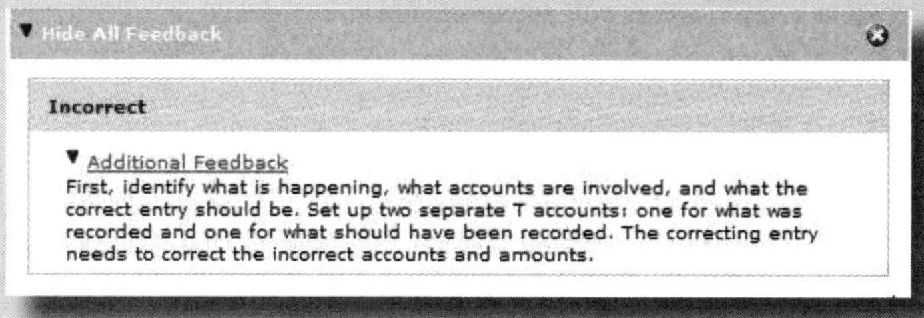

Assignable Study Tools

These resources can be used for self-study or assigned as an assignment for a grade. They help students focus on where they need the most help and provide valuable exam prep.

Pre-Test: Assesses where students are at that moment in time by asking mostly conceptual, multiple-choice questions.

Personalized Study Plan: A diagnostic tool that suggests readings and study resources based on a student's areas of weakness so that he or she can focus his or her study.

Post-Test: This can be taken over and over by the student until he or she has mastered the concepts. The personalized study plan will continue to evolve based on the student's changing comprehension.

To assign any or all parts of ***Assignable Study Tools****, choose this "type" of assignment in the assignment creation process.*

Blueprint Problems: Taking Students to a whole new level!

Blueprint Problems are designed to help students understand the fundamental accounting concepts and their associated building blocks and not just the formulas or journal entries required for a single concept. This allows students to get the overall big picture and to begin to see how accounting concepts are interrelated in one succinct discussion.

How Can Blueprint Problems Be Used?

- As review either during or after a student reads a chapter
- To prepare students for lecture
- To reinforce concepts for students who are struggling with specific topics
- As material that goes beyond standard end-of-chapter and challenges students to think critically
- To initiate classroom discussion
- To function as review module for exam prep
- As a group quiz or assignment, allowing students to discuss amongst themselves

To assign a Blueprint Problem, choose the Homework bank when creating an assignment. Once you expand the menu, you can select from the Blueprint Problem question bank.

Assessing Student Learning/Reporting on Outcomes

CengageNOW has built-in reports you can run to determine how well your students are performing in relation to various measures. You can also create custom reports. Since the content in CengageNOW is tied to multiple types of outcomes, you can choose the measures that matter most to you. Content is tagged by:

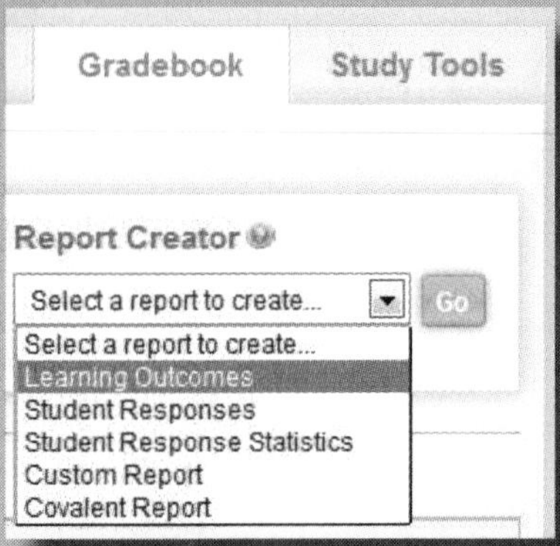

- AACSB
- ACBSP
- Learning Objective
- Blooms Taxonomy
- Difficulty Level
- Average Completion Time
- And more, allowing you to use these reports for accreditation or for internal reporting purposes.

Summary of student performance by concept

Name:	AACSB Analytic	AACSB Reflective Thinking	AACSB Communication	AICPA FN-Reporting	AICPA FN-Measurement
Borst, Kevin	%100	%100	%25	%57	- -
Doe, Jane	%50	%0	%0	%14	%100
Howell, Nick	%100	%100	%25	%57	%50
Smith, John	%50	%100	%75	%71	%100

Getting Ready for a New Term

Once you have created your course the way you want it, the next term is a piece of cake to set up!

First, **copy over the course.** Do this by selecting the box next to the course you want to copy and under the **Courses and Sections** drop-down menu, select **Copy**, then **Go**. Next, under the **Folders** menu, select **Paste Course**, then **Go**. Finally, make sure the course is correct and choose **Paste Selected Items**. You will now see a copy of your previous course in your course list.

Next, **change your due dates**. From the assignments page of your newly copied course, select all the assignments that have dates that need changed. Click on the **Modify Dates**, then **Specify Dates for Each**. Now you can change the dates to match your current term, and you are ready to go!

CengageNOW Student Study Tools Guide

What's Inside

ACCT has many resources to help you succeed in the course! See below for the valuable assets you will find in the Study Tools tab of CengageNOW.

Animations

Built from examples in selected chapters of the book, these animations bring the examples and underlying concepts to life. If you are a visual learner or you need some review on this particular topic, Animations will be a great resource for you.

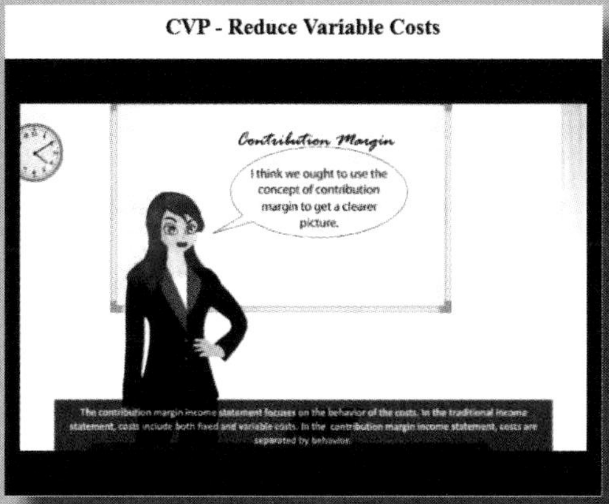

Electures

Need something that will help you review concepts if you miss class or need additional help in an audio-visual format? These refreshers on the concepts for each chapter mirror the classroom experience and are PowerPoints with recorded audio walking you through concepts like a live lecture.

Crossword Puzzle

These fun puzzles help you review key vocabulary and definitions from the chapters.

PowerPoint Slides

These slides summarize key concepts and help you organize your review for enhanced understanding and exam and quiz prep.

Beat the Clock

This game quizzes you on important aspects of each chapter and helps you practice answering questions while the clock is ticking.

Quiz Bowl

This "Jeopardy-style" game is a fun way to review concepts and key terms. Regardless of whether you get the answer right or wrong, you will receive feedback on the correct answer so that you learn through the process.

Quizzing

Want to prep for your upcoming quiz or exam? Students often ask for practice with multiple-choice questions like those that often show up on tests and exams. Get used to answering multiple-choice accounting questions by quizzing yourself!

What's Inside

Using the *Personalized Study Plan* and *Interactive eBook*:
In addition to housing all of the study resources available to you, the ***Study Tools*** tab is where you will find access to your interactive eBook as well as your ***Personalized Study Plan***. This card will explain how to use these powerful learning tools.

Using the Personalized Study Plan

First, take the Pre-Test.
While on the ***Study Tools*** tab, click on ***Study Plan View*** on the right to access the pre-test. This will help you gauge what you understand right now about chapter topics. When finished, view your graded pre-test & feedback by clicking on your score under ***Result.*** Click on ***Home*** to go back to the ***Study Plan View***.

Next, view your Personalized Study Plan.
The ***Personalized Study Plan*** will suggest readings or study tools based on your pre-test results to help you focus your study. To access, click on ***View*** under the ***Study Tools*** column.

Finally, take the Post-Test and review your Revised Study Plan.
The post-test can be taken again and again until you have mastered the concepts. Click on the link to take the ***Post-Test***. The personalized study plan will continue to revise based on your pre-test results.

Using Your Interactive eBook

ACCT offers a dynamic eBook that will help you interact with accounting content while on the go! Check out how you can read & study with your eBook.

Table of Contents:
Easily navigate to various chapters or to specific learning objectives within a chapter with the ***Table of Contents*** tab on the left.

Search:
Looking for all content related to a specific word or phrase? Use the ***Search*** bar to find all mentions of your search term throughout the eBook.

Index:
Another way to find exactly what you are looking for is to click on the ***Index*** tab, which will take you directly to the pages where a term or concept is covered.

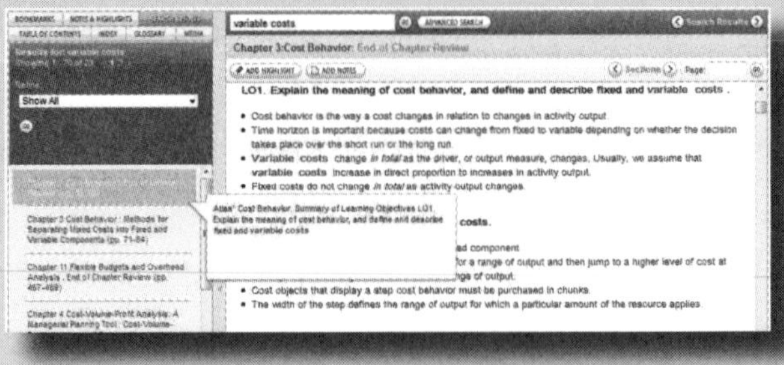

Glossary:
To find the definition of a key term in the text, go straight to the ***Glossary*** or hover over the term in the text.

Notes:
As you move through the eBook, you can write notes to yourself next to certain parts of the text. Click on the ***Add Notes*** button at the top.

Highlights:
To highlight sections of text, click on the ***Add Highlight*** button at the top and drag your mouse over the section you want to highlight.

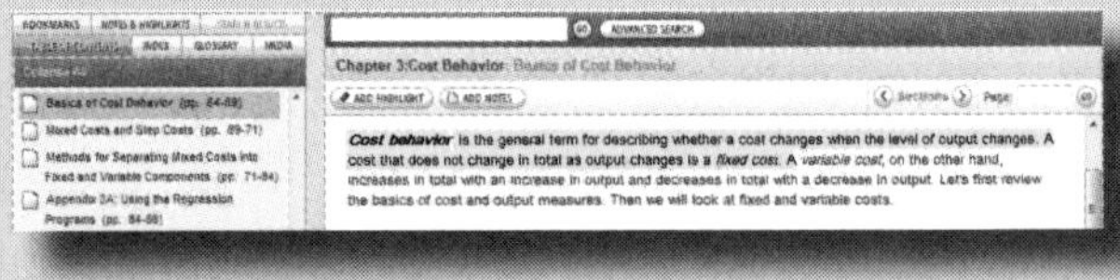

Notes & Highlights:
All of your notes and highlights are captured for you in one easy place under the ***Notes & Highlights*** tab. Use this as your "virtual study guide" to focus on what you have deemed the most important parts of the chapter.

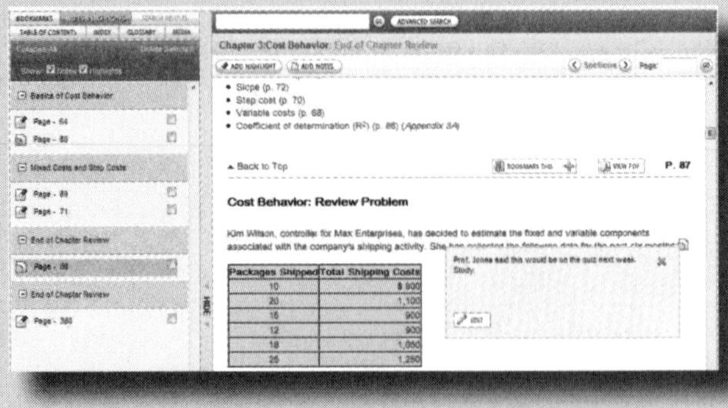

comprehensive chart of accounts

Assets

- Cash
- Petty cash
- Accounts receivable
- Allowance for bad debts
- Fuel
- Interest receivable
- Inventory
- Notes receivable
- Office supplies
- Prepaid insurance
- Prepaid rent
- Short-term investments
- Supplies
- Long-term investments
- Buildings
- Equipment
- Land
- Accumulated depreciation
- Copyrights
- Goodwill
- Patents

Liabilities

- Accounts payable
- Dividends payable
- Dividends payable—common
- Dividends payable—preferred
- Federal tax withholdings payable
- FICA taxes payable
- Income tax payable
- Interest payable
- Notes payable
- Salaries payable
- Sales tax payable
- State tax withholdings payable
- Unearned revenue
- Utilities Payable
- Bonds payable
- Discount on bonds payable
- Premium on bonds payable
- Mortgage payable

Equity

- Additional paid in capital
- Capital stock
- Common stock
- Common Stock to be Distributed
- Contributed capital
- Dividends
- Preferred stock
- Retained earnings
- Treasury stock

Revenues

- Sales
- Sales discounts
- Sales returns and allowances
- Service revenue
- Interest revenue
- Gain on disposal
- Gain on redemption

Expenses

- Administrative expense
- Advertising expense
- Amortization expense
- Bad debt expense
- Cash over and short
- Cost of goods sold
- Depreciation expense
- Fuel expense
- Income tax expense
- Insurance expense
- Interest expense
- Loss on disposal
- Loss on impairment
- Loss on redemption
- Maintenance expense
- Miscellaneous expense
- Payroll tax expense
- Postage expense
- Purchases
- Purchase discounts
- Purchase returns and allowances
- Rent expense
- Salaries expense
- Service charge expense
- Supplies expense
- Transportation-in
- Utilities expense